Radio's Civic Ambition
American Broadcasting
and Democracy in the 1930s

David Goodman

OXFORD
UNIVERSITY PRESS

OXFORD
UNIVERSITY PRESS

Oxford University Press, Inc., publishes works that further
Oxford University's objective of excellence
in research, scholarship, and education.

Oxford   New York
Auckland   Cape Town   Dar es Salaam   Hong Kong   Karachi
Kuala Lumpur   Madrid   Melbourne   Mexico City   Nairobi
New Delhi   Shanghai   Taipei   Toronto

With offices in
Argentina   Austria   Brazil   Chile   Czech Republic   France   Greece
Guatemala   Hungary   Italy   Japan   Poland   Portugal   Singapore
South Korea   Switzerland   Thailand   Turkey   Ukraine   Vietnam

Published by Oxford University Press, Inc.
198 Madison Avenue, New York, New York 10016

www.oup.com

Oxford is a registered trademark of Oxford University Press

Library of Congress Cataloging-in-Publication Data
Goodman, David, 1957–
Radio's civic ambition : American broadcasting and
democracy in the 1930s / David Goodman.
    p.   cm.
Includes bibliographical references and index.
ISBN 978-0-19-539408-5 (alk. paper)
1. Radio broadcasting—United States—History—20th century.
2. Public radio—United States—History—20th century.
3. Radio broadcasting—Political aspects—United States—20th century.
4. Radio broadcasting—Social aspects—United States—20th century.   I. Title.
HE8698.G66 2011
384.540973'09043—dc22
2010014001

Oxford Web Music (🔊)
Visit the companion website at: www.oup.com/us/radioscivicambition
For more information on Oxford Web Music, visit www.oxfordwebmusic.com

1 3 5 7 9 8 6 4 2

Printed in the United States of America
on acid-free paper

Contents

Library and Archive Abbreviations

CRBM—Columbia University Library, Rare Book and Manuscript Library
LOC—Library of Congress
NYPL—New York Public Library
NACP—National Archives College Park
OHS—Ohio Historical Society
RAC—Rockefeller Archive Center
UCSC—Special Collections Research Center, University of Chicago library
WHS—Wisconsin Historical Society

Acknowledgments

There has been a significant flourishing of American radio history in the past decade or so, and this book has been both delayed and immeasurably improved by the quickening of research and refining of argument in the field. I have benefited from several years of conversations with a wonderful circle of American radio history scholars, including Susan Smulyan, Michele Hilmes, Elena Razlogova, Derek Vaillant, Jason Loviglio, Bill Kirkpatrick, Len Kuffert, Michael Socolow, Alex Russo, David Suisman, and Douglas Craig. Colleagues in the School of Historical Studies at the University of Melbourne, and in the Australian and New Zealand American Studies Association, have been unfailingly supportive. I am grateful to the Australian Research Council for Large Research Grant A59601212 for a project on "Conformity, Diversity and Citizenship," which started me on the path to this book. That is more than a formulaic thanks—ARC support has allowed me to participate in international research and scholarship in a way that simply would not have been possible otherwise. Research assistants, including Tim Verhoeven and Jasper Collier, helped me locate and organize material. I also want to thank the research libraries and archives that have facilitated the research for this book—in particular the Wisconsin Historical Society, the Library of Congress, the Library of American Broadcasting at the University of Maryland, the National Archives at College Park, the Columbia University Library, the University of Chicago library, the Rockefeller Archive Center, and the New York Public Library. For specific permissions to quote or reproduce archival materials, I thank the BBC Written Archives Center, the Rare Book and Manuscript Department at the Columbia University Library, the Rockefeller Archive Center, NBC Universal, and CBS. Finally, Julie McLeod and I spent two of our sabbaticals with our daughters Clara and Eva in Madison, Wisconsin, making possible extended research in the rich broadcasting collections there. Julie has been an astute in-house reader and critic; together my family has always provided just the right mixture of interest and impatience to see this project completed.

About the Companion Website

www.oup.com/us/radioscivicambition

Oxford has created a password-protected website to accompany *Radio's Civic Ambition*. It contains some additional text and illustrations, and web links to online material and sound files that will enhance a reading of the text. The relevant web materials are signposted in the text with this symbol: ◕

Preface

The generation that came of age in the late 1920s was the first to live a whole life amidst the new soundscape of the broadcast era. It experienced the shock of discovering, as one contemporary observer marveled, "the difference it makes to the earth and its inhabitants when anything uttered anywhere is audible everywhere at will."[1] Radio was indeed a revolutionary device. It altered conversational patterns, provided a new social and symbolic center to the home and a new kind of background noise. It rapidly became one of the most important institutions of American life. Talk and music, so often previously scarce and even precious resources, came flooding out of the box in endless supply. Radio told stories, provided current news, and regularly brought professionally performed music into lives that had seldom known it before. [Figure 0.1.] Homes were filled with cheerful and persuasive voices. We who have lived through the remarkably rapid revolutions of the digital era can identify with some of the euphoria that greeted radio, the sense of extraordinary new possibilities, and greatly expanded horizons. But there were also worries. Radio's unceasing chatter prompted new concerns about the quality of listening—would people listen distractedly rather than attentively and critically? The new abundance of home entertainment also provoked anxieties about radio's effects on public and civic life—would radio make Americans more passive, less inclined to go out, less likely to think independently, to develop and voice opinions of their own? The anxieties no less than the hopes and wonders are a part of radio history, because they also shaped what radio became.

The dominant memory of American radio in its golden age—reinforced in the nostalgia for old-time radio as well as in passing references in the work of countless social and cultural historians—is that it functioned primarily as entertainment, and as something that brought the nation together as never before.[2] What is remembered and mythologized in old-time radio nostalgia is the national community created by the shared and simultaneous experience of listening to the fireside chats or Jack Benny.[3] Radio has entered the textbooks as an instrument of cheap and distracting mass entertainment that fortuitously

1. Anne O'Hare McCormick, "The Radio: A Great Unknown Force," *New York Times*, March 27, 1932: SM1.
2. The "golden age" can be roughly defined as the period after networking and before television—i.e., early 1930s to mid-1940s.
3. See, e.g., Gerald Nachman, *Raised on Radio* (New York: Pantheon Books, 1998); Leonard Maltin, *The Great American Broadcast: A Celebration of Radio's Golden Age* (New York: Dutton, 1997).

Figure 0.1. Photographers were fascinated by the way that radio had become an intimate part of family life. John Frost and daughter listening to radio in their home, Tehama County, California, 1940. Photographer: Russell Lee. FSA-OWI Collection, Library of Congress, LC-DIG-fsa-8b00054 D.

arrived just in time for the Depression, when the nation most needed cheap and cheerful entertainment.[4]

As so often in history, this view is not wrong; it is just that through sheer repetition, it begins to prevent other important perspectives from being noticed. A series of oppositions runs through the history of radio—between entertainment and education, commercial and civic roles, passive and active listening, compliant and resistant audiences. Each of these oppositions was, however, also debated extensively in the 1930s. Radio history needs to pay close attention to the meanings and debates of the time, to be reflective about *their* categories of understanding. The danger is not simply the presentism of imposing our categories—to pick examples from opposite ends of the histori-

4. Good summaries of this view include Tom Lewis, "'A Godlike Presence': The Impact of Radio on the 1920s and 1930s," *OAH Magazine of History* 6, no. 4 (Spring 1992); Erik Barnouw, *A Tower in Babel: A History of Broadcasting in the United States, to* 1933 (New York: Oxford University Press, 1966); Erik Barnouw, *The Golden Web: A History of Broadcasting in the United States,* 1933 *to* 1953 (New York: Oxford University Press, 1968).

ography, entertainment, or active audiences—on the past. In using our terms rather than beginning by reflecting on theirs, we can obscure the extent to which our ideas about the social and civic role of media derive from—advance or not from—those of the 1930s. It is also only by attending to the extensive debates of the time about broadcasting and its effects that we will understand the many ways in which radio divided as well as united Americans. So this is an embedded cultural history, which aims to show how crucial understanding the terms of contemporary debate is to a cultural history of radio. Such contemporary debate is to be found not just in formal public argument, where programmatic and often predictable statements were traded, but also along the way, dramatized in action and story.

This book is then about the ways in which American radio in its golden age attempted to do more than entertain. It is, however, neither a comprehensive history of the many attempts to use radio for education, nor of the important ways in which the educational radio lobby shaped early debates about radio regulation.[5] It is, rather, about the endemic creative tension between American radio's entertainment and its educational and civic purposes. American radio, I argue, had—distinctively—a civic legitimation and a commercial function, which meant that it was always attempting to change ideas and behavior, striving to create active and informed listeners, as well as to entertain. This book analyses some of the ways in which American radio carried out its civic functions in the years before World War II; it seeks to identify and interpret rather than denounce the tensions and contradictions within American broadcasting, to acknowledge their productive as well as disabling aspects.

While historians have been very interested in how the United States acquired a predominantly commercial broadcasting system in the 1920s and 1930s, there has been less work that has explored the characteristic tensions and capacities of that system. Other nations had monopoly national, public service broadcasters, or dual systems in which public service broadcasters operated alongside commercial broadcasters. But in the United States, it was the commercial broadcasters that had to acknowledge and work with the high expectations of the era about what radio might do for national life, even as they operated as businesses seeking profit. The resulting system looks in comparative terms like a curious hybrid—overwhelmingly commercial, but straining to be seen to perform the tasks of national and public service broadcasting. The effects of this structural situation have thus far been little explored in U.S. radio history.

Radio was important in most Western nations in the 1930s, but nowhere more so than in the United States.[6] Census figures show that purchase of radio sets through the nation was rapid but uneven from the 1930s. The graph of national trends shows a very steep upward curve. By 1937, more than half the radio sets in the world were in the United

5. On the latter topic, see Robert McChesney, *Telecommunications, Mass Media, and Democracy: The Battle for the Control of U.S. Broadcasting, 1928–1935* (New York: Oxford University Press, 1993); see also Eugene E. Leach, "Tuning Out Education: The Cooperation Doctrine in Radio, 1922–38," which originally appeared in *Current* in January, February, and March 1983. Available: http://www.current. org/coop/index.shtml. [Jan. 27, 2010].

6. See Douglas B. Craig, *Fireside Politics: Radio and Political Culture in the United States, 1920–1940* (Baltimore: Johns Hopkins University Press, 2000): 12, for comparative figures.

States—one for every 4.2 persons—and in the nation's expanding cities, there was a radio in over 90% of homes. Younger Americans came to regard radio as a necessity, and as a focal point of social interaction.[7] The diffusion of radio sets allowed for the virtual assembly of a mass audience—at least 10 times President Roosevelt addressed radio audiences estimated at 40 million, and entertainment programs reached audiences in excess of 30 million.[8] But broken down by region, race, and class, important differences emerge. The 1940 census found the percentage of radio-equipped dwellings ranged all the way from 39.9% in Mississippi to 96.2% in Massachusetts. It also found that while 86.8% of white households in the United States had a radio, only 43.3% of nonwhite households did.[9] The South in general was significantly less tuned in to radio than the rest of the nation, and Southern blacks were the least likely of any group to have a radio before 1950.[10] Meanwhile the wealthy had less time to listen but gave themselves more opportunities to do so—an increasing number of American households had two radio sets, and there was by the mid-1930s a small but rapidly growing minority of Americans who also had a radio in their cars.[11]

Focusing on national aggregates rather than these uneven rates of adoption, radio seemed to many Americans at the time a profoundly democratic technology. It was certainly not only the wealthy who could own a radio and enjoy the stream of free entertainment and information that came from it. Annoyed at President Roosevelt's second inaugural evocation of the one-third of a nation "ill-housed, ill-clad, ill-nourished," the *Chicago Tribune* editorialized that, on the contrary, mass radio ownership was evidence that modern industrial capitalism fostered democratic equality: "Possession of a radio . . . does give a fair indication of the extent to which the common man shares in the fruits of industrial civilization."[12] Not all were as sanguine as the *Tribune*, however, about the democratic potential of radio's industrialization of entertainment and its centralized mass distribution of information. Alerted by populist warnings about the dangers of centralization and monopoly, many other Americans worried about networked radio's transformation of social and civic life. Nobody knew for certain just what the impact of radio would be, but something so widely diffused and so much in use could plausibly be expected to have large and enduring effects.

A 1938 *New Yorker* cartoon depicted a scientist in his lab full of monkeys explaining proudly to a visitor, "As you can see, the one I injected now takes a normal, healthy interest in everyday affairs."[13] The monkey in question sits in an armchair, reading a newspaper.

7. F. Holter, "Radio among the Unemployed," *Journal of Applied Psychology* 23, no. 1 (1939): 166–67.

8. William C. Ackerman, "The Dimensions of American Broadcasting," *Public Opinion Quarterly* 9, no. 1 (Spring 1945): 7.

9. Ackerman, "The Dimensions of American Broadcasting": 3; "43.3% Have Radios among Non-Whites," *Broadcasting* 23, no. 21 (Nov. 23, 1942): 14.

10. Steve Craig, "How America Adopted Radio: Demographic Differences in Set Ownership Reported in the 1930–1950 U.S. Censuses," *Journal of Broadcasting & Electronic Media* 48, no. 2 (Jun. 2004): 179–96.

11. "Study Shows Rapid Rise of Radio," *Los Angeles Times*, March 12, 1935: 14; E. A. Suchman, "Radio Listening and Automobiles," *Journal of Applied Psychology* 23, no. 1 (1939): 148–67.

12. "Life in America," *Chicago Daily Tribune*, August 28, 1937: 10.

13. George Price cartoon, *New Yorker*, June 4, 1938: 14.

A large radio set is blaring, and the contented-looking monkey appears to be reaching over to turn up the volume. The cartoon puts the mass-mediated forms of that "normal, healthy interest in everyday affairs" under some comic suspicion, neatly posing the question of how one could claim to have an active interest in public affairs while sitting comfortably cocooned at home. The image makes sense only against the background of concern that still surrounded radio's civic role. Was an engagement with public life mediated through a one-way radio in some ways counterfeit or civically negligent?

A few months later in 1938, émigré German philosopher Theodor Adorno was in New York conducting research on American radio. Something puzzled him. Reading through files of letters written by listeners to radio stations, he found them surprisingly "full of reference to the writer's personality." Why, he wondered, would listeners feel that it was useful or appropriate to write so personally to a large commercial organization? Adorno found it rationally inexplicable that an individual would write in such a manner "when he knows that he cannot expect any real personal interest" in return. And yet "not only obviously neurotic persons but also some who are apparently quite sensible talk about themselves, their age, their profession and their outlooks." For Adorno, the most extraordinary thing was that "they seem to justify their suggestions by considering their particular viewpoints as expressions of their particular personalities." What could have provoked such apparently inappropriate writings? Perhaps, Adorno speculated, the letter writers could find no other way to deal with their feelings of being "lost and neglected" by radio and its "ubiquity-standardization"? Perhaps they felt ashamed of their letters? Perhaps the listener, although "aware of the futility of his attempt to pit his personality against the power of a radio network," was trying "to compensate by emphasizing his uniqueness"?[14] The insistent explication by listeners of the relationship between their "particular viewpoints" and their "particular personalities" might itself be a form of resistance, Adorno speculated, to radio's standardizing and homogenizing pull.

Adorno was in many ways an astute observer of American radio and American life.[15] Although he had arrived in the United States only in 1938, he had already identified a genuinely intriguing and interesting phenomenon. In thinking, however, of the problem primarily as an issue of psychological adjustment to late capitalism, and in terms of audience surrender or resistance to the "ubiquity-standardization" of radio, Adorno had failed to notice other and contrary dynamics. Much recent media audience scholarship has been dedicated to reversing his thought, to emphasizing audience agency rather than broadcaster hegemony.[16] But this cultural, communications, and media studies scholarship shares a fundamental assumption with Adorno's pessimistic critique—an understanding that acceptance of media messages was a form of passive conformity, that rejection or active appropriation of them for one's own ends was individual assertion, that in short, active audiences were resistant and passive ones compliant.

14. Theodor Adorno, "Radio Physiognomies" [1939], in Robert Hullot-Kentor (ed.), *Theodor Adorno: Current of Music: Elements of a Radio Theory* (Cambridge: Polity, 2009): 106–8.

15. For the most recent assessment of Adorno's American years, see David Jeneman, *Adorno in America* (Minneapolis: University of Minnesota Press, 2007).

16. See, e.g., Will Brooker and Deborah Jermyn (eds.), *The Audience Studies Reader* (London: Routledge, 2003).

I want to disrupt this now conventional mapping, and to argue instead that in the 1930s, broadcasting in the United States was officially intended to incite and create an active audience, so that the active audience was actually the compliant one. The impulse to make active audiences came from a distinctively American intersection of regulatory expectations, political pressures, and commercial imperatives, and was one of the key responses to the endemic underlying tension between commercial and public service imperatives in American broadcasting. What Adorno did not perceive in 1938, then, was the extent to which American radio was constructed around a dual civic and commercial paradigm of active listening and individual response. His letter writers were obedient to the call of an institution that sought, not silent uniformity, but individual testimony about active and differentiated listening. The individualized identity of listeners was, in other words, to be socially produced. Americans understood that radio in other nations was deployed to create conformity, but they knew that in the United States it was supposed to be a machine for producing individuals and individualism. A Newark high school teacher designing a curriculum in radio appreciation suggested that students research radio in other countries: "Are programs regulated to secure greater cultural values? To produce rigid uniformity?"[17] The implicit message to American pupils was that, in contrast, American radio stimulated diversity and individualism. It was a theme widely echoed in public discussion of radio in the United States in the 1930s.

This book both describes and admires the cultural ambition of golden age American radio. It offers in that sense an optimistic analysis, a glimpse of what one mass medium once was and hence could be again. But it is also—and inevitably—ultimately a story of failure. While the first part of the book explores the high hopes that surrounded radio, the second examines some of the ways in which the characteristic nagging structural conflicts within American radio—civic yet commercial, supplying what the people wanted yet uplifting and improving them, appealing to people as they were yet attempting to make them better and more tolerant citizens—eventually enmired its ambitions.

The book has three—related—revisionist arguments. First, that American radio in the 1930s was dominated by a civic paradigm, central to which was the ideal of an active, responsive, opinionated, and individualized audience. Second, that the civic paradigm was a product of state intervention, of the federal regulation of broadcasting through the Federal Communications Commission. Third, that as a direct consequence of this domination by civic values that were also cosmopolitan and pluralist, radio spoke to a class-divided audience. The focus on class here does not reflect a belief that ethnic, race, or gender divides have been any less prevalent or less important in U.S. radio history; my specific argument is, however, that what I identify as the civic paradigm in the United States called forth class-defined more than it did ethnic-, race-, or gender-based resistance.

The chapters of the book explore aspects of this culturally ambitious but ultimately divisive civic paradigm. Chapter 1, "The American System," argues that the American system was never completely free from government influence and control, and that FCC

17. Max J. Herzberg, "Tentative Units in Radio Program Appreciation," *English Journal* 24, no. 7. (September 1935): 548.

regulation—despite its weakness, inconsistency, and party political maneuvering—had demonstrable and arguably beneficial effects on broadcasting practice. After 1934, politically alert broadcasters continued to fear government competition in broadcasting, or the imposition of a more demanding regulatory regime, and networks were concerned about trust-busting attention to their commercial dominance. We know this because there was as a consequence far more high cultural, educational, and civic programming on American radio than commercial broadcasters left to themselves would have provided. Chapter 2, "The Civic Paradigm," elaborates the first and second of the three arguments about the civil paradigm—establishing that there was such a dominant cluster of ideas, and that it centered upon the figure of the active, critical, but empathetic listener. Chapter 3, "The Promise of Broadcast Classical Music," explores the question of why there was so much classical music on 1930s American radio. Radio's engagement with the ideas of 1930s music educators led to an emphasis on the added effort that would be necessary to turn music listening into genuine music appreciation. Local performers, amateurs talking about their musical hobby, broadcast music lessons, composition competitions, and play-along programs all evidenced and emphasized links to an active musical culture and demonstrated why broadcast classical music was so important a part of civic paradigm radio. Chapter 4, "Democratic Radio," analyzes the important radio forum programs, which imagined, and to some extent helped to create, an audience that was rational, discursive, open to persuasion, critical, wedded to the process of truth seeking rather than to any particular beliefs—and above all willing to change its mind.

The second half of the book is about social and cultural divisions that were accentuated by the civic paradigm. It describes how the civic ideal of radio ended by alienating those Americans in whom the pluralist virtues of tolerance, openness, and empathy aroused suspicion rather than trust. Chapter 5, "Class, Cosmopolitanism, and Division," argues that while radio was a nationalizing and cosmopolitan force that brought Americans together in unprecedented national and international simultaneity, it was also for those very reasons the site of a sustained culture war. Chapter 6, "Radio and the Intelligent Listener: The *War of the Worlds* Panic," sets the famous 1938 broadcast in the context of pervasive contemporary concern about propaganda and the intelligence of the population. A key component of the civic ideal was the imperative that listeners take responsibility for their own listening and the formation of their own opinions and beliefs. Anxiety about propaganda on the radio in the late 1930s created a cultural and intellectual climate in which the credulity and intelligence of the American population was under intense scrutiny. The civic paradigm proved divisive in practice, as the panicked listeners to the Martian broadcast were repeatedly and aggressively blamed for their failure as citizens to listen correctly. Chapter 7, "Populism, War, and the American System," examines populist challenges to the American system of broadcasting from the late 1930s, and argues that the civic paradigm compact was beginning to fray in the conditions of WWII, as quite different demands were made of broadcasters by government. A postlude looks at some immediately postwar evaluations of American radio, such as the FCC's "Blue Book" and the discussions of radio by the Commission on the Freedom of the Press, chaired by University of Chicago president Robert Hutchins.

One of the important things about recent work in U.S. radio history has been the very productive interaction between communications, media, and American studies work and that produced by historians. Out of this stimulating nexus has come a body of recent work that goes well beyond narrating what happened in radio history, and takes on the burden of demonstrating rather than assuming radio's broader social and cultural importance. I have increasingly come to believe that the need now is indeed for a radio history in which the radio sits somewhere in the middle distance—showing how radio was incorporated into and in turn transformed aspects of American life.

I came to this project with an interest in comparative history, and as an Australian who teaches and researches U.S. history from outside American borders. I have tried throughout, perhaps more than has been usual in the recent wave of scholarship, to venture some arguments about the distinctiveness of American broadcasting. As always, because of the great influence of American media practices in the rest of the world, isolating an American model for analysis can be extremely difficult—there is no static comparative laboratory for comparative historical work, just a dynamic world in which ideas, particularly American ideas, are constantly translated into other contexts. Much more comparative investigation remains for someone else—or rather many someone elses—but I have tried here at least to suggest some themes that future comparative and transnational work in radio history might take up. Finally, I should note that—like most of the U.S. radio history written in recent decades—this book is better informed about the inner workings of NBC than about the other networks, because major NBC archival collections have long been available to researchers at the Wisconsin Historical Society and the Library of Congress, and there has been no comparable access to archival material about the CBS or (until recently) Mutual networks.[18]

18. The Library of Congress also has the WOR collection, which will eventually shed further light on the Mutual network.

Part 1
Ambition

1

The American System

PROLOGUE: THE SETTLEMENT OF 1934

In late 1934, the future of the American system of broadcasting was being decided. In the endgame of a complicated series of legislative and activist skirmishes between radio reformers and the broadcasting industry, Senators Robert Wagner of New York and Henry Hatfield of West Virginia had proposed an amendment to the legislation setting up the new Federal Communications Commission that would have set aside 25% of all radio facilities for the use of "educational, religious, agricultural, labor, co-operative and similar non-profit-making associations."[1] The proposal gained strong support from nonprofit broadcasters, who had been contesting the commercial dominance of the public resource of the airwaves for a decade or more, and who had several times before advocated set-aside proposals.[2] Indeed, for many radio reformers, a reservation of a portion of radio's frequencies or hours for nonprofit uses was itself a modest compromise, a step back from the more thoroughgoing demands emanating from what critic James Rorty had described in 1931 as the "increasingly articulate movement for public ownership and operation of essential public services."[3]

By 1934, on all sides, the battle over U.S. broadcasting was understood to be entering a critical and probably decisive phase. One reformer warned that in no realm of social life was "private control more menacing to the common interests of mankind."[4] Father John Harney, from the Paulist Fathers' station WLWL in New York, unhappy with the way the

1. This complex story is well told in McChesney, *Telecommunications, Mass Media, and Democracy*, ch. 8; in Susan Smulyan, *Selling Radio: The Commercialization of American Broadcasting 1920–1934* (Washington DC: Smithsonian Institution Press, 1994), ch. 5; and Barnouw, *The Golden Web*: 22–28.

2. Senator Simeon Fess had unsuccessfully introduced a bill in 1931 to reserve 15% of radio channels for nonprofit, educational broadcasting. On the history of set-aside proposals, see McChesney, *Telecommunications, Mass Media and Democracy*; and Louise M. Benjamin, *Freedom of the Air and the Public Interest: First Amendment Rights in Broadcasting to 1935* (Carbondale: Southern Illinois University Press, 2001), ch. 12.

3. James Rorty, "The Impending Radio War," *Harpers Magazine* 163 (November 1931): 714–15.

4. Gross W. Alexander of the Pacific-Western Broadcasting Federation in, *Hearings Before the Committee on Interstate and Foreign Commerce, House of Representatives, 73rd Congress, 2nd session, on HR 8301*: 281–91.

Federal Radio Commission had forced his station to cede some of its broadcasting hours to commercial stations, had successfully mobilized a coalition of Catholic and other protesters. They wanted legislation to protect noncommercial broadcasting from a Federal Radio Commission whose decisions seemed to them permanently tilted in favor of the commercial broadcasters.[5] Harney optimistically told a House committee that reserving a quarter of radio frequencies for "human welfare agencies, education, religion, labor organizations, agricultural, cooperative, fraternal organizations," rather than "handing them over to purely commercial interests for exploitation," was a principle that none could dare oppose.[6]

The broadcasting industry argued that such an extensive set-aside would destroy American radio, necessarily taking licenses away from established broadcasters. The National Association of Broadcasters pointed out that under the 1927 Radio Act, its members were already legally required to broadcast in the "public interest, convenience, or necessity," and it characterized set-asides as benefits for special interests that should be resisted on behalf of the "public as a whole"—in whose name they claimed to speak.[7] Harney memorably put the opposing case, objecting to any casting of the coalition of education, labor, and religious groups as "special interests": "I say it is not a special interest, unless you want to say that those who are working for human welfare are pursuing special interests and that the gentlemen who are working for their own pockets are not."[8] At issue here was a fundamental and recurring question in the history of American broadcasting—could the diversity of American society be adequately represented in comprehensive, something-for-everyone radio programming, or only by giving all who wanted it access to a broadcasting outlet that would make self-representation possible?

The Wagner-Hatfield amendment was defeated in the Senate, but Section 307(c) of the 1934 Communications Act did stipulate that the newly created FCC must hold hearings on the desirability of frequency set-asides for nonprofit broadcasters. The FCC duly held the inquiry in October and November 1934, amassing nearly 14,000 pages of testimony in the process. In these hearings, the broadcasting industry argued that it was cooperating productively with educators and had been providing the nation with a steady diet of public service programming. Extensive testimony detailed network achievements in religion and public affairs, and in the broadcasting of classical music, always a touchstone for those who held high hopes for radio's culturally transforming and improving capacity. CBS president William Paley reported proudly, as part of his defense of the status quo, that jazz programs were less in demand than previously, and that there was

5. Hugh Slotten, *Radio's Hidden Voice: The Origins of Public Broadcasting in the United States* (Urbana: University of Illinois Press, 2009), ch. 4.

6. *Hearings Before the Committee on Interstate and Foreign Commerce, House of Representatives, 73rd Congress, 2nd session, on HR 8301*: 147–53.

7. "Supplementary Statement by the National Association of Broadcasters Regarding the Amendment to HR8301," *Hearings Before the Committee on Interstate and Foreign Commerce, House of Representatives, 73rd Congress, 2nd session, on HR 8301*: 116–17.

8. *Hearings Before the Committee on Interstate and Foreign Commerce, House of Representatives, Seventy-Third Congress, 2nd session, on HR 8301*: 161.

increasing audience interest in symphonic music and opera.[9] [Figure 1.1.] The networks, understanding the strength of the political challenge they faced, went to considerable trouble and expense to document all the ways in which they already were national and public service broadcasters.

The educators and radio reformers for their part were very restrained in the hearings, offering little contestation of the continued commercial dominance of American radio. Most did not even raise the question of the creation of an American national public broadcaster on the model of the BBC. Two state university presidents privately expressed interest in a scheme that would give states, perhaps through their universities, responsibility for some portion of the broadcast day.[10] Floyd Reeves of the Tennessee Valley Authority said publicly that he thought the U.S. government should "own and operate a national chain of radio stations," but he was quickly corrected by the TVA chair who confirmed (after prompting from the White House) that the TVA did not favor "government

Figure 1.1. Dapper CBS president William S. Paley in 1939. Harris and Ewing collection, Library of Congress: LC-H22-D- 5684.

9. "W. S. Paley, Against 'Forced' Programs," *New York Times*, October 18, 1934: 26.
10. Orrin Dunlap, "Congress Wants It," *New York Times*, October 14, 1934: XII; Henry K. Norton to William Hard, October 1, 1934, folder 28, box 26, NBC records, WHS.

administration of radio programs."[11] Overall, NBC's H. K. Norton heard "very little in the way of serious attack upon the business as now conducted."[12] He noted with evident relief that at the hearings "the question of government control did not arise; nor was there any suggestion of stations to be operated on a commercial but non-profit basis."[13]

The FCC recommended to Congress in January 1935 that no set-asides be made. "Flexibility" was to be preferred; educational organizations would be better off cooperating with commercial broadcasters, using existing facilities with their "costly and efficient equipment" rather than seeking their own stations. "Cooperation in good faith" was to be required from the broadcasters, and this cooperation should be "under the direction, and the supervision of the Commission."[14] To promote and study this cooperation, the FCC set up the Federal Radio Education Committee (FREC), to be chaired by John Studebaker, the U.S. commissioner of education.[15]

The story of the public contest over radio in 1934 has most often previously been told as the end of something, as the final act of the "battle for control of U.S. broadcasting."[16] Barnouw called the hearings and report the "formal interment" of the reform cause.[17] McChesney argued that the FCC's January 1935 report marked "the death of the movement for broadcast reform", and that before long the "previous fifteen years of struggle and debate over the control and structure of U.S. broadcasting had been erased from history" and from memory.[18]

It is certainly true that after 1934 few informed observers in the United States seriously countenanced the creation of an American BBC. The setting aside of frequencies on the now crowded AM band was henceforth politically inconceivable (although in 1940, and again in 1945, the FCC did set aside frequencies on the FM band for noncommercial educational stations).[19] But it is also true that for at least a decade after 1934, commercial broadcasters remained anxious about the terms of their tenure of the airwaves. The industry journal *Broadcasting* warned at the start of 1936 that "alertness rather than smugness" had to be the watchword, and that those broadcasters who wanted to make of radio "a mere adjunct of show business, with all its ballyhoo and blatancy," could prove fatal to all.[20]

---

11. "Tennessee Valley Authority Urges Federal Chain," *Education by Radio* 4, no. 12 (October 25, 1934): 45; Eugene E. Leach, *Tuning Out Education: The Cooperation Doctrine in Radio, 1922–38*, http://www.current.org/coop/coop5.html; McChesney, *Telecommunications, Mass Media, and Democracy*: 217–20.

12. Henry K. Norton to R. C. Patterson Jr., October 4, 1934, folder 28, box 26, NBC records, WHS.

13. H. K. Norton to William Hard, October 1, 1934, folder 28, box 26, NBC records, WHS.

14. FCC press release, December 18, 1935, folder 24, box 68, NBC records, WHS.

15. "Joint Committee to Lay Plans for Educational Cooperation," *Broadcasting* 10, no. 1 (January 1, 1936): 22.

16. Accounts that end with Wagner-Hatfield include most prominently McChesney, *Telecommunications, Mass Media, and Democracy*; Smulyan, *Selling Radio*; and Benjamin, *Freedom of the Air* .

17. Barnouw, *The Golden Web*: 26.

18. McChesney, *Telecommunications, Mass Media, and Democracy*: 226, 224, 242.

19. Smulyan, *Selling Radio*: 130.

20. "1936 and Public Service," *Broadcasting* 10, no. 1 (January 1, 1936): 32.

The end of one story is, however, always the beginning of another, and in this case it is a much less explored one. In focusing on the leadership of the organized broadcast reform movement, on the either/or question of public or private ownership, and in looking for decisive legislative outcomes, historians have been too quick to announce the total victory of the commercial broadcasters and the complete evaporation of the way of thinking that saw the free market and the public interest in radio as in permanent tension. If we shift our attention from political economic questions of public or private ownership to cultural and social questions about radio's civic role, the Faustian aspect of the 1934 settlement becomes clearer.

The American radio system in the second half of the 1930s was profoundly shaped by broadcaster anxiety about possible reform. Little about the system makes sense if we attempt to understand broadcasting simply as a business like any other. The networks in particular were working hard to placate influential critics who continued to worry that a merely commercial broadcasting system would neglect high culture, education, and civic life. They had to be seen to cooperate with entities such as the FREC, set up to "eliminate controversy and misunderstanding" between educators and broadcasters and to "promote actual cooperative arrangements." FREC's budget came half from broadcasters through the NAB and half from the large foundations.[21] Behind the scenes, there was anxious negotiation—NBC's Frank Russell reported that the industry representatives had made it very clear that they would not subscribe their share of the budget "until we definitely know that the instructions to the Committee are satisfactory to us." The requested adjustments included striking out provisions that required the committee to inquire into "ways and means of preserving the air as a public forum," and into other national systems of broadcasting. This reaffirmed that the battle of 1934 had been won by the broadcasters, and that structural reform was off the table. The FCC in its report to Congress had, Russell happily reported, "thoroughly and completely upheld the American System of broadcasting."[22] But there was still a great deal for the broadcasters to worry about in the ongoing public discussion of radio's civic responsibilities.

FREC's official position was that the solution to the radio problem was cooperation, but that more research was needed into just how cooperation would work. Research was sponsored in areas such as the training of teachers in the educational uses of radio. An experimental script and idea exchange was established, which by late 1939 had distributed 250,000 copies of educational radio scripts to stations around the country.[23] On the foundation side, Rockefeller's General Education Board gave money for an evaluation of educational radio programs at Ohio State University and a study of the *Wisconsin School of the Air* , as well as for a major radio research project at Princeton University.[24] Carnegie

---

21. "Joint Committee to Lay Plans for Educational Cooperation," *Broadcasting* 10, no. 1 (January 1, 1936): 22.

22. Frank Russell to R. C. Patterson Jr., September 21, 1935, folder 42, box 91, NBC records, WHS.

23. "Minutes of the Meeting of the Executive Committee of the Federal Radio Education Committee September 29, 1939," folder 24, box 68, NBC records, WHS.

24. Paul Seattler, *The Evolution of American Educational Technology* (Mahwah, NJ: L. Erlbaum, 2005): 238–43.

funded a study of radio listening groups.[25] The foundations had by early 1939 pledged a total of $355,000, making them major players in the drama of reconciliation between education and commercial radio.[26] Meanwhile the broadcasters themselves were to fund further FREC research on topics such as publicizing educational radio programs and listener ideas of what was educational.

FREC's activities soon faded from public view, leading Barnouw to conclude that the reformers had been "skillfully shunted into busy-work." But, he astutely observed, that was not the whole story: "In winning their victory, networks and stations had made promises that were hostages."[27] In December 1938, Levering Tyson, a veteran radio reformer known as an advocate of cooperation with the networks, wrote to Neville Miller of the NAB, reemphasizing the importance of industry cooperation with radio reform moderates: "Really responsible educators and top-flight men in the profession," he said, were in agreement that cooperation, rather than separate public or educational stations, was the solution. But the industry had to take self-regulation more seriously, Tyson warned, really "establish standards and maintain them," or

> one of these days all of us are going to wake up and find that a loony Congress has taken over broadcasting…and I don't mean maybe. A great many people, intelligent members of different branches of society, who do not believe in government control and who know of and applaud the obvious public services radio has performed (such as flood relief), who admire the fine things which we get on air (like the Philharmonic and Toscanini programs)…nevertheless, are disgusted with the average and less than average programs and practices of broadcasters; they openly state they would prefer a government system to what we have now.

With the "jittery feeling abroad today," Tyson concluded, "you cannot tell what a crazy Congress might do."[28] Responsive to fears such as these, network executives were in many cases quite prepared to authorize significant investment in high cultural, civic, and educational programming, just as they were more than happy to open their microphones to elected leaders. In particular, they were eager to cooperate with the federal government, lest New Deal reform activism should spill over into a plan for a national public broadcaster; the presidents of both NBC and CBS telegraphed President Roosevelt just after his inaugural address, for example, to offer him access to their networks whenever he

25. Frank Ernest Hill, *Radio's Listening Groups: The United States and Great Britain* (New York: Columbia University Press, 1941).

26. National Association of Broadcasters, "The FREC? What Does It Mean to the Broadcaster?," folder 24, box 68, NBC records, WHS; William J. Buxton, "The Political Economy of Communications Research," in Robert E. Babe (ed.), *Information and Communication in Economics* (Boston: Kluwer Academic, 1994): 168, sees the Rockefeller Foundation acting as "a de facto agent of the state."

27. Barnouw, *The Golden Web*: 26–27.

28. Levering Tyson to Neville Miller, December 9, 1938, folder 66, box 62, NBC records, WHS. Tyson had been director of the Carnegie-funded National Advisory Council on Radio in Education, which worked for cooperation between education and the commercial broadcasters, but was becoming disillusioned with the commercial broadcasters—see Slotten, *Radio's Hidden Voice*: 177.

wished.[29] Inasmuch as this was a pragmatic strategy designed to blunt the criticisms of reformers seeking a larger reshaping of American broadcasting, it succeeded. But it was a strategy openly acknowledged only behind the scenes. In public, American radio trumpeted a different story—that only in the United States was radio free.

FREEDOM ON THE AIR

Herbert Hoover, as U.S. secretary of commerce, told a congressional committee in 1924 that radio was "a public concern...to be considered primarily from the standpoint of public trust." Hoover said that radio was too important to be carried on merely as a business "for private gain, for private advertisement, or for the entertainment of the curious."[30] Historians of American radio usually quote these words in elegiac voice, lamenting what might have been. Within 10 years, the industry orthodoxy in the United States—and arguably the dominant public opinion—was that freedom of the air could be maintained only by a commercial system, free from government interference or propaganda. "I have seen no inclination on the part of our government or lawmakers to interfere with freedom of expression on the radio," observed RCA president David Sarnoff in 1935. "This is not true in many other countries."[31] [Figure 1.2.] The role of government, in the golden age of American radio, was to be understood only negatively, as censorship, and conversely radio's freedom was understood to rest upon government restraint or inaction.

That was in comparative terms a striking outcome. Indeed, in "many other countries," Hoover's 1925 view remained the orthodoxy—that radio was simply too important to be

Figure 1.2. RCA president and NBC chairman of the board David Sarnoff in 1939. Harris and Ewing collection, Library of Congress, LC-H22-D- 5686.

29. President's Personal File 75, Franklin D. Roosevelt Presidential Library, Hyde Park, NY.

30. In Marvin R. Bensman, *The Beginning of Broadcast Regulation in the Twentieth Century* (Jefferson, NC: McFarland, 2000): 99.

31. Orrin E. Dunlap Jr., "Sarnoff Scans the Radio World," *New York Times*, October 27, 1935: SM 5.

left to the market and the profit-making imperative. The Canadian Radio League, set up by nationalist young men, argued that radio was so vital that "no other agency than the State should ultimately be responsible for its operation and control."[32] Graham Spry, of the League, argued that to permit commercial interests in broadcasting "is tantamount to abandoning the rash but noble hope for democratic government."[33] The boldness of the attempt south of the border to establish exactly the opposite as the common sense of the matter is thrown into sharp relief in this comparative perspective.

The tale of the U.S. radio industry's continuing attempts to legitimate itself after 1934 can in one sense easily be told. There were still some Americans who obstinately and publicly persisted in seeing the economic power of the big broadcasters as inimical to freedom of speech on radio and to the proper educational, cultural, and civic use of the medium. That view—now cast as radical—gained little time on the air. [34] It did, however, retain its power to haunt the industry, to shape its sense of what it had to do to defend the status quo of American broadcasting. Persuading Americans that the growing economic might and cultural influence of commercial radio was not just a good thing, but a distinctively American good thing, would clearly be to their advantage.

In the later 1930s, a sustained and sophisticated public relations campaign was aimed at building nationalist pride in the retention of a predominantly commercial broadcasting sector. To that end, the U.S. radio industry in the 1930s talked insistently and often of the "American system" of broadcasting, cloaking the status quo in a patriotic haze. The term *American system* had a long history in U.S. nationalism, from advocates of tariff protection in the early 19th century to conservative opponents of the New Deal in the twentieth.[35] When NBC's Franklin Dunham spent an evening with progressive academics from Columbia University in 1936, debating radio and education, he came away with the strong impression that "those who were opposed to the present system of broadcasting are also fundamentally opposed to the present system of American government."[36] Within the network, Dunham was at the liberal end, but even he by 1936 had come to see the question of support for American commercial broadcasting as a matter of national loyalty.

The "American system" of broadcasting was most commonly described by its advocates as "free." "There is no radio freedom in all the world like that of the United States," NBC vice president John Royal reported happily, after returning from a 1938 European tour.[37] [Companion website link 1.1.] America's free radio, RCA president David Sarnoff

32. Marc Raboy, *Missed Opportunities: The Story of Canada's Broadcasting Policy* (Montreal: McGill-Queens University Press, 1990): 43.

33. Quoted in Mary Vipond, *Listening In: The First Decade of Canadian Broadcasting 1922–1932* (Montreal: McGill-Queen's University Press, 1992): 228.

34. See, e.g., Ruth Brindze, *The Truth About Radio—Not to Be Broadcast* (New York: Vanguard, 1937); Nathan Godfried, *WCFL, Chicago's Voice of Labor, 1926–78* (Urbana: University of Illinois Press, 1997); National Advisory Council on Radio in Education, Committee on Civic Education by Radio, and American Political Science Association, *Four Years of Network Broadcasting: A Report* (Chicago: University of Chicago Press, 1937).

35. See, e.g., *Facts—The New Deal versus American System* (Chicago: Republican National Committee, 1936).

36. Franklin Dunham to John Royal, March 3, 1936, folder 6, box 92, NBC records, WHS.

37. Orrin Dunlap, "An American Showman's View," *New York Times*, May 29, 1938.

explained, paid its own way through commercial advertising and broadcast the "best programs produced anywhere," thus supplementing existing freedoms of religion and speech and press with the new freedom of radio.[38] The idea of freedom has had extraordinary currency and centrality in American society—Foner argues that "no idea is more fundamental to Americans' sense of themselves as individuals and as a nation."[39] It is thus little surprise that American radio was widely understood as peculiarly free. But what was meant by free radio? There were two main themes to the discussion through the 1930s. The first was the absence of government control. Industry spokesmen constantly stressed government censorship as the most potent enemy of radio freedom.[40] They worked hard to establish as common sense the view that the main threat to free radio came from government—either from the possibility of government entering the broadcasting field as a competitor or from the heavy hand of official censorship and regulation. Edward M. Kirby, then director of public relations for Nashville station WSM, wrote a credo for the American listener in 1940: "No person decrees to what I shall listen; no government taxes me. In America radio is free."[41] [Figure 1.3.] Freedom was understood here as something wrested from government, to be defended by individual listeners. The second important theme was a claim about the democratic consequences of the commercial basis of American broadcasting—that the necessary responsiveness of commercial radio to audience preferences was a source and a sign of democratic freedom.[42] "Democratic control of programs," explained radio advertising expert Herman Hettinger, "implies control by the listening majority."[43]

On the other side, radio reformers disputed the idea that there existed anything as organized or rational as an American "system"—"there is actually no system in the ordinary sense of the term," observed BBC director general John Reith in 1931.[44] Radio reformer Joy Elmer Morgan wrote that radio broadcasting in the United States was "the exact opposite of a system"; it was rather "one mad scramble of powerful commercial interests to gain control of this new means of reaching the human mind." He stressed the continuing "chaos" of American radio—the same language used by British critics.[45] John Reith also went out of his way in 1937 to question simple American claims about radio and freedom. "A great deal is said about freedom of this and that," he told a conference in London. "A great deal of nonsense too." He argued that either government or commercial control could curtail a broadcaster's freedom.[46]

38. "Radio Self-Rule Urged by Sarnoff," *New York Times*, November 15, 1938: 19.

39. Eric Foner, *The Story of American Freedom* (New York: W. W. Norton, 1998): xii.

40. McChesney, *Telecommunications, Mass Media, and Democracy*: 239–51.

41. Quoted in Paul F. Peter, "The American Listener in 1940," *Annals of the American Academy of Political and Social Science* 213, no. 1 (January 1941): 1.

42. Craig names this principle "listener sovereignty": *Fireside Politics*: xvii.

43. Herman S. Hettinger, "Broadcasting in the United States," *Annals of the American Academy of Political and Social Science* 177 (January 1935): 11.

44. J. C. W. Reith, "Broadcasting in America," *Nineteenth Century* 110 (August 1931), reprinted in E. C. Buehler (ed.), *American vs. British System of Radio Control* (New York: H. W. Wilson, 1933): 282.

45. Joy Elmer Morgan, "The New American Plan for Radio," in Bower Aly and Gerald D. Shively (eds.), *Debate Handbook: Radio Control* (Columbia, MO: Staples, 1933): 82.

46. "Sir John's View of News," *New York Times*, June 27, 1937: 146.

I'm GLAD AMERICAN Air IS FREE*!*

I BOUGHT a radio for Christmas.

It's a beauty, too, with an all-wave receiver.

These cold winter days I tune-in the world.

But I hear strange things.

Things I never hear in American radio.

Some of the programs are good, all right. They seem to know their music over there.

But foreign radio is so different, so tense. Surrounding each broadcast there seems to be an atmosphere of awful dread, of fierce control.

That sense of freedom to which we are accustomed just isn't there.

Much of the air is oratory, inflamed and destructive. Neighbors seem to be set against neighbors. They are selling hatred.

Maybe I don't understand the language, but the words, the tones, the manner of delivery can be understood by anyone with ears to listen.

That isn't our conception of radio's place in the world.

We don't do that here.

No one on the American air dares tell us to hate one another because of race or religion.

No one dares use the air to drive us apart. *In America radio brings us closer together.*

American radio enjoys freedom in which to contribute the greatest service to the American listener, to develop the art to its widest possibilities. Here its purpose is to entertain, to inform, to serve.

We are free to turn the dial until we find the message, the service, or the music to match the mood we feel. The only dictator we know in America is the dictate of our own desire.

I'm glad the American Air is free.

I'm glad particularly now, because American radio is free to bring us again the Christmas message: *Peace on Earth, Good-will toward Men.*

This is the American system of broadcasting.

A message in the interests of the American system of broadcasting by one proud to be a part thereof; by one privileged from time to time to have contributed to its progress, by one seeking new ways to broaden its service to the American listener.

W S M

The Air Castle of the South

50,000 WATTS

E. W. CRAIG, *Vice-President* ● IN CHARGE OF RADIO
HARRY STONE, *General Manager*

OWNED AND OPERATED BY

THE NATIONAL LIFE AND ACCIDENT INSURANCE COMPANY, INC., NASHVILLE, TENNESSEE

Figure 1.3. The American system compared. Edward M. Kirby perhaps also had a hand in this eloquent 1937 WSM advertisement in the trade journal *Broadcasting*, with its striking claim that "The only dictator we know in America is the dictate of our desire." WSM advertisement, "I'm Glad AMERICAN Air IS FREE," *Broadcasting* 12, no. 12 (Dec. 15, 1937): 43. Reprinted by permission of Gaylord Entertainment Company.

Events in Europe seemed to provide more and more supporting evidence for the exceptionalist claim that nowhere else was radio so free. The historical coincidence of the resurgence of undemocratic forms of government in Europe and the entrenchment of commercial broadcasting in the United States encouraged many industry defenders to posit a connection—to argue that it was the commercial basis of American broadcasting that accounted for its freedom. A Chicago radio manufacturer returned home from Europe in 1937 with a renewed sense of "how lucky we are in our American radio situation," and observed that those Americans who were "forever grumbling and grouching about our commercial announcements would, I think, be willing to take twice as much if the alternative were to listen daily to the propaganda dished out" by the government broadcasters of Europe.[47] New England radio commentator Marion Hertha Clarke was voicing conventional wisdom when she claimed in early 1941 that the United States had the "last free radio system in the world."[48] Those who complained about advertising on radio could increasingly be portrayed as naïve and even parochial in outlook.

The genius of industry arguments in defense of the "American system"—in this environment—thus lay in the assertion that it was the commercial organization of American radio that made it both free and democratic. The market in commercial radio broadcasting was the guarantee that the people rather than the government ruled the airwaves, that their preferences actively and continually shaped the content of broadcasts, thus ensuring freedom of speech on the air. NBC president Niles Trammell argued strikingly in 1946 that advertising was not only in the public interest, it was "the very expression of that interest." Freedom and commercial competition were inseparable, he insisted: "There can be no freedom without competition and no competition without freedom."[49]

Freedom of the air and the commercial basis for broadcasting thus became twinned ideals, both in need of constant defense. Neville Miller, president of the National Association of Broadcasters, warned in 1938 that "invasion of our free, competitive system of American broadcasting from any quarter whatsoever will be met with all the determined resistance at my command, and I believe as well with the determined resistance of the people who own and use the thirty million radio sets operative throughout America."[50] A commercial radio system became, in this increasingly persuasive way of thinking, an essential precondition of democracy and true liberty. The freedom that American broadcasters so insistently defended was first of all an economic freedom—the right of broadcasters to operate radio as a business, the right of listeners to choice and variety of programs—and then a political freedom, the right to hear broadcast speech uncensored or unintimidated by government. The insistent message of the industry was that these things were linked—that one could not exist without the other—even that they were ultimately indistinguishable. It was an argumentative strategy both breathtakingly bold and brilliantly executed. It worked as well as it did because the languages of freedom and resistance to tyrannical government resonated through American history, but also because the industry succeeded in depicting the choice as between only two clearly defined possibilities.

47. "Lucky U.S., Says Radio Man After Trip to Europe," *Chicago Tribune*, August 22, 1937: W4.

48. "Clubwomen Are Told Public at Fault for Poor Radio Programs," *Lowell Sun*, March 4, 1941: 4.

49. Niles Trammell, "Advertising in the Public Interest," *National Association of Broadcasters—Information Bulletin—Convention* 14, no. 16 (November 25, 1946), box 5B, NAB collection, WHS.

50. Neville Miller, "The Place of Radio in American Life: A Free People Can Never Tolerate Government Control," *Vital Speeches of the Day* 4, no. 23 (September 1936): 715.

STARK ALTERNATIVES

The nationalist language of justification of the freedom of the American system rested upon a series of stark oppositions, between government control and individual liberty, old world and new. These binary oppositions dominated thinking and public discourse about broadcasting through the turbulent 1930s. As the decade progressed, it became more and more difficult to imagine desirable alternatives to the American system. The mounting evidence of the control of radio by the state in fascist and communist nations made government broadcasting less and less politically plausible an option in the United States, and industry spokesmen made much of the contrast. NAB president Neville Miller warned in August 1938 that if "an agency of government seeks to dictate what shall and what shall not be broadcast…that agency is abandoning the democratic pattern and is assuming the technique of the totalitarian state which determines what people shall hear, what they shall say, what they shall read and think."[51] The strategy of industry publicists was to make the choice about radio sharply defined and simple, to depict the broadcasting question as an all-or-nothing fight for freedom parallel to the broader struggle of the democracies against their dictator enemies. The American public had to be persuaded that it faced only two very stark alternatives. The sharply polarized politics of the era helped broadcasters suggest that there could be no compromise for radio, no midpoint between complete freedom and wholesale surrender to government control.

Ed Kirby, director of public relations at the National Association of Broadcasters, wrote to NBC president Lenox Lohr's assistant in November 1938, rehearsing the argument that he thought the American broadcasting industry needed to be making in its own defense:

> I do not believe the American public realizes the full significance of the commercial structure of radio in this country; it does not realize that if economic support for radio did not come from the advertisers, then an assessment would have to be made to pay the bill; and this is nothing short of a tax, and a tax is nothing short of government domination, political control and loss of the American radio freedom of expression.[52]

The length of the sentence emphasized the series of slides from one point to another—the effect of the industry case was to render invisible any resting place between the market freedom of commercial broadcasting on the one hand, and totalitarian governmental control and loss of freedom of speech on the other. Commercial broadcasting was here aligned with the spirit of the American Revolution, as a defense of freedom against government tyranny. For defenders of the American system, publicly funded radio was inevitably "government-controlled," politically partisan and intolerant, while for-profit commercial broadcasting delivered freedom for all. No distinction between public funding and government "control" could be admitted.

Actually the radio world of the 1930s was a good deal more variegated and complicated than that. Until the formation of National Public Radio in 1970, the United States

---

51. *Broadcasting* 15, no. 5 (September 1, 1938): 14.
52. Ed Kirby to Martha McGrew, November 26, 1938, folder 66, box 62, NBC records, WHS.

did not have a national public broadcaster, and we can describe its national broadcast system after the 1920s as predominantly commercial. There had been an important not-for-profit broadcasting sector in the 1920s, when educational institutions, labor unions, churches, and other welfare bodies had moved quickly to attempt to harness the wonderful capacities of broadcasting for their own purposes. But only a small proportion of these stations survived into the 1930s. A 1937 study found that, of 202 broadcasting licenses issued to educational institutions, only 38 remained at the beginning of 1937, and many of those were struggling to find adequate means of support.[53] Some of the survivors from this nonprofit sector grew stronger in the 1930s but served nevertheless as a reminder, with their distinctive public service missions, of the massive economic and political dominance of commercial broadcasting in the United States.

Before World War II, this way of organizing broadcasting was unusual but not unique. Some Latin American nations—Bolivia and Chile, for example—followed this predominantly commercial path, with U.S. encouragement.[54] It was true that almost all of Europe—every nation except Luxembourg—had some form of state involvement in broadcasting. The Netherlands was a partial exception; it had only nonprofit broadcasting, but no state funding for the several broadcasters, which represented Protestant, Catholic, and socialist constituencies, and then AVRO, the general or nonpartisan broadcaster.[55] In some countries, the national broadcaster held a monopoly of radio: the BBC in Britain was the most well known example in the United States, but Germany, Japan, the Soviet Union and Iceland also had state broadcasting monopolies. Fascist and communist regimes demonstrated the propaganda potential of the new medium in the hands of partisan state broadcasters. But in much of the world, as in the region, national governments took a more indirect role in broadcasting through the creation of a publicly funded national broadcaster—again, the BBC was the most prominent model—or through licensing a dominant or monopoly non–state broadcaster, as in Turkey, Norway, Estonia and Rumania.[56]

The assertion that the commercial "American system" was the only form of broadcasting befitting a free people could thus be sustained only by a highly selective glance at the rest of the world. In nearby Canada, as well as in distant Australia, South Africa, and France, there were mixed systems, in which the national public broadcaster sat alongside commercial broadcasters. Mixed systems flourished in many nations, large and small—including Ireland, Norway, Poland, Brazil, Mexico, Argentina, and Uruguay. American broadcasters invoked the state monopolies in the fascist and communist nations on the one hand, and went out of their way to discredit the BBC on the other, as the one high-status and potentially appealing state monopoly. About mixed systems they were silent, or even mendacious. The United States, CBS president William S. Paley proclaimed in

53. See S. E. Frost Jr., *Education's Own Stations* (Chicago: University of Chicago Press, 1937): 4–5.

54. See James Schwoch, *The American Radio Industry and Its Latin American Activities 1900–1939* (Urbana: University of Illinois Press, 1990).

55. J. C. H. Blom and Emiel Lamberts (eds.), *History of the Low Countries* (Providence, RI: Berghahn, 1999): 430.

56. Armstrong Perry, "Radio Broadcasting in Europe," *Education by Radio* (February 1932), reprinted in Buehler (ed.), *American vs. British System of Radio Control*: 115–30.

1935, "is the one important nation in which broadcasting has not been made a government monopoly."[57] Only the adjective *important* saved that from being a simple untruth. Paley's statement certainly concealed the fact that some quite substantial Western nations were operating mixed systems with apparent satisfaction. This was what the U.S. broadcasting industry did not want known or understood. When University of Wyoming president and National Committee on Education by Radio chairman Arthur Crane proposed a mixed system for the United States—a "combination plan" with a "government chain paralleling the present commercial chain"—he stressed that paralleling meant "supplementing but not supplanting, not displacing" commercial broadcasting. NBC's Frank Russell astutely noted that this was "the most dangerous thought today on the subject."[58]

The term *mixed system* (or *dual* or *hybrid broadcasting systems*—no firm terminology seems to have evolved, reflecting perhaps the oddly uncertain status of what was in fact a common solution to the radio problem) perhaps falsely suggests a clear and organized division of labor between a noncommercial national public broadcaster and a commercial sector. In fact, the label conceals much further diversity and complexity. There were almost endless national variations on the theme of mixed broadcasting systems through the 1930s, particularly in New World nations. In Canada, the national broadcaster carried advertisements, because it operated in large part through affiliation with existing commercial stations; Vipond has argued that this Canadian arrangement placed the public and commercial broadcasting systems "in a symbiotic relationship, mutually dependent."[59] In Australia, the Australian Broadcasting Commission was established in 1932, the same year as the Canadian Radio Broadcasting Commission, but never carried advertising.[60] Before 1936, private stations existed in New Zealand but were forbidden to carry advertising; after 1936, the national broadcaster operated both the noncommercial national service and local commercial stations that aimed to provide a "high standard" of popular entertainment and to maximize advertising revenue—this was a public broadcasting monopoly with mixed revenue sources.[61] In Brazil, there was a small government-run educational broadcasting service and a larger commercial sector, but the government in the 1930s attempted considerable management through regulation of the programming of the commercial stations.[62] In Mexico, while there were in the 1930s three government-run stations, radio was mainly commercial, with many stations having connections

57. William S. Paley, "Radio and the Humanities," *Annals of the American Academy of Political and Social Science* 177, no. 1 (January 1935): 94.

58. Frank Russell to R. C. Patterson Jr., "Statement of Dr. Arthur G. Crane," folder 38, box 36, NBC records, WHS.

59. W. H. N. Hull, "The Public Control of Broadcasting: The Canadian and Australian Experiences," *Canadian Journal of Economics and Political Science/Revue Canadienne d'Economique et de Science Politique* 28, no. 1 (February 1962): 114–26; Mary Vipond, "British or American? Canada's 'Mixed' Broadcasting System in the 1930s," *Radio Journal* 2, no. 2 (2004): 91.

60. The Canadian Broadcasting Corporation replaced the CRBC in 1936.

61. Patrick Day, *The Radio Years: A History of Broadcasting in New Zealand* (Auckland: Auckland University Press): 229.

62. Daryle Williams, *Culture Wars in Brazil: The First Vargas Regime, 1930–1945* (Durham: Duke University Press, 2001): 85.

to the U.S. radio networks; these commercial stations were, however, subject to extensive nationalist government regulation designed to ensure Mexican content and avoidance of controversial material, and the government could claim access to airtime on them for direct broadcasts.[63] In Venezuela, commercial broadcasting began in 1930, but a state-run national service was established alongside it in 1936.[64] Remarkable variation existed then in dual systems—variation in degree of separation between public and private broadcasters, in funding arrangements, and in the amount of regulation practiced on the commercial sector. In the actual world of 1930s broadcasting, there were not stark choices, simple oppositions between freedom and tyranny, or between market and government solutions. Nations inventively found many different resting places between these polar extremes.

In at least some of the nations with dual systems, the existence of a national broadcaster liberated commercial stations from any too onerous civic or national responsibilities, leaving them free simply to act as purveyors of decent entertainment, while the public broadcasters took on the self-consciously nation-building roles. In Australia, for example, the commercial stations in the 1920s were not expected to supply the comprehensive service required of the taxpayer-supported national stations. They were, Lesley Johnson notes, "unfettered by notions of the public interest or national service." On the other side, some at the Australian Broadcasting Commission could argue that the existence of commercial stations freed their organization from the need to cater to popular tastes.[65] Dual systems could allow this kind of bifurcation—education, self-improvement, nation-building from the public broadcaster, and popular entertainment from the commercials. When the president of the Australian Federation of Broadcasting Stations visited the United States in 1935, he explained frankly to the American industry that there were real advantages to such a dual system. "Actually, the government system is a boon to commercial operators," he reported. "It keeps the wailing crusaders off our necks and leaves us free to produce programs without interference from outsiders."[66] But this was not a message the U.S. industry generally was prepared to hear; it did not want to acknowledge that any such compromise was possible.

The occasional press article that did discuss the existence of mixed systems tended to explain them away as the product of peculiar national circumstances—in the cases of Canada and Australia, for example, of small populations and large distances.[67] Far more

63. Michael S. Werner (ed.), *Concise Encyclopedia of Mexico* (London: Fitzroy Dearborn, 2001): 663–66.

64. Mark Dineen, *Culture and Customs of Venezuela* (Westport, CT: Greenwood, 2001): 75–76.

65. Lesley Johnson, *The Unseen Voice: A Cultural Study of Early Australian Radio* (London: Routledge, 1988): 61, 151. On the Australian hybrid system, see also Bridget Griffen-Foley, "The Birth of a Hybrid: The Shaping of the Australian Radio Industry," *Radio Journal* 2, no. 3 (2004): 153–69; Bridget Griffen-Foley, *Changing Stations: The Story of Australian Commercial Radio* (Sydney: University of NSW Press, 2009).

66. "Public Operation Not Suitable Here Says Anzac Chief," *Broadcasting* 8, no. 12 (June 15, 1935): 38.

67. See, for example, Orrin Dunlap on Canadian broadcasting: "Radio Reciprocity—Science and Geography Lead the Dominion to Combine American and British Radio," *New York Times*, March 6, 1938: 160, and Larry Wolters on Australian radio: "Radio Stops for Tea—and Beer in Australia," *Chicago Tribune*, June 26, 1938: SW4.

often, however, attention was focused on the dramatic contrast of freedom and compulsion that could be generated by a simple comparison of the United States and a generalized "Europe." "We desire to emphasize the freedom of speech without any restriction on the part of the party in power," explained FCC chair Anning Prall in 1936. Other nations had chosen an opposite course, but "our country has decided upon the so-called American system. In this country, we believe that broadcasting can be a medium for promoting good or evil, depending upon the manner in which it is used."[68] Prall's stark oppositions perfectly expressed the dominant understanding of radio in the United States.

My argument is that the structure of national broadcasting systems and regulatory environments had significant effects, often invisible to those inside the system, on the kind of programming that occurred within them. In the various national contexts, the mainstream historiography narrates the evolution of the national broadcasting system as a story of progress and development, while the more critical historiography stresses the contingency of the eventual outcome. So McChesney recaptures the moment in the early 1930s when the United States might have had a national public broadcaster, and Canadian and Australian radio historians emphasize the happenstance of directions taken as a result of initial appointments to the CRBC and ABC. Reminding us that things might have worked out differently is an important function of critical history. But so is considering the structural effects of the various outcomes that did prevail, and there has been much less of that in each of the national historiographies. Those who wrote about U.S. radio in the 1930s, and many of the historians who have written about it since, assumed more than they investigated the uniqueness of American radio. My central assertion is that the distinctiveness of the American system lay in its combining of commercial and civic-national functions. The same broadcasters had to perform both roles. That gave rise, I argue, to some very distinctive tensions within American broadcasting.

CONSENSUAL NATIONAL SYSTEMS

Surprisingly, given the actual diversity of national broadcasting systems, and the enormous importance of broadcasting to both populations and governments, the arrangements chosen for radio within each nation were generally adopted without controversy. In Britain, the establishment of the BBC's monopoly was not politically controversial—the Crawford committee in 1925 and 1926 heard from witnesses who "however different the interests they represented, generally agreed that there should be a single broadcasting authority subject not to trade but to public control."[69] In New Zealand, a Labour government created the national broadcaster, but both sides of politics when in power supported the idea. In Australia, the plan for the ABC came from a Labor government but was enacted by its conservative successor. There was only one dissenting vote in the Canadian House of Commons on the bill to establish the CRBC.

68. "Hopes of the Future," *New York Times*, November 15, 1936: X10.

69. D. L. Le Mahieu, *A Culture for Democracy: Mass Communication and the Cultivated Mind in Britain Between the Wars* (Oxford: Clarendon Press, 1988): 151; Asa Briggs, *History of Broadcasting in the United Kingdom: Volume I: The Birth of Broadcasting* (Oxford: Oxford University Press, 1995): 300.

Once particular national arrangements were in place, dissent was even less likely. The arrangement of a national broadcasting system soon came to seem natural, obvious, and somehow peculiarly attuned to the national character. The Aird Commission in Canada prominently invoked public opinion to legitimate its call for a national broadcasting system—it was what Canadians wanted.[70] "While other and alternative systems might suit the requirements of other countries," observed the first chairman of the CRBC, "in Canada the system which could be most profitably employed was one which responded most directly to the popular will and the national need."[71] Elsewhere too, the quite disparate dual systems came to represent acceptable compromises, rarely challenged politically. Geographic determinism was contradictorily invoked on all sides as part of this naturalizing of the choice of broadcast system. *New York Times* radio columnist Orrin Dunlap opined that "the main argument" was whether a "radio plan suitable to the relatively small area of the British Isles could serve the wide territory of the United States with equal utility."[72] Other commentators asserted, on the contrary, that it was the large territories of Canada and Australia that made them turn both to the state and to private enterprise for their radio service.

In the United States too, the complicated outcomes of choices made about broadcasting policy and practice soon came to seem natural and obvious, and perfectly tailored to the national character. "I think our system of broadcasting is typically American," Harold LaFount of the U.S. Federal Radio Commission observed in 1933, "and that it suits our democratic temperament as no other system I have yet encountered would."[73] Explaining the radio question to high school debaters, speech educator Ezra Buehler wrote, "Since, in the past, it has been an essential characteristic of the American public to frown upon the idea of governmental interference with the natural developments of business, it was only natural therefore that commercial interests under free competition should exercise full control of the broadcasting of radio programs."[74] Anning Prall, FCC chairman in 1936, expressed the view that Americans would not agree to a tax or licensing fee: "It is my personal opinion that American listeners would not stand for the payment of a receiving set tax....It is not the American way of accomplishing things."[75] The American system was thus rapidly assimilated to the perceived national character—Americans had chosen this way of doing things because they were the kind of people they were.

It is very striking then—given how innovative and complex were the solutions arrived at—just how uncontroversial each national solution to the problem of national broadcasting policy proved to be. McChesney claims American distinctiveness because in the

70. Mike Gasher, "Invoking Public Support for Public Broadcasting: The Aird Commission Revisited," *Canadian Journal of Communication* 23, no. 2 (1998). Available: http://www.cjc-online.ca/index.php/journal/article/view/1032. [January 27, 2010].

71. Hector Charlesworth, "Broadcasting in Canada," *Annals of the American Academy of Political and Social Science* 177 (January 1935): 47.

72. Orrin Dunlap, "What Is the Ideal System?" *New York Times*, December 17, 1933: X15.

73. Harold Lafount, "Should the US Adopt the British System of Radio Control?" *Congressional Digest* 12, nos. 8/9 (August/September 1933): 205.

74. E. C. Buehler, "Analytical Discussion," in Aly and Shively (eds.), *Debate Handbook*: 45.

75. "Educators Urge Freedom of Radio," *New York Times*, December 11, 1936: 28.

United States, unlike he says in "most other nations," there has been a lack of fundamental public debate about the media system since the mid-1930s.[76] But in broader comparative perspective, the consensus in the United States appears unexceptional. National media landscapes, no matter how arbitrary or unusual they might have seemed to visitors, quickly took on a semblance of inevitability to those for whom they had become a part of everyday experience. As many in the 1930s hoped or feared, radio entered the commonsense world and shaped it. Radio everywhere succeeded, with extraordinary rapidity, in becoming a taken-for-granted part of life. Scannell writes that broadcasting in Britain lent public life "an ordered, orderly, familiar, knowable appearance by virtue of an unobtrusively unfolding temporal sequence of events that gave substance and structure to everyday life."[77] One measure of the deep imbrication of radio in Americans' lives was the research finding that about a third of American children had dreamed of radio plots.[78] To step outside such deep influence and ask whether another system of radio might be better was not something that most Americans would have had the knowledge or inclination to do. Radio researcher Paul Lazarsfeld, introducing in 1946 the results of a major survey of American listeners' attitudes to radio, drew the conclusion that "within certain limits it is a recognized fact that people like what they get."[79] Former BBC executive and then FCC advisor Charles Siepmann remarked more acerbically that "if the merit or superiority of a broadcast system is to be determined solely by the apparent satisfaction it offers to its listeners...then all systems are sound and superior to all other systems—which is absurd." He noted that "lacking knowledge of any other system, the listener everywhere tends to adapt himself to what he hears."[80] At least some of the passion of the radio reformers arose from this realization that a commercial radio system would soon begin shaping the common sense of the population. Joy Elmer Morgan wrote that radio programs "affect our attitudes, influence our speech, and help to determine our purposes and ideals." Somewhat melodramatically, he concluded that commercialized broadcasting "may threaten the very life of civilization, by subjecting the human mind to all sorts of new pressures and selfish exploitations. It may easily destroy all that the best homes and churches and schools have built up thru the centuries."[81] To critics alert to the ways in which radio listening was embedding itself in, shaping, and structuring everyday life, the organization of the national broadcasting system, its funding basis and civic role, were momentous matters.

76. McChesney, *Telecommunications, Mass Media and Democracy*: 4.

77. Paddy Scannell, *Radio, Television and Everyday Life: A Phenomenological Approach* (Oxford: Blackwell, 1996): 153.

78. Hadley Cantril and Gordon W. Allport, *The Psychology of Radio* (New York: Harper and Brothers, 1935): 34.

79. Columbia University Bureau of Applied Social Research, Paul Felix Lazarsfeld, Harry Hubert Field, National Opinion Research Center, and National Association of Broadcasters, *The People Look at Radio* (Chapel Hill: University of North Carolina Press, 1946): 11.

80. Charles A. Siepmann, *Radio, Television and Society* (New York: Oxford University Press, 1950): 111–12.

81. Joy Elmer Morgan, "The New American Plan for Radio," in Aly and Shively (eds.), *Debate Handbook: Radio Control*: 93.

THE BBC MODEL

When the National Advisory Council on Radio in Education proposed a national debate on radio in 1933, focused on whether the United States should have a "governmentally owned and operated" system, the University Extension Association framed it as a question of whether "the United States should adopt the essential features of the British system of radio control and operation." Thousands of schools and colleges in 33 states debated that topic; perhaps 2.5 million Americans heard the arguments on both sides.[82] There was a network broadcast of a debate on the question, featuring three professors on each side.[83] Handbooks were published to assist debaters.[84] The NAB issued its own booklet, attempting to focus the debate on the shortcomings of the British system rather than on the problems of the American.[85] One of the issues in the background of the broader public discussion about the future of American radio was whether the BBC ought to be understood as "government radio." The BBC was formally a "quasi-public corporation," funded by government but independent of it. In one of the 1933 debate handbooks was reprinted an article by Sir John Reith, in which he emphatically denied that the BBC was a government radio network, and asserted that "in ordinary matters of policy and in management," the BBC was not only "practically autonomous," it had in fact "commercial freedom" to run its affairs.[86] But one of the American debate handbooks, brushing aside such subtle distinctions, advised students that "for the purpose of debate the same type of arguments may be applied as if it were stated that the British government owned and operated its radio system."[87] Looking back, former BBC director of talks Charles Siepmann concluded in 1950 that the idea that the BBC was government-controlled had been "maliciously propagated" in the United States.[88] Assimilating the BBC to the category of "government radio" should have made the negative case an easy winner in the American debates, yet in several reported cases, the affirmative side won.[89]

The BBC could not be ignored in the United States because it represented the most credible and respected alternative to the American system. Michele Hilmes draws attention to the almost obsessive trans-Atlantic dialogue that dominated whatever attention Americans paid to foreign radio before World War II. Both Britain and the United States, she argues, "used the idea of the other as the only conceivable alternative,"

---

82. "Schools in 33 States to Debate Merits of American–British Radio," *New York Times*, October 1, 1933: X9.

83. "Columbia Hails Chicago Station," *Los Angeles Times*, November 1, 1933: 18. Among the speakers for the affirmative were speech professors H. L. Ewbank of Wisconsin and Ezra Buehler of Kansas, both cited elsewhere in this chapter.

84. Aly and Shively (eds.), *Debate Handbook: Radio Control*; Buehler (ed.), *American vs. British System of Radio Control* .

85. McChesney, *Telecommunications, Mass Media, and Democracy*: 160–62.

86. John Reith, "What Europe's Experience Can Offer America" in Bower Aly and Gerald D. Shively (eds.), *A Debate Handbook Supplement on Radio Control and Operation* (Columbia, MO: Staples, 1933): 8.

87. E. C. Buehler, "Analytical Discussion," in Aly and Shively (eds.), *Debate Handbook: Radio Control*: 47.

88. Siepmann, *Radio, Television and Society*: 118.

89. See, for example, Oakland High's defeat of Berkeley High School: *Oakland Tribune*, March 9, 1934: 6; and Purdue's defeat of University of Illinois: *Hammond Times*, December 14, 1933: 10.

thus closing off consideration of any more genuinely popular possibilities. In the United Kingdom, British "quality" was opposed to "the commercial, the local and the popular, with American broadcasting always providing the primary negative example."[90] There was both admiration for aspects of American radio and an overriding concern to limit the Americanization of BBC programs—to develop, for example, truly British forms of light entertainment.[91] The educational side of U.S. radio was less well perceived or understood across the Atlantic. The *Radio Times* observed in 1933 that "we are apt to think of American radio as entirely frivolous" and it noted with some surprise that NBC claimed that 24 percent of its programs were educational.[92]

The existence of the BBC—as a publicly funded national broadcaster formally independent of government—had at least the potential to disrupt the idea that there were only two stark alternatives, commercial freedom or submission to government tyranny and propaganda. There was for that reason considerable public discussion from industry sources in the United States of the shortcomings of the British system. Felix Greene, the BBC's first North American representative, reported that in the United States the "forces entrenched against the proper use of this new medium are so immense" that his problem was not just countering ignorance of the BBC but "the *wrong* information which they have about us (and cling to so tenaciously)."[93] While the BBC could not readily be said to be just an outlet for government propaganda, it could almost as a consequence, however, be vulnerable on another front. One word dominated American discussion of British radio: the *dullness* of British programs became an article of faith among supporters of the American system. A Chicagoan might find radio fare in Britain, predicted radio manufacturer E. H. Scott in 1937, "rather dullish."[94] Articles about the BBC usually began with acknowledgment that some Americans might imagine that radio without commercial interruption would be appealing, but then argued that on closer acquaintance, few Americans would find anything attractive about the lack of choice in British broadcasting. Some Americans thought they wanted the British system of radio because they did not like listening to "long-winded announcements," reported a 1938 article in *Radio Guide*, but did these listeners really want all the things that went with the British system: "Dull programs because of a lack of competition, too high a percentage of what we would call 'sustaining shows'. Frequent changes in program time, unexplained 'dead' time on the air, and so forth."[95] Conceding that the BBC excelled at radio drama and "good music," the *Chicago Tribune*'s radio critic, Larry Wolters, also came, on the

90. Michele Hilmes, "British Quality, American Chaos: Historical Dualisms and What They Leave Out," *Radio Journal* 1, no. 1 (2003): 14.

91. See Simon Frith, "The Pleasures of the Hearth: The Making of BBC Light Entertainment," in Fredric Jameson, Victor Burgin and Tony Bennett (eds.), *Formations of Pleasure* (London: Routledge, 1983): 101–23.

92. Quoted in Valeria Camporesi, *Mass Culture and National Traditions: The BBC and American Broadcasting 1922–1954* (Florence: European Press, 2000): 178.

93. Felix Greene, Confidential Report "USA," March 1, 1936, BBC Written Archives Centre File E1/113/2.

94. "Lucky U.S., Says Radio Man after Trip to Europe," *Chicago Tribune*, August 22, 1937: W4.

95. "Will FDR Be the First Radio Czar?" *Radio Guide*, November 26, 1938: 2.

basis of conversations with a score of British acquaintances, to the reassuring conclusion that most British programs were "pretty dull."[96]

On the other side, U.S. radio reformers were almost equally likely to focus attention on the BBC as the only possible alternative, and to believe that the United States alone in the world had resisted state broadcasting. In 1929, John Reith asserted that "broadcasting should be conducted as a public service and nothing else," describing the "the commercial motive" as "most undesirable."[97] That uncompromising stance had great appeal to many U.S. educators and others dissatisfied with the existing forms of American radio. For reformers in the United States, and for those charged with designing sustaining (non-sponsored) programs, Hilmes argues, "the British model was used...to stand in for any and all possible alternatives to the existing commercial network model."[98] Cornelia Rose, in *National Policy for Radio Broadcasting*, wrote that "elsewhere, with few exceptions, broadcasting facilities are either publicly owned or governmentally controlled."[99] So many analysts of American radio wrote in this mode, as though the distinctiveness of American radio before World War II lay in its not being a government-controlled or government-monopoly system, and the BBC's monopoly typified the rest of the world's radio.

Radio reformers in the United States after 1934 remained very interested in the BBC model, although they found it difficult to get favorable public attention for the issue in the face of the increasingly successful identification of commercial broadcasting as intrinsically American, and as exemplifying fundamental national freedoms. Behind the scenes, the networks even attempted to manage the relationship between American radio reformers and the BBC. John Royal was angry in 1937 when he saw the program for a "Social Control of Broadcasting" conference at Princeton that listed the BBC representative, Felix Greene, as "conference consultant." Greene reported home that, aware as he had been that "the companies have from my first arrival shown nervousness as to any of my activities which even remotely may strengthen the hands of their 'opponents,'" he had carefully declined an invitation to speak at the event, agreeing instead "to meet those especially interested in the B.B.C. in a discussion during which they could ask me questions."[100] Royal admitted no such diplomatic niceties, fuming in turn to Fred Bate, NBC's man in London: "I would like to know how far the BBC is going in this sort of thing in America. We are not doing it in England, and, as you know, you are under instructions not to participate in this sort of thing. Maybe we should do it in England."[101] NBC officials also worried about attempts to bring Sir John Reith to the United States to address the 1937 National Conference on Educational Broadcasting in Chicago—"it will

96. Larry Wolters, "Britain Bars Ads for Decade: Dull Airfare Assured," *Chicago Tribune*, August 2, 1936: 1.

97. "State Control of Broadcasting: Sir John Reith's View," *Times*, July 29, 1930: 12.

98. Michele Hilmes, "*Front Line Family*: 'Women's Culture' Comes to the BBC," *Media, Culture and Society* 29, no. 1 (2006): 7.

99. Cornelia B. Rose, *National Policy for Radio Broadcasting* (New York: Harper and Brothers, 1940): 47.

100. Greene confidential report, May 19, 1937, BBC Written Archives Centre File E1/212/2.

101. John Royal to Fred Bate, March 13, 1937, folder 33, box 93, NBC records, WHS.

not be important enough to warrant Sir John making such a trip," John Royal primed Bate. He reminded NBC president Lenox Lohr that "such conferences are a waste of time and unnecessary, and definitely meddlesome."[102] That the networks were trying to limit American reformers' exposure to the BBC was one good sign of their continuing anxiety about the survival of the "American system." They failed to prevent continuing dialogue and exchange of ideas across the Atlantic. But the underlying cultures of the British and American national systems remained very different.

MODES OF ADDRESS

The BBC provided one strong model of the way a national public broadcaster could talk to its audience—authoritatively, and from a position above controversy. Imitation of the BBC was a significant factor in broadcasting in other English-language systems, just as the BBC continued to provide a defining and enduring point of contrast for U.S. broadcasting. In the United States, intimacy and familiarity were discovered to be the most effective modes in both commercial and other program settings, while the BBC chose impersonal authority.[103] The U.S. networks' early efforts at standardizing voice and producing impersonal distance were overwhelmed by the sheer diversity and linguistic inventiveness of the content of programs, while the BBC had a little more success in standardizing broadcast speech.

The BBC from the mid-1920s insisted on anonymous announcers, in order to create a sense of the organization's "collective personality." The "distanced, anonymous, collective voice" of the BBC, Asa Briggs explains, signified "the authority and respectability of radio."[104] BBC officials were alert to the intrusion both of American expressions and of an American style of address that was considered too informal and cheery—they self-consciously avoided, as Scannell and Cardiff put it, "a democracy of manner and outlook which was as much a matter of communicative style as of content."[105] A report in the *New York Times* in 1930 marveled at the way BBC announcers, "paragons of decorum and good taste," remained "completely unknown," did not become "personalities."[106] Hilda Matheson, the BBC's head of talks from 1926, understood the preference for impersonality in national character terms: "It seems that the British listener prefers that the personalities of those who read his news and his weather reports and announce the items in his programmes should not be unduly conspicuous." Matheson noted approvingly that while the policy of anonymity did not "extinguish" fan mail, it did reduce it "enormously."[107]

102. John Royal to Fred Bate, May 22, 1937, folder 22, box 53, NBC records, WHS.

103. See chapter 2 for a more extended discussion of the widespread perception that U.S. radio was an intimate medium.

104. Asa Briggs, *The Birth of Broadcasting*: 267; Paddy Scannell and David Cardiff, *A Social History of British Broadcasting: Volume One 1922–1939—Serving the Nation* (Oxford: Basil Blackwell, 1991): 317.

105. Scannell and Cardiff, *A Social History*: 293, 298.

106. George Fyfe, "Sidelights on England's Radio," *New York Times*, November 9, 1930: 22.

107. Hilda Matheson, *Broadcasting* (London: Thornton Butterworth, 1933): 54.

Radio listeners in Britain did not write many letters, John Reith observed. "They are not encouraged or invited to communicate," he reported in 1931. The BBC then received barely 100,000 letters a year, and in its early years, unlike its American commercial counterparts, it disdained research on listeners.[108] Finally conceding the need for systematic knowledge of who was listening, the BBC established its Listener Research Department in 1936. The ABC in Australia talked about listener research in 1938, but decided even that late in the decade that it was unnecessary, perhaps even undesirable, on the grounds that even if the majority proved to have lowbrow tastes, that ought not influence the commission's programming.[109] The New Zealand Broadcasting Board conducted one listener questionnaire in 1932, but made no further attempts to study listener preferences.[110]

For national broadcasters in dual systems, where listeners had a choice, the BBC mode had different implications. In Australia and New Zealand, the aspiring national broadcasters imitated the BBC in style, even as they inevitably failed to match its resources or monopolistic, heart-of-empire self-confidence. Lesley Johnson notes that the "formality of tone, correctness of pronunciation and the air of distance" of ABC announcers was in part an attempt to distance the ABC from the "indiscreetness and the over-intimacy" of the commercial stations.[111] The ABC's insistence that its announcers remained anonymous, in contrast to the named and known personalities already becoming popular on Australian commercial radio, contributed to the perception that the national broadcaster was austere and unwelcoming. In New Zealand too, the NZBB strictly limited the projection of individual personality by its announcers—they were addressed on air as "Mr Announcer."[112]

The cultural authority of the BBC was also initially at least thought to rest upon remaining above controversy—controversial discussions were banned until 1928. The dominion broadcasters held to the avoidance of controversy for even longer. The ABC began actively programming controversial talks only in 1935, while in New Zealand the ban on controversial material lasted until 1947.[113] In the United States, in clear contrast, the public interest obligations of the licensing regime ensured that broadcasters did attempt to represent divergent views. Craig concludes that American radio offered "the most voluminous and diverse diet of political advertisements and programming in the world"—reluctantly even including airtime for communists and socialists—although stations and networks moved to forbid sale of time for controversial programming.[114]

108. "Radio Differs Across the Sea," *New York Times*, May 31, 1931: XX9. See also Camporesi, *Mass Culture and National Traditions*, ch. 3.

109. Commercial audience surveys found that only a small minority of listeners—around 20%—listened to the ABC rather than to the commercial stations. K. S. Inglis, *This Is the ABC: The Australian Broadcasting Commission 1932–1983* (Carlton: Melbourne University Press, 1983): 75.

110. Day, *The Radio Years*: 163–64.

111. Lesley Johnson, "The Intimate Voice of Australian Radio," *Historical Journal of Film, Radio and Television* 3, no. 1 (1983): 46.

112. Day, *The Radio Years*: 165.

113. Johnson, *The Unseen Voice*: 190; Day, *The Radio Years*: 288–89.

114. Craig, *Fireside Politics*: 184.

Radio speech everywhere aroused new interest in questions of accent, dialect, tone. Hilda Matheson observed as early as 1933 that "in every broadcasting country," radio had brought about an "education of the ear," and hence a "new self-consciousness," a greater sensitivity toward sounds and accents.[115] The BBC model was in part a matter of voice— exemplary diction, standard pronunciation. The British broadcaster's choice of educated southern English speakers as announcers on its national programs provoked praise but also criticism within the United Kingdom, a contestation of the implied hierarchy in which regional accents were deemed suitable only for local consumption and entered the national public sphere mainly as material for comedy.[116] In Australia too, the issue of accent dogged the national broadcaster. In 1937, 10 of the ABC's 34 announcers were British-born men who spoke the BBC English that the Australian organization deemed most appropriate for broadcasting, to the sustained resentment of Australian nationalists and Labor members of parliament, who more than once attempted to make a political issue of the question.[117] In New Zealand, there were complaints in parliament about the intrusion of American accents and expressions on the air.[118]

Part of the structural reason then that the BBC model eventually seemed so self-evidently wrong for the United States was that the distancing strategies possible in monopoly public or dual systems were simply not possible in the U.S. market-based system. The American networks had the double task of establishing themselves as authoritative national institutions, and of appealing broadly to the people. That made their choice of representative voices even more difficult and contested; their voices of authority had also to be popular. We cannot understand the history of American network broadcasting in the 1930s unless we recognize both the extent to which the networks strove for a national institutional authority and identity comparable to that of the BBC—partly from influence, partly from a largely shared set of elite ideals about culture and language—but also the way that they had to make that attempt from within the very different structural conditions of the American system.

In the United States, radio also stimulated considerable new interest in pronunciation and speech. Radio stations were flooded with inquiries about correct pronunciation.[119] Margaret Cuthbert at NBC claimed in 1935 that radio had led to an "amazing revival of interest in public speaking and debating in our High Schools," and that it had been responsible for an increase in vocabulary, clearer enunciation, and even a speeding up of speech among young people.[120] This heightened interest in correct speech also provided business opportunities. The Better Speech Institute of America began the NBC network

115. Matheson, *Broadcasting*: 62.

116. Lynda Mugglestone, *Talking Proper: The Rise of Accent as Social Symbol*: 276–77; Scannell and Cardiff, *A Social History* .

117. Inglis, *This Is the ABC*: 70. Joy Damousi shows how in Australia this sensitivity to accent (in particular an elite rejection of the sound of American voices) surrounded the introduction of talking films and then radio: "'The Filthy American Twang': Elocution, the Advent of American 'Talkies,' and Australian Cultural Identity," *American Historical Review* 112, no. 2 (April 2007): 394–416.

118. Day, *The Radio Years*: 126.

119. "Educators Plan to Improve Programs," *Broadcasting* 11, no. 12 (December 15, 1936): 72.

120. "Address by Margaret Cuthbert to the General Foundation of Women's Clubs, San Francisco, March 11, 1935," folder 51, box 68, NBC records, WHS.

program "Your English" in 1935, selling a 10-cent pamphlet that listed 500 frequently mis-pronounced words; by 1936, the institute had sold over 100,000 copies of its "Self-Teaching Course in Practical English and Effective Speech."[121]

The American networks in the 1930s sought to train their announcers in correct and standard pronunciation. English-born Frank Vizetelly had worked on numerous dictionaries and language advice books—including *A Desk-Book of Twenty-Five Thousand Words Frequently Mispronounced* .[122] He wrote *How to Speak English Effectively* in 1933 for the CBS announcing staff. Vizetelly professed to admire the "plain talk" of ordinary Americans, but his populism had its own prescriptive and exclusive edge. He began his book with the claim that never in American history had there been such a need for "active steps to establish and maintain the purity of our language," which was under threat from immigrants and their foreign languages and accents.[123] Vizetelly was hopeful that radio would play a homogenizing role, to "iron out certain jarring irregularities common to various sections." He looked forward to achieving "harmony in the pronunciation of words by all announcers."[124] William Cabell Greet, professor of speech at Columbia University, became the CBS language advisor after Vizetelly. He, on the contrary, accepted that radio had not standardized American English, and in fact perceived radio as part of the cause of continuing language diversity, as "we hear over the air all the varieties of American English."[125] At NBC, language advice came from Vida Ravenscroft Sutton, who was born in California and raised in Helena, Montana, before she studied philosophy at the University of Chicago.[126] She presented *The Magic of Speech* on NBC from 1929 until 1937, and trained NBC announcers in pronunciation and speech. Sutton regarded regional "good usage" as perfectly acceptable on the air, but did think that standardization was under way of its own accord: "We are evolving a standard in the United States that promises to unite the most desirable attribute of various sections."[127] The networks took their national and exemplary role seriously, and knew that the network voice had to sound authoritative and correct to most Americans.

The networks early on made a significant effort to recruit college graduates as announcers, projecting a level of class and decorum that they then struggled to maintain within programs. "If our announcers are guilty of mispronunciation," NBC vice president John Royal assured one complainant in 1936, "it is not because they are lacking in education, because more than eighty percent of them are college men."[128] The aspirations in this direction led some early network executives to praise the BBC voice. In 1931, CBS vice

121. "A Market for Words Is Developed by Radio," *Broadcasting* 12, no. 8 (April 15, 1937): 15.

122. Frank Vizetelly, *A Desk-Book of Twenty-Five Thousand Words Frequently Mispronounced* (New York: Funk and Wagnall, 1917).

123. Quoted in Thomas Paul Bonfiglio, *Race and the Rise of Standard American* (New York: Mouton de Gruyter, 2002): 164.

124. "Expert Urges American Speech," *Syracuse Herald*, October 18, 1931: 11.

125. W. Cabell Greet, "A Standard American Language?" *New Republic* 95 (May 25, 1938): 69–70.

126. "Vida R. Sutton, Former Helena Resident, Dies," *Helena Independent Record*, August 5, 1956: 3.

127. Vida Ravenscroft Sutton, "Speech at the National Broadcasting Company" *English Journal* 22, no. 6 (June 1933): 457.

128. John Royal to Colonel H. B. Hayden, February 6, 1936, folder 4, box 108, NBC records, WHS.

president Henry Adams Bellows told a conference that his announcers needed scripts because they were not yet all college-educated. "British program announcing is a good deal better than ours," he asserted, "because the announcers over there are all honor graduates of Oxford and Cambridge." Only when all American announcers were "college men and women of high standing," he concluded, "will we be able to allow them to speak for themselves."[129] Bellows himself had a Harvard PhD in English literature, and had given up his assistant professorship in rhetoric at the University of Minnesota for a career in publishing and then broadcasting; he wrote the program notes for the Minneapolis Symphony and a music column for the *Minneapolis Daily News* in his spare time. *Broadcasting* noted admiringly that Bellows brought to his work in radio "a mind trained in cultural values, a fine perception of radio's place in the social order."[130] Bellows wrote a controversial article on radio for *Harpers* in 1935, in which he called for the "replacement of such executives as see in radio simply a means for making money by persons with a truer sense of their obligations to society."[131] He had, however, left the industry by 1935, with the feeling that radio was not proving to be the domain for educated and talented men he had hoped for.[132]

Women announcers were rare in most English-speaking nations in the 1930s.[133] In the United States, women were seldom employed as station or network announcers. Women's voices were, however, frequently heard on American daytime radio, in serial drama, on homemaker and children's programs, and at all hours as singers.[134] There were commercial reasons for this gender segregation, as a newspaper explained in 1933: "The fact that the radio uses a majority of women announcers and entertainers on the morning and afternoon programs is due not only to the fact the programs involved interest the women more, but listeners to the evening and night programs have objected to the women announcers."[135] There were enough female voices on American radio that visitors noted them as something distinctive. When Alfred Edward Bennett, the president of Australian Federation of Broadcasting Stations, visited the United States in 1935, he made clear his view that radio should be reserved for strong male voices and reported proudly that in Australia, "we don't allow the women to run the country, dominate the men or get too much of a foothold in radio."[136] In Canada too, there was some derision of the very idea of women making serious announcements on the air. In 1937, E. L. Bushnell, the CBC's program director, was interviewed about women announcers:

129. "U.S. Language Follows Radio and Talkies," *Charles City Daily Press*, January 23, 1931: 5.

130. "We Pay Our Respects To—Henry Adams Bellows," *Broadcasting* 3, no. 8 (October 15, 1932): 17.

131. "Bellows Charges FCC, Broadcasters Censor Radio," *Broadcasting* 9, no. 9 (November 1, 1935): 44.

132. See his 1935 correspondence with NBC president M. H. Aylesworth, folder 1, box 34, NBC records, WHS.

133. Anne McKay, "Speaking Up: Voice Amplification and Women's Struggle for Public Expression," in Cheris Kramarae (ed.), *Technology and Women's Voices: Keeping in Touch* (New York: Routledge, 1988): 198–203.

134. See Donna Halper, *Invisible Stars: A Social History of Women in American Broadcasting* (Armonk, NY: M. E. Sharpe, 2001): ch. 3.

135. "Man's Voice Clearer and More Distinct over Telephone and Radio," *Syracuse Herald*, August 27, 1933: 4.

136. "Public Operation Not Suitable Here Says Anzac Chief," *Broadcasting* 8, no. 12 (June 15, 1935): 38.

"But there are some things that women can do very nicely," he said. "A woman might announce a nice symphonic programme if her voice is appealing, or talk to women on home economics or interior decorating."

"Will women announce on news broadcasts?"

"No," he laughed, "I don't think they'll announce on news broadcasts."[137]

Both major U.S. networks in the early 1930s endorsed the view that women would not make suitable announcers. Supervisor of announcers at NBC, P. J. Kelly, believed women "would not be equal to the nervous strain" of announcing, while John Carlile of the CBS production department believed that women's voices were "not impersonal enough" for network announcing. Vida Ravenscroft Sutton also maintained that men were more suited to radio announcing than women—their voices were "better, more even and resonant."[138] There is some evidence that the broadcasters did reflect public opinion in these views. Psychologists Hadley Cantril and Gordon Allport in their 1935 book *The Psychology of Radio* reported that both men and women preferred male voices on the radio. Their research revealed a set of highly gendered expectations and assumptions about male and female voices. Those surveyed found men more natural and more persuasive, particularly when talking about politics, news, or the weather, but expressed a strong preference for women's voices reading poetry.[139]

The ideal of the early network era then was of an educated, authoritative, male announcer employing correct and standard pronunciation. The question of accent was discussed in the 1930s in the United States, and it was widely predicted that, as one newspaper put it, "If we ever attain uniformity in pronunciation, it will be radio that accomplishes it."[140] There was some evidence that radio and other forms of communication and travel were eroding regional differences. Researchers at Brown University reported in 1935, for example, that New Englanders were adopting the pronounced "r" of most other regions of the United States, losing at least some of their distinctive regional accent.[141]

Accented and dialect English was frequently heard on network radio's comedy programs, where regional and ethnic voices were caricatured for laughs, at the very time that the opportunities for actual ethnic or foreign-language broadcasting on smaller, local stations were diminishing. Famously, the first network hit was the minstrelsy of *Amos 'n Andy* from 1929, but there were few occasions before World War II when African American speakers could be heard on radio as themselves.[142] African Americans, Derek Vaillant

137. "No Replacements," *Winnipeg Free Press*, October 25, 1937: 8.

138. "Women Not Wanted as Announcers," *Zanesville Times Recorder*, October 16, 1931: 9.

139. Cantril and Allport, *The Psychology of Radio*: 127–32.

140. "Pronunciation," *Moberly Monitor-Index*, October 26, 1929: 4.

141. "Uniformity of Speech Passing," *North Adams Transcript*, December 20, 1935: 10. Vizetelly thought the pronounced American "r" was a sign of linguistic virility so would not have been pleased by such a change: Bonfiglio, *Race and the Rise of Standard American*: 167.

142. William Barlow, *Voice Over: The Making of Black Radio* (Philadelphia: Temple University Press, 1999): ch. 2; Melvin Patrick Ely, *The Adventures of Amos 'n Andy: A Social History of an American Phenomenon* (New York: Free Press, 1991); Murray Forman, "Employment and Blue Pencils: NBC, Race and Representation 1926–55," in Michele Hilmes (ed.), *NBC: America's Network* (Berkeley: University of California Press, 2007): 117–20.

concluded in his study of Chicago, "were unable to control their radio representations to the extent that others could," and often the African American music being broadcast from venues across the city was played by white musicians.[143] The first successful African American radio announcer, Chicago radio entrepreneur Jack Cooper, spoke standard English rather than black vernacular, after having made his name as a comedian whose routine included a range of ethnic voices. Black actors in comedy roles had sometimes to be taught the minstrel accent. Black musicians, on the other hand, appeared frequently on radio—Duke Ellington had his own NBC network show from 1936, Louis Armstrong from 1937.[144] But it was only after World War II, as advertisers discovered the African American market, that black voices and accents could regularly be heard on American radio. In 1941, the *King Biscuit Time* show began on KFFA in Helena, Arkansas, featuring live performances from blues players Sonny Boy Williamson and Robert Junior Lockwood each lunch hour. Its success demonstrated the existence of a market for vernacular African American speech and music; by 1949, over a hundred black DJs were working on U.S. local radio.[145]

Despite all the efforts of network broadcasters and their linguistic advisers, standardized pronunciation was never achieved either in or out of the studio. Many Americans were pleased to retain their language diversity. "In 1927," wrote William Cabell Greet, looking back a decade later, "many of us thought and said that in ten years radio would have brought one standard English to America. This has not happened."[146] One newspaper noted in 1940 that, while it was "regrettable that greater confidence cannot be placed in the correctness of radio pronunciation and use of words," there was little to be gained from complete standardization of language and consequent loss of "beauty and individuality."[147] An Iowa newspaper editorialized in 1938 that

> in truth it would be a pity were there to be anything like "standard American." It adds variety and interest to our speech that there can co-exist the nasal twang of Upper New England, the precocity of Boston, the soft slur of the South and the hard consonants of the northwest. We are a various people—it is one of our defenses and not least of our virtues.[148]

American radio, in fact, contributed to nonstandard speech because caricatures of nonstandard speech patterns also effectively publicized and celebrated them, and made

143. Derek Vaillant, *Sounds of Reform: Progressivism and Music in Chicago, 1873–1935* (Chapel Hill: University of North Carolina Press, 2003): 236–46.

144. J. Fred Macdonald, *Don't Touch That Dial! Radio Programming in American Life 1920–1960*: Available: http://www.jfredmacdonald.com/blacks.htm. [January 27, 2010].

145. Barlow, *Voice Over: The Making of Black Radio*: 57, 96–98; Kathy Newman, "The Forgotten Fifteen Million: Black Radio, the 'Negro Market' and the Civil Rights Movement," *Radical History Review* 76 (2000): 115–35; Bob Hunter, "74 and Blind, Jack L. Cooper, First Negro Deejay, Still Airs Radio Show," *Chicago Defender*, May 14, 1963: 9.

146. Quoted in "Educators Plan to Improve Programs," *Broadcasting* 11, no. 12 (December 15, 1936): 72.

147. "Variations in Speech," *Mansfield News Journal*, January 24, 1940: 4.

148. "Variable Language," *Mason City Globe Gazette*, September 2, 1938: 4.

linguistic difference a national fascination. Susan Douglas has explored the ways in which dialect, accent, and "linguistic rebellion" became the staples of comedy, radio's most popular entertainment, even as network announcers were, like their counterparts in other nations, being disciplined and taught standard pronunciations.[149] Commercial radio programs and advertisements produced a spoken English marked by speed, exaggeration and the quest for distinctive pronunciation or inflection. As Douglas puts it, linguistic decorum and insubordination "took turns" on American radio.[150] If the formal network announcers aspired to correctness, the comedians who followed them strove to trademark language eccentricities—drawing upon and developing the already rich language traditions of vaudeville, minstrelsy, and ethnic comedy. As network radio drew audiences away from smaller, local, and ethnic stations, actual ethnic voices were replaced in many living rooms by caricatures of them.[151] Hilmes has argued that there was something almost obsessive in the rehearsing of linguistic distinctions—"endlessly circulating and performing structured representations of ethnicity, race, gender…all through language, dialect, and carefully selected aural context," as part of the process by which radio defined the boundaries of national inclusion.[152]

When the secretary of the BBC's Advisory Committee on Spoken English, professor Arthur Lloyd James, visited the United States in 1936, he contrasted the unemotional and impersonal recital of news on the BBC with the "racy journalistic style" of American radio news, "full of metaphor, emotional adjectives and adverbs, and frank criticism." But Lloyd James was also struck by the linguistic distortions introduced by commercial announcement readers: "They use a form of speech accent reinforced almost beyond recognition in their attempt to stress the point at issue." Lloyd James had played a significant role in convincing the BBC of the merits of a standard English pronunciation, and he was happy to share his advice with Americans, recommending that the "hysterical plugging of isolated words be abandoned" and replaced by "normally spoken English with natural accents."[153]

Some of the leaders of American broadcasting certainly agreed with Lloyd James. But American radio needed its linguistic eccentricities, rebellions, and playfulnesses. Radio's making of distinctions had always to be inclusive, creating a new mass community of radio insiders. Beginning with Amos and Andy's malapropisms at the end of the 1920s, and developing through the recurring taglines of key characters in so many of the 1930s ensemble radio comedies, Douglas argues that "linguistic slapstick" enabled listeners to feel as though they had the "password into a club."[154] This process

149. Susan Douglas, *Listening In: Radio and the American Imagination* (New York: Times Books, 1999): 102–103.

150. Douglas, *Listening In*: 101.

151. Lizabeth Cohen, *Making a New Deal: Industrial Workers in Chicago, 1919–1939* (New York: Cambridge University Press, 1991): 328.

152. Michele Hilmes, *Radio Voices: American Broadcasting, 1922–1952* (Minneapolis: University of Minnesota Press, 1997): 21.

153. "Some Sales Tips by Prof. Lloyd Jones," *Broadcasting* 10, no. 7 (April 1, 1936): 18; Mugglestone, *Talking Proper*: 273–75.

154. Douglas, *Listening In*: 111.

of creating a new community around shared linguistic novelty was an important function of national radio in a nation as large and diverse as the United States. Network programs emanated from Hollywood, Chicago, and New York, and there were complaints that humor too local to those places did not travel well. NBC's Phillips Carlin reported on this in 1938: "It was called to my attention that an out of town station resented the fact that in many of our programs local situations and gags are used which have no significance to a person outside of the city from which the broadcast originates.... The audience in the studio will give the gag a big laugh but to the rest of the country it means little if anything."[155] Linguistic humor internal to the program was far more likely to succeed with large, diverse national audiences. It was also a by-product of the commercial structure of American radio—comic taglines had a clear commercial function on a crowded dial. As one perceptive newspaper radio columnist put it, "A silly selection of words, voiced in a comic manner, makes money for sponsors and actors and networks."[156] American radio in its commercial mode had a constant need for means of identification and distinction in an aural environment in which there were always competitors and choices, even as in its national mode it needed to strive for BBC-like authority and uniformity. American radio was, it might be said, at war with itself—except that the tensions were as often productive, even creative, as they were disabling.

PUBLIC SERVICE AND HIGH CULTURAL BROADCASTING

Later consideration of American radio in its golden age has too readily accepted the existence of a sharp dichotomy between U.S. and all other radio, a dichotomy itself in part the product of the 1930s American broadcasting industry polemics described above. American radio was distinctive, but not for the very simple reasons adduced by industry apologists—not, that is, because it was the opposite of national, public service broadcasting—but because it had to incorporate national and public service functions *within* a commercial and entertainment structure. When seeking a quick way to differentiate American radio from British, U.S. broadcasters most often said that American radio gave the people what they wanted while British radio gave its people what the government thought they ought to have. But actually the distinction was never quite that clear.

"Ringing in the ears of the broadcasters as they come face to face with the crusaders," the *New York Times* radio columnist predicted in 1934, "will be the formula that to survive they must adhere to 'public interest, convenience and necessity.'"[157] The ideological and cultural work of establishing that the networks could simultaneously be public service broadcasters and profitable commercial entertainers was far from over at the end of 1934. The networks began new public service programs to demonstrate that they were keeping

155. Memo from Phillips Carlin, August 22, 1938, folder 59, box 93, NBC records, WHS.
156. "Slangy Taglines Spell Success," *Fresno Bee*, September 28, 1941.
157. "'Court' Opens Tomorrow," *New York Times*, September 30, 1934: 12.

their side of the bargain. The more politically alert broadcasting executives were keenly aware that they had to appear as often as possible as providers of public service radio. "A good radio station must do more than merely entertain," powerful Cincinnati station WLW proclaimed in a full-page 1938 advertisement in *Broadcasting* . "It must also provide knowledge and information."[158]

American broadcasters were not free simply to give listeners what they wanted, to become just skilled purveyors of entertainment and sellers of airtime for profit. They were constrained by the regulatory system and the political environment to offer what seems now an extraordinary range of civic, educational, and high cultural programming, as the price of their freedom from government competition. They had constantly to maintain the appearance of being public service broadcasters with a keen sense both of national and of local needs, committed to the goals of education and uplift. The existing historiography acknowledges the importance of civic ideals to network radio in the early days of NBC, from 1926, but argues that, from the formation of CBS in 1928, a more ruthless commercialism prevailed, and that the ideals of the early period were then rapidly abandoned.[159] Once there was competition between networks, commercial programming increased as a proportion of the broadcast day at the expense of sustaining programs, and the time allocated to classical music declined. And when in the early 1930s advertising agencies took over the production of many commercial network programs, historians have concluded, civic values diminished even further in importance. Barnouw argued that there was a connection between advertiser dominance of program production and the decline of civically worthy content. As advertisers sought to avoid offending any audience segment, they gravitated toward vaudeville entertainment rather than programs dealing with current social or political issues.[160] Economics dictated, Hilmes maintained, that with two competing networks, "the lofty public service goals put forth by the FRC and backed by RCA must give way to a more profit-oriented view." She cites figures from Llewellyn White's 1947 study *The American Radio* showing that NBC went from 76% sustaining shows in 1933 to 50% in 1944, and that the time devoted to "classical and semiclassical music" dropped from 26% to 12% over the same period.

This decline was real and dramatic. But the public service glass remained half full. There were still very many public service programs and a great deal of classical music on American commercial radio through the 1930s. And the decadelong decline conceals a large spike in the later 1930s, when the numbers of both sustaining shows and classical music broadcasts increased significantly. Heistad's year-by-year analysis showed that the number of sustaining public service programs and the quantity of broadcast classical music fell a little in 1934 and 1935, but then rose considerably during the later 1930s, before declining again during World War II. Over the whole period 1928 to 1952, he calculated, public service programs made up on average one-third of the program schedule. Each of Heistad's graphs of numbers of sustaining and public service programs shows the same

158. WLW advertisement, *Broadcasting* 15, no. 1 (July 1, 1938): 67.

159. See for example Michele Hilmes, *Hollywood and Broadcasting: From Radio to Cable* (Urbana: University of Illinois Press, 1990): 51–52; Hilmes, *Radio Voices*: 97; Daniel J. Czitrom, *Media and the American Mind: From Morse to McLuhan* (Chapel Hill: University of North Carolina Press, 1982): 80–81.

160. Barnouw, *The Golden Web*: 17.

peak in the later 1930s and then a pronounced dip during World War II, when advertising dollars abounded but products for sale were scarce, so that sponsorship of all kinds of programming seemed newly attractive.[161] I want to try to explain why there was so much, rather than why there was so little, public service programming, because the answer to that question seems to me to get at much of what was structurally and comparatively distinctive about American broadcasting in this period. Nowhere else did a commercial radio system carry such a burden of cultural and civic expectations, and nowhere else was there such a creative but unstable fusion of civic and commercial imperatives. My argument is that the distinctiveness of American radio was located not in its commercialism or its pep or its personalities, but rather in the working out of the productive tension between entertainment and public service roles, the commercial and the national faces of the networks. The nostalgists for old-time radio do accurately identify the musical and comedy and drama programs to which most Americans listened most of the time. But the fact that those popular programs sat cheek by jowl on the schedule with a lot of classical music and educational and public service programming was a constitutive quality of the American system. Unresolved cultural tension was one of the defining features, and an important part of the appeal of, American radio. The American system in its golden years was best defined by its creative instability—its constant need to juggle the incompatible demands of popularity and commercial success, respectability and elevation.

If we think of entertainment and education only as opposed categories, it is difficult to understand the excitement that radio provoked. Theodor Adorno astutely noted in 1938 that "even the question of whether the commercial interests represent the reactionary side of radio and the educational interests represent the progressive side of radio is not nearly so easy as it appears on the surface."[162] There was much public discussion in the early 1930s about the role of education on radio—education understood broadly as involving something beyond the use of radio as a schoolroom supplement or a way of learning French at home. Educational radio became the rallying point for all of those who wanted something more from the miracle of broadcasting than commercial entertainment.[163] The requirement of the Radio Act of 1927 and Communications Act of 1934 that radio broadcast "in the public interest," and the interpretation of that phrase in the licensing processes of the Federal Radio Commission (FRC, 1927–1934) and then Federal Communications Commission (FCC, 1934–), meant that the largely commercial American radio sector was in its early decades forced to think creatively about how to combine mass appeal and hence profitability with identifiable educational and public service programming.

161. Mark Jonathan Heistad, "Radio without Sponsors: Public Service Programming in Network Sustaining Time, 1928–1952" (PhD diss., University of Minnesota, 1998): 132.

162. Theodore Wiesengrund-Adorno, "Memorandum: Music in Radio," typescript in Paul F. Lazarsfeld papers, CRBM: 7.

163. See McChesney, *Telecommunications, Mass Media, and Democracy* . The National Committee on Education by Radio produced its journal *Education by Radio* from 1931 to 1941—which was the period when educational radio stood as a cause much broader and more political than simply discussion of radio programming and classroom pedagogy.

For listeners too, the lines between entertainment and instruction were blurred. Radio educator Lyman Bryson advocated the use of popular soap operas in adult education classes: "The minute a person feels sympathetic interest in a character, he has already to some extent identified himself with that character, and has already taken part in a decision on what is right and what is wrong for that character to do in a given situation."[164] The early researchers into radio audiences repeatedly made this discovery that listeners found entertainment in programs that seemed to offer them commentary on the conduct of life. Listeners interviewed in the late 1930s reported that soap operas were directly useful guides for living: "I like to continue listening to the story because I can learn from it"; "I can use some of the things he does in my own home."[165] One study noted that "most of the daytime serials deal with people who get into some kind of trouble, and the plot is concerned with the way the characters solve their problems.... Many listeners match their own difficulties with those of the main characters and use the story as advice and guidance for their own behavior."[166] American radio was popular in part as an escape and a distraction, but it was also popular because it was innovative in finding ways to entertain and instruct at the same time.

PUBLIC SERVICE PROGRAMMING AS INSURANCE

To the broadcasters, and especially the networks, the considerable investment in cultural and educational programming represented a kind of insurance policy in uncertain times against the possibility of government deciding to establish a national public broadcaster. The broadcasting industry at its highest levels understood cultural and civic programs to be the political legitimation of the whole system, the main defense against government intervention or reform.

Of course critics, reformers, and educationalists through the 1930s always wanted more public service from radio. But to early 21st-century radio listeners, the diversity and cultural range of prewar commercial American radio seems astonishing. Deems Taylor counted the following on one weekday 12-hour period in 1934, on the four main network stations in New York City: 17.5 hours of symphonic music, 14 hours of lectures and discussions, 4.5 hours each of opera and vocal or instrumental recitals, and 2.75 hours of chamber music.[167] On December 4, 1938, a New York radio listener could have heard six symphony orchestra programs, a live opera broadcast, two radio plays—one with Orson Welles and one with Clark Gable—a live broadcast of the French Minister of Finance from Paris, three forum discussion programs, and a broadcast of Edward Bernays speaking at Cooper Union on "Public and Private Interest." That was New York, but many of these programs were networked. American commercial radio listeners in the 1930s had available to them a quite remarkable array of cultural and educational programming.

---

164. Lyman Bryson, "Daytime Serials" typescript talk 1942, box 29, Lyman Bryson papers, LOC.

165. Paul F. Lazarsfeld, *Radio and the Printed Page—An Introduction to the Study of Radio and Its Role in the Communication of Ideas* (New York: Duell, Sloan and Pearce, 1940): 52.

166. Paul F. Lazarsfeld, *Should She Have Music?* (New York: Bureau of Applied Social Research, 1942): 8.

167. Deems Taylor, "Radio: A Brief for the Defense," *Harpers Magazine* 166 (April 1933): 557.

In their public service programming, in educational broadcasts designed for the classroom, in the discussion programs that had links to a broader adult education forum movement, in classical music programming aimed at inducting a mass audience into the protocols of appreciation of "serious" music, in religious broadcasts, in the practical advice that proliferated on home and farm and garden programs, and even in the moral tone of many of the soap operas, the American radio networks in the 1930s took on many of the civic and national tasks that in other nations were the responsibility of publicly funded national broadcasters. They provided airtime when requested by senior government officials.[168] Those responsible for network public service programming tried to imagine and address an inclusive nation, together as well as in its constituent parts.

Despite the reflex rhetoric distancing American radio from the prescriptive Reithian ideal, it was quite clear that while the entertainment face of the networks was dedicated to giving the people what they wanted, the public service face was attempting instead to refashion the listening population—to make more active, responsive citizens, more able to participate in democratic conversations, more familiar with some of the high points of the Western European cultural tradition, more rational, productive, and autonomous. The advertising underpinnings of American broadcasting perhaps made those who shaped it more habituated to working at the transformation of behavior, at persuasion and exhortation, than public service broadcasters elsewhere.

The pressure the broadcasters perceived about public service and civic programming continued and even intensified in the later 1930s. NBC president M. H. Aylesworth described in 1935 a private conversation with FCC chair Anning Prall: "Chairman Prall stated confidentially there was a small group in Washington who would like to have more drastic control of radio broadcasting and that he opposed it. He suggested that if we continue to do the job as we are now there will be little support for further control of radio broadcasting."[169] Broadcasters knew that a crucial part of "the job" in this context was educational and public service programming, and they were frank with one another about their reasons for both broadcasting and publicizing it. NBC programs vice president John Royal, in a 1937 memo discussing whether NBC should send a representative to the World Federation of Education Associations meeting in Tokyo, said that while it might "at first observation" appear unnecessary to send someone, he thought NBC should if CBS did, "and even if they don't it might be well for us to do so.... In this battle for prestige we are probably going to do a lot of things we ordinarily wouldn't do."[170] The American networks took on, in this defensive and prophylactic mood, a great deal of public service broadcasting—in the later 1930s competing with each other for the "prestige" and political advantage they thought could be won in this way.

Awareness of the political importance of this "battle for prestige" was stronger at the top of American broadcasting than down the ranks. NBC president Lenox Lohr told a conference of NBC station and network educational directors in 1939, "I have taken a very

168. During 1937, there were 223 hours and 45 minutes on NBC of speaking time for federal officials—including the president, vice president, cabinet members, senators, and representatives. H. M. Beville, NBC Statistician, Memo May 25, 1938, box 94, folder 34, NBC records, WHS.

169. M. H. Aylesworth to R.C. Patterson, March 26, 1935, folder 36, box 36, NBC records, WHS.

170. John Royal to Lenox Lohr, April 19, 1937, folder 10, box 108, NBC records, WHS.

keen interest in our public service programs, because as I look upon them, in the final analysis, our whole system of American broadcasting may depend on how well we do that particular job."[171] To the men heading the networks, that was a pragmatic political reality. But the urgency of the task was not always well communicated to those below. NBC education counselor James Angell wrote to John Royal in 1938:

> I think it is fair to say, in the bosom of the family, that, generally speaking, education has been a terrible headache for the broadcasting industry and it is my candid judgment that only a handful of men connected with this—these, fortunately, in high position—have any sincere appreciation of the obligation which broadcasting owes to education or any full understanding of the central position which education must occupy in a democracy.[172]

Royal was, at least after 1934, very clearly and pragmatically aware of the need for prominent civic, cultural, and educational programming.[173] He recalled later that "in the very early days when I came here we put on a lot of Shakespeare.... Now, we didn't put it on because we were great enthusiasts for Shakespeare. To be strictly honest, we put it on for Exhibit A, to show educators etc. that we were adding something to culture."[174] Speaking among themselves at the time, network executives were equally direct about their motives for emphasizing educational and high cultural fare. The NBC official who was most acutely aware of the necessity for continued defensive measures was Washington vice president Frank Russell, who wrote a 1940 letter (marked "Confidential—No Record Kept—Please Destroy") to NBC president Lenox Lohr, reminding him quite bluntly that "RCA-NBC inaugurated public service broadcasting in all the various fields because we wanted to demonstrate beyond any question of doubt that radio should remain in the hands of private interests and that RCA-NBC, quite apart from its millions of dollars invested, was managed and operated on a high plane of public service."[175]

When the American system seemed threatened by government regulation or competition, the broadcasters' principal tactic was to proclaim that uplifting public service programs would be the first victims of government interference. The FCC introduced new regulations on network broadcasting in 1941, and in response NBC's president issued a

171. "Proceedings—Educational Directors' Meeting, National Broadcasting Company," December 5, 1939, Drake Hotel, Chicago, folder 61, box 94, NBC records, WHS.

172. James Angell to Lenox Lohr, June 28, 1939, folder 60, box 94, NBC records, WHS.

173. Royal had though not always been so aware of the importance of the cultural strategy. At an early meeting of the University of Chicago Radio Committee in 1932, NBC Chicago executive Judith Waller warned that within NBC there were two attitudes to educational radio: "One is represented by John Royal, Program Director, and one time actor who has no respect for educational features and who, in fact, seems lacking in appreciation of anything cultural...those favoring education are in the minority." Minutes of University of Chicago Radio Committee, February 1932, Allen Miller papers, WHS.

174. Interview with John Royal (1964): 16, folder 3, box 3, William Hedges papers, WHS.

175. Frank Russell to Lenox Lohr, January 21, 1940, folder 474, NBC history files, LOC.

press release saying that to meet the new regulations of the commission, the network might be "forced to sacrifice such outstanding programs as the 'Town Meeting of the Air,' the 'Toscanini Symphony Concerts,' the 'Farm and Home Hour,' the 'NBC Music Appreciation Hour,' the 'Metropolitan Opera' and outstanding religious and educational programs."[176] Only network-scale profits, NBC insisted, made such programming possible, and conversely, the provision of these high-status programs provided the legitimation for the continued existence of the commercial networks.

Not all within the networks shared the understanding of the political importance of cultural and educational programming. The result was that, despite the high publicity given to public service programming, it was often not well treated in the network schedule. Reformers charged—accurately—that network educational programs were given the least commercially desirable times, and were shifted around if commercial programs wanted their spots. Franklin Dunham, of the educational division of NBC, complained in 1938 about the treatment of the program *The World Is Yours*, which had been he said "kicked around badly." It was not only that 300,000 announcements about the program had recently been sent out under government frank, but also that the network would be open to "the most severe kind of criticism" from U.S. commissioner of education John Studebaker: "We are rapidly losing our reputation to cooperate with existing educational agencies."[177] Public service programs were not necessarily broadcast by even local stations, if they could find a paying local alternative.[178] In "a disturbing number of cases," James Angell noted in 1938, local stations were indisposed to or unable to take sustaining programs.[179] The networks had limited capacity to force affiliates to broadcast these programs. Faced with the choice between taking free but nonrevenue earning sustaining programs or selling time for a local commercial program, local network affiliates would often take the money. As researcher Llewellyn White explained to the Commission on the Freedom of the Press, because stations were not obligated to carry network sustaining programs, "as a result most of them don't; they go around the corner and get Sol's Toggery for fifteen minutes and pick up a little change."[180] Thus, nationally known shows broadcast on the networks did not necessarily reach the whole country. Noting this, James Rowland Angell at NBC asked then program vice president Sidney Strotz in 1941 if he could check up more often whether stations were or were not carrying public service programming. Strotz replied testily:

Checking the stations doesn't make them carry the programs. The merit of the program itself and the interest to the public as a whole plus the selling job that is

176. Press release, Niles Trammell, May 4, 1941, folder 5, box 83, NBC records, WHS.

177. Franklin Dunham to Phillips Carlin, January 18, 1938, folder 39, box 60, NBC records, WHS.

178. See, for example, Committee on Civic Education by Radio of the National Advisory Council on Radio in Education and the American Political Science Association, *Four Years of Network Broadcasting* (Chicago: University of Chicago Press, 1937).

179. "Memorandum of Matters on Dr. Angell's Desk as of July 1, 1938," folder 57, box 93, NBC records, WHS.

180. "Preliminary Report by White on Radio Regulation": 65, folder 10, box 3, Commission on Freedom of Press Records, UCSC.

done by the Program Department through the Station Relations Department is frankly the answer. I find that such programs as Defense for America, Town Meeting of the Air, University of Chicago Round Table, and those programs really having merit do enjoy a substantial station line-up and those that really haven't any merit or are not of particular interest to the public in turn have a very small station line-up.[181]

The advertiser, rather than the network, decided just how much national coverage to pay for. The stations most often left off networked broadcasts were in the South, but coverage in the West was also often partial.[182] The uncertainty about station coverage was a continual frustration and embarrassment to the network staff concerned with public service programming. NBC's Judith Waller complained in an internal memo, "It does seem senseless that so much time and effort should go into the building of unusual and interesting sustaining programs both from Europe and America, only to have them booked on a handful of stations—and not even our own outside of New York."[183]

There was yet another reason that public service programs on NBC reached smaller than possible audiences. NBC maintained two networks through the 1930s—the Red and the Blue. The Red network was the bigger and more valuable chain, carrying the most commercially profitable shows. The Blue network was then available to NBC for trying out new shows, allowing them time to find a sponsor and move to the Red network if successful. The Blue network schedule also operated as a residual space for sustaining and public service programs. Frank Russell complained in 1936: "Today our 'must sustaining' programs, including a wide variety of talks and other programs which lack listener interest, are automatically shunted to the Blue. There is a normal and natural ambition to keep the Red ahead of Columbia at any cost. The Blue necessarily suffers....."[184] The result of these complexities in the actual operation of networks was that the public service programs were not as widely disseminated as network publicity might have led people to believe.

Those insiders most alert to the importance of the perception of the networks as public service providers were acutely conscious of the destructiveness of any bad publicity in this area. In 1936 the Committee on Civic Education by Radio, looking back on four years of broadcasting on NBC, concluded pessimistically that "in view of the double conflict between commercial and educational interests and between the chains and their individual stations, it is useless at this time to attempt systematic education by national network broadcasting at hours when it will be available to large adult audiences."[185] These were highly damaging claims, because the networks habitually used their high cultural

181. Strotz to Angell, April 25, 1941, folder 1, box 354, NBC records, WHS.

182. The best discussion of this phenomenon is in Michael J. Socolow, "To Network a Nation: NBC, CBS, and the Development of National Network Radio in the United States, 1925–1950" (PhD diss., Georgetown University, 2001), ch. 2.

183. She was referring to the network's "owned and operated" stations. Judith Waller to John Royal November 3, 1936, folder 6, box 92, NBC records, WHS.

184. Frank Russell to Lenox Lohr, September 29, 1936, folder 31, box 92, NBC records, WHS.

185. Committee on Civic Education, Four Years of Network Broadcasting: 73.

and civic programming as legitimation of the whole American system. John Royal sent NBC president Lenox Lohr a copy of the book and advised that both he and RCA president David Sarnoff read it in its entirety: "It shows how serious this educational matter can be."[186] The conflict between commercial and public service goals was never solved, but it was out of this contradiction that the distinctiveness of American radio was produced.

PUBLIC SERVICE VERSUS ENTERTAINMENT

The tensions between the public and commercial roles of the broadcasters—between their presentation of themselves as primarily servants of the public interest, and their defense of lightly regulated, free enterprise, profit-making broadcasting—were constantly evident. Inevitably, some of these tensions had a gendered dimension. One reading of gender and mass culture in the field of radio history flows from Andreas Huyssen's now classic essay "Mass Culture as Woman: Modernism's Other," with its provocative and persuasive contention that mass culture in the modernist era was attributed feminine characteristics.[187] Hilmes argues that U.S. broadcasters in the 1930s had the twin tasks of making money from "an economic base that clearly rested on the female purchaser of household products" and at the same time convincing regulators that their broadcasting practice "consisted as much of public service programming as of sheer commercialism." Broadcasters, Hilmes observes, did this by differentiating daytime programming that was "debased...commercialized, feminized," from the more "sophisticated, respectable, and masculine-characterized arena of prime time."[188] Within the networks, however, the gendering could also be reversed. Public service broadcasting, in the form of "sustaining" educational and high cultural programs, clearly had a more feminine character than the tougher, moneymaking side of operations. This was because of the association with the arts, but also perhaps because of the strategies of improvement that lay behind educational radio: cajoling, nagging, and exhorting into things that were good for you was a feminine role (as in the characterization of the BBC as "auntie"). The Women's National Radio Committee played an important lobbying role for educational and cultural programming—NBC president Merlin Aylesworth noted gruffly that they were interested in "children's programs and cultural stuff."[189] Of the few senior women in broadcasting, several—such as NBC's Judith Waller and Margaret Cuthbert, and CBS's Marian Carter—worked in the educational and public service area. The business side of network broadcasting had a demonstrably more masculine air to it—staffed by men, whose golf-playing camaraderie was evident in photos of NAB convention gatherings.[190] Figure 1.4. And even

186. John Royal to Lenox Lohr, December 23, 1936, folder 6, box 108, NBC records, WHS.

187. In Andreas Huyssen, *After the Great Divide: Modernism, Mass Culture, Postmodernism* (Bloomington: Indiana University Press, 1986).

188. Hilmes, *Radio Voices*: 153–54.

189. M. H. Aylesworth to R. C. Patterson Jr., March 26, 1935, folder 36, box 36, NBC records, WHS.

190. Donna Halper concludes that the broadcast organizations such as NAB were "run by men and oriented around the opinions of their male members": Donna Halper, *Invisible Stars: A Social History of Women in American Broadcasting* (Armonk, NY: M. E. Sharpe, 2001): 79.

Figure 1.4. *Broadcasting* magazine council. Left to right: Thad Holt, WAPJ; Lindsay Wellington, BBC; Harry Butcher, CBS; Paul Porter, CBS; Indian Springs Golf Club, March 22, 1938. Harris and Ewing collection, Library of Congress, LC-H22-D- 3554.

here the gender situation was complex, for the popular entertainment shows these men were selling treated gender boundaries in unorthodox ways. The content of the top-rating commercial comedy shows, as has been explicated by several astute cultural historians, was surprisingly often devoted to somewhat unsettling explorations of dominant gender norms, in particular of conventional masculinity. Male characters played "swish," and what Susan Douglas has dubbed "vocal cross-dressing," was central to the jokes and on-air personalities of several of the top radio comedians of the 1930s.[191] So prevalent was

191. Douglas, *Listening In*: 111. See also Margaret T. McFadden, "'America's Boy Friend Who Can't Get a Date': Gender, Race, and the Cultural Work of the Jack Benny Program, 1932–1946," *Journal of American History* 80, no. 1 (June 1993): 113–34; Margaret T. McFadden, "'Anything Goes': Gender and Knowledge in the Comic Popular Culture of the 1930s" (PhD diss., Yale University, 1996); Matthew Murray, "'The Tendency to Deprave and Corrupt Morals': Regulation and Irregular Sexuality in Golden Age Radio Comedy," in Hilmes and Loviglio (eds.), *Radio Reader*: 135–56.

the comic portrayal of what NBC's Janet MacRorie called "effeminate or sex-perverted characters" that the network issued an internal directive "banning all characterizations verging on this from the air."[192] So a history of the divided self, of the dual identities of American radio, has to acknowledge that the gendering of radio was complex. Nevertheless the clash within the networks between those with responsibility for the commercial side of broadcasting and those in charge of its cultural and educational mission reveals a cultural conflict that had some relatively clear gender and class dimensions.

NBC executive Frank Mullen explained the American system of broadcasting to a Republican congressman in 1942:

Mr. Charles Wolverton [Republican, New Jersey]: What did you mean by that—"the American system?"

Mr. Frank E. Mullen [Vice President and General Manager, NBC]: The American system.

Mr. Wolverton: Did you use that term to distinguish from some other system?

Mr. Mullen: Yes, sir; the American system of broadcasting is a system supported by private enterprise, free enterprise with democratic principles and freedom of speech. No other country in the world has that kind of system.

Mr. Wolverton: Could you illustrate by contrasting the systems?

Mr. Mullen: The English system, to take one illustration, is controlled by the British Government. It is supported by taxes on receiving sets. There are no advertising programs in England.

Mr. Wolverton: Under such a system as that, who provides the programs?

Mr. Mullen: The British Broadcasting Corporation, which is a subsidiary of the British Post Office.

Mr. Wolverton: I am inclined to agree with you that there is some importance to the statement you made when you stated that we should preserve the American system of broadcasting. I certainly would not like to see it get to the point where the Government itself provides the programs for us over the air.[193]

Mullen here provided the inquiring congressman with an exemplary statement of the twin virtues of the American system—its free enterprise and freedom of speech—and an elaboration of the belief that the former was the cause and support of the latter. He further asserted that the greatest threat to that bundle of freedoms came from government. Mullen made the transitions absolutely seamless, to produce the one coherent entity "free enterprise with democratic principles and freedom of speech."

But what if the American system, so imbued with and reflective of freedom, could be maintained only by forms of programming that did not accept the sovereignty of listeners as they were, but instead attempted to improve and remake them? And what if the

192. Janet MacRorie to Witmer and Kobak, December 19, 1940, folder 14, box 95, NBC records, WHS.

193. *Proposed Changes in the Communications Act of 1934, Hearings Before the Committee on Interstate and Foreign Commerce House of Representatives, 77th Congress, 2nd session, 1942*: 195.

cost of such programs dented the profitability of the network? Here is a glimpse of the same Frank Mullen in 1939:

> Yesterday I was the first to arrive for luncheon at the RCA Dining Room. Frank Mullen came in next, shaveless and looking as if he had been on an all-night bat. He asked me just what I was doing. He next asked how much we spend on educational programs. I told him I thought it was between 200 and 250,000 per year. Colonel Davis came in next and Mullen turned to him and said: "Do you realize that NBC spends almost one quarter of a million for educational programs, not including the time?" Mullen then asked me: "Do you look upon this as the minimum or the maximum?" I told him it was a minimum. Other people then came in and the subject was changed. Mullen was in a hell-raising mood and was particularly critical of NBC for allowing Mutual to sell the exclusive rights to the World Series Baseball broadcasts. I hope that this does not mean that he will start to shoot at what little monies we now have for our educational programs.[194]

There were, as this vignette so clearly suggests, two very different cultures within the network. Conflict between commercial executives focused on the business of broadcasting and educational executives focused on the pedagogical and cultural possibilities of the new medium was endemic at NBC. Both sides thought they were acting in the best interests of the company. Mullen's sense that educational programs were too expensive, depleting the network's ability to compete for top-level sports broadcasts, has a gender implication—the "shaveless" Mullen feared, it seemed, an emasculation of the network by the proponents of educational programming. But there was also a class dimension to this internal conflict. The above report of Mullen's outburst was written by Walter Preston, education division chief in the program department at NBC, in a confidential memo to James Rowland Angell, until recently the president of Yale University, and now NBC's education counselor. Preston had been educated at Phillips, Andover, and Yale, had undertaken graduate work at Creighton, Chicago, and Cincinnati, before taking a job as assistant to University of Chicago president Robert Hutchins.[195] While at NBC, he was also serving as president of the Class Secretaries Association of the Yale alumni.[196] Preston understood clearly that there were many within NBC management who would have liked to cut the public service programming budget and the number of hours devoted to it. "I am convinced that the money-making attitude of the Management," he reported to Angell, "can mean only that we are going to have less time and poorer hours for our public service shows."[197]

Frank Mullen, on the other hand, had grown up on farms in Kansas and South Dakota—his father was a lawyer and county judge. He attended the Agricultural College

---

194. Walter Preston to James Rowland Angell, August 19, 1939, folder 59, box 94, NBC records, WHS.

195. "Preston Appointed to Assist Royal," *Broadcasting* 15, no. 3 (August 1, 1938): 26.

196. Sadly, Preston's career was cut short. Newspapers of the morning of Sunday, December 7, 1941, the day of the attack on Pearl Harbor, carried news of his suicide—he was only 39 years old. "NBC Official Found Dead on Floor of Home," *Lima News*, December 7, 1941: 35.

197. Preston to Angell, August 3, 1939, folder 59, box 94, NBC records, WHS.

of Iowa State at Ames, where he majored in agricultural journalism, and worked part time as assistant editor of *Swine World*. Mullen fought in France in World War I, and took his first job as the farm page editor of the *Sioux City Journal*. He then worked in radio at station WMAQ in Chicago, where he pioneered programming for farmers, before becoming NBC's national director of agricultural programs, including its long-running *Farm and Home Hour*.[198] A newspaper profile in 1930 described him as "still just a farmer," who understood the importance to farmers of weather and market information, and of old-time fiddle and hillbilly music.[199] Perhaps to Mullen, NBC's emphasis and expenditure on educational programming seemed a violation of its commitment to "free enterprise with democratic principles and freedom of speech." He was clearly unable to see why it was in the interests of the company to be spending so much on education.

Mullen was a loyal and able NBC executive. On the regulation of radio, he took an uncompromising line in defense of the "American system," and saw danger in even the minimal government oversight involved in the licensing system. Licensing meant that the broadcasting industry "is subject to a certain amount of governmental control, which presents an ever-present danger unless zealously held within bounds by the citizens."[200] Reaffirming in 1944 that the United States had the only free radio in the world, Mullen pointed to the dangers of covert censorship through the licensing system:

We have a system. What is there that makes it distinctively an American system? The answer can be summed up in four words: free speech and free enterprise.... Most of us never stop to think that ours is the only country in the world in which radio programs are not under government control. Yet our lack of concern on this score is in itself a source of potential danger. It is apt to make us blind to encroachments on the freedom of radio which should serve us as warning signals. For while we in the United States do not have direct censorship of programs, the very fact that station licenses are issued, and can be revoked, by a Government bureau makes possible a form of censorship that is no less effective for being indirect.[201]

There was a very considerable element of self-blindness to this. Mullen had made his name on NBC's *Farm and Home Hour*, which was a program produced in collaboration between a government department and the commercial network. His own career belied the notion that the only conceivable role for government in broadcasting would be a negative, censoring, freedom-denying one.

198. Information contained in Mullen speech over WHY Schenectady, November 1, 1940, document 160-G in Library of American Broadcasting, University of Maryland, and in "We Pay Our Respects To—Frank Ernest Mullen," *Broadcasting* 7, no. 11 (December 1, 1934): 14.

199. "Frank Mullen Helped in Making Radio Valuable to Farm Folk of Continent," *Decatur Herald*, September 21, 1930: 18.

200. Frank Mullen, "Free Radio, An American Institution," address to the National Society of the Daughters of the American Revolution, New York, April 18, 1944: 7, document 160B, Library of American Broadcasting, University of Maryland.

201. Frank Mullen, *The American System of Broadcasting* (New York, 1944): 12–13.

There were many leaders of commercial broadcasting, particularly in local stations, who agreed with Mullen, who believed in the free market qualities of the American system, and who thought that the right amount of improving high cultural and educational programming was whatever quantity the American people wanted. NAB president Mark Ethridge observed in 1938, "I confess to a total inability to understand how any group of men and women would be able to draw a cultural pattern in a democratic country." Radio mirrored the "talent, the genius and the thought" of the American people, and its level "can be no higher than the general level of culture and the appreciation of cultural things in the country."[202] That pointed comment neatly captured one of the endemic tensions within American radio, between its claiming complete freedom from government and its adoption of an effectively governmental role in education and civic advice.

Public service programming was strategically important to the networks, but it was also under constant scrutiny. There was never a time when individual programs were safe from cost-cutting by skeptical network executives with commercial backgrounds and an appropriate zeal for profit. Frank Mullen acknowledged the tension between the commercial and public service functions of the network but argued that each side was "intelligent enough" to see that the other was necessary: "We wouldn't have a healthy organization if the commercial department didn't feel that it was No. 1 and the public service department wasn't likewise fairly certain that it delivered the audiences for the sales department to sell."[203]

The construction of the commercial, national, public service programming of the networks was thus a fraught and complex exercise, internally as well as externally contested. This becomes clearer if we examine a little more closely the role of James Rowland Angell in assisting NBC with the delicate task of explaining how a commercial network that sold entertainment could also function as a credible, authoritative national institution dedicated to serving the public interest. NBC's shrewd choice of Angell, and his strategic advice to the network, illuminate both the complexities of and the tensions within the American networks' role.

ANGELL'S DILEMMAS

John Royal was sent in early 1937 to talk to retiring Yale president James Rowland Angell about a position at NBC. He found that Angell had already been offered three other positions, but that at 68 he was still active and looking for "something with a spark of excitement." Royal reported, "I explained that we were facing a very serious problem and needed help to solve it." Heartened by the five radios in the house, and by Angell's spontaneously offering the observation that he did not think the British system of radio would be successful in the United States, Royal left with some optimism.[204] Angell did accept, telling NBC president Lenox Lohr that he knew nothing about broadcasting: "I'm a

202. Testimony of Mark Ethridge, President of the National Association of Broadcasters, before the FCC, Washington DC, June 6, 1938, box 1, NAB Collection, WHS.
203. "NBC Decision to Sell Service Shows Not Set," *Billboard*, August 26, 1944: 8.
204. John Royal to Lenox Lohr, March 8, 1937, folder 64, box 92, NBC records, WHS.

freshman." But Lohr recalled that, despite Angell's age, "the thing that amazed me was the alertness of a young mind that was willing to start right from scratch on a brand new subject and learn broadcasting."[205] NBC announced in a blaze of publicity that it had hired Angell as its network education counselor.[206] NBC said the appointment grew from its "constant recognition of a deep obligation to foster the broadest range of educational and cultural interests of the public."[207] Angell understood with some clarity the task that confronted NBC, of constructing and legitimating a great, national public service organization that was also a business. There were few models to look to. But in some ways NBC had been astute in choosing a leader of an Ivy League institution—they too were private entities with an established national public service role. Angell had also in 1920–21 served as president of the philanthropic Carnegie Corporation of New York—another private body with a national and international cultural mission.

Angell, academically trained in psychology, came to NBC from leading Yale through the Depression and New Deal, with a record of reflection on the relation of private and public American institutions, and on the coexistence of democracy with elite leadership and guidance. Like many of his generation, he understood the instinct for just the right amount of democracy as ultimately racial in origin. "In our racial line of descent," he told the Yale graduating class of 1936, "we are derived from stock which has been peculiarly jealous of personal liberty, but which has nevertheless managed to work out a type of social control which we term democratic, although in form it is a constitutional republic, with the tradition of private property deeply imbedded in its social structure." This balance could be maintained only if there was sufficiently "generous and humane administration of the great enterprises" of society to ensure that they were not endangered by "too little foresight and imagination and too great selfishness." The "ethical corollary of freedom is moral responsibility," Angell warned.[208] This business version of *noblesse oblige* was articulated for the benefit of the graduates of Yale upon whom some of the responsibility for maintaining the balance of democracy and private property—the "type of social control which we term democratic"—would fall. Once at NBC, Angell's public utterances were a little more constrained—although he did give a commencement address in 1938 condemning the "self-complacent vanity" of New Deal planning.[209] From his relatively conservative perspective, individualism and self-government were always the solution—they had to be championed against excessive centralization, planning, and executive control. High national morale, Angell wrote in 1941, rests upon "a general belief that the government is in safe hands with intelligent men of integrity in charge."[210]

205. "Proceedings—Educational Directors' Meeting National Broadcasting Company," December 5, 1939, Drake Hotel, Chicago, folder 61, box 94, NBC records, WHS.

206. He was to be paid $25,000 a year: announcement in folder 64, box 92, NBC records, WHS.

207. "Angell to Be Radio Educational Counsellor: Takes NBC Post as Avenue to Wide Service," *New York Times*, June 28, 1937: 1.

208. James Rowland Angell, "The Moral Crisis of Democracy," *Vital Speeches of the Day* 2, no. 22 (August 1936): 671–72.

209. "Angell Calls FDR Policies Undemocratic," *Middletown Times Herald*, June 15, 1938: 2.

210. James Rowland Angell, "Radio and National Morale," *American Journal of Sociology* 47, no. 3 (November 1941): 352.

At least some of the executives of the networks were graduates of elite private universities and colleges, which probably did have something to do with their ability to conceptualize the possibility of a private corporation engaged in public service. It was an argument the leaders of the elite universities had been making vigorously. Angell had told the National Education Association, "It is easy to exaggerate the importance of the source from which educational resources are derived."[211] "The distinction is not between public and private," argued Columbia's Nicholas Murray Butler, "but between official and unofficial."[212] It was very important to establish that there could be nongovernmental institutions of public service. In many ways then, Angell was perfectly prepared intellectually to understand the delicacy of the task that NBC had in mind for him. Preserving the commercial basis of American broadcasting involved demonstrating that the networks could exercise just the kind of enlightened and public-spirited leadership and self-regulatory capacity that Angell had spoken of while at Yale. The "ethical corollary of freedom" in free enterprise, commercial broadcasting was also moral responsibility and a constant vigilance.

The network broadcaster needed, it was clear to Angell, to ensure that it offered leadership, foresight, and imagination. Unless it could be seen to display a generous and humane sense of the public good as well as concern for its own profits, greater public control of broadcasting would certainly be demanded. A national broadcaster would have to meet these expectations of leadership and enlightenment, and convince the public that its management was public-spirited and self-regulating. Angell asked in a 1934 address, ""Can we *impose on ourselves* a severity of discipline adequate to cope with the imperative social and economic demands of the time?"[213] In commercial broadcasting, as in business life more generally, self-discipline and a kind of inner moral autonomy were crucial for survival.

Angell was a canny choice of educational figurehead for NBC as it attempted to fashion itself as a self-disciplining national broadcaster, fully able to reconcile the tensions between profit and public service. NBC aspired to earn the kind of trust that would place it quite beyond the need for government interference or competition. Angell understood that network broadcasting was itself a form of governing that involved shaping citizens as well as giving them what they wanted, and that it could thus function as an exemplary form of democratic social control. This was an American articulation of the role of a national broadcaster—Angell did not, notably, advocate further emulation of the BBC. He discerned well the very particular circumstances of the broadcasting networks in the social, political, and cultural environment of the United States.

Angell was careful in his own public statements to stress that while American broadcasting was "fundamentally commercial" and not a "philanthropic enterprise," it

211. James Rowland Angell, "The Endowed Institution of Higher Education and Its Relation to Public Education," in James Rowland Angell, *American Education: Addresses and Articles* (New Haven: Yale University Press, 1937): 31.

212. Nicholas Murray Butler, "Democracy in Danger: Without Vision, the People Perish," *Vital Speeches of the Day* 2, no. 23 (September 1938): 709.

213. James Rowland Angell, "Moral Implications of Contemporary Special Trends," in Angell, *American Education*: 227.

recognized that "as its financial resources derived from the public, it cannot hope permanently to retain the confidence of that public unless it ministers to as many as possible of their essential interests and needs."[214] The last phrase most skillfully evaded the question—so fraught in justifications of the American system—of whether the American public was self-consciously aware of its "essential interests and needs," or if these were to be diagnosed for it. Was the public being given what it wanted, or what was good for it, or were the two were somehow happily coincident?

There was some anxiety at NBC after his appointment that Angell not become too enamored of the BBC model. NBC agreed to send him on a European study tour. Felix Greene, the BBC's North American representative, reported to London that, as a man of "national reputation," Angell "may be able to change the pattern of thinking in American broadcasting to a far larger extent than we now believe possible": "You will at first find him despairingly dull," Greene warned, "but after a while through his dullness and rather pompous speech rather happier qualities emerge."[215] Meanwhile John Royal issued some blunt instructions to Fred Bate, NBC's London representative: "When you talk with Angell, show him the weaknesses of the BBC educational system...Give him all the dirt you have."[216] Bate replied reassuringly that Angell was "under no delusions at all as to the efficacy of the education-for-education's sake type of broadcasting," and that Reith had spoken very frankly to him about the difficulties of educational radio. Angell met with section heads at the BBC, and also visited schools to see BBC schools broadcasts in action.[217] The next month, New Zealand–born Mary Somerville, the BBC's director of schools broadcasting, was in the United States. She made some critical public remarks about American educational radio, which angered John Royal. He asked Fred Bate to complain officially to Reith, and fumed about BBC propaganda and what he could say but would not about "their very dull and stupid programs."[218] A few months later, still apparently irate, Royal was instructing Bate to try to secure some recordings of BBC variety programs in which there were "little off-color jokes."[219] NBC was very concerned to ensure that public perceptions of the BBC as providing entirely superior educational and cultural radio be challenged.

There was continuing discussion at NBC about the most strategic way to name its public service programming. Because of the strength of the lobby for educational radio in the early 1930s, there was a lingering tendency to want to subsume a great deal of it under the heading of "educational" broadcasting, and to push out as generously as possible the boundaries of what might be considered educational. In preparing the company brief for the FCC hearings on radio in 1934, for example, NBC's Franklin Dunham advised public relations consultant William Hard that "all music in the upper brackets through and including semi-classical, should be automatically considered of education

214. James Rowland Angell, "Listening to Learn," *New York Times*, February 2, 1941: X10.

215. Felix Greene to C. G. Graves, September 24, 1937, BBC Written Archives Centre File E1/115.

216. John Royal to Fred Bate, October 5, 1937, folder 64, box 92, NBC records, WHS.

217. Fred Bate to John Royal, October 21, 1937, folder 64, box 92, NBC records, WHS.

218. John Royal to Lenox Lohr, and John Royal to Fred Bate, October 6, 1937, folder 15, box 108, NBC records, WHS.

219. John Royal to Fred Bate, February 24, 1938, folder 19, box 18, NBC records, WHS.

developmental value."[220] Once he had assessed the situation, however, Angell began calling internally for some greater moderation and realism in the claims made for the network's cultural and educational programming. He noted in 1937 of the NBC Educational Bulletins that "a good deal of material is printed in the schedule which is only educational in a rather loose sense of the phrase."[221] In 1939, he read through one draft of a proposed publicity brochure and wrote to NBC's president:

> I am again fearful that ill-natured newspaper radio people may seize on the some-what philanthropic and altruistic tone of the whole document to point out that the company has been one of the biggest money-earners in terms of the capital invested to be found among modern American industries. Perhaps, at one or two points, a somewhat franker recognition of the fact that there are large numbers of stockholders eager to receive a return on their investment may be wise.[222]

Angell was not alone in suggesting that the network show a little more tact and subtlety in making the public service case—Frank Russell commented to NBC's director of publicity in 1937, "I never like to see NBC make a statement such as 'entirely altruistic.'"[223]

Angell began to argue that NBC ought to replace the label *educational* with *public service* —so an educational program would conclude with the announcement: "This has been a public service feature of the National Broadcasting Company."[224] In response, NBC Washington Vice President Frank Russell warned that "public service" had some very unfortunate public utility connotations for an industry that was always at pains to argue that broadcasters should not be regarded as, and hence regulated like, common carriers such as telephone service providers or utilities such as gas or water: "It would be unfortunate, it seems to me, for us to accept a term capable of this definition." Russell suggested instead the phrase "broadcast in the public interest," to echo the language of the 1934 Communications Act.[225] Angell conceded that "there is no doubt of the objection to the phrase," but thought it might be the lesser of several evils. He asked Russell what he thought of "programs offered in the service of the public" or "in the interests of the public"—the clumsy locutions testimony to the difficulty the broadcasters had in formulating their civic role in acceptable yet strategic ways.[226] Angell's original suggestion was eventually adopted, and publicized as an example of the broadcasters' realization that "listeners tune in to be amused not to be educated," and that hence "to teach on air they

220. Franklin Dunham to William Hard, September 24, 1934, folder 28, box 26, NBC records, WHS.
221. James Rowland Angell to John Royal, December 13, 1937, folder 64, box 92, NBC records, WHS.
222. Angell to Lohr, May 15, 1939, folder 60, box 94, NBC records, WHS.
223. Frank Russell to Clay Morgan, May 18, 1937, folder 26, box 93, NBC records, WHS.
224. James Angell to John Royal, October 18, 1938, folder 57, box 93, NBC records, WHS.
225. Frank Russell to John Royal, October 28, 1938, folder 57, box 93, NBC records, WHS. Russell's views are also discussed in Walter Preston to Judith Waller, November 2, 1938, folder 477, NBC history files, LOC.
226. James Angell to John Royal, November 1, 1938, folder 57, box 93, NBC records, WHS.

must entertain."[227] In 1939, Angell observed to a meeting of NBC station educational directors that he was happy with the public service label: "It seems the best single term that we have been able to hit upon."[228] The uncertainty about naming the public service function of the commercial networks captured perfectly the tension inherent in the "American system"—how to run a business whose condition of profitability was to appear to be not just a business.

It took some skill and political acuity to think through in each case how programming decisions might be interpreted. Walter Koons seemed to be on the right track when in 1937 he enthusiastically proposed to his fellow executives that the network set up an NBC Music Foundation that would "further dignify and place above all 'commercial suspicion' our broadcasting of art music." The foundation would also accept donations to assist with the costs of broadcasting such music. There were precedents—the Philharmonic Society of New York enrolled radio members who helped support the CBS broadcasts of the New York Philharmonic. Koons thought of the foundation as part of "our front line defense of private ownership of radio." He wrote that he could "conceive of no better way of strengthening our position with the public than by developing this spirit of public participation in broadcasting, its sense of possession in our private corporate ownership."[229] The language here immediately betrays the complexity of the public relations task the networks faced—cultivating a "sense" of possession of something that was actually corporately owned.[230] Walter Preston was also enthusiastic: "The appointments of men like Dr. Angell, Maestro Toscanini, and the establishment of such a foundation as this are contributions of radio to the public service which are, very possibly, of greater value than the most enthusiastic of us realize."[231] But the music foundation idea was soon squashed further up the organizational ladder, by men with a sharper political sense. The formation of such a foundation, A. L. Ashby warned, "might also be used against us as an argument for government ownership." It could be perceived that NBC was saying that it could not finance the best possible programs on its own or, more damagingly, that "this is an effort on our part to pass on a part of our sustaining program costs to the public in order to increase the net profit of NBC."[232]

The point here is not, I think, to enter into discussion about how well the networks carried out their self-proclaimed public service mission, or to conclude with the revelation that actually they cared more about profits. The significant point is that they felt the necessity of being seen to carry out these tasks, and that through the 1930s they—accurately—perceived public service as being quite central to their legitimacy and viability as national broadcasters. They felt they had continually to justify and demonstrate that

227. "Radio Finds a New Word for Education," *New York Times*, February 11, 1940: 138.

228. "Proceedings—Educational Directors' Meeting National Broadcasting Company," December 5, 1939, Drake Hotel, Chicago, folder 61, box 94, NBC records, WHS.

229. Walter Koons, "Proposal for an NBC Music Foundation," June 22, 1937, folder 222, NBC history files, LOC.

230. On strategies of large corporate advertising in this period, see Roland Marchand, *Creating the Corporate Soul: The Rise of Public Relations and Corporate Imagery in American Big Business* (Berkeley: University of California Press, 1998).

231. W. G. Preston to Clay Morgan, September 15, 1937, folder 222, NBC history files, LOC.

232. A. L. Ashby to Clay Morgan, September 23, 1937, folder 222, NBC history files, LOC.

legitimacy, and they knew that government and reformers, and national and international opinion makers, were watching them. It was in this way that the ideal of public service broadcasting had real effects in the United States—not as something that might have been, a lost cause, but as something that constantly shaped the actual practices and self-definition of the commercial, national and networked broadcasters that were the cornerstones of the American system.

The public service ideal was an internationally shared ideal, but the tensions between it and the commercial and entertainment functions of radio were distinctive to American broadcasting. James Angell acknowledged in a report to Frank Mullen in 1945 that "radio is part theater, part concert hall, part newspaper, part school, part pulpit, part public platform and to drive all this team abreast, or tandem, or how you will, is a very difficult practical problem."[233] As Angell well recognized, one of the striking characteristics of the American system was the jostling together on commercial network schedules and budgets of commercially sponsored popular entertainment and unsponsored public service programming.

PUBLIC SERVICE WITH "SHOWMANSHIP"

One of the most oft-claimed qualities of American radio was "showmanship." Broadcasters earned their living selling showmanship to advertisers. WSM in Nashville, for example, promised advertisers that it had a "unique conception of showmanship": "To the power of the giant from the tall timber, the shrewd circus man adds a leopard skin and a bit of bally-hoo."[234] The official doctrine of cooperation between educators and broadcasters was frequently expressed as the view that educators needed assistance from professional showmen. The 1935 FCC inquiry concluded that there was a need to combine the "educational experiences of the educators with the program technic of the broadcasters."[235] John Studebaker, U.S. commissioner of education, a keen advocate of cooperation, affirmed that educational broadcasting had not kept pace with the development of entertainment radio, and that educational program makers needed to "do the job of educating over the air as effectively for our purposes as the commercial broadcasters do their job of entertaining."[236] Any failures of educators to communicate effectively and entertainingly were rendered more obvious when they were broadcast on commercial stations alongside popular entertainment programs. Early university broadcasts had often been simply broadcast lectures. From the mid-1920s, for example, the University of Chicago broadcast over commercial stations WMAQ and WLS whole courses of lectures ("Aspects of American Life," "Readings in Modern Literature"), as well as basketball games and live chapel services. In the détente of "cooperation," what the broadcasters brought to the table was their skill and experience in discerning and producing showmanship. The aim was now to transform educational radio into something more effectively pedagogical but less lecture-like.

233. James Angell to Frank Mullen, June 1, 1945, folder 69, box 114, NBC records, WHS.
234. "The Leopard Skin Puts Him Across," *Broadcasting* 11, no. 10 (November 15, 1936): 38.
235. Quoted in McChesney, *Telecommunications, Mass Media, and Democracy*: 223.
236. "Education's Future," *Broadcasting* 11, no. 12 (December 15, 1936): 73.

The network argument was that they knew how best to produce cultural and educational programs that were attractive to American audiences. The message was repeated again and again, both internally and in publicity. At NBC, long-serving Chicago educational director Judith Waller advised John Royal in 1936 that their goal should be to "strive to make programs built primarily for the 15% interesting enough to win the 85%."[237] "The Value of an Educational Program Depends on Its Audience" proclaimed a full-page 1938 NBC advertisement in *Broadcasting*: "the most painstakingly arranged program is worthless if not built to hold listeners."[238] CBS vice president Paul Kesten explained in 1945 that CBS understood one of its tasks to be presenting educational and cultural programs to which more people would want to listen.[239]

There was on all sides by the mid-1930s said to be a need to dramatize and enliven educational material with some of the verbal skill and energy that pervaded the most popular commercial shows. The industry-friendly National Advisory Council on Radio in Education (NACRE) specifically advocated cooperation between commercial broadcasters and educators on just these grounds. NACRE director Levering Tyson went so far as to argue that "there is no great difference between showmanship and education."[240] Paul Lazarsfeld, the most influential early scholar of mass communications, often advocated the educational potential of the quiz show format.[241] There was then remarkable unanimity of sentiment on this idea in the mid-1930s, from both the broadcaster and educator sides, that showmanship would be the future and salvation of educational radio. This conclusion fitted with a revision of the understanding of the role of educational radio. The key function of radio in education was now said to be not systematic instruction but provoking a desire to learn—just as the function of an advertisement was not comprehensive education about the product but sparking interest and desire. University of California president Robert Gordon Sproul argued in this way in 1934 that the role of educational radio was to "arouse in the average citizen a desire for intellectual and spiritual growth."[242]

Within the commercial broadcasting industry there was constant discussion of and experimentation with techniques to capture and hold listener interest. Aware of the prevalence of distracted radio listening, advertisers and broadcasters scrambled to develop programs that encouraged and rewarded concentration. "To enjoy the 'Cream of Wheat' broadcast," a J. Walter Thompson advertising executive explained in 1935, "attention must be focused very closely. Bridge, talking, dancing or other household diversions are laid

237. Judith Waller to John Royal, November 3, 1936, folder 6, box 92, NBC records, WHS.

238. *Broadcasting* 15, no. 3 (August 1, 1938): 7.

239. Llewellyn White interview with Paul W. Kesten, August 26, 1945, folder 1, box 4, Commission on Freedom of Press Records, UCSC.

240. Quoted in Edmund Leach, "Tuning Out Education: The Cooperation Doctrine in Radio, 1922–1938," Part 4: 2, available at http://www.current.org/coop/coop4.html.

241. For some of the work of the radio research project in this area, see Herta Herzog, "Professor Quiz: A Gratifications Study," in P. F. Lazarsfeld and F. N. Stanton (eds.), *Radio Research 1941* (New York: Duell, Sloan and Pearce, 1941).

242. R. G. Sproul in *Radio and Education* 1934, quoted in William Albig, *Public Opinion* (New York: McGraw Hill, 1939): 353.

aside until the program is ended." The commercial message, he proclaimed, "is so woven into the broadcast that there is no choice but to listen."[243] It was this kind of practical wisdom that lay behind the insistence of industry spokesmen that educational radio had to be entertaining. "The public wants to be educated," asserted a 1940 NBC brochure on public service broadcasting, "but it wants its education 'sugar-coated.'"[244] Philip G. Loucks, the managing director of the NAB, chose his words carefully when he told educators that education by radio had to be "interesting and unbiased as well as democratic in its concept and supplementary in its purpose."[245]

The networks put on their own educational programs in sustaining time, and these were among the most trumpeted of all radio's educational offerings. Walter Damrosch's *Music Appreciation Hour* on NBC and Alice Keith's *American School of the Air* at CBS were very important flagship programs. With these programs, the networks wanted to demonstrate their capacity to do serious, classroom education. The *Music Appreciation Hour* survived until 1942, and the CBS *American School of the Air* until 1948, but they were not joined by other network-level school of the air programs. Figure 1.5. State and

Figure 1.5. Frank Ernest Hill and others during *This Living World*, part of the CBS *American School of the Air*, December 31, 1943. On this program a problem was dramatized and then, in the final 10 minutes, students participated in discussion of it. CBS/Landov.

243. Herschel V. Williams Jr., "Skimming the Cream off the Air Audience," *Broadcasting* 8, no. 4 (February 15, 1935): 9.

244. *NBC Interprets Public Service in Radio Broadcasting* (New York: NBC, 1940): 5.

245. "Educators Oppose Upheaval of Radio at Ohio Sessions," *Broadcasting* 8, no. 10 (May 15, 1935): 46–47.

local government and educational institutions were more likely than networks to run directly pedagogic school of the air programs.[246] The network educational programs were less formally innovative than some of the programs produced in collaboration with outside cultural agencies or government, in which the emerging orthodoxy about radio's role as sparking interest found clearest expression. It might, of course, be noted that the networks' declared lack of interest in direct classroom broadcasting coincided with the rise of the soap opera and the increased commercial value of daytime radio hours.

At NBC, almost inevitably once entertaining public service programs had built an audience, there was talk of selling them to advertisers. Could educational programming be sold? A questionnaire sent to members of the FREC revealed that its members were divided on the question.[247] The question remained controversial, but unsurprisingly the networks came around to the view that sponsored educational or public service programming would be acceptable. The Standard Oil Company of California produced educational programs under its own sponsorship—the *Standard School Broadcast* began in 1928, and the *Standard Symphony Hour* in 1926. Both were presented free of advertising as a "means of making new friends for the company." Follow-up newspaper advertisements boasted that "we never meant it to sell anything—only to say 'Thank you' to our friends and patrons."[248]

Angell was not opposed in principle to selling NBC educational programs—he told NBC educational directors in 1939 that "there is no earthly reason why material that has general public service qualities or educational qualities should be confined to sustaining programs that the company puts on at its own expense."[249] A 1944 memo reported that Angell had decided that NBC public service programs, except for religious programs, could be sold to "dignified sponsors." He was quoted in *Billboard* as saying the decision was based on a recognition that a sustaining program might air on only 50 to 75 NBC stations, while a sponsored one had some chance of getting all 150 stations.[250] At CBS too, it was argued that there was no necessary incompatibility between first-rate educational and cultural features and commercial sponsorship.[251] But the underlying conflict between commercial and public service functions remained, and feelings remained high on this question—acknowledged as a public, not just a company, issue.

246. For a detailed history of the schools of the air at national, state, and local levels, see William Bianchi, *Schools of the Air: A History of Instructional Programs on Radio in the United States* (Jefferson, NC: McFarland, 2008).

247. "Joint Committee Seeks $142,000 Fund," *Broadcasting* 10, no. 5 (March 1, 1936): 46.

248. "The School Broadcasts of Standard Oil Company," *Broadcasting* 9, no. 6 (September 15, 1935): 11; Standard Oil advertisement, *Fresno Bee*, September 18, 1939: 3.

249. "Proceedings—Educational Directors' Meeting National Broadcasting Company," December 5, 1939, Drake Hotel, Chicago, folder 61, box 94, NBC records, WHS.

250. Memo Dwight Herrick to Bertha Brainard, October 6, 1944, folder 476, NBC history files, LOC; "NBC Decision to Sell Service Shows Not Set," *Billboard*, August 26, 1944: 8.

251. Llewellyn White interview with Paul W. Kesten, August 26, 1945, folder 1, box 4, Commission on Freedom of Press Records, UCSC.

COOPERATION IN PRACTICE

In 1939, NBC was cooperating with 22 different nonprofit groups in the making of public service and educational programs.[252] These cooperations were very important to the networks, particularly NBC. Walter Preston told James Angell frankly in 1939 that he thought "we have in the past followed the easy path by giving time and by putting on any old type of program with a pressure group just to satisfy the requests of the national officers of the pressure groups." This was particularly damaging, he felt, because "we have put it on and then promptly forgotten it as far as production is concerned but we have not forgotten to go around the country bragging about it."[253]

The extent of government radio production was one important reason that the industry story of an American system defined solely by its independence from government was a misrepresentation. The New Deal era of heightened government activism, and its historically novel attempts to integrate government into everyday life, led to a natural interest on the part of many government departments and agencies in using radio. Researcher Jeanette Sayre counted 42 federal agencies broadcasting in some form in 1940.[254] Government programming—in the form of live and recorded programs, as well as scripts for local broadcast performance—formed a significant minority among the networks' public service offerings through the 1930s. Many federal agencies—the Federal Housing Administration, the Department of Commerce, the Office of Education, the Works Progress Administration, the Department of Labor—made or contributed to programs. The WPA Federal Theater project had a radio section, which developed many drama and musical shows, including *Professional Parade* on NBC, featuring out-of-work actors and musicians performing musicals and other stage shows. The Department of the Interior in 1938 acquired its own broadcast studios in its Washington building—alarming many in the industry, and prompting the *Chicago Tribune* to warn of the danger of government "setting up radio divisions for systematic pirating of the airways for propaganda purposes."[255]

These government programs exemplified the 1930s belief that radio's real contribution to learning would lie in the blend of educational content and entertainment form. The U.S. Office of Education established a radio unit in 1930, which initially received funding from Carnegie and other philanthropic foundations. From 1936 the Emergency Educational Program trained radio writers and producers in an educational radio workshop. They had a brief to experiment with educational radio techniques, to find ways to combine educational content and entertainment technique in new and imaginative combinations. An advisory committee with industry representation oversaw the Office of Education productions—Franklin Dunham represented NBC and Edward R. Murrow, CBS. By 1940, the unit employed close to 200 people working on radio production.

252. Heistad, "Radio without Sponsors": 199.
253. Walter Preston to J. R. Angell, August 23, 1939, folder 59, box 94, NBC records, WHS.
254. Jeanette Sayre, *An Analysis of the Radiobroadcasting Activities of Federal Agencies* (Studies in the Control of Radio, no. 3) (Cambridge, MA: Radiobroadcasting Research Project at the Littauer Center, Harvard University, 1941): 8–16.
255. Walter Trohan, "See Roosevelt Regime Threat to Air Freedom," *Chicago Tribune*, February 16, 1939: 11.

The Office of Education concluded early that radio was not a good medium for detailed instruction, but that it was a good way to stimulate interest in a subject.[256] Office projects were self-consciously demonstrations of the possibilities of producing programs with educational value *and* entertainment appeal. NBC boasted in 1937 four series produced in cooperation with the Office of Education that "were designed to disseminate information in the form of dramatizations, games and round-table discussions"—shows such as *Have You Heard*, which featured dinner party conversations about scientific discoveries and *Answer Me This*, a social-science-based question-and answer-program.[257] The Office of Education made some other important series—perhaps most prominently *Americans All, Immigrants All* (CBS), dedicated to the "promotion and practice of the spirit of racial and group tolerance by all Americans."[258] Other Office series included *Let Freedom Ring* (CBS) on civil liberties, *Democracy in Action* (CBS) on the work of government, *Gallant American Women* (NBC), and *Brave New World* (CBS) in cooperation with the Pan-American Union. These cooperative endeavors—the networks supplying free time and access to talent, the government agencies producing scripts and ideas—were sometimes ambitious and complex productions, with elements of drama, narration, and music.

The *National Farm and Home Hour* —the program originally led from the network end by Frank Mullen—ran six days a week on NBC from 1928 to 1958. What was heard on air was a mix of music and entertainment supplied by the network, and information direct from the U.S. Department of Agriculture.[259] The *Hour* became an institution, had a loyal audience in both rural and urban areas, and was regarded as untouchable by the network. It was also a practical demonstration of cooperation. But when the USDA suggested in 1936 that it might be more convenient if it built its own broadcasting studio, Frank Russell at NBC was alarmed: "The construction of government studios is a step in the wrong direction. It would not be long before they started action to get control of broadcasting facilities."[260] The USDA also produced *Housekeepers' Chat*, and *Your Child*, for which the content was supplied by the Children's Bureau of the Department of Labor. Other USDA programs were distributed to stations in script form, to be read by local staff. Figure 1.6.

The government programs were one of the reasons that the simple idea of an American system of broadcasting as something quite independent of government misrepresented the actual situation of American radio in the 1930s. Government was involved with radio at many levels—from the licensing and regulatory system all the way to cooperative program production. The line between public and private broadcasting was actually as blurred and complicated in the United States as it was in many other nations. Sometimes, for example, government programs could be commercially sponsored. NBC

256. Sayre, *An Analysis of the Radiobroadcasting Activities of Federal Agencies*: 80.

257. *The NBC 1937 Yearbook: A Report of the National Broadcasting Company's Service to the Public in Its Eleventh Year* (New York: NBC, 1938), unpaginated.

258. "Americans All—Immigrants All, Purpose and Objectives," in Office of Education files, box 1, Entry 174, RG 12, NACP.

259. "Uncle Sam on the Air—with Donated Time," *Broadcasting* 10, no. 8 (April 15, 1936): 56.

260. Frank Russell to Niles Trammell, August 13, 1936, box 92, folder 31, NBC records, WHS.

Figure 1.6. Secretary of agriculture Henry A. Wallace speaking over the Farm and Home Hour on June 27, 1938, to mark the 3,000th hour of the program on the air. The Hour was at that moment claimed to be the world's oldest radio program, as measured in hours on the air. Harris and Ewing collection, Library of Congress.

sold 15 minutes of the *National Home and Farm Hour* from 1938.[261] The Federal Housing Authority produced series of programs for radio designed simply to promote the idea of home ownership—they were ready-made commercial programs with spaces for sponsors' advertisements and music as entertainment. Jeanette Sayre observed, "There is no doubt that the happy combination of performing a public service and making money for radio at the same time has enhanced the popularity of the FHA program with the stations."[262]

Perhaps inevitably, the federal radio programs came in for criticism from the industry. There was some carping about production standards—the budgets available to the government agencies were small in industry terms. Sayre contrasted the government's efforts with the intermission talks by William J. Cameron in the *Ford Sunday Evening Hour* from 1934: "What bureau or agency can afford the Detroit Symphony Orchestra to lure listeners to hear the capsuled political philosophy of an Administration as Mr. Ford can for his point of view?"[263] The federal government sometimes thus appeared as the poor cousin of radio production, in clear contrast to the situation of government broadcasters in other nations.

Stations also complained at times about the expectation that they should carry government shows free as part of their public service. By mid-1936, *Broadcasting* was reporting that "not only network shows, but scripts, spot announcements and even transcriptions are emanating regularly from New Deal agencies and sent directly to stations, many of which have already begun to complain that they do not have enough time

261. Sayre, *An Analysis of the Radiobroadcasting Activities of Federal Agencies*: 53.

262. Sayre, *An Analysis of the Radiobroadcasting Activities of Federal Agencies*: 63, 66.

263. Sayre, *An Analysis of the Radiobroadcasting Activities of Federal Agencies*: 115. On Ford's radio activities, see David Lewis, *The Public Image of Henry Ford: An American Folk Hero and His Company* (Detroit: Wayne State University Press, 1976), ch. 19.

available to carry them."[264] Behind the scenes, NBC's Frank Russell began discussions with the FCC about the burden the government programs imposed on the network. During 1935, he reported, NBC had broadcast 556 hours of federal government programs. In addition, each government agency, Russell complained, sent out "thousands of mimeographed speeches and scripts and electrical transcriptions."[265]

These were annoyances, but the American broadcasters' biggest concern was of course that government activity in radio might presage more fundamental reform of the American system. The BBC's representative Felix Greene reported to London in 1937 that the U.S. government, "pleased with the success of the programmes it has itself launched through its relief agencies, is preparing plans for a further tightening of Government control and extension of direct Government activity in broadcasting."[266] The broadcasters regarded the Office of Education's John W. Studebaker as a "dangerous" man for the industry, and it seems clear that Studebaker was in 1937 seriously entertaining the idea of a government radio network—to the extent that one of his closest colleagues, Chester S. Williams, felt it necessary to criticize the idea. Williams argued back to Studebaker that "the federal Government need not establish a network of its own. It would only have to establish a central broadcasting station and then buy time from the local stations."[267] That same month Studebaker sent a statement to the network presidents, asserting that the Office of Education had a legitimate interest in broadcasting and that he was quite prepared to invoke his oversight of the nation's educational welfare as ground for an intervention into broadcasting:

> There is no socially sound reason why there should be adequate, systematic and sustained provision for an assured, regular, national coverage for ideas concerning articles for sale, while at the same time there is no similar provision for the dissemination of knowledge, ideas, ideals and inspiration which serve the sole purpose of lifting the general level of enlightenment and culture.[268]

From a high federal official, these were fighting words. Studebaker wanted NBC and CBS to form an American Academy of Educational Broadcasting, to produce educational programs for national broadcast. He addressed the Institute for Radio in Education conference in May 1937, and identified three grounds on which the federal government had a legitimate and active interest in radio:

> To safeguard the use of radio frequencies to insure the maximum of public service; to use radio to acquaint the public with the work of government; and to keep the public posted concerning the services it should expect of radio, and to persuade and assist broadcasters to provide those services.

264. "Uncle Sam on the Air—with Donated Time," *Broadcasting* 10, no. 8 (April 15, 1936): 11.

265. Frank Russell to Anning Prall, May 11, 1936, box 45, folder 71, NBC records, WHS.

266. Felix Greene confidential report, May 19, 1937, BBC Written Archives Centre File E1/212/2.

267. Memo Williams to Studebaker, April 13, 1937, Federal Forum Project, box 1, RG 12, Entry 190, NACP.

268. J. W. Studebaker, "How Can a Real System of Educational Broadcasting Be Established in the United States?" April 6, 1937, folder 18, box 53, NBC records, WHS.

Studebaker argued that popularity could not stand as the only measure of the public interest in broadcasting: "American broadcasts are generally popular with American audiences. It is hard to conceive, however, that nearly all radio channels in the broadcast band should be placed permanently in the hands of commercial companies even though they are charged to use them in the public interest, convenience, and necessity." And as a final parting shot, "The airways belong to the people and the right to use them can be taken away by the people's agency of government as easily as the right is given."[269] This was the most alarming thing the broadcasting industry had heard for some time. John Royal wrote to Lenox Lohr, "These opinions by Dr. Studebaker are very serious."[270] *Broadcasting* printed the speech in full, with an introduction that warned that Studebaker's outline of federal aims in radio "may possibly augur administration policy of the future toward the existing radio system."[271] Royal continued to watch Studebaker carefully, scrutinizing his public utterances for signs of a move on commercial radio. In 1940, Studebaker issued a report on the activities of the FREC, which observed in passing that radio "belonged to the people; it should be developed and regulated by the people, in the public interest."[272] Royal detected a "slightly dangerous tinge" to the comment. He wrote to RCA president David Sarnoff that "a number of interpretations can be put on this, and I am not sure that Mr. Studebaker's interpretation is wholly for our best interests."[273] The threat of a government educational broadcaster was quite real enough to keep the networks anxious, but also cooperative within the terms of the 1934 settlement.

NATIONAL VERSUS COMMERCIAL

The nation-building expectations of radio were perhaps most obvious in the smaller nations, which looked to national broadcasting systems both to create and to defend national cultures. The Canadian Radio League adopted the aim of "protecting Canada from a radio system like that of the US" and from excessive American content.[274] When formed, the Canadian public broadcaster took on a national role, while commercial broadcasters were more local in orientation.[275] Canada's Aird Royal Commission in 1929 understood radio as a national medium, and predicted that once a Canadian system had been established, radio would "undoubtedly become a great force in fostering a national spirit and interpreting national citizenship."[276]

269. J. W. Studebaker, "The Government's Responsibility for Education by Radio," Speech at 8th Institute on Education by Radio, May 4, 1937, Columbus, Ohio, unprocessed collection: Institute for Education by Radio and Television, Ohio State University Archives.

270. John Royal to Lenox Lohr, May 10, 1937, folder 18, box 53, NBC records, WHS.

271. "Federal Aims in Education by Radio," *Broadcasting* 12, no. 10 (May 15, 1937): 17.

272. John Studebaker report on FREC, December 19, 1939, folder 3, box 77, NBC records, WHS.

273. John Royal to David Sarnoff, January 13, 1940, folder 3, box 77, NBC records, WHS.

274. Quoted in Marc Raboy, *Missed Opportunities*: 31.

275. Mary Vipond, "British or American? Canada's 'Mixed' Broadcasting System in the 1930s," *Radio Journal* 2, no. 2 (2004): 92.

276. Aird Commission report quoted in Hector Charlesworth, "Broadcasting in Canada," in *Radio the Fifth Estate, Annals of the American Academy of Political and Social Science*, 177, (January 1935): 42.

Nation-states intervened to defend their people against the newly mobile cultural forms and products of the broadcast age—for the technologial means of nation-building were also effective in disseminating cultural product transnationally.[277] Levels of national content became a political and governmental issue in many countries in the 1930s—particularly in those English or Spanish-speaking nations that lacked a natural barrier of linguistic protection from foreign programming. "Nationalization gets its strongest advocates," the *New York Times* reported of Canada, "out of those who resent domination of the air by American programs of jazz, crooners, American oratory and infinitely wearisome advertising blurbs."[278] In Australia, Canada, and New Zealand, broadcasters played American programs and took BBC Empire programs, but governments worried about protecting the national culture. There were no simple answers. As Orrin Dunlap noted in the *New York Times*, the Canadian audience was itself conflicted: "In sentiment the Canadian is predominantly British: in habit American. He listens to Jack Benny and he believes in the British constitutional monarchy."[279]

Putting U.S. radio history alongside the other national broadcasting histories makes clearer that in the United States too, radio had important national functions, but they were made more complicated by broadcasting's commercial structure. The nation-building role of U.S. radio has been less explored than those of national broadcasters in smaller nations. This is another instance in which the focus, in the 1930s and since, on the broadest contrasts between the largest English-speaking nations, comparing British and American radio, obscures broader patterns. Radio in the United States and United Kingdom could and did fill its broadcasting schedules almost entirely with homegrown product—the exceptions being deliberately chosen special events programming from abroad. There was no need for the national content quotas introduced in smaller nations to protect indigenous culture and performers. But although not expressed in mandated quotas, there was a clear nationalist and nation-building role for the national networks in the United Kingdom and the United States—evident, for example, in their special attention to national musics, the growing importance of a national news service, and their explicit or implicit efforts to incorporate or assimilate classes and ethnicities and regions into a national culture. Hilmes argues that the networks worked to "centralize and unify American cultural experience and identity as no other medium had ever attempted."[280] The American networks were eager to portray themselves as national broadcasters—in their broadcast of talks from a range of federal officials, of debates and forums about national issues, of news from distant parts of the nation. The 1937 NBC Year Book, lavishly illustrated, contained photographs of President Roosevelt and other U.S. government officials speaking through NBC (and other surprisingly unlabeled) microphones. The brochure explained that the "ultra-modern" NBC studios in Washington DC were "easily accessible to officials, diplomats and lawmakers." CBS also

277. See discussion of this point in Eric Thomas, "Canadian Broadcasting and Multiculturalism: Attempts to Accommodate Ethnic Minorities," *Canadian Journal of Communication* 17, no. 3 (1992). Available: http://www.cjc-online.ca/index.php/journal/article/view/676/582. [January 27, 2010].

278. "Canada Seeks Plan for Radio Control," *New York Times*, February 21, 1932: E6.

279. Orrin Dunlap, "Radio Reciprocity," *New York Times*, March 6, 1938: 160.

280. Hilmes, *Radio Voices*: 22.

stressed its national functions—William Paley claimed that "all broadcasts which tend to develop in our Nation a unity of national sense and feeling may be considered to have important educational value."[281] That network radio made the nation more real to ordinary Americans is now a well-known historical fact—the fireside chats famously made a powerful connection in many minds between the radio networks and the nation.

But the American networks in the 1930s stood in a completely different relation to their programs than did the BBC. They increasingly handed over production of programs to advertisers, even as they strove to exercise control over content. The networks regretted their situation, but found it difficult to change. CBS president William Paley confided to University of Chicago president Robert M. Hutchins some time in the late 1930s that the broadcasters had made a "terrible mistake" in allowing advertisers to take over program production.[282]

The networks' lack of direct control over programs became a particular issue at moments of national significance and solemnity. When in 1935 internationally known social reformer and peace activist Jane Addams died, there was some dismay and subsequent internal correspondence at NBC about the way the death was announced on air. The bulletin mentioned the cause of death—cancer—which had been kept secret even from Addams herself. Sidney Strotz at NBC Chicago apologized to John Royal in New York for "muffing" the announcement, which had been made not by a staff announcer, but by a "special announcer engaged for a commercial show."[283] Even NBC's own executives felt that the national voice and the commercial voice ought to be different in tone, and were uneasy with the results of the mixing that was inevitably occurring. Truly national symbols had to be associated with the network, not with advertisers. The national anthem, for example, had to be linked to the network identification, not the advertiser, so at NBC, "it has been a policy of the Company not to permit any producer credits or commercials after the National Anthem. . . . In other words, we do not permit the National Anthem to be tied up with a commercial."[284]

Listeners wrote to the FCC to complain about the incongruity of having important national speakers cut short for advertisements. "I have heard many national figures talking," reported a Montana listener, "only to have them cut off in the most interesting part for some silly advertisement."[285] Some listeners heard commercial comedy programs being disrespectful to the nation. An Ohio woman in 1942 was "disgusted" to hear George Burns and Gracie Allen use the name of Lincoln and parts of the Gettysburg Address "very lightly." "It seems to me," she wrote, "that in serious times like these the last thing we want is our heroes and the fine things they left us treated in a disrespectful manner."[286] The American system of radio was characterized by this tension between the national

281. William S. Paley, "Radio and the Humanities," *Annals of the American Academy of Political and Social Science*, 177 (January 1935): 96.

282. Folder 10, box 3: 90, Commission on Freedom of Press Records, UCSC.

283. Sidney Strotz to John Royal, folder 49, box 33, NBC records, WHS.

284. Sidney Strotz to Niles Trammell, December 15, 1941, folder 9, box 354, WHS, NBC papers.

285. Letter to FCC, June 25, 1938, box 184, RG 173, FCC, Office of the Executive Director, General Correspondence 1927–46, 44–3, NACP.

286. Letter to FCC, February 13, 1942, box 194, RG 173, NACP.

voice and the commercial one. Listeners experienced dissonance as they heard one rapidly after the other, one impersonating or making fun of the other.

Time given to national leaders and representatives was a major plank in the civic and public service programming of the networks, and something they boasted about in publicity. The time involved was quite significant. NBC statisticians counted 223 hours and 45 minutes given over to federal officials—including the president and vice president, cabinet members, senators, and representatives—in 1937.[287] President Roosevelt himself was at times a prolific broadcaster, quite apart from the famous, set-piece fireside chats, of which there were a limited number. In July 1938, for example, Roosevelt spoke five times over NBC—dedicating monuments and discussing the work of his administration.[288] The normal procedure at NBC was to try to place talks by national leaders and representatives in unsold time, to minimize the cost to the network. An internal memo in late 1936 praised one executive who had succeeded splendidly at this task, without apparently alerting the speakers too bluntly to the commercial imperatives behind the scheduling: "In addition to the fact that Morton maneuvered about 80% of all political broadcasts into open time," reported Frank Russell, "he also handled the different groups with unusual and consummate tact and finesse."[289]

The commercial success and profitability of network radio, however, only exacerbated the tensions between national public service of this kind and normal commercial functioning. As more and more time was sold, the number of open slots in the schedule diminished. Sidney Strotz wrote to the NBC sales vice president in 1941, pointing out the way in which commercial success could imperil national service:

> You and your Sales department have done such a swell job on selling the Red that it has resulted in the Red having only the following open spots: Saturday, 7.00–7.30, and the three limited splits—Monday and Friday, 10.30–11.00, and Saturday, 10.00–10.30.
>
> Having done such a swell job you are now faced with the problem that if the President of the United States or others of less importance ask for time, it will probably be necessary for us to cancel commercials time....[290]

If a major political event or crisis motivated unusual numbers of legislators to request time to speak on the radio, the networks could not avoid making a loss in honoring their civic responsibilities. During the court-packing debate in 1937, NBC calculated its net loss from cancellation of commercial programs to provide time for Supreme Court related discussions at—precisely—$13,611.76.[291] In late August and early September 1939, as war broke out in Europe, NBC canceled numbers of commercial programs to cover the news,

287. Memo from H. M. Beville, May 25, 1938, folder 34, box 94, NBC records, WHS.
288. "Appearances of President Franklin D. Roosevelt on NBC Red and Blue Networks 1938," folder 84, box 63, NBC records, WHS.
289. Frank Russell to Lenox Lohr November 5, 1936, folder 31, box 92, NBC records, WHS.
290. Sidney Strotz to Roy Witmer, August 11, 1941, folder 5, box 354, NBC records, WHS.
291. Mark Woods to Frank Russell, March 16, 1937, folder 26, box 93, NBC records, WHS.

at a total reported cost to the network of $22, 706.72.[292] Such costs could be finely calcu-lated, while the benefits were less quantifiable—partly a matter of risk analysis, but also involving assessment of the audiences gained—which made the task of those executives such as Frank Russell, whose job it was to monitor the political threats to the continued functioning of the "American system," all the more difficult.

On December 7, 1941, a few minutes after the broadcast announcement of the attack on Pearl Harbor, RCA president and NBC board chairman David Sarnoff sent a tele-gram to President Roosevelt saying, "All our facilities and personnel are ready and at your instant service. We await your commands." This was a preemptive declaration that the network was already a national broadcaster, in no need of federal emergency inter-vention. The networks immediately went on to 24-hour transmission. News "flashes" regularly interrupted programs to keep listeners informed about the attack and the dec-larations of war during the following days of crisis. Some scheduled programs were abandoned altogether. One radio columnist wrote approvingly that "all regular pro-grams were put into a secondary category to make way for the tremendous news from the Pacific."[293]

The interruption of so many programs to carry news of Pearl Harbor was, however, very disruptive to the commercial operation of the networks. NBC attempted to limit the commercial impact by running "scheduled news flashes" in the first minute of each 15-minute program and the first two minutes of every half-hour program. The NBC archive allows us a glimpse of the house divided inside the network, as executives with commercial responsibilities clashed even on this solemn occasion with those in charge of programming. One senior sales executive wrote to another in January 1942 that there had been great difficulty making satisfactory explanations and adjustments with clients who had lost program time to news flashes, and that he thought that scheduled news flashes should never be used again.[294] Clarence Menser, then vice president for programming, did not agree:

> I believe two favorable things were accomplished. The first is that it probably held audience, if not indeed increased audience, for the shows from which the time was taken because in a short time that audience became acquainted with the reg-ularity of the news and knew they didn't have to go fishing all over the dial for news flashes. The second thing was that it gave an opportunity for the client to get both his commercials into the program without interruption and at the same time allowed the audience to get the full story.....[295]

The tension between the roles of national broadcaster and seller of valuable time to advertising agencies was again clearly dramatized in this moment of national crisis. One radio columnist thought there was an "essential contradiction between wartime

292. Charles Rynd to R. C. Witmer, September 20, 1939, folder 13, box 68, NBC records, WHS.

293. Larry Wolters, "War News Puts Stations on 24 Hour Basis," *Chicago Tribune*, December 14, 1941: N10.

294. Roy Witmer to Frank Mullen, January 1942, folder 10, box 354, NBC records, WHS.

295. C. L. Menser to Roy Witmer January 19, 1942, folder 10, box 354, NBC records, WHS.

radio as a national instrumentality and the methods of peacetime commercial broadcasting."[296]

If we take American radio at its word, and attempt to understand it simply as the opposite of the BBC, many aspects of it will make little sense. Radio after 1934 was shaped by the regulatory framework and by apprehensions about the political environment. American networks, in particular, had to maintain a whole series of dual identities—as entertainers and educators, as cooperative providers of just what the people wanted and vehicles for uplift and improvement, as smart commercial operators and authoritative national institutions. The broadcasters did not have the luxury of treating any of these as either/or options. These continuing tensions, rather than some essential quality of "freedom," were the truly distinctive thing about American radio.

The broadcasters soon came to realize, however, that educational and high cultural programming, despite its great political efficacy, would not be enough to solve all of their problems of legitimation. While the radio reform movement, which foregrounded education, was defeated in 1934, the game soon moved on. In the era of propaganda, centrally diffused education came to seem a less urgent need, and even a less desirable thing, than the production of rational, skeptical, and self-aware citizens. Broadcasters thus needed, in addition to education and high culture, to address a third crucial area—civics—and to develop programming that made more active and critical citizens. The defeat of set-aside educational radio was actually the birth of something else, something much less noticed by historians. The next chapter moves from the story of defeat to an account of the emergence of radio's civic paradigm.

296. John Coburn Turner, "Why Not One Network Solely for News Bulletins?" *Washington Post*, December 14, 1941: L5.

2

The Civic Paradigm

PROLOGUE: STORIES OF DEFEAT

Dr. John R. Sampey was president of the Southern Baptist Convention. He was a very senior church figure, who had taught at the Southern Baptist Theological Seminary in Louisville, Kentucky, since the 1880s, and been its president since 1929.[1] He was, in 1938, late in life, just discovering radio and his own skill at communicating with it. "Friends far and wide," he recalled, "have told me that I have a good radio voice."[2] Sampey was to become a regular broadcaster who, from 1939 to 1945, would preach on the second Sunday of every month on the *Baptist Hour* on Louisville radio.[3]

In January 1938, in Macon, Georgia, Sampey delivered an angry sermon about radio. There was urgency in his message. He criticized American radio for "wasting time advertising somebody's soap and tooth paste." In a subsequent newspaper interview, he went further. If he had his way, he told the reporter, broadcasting stations would be operated by a federal board, and supported by licenses. He said that he would prefer that radio was used for educational purposes, as in England, "rather than for commercial purposes, as in America." He hastened to add that there was nothing wrong with the technology itself: "Many a fine institution is sometimes perverted to wrong use. For example, the airplane carries serum to suffering humanity, and at the same time the airplane drops bombs in China."[4]

Sampey's Macon sermon was broadcast over WMAZ. The station had begun as a project of the physics department at Mercer University, a Baptist institution—the studio had been constructed in the tower of the university chapel in 1922. But, as at many colleges, after the initial enthusiasm subsided, Mercer found it difficult to sustain a regular schedule for the broadcast day.[5] Facing additional expenses to modernize the equipment

---

1. James Duane Bolin, *Kentucky Baptists 1925–2000: A Story of Cooperation* (Brentwood, TN: Southern Baptist Historical Society, 2000): 105.

2. *Memoirs of John R. Sampey* (Nashville: Broadman Press, 1947): 270.

3. *Memoirs of John R. Sampey*: 269. See also biographical information, available at http://www.ageslibrary.com/authordb/S/sampey.html. [January 27, 2010].

4. "Baptist Leader Voices Surprise", *Charleston News and Courier* January 28, 1938: 2.

5. On the decline of college and educational broadcasting, see Llewellyn White, *The American Radio: A Report on the Broadcasting Industry in the United States from the Commission on Freedom of the Press* (Chicago: University of Chicago Press, 1947), ch. 5; and Hugh Slotten, "Universities, Public Service Experimentation, and the Origins of Radio Broadcasting in the United States, 1900–1920," *Historical Journal of Film, Radio and Television* 26, no. 4 (October 2006): 485–504.

of the station, in 1926 the university's board of trustees decided to lease, and then in 1929 to sell, the station to the Macon Chamber of Commerce.[6] Station manager E. K. Cargill and three other local businessmen leased the station from the chamber in 1929, and bought it in 1936. So, by stages, the educational station became a commercial one.

Born in nearby Eufaula, Alabama, E. K. Cargill thus became president and manager of WMAZ. He belonged to the first generation of Americans to have built a whole career in radio—first as an entertainer, then from 1927 managing and finally owning WMAZ. In April 1937, Cargill and his associates affiliated WMAZ with CBS. Now in charge of an important network station, he was offended by Sampey's sermon. It seemed to him that Sampey had shown "very poor judgment in saying what he did," after WMAZ had arranged a "courtesy broadcast" of the sermon. Cargill wrote to the pastor of the First Baptist Church of Macon, Dr. J. P. Boone, to say so. Boone, strikingly, decided that he agreed with the radio station owner rather than with his own senior church colleague, and promptly expressed his disappointment at Sampey's criticisms of radio. He offered his "appreciation of the courtesy extended by WMAZ" and deeply regretted that anything was said that "gave offense to our local radio station."[7] Sampey was defiant: "I said nothing to apologize for and I would say the same thing a thousand times over."[8]

By the late 1930s, principled public resistance to the commercialized American system of radio had become both personally and politically difficult. Broadcasters wielded growing influence in many American communities. Perhaps Sampey was galled by the need to be grateful for a "courtesy" broadcast on a station that had so recently been owned and operated by the Baptists. The increasing dominance of commercial and network broadcasting was a part of his own experience. Sampey was old enough, senior and out-of-town enough, that he was oblivious to the displeasure of the owners of the Macon station. That indifference was not possible for Boone, who had to live and work in Macon, and who needed the goodwill of the station owners.[9] Boone had to acknowledge publicly the persuasiveness of their advocacy of the "American system," with its promise of friendly cooperation with educational, religious, and other community groups.

FROM EDUCATION TO THE CIVIC PARADIGM

Sampey's story helps us understand why, despite some high profile critics—often from the consumer movement, contesting the execution rather than the principle of commercial radio—fundamental criticism of the commercial basis of the American system of

6. James Adams Lester, *A History of the Georgia Baptist Convention 1822–1972* (Nashville: Curtley Printing, 1972): 517; Joseph G. Jackson, "Vintage Broadcasting: The End of An Era—WMAZ AM (1921–1996)," *Antique Radio Classified* 15, no. 3 (March 1998). Available: http://www.antiqueradio.com/wmaz_03-98.html. [January 27, 2010]; S. E. Frost Jr., *Education's Own Stations: The History of Broadcast Licenses Issued to Educational Institutions* (Chicago: University of Chicago Press, 1937): 197–98.

7. *Florence Morning News*, January 28, 1938: 3.

8. *Charleston News and Courier*, January 28, 1938: 2.

9. In October, Boone resigned from the position of pastor in Macon, and returned to Waxahachie, Texas. H. Lewis Batts, *History of the First Baptist Church at Macon* (Macon: Southern Press, 1968): 180.

broadcasting had become by the late 1930s a fugitive thing.[10] The broadcast reform movement's arguments about the need for more education and civic and high cultural programming on the air were easily co-opted by the broadcasters, who earned much political capital from their cooperative efforts in these directions. The doctrine of cooperation – that educational programming was best delivered interspersed with entertainment by skilled commercial broadcasters—had for a time ended the argument about separate facilities for nonprofit and educational broadcasting. Meanwhile, the power and influence of commercial broadcasters in local communities was growing. Radio was popular, and many of its programs were already well-loved friends. The alternative—state-run broadcasting as practiced in Europe in the age of propaganda—seemed less and less appealing or plausible an alternative for the United States. The BBC functioned with diminishing frequency as a visible and appealing alternative to the American system, and Britain itself was a less viable role model as the isolationist majority's suspicion of British motives in foreign policy spilled over into a more general critique of British values and institutions.

The radio and education reformers were indeed by the later 1930s losing heart about the prospects of systemic reform of broadcasting. The broadcasting industry was using its considerable public relations capacities to persuade Americans that the major threat to free speech came from government censorship rather than from commercial control of the air. The international examples of government control of radio under fascism and communism were acknowledged on all sides in the United States as frightening. Few Americans cared even to attempt to make the difficult case distinguishing public funding from direct government control. Once-prominent critics of commercial network broadcasting began to use the pejorative language of "government" rather than "public" broadcasting, which conceded a great deal to those who saw an inevitable slide from government funding to censorship and propaganda. The American Civil Liberties Union, for example, shifted from concern about the threat to free speech posed by the commercial broadcasting system, to a focus on government censorship and an acceptance that radio stations were "private enterprises" not themselves susceptible to charges of censorship.[11] Roger Baldwin of the ACLU made it clear in 1939 that he and his organization did not support the principle of government ownership of radio—an issue that, he said, had already been "frequently before the public."[12] S. Howard Evans of the National Committee on Education by Radio, formerly the most oppositional of the educational broadcast reform organizations, had also come to a reluctant acceptance of the status quo, and a belief that better regulation rather than structural reform was the most that could be hoped for.[13] Evans conceded that "recent experience with radio in European countries suggests that there is a real danger to democracy in turning over to any central government more than the minimum of authority over what shall be spoken on the air."[14]

10. See Kathy M. Newman, *Radio Active: Advertising and Consumer Activism, 1935–1947* (Berkeley: University of California Press, 2004), ch. 2 for discussion of 'radio activists'.

11. Robert McChesney, *Telecommunications, Mass Media, and Democracy: The Battle for the Control of U.S. Broadcasting, 1928–1935* (New York: Oxford University Press, 1993): 82–86, 236–39.

12. Roger Baldwin interview, FCC hearings, docket 5060, box 1413, RG 173, NACP: 6504.

13. McChesney, *Telecommunications, Mass Media, and Democracy*: 232–33.

14. Howard Evans interview, FCC hearings, docket 5060, box 1413, RG 173, NACP: 6571.

The early 1930s radio reform movement had been led and dominated by educators, with religious and labor leaders also playing very important roles. The broadcasting industry had thus long identified the "educational problem" as one of the clouds on its horizon. *Broadcasting* reminded readers in 1936 that the "educational problem" had underlain the Wagner-Hatfield and other set-aside proposals. Concern about education had "caused many members of Congress to burst forth in attacks upon radio generally" and had provided "the vehicle upon which many a reformer and agitator has ridden into the limelight."[15] So the immediate broadcasting industry response to victory in 1934 was that concessions to education and religion would continue to be necessary. NBC's John Royal wrote confidentially of the FCC report, "The tone...very definitely sounds a note of warning to us. It is very apparent that the Commission feels that education and religion should be given consideration by the present radio set-up." Fellow NBC executive, Richard Patterson, agreed: "Absolutely—let us take care."[16] The message many broadcasters heard most clearly was thus that educational, high cultural and religious programming had to be given time on the air. About labor there was always more reluctance—no doubt because of broadcasters' need to court corporate advertisers, labor's message was classified as "controversial" rather than improving.[17]

But the terms of the public discussion in the United States about radio's social purposes were subtly changing. The debate in 1934 looked back to a recent past in which the arguments about broadcasting were dominated by issues about access. Could educational institutions, churches, labor unions, and ethnic organizations own and operate their own radio stations? On what terms could they gain time on existing stations to represent themselves? But as the Sampey story illustrates, the battle for direct access through diffusion of station ownership amongst diverse groups in American society had largely been lost by the mid-1930s.

The legal frame for the access debate was the question of whether radio stations could be or should be considered as public utilities, like water or electricity supplies, available without discrimination at a known price to all who wished to use them? Or even further, should radio be considered a common carrier like telegraph and telephone, so all had a right not just to receive but to send messages on known and equal terms? The Communications Act of 1934, like the 1927 Radio Act, borrowed language from public utility regulation but clearly specified that broadcasting stations were not to be deemed common carriers. The idea that broadcasters should be considered as public utilities or even common carriers however remained in the air in the 1930s, revived in spirit or in name by numbers of populist reformers and by those frustrated in their attempts to broadcast. When Frank McNinch took over as FCC chairman in 1937, from a background in public utility regulation at the Federal Power Commission, he made it clear that, while radio might not be a common carrier, he did consider it a public utility and intended to regulate it as such.[18] A legal scholar could still with some justification conclude in 1940 that "broadcasting has

15. "Educated Cooperation," *Broadcasting* 10, no. 1 (January 1, 1936): 32.

16. John F. Royal to Richard C. Patterson Jr., January 23, 1935, folder 26, box 26, NBC records, WHS.

17. Elizabeth Fones-Wolf, "Promoting a Labor Perspective in the American Mass Media: Unions and Radio in the CIO Era, 1936–56," *Media, Culture & Society* 22, no.3 (2000): 288.

18. "Mr. McNinch Talks about Radio," *New York Times*, October 10, 1937: 184.

been generally described as a public utility by prominent legislators, radio commissioners and legal writers."[19]

By the later 1930s, however, this set of questions about access to broadcasting facilities was subordinated to a cluster of claims about individuals in their role as audience. This happened in part for the reason McChesney and others have identified—that the radio reformers who wanted more education, religion, and labor on radio had largely given up hope of major reform of the American system of broadcasting and were no longer a potent political force. But it also happened because there was a quite different national and world political and cultural situation by the mid to late 1930s. The mounting fear of the influence of propaganda on the national population provided a powerful new motivation to develop a broadcasting system that produced active, critical audiences. Thus civically desirable qualities of individual citizens, such as self-improvement, self-government, empathy, tolerance, and rationality, joined the uncontroversial goods of education and high culture and mainstream religion, as the goals of radio's public service programming.

The Sampey story thus dramatizes one of the fundamental shifts from the debates of the late 1920s and early 1930s, to the terrain of argument after that. In the earlier period, the biggest aspiration of reformers was to have their own broadcasting facilities, nonprofit radio stations run for and by educational institutions, labor unions, churches, or ethnic organizations. But over time, many nonprofit groups struggled to maintain their stations, to fill the hours of the week with programming, and to pay the bills and maintain equipment to the standard the FCC required. The dream of direct access, each group with its own broadcasting outlet, was aggressively opposed by the broadcasting industry, and undermined by the FRC and then FCC as they enacted the policy of favoring general interest over single issue or identity stations. The future of broadcasting was now most often said to be as a representative institution, not as a common carrier to which all could claim access to speak for themselves. Stations were to invite in community representatives of all kinds and hence in theory offer something for everyone—the generalist station would appeal to many different audiences over the course of a day, and thus introduce different community sectors to one another. Early in his tenure as U.S. commissioner of education and chair of FREC, John Studebaker succinctly described the shift that he and many others had made away from questioning the American system, toward trying to make good the promise of representation and cooperation. Our system of communication is privately owned and operated, he noted, but "regardless of who owns these lines of communication or what authority operates them at any given time, it is essential to the preservation of our democracy that they be used to *REPRESENT* the American people and not to *DICTATE* to them."[20] The "public interest" responsibilities of the broadcasters were to be exercised by knowing their local community and facilitating the process by which the community as a whole represented itself to itself. There were endless complexities to this, perhaps the most important of them the way that broadcasting and

19. "Notes: Radio," *Air Law Review* 11, no.2 (April 1940): 181.
20. John Studebaker, "Educational Broadcasting in a Democracy," speech given May 15, 1935, folder 36, box 36, NBC records, WHS.

broadcasting policy privileged place-based community, the "local." Broadly however, the decade after 1934 was dominated by regulatory expectations of service to a local community, and by the demand that the diversity of that local community be hearable on radio.

Lest the move from a dream of direct access to the promise of representation—an hour or two here and there on a crowded schedule—seem just a loss, another case had to be developed, about the effects of exposure to such diversity on the listener. The ground of the argument shifted from the rights of groups representing themselves, to the rights of audience members. Increasingly, the public interest claims of the broadcasters rested upon the benefit to the listener of being exposed to diversity, of hearing many points of view, many kinds of people, and many types of music, on their radios. Listening to that diversity, rather than broadcasting yourself, was coming to be thought of as a right by the later 1930s. At a time when newspapers were still often openly and stridently partisan, radio's modern promise was of a general and responsible representativeness. Studebaker argued that "the people have an inalienable right to hear every important point of view."[21] For their own reasons, broadcasters, the FCC, and many articulate and educated listeners joined in endorsing this representative ideal as a solution to the conflict over radio's public purpose. A dissident populist chorus, for example, among the many supporters of Charles Coughlin the radio priest, did keep alive the older public utility claims for a right of direct access, and while they ultimately lost this long battle about radio's public sphere, they did succeed in providing a sustained, vigorous, and pointed opposition to the didactic pluralism and managed representativeness of what became the dominant ideas about radio's public sphere.

The representative model of broadcasting seemed the way of the future. It was one key component of what I am calling the "civic paradigm" for radio, a specific solution to the issues and conflicts so visible in 1934. The civic paradigm replaced the direct access ideal as the dominant—at once liberal and elite—way of thinking about broadcasting's public role in American society. The civic paradigm as I define it included most importantly the following beliefs:

- Radio stations should represent the diversity of their local community.
- Listeners had a right to hear that diversity represented.
- Listeners became better citizens through listening to these diverse voices and points of view.
- The ideal listener was active, rational, and critical, as well as tolerant and empathetic, and individually responsible for her/his listening.
- Such ideal listeners were as much made as found, and broadcasters shared with government a responsibility to transform radio listening into more than a passive recreation.
- Citizen listeners in a democracy and in an age of propaganda had, as the culmination of listening, the task of forming and articulating their own personal opinions.

This is my blunt summation of the ideas that I will be arguing constituted the official orthodoxy of American broadcasting for a decade or more after 1934. The big broadcasters

21. Studebaker, "Educational Broadcasting in a Democracy."

won the right to continue their profitable operations free from government competition, but only within the terms of this civic paradigm. For them, the civic paradigm was demanding but much more possible to live with than demands for direct access. The civic paradigm sat alongside, and gave a particular inflection to, commitment to educational and high cultural broadcasting. For government, the FCC, and the many listeners who shared the pluralist values implied in the civic paradigm, this was the most viable, most acceptable aspirational answer to the problem of radio's public role.

FROM EDUCATION TO CITIZENSHIP

While education, religion, labor, and the special needs of rural areas remained topics of concern in public discussion of radio in the later 1930s, there was, in addition, an increasing and new emphasis on citizenship, democracy, and the dangerous power of propaganda, which had quite different effects. NBC's Henry Norton observed, astutely, that it was Henry Lee Ewbank of the University of Wisconsin who had at the 1934 FCC hearings "stated the case against us as strongly as it is likely to be stated." Ewbank's theme was the necessary conditions for modern citizenship. He provided a succinct statement of the cluster of beliefs I am calling radio's civic paradigm. "If democracy is to endure," he told the commission, "we must have a citizenry alive to the problems that are pressing for solution, and able to express, both at election times and between times, an intelligent opinion on these issues." Ewbank called for the "unhampered, intimate, and sustained discussion of public issues" on noncommercial radio stations, because commercial stations were "inherently prejudiced as a source of information on controversial subjects."[22] This was, NBC's Norton perceived, the ground on which the broadcasting industry would have to legitimate itself in the future—to demonstrate that a commercial radio system could produce a citizenry capable of forming and expressing "intelligent opinion." Radio listeners were imagined now as consumers of a service rather than as active participants in broadcasting, but the demand that their listening turn them into active and opinion-forming citizens had to be taken seriously.

What followed 1934 then was a decade or more in which the language of civic responsibility and citizen formation dominated discussion of radio's place in American society. The civic paradigm was a way of thinking about radio as representative, as both reflecting and producing diversity, and hence as producing citizens who listened to the contrasting opinions of others and formed their own individual opinion, who were civically aware, cosmopolitan, yet locally active. American radio in its golden age was thus widely understood as a governmental technique for producing new kinds of persons—self-aware and self-governing, active, rational, reflective, culturally literate, tolerant, articulate, opinion-forming, and empathetic—all of them key qualities within 1930s liberalism.

Representatives of government and the broadcasting industry, when asked to speak publicly about radio, often spoke of citizen formation. Kansas Republican Harold McGugin told the House of Representatives in 1932, "I firmly believe that in considering radio we are considering something far more vital than entertainment, because its role in

22. "Brief for H. L. Ewbank's Remarks before Communications Commission," folder 38, box 26, NBC records, WHS; "More Education over Radio Asked," *New York Times*, October 2, 1934: 16.

forming citizens is increasingly apparent. I believe we are considering something which strikes at the very roots of government itself."[23] What had been one issue among many in 1932 became, by the later 1930s, the dominant legitimating language for discussing American broadcasting. FCC commissioner E. O. Sykes told the National Association of Broadcasters in 1937 that the main object and purpose of broadcasting was public service and that the sale of commercial time was "but an incident." Radio programs, he said, reached the men, women, and children of the entire nation, including those who were being "trained to assume the reins of government when the present actors pass from the stage." The younger generation listening to the radio "should be improved and be better equipped for their responsibility to be so soon assumed by them."[24] President Roosevelt sent the 1938 NAB convention a message that talked about broadcasting as a new field of public service and of his expectation that it would increasingly contribute to "our social as well as our economic advancement." Broadcasters, he said, had a responsibility to see that radio "is made to serve the high purposes of a democracy."[25] It would be a mistake to dismiss such statements as bland, universally accepted truths. This was a historically particular legitimating language and it had real effects. Radio was talked about, valued, reviled, and regulated as if it were not just a noisy means of entertainment, but an important civic instrument.

MAKING ACTIVE AUDIENCES: LYMAN BRYSON

The People's Platform, hosted by Lyman Bryson, was broadcast on CBS from 1938.[26] Each episode featured four guests who were served dinner in a CBS dining room and whose subsequent conversation was picked up by hidden microphones. "For a half hour," network publicity boasted, "spontaneously expressed opinions and beliefs—and sometimes heated arguments—are broadcast from coast to coast." The conversations were said to represent and reveal American differences: "Unrehearsed and informal, they reveal a cross-section of American ideas, the ideas of different occupations, different party affiliations, different economic levels," thus providing an "immediate reflection of American thinking and American feeling."[27] [Figure 2.1.]

Bryson was during this period also professor of education at Teachers College in New York and chairman of CBS's Adult Education Board. He was one of the key figures defining the relations of radio and education in the second half of the 1930s. He described *The People's Platform* as modeling good civic behavior: "we give people an example of lively difference of opinion and vigorous discussion that is never unfriendly." The "very unfinished nature of the broadcast stimulates discussion among listeners at home when it is over." The modeling was enhanced by the fact that, while one or two of the guests were usually prominent public figures, the other two were chosen from everyday life—ordinary people (identified by occupation, such as taxi driver, housewife, plumber) who would

23. Debate on HR 7715, *Congressional Record—House of Representatives*, February 10, 1932: 3692.
24. "Radio Warned of Obligation," *New York Times*, June 27, 1937: 146.
25. "Broadcasters Act to Clean Up Radio," *New York Times*, February 15, 1938: 4.
26. The program ran until 1952; Bryson was the host 1938–46.
27. CBS advertisement "Columbia Sets the Table," *Broadcasting* 15, no. 12 (December 15, 1938): 4–5.

Figure 2.1. "Columbia Sets the Table…," *Broadcasting* 15, no. 12 (Dec. 15, 1938): 4–5.

discuss and argue with the experts. Bryson's recipe for selecting guests was: one big name, one person who knows something about the topic, a woman, and then "somebody from the street. He had to be a cab driver or a shoe clerk or a small bookkeeper or somebody."[28] The latter "representative of the American public" was present, Bryson explained, "not only for his own sake but because he compels the expert to talk to the layman in his own language."[29] The task of these people was to dramatize their different perspectives, along the way contextualizing their contrasting opinions within their own biographies. Bryson saw his own role as assisting with this self-dramatization. He recalled, "I began to see my job, as time went on, as a kind of a dramatist of the moment. I studied the dialogue of plays a good deal.… I've always been a devotee of the theater."[30] [Figure 2.2.]

Bryson shared to a certain extent the pluralist perspective of progressive education— that knowledge was individual and grew from experience. Some of this came from his own life experience. Having worked as a journalist, and taught journalism and rhetoric

28. "Reminiscences of Lyman Bryson," typescript of oral history interview with Frank Ernest Hill, 1951, Oral History Research Unit, Columbia University, in box 40, Lyman Bryson papers, LOC: 121. Sometimes there was more than one woman—but the formula clearly rested upon the assumption that normally the expert, the big name and the "man on the street" would not be women.

29. "Are We Victims of Propaganda: A Program in the Manner of 'The People's Platform'" in Josephine H. MacLatchy (ed.), *Education on the Air: Eleventh Yearbook of the Institute for Education by Radio* (Columbus: Ohio State University, 1940): 41.

30. "Reminiscences of Lyman Bryson": 136.

Figure 2.2. The intellectual on network radio—formal portrait of Lyman Bryson, December 30, 1937. CBS/Landov.

at the University of Michigan, he worked for the Red Cross in Europe from 1919 to 1924, some of the time as assistant to Ivy Lee, the director of public relations for the Red Cross—thus gaining exposure to the ideas of the nascent profession of public opinion management. The years in Europe gave Bryson some critical distance on American life. He said of his return to the United States in 1924 that "you become conscious of what it is to be an American, and yet you are not uncomfortable if you are where other people aren't Americans, which I suppose is really becoming somewhat cosmopolitanized."[31] Moving to San Diego and attempting to make a career as a writer, in 1928 he accepted a half-time position as associate director of the San Diego anthropology museum, a position that also involved teaching anthropology subjects at the state teachers college in San Diego. With little previous background in anthropology, Bryson recalled, "I plunged up to my neck in anthropological reading": "I found myself pretty heavily involved then in an entirely new line of thinking."[32] Anthropological thinking at this time would also, we might reasonably speculate, have had a cosmopolitanizing effect on Bryson, offering

31. "Reminiscences of Lyman Bryson": 64.

32. "Reminiscences of Lyman Bryson": 68–69; "Dr. Lyman Bryson of Columbia Dead," *New York Times*, November 26, 1959: 37.

another mode of contrasting "our" way of doing things with the vast diversity of human belief and behavior.

In 1929, just in time for the challenges of the Depression, Bryson began working in the newly important field of adult education, as director of the Carnegie-funded California Association for Adult Education. From there, his connections with Frederick Keppel and Morse Cartwright at the Carnegie Corporation helped propel him to a national career in adult education. In 1932 he moved to Des Moines, Iowa, to work on a showpiece Carnegie project, directed by an old friend from Junior Red Cross and WWI days, John Studebaker, then superintendent of schools in Des Moines. The Carnegie demonstration project was to establish evening adult discussion forums in the public school system.[33] [Companion website link 2.1.] From Des Moines, Studebaker was appointed commissioner of the U.S. Office of Education in 1934, and Bryson went on in the same year to a position in adult education at Teachers College in New York. There was to some extent a parting of the ways here. Studebaker took his forum ideas to a national level and inaugurated the Federal Forum program.[34] Bryson continued to advocate forums, but was wary of government involvement. At a 1935 conference at Columbia University he cited the fact that the United States commissioner of education was seeking federal appropriations to set up public forums throughout the country as one of five pieces of evidence that there was a "terrific danger" of fascism in education in the United States.[35]

All of these influences and experiences added to Bryson's education in the perspectivalist, even relativist, currents of thought of the time. As an adult educator, he was always conscious of the value of exposing people to other ways of thinking, to confronting them with the contingency of their own cultural formation. Within the context of Teachers College, where he was a faculty member from 1934, Bryson identified himself as more conservative than those colleagues who were the acknowledged leaders of the social reconstructionist wing of the progressive education movement, who thought the end of adult education should be social change.[36] Bryson did however share the progressive sense that real knowledge grew from experience, and that people needed to be open and receptive to new ideas, ready for change—"the people who seem to get the most out of life are those who keep open-minded." Democracy could not be made a successful form of government, he argued, "unless the self-governing citizens who are responsible for its working keep themselves informed as to what is going on." They "must be willing to examine their most cherished opinions frequently" to check that they are still valid.[37]

33. On Des Moines, see William M. Keith, *Democracy as Discussion: Civil Education and the American Forum Movement* (Lanham, MD: Lexington Books, 2007): 277–86.

34. On the Federal Forum project, see David Goodman, "Democracy and Public Discussion in the Progressive and New Deal Eras: From Civic Competence to the Expression of Opinion," *Studies in American Political Development* 18, no. 2 (Fall 2004): 81–111; and Keith, *Democracy as Discussion*, ch. 9.

35. "Fascism Danger Faces Education, Declares Bryson," *Teachers College Record* 37, no. 1 (1935): 79–80.

36. Lyman Bryson to Morse Cartwright, March 5, 1934, box 3, Lyman Bryson papers, LOC.

37. Lyman Bryson, "Adult Education," talk over NBC Red network, August 14, 1934, box 20, Lyman Bryson Papers, LOC.

Like James Rowland Angell, Bryson distinguished democracy from mere majority rule. "The protection and the nurture of diverse opinions is a much more crucial test of democratic action," he argued. He insisted that democracy was an educational form of government, designed to "subject all its citizens to experiences that will bring out of them their best qualities, build up their powers, and force them into growth."[38] That is in many ways a remarkable—and Deweyan—formulation. The final imperative was crucial—the progressive educator's democracy was to be one in which citizens were forced into personal growth and change. Hearing and understanding that note of compulsion is fundamental, I will be arguing, to understanding radio's civic function in the United States after 1934. The civic vision that saw active participation in democratic life as a form of continuing education was a significant component of American radio's civic paradigm. Radio and "adult education" seemed made for each other—both involved a significant broadening of conventional understandings of education into something that was endless, always about growth and change.

Bryson believed that individualism was waning in America, that there was a standardization and "sameness" spreading across the continent which was working against "the original conception of individualism and democracy." This standardization, itself a product of "radio civilization," was so pervasive that in the future, he worried, "independence may cease to be a doctrine, as it gradually ceases to be a possibility."[39] It is striking that Bryson, and many of his educated contemporaries, could see radio both as part of the cause and of the solution to standardization—this is an important point because the fear of radio propaganda has generally been much better remembered than the proposed remedy. It was clear from Bryson's work at CBS—as well as being chair of its Adult Education Board, he moderated programs such as *School of the Air*, *Church of the Air*, and *Of Men and Books*—that he believed that a different use of radio, as a model of and prompt for dialogue, could begin the process of reindividualizing Americans and of leading them constantly to nurture and reflect upon their own opinions. *The People's Platform* was educational and individualizing, Bryson maintained, because it "ensnared" people into listening to things with which they did not agree: "When you get them listening to a dinner party where the opinions are all tangled up, they have to listen. They can't get away from it." This not only summarized the educational philosophy of this particular discussion program, it also expressed the underlying ethos of much of the public service programming on network radio in the 1930s. "Education should not confirm us in our prejudices and previous ideas," Bryson explained, "It should be a little bit exasperating."[40] Individuals were to form their own opinions but were to do so only after exposure to a range of different views. This civic philosophy committed citizens to the unsettling free play of ideas, to the virtues of tolerance and empathy rather than to a singular idea of truth. "Mutual recognition of the validity of the other fellow's ideas," explained one laudatory newspaper review, "is the ultimate aim of 'The People's Platform.'"

38. Lyman Bryson, "Education, Citizenship and Character," *Teachers College Record* 42, no. 4 (1941): 298, 300.

39. "Educator Finds Individual Thinking Waning," *New York Times*, February 24, 1935: N1.

40. Lester Bernstein, "Victory on the Side of Education," *New York Times*, September 1, 1940: X10.

The show was to be a perspective-shifting forum, not a debate with a single victor, or a mere "chat" or "talk" show in the late 20th-century sense.[41] It had a stated goal of inducting—forcing—people into the pluralist world of opinions and the relativist understanding that because opinions arose from experience and people's life circumstances differed, the opinions of others had to be engaged with empathetically as well as judgmentally. And at its best it did fulfill the hopes of those who said that educational programs could also entertain. Critically reviewing Ed Sullivan's new celebrity interview radio show in 1943, *Billboard* recommended that he "listen to *The People's Platform* someday" to learn "just how to make people sitting around a table sound like human beings."[42]

Beyond "the Best that Has Been Thought and Said": American Radio and the Production of Personal Opinion

The language of the debate about radio in different nations can look at first rather similar. Everywhere in the Western world in the 1920s and 1930s, for example, there was a battle between proponents of broadcasting classical music and those of jazz and popular music; everywhere those who thought radio would most importantly be an instrument of mass enlightenment and improvement fought those who saw it primarily as an historic opportunity for cheap entertainment for ordinary people. Some of the praise of educational broadcasting and condemnation of popular programming, or the rejection of highbrow seriousness in the name of popular entertainment, was generic, and could readily be imported into different national contexts. There was a shared currency in the English-speaking world of Arnoldian ideas of uplift and improvement, a belief that bringing forms of high culture to the masses via radio would have dramatic social effects.

Look a little deeper in each nation, however, and the inflections of the debate, and the range of politically possible outcomes, are different. For example the ways in which the divide between the educational and the popular was understood and managed could differ significantly, as could the local gender, race, ethnic and class resonances of the cultural conflict over radio. For Reith, the mission of broadcasting was explicitly the Arnoldian one of bringing the "best that has been thought and said" to the greatest number. In his 1924 book *Broadcast Over Britain*, he defined the responsibility of the BBC as "to carry into the greatest possible number of homes everything that is best in every department of human knowledge, endeavor and achievement, and to avoid the things which are, or may be, hurtful."[43] The ultimate criterion was truth—the search for truth, he wrote, was "the highest function of man." He quoted Matthew Arnold on this search, urging listeners "to try to approach truth on one side after another." Reith lamented that "we cannot help feeling at times that after all there are no competent, impartial and established judges to whom we may finally submit our efforts for approval or condemnation," and thus "we are driven back upon ourselves." Broadcasting aims to assist in the search for truth; truth must be approached from many directions because there are no established

41. "After-Dinner Radio Forum," *Christian Science Monitor*, March 21, 1939: 11.
42. "Ed Sullivan Entertains," *Billboard*, October 2, 1943: 13.
43. J. C. W. Reith, *Broadcast Over Britain* (London: Hodder and Stoughton, 1924): 34.

authorities; but the truth that is sought is singular. The task of the broadcaster is to reach for this singular truth and to come as close as possible to it. Broadcasting different points of view is here very clearly part of the process of winnowing truth, not an end in itself.

The Arnoldian mission was consistent with a highly centralized broadcasting system. Scannell and Cardiff report that at the BBC the "standards and values of metropolitan culture were taken for granted"—it seemed "self-evident that London could provide better quality in musical performance, bigger stars for entertainers, more important speakers than the rest of the country."[44] Even at those points at which audience participation was requested, standards of excellence had to be maintained. In December 1932, the BBC's director of talks invited listeners to send in poems for broadcasting. The BBC publication *The Listener* reported bluntly that "the huge mass of verse showed an astonishing absence of any understanding of the business of writing poetry," and that the submitted efforts were "on the whole very conservative" in form.[45] They were being judged against the standard of the best of the time and found wanting. The national broadcaster's role was to enable more people to understand what the best was and how their own efforts measured up against it.

Perhaps the most quoted and misquoted words John Reith ever wrote were "it is occasionally indicated to us that we are apparently setting out to give the public what we think they need—and not what they want, but few know what they want, and very few what they need."[46] There were two lines of American response. The first, and the most well known, as we have seen, was to say that the American system gave listeners what they wanted not what the government thought they should have. That proposition became the basis of the defense of the democratic and free nature of American commercial radio. William Berchtold repeated this industry orthodoxy when he wrote in 1935 that the BBC was "assuming the attitude that it knows best what is good for the British audience. With no incentive for competition such as exists on the commercially sponsored chain programs…in the United States, the BBC programs have, unfortunately, become increasingly anaemic."[47] This contrast was made again and again by defenders of the broadcasting status quo, in their efforts to recruit American radio listeners to their way of seeing things. Industry representatives almost always defined American radio in opposition to British by saying that their role was to give the people what they wanted. FRC commissioner Harold Lafount wrote in 1929 that "any comprehensive plan for general improvement of radio programs in the United States necessarily resolves itself into a procedure whereby more persons will receive more of what they want, when they want it." The question of what constitutes a desirable program, he asserted, "is obviously one of individual prejudice, and opinion is of little value except in the mass."[48] That was a statement as representative in its way as Reith's on the other side. In a commercial system, numbers mattered, and the most important preferences and opinions were those held by the largest number of people.

44. Paddy Scannell and David Cardiff, *A Social History of British Broadcasting*: 16.

45. "Week by Week," *Listener*, June 7, 1933: 892.

46. Reith, *Broadcast Over Britain*: 34.

47. William E. Berchtold, "Battle of the Wave Lengths," *New Outlook* (March 1935): 25.

48. Harold A. Lafount, "Lafount Tells Way to Better Radio Programs," *Chicago Tribune*, October 20, 1929: J10.

The second line of American response has however not been so well identified, as it was often implicit rather than explicit in American broadcasting philosophy and practice. This was a belief that presenting a multiplicity of views was a public good in itself, not just a necessary step toward eventually discerning truth. Part of that case was to assert a more pluralist understanding of the public sphere, to say that, as CBS president William S. Paley put it so succinctly, "there is no 'public'; there are publics."[49] In this way of thinking, it was not one singular truth or the numerically dominant opinion that was most important. The crucial fact was the existence of a diversity of opinion, and the belief that empathetically engaging with that diversity was the only transcendent value. Correspondent Edward Acheson assured readers of the *Washington Post*: "By its very definition, a government-owned radio system cannot tolerate the other side of any political question." So, he concluded, its charms would not be translatable to the United States, "for America 'revels' in other sides."[50] Acheson did identify here something important about American radio's understanding of public service—that it was as much about exposing audiences to different perspectives as it was about disseminating "the best" to the masses. Franklin Dunham, who was in 1938 NBC's director of educational and religious programming, justified the network's religious programming in these terms: "We feel that the best thing accomplished in this manner of religious programming is the mutual respect and understanding of the other person's point of view which has come about as a result of it." Religion on the radio had, he said, made it possible for "people to know how others think."[51] The justification was to do with exposure to different points of view, about the encouragement of tolerance and empathy. This was the American version of Reithian prescription—what the people needed was exposure to multiple perspectives.

Where did this American interest in perspective and different points of view come from? The ideas of progressive education, and more broadly of cultural pluralism deriving in part from cultural anthropology, had an important influence on American radio's understanding of its civic mission in the 1930s. Forms of cultural pluralism and cultural relativism were significant in the United States in the 1930s in other contexts, although we are yet to have a full history of these ideas. The New Deal itself was one important seedbed of pluralist thought—the historically novel engagement of the central government in fostering appreciation of cultural diversity within the nation. Jerrold Hirsch, in his history of the Federal Writers Project, argues that "the creation of an environment in which cultural pluralism could develop was a triumph of New Deal nationalism"; the New Deal turned "diversity into a virtue."[52] Historians of interwar anthropology point to the rise to intellectual respectability, even cultural dominance, of the scientific critique of racialism and the relativism embedded in cultural

49. William S. Paley, "Broadcasting and American Society," *Annals of the American Academy of Social and Political Sciences* 213, no. 1 (January 1941) p. 65.

50. Edward Acheson, "Britain Sees US Broadcasting Soon Under Government Control," *Washington Post*, December 9, 1934: B5.

51. Quoted in Elizabeth Benneche Petersen, "Religion in the Armchair," *Radio Stars* (August 1938): 68.

52. Jerrold Hirsch, *Portrait of America: A Cultural History of the Federal Writers Project* (Chapel Hill: University of North Carolina Press, 2003): 18.

anthropology. By the later 1930s, Stocking argues, "the new era had begun in which Boasian anthropology was to speak to educated Americans as 'the voice of science' on matters of race and culture."[53] It was not just the critique of racialism that was important here, but the substitution of a thoroughgoing cultural relativism—the doctrine that was codified and evangelized by Franz Boas's students, most prominently Ruth Benedict, Margaret Mead, and Melville Herskovits. This involved a shift from talk of culture in the singular to the plural—cultures. The cultural anthropologists sought to situate and in a sense denaturalize Western common sense within the rich sea of cultural difference.

Arguably the discourse of progressive education—with its emphasis on individual personality and opinion, on child-centered learning, on imaginative pedagogy and active learning—even as it was resisted by many Americans, had greater social and cultural effect in the United States than elsewhere. With their emphasis on active learning and child-centered pedagogy, progressive educators sought relevance, creativity, and self-expression, and insisted that knowledge came from activity and experience. Schooling was to be part of an effort to "develop the child's total personality."[54] While these ideas had a long ancestry in Romantic individualist thought going back to 18th-century Europe, they were given a new lease of life and found new institutional expression in the United States in the 1920s and 1930s, particularly of course through the work and influence of John Dewey.[55] Cremin locates the high-water mark of the progressive education movement in the United States in the years just before World War II.[56]

While it is debatable—despite the lamentations of educational conservatives—how far the practices advocated by progressive educationalists actually reached into the public school system, the combined effect, Reese argues, of the battle between Romantic, individualist progressive educators and utilitarian, testing-oriented social efficiency advocates was the "powerful" way in which "the language of human differences" entered American schools.[57] Brehony argues, in contrast, that "in England progressive education was a social construction that did not emerge until the 1960s and 1970s."[58] There was in the U.S. a further significant link between ideas about progressive education and ideas about radio listening in the funding priorities of the major philanthropic trusts, the Carnegie Corporation and the Rockefeller Foundation, both of which funded

53. George Stocking, "Introduction: Thoughts toward a History of the Interwar Years," in Stocking (ed.), *Papers from the American Anthropologist* (Lincoln: University of Nebraska Press, 2002): 48.

54. Harold Rugg and Ann Schumaker, *The Child-Centered School* (1928) as quoted in Maurice R. Berube, *American School Reform: Progressive, Equity, and Excellence Movements, 1883–1993* (Westport, CT: Praeger, 1994): 14.

55. On the romantic origins of progressive education, see William J. Reese, "The Origins of Progressive Education," *History of Education Quarterly* 41, no. 1 (Spring 2001): 1–24.

56. Lawrence A. Cremin, *The Transformation of the School: Progressivism in American Education, 1876–1957* (New York: Alfred A. Knopf, 1964): 324.

57. William J. Reese, *America's Public Schools: From the Common School to "No Child Left Behind"* (Baltimore: Johns Hopkins University Press, 2005): 179.

58. Kevin J. Brehony, "From the Particular to the General, the Continuous to the Discontinuous: Progressive Education Revisited," *History of Education* 30, no. 5 (2001): 414.

educational research, and research on the social and educational possibilities of radio listening.[59]

Of course an emphasis on active learning characterized talk about radio education in many nations. John Reith believed that young people needed to "develop their own personality and character to the greatest extent."[60] He believed that radio listening had to be an active process, "an act of will."[61] But there was in the United States a set of ideas about radio's civic role that went beyond those important shared ideas to (1) an emphasis on perspectivalism and point of view in public life and (2) a belief that the proper culmination of radio's civic education would be the formation of citizens with informed, articulable, and always provisional personal opinions. I am arguing that both the perspectivalism and the consequent stress on the need to develop personal opinion as a result of radio listening resonated with, and gained credence from, the contemporary ideas of progressive education.

The strand of progressive education that I am drawing attention to here placed relentless emphasis on individual difference and the individual benefits of engaging with the diversity of ways of comprehending the world. Here is a progressive educator writing in 1936: "In the process of discovering the bases of his own integration with society, the student will discover that social interests and purposes are enormously heterogeneous and chaotic, and that there is nowhere any unified understanding of methods by which those interests and purposes are to be served."[62] Here is another progressive educator writing in 1938: "We need to find out what we mean by the word *normal*. We need to look at the people all over the world and with the help of this perspective find out whence our images of ourselves were derived."[63] This is a long way from Arnoldian sweetness and light—it involves confronting rather than escaping diversity. Imperatives dominate the language of progressive individualism—we *need* to relativize our understanding, people *must* come to acknowledge the plurality of ways of thinking and feeling. The potential of a mass medium like radio to illustrate, confirm, and reinforce views like these was considerable.

Radio could bring a range of different points of view into the home, and confront each citizen with the extent of difference in their society. In his 1938 *Is American Radio Democratic?*, S. E. Frost made the case for a democratic radio in just these individualized, pluralist, and perspectival terms. "Any institution of society is democratic," he wrote, "to the degree that it actively and consciously functions so that all individuals may 1) experience broad, wide, varied, and rich shared contacts with their physical environment and with others and 2) develop an attitude of open-mindedness or

59. On Rockefeller and progressive education, see Theresa Richardson, "Rethinking Progressive High School Reform in the 1930s," *American Educational History Journal* 33, no. 1 (2006): 77–87; and Ellen Condliffe Lagemann, *An Elusive Science: The Troubling History of Education Research* (Chicago: University of Chicago Press, 2002): 130–34.

60. "Sir John Reith on Education," *The Times*, October 9, 1928: 9.

61. Quoted in James Donald, *Sentimental Education—Schooling, Popular Culture and the Regulation of Liberty* (London: Verso, 1992): 75.

62. Lester Dix, "Integration in the Lincoln School Philosophy," *Teachers College Record* 37, no. 5 (February 1936): 369.

63. Alice V. Keliher, *Life and Growth* (New York: D. Appleton-Century, 1938): 4.

willingness to consider possible consequences of proposed activity and 3) develop a flexibility of thought and action such that they live constructively in a changing environment."[64] Frost was a progressive educationalist and philosopher steeped in the ideas of his time. The importance of experiencing difference and of remaining flexible and open-minded were common themes in his work. This was, he perceived, one of the ways that radio could assist in shaping modern citizens. Frost summarized ideas widely held by the most influential shapers of the interactions of radio and education. [Companion website link 2.2.]

John Studebaker, U.S. commissioner of education, was probably the most powerful radio and education advocate in the United States, and he too was steeped in these progressive ideas—he had completed a master's degree at Teachers College under the supervision of William Kilpatrick, a committed Deweyan. Studebaker defined the task of liberal education in his 1936 book *Plain Talk* as "to liberate the minds of individuals to function effectively in the democratic control of their social life, and to prepare them for and to induce continuous growth in personal self-expression and personal efficiency."[65] He wrote in a 1939 report on FREC that U.S. education proceeded on the assumption that "under the American form of government, the individual should be encouraged toward the fullest self-expression," and that it endeavored "to guide him toward a type of self-expression which will be constructive and in the best interests of the whole body of citizens."[66] These ideas were common currency among radio and education activists, but Studebaker could do more to put them into practice than most. The director of the Department of Extension Teaching at the University of Wisconsin said that the greatest thing about radio in education was its role in "breaking down errors and prejudices and other evils through the broadening and illuminating of men's horizons."[67] Radio reformer Joy Elmer Morgan, chairman of the National Committee on Education by Radio, also shared much of this way of thinking. Education was a permanent necessity: "There must be continuing daily discussion of important local, state and national enterprises so that the people will be familiar with the management of their own household."[68] This imperative tone—there must be daily discussion; the evil of prejudice will need to be corrected by broadening of horizons—pervaded 1930s polemics on the place of radio in education.

In many nations in the 1930s, of course, radio was understood to be a democratic medium. Scannell and Cardiff note that in Britain the establishment of broadcasting coincided with "the moment that the vote was finally conceded to all adult men and women, and the development of mass democracy is closely connected with broadcasting's role in that process."[69] Reith on his 1931 American visit predicted that the United States would one day adopt the British model of broadcasting. Radio, he said, "is peculiarly

---

64. Frost, *Is American Radio Democratic?*: 156.
65. John W. Studebaker, *Plain Talk* (Washington DC: National Home Library Foundation, 1936): 87.
66. John Studebaker report on FREC, December 19, 1939, folder 3, box 77, NBC records, WHS.
67. Quoted in undated Judith Waller talk, folder 32, box 26, NBC records, WHS.
68. Joy Elmer Morgan, "The New American Plan for Radio" in Bower Aly and Gerald D. Shively (eds.), *Debate Handbook: Radio Control* (Columbia, MO: Staples, 1933): 81.
69. Scannell and Cardiff, *A Social History*: 10–11.

fitted to unlock in human beings everywhere the specific aptitude that local circumstances may have inhibited. It can, in fact, make democracy safe for the world."[70] That un-American inversion betrayed, as well as a faith in education and uplift, a sense that democracy was dangerous and needed managing. Plenty of elite Americans may have shared the sentiment, but such thoughts were no longer publicly sayable in the United States. What could be said in the United States, and was repeatedly said, was that the flourishing of individual opinion was a precondition of democracy.

CBS president William S. Paley elaborated the central idea about democracy and personal opinion further when he wrote in 1935 that "our Nation's economic and political thought is connected very closely with the very personal concepts of each individual concerning those things which he considers related to his welfare." Paley, one of the most powerful men in the broadcasting industry, argued that radio was playing a very important part in American life, and emphasized two things—that American life itself was changing fast ("the fluxing American life of today") and that it was "Man's desires concerning very small and personal things" that "determine the course of whole societies."[71] To say that that was not the way Sir John Reith habitually talked is to state the obvious. But previous scholarship has not noted, comparatively, the way the twin progressive themes of individual desires, preferences, and opinions, and the perception of the social as made up most importantly of individuals learning to adapt to change, mark the American discussion of radio in the 1930s.

The sketch I am making here is to show a sharp contrast with the BBC and its Arnoldian, top-down philosophy of radio's role in civic education. There was some expression of that idea in the United States too—in 1933, for example, federal radio commissioner Harold Lafount predicted that in the near future, educational programs would be broadcast "by the Government itself over a few powerful short-wave stations" so that "the whole Nation would be taught by one teacher."[72] That strand in American radio has arguably not been adequately recognized.[73] But nor has this other, progressive, civic paradigm strand. In the United States, the individualist orthodoxy was that radio would be important because it could develop individuals who displayed "continuous growth in personal self-expression" and who were yet personally efficient; people who were adept at self-management, but also submissive to Morgan's imperative that "there must be" daily discussion of public affairs. The set of ideas that dominated American radio's proclaimed civic mission was at once progressive and coercive—full of talk about individual difference and personal growth, yet imperative and unyielding about the need for these things.

I am certainly not arguing that network executives were all open advocates of progressive ideas or avid progressive New Dealers. Many were indeed conservative Republicans, hostile to the New Deal and all that it stood for. But the climate of reform

70. "Radio Differs across the Sea," *New York Times*, May 31, 1931: 9.

71. William S. Paley, "Radio and the Humanities," *Annals of the American Academy of Political and Social Science* 177 (January 1935): 94–95.

72. Harold Lafount press release, May 19, 1933, folder 35, box 17, NBC records, WHS.

73. Although, see William Bianchi, *Schools of the Air: A History of Instructional Programs on Radio in the United States* (Jefferson, NC: McFarland, 2008).

ideas meant that these politically astute men knew where to turn for advice, knew the kinds of reform activities that would lend credibility and dignity to radio, make it seem like a progressive and socially responsible as well as a profitable medium. When they collaborated with educators to make programs, when they sought expert advice on the civic role of radio in the age of propaganda, they were most likely encountering the set of progressive and perspectival ideas I have just described. And that had discernible effects on radio and its understanding of its civic mission.

FORMING OPINIONS IN THE AGE OF PROPAGANDA

There was concern on all sides through the 1930s about the persuasive capacity of broadcasting, and the power that could flow to those who controlled it. A Los Angeles broadcaster warned ominously that "these machines of communication" should remain "a public possession, a racial utility, a human protectorate," because "whoever controls them is virtually in a position to control human society."[74] In order to understand the dominance of the idea, central to the civic paradigm, that radio's mission was to facilitate individual opinion formation, we need some sense of the problem—propaganda-induced conformity—that strategy was meant to correct.

The interwar American propaganda scare stemmed most directly from assessments of the effects of propaganda—British propaganda as well as that of George Creel's Committee on Public Information—during WWI. In the early 1930s discussion of propaganda and radio within the United States focused most intensely on domestic political figures such as Franklin Roosevelt, Father Charles Coughlin, and Huey Long. Coughlin was the primary American exemplar of a propagandist. In 1939, Alfred McClung Lee and Elizabeth Briant Lee published a book-length study of Coughlin's oratory, *The Fine Art of Propaganda*, which found within Coughlin's rhetoric examples of all the major strategies of propagandists. Radio propaganda seemed to many of those who studied it to threaten not only individualism, but democracy.[75] By the later 1930s, as an international propaganda war erupted on shortwave radio, Hitler and Mussolini were also central to these discussions. Radio, Sigmund Neumann warned in 1938, "opens new possibilities for demagogic leadership."[76]

Concern about propaganda traversed the political spectrum. Radicals saw propaganda everywhere in modern American society, and they feared the increasing political activism of conservative and far-right groups within the United States. But for many on the left, the most powerful and insidious propaganda was commercial rather than political. James Rorty argued that it was a necessary consequence of the capitalist organization of the media

74. Gross W. Alexander of the Pacific-Western Broadcasting Federation in, *Hearings Before the Committee on Interstate and Foreign Commerce, House of Representatives, 73rd Congress, 2nd session on HR 8301*: 281.

75. Influential works of propaganda analysis included Leonard William Doob, *Propaganda; Its Psychology and Technique* (New York: H. Holt, 1935); Alfred McClung Lee and Elizabeth Briant Lee, *The Fine Art of Propaganda: a Study of Father Coughlin's Speeches* (New York: Harcourt Brace, 1939).

76. Sigmund Neumann, "The Rule of the Demagogue," *American Sociological Review* 3, no. 4 (August 1938): 497.

that the owners of press and radio used "our major instruments of social communication, whose free and disinterested functioning is embodied in the concept of a democracy, to serve the profit interests of the advertisers who employ and pay them." Advertising expressed "the central acquisitive drive of the culture" and influenced the lives of radio listeners "infinitely more than the relatively microscopic amount" of education featured on the air.[77] More comprehensively still, the intellectuals of the émigré Frankfurt School were arguing from the later 1930s that American mass culture as such was indistinguishable from propaganda—that it was, as Adorno and Horkheimer were to put it, propaganda for a way of life in which "something is provided for all so that none may escape."[78]

Liberals worried that propaganda would diminish democracy by negating individualism, so that when Americans came out to vote, their opinions would not be their own. Part of the liberal concern about the insidiousness of radio propaganda was that, entering the living rooms of America, it might induce conformity of belief and demeanor on a scale never before experienced. If propaganda began at home, where citizens formed their opinions in private, what meaning could democracy have? Liberals, like radicals, worried about the insurgent populism of Charles Coughlin and the militant employer propaganda of the second New Deal period. Liberal concerns about propaganda were primarily political—about the future of democracy—but they extended to the cultural sphere, to anxieties about the political consequences of social and cultural conformity. In 1938, economist Harry Gideonse warned undergraduate students at Barnard College about the dangers of swing music. "Swing is musical Hitlerism," he said, "There is a mass sense of 'letting oneself go.'" Gideonse thought the emotion thus released was dangerous because it was generally not acknowledged in modern society: "Modern man is a vacuum emotionally."[79] He worried that radio debate too often "degenerates into emotional appeals": "The result is I very frequently have the feeling that while programs like that are very exciting and you get evidence that many people listen, it is not an intellectual experience. It is rather of a very different order; it is emotional. People get very stirred up."[80] Gideonse thus warned of the intrusion of emotion into rational public debate; he worried too that academic analysis was in danger of so comprehensively filtering out and setting aside emotion that it would remain ignorant of some of the most powerful forces in society.

The conservative concern with propaganda in the 1930s had initially most to do with the New Deal, and with fears that the federal government was acquiring the kind of power over the flow of information that would allow it to install Roosevelt as a dictator.[81] Republicans—prominent among them Charles Tobey of New Hampshire—raised the

77. James Rorty, *Our Master's Voice: Advertising* (New York: John Day, 1934): 14, 274.

78. Max Horkheimer and Theodor W. Adorno, *Dialectic of Enlightenment* (1944; reprint, London: Allen Lane, 1973): 123.

79. "Swing Viewed as 'Musical Hitlerism,'" *New York Times*, November 2, 1938: 25.

80. Transcripts of discussion at the Second National Conference on Educational Broadcasting, Chicago November/December 1937, Records Relating to National Conferences on Educational Broadcasting, 1936–37, box 2, RG 12, NACP.

81. See Barry Karl, *The Uneasy State: The United States from 1915 to 1945* (Chicago: University of Chicago Press, 1983).

issue of monopoly in broadcasting repeatedly in the later 1930s, trying to prove connections between the big networks and the Democratic Party.[82] By the later 1930s, conservative concern about propaganda was increasingly centered on Communism and the threat that disguised and apparently reasonable forms of Communism posed to ordinary Americans in the popular front era.

While critics of propaganda thus held diverse political views, they had in common a sense that the technologies of mass communication had created an unprecedented capacity to manipulate public opinion. They believed that existing modes of political deliberation must inevitably be transformed by the use of these technologies, and that the American people as a whole were dangerously unprepared to deal with the flow of propagandas they would encounter every day. The only possible response to this concern was a call for better education about and against propaganda. Propaganda critics feared the capacity of the media to change opinions, and they concluded that democracy could survive in the United States only if concerted efforts were made to educate the people to the workings of propaganda.

By the mid-1930s, Lyman Bryson believed that the reason the public service and educational role of radio mattered so much was the threat of propaganda. He told the first National Conference on Educational Broadcasting in 1936 that it was the responsibility of educators "to equip all people, at all levels of their education, and at all ages, with a sufficient rational skepticism to defeat propaganda in its effort to confuse or misinform." Universal skeptical education was the only solution because truth was perspectival. If propaganda was lies and education truth, the matter would be very simple—radio should banish propaganda. The problem, Bryson argued, was, however, that propaganda was just "the other fellow's education." It was on that challenging perspectivalist basis that Bryson constructed his radio education work. That was what made him such an emblematic American radio and education figure in his concern with fostering personal opinion.[83]

When interwar intellectuals directed their attention to radio, the most urgent issues were mass persuasion and the consequent looming possibility of historically unprecedented levels of conformity.[84] A chorus of commentary through the 1930s predicted that radio would create conformity, homogenize and standardize opinion. The capacity of network radio to bring the same aural experience to masses of people at the same time provoked both utopian and dystopian predictions of an imminent future in which independence and diversity of thought would have greatly diminished.

Not all Americans who thought about propaganda were afraid of it. Public relations expert Edward Bernays argued in 1928 that "the manipulation of the public mind ... serves a social purpose," and he wrote enthusiastically of the new techniques and technologies

82. On the monopoly concern generally, see Socolow, "To Network a Nation": ch. 3.

83. Typescript summary, Session U, National Conference on Educational Radio 1936, box 29, Lyman Bryson papers, LOC.

84. See Eugene E. Leach, "'Voices out of the Night': Radio Research and Ideas about Mass Behavior in the United States, 1920–1950," *Canadian Review of American Studies* 20 (1989): 191–209; Gerd Horten, *Radio Goes to War: The Cultural Politics of Propaganda during World War II* (Berkeley: University of California Press, 2002): ch. 1; J. Michael Sproule, *Propaganda and Democracy: The American Experience of Media and Mass Persuasion* (New York: Cambridge University Press, 1997).

available for the "mass distribution of ideas."[85] Harold Lafount believed that radio promoted national unity and that "common sources of entertainment, common economic interests, common ideals, problems and dangers constitute bonds for making our people homogenous."[86] Lafount could, however, see only positives, most importantly a good kind of social stability, flowing from this uniformity.[87] Psychologists Hadley Cantril and Gordon Allport, in their 1935 *The Psychology of Radio*, one of the first and most perceptive academic studies of broadcasting, argued that radio tended to "standardize and stereotype mental life." They predicted that radio would create "further standardization of our habits of living." They too saw many advantages to this increasing commonality. Radio promoted "social solidarity," and it was already making Americans more socially integrated, more in touch with expert advice, and more punctual.[88] Cantril subsequently pointed out a further optimistic possibility—the standardization of life was he thought a sign of the breaking down of inequalities, of the more equal opportunities Americans had for social participation.[89] Sociologist Howard Odum was also hopeful that radio would help bring about that "homogeneity of ideas and understanding, through which a better designed America may emerge."[90] James Rowland Angell, while employed at NBC, looked forward to the deployment of broadcasting as an instrument of social engineering—he praised radio in 1938, saying that "the world has never known any agency of comparable importance for the direction and control of human relations."[91] The possibility of a more coordinated, and controlled society thus had considerable and understandable appeal to a spectrum of American intellectuals amidst the disorder of the Depression years. To those still holding to some of the hopes of Progressive planned social improvement, radio—and particularly networked radio—seemed quite miraculously to offer a cost-effective means to that somewhat elusive end.

The fears about broadcast propaganda are probably more familiar today than the hopes. Intellectuals worried that the mass address of radio was necessarily aimed at broad categories of taste and opinion, and might lead not just to rational coordination of society, but to a dull and dangerous conformity. Cantril and Allport noted that broadcasters worked with very broad categories of opinion and musical taste, and that listeners had to make do with the nearest approximation to their own preferences: "I constantly sacrifice my individuality so that I may fit into one of the common molds that radio offers. If I

85. Edward L. Bernays, "Manipulating Public Opinion: The Why and the How," *American Journal of Sociology* 33, no. 6 (May 1928): 959, 971.

86. Harold Lafount, "Radio Control in the United States," folder 35, box 17, NBC records, WHS.

87. "Extract of Remarks Made by Commissioner Harold Lafount," May 19, 1933, folder 34, box 17, NBC records, WHS.

88. Hadley Cantril and Gordon W. Allport, *The Psychology of Radio* (New York: Harper and Brothers, 1935): 22–24. On Cantril and Allport, see Katherine Pandora, "'Mapping the New Mental World Created by Radio': Media Messages, Cultural Politics, and Cantril and Allport's *The Psychology of Radio*," *Journal of Social Issues* 54, no. 1 (Spring 1998): 7–27.

89. Hadley Cantril, "The Effect of Modern Technology and Organization upon Social Behavior," *Social Forces* 15, no. 4 (May 1937): 494.

90. "Radio Augurs World Peace, Parley Hears," *Washington Post*, December 12, 1936: X17.

91. James Rowland Angell, "The Influence of Radio," in Federal Council of the Churches of Christ in America, *Broadcasting and the Public: A Case Study in Social Ethics* (New York: Abingdon, 1938): 13.

insist on remaining an individualist, I shall dislike nearly all radio programs."[92] While in musical taste the costs of conformity were not perhaps immediately socially consequential, advice about the conduct of life was another matter. In 1943 radio researcher Marjorie Fiske discussed the way radio "provides people with ready-made standards of judgment which help them to make decisions about their personal conduct."[93] Radio's prefabricated advice and stories seemed to some intellectuals a poor substitute for developed engagement with other people. It was only a few steps from this kind of concern about standardized opinions and judgments to more strident warnings about the political consequences of broadcast propaganda. Researcher Herta Herzog asked some disturbing questions about the emotional effects of radio on children and its civic consequences: "What does it mean for the emotional development of a personality if, in their early youth, children are conditioned to live on borrowed experience? To what extent will they be trained this way, later on always to look for somebody else to provide excitement for them and thus fall easy prey to any kind of propaganda which makes use of their emotional starvation?"[94] Here the discussion moved from the problem of retaining individuality, to the issue of manipulation and loss of rational control over one's own thoughts and feelings. What meaning could democracy have, if opinions were to be shaped and manipulated by centralized, even deliberately coercive means? If propaganda invaded the home, and the opinions citizens spoke were not necessarily their own, then the democratic process was disturbingly manipulable. This threat received increasing attention through the 1930s and beyond, to the point that sociologists Lazarsfeld and Merton could observe in 1948 that Americans stood in "peculiar dread of the power of propaganda."[95]

Another kind of propaganda was all around, central to the American system. Radio networks had appeared in the later 1920s just in time to catch the rising tide of national advertising. Psychological research suggested, to the great satisfaction of the broadcasting industry, that things heard were much better remembered than things seen—a radio advertisement was more satisfactorily recalled than one viewed in a magazine, and the memory gap increased as time passed.[96] Radio, observed Herman Hettinger, the nation's leading expert on radio advertising, possessed "all the emotional appeal and persuasiveness

92. Cantril and Allport, *The Psychology of Radio*: 22–23.

93. Marjorie Fiske, "Survey of Materials on the Psychology of Radio Listening" (New York: Office of Radio Research, 1943), typescript paper B0185, in *Reports of the Bureau of Applied Social Research on Microfiche* (New York: Clearwater, 1981): 44.

94. Herta Herzog, "Children and Their Leisure Time Listening to the Radio" (New York: Office of Radio Research, 1941): 44.

95. Paul F. Lazarsfeld and Robert K. Merton, "Mass Communication, Popular Taste and Organized Social Action," in Lyman Bryson (ed.), *The Communication of Ideas* (New York: Harper and Brothers, 1948): 95.

96. John J. Karol, "Notes on Further Psychological Research in Radio," *Journal of Marketing* 1, no. 2 (October 1936): 150; H. N. De Wick, "The Relative Recall Effectiveness of Visual and Auditory Presentation of Advertising Material," *Journal of Applied Psychology* 19, no.3 (June 1935): 245–64; "Memory for Advertising Copy Presented Visually vs. Orally," *Journal of Applied Psychology* 18, no. 1 (February 1934): 45–64.

of the voice," giving it a "power which cold print cannot equal."[97] In the 1930s, advertising and marketing were said by industry enthusiasts to be incipient sciences and the hope was that the whole selling process could eventually become a matter of "systematized scientific persuasion."[98]

New Deal era academic critics who thought about broadcast propaganda sooner or later arrived at the insight that commercial radio depended for its very existence on advertising propaganda little different in form to political propaganda, and similarly skillfully designed to produce conformity of belief and action.[99] "The technique of manipulating large masses of people is developed in the business world and from there permeates our whole culture," Paul Lazarsfeld observed.[100] Cantril and Allport made no categorical distinction between commercial propaganda for Pepsodent or Chesterfields, and political propaganda for Hitler or Coughlin.[101] Part of the reason that propaganda criticism as a nascent branch of social science always had a liberal or leftist tinge to it was the inevitability of this turn—the very category of "propaganda" invited reflection on the relation of commercial and political techniques of persuasion.

Broadcasters had to keep alive two mutually contradictory stories about the radio audience. When talking to listeners and political leaders, they argued that in America listener preferences determined what was broadcast—and in the letters they wrote to radio fan magazines, it seemed that many keen radio listeners accepted the role.[102] In their appeals to potential advertising customers, broadcasters boasted of their persuasive power. A brochure put out by CBS in 1935, directed at potential advertisers, claimed, "Seven times, Eight times, Nine times out of ten, People do what they're told."[103] This claim was elaborated in a follow-up advertisement in *Broadcasting*, which explained how responsive American families were to advertiser suggestions about what they should eat. [Figure 2.3.] When NBC president Lenox Lohr addressed the U.S. Chamber of Commerce in 1938, he stressed radio's "appeal to the emotions as well as to the intellect." He told a story about a daytime serial depicting the home life of a simple American family, who in one episode planted a garden. The announcer invited listeners to send in 10 cents so that a character in the serial could send them "some of her own petunia seeds." "It is interesting here," said Lohr, "to analyze the emotions of the hearers":

97. Herman S. Hettinger, "Broadcasting in the United States," *Annals of the American Academy of Political and Social Science* 177, no. 1 (January 1935): 3.

98. John T. A. Ely and Daniel Starch, *Salesmanship for Everybody* (New York: Gregg, 1936); T. J. Jackson Lears, *Fables of Abundance: A Cultural History of Advertising in America* (New York: Basic Books, 1994): 225–26.

99. See Kathy Newman, *Radio Active: Advertising and Consumer Activism, 1935–1947* (Berkeley: University of California Press, 2004): chs. 1 and 2; Bruce Lenthall, *Radio's America: The Great Depression and the Rise of Modern Mass Culture* (Chicago: University of Chicago Press, 2007): Ch. 1.

100. Paul Lazarsfeld, "Remarks on Administrative and Critical Communications Research," *Studies in Philosophy and Social Science* 9 (1941): 9.

101. Cantril and Allport, *The Psychology of Radio*: 59–64.

102. Craig, *Fireside Politics*: xvii. On fans as accepting the role, Elena Razlogova, *The Listener's Voice: Early Radio and the American Public* (Philadelphia: University of Pennsylvania Press, 2011).

103. Barnouw, *The Golden Web*: 62.

She does what she's *told* . . . .

This started out to be a story about the lady-who-listens-in-the-kitchen, jotting down the CBS recipes she hears.* But how about Dad? He's not shown here, but he *won't* be left out of the radio picture. *He* tells her of a soup he wants to try—because *he's* been listening evenings.* And there's Johnny and Judy, of course. For the first time in their lives, they're actually *excited* about cereals and milk*—because their favorite voices on the air tell them they're good. ● The whole family listens—and does what it's *told*—when the telling is as easy-to-take as the family's favorite CBS programs. Little wonder CBS food advertisers doubled their schedules in '34. Or that in January they're already 20% ahead of last year. ● So are cigarette and automobile advertising on CBS—and almost everything else in the price-brackets between. The world's largest radio network is a swift and lively route to twenty-million families—who buy the things they're *told* to buy!*

*We'll be glad to show you proof...*and proof...*and proof...

● America's Little House — exclusive broadcasting facilities from the "Little House" are available to CBS clients.

COLUMBIA BROADCASTING SYSTEM

485 MADISON AVE., NEW YORK • 410 N. MICHIGAN AVE., CHICAGO, ILLINOIS
WORLD'S LARGEST RADIO NETWORK • 97 STATIONS IN 95 CITIES

● Thousands of women each week visit in person this kitchen in America's Little House. Millions of women listen, in their own kitchens and living rooms, to the Columbia Network programs broadcast regularly from the special studio in the "Little House."

Figure 2.3. "She does what she's told…," *Broadcasting* 8, no. 3 (Feb. 1, 1935): 2–3.

To them, the characters in the story were as real and alive as their next door neighbors. That the petunia seeds and the garden were but the fiction of a script writer read by actors in a studio, did not occur to them. They did not stop to consider that, even had there been such a garden, their well-loved character could not have fulfilled their wants, but their seeds, acquired from a wholesaler, would be sent by a staff of people assembled for that purpose. But, so great was the emotional appeal, that the listeners were motivated to the rather complicated action of writing a letter, enclosing a dime and mailing the envelope. And yet, from this offer, there came in over a million dimes and more than a hundred thousand dollars worth of petunia seeds were dispatched.

Talking directly to the potential buyers of time on his network, Lohr had no qualms about portraying network listeners as unreflective dupes of broadcast aural fictions: "So keen was their interest in the characters, so much a part of their life had they become, that the words which reached the listening ears went directly to their hearts, by-passing normal mental processes, for surely under the urge of cold logic, few dimes would have been sent in."[104] If that were true, all the better for the advertisers. But for those with broader civic concerns, such reports of demonstrated impressionability were highly disturbing.

---

104. Lenox R. Lohr, *Some Social and Political Aspects of Broadcasting* (Washington, DC: United States Chamber of Commerce, 1938): 9.

RADIO'S INTIMACY

Radio was central to discussions of propaganda because of certain characteristics of the medium. Radio allowed outside voices to enter the home, to speak to people as they relaxed. One of the great discoveries of the 1930s—attested to again and again—was that radio was an intimate medium. Radio spoke to a mass audience, but in small groups, in living rooms all over the nation. Neville Miller, president of the National Association of Broadcasters, boasted in a speech broadcast in 1939 that one of the unique characteristics of radio was that "it comes to visit you in your home, it is almost human—it is persuasive, cajoling, commanding—always intimate, its spoken word simultaneously makes its impact on millions of people."[105] Cecil B. de Mille too commented in 1938 on the intimacy of radio—"It is the most intimate of all mediums," he said. "It is the closest contact that I have ever felt in my professional experience. And it is a great responsibility that rests upon us, for we enter the listeners' home and join them at the fireside to weave the pattern of our story."[106]

The key discovery made by advertisers was then not a scientific but a performative one—that radio's persuasiveness was related to its intimacy, and that listeners at home were most effectively addressed in a personal or even intimate voice.[107] It is a point repeated to this day in broadcasting textbooks, with little apparent sense of the veteran status of the idea.[108] Hettinger in 1934 praised recent commercials on radio for their "quieter, more persuasive, more sophisticated" tone. Radio, he explained, "is conversation between the announcer and each individual listener, not between one person and massed millions."[109] As advertising agencies moved into the actual making of programs, entertainment programs themselves came to be conceived within the industry quite explicitly as an intimate means to reach customers for the advertised products. Station WXYZ Detroit advertised its own local daytime serial *Ann Worth, Housewife* in the industry journal *Broadcasting*, boasting quite frankly that the program, with its "exceptionally convincing" lead character, had been "specially planned to break down the barriers that make direct to home selling very difficult in Detroit's highly competitive market." The simple message was that "when women listen…they buy!!"[110] The intimacy and persuasiveness of radio was within the industry clearly understood to be a tactic for selling, part of an emotional rather than rational appeal to listeners. Outside the broadcasting and advertising industries, however, that was a frightening conclusion.

105. Neville Miller, *The Code Preserves Free Speech* (Washington, DC: National Association of Broadcasters, 1939): 3.

106. *New York Times*, January 23, 1938: 12.

107. Roland Marchand makes the analogy between this intimate address and the rise of crooning as a radio singing style: see his *Advertising the American Dream: Making Way for Modernity, 1920–1940* (Berkeley: University of California Press, 1985): 108–10.

108. "Radio is arguably the most intimate medium": Charles Warner, *Media Selling: Broadcast, Cable, Print and Interactive* (Oxford: Blackwell, 2003): 389.

109. Herman S. Hettinger, "The Future of Radio as an Advertising Medium," *Journal of Business of the University of Chicago* 7, no. 4. (October 1934): 286, 290.

110. WXYZ advertisement, *Broadcasting* 12, no. 2 (January 15, 1937): 34.

If it was advertisers who made the primary discovery about the efficacy of radio's intimate voice, it was president Franklin Roosevelt who most famously utilized that insight in political broadcasting, delivering "fireside chats" as well as formal or declamatory speeches, addressing his national audience as "my friends." But what if a bad leader should employ such intimate and appealing techniques? The debate about propaganda in the 1930s almost always hinged on its two-edged capacities, and the question of whether or how the techniques could be confined to democratic and benign commercial uses.

In 1930s debates about broadcast propaganda, radio was thus spoken of as a technology of political domination and control that worked not by violence and coercion, but by enticement and persuasion. It was understood that the power and the danger of radio lay in its penetration of, even destruction of, public/private boundaries. Radio brought the oratory of the political platform, the raucous pitch of the salesman, the bawdy humor of the popular stage, the abrupt news of disaster, right into the living room. It was an intimate medium, which addressed family members at home, in their most relaxed and private moments. Radio's intimacy brought seductive charm and danger, as well as hopes and plans for improvement.[111] American broadcasters were not unique in discovering the crucial role of intimate address in radio—a Czech broadcasting official told an international conference in 1938 about how "sensitive the listener is to the talk that seems to be addressed particularly to him, where use is made of such expressions as 'I'm thinking of you,' or 'you, listeners of the Tatras,' or again 'you who are listening in Moravia,' etc. That is why the form adopted by the platform speakers is so much less successful."[112] American broadcasting industry leaders, entertainment makers, and political leaders, concurred—radio's sometime frightening power was a product of its intimacy. The potential influence of a technology that allowed for mass address, but would be experienced as intimate and personal, seemed immense.

The intellectual concern with propaganda is traced in innumerable studies back to Walter Lippmann's views on public opinion and democracy (discussed in more detail in chapter 4) in his *Public Opinion* (1922) and *The Phantom Public* (1925). Lippmann saw that propaganda could be useful to a scientific policymaking elite that could engineer consent about the policies that it knew would be of most benefit to the public: "The knowledge of how to create consent will alter every political calculation and modify every political premise."[113] John Dewey replied in his 1927 *The Public and Its Problems*, defending the wisdom of the public and the viability of popular sovereignty in the modern age. The debate between these two articulate liberal intellectuals has received the most prominent place in the historiography on questions of public opinion and its manipulation. They have come to represent the two major strands of the debate—the Deweyan tradition leading to the attempts to give the public a critical education about

111. On radio's public/private address, see especially Jason Loviglio, *Radio's Intimate Public: Network Broadcasting and Mass-Mediated Democracy* (Minneapolis: University of Minnesota Press, 2005).

112. Otakar Matousek [professor at Prague University; director of Czechoslovak Broadcast Talks], "Wireless Listening Groups," preparatory document for Union Internationale de Radiodiffusion, Geneve, Conference of Experts in Broadcast Talks, 1938, Radio Broadcasting Collection, Princeton University Library.

113. Walter Lippmann, *Public Opinion* (New York: Harcourt, Brace, 1922): 248.

propaganda, and the Lippmann tradition leading to the belief that propaganda was an inevitable and even desirable feature of modern society and that it ought to be used for good.

Historians of the propaganda idea argue that by the 1940s the Lippmann tradition had triumphed in the United States.[114] But for the history of radio's civic paradigm, the most important point is that the American radio system always had both these ideas before it—the interest in how to influence *and* the civic goal of how to create critical, propaganda-proof individuals capable of making up their own minds. Evidence that individuals were persuaded by what they heard on air was vital to the business health of radio, but evidence that personal opinion formation was surviving the onslaught of broadcast propagandas was absolutely crucial through most of the 1930s to the public and political legitimation of the American system.

RADIO'S OBEDIENTLY ACTIVE AUDIENCES

Radio, it has long been recognized, troubled and complicated public/private divisions.[115] As Mary Douglas argued long ago, cultures are obliged to confront anomalies and ambiguities, to surround them with reinforced or revised rules.[116] Radio's danger as a technology arose from its breaching of public/private boundaries. It was in a context of concern about radio's ability to bring public voices into private spaces that the U.S. government, through its regulatory agency the FCC, sought to shape the largely commercial U.S. broadcasting sector into something that had a specific and demonstrable civic role. Broadcasting technology offered quite revolutionarily new possibilities for thinking about the relationship between public and private life. What if the one-way mass distribution technology of broadcasting could be used not to produce conformity, but to create individualism—mass-produced individualism? In the United States, many shared the hope that this new device would permit a new, better, more democratic, and more participatory civic life, based on an enhanced individualism.

What U.S. communications scholarship has remembered about the 1930s has been mainly the importance of propaganda theory. The fear has been remembered but not the response, leaving us with an image of the 1930s as far more credulous than it was. The influential theory developed by media scholars in the 1940s that mass communications had only "limited effects" on audiences led them to exaggerate the extent to which 1930s scholars of media believed in the propaganda or "hypodermic needle" theory of mass communications. The idea became implanted in postwar mass communications study that in the 1920s and 30s there had been a general and simple belief that media audiences were extremely vulnerable to propaganda. Katz and Lazarsfeld argued bluntly, for example, in their 1955 study *Personal Influence* that propaganda critics in the 1920s and

---

114. See Brett Gary, *The Nervous Liberals: Propaganda Anxieties from World War I to the Cold War* (New York: Columbia University Press, 1999).

115. Loviglio, *Radio's Intimate Public*.

116. Mary Douglas, *Purity and Danger: An Analysis of Concept of Pollution and Taboo* (1966; reprint, London: Routledge, 2002): 48.

1930s had in common a picturing of "every Message as a direct and powerful stimulus to action which would elicit immediate response."[117]

Since the 1970s, the debate about media audiences has been condensed in media and cultural studies to the reductive question—do the broadcast media render audiences passive, or can they be critical, active, even resistant? The claim that audiences were naturally active rather than passive, once elevated to orthodoxy, was vulnerable to further simplification and promotion to the status of timeless truth rather than historically specific argument.[118] Invocations of the active audience also often rested upon a caricature of earlier thought, and an exaggeration of the broader influence of pessimistic Frankfurt School mass culture theories. A recent anthology on audience studies traces what has become the conventional genealogy: it was in the "1920s and 1930s that the mass-society or mass-culture thesis arose"; then the Frankfurt School proposed that "culture was imposed from 'above' on to a passive and malleable audience", and the "effects" school of audience research proposed a "hypodermic needle" model and presumed that audiences could "be straightforwardly 'injected' with a message."[119] This story works as a legitimating genealogy of present-day active audience theory, but rather less well as history. Meyrowitz maintains, "The old 'hypodermic needle' theory (popular in the 1920s) has been abandoned by almost all researchers."[120] In fact, significant doubt has been cast on whether anybody ever actually held the passive audience view in its simplest form. The hypodermic "theory" was perhaps always a straw person, something used by Lazarsfeld and his colleagues to distinguish more dramatically their limited effects model of the media from its competitors.[121] It was a summary of conventional wisdom rather than anybody's formulation in particular—a distillation of the common sense of the time, Chaffee argues, and an explanation of the "observable fact of rapid and radical political change in Europe."[122] So many things about the 1930s suggested that radio could bring about, as sociologist Robert K. Merton put it in 1946, "the quick persuasion of masses of

117. Elihu Katz and Paul F. Lazarsfeld, *Personal Influence; the Part Played by People in the Flow of Mass Communications* (Glencoe, IL: Free Press, 1955): 16.

118. On the limitations of this debate as it developed in the 1980s and early 1990s, see Meaghan Morris, "Banality in Cultural Studies," in Patricia Mellencamp (ed.), *Logics of Television* (Bloomington: Indiana University Press, 1990): 14–43; David Morley, "Active Audience Theory: Pendulums and Pitfalls," *Journal of Communication* 43, no. 4 (Autumn 1993): 13–20.

119. "Introduction: Paradigm Shift," in Will Brooker and Deborah Jermyn (eds.), *The Audience Studies Reader* (London: Routledge, 2003): 5–6.

120. Joshua Meyrowitz, "Media and Behavior: A Missing Link," in Denis McQuail (ed.), *McQuail's Reader in Mass Communication Theory* (London: Sage, 2002): 100.

121. But see Jeffrey Bineham, "A Historical Account of the Hypodermic Model," *Mass Communication* 55, no. 3 (September 1988): 230–47.

122. Steven H. Chaffee, "Differentiating the Hypodermic Model from Empirical Research: A Comment on Bineham's Commentaries," *Communication Monographs* 55, no. 3 (September 1988): 247–50. A similar argument is made in Ellen Wartella, "The History Reconsidered," in Everette E. Dennis and Ellen Wartella, *American Communication Research: The Remembered History* (Mahwah, NJ: Lawrence Erlbaum, 1996): 172. Chaffee and Hocheimer argued that Lasswell, for example, never used the term: S. H. Chaffee and J. L. Hochheimer, "The Beginnings of Political Communication Research in the United States: Origins of the 'Limited Effects' Model," *Mass Communication Review Yearbook* 5 (1985): 75–104.

people."[123] However the limited effects paradigm advocated in the 1940s and 1950s by pioneer radio researchers including Merton, Lazarsfeld, and others led a generation to exaggerate and simplify 1930s understandings of when and how propaganda worked on audiences.[124]

Lazarsfeld was well aware that *limited effects* was not a timeless truth, but rather a summary of the experience of American broadcasting to date. The argument was not that broadcasting always and everywhere had limited effects on audiences, but that the effects would be limited unless certain optimal conditions were present.[125] In their classic 1948 article "Mass Communication, Popular Taste and Organized Social Action," Lazarsfeld and Merton specified that at least one of three conditions must be met if propaganda was to be effective—the existence of a monopoly of the mass media; that the propaganda was, like most commercial advertising, attempting only a "canalization" of existing attitudes rather than an invention of new ones; or that the broadcast propaganda was "supplemented" with face to face contacts—"local discussions serve to reinforce the content of mass propaganda."[126] That propaganda worked only under these ideal conditions was a reassuring discovery. Americans were, it turned out, not nearly as vulnerable to propaganda and media-produced conformity as had been feared.

We need to read the intellectual history of ideas about communication against the cultural history of communication practices. Lazarsfeld and his colleagues in 1948 knew very well that American radio had for two decades been attempting in systematic and self-conscious ways to counter audience passivity with structured incitements to opinion formation and action. In response to concerns about radio-induced passivity, conformity, and inauthenticity, the regulators of American broadcasting and the public constantly sought reassuring evidence that radio was both reflecting and stimulating communal life. American broadcasting as a system was constructed to counter fears about passive conformity. Brett Gary concludes from study of the record of intellectual debate that the fear of propaganda fed a strengthening belief in the irrationality of the public, creating a perception by the late 1930s that "human reason and intellect could not withstand the onslaught

123. Robert K. Merton, *Mass Persuasion: The Social Psychology of a War Bond Drive* (New York: Harper and Brothers, 1946): 1.

124. See Peter Simonson and Gabriel Weiman, "Critical Research at Columbia: Lazarsfeld's and Merton's 'Mass Communication, Popular Taste, and Organized Social Action,'" in Elihu Katz, John Durham Peters, Tamar Liebes, and Avril Orloff (eds.), *Canonic Texts in Media Research: Are There Any? Should There Be? How about These?* (Cambridge: Polity, 2003): 12–38.

125. A point not always noted by critics. See Todd Gitlin, "Media Sociology: The Dominant Paradigm," *Theory and Society* 6, no. 2 (1978): 205–53; Robert McChesney, *Rich Media, Poor Democracy: Communication Politics in Dubious Times, The History of Communication* (Urbana: University of Illinois Press, 1999), who have developed arguments about the political consequences of media studies paradigms. Gitlin argued that the 1940s and 1950s communications researchers' conclusion that the media had only limited effects was suspiciously congruent with broadcasters' interest in downplaying the need for regulation; McChesney similarly points to the complicity of active audience theory today with the corporate media's desire to camouflage its social and economic power.

126. Paul F. Lazarsfeld and Robert K. Merton, "Mass Communication, Popular Taste and Organized Social Action," in Lyman Bryson (ed.), *The Communication of Ideas* (New York: Harper and Brothers, 1948): 113–16.

of mass-mediated images and slogans." Gary extrapolates from this idea that "powerful propagandas combined with public naivete" posed a threat to American institutions, to the conclusion that this "resulted in a much diminished belief in public capabilities."[127] This observation is however mainly based on scrutiny of the views of those intellectuals interested in propaganda as a form of social management. A different set of beliefs and strategies about the public and its capacity to develop critical and rational capacities in the face of broadcast propaganda can be derived from study of radio's practice.

John Durham Peters's intellectual history of mass communication theory argues against the older orthodoxy, which held that early communications scholarship was wholly in the grip of mass society theory and a deep pessimism about individuals' capacity to withstand manipulative communication. Broadcast culture in the 1930s, Peters observes, "was quite self-conscious about overcoming the specters of (a) a mass audience without mutual interaction or awareness, (b) a one-way flow and (c) anonymous forms of address."[128] Peters's argument is that many elements of 1930s "broadcast culture" were self-consciously designed to counteract what were feared to be the passive and alienating characteristics of mass communication. Interwar intellectuals who thought about broadcasting, he argues, were "attentive to the potential for interchange within large-scale communication" and were both "fascinated and alarmed by radio's apparent intimacy, its penetration of private spaces, and its ability to stage dialogues and personal relationships with listeners."[129] Radio simulated audience presence in so many ways in order to overcome the always-felt absence of the actual audience:

> By defining broadcasting in terms of the public interest, the 1934 Communications Act articulated a vision of the audience—a civic one, the audience as disinterested public—that fit the technology's lack of confidentiality, and gave a lofty lineage to a set of practices that owed as much to the circus as to the polis.... The brief shining moment of dissemination was washed over by a flood of dialogism.[130]

It is a very suggestive and important passage, one whose implications are only touched upon in Peters's book, which is not a cultural history of broadcasting but an intellectual history of the "idea of communication." Where I diverge from Peters is over his view of the civic role of American radio as ideally involving central dissemination of knowledge to a disinterested audience, and his *contrast* of this to the dialogic, intimate voice that commercial entertainment radio successfully developed to help simulate presence: "crooning, direct address of listeners, dramatic dialogue, 'feuds' between stars, fan letters, fan clubs, contests and promotional giveaways, or radio comedy."[131] For Peters the "flood

127. Gary, *The Nervous Liberals*: 3, 11.

128. John Durham Peters, "The Uncanniness of Mass Communication in Interwar Social Thought," *Journal of Communications* 46, no. 3 (Summer 1996): 111–12.

129. Peters, "The Uncanniness of Mass Communication": 109–13.

130. John Durham Peters, *Speaking into the Air: A History of the Idea of Communication* (Chicago: University of Chicago Press, 1999): 211.

131. Peters, *Speaking into the Air*: 216.

of dialogism" is a different thing from the civic ideal of top-down dissemination. But my argument is, on the contrary, that American radio's civic paradigm was always as much about producing personal opinions, and hence about simulating dialogue, as it was about disseminating education and culture as prepackaged truths. The commitment to individual opinion formation as the bedrock of rational citizenship in an age of propaganda is much clearer in the cultural history of broadcasting practice than in the record of high intellectual debate.

One of the legacies of the past few decades of active audience theory has been a habitual understanding of active audiences as resistant, and passive ones as compliant. Susan Douglas in 1992, for example, called for a history of media audiences focused on the question of "the extent to which people acquiesced to—or resisted—the homogenization and taming pull of the culture industry."[132] This stream of thought in contemporary cultural studies goes back at least to the work of Stuart Hall and the Birmingham Centre for Contemporary Cultural Studies in the 1970s, which sought to "link the active audience with resistance to ideology."[133] I want to qualify this now conventional mapping of active/passive onto resistant/compliant audiences by arguing that in the 1930s the whole official apparatus of broadcasting in the United States was intended to incite and create an active audience. That active audience—inasmuch as it was being critical, opinionated, outspoken in an individual mode—was not resisting but complying with the individualizing demands of the system.

Historical work can thus help us see a way around the current impasse in media studies between revivers of simple propaganda theory about media power, and overoptimistic celebrants of audience agency.[134] In the 1930s, there was not this simple opposition between pessimistic belief in the media's propaganda power and redemptive belief in the audience's critical activity and agency. In an environment made self-conscious about listener response by propaganda theory, audience activity was much more often understood to be the product of cultural work. Active audiences were not expected to appear spontaneously—they were very clearly understood, for example, by Lazarsfeld and Merton, as things that needed to be created, educated, and instructed into being.

How would we know that past audiences thought of themselves as active? So many millions of Americans took the trouble to write letters to tell broadcasters or government or the newspapers how they felt about what they had heard.[135] Radio seemed important enough that it was worth protesting if something incorrect or outrageous or ill-mannered or un-American or blasphemous was said on the air. Listeners would write to

132. Susan J. Douglas, "Notes toward a History of Media Audiences," *Radical History Review* 54 (Fall 1992): 127.

133. See Chris Barker, *Cultural Studies: Theory and Practice* (London: Sage, 2003): 329. The work of John Fiske in television studies represented one influential version of this: John Fiske, "TV: Re-situating the Popular in the People," *Continuum* 1, no. 2 (1987), and his *Television Culture* (London: Methuen, 1987).

134. On the contemporary dilemma of media studies about audiences, see Susan J. Douglas, "Mass Media: From 1945 to the Present," in Jean Christophe Agnew and Roy Rosenzweig (eds.), *A Companion to Post-1945 America* (Oxford: Blackwell, 2002): 89–90.

135. The most sophisticated study of listener letters to date is Razlogova, *The Listener's Voice*.

complain, to congratulate. But they also—importantly—wrote to tell about themselves, and to describe the mood and context of their listening. They wrote in simply astonishing numbers—most famously, of course, the millions who wrote to President Roosevelt in response to his radio "fireside chats."[136] The use made of radio by President Roosevelt, and by the various New Deal agencies, to make known the measures underway to ameliorate the effects of depression, constituted a new use of radio for government—"the radio emerged an instrument of participating democracy."[137] Roosevelt said in his July 1933 chat, "When I am asked whether the American people will pull themselves out of this depression, I answer 'They will if they want to'"—the broadcast words seemed to call for some testimony in response, some account of individual willingness to act. The early fireside chats stimulated such an avalanche of mail that many assistants had to be hired; during March 1933 alone, half a million letters were written to the president, often addressing him personally and narrating the authors' own experiences. When CBS in 1931 tried to stop Detroit's "radio priest," Father Charles Coughlin, from broadcasting on political topics, it received 1.25 million items of mail in protest at the attempted "censorship." By 1933, Coughlin was said to be receiving 12,000 letters a day; by 1935, he was employing 150 stenographers to reply to his mail and it was said that he received more mail than anyone else in America.[138] After broadcasts in 1935, Huey Long was receiving between 8,000 and 15,000 pieces of mail a day, and employed a staff of at least a dozen to open the mail and reply to requests for copies of speeches.[139] In 1938, NBC claimed to have received more than 6 million letters and 50,000 telegrams from listeners commenting on programs.[140]

These facts are familiar from repetition now, but in the textbooks few conclusions are drawn from them. Here I argue that radio—both local and networked, in their different ways—incited its audience to speak, to testify to their listening, to document what and how they heard. Many radio programs were indeed specifically designed to elicit personal opinion—about soap opera characters' dilemmas, popular songs, and public issues. The letters pages of radio fan magazines provided spaces for the expression of personal opinions about programs. The responsible formation of individual opinion, stimulated by the information and opinion already in circulation, was one of the tasks of the modern democratic citizen. NBC commentator and radio industry defender William Hard summarized the legitimating ideology of the American system of broadcasting when he wrote

136. On the fireside chats, see Loviglio, *Radio's Intimate Public*, ch. 1; Lawrence W. Levine and Cornelia R. Levine, *The People and the President: America's Conversation with FDR* (Boston: Beacon Press, 2002); Edward D. Miller, *Emergency Broadcasting and 1930s American Radio* (Philadelphia: Temple University Press, 2003).

137. Louis E. Kirstein, "Radio and Social Welfare," *Annals of the American Academy of Political and Social Science* 177 (January 1935): 130.

138. John M. Carlisle, "Priest of a Parish of the Air Waves," *New York Times*, October 29, 1933: SM8; "American Messiahs," *Washington Post*, May 21, 1935: 1; "War of Words," *New York Times*, March 10, 1935: E1; Donald Warren, *Radio Priest: Charles Coughlin the Father of Hate Radio* (New York: Free Press, 1996).

139. Frank Russell to R. C. Patterson February 14, 1935, folder 40, box 91, NBC records, WHS.

140. Typescript "Broadcast Policies," January 27, 1939, folder 336, NBC history files, LOC.

that the highest duty of the broadcaster was to "admit all schools of thought to his studios and to permit them to convey their orthodoxies or heresies to the listeners, who will themselves decide what they think."[141] This ideology informed the regulation of radio, program construction, and listeners' self-understanding. It offered a model of broadcasting in which the power of radio was used to create individualism not uniformity, activity not passivity. Even advertising was designed to elicit not blind conformity, but strong opinions about ostensibly similar products—Newman argues that advertisers wanted active not passive consumers, people positively motivated and prepared to act on the basis of what they had heard.[142]

It was because of this general emphasis on the role of broadcasting in the formation of critical individual citizens that Americans expected their radio to have a broadly civic and educational as well as an entertainment role. When asked in a 1945 survey whether it was important that a radio station broadcast at least one "serious or educational" program every evening, 74% of respondents said yes—there was "general agreement that the discussion of public affairs is one of the most distinctive and impressive features of the American system of broadcasting."[143] The civic and educational role of radio was almost always understood to culminate in the production of listeners who were self-consciously opinion formers, individuals who took in the diverse comment and information broadcast on the radio and made their own critical assessment of it.

Most Americans knew of the fear that radio would reduce the population to armchair passivity, and letter writing was at times a self-conscious refutation of that view. It would be a mistake, then, to cite 1930s radio listeners' letters simply as evidence of the existence of active listeners who were resisting the homogenizing messages of mass communication. There would be something ahistorical about applying such terms of analysis back onto the past without acknowledging that a self-conscious relationship to those very issues was a part of the historical reality being analyzed. When 1930s listeners wrote back to the voices on their radios, either to praise or to criticize, they were not resisting the demands of mass culture, but obeying its call to respond, to take responsibility for and to speak about themselves and their listening and opinions, to define themselves self-consciously both as individuals and as members of a population and an audience—evidence of what Loviglio has so aptly termed the "self-reflexive and self-abstracting" nature of listener letters.[144]

Not only did listeners write letters, they joined organizations whose purpose was to provide them with a forum to speak or write about their listening. The Women's National Radio Committee claimed in 1937 to have more than 10 million women affiliated to it, who participated in voting for its "radio program of the year" awards.[145] Radio listeners

141. William Hard, "Radio and Public Opinion," *Annals of the American Academy of Political and Social Science* 177 (January 1935): 106.

142. Newman, *Radio Active*: 27–30.

143. Paul F. Lazarsfeld and Harry Hubert Field, *The People Look at Radio: Report on a Survey* (Chapel Hill: University of North Carolina Press, 1946): 54, 58.

144. Loviglio, *Radio's Intimate Public*: 7.

145. *New York Times*, April 1, 1937: 25.

also wrote to government, and commentators marveled at the new relationship of citizens to government that radio seemed to be creating: "He is stopped by no consideration of class, time or space. As a citizen of this democracy, he has no hesitation in addressing his pleas or his demands to any officer in the land."[146] Listeners wrote freely to the voices they heard on their radios, whoever and wherever they were, expressing their feelings and responses, confident that their opinions would be heard.[147] Enlivened by the new simultaneity—taking up their pens during or immediately after a broadcast, American listeners felt themselves to be joining the world in time just as the broadcast sound traversed space.

In an era suffused with anxiety about propaganda, then, the dominant people and institutions in U.S. broadcasting set out to shape a broadcasting system that worked in exactly the opposite way. Aware that the mass medium of broadcasting could be employed to create uniformity and homogeneity of belief—whether about political or consumer affairs—those setting the policy directions for the American broadcasting system attempted to make of radio a sort of antipropaganda machine, one that was intended to ensure that broadcasting's mass-distributed messages were individually received and interpreted. Radio's public sphere was to be rational, but pluralist. Ideal listeners were to respond critically in order to combat propaganda, but also empathetically, tolerant of the point of view of others, to combat extremism and prejudice.

PRODUCED BY STATE REGULATION

The civic paradigm was an artifact of state regulation. John Reith looked at American broadcasting in 1931 and saw it hampered by a "lack of institutions," those stable institutions that should be providing "protection for the social activity of right-minded men."[148] But there were institutions and regulations demonstrably producing effects on American radio. As Thomas Streeter has argued, it makes little sense to think of American broadcasting as a purely commercial phenomenon whose growth was simply the product of an absence of social and political regulation—it was "more a product of deliberate political activity than a lack of it."[149] The civic goals of the American broadcasting system can be described because broadcasting in the United States was governed between 1927 and 1981 through a regulatory regime whose central premise was that a government authority was capable of making judgments about civic effects, and thus could make decisions to shape a broadcasting sector that would operate "in the public interest." Broadcasters submitted to this public interest requirement in return for a barrier to new entrants into their broadcasting market and for the absence of a taxpayer funded public broadcaster. Radio's civic paradigm was thus not a spontaneous efflorescence of American high-mindedness, but a product of state intervention and

146. Mildred Adams Washington, "We the People Speak," *New York Times*, June 30, 1935: SM 9.

147. Elena Razlogova, "True Crime Radio and Listener Disenchantment with Network Broadcasting, 1935–1946," *American Quarterly* 58, no.1 (2006): 137–58.

148. "British and US Broadcasting," *Times*, May 25, 1931: 9.

149. Thomas Streeter, *Selling the Air: A Critique of the Policy of Commercial Broadcasting in the United States* (Chicago: University of Chicago Press, 1996): xii.

regulation. The civic paradigm was the result of a political process and it had real effects through the operation of the regulatory system.[150]

The history of this public interest regulatory regime can now be written in comparative and retrospective fashion, as it has more recently been replaced by something else. The premise that a government agency can recognize public interest when it sees it has largely been abandoned in the United States. From 1981 a lottery, and from 1994 auctioning of licenses for new telecommunications services were introduced. In 1999, the FCC reaffirmed its decision that auctions would be a "speedier and fairer" way of resolving competing commercial broadcast license applications than the old system of comparative hearings and a decision on public interest grounds.[151] In 2004, the agency held a major auction for 258 broadcast FM construction permits, explaining that "spectrum auctions more effectively assign licenses than either comparative hearings or lotteries."[152] In the long tussle between public interest and private property modes of understanding and regulating broadcasting, the scales had very clearly tipped toward broadcaster claims of property in spectrum.[153] These late 20th-century events make even clearer that 1934 in contrast was a qualified not a total victory for free market broadcasting.

Those who want to skip to the end to find out who won may not find the details of the qualifications so significant in the biggest picture and the longest run. The argument of this book is, however, that it matters that we understand that it was state regulation as well as corporate advertising that produced the golden age of American radio. This is not to idealize or exaggerate the role of the FCC, which was in many ways the weak and ineffective regulator its critics claimed it to be. It was indeed in part because of rather than despite the FCC's vulnerability to political influence and ideological infighting that it had to be taken seriously by broadcasters, because it was always a little restless and unpredictable—and hence potentially dangerous—in the way it might interpret its mandate to ensure that broadcasters operated "in the public interest."[154]

State regulation of broadcasting in the United States has had some demonstrably significant and beneficial effects. There has been a tendency on all sides to minimize this role—on the left to lament its weakness and capture by the industry, on the right to celebrate the operation of the free market, and in comparative perspective to stress the relative weakness of U.S. state regulation. An economic rationalist historiography has grown up to defend the notion that selling licenses to the highest bidder in an open market is so obviously the best and fairest way to run a broadcasting system that the only puzzle requiring historical explanation is how it took so long for this fundamental truth

150. The historical role of the state in shaping American broadcasting has not engaged the attention of many scholars, though see Hugh Slotten, *Radio and Television Regulation: Broadcast Technology in the United States, 1920–1960* (Baltimore: Johns Hopkins University Press, 2000).

151. *FCC News*, April 15, 1999.

152. Http://wireless.fcc.gov/auctions/default.htm?job=about_auctions, accessed September 1, 2007.

153. Krystilyn Corbett, "The Rise of Private Property Rights in the Broadcast Spectrum," *Duke Law Journal* 46, no. 3 (December 1996): 611–50.

154. The wording was carried over from the 1927 Radio Act to the 1934 Communications Act.

to be perceived.[155] Legal scholars generally conclude that the idea of property rights in the radio spectrum had not developed by the 1930s.[156] But there are certainly glimpses of such argument in the record—evidence that the firm statements in the 1927 and 1934 acts that a broadcasting license gave right to the use but not the ownership of a frequency was indeed a response to demands or expectations to the contrary.[157] Continuing regulatory anxiety about the high prices fetched by radio stations, which might be said to involve tacit selling of licenses, is also evidence that the idea of spectrum as property was a familiar but generally rejected one in the 1930s.[158] Heads of networks were careful always to go along in public argument with the spirit of the public interest licensing regime. Only less cautious broadcasting interests argued openly for property rights in spectrum. The *Chicago Tribune*—itself the owner of a radio station (WGN)—provided ongoing conservative opposition to the American broadcast licensing system, arguing openly for property rights: "Those who originated wave lengths had a natural right to them, and a natural right to transfer them." The *Tribune* argued that the right to buy and sell wave-lengths would ensure that they would "gravitate to those who give the public what the listeners want."[159] Such open defenses of the idea of broadcasting licenses as property were relatively uncommon in the later 1930s, further evidence of the dominance of the civic paradigm. It was very difficult in the 1930s to maintain publicly that broadcaster rights were more important than listener ones, in part because of the negotiated settlement of 1934, but also because of widespread concern about the vulnerability of listeners to propaganda.

THE PROMISE OF REPRESENTATION

While debate about broadcasting as a public utility continued, the rival representative model of thinking about radio and its public was becoming more solidly entrenched as consensus and official doctrine. The representative model said that the broadcaster's responsibility was not to provide access to all but rather to represent the diversity of the local community. The most well known and influential early articulation of this representative model came from the Federal Radio Commission in its 1929 *Great Lakes* decision. The commission began with a ritual renunciation of the common carrier model; if that analogy was pursued, it argued, "a broadcasting station would have to accept and transmit for all persons on an equal basis without discrimination in charge,

155. See, e.g., Thomas W. Hazlett, "Assigning Property Rights to Radio Spectrum Users: Why Did FCC License Auctions Take 67 Years?" *Journal of Law and Economics* 41, no. 2 (October 1998): 529–75; Peter Cramton, "The Efficiency of the FCC Spectrum Auctions," *Journal of Law and Economics* 41, no. 2 (October 1998): 727–36.

156. See, e.g., Glen O. Robinson, "The Federal Communications Act: An Essay on Origins and Regulatory Purpose," in Max D. Paglin (ed.), *A Legislative History of the Communications Act of 1934* (New York: Oxford University Press, 1989): 11.

157. And see Thomas W. Hazlett, "The Rationality of U.S. Regulation of the Broadcast Spectrum," *Journal of Law and Economics* 33, no. 1 (April 1990): 133–75.

158. Streeter, *Selling the Air*, ch. 6.

159. "Wave Lengths as Property," *Chicago Tribune*, May 25, 1938: 10.

and according to rates fixed by a governmental body" and "this obligation would extend to anything and everything any member of the public might desire to communicate to the listening public, whether it consists of music, propaganda, reading, advertising or what-not." That situation would be intolerable and impractical—"thousands of new stations" would be necessary to cater for all of those who might "insist on airing their views through the microphone," and listeners trying to choose a program would face an "insoluble problem."

Having thus briskly disposed of the open access model, the FRC then argued that the emphasis in broadcasting policy should actually be on the receiver rather than the sender of messages. This elevation of the listener was its most decisive and creative intervention, at once expanding and contracting radio's public sphere. The representative model redefined the public as radio consumers rather than performers, listeners rather than potential broadcasters. But in confining them to that role, it gave them a broad, ambitious, contentious, and often unwelcome right—the right to hear their whole community represented over the air. Radio, the commission stated, should be seen not as a common carrier like telegraphs or railroads, but rather as a utility akin to those "engaged in purveying commodities to the general public," such as electricity or water. The public interest in broadcasting centered on the listener who had a right to a representative service and thus required "ample play for the free and fair competition of opposing views." A broadcaster would need to make programs addressed to the "entire listening public within the service area," meaning that "the tastes, needs and desires of all substantial groups among the listening public should be met, in some proportion, by a well-rounded program, in which entertainment, consisting of music of both classical and lighter grades, religion, education and instruction, important public events, discussions of public questions, weather, market reports, and news, and matters of interest to all members of the family find a place." This representative programming stood in contrast to that on the "propaganda" station, which was committed to the broadcasting of only some views. Propaganda stations were "not consistent with the most beneficial sort of discussion of public questions."[160]

As several historians have pointed out, this policy preference for a general and representative broadcasting schedule, as opposed to one representing one group in particular, was high among the reasons that FRC decisions favored commercial stations over nonprofit stations run by religious, ethnic, labor, and other organizations.[161] What has been less noted in the history is the other side of this bargain—that in return for protection from common carrier status, commercial radio stations were being required to demonstrate that they were in fact offering something for everyone, that they were adequately representing social diversity. The official legitimation of radio rested upon the representative model. The FCC repeatedly referred to this philosophy as justification for its decisions. In 1938, for example, explaining why Pittsburgh did not need a radio station dedicated to foreign-language broadcasting, the commission reiterated that it

160. *Third Annual Report of the Federal Radio Commission* (Washington DC: United States Government Printing Office, 1929): 32–34.

161. Craig, *Fireside Politics*: 71–75; Streeter, *Selling the Air*: 94; Vaillant, *Sounds of reform*: 262–69.

was "an essential practice in the continued successful operation of the American system of broadcasting" that licensees make their stations reasonably available to "all groups of society and all legitimate schools of thought" on a fair and equitable basis and regardless of race and creed, in a way that was "consistent with the rendition of a balanced program service which will be interesting and in the interest of the public as a whole in that community."[162]

That package of expectations—the orthodoxy of 1930s broadcast regulation in the United States—was the result of some particularly American cultural and political struggles, and it was, if taken seriously, quite demanding. The representative model raised very different and even more complex questions than the ones about direct access to broadcasting facilities for education, religion, labor, and rural communities. But it is only if this representative model is understood in its context as a key component of the civic paradigm that its real significance becomes clear. Crucially, in the civic paradigm, diversity was understood to be important not just for the groups gaining small amounts of airtime, but for the public as a whole, whose interests were held to best be served by exposure to diverse programming.

This was, to be clear, not "multiculturalism" in the post-1960s sense. The FCC often seemed to understand the point of foreign-language broadcasting, for example, in terms of the desirability of "Americanization." But rather than dwelling on the very obvious limits of the commission's understanding of or sympathy for actual minorities, I stress here its adherence to the potentially controversial doctrine that diversity of programming was intrinsically "in the public interest." That doctrine was a severe constraint to minorities, in that speakers hoping to be heard over radio had to be deemed not just representative, but interesting to the public as a whole. It was now held to be in the public's interest, not just minorities', that community diversity be heard on the air, that "all legitimate schools of thought" be aired side by side on mainstream radio. Radio was—in Habermas's terms—being asked to form one big public sphere, not a multitude of smaller ones.

The reformers were thus defeated at every turn on the supply side of radio. There was to be no guarantee of equal access to radio, of a right to broadcast or common carrier status. Instead, diversity on radio was to become established as a consumer right. The landmark 1941 FCC decision in the case of the Mayflower Broadcasting Corporation is most remembered for its disapproval of station editorializing, but it was also a strong affirmation of the listener's right to hear presented "all sides of important public questions, fairly, objectively, and without bias."[163] The FCC's Fairness Doctrine in 1949, the end point of this policy trajectory, while reversing the ban on editorializing, required that broadcasters devote time to public affairs, and formalized not the right of minorities to be heard, but "the paramount right of the public in a free society to be informed and to have presented to it for acceptance or rejection the different attitudes and viewpoints concerning these vital and often controversial issues which are held by the various groups

162. "In Re Docket 4758," *Federal Communications Commission Reports* 6 (Washington DC: U.S. Government Printing Office, 1940): 372.

163. Mayflower Broadcasting Corp., Proposed Finding of Fact and Conclusions of the Commission, 8 FCC 333: 340.

which make up the community."[164] The passive voice is significant. The public is imagined here as audience and as a consumer of radio rather than a producer of it; it thus has a right to have diversity "presented to it" rather than a right to speak. The Fairness Doctrine codified the representative demands of the civic paradigm, attempting to enforce in policy the ideal of radio as all-in-one representative of a diverse community. A right to listen to all points of view was in many ways the least radical of the options debated in the 1920s and 1930s, but it became the focus of left and liberal activism about radio from the 1940s, and had even come by the 1980s to seem an intolerably liberal, big-government imposition—the Fairness Doctrine was abolished by the FCC in the Reagan era.[165] But while the Fairness Doctrine is in all the textbooks, the longer history of the representative model is not. My argument here is that the representative model was a key part of a bargain and a compromise by which broadcasters gained protection from public utility status in return for a commitment to representing diversity and signing on to the civic paradigm, which understood listening to diversity to be a civic good.

CENTRAL STATE REGULATION ENFORCES LOCALISM

Because the idea of active rather than passive audiences was so central, the governance of 1930s radio was always more concerned with local than national audiences. State regulation of radio in the United States in this period was most importantly about national policy regulating localism. Applicants for new licenses had to persuade the FCC in Washington not that they had some novel form of entertainment in mind, but that they would provide local public service of a kind not already offered by other broadcasters. In calling forth representative voices, in seeking out local talent and local opinion, radio became a part of modern democratic government, which needed individual, autonomous, rational, opinion-forming, and opinion-trading individuals, and communities that were representable. The civic paradigm was in part a shared fiction about the relation of radio to its local community, but it was a governing fiction that decisively shaped broadcasting in the United States.

The paradox of American radio as a rapidly centralizing technology that was governed by a regulatory regime in which the highest currency was local service to a place-based community has often been noted. The premise upon which the 1934 act rested—that broadcasting was a local responsibility exercised by individual licensees—was, Barnouw argued, "obsolete in 1927 and by 1934 totally invalid."[166] Radio regulation was all about local stations and local service, at a time when more and more Americans were listening to nationally networked programs. To those committed to improving efficiency and organization in national life, that seemed to be a serious mistake. A 1940 report from the National Economic and Social Planning Association argued that the network systems

164. Federal Communications Commission, *Editorializing by Broadcast Licensees*, 13 FCC 1246 (1949) cited in FCC, *Fifteenth Annual Report* (Washington DC: U.S. Government Printing Office, 1950): 33.

165. On the policy trajectory from Mayflower to Fairness Doctrine and beyond, see Amy Toro, "Standing Up for Listeners' Rights: A History of Public Participation at the Federal Communications Commission" (PhD diss., University of California–Berkeley, 2000): 81–102.

166. Barnouw, *The Golden Web*: 33.

should be the basis of the governance of American radio. The method of regulation of individual stations that assumed that a station existed primarily to serve the interests of its local community was, the report concluded, "obsolescent, if not already obsolete," and the "reality of network domination" needed to be recognized in public policy.[167] But the privileging of local service could not so easily be excised. The prevalence of populism and the fear of centralized propaganda meant that saying that radio was primarily local had significant ideological resonance in the United States, although from the formation of NBC in 1926 and CBS in 1927, the networks actually continued to grow in audience share and profitability.[168] In 1932, network advertising revenue was $39 million; by 1935, $49 million, and by 1939, $83 million.[169] The networks through the 1930s received more than half of the total of radio advertising revenue. The proportion of stations affiliated with networks increased from 21% in 1930 to 59% by 1940. Network dominance was, however, greater than those figures alone would convey, because network affiliates included most of the more powerful stations in the nation.[170] The FCC's decade-end inquiry into chain broadcasting reported that, by 1938, the network stations "used 97.9% of the total night-time broadcasting power of the United States."[171]

Networks, then, were undeniably important, but they have disproportionately dominated radio history in part because they are better documented than local stations.[172] It was only after 1938 that more than half of U.S. radio stations had a network affiliation. Local stations remained important, as did the local programming of networked stations. Then, listeners to networked stations did not always hear identical programming. "Split networks" were often sold to advertisers, so that different regions (most often the South or the West Coast) received different programs. Recent research has made clear that the relations between local, regional, and national broadcasters were far more complex, entangled, and antagonistic than earlier histories of radio had allowed.[173] Nevertheless, the general momentum of audiences and stations toward networked content and away from localism was clear.

The local civic ideal was articulated in its purest form when stations presented their case to the FCC seeking a new or renewed license. The model station invoked in such— sometimes semifictional—presentations devoted a large share of its airtime to "sustaining" rather than commercial programs, favored local rather than networked programming, was embedded in and reflective of its community, gave time on the air to

167. C. B. Rose, *National Policy for Radio Broadcasting* (New York: Harper and Brothers, 1940): 268.

168. See discussion in Craig, *Fireside Politics*: ch.2.

169. Herman S. Hettinger, "Broadcasting in the United States," *Annals of the American Academy of Political and Social Science* 177 (January 1935): 2; Paul F. Peter, "The American Listener in 1940," *Annals of the American Academy of Political and Social Science* 213 (January 1941): 5.

170. See tables in Christopher H. Sterling and John M. Kittross, *Stay Tuned: A Concise History of American Broadcasting* (Belmont, CA: Wadsworth, 1978): 516, 512.

171. Federal Communications Commission, *Report on Chain Broadcasting* (Washington DC: U.S. Govt. Printing Office, 1941): 77.

172. Clifford Doerksen, *American Babel: Rogue Radio Broadcasters of the Jazz Age* (Philadelphia: University of Pennsylvania Press, 2005): viii.

173. Socolow, "To Network a Nation": 88–112. See also Bill Kirkpatrick, "Localism in American Media 1920–1934" (PhD diss., University of Wisconsin–Madison, 2006); Alexander Russo, *Points on the Dial: Golden Age Radio beyond the Networks* (Durham, NC: Duke University Press, 2010).

a range of community organizations, broadcast live rather than recorded music, and drew upon and fostered local performing talent. The model local broadcaster understood, in short, that radio was a way of producing a more aware, rational, tolerant, and active citizenry, and that a national culture rested on the strength of its local roots.

The FCC defined a local station as one that could serve "to present programs of local interest to the residents of that community; to utilize and develop local entertainment talent which the record indicates is available; to serve local, religious, educational, civic, patriotic, and other organizations; to broadcast local news; and to generally provide a means of local public expression and a local broadcast service to listeners in that area."[174] Recognizing the strength of localist sentiment in particular regions, the commission often maintained that licensees needed to be knowledgeable about their community, sometimes that they needed to be locals.[175] FCC commissioner E. O. Sykes, a Mississippian, emphasized to the NAB in 1936 that "a local station is to serve a particular community and that, if possible, it should be owned and controlled by the people of that community and not outsiders."[176] The FCC asserted this principle in several decisions, denying licenses on the ground that the applicants were not sufficiently local, were "strangers" to the community they proposed to serve, and hence unacquainted with the talent available there.[177] A man from South Carolina sought to establish a station in Gastonia, North Carolina, in 1937, but the FCC could not find that his proposed station would broadcast in the public interest, in part because he had never lived in Gastonia and he had "not demonstrated sufficient knowledge of, and familiarity with, the needs of the area proposed to be served."[178] The national civic aims of radio were to be achieved locally, and the FCC was at times prepared to administer the licensing regime to ensure that such local service was provided.

This ethos of active, civic participation and improvement conveyed a belief that radio should reflect and represent, as well as engage and improve, its community. *The Great Lakes* decision had established the principle that "a broadcasting station may be considered

174. "In the Matter of the Okmulgee Broadcasting Corporation," *Federal Communications Commission Reports* 4 (Washington: Government Printing Office, 1938): 302.

175. In 1937 the commission turned down an application for a local station in Pottsville, Pennsylvania, mentioning among its reasons that the applicant "did not show himself acquainted, in any way, with the area proposed to be served or familiar with the needs of the listening audience in that region": Docket 4071 "In the Matter of The Pottsville Broadcasting Company," *Federal Communications Commission Reports* 4 (Washington, DC: U.S. Government Printing Office, 1938): 319. The DC Appeals Court overturned the decision in 1939, noting that the FCC had "not adopted a fixed and definite policy in that respect": *Pottsville Broadcasting Company v. FCC*, 70 App. D.C., 157.

176. "Aims of the FCC," *New York Times*, July 12, 1936: XX14.

177. See the striking formulation "he is a stranger to the community" in an unsuccessful application in Indiana: "In the Matter of L. M. Kennett, Docket no. 2613," *Federal Communications Commission Reports* 2 (Washington DC: U.S. Government Printing Office, 1937): 275. This local requirement was described by one legal scholar in 1941 as the "settled policy" of the commission: Giles H. Penstone, "Meaning of the Term 'Public Interest, Convenience or Necessity' under the Communications Act of 1934," *George Washington Law Review* 9, no. 8 (June 1941): 894.

178. "In the Matter of J. B. Roberts, Docket no. 4215," *Federal Communications Commission Reports* 4 (Washington DC: U.S. Government Printing Office, 1938): 565.

Figure 2.4. John Royal, NBC vice president for programs, testifies before the FCC inquiry into monopoly in network broadcasting, November 17, 1938. Harris and Ewing collection, Library of Congress, LC-H22-D-4967.

as a sort of mouthpiece on the air for the community it serves." More assertively, if "the station performs its duty in furnishing a well-rounded program, the rights of the community have been achieved."[179] "Rights" was strong language. The FRC and then FCC made it clear that they wanted to hear about broadcasting that was live and local. Knowledge of these expectations produced promises of local and civic programming from broadcasters. There was a strong strain of thought informing FCC philosophy that said that putting the local choir live on the radio was public service, but playing a recording of an excellent choir from somewhere else might not be. The networks professed to take the official preference for live broadcasting very seriously. NBC's vice president for programs John Royal shared with the FCC in 1938 his belief that recorded programming was both inferior and inauthentic—that "the difference between a live program and a transcribed program is the difference between a pretty girl and her picture."[180] [Figure 2.4.]

179. In re Great Lakes Broadcasting Co., FRC Docket no. 4900, quoted in Federal Communications Commission, *Public Service Responsibilities of Broadcast Licensees* (Washington DC: FCC, 1946): 12.

180. FCC Hearings, docket 5060, box 1400, RG 173.5, NACP: 511. He also assured the commission that NBC policy was that "there shall not be any ad-libbing"—scripted but live programs were understood to be the means of maintaining both decorum and standards. Ibid.: 542.

The talk at the station licensing hearings was not only about local programming and local needs, but also about local people as radio performers. At issue was how aware the proposed station licensees were of local talent, how they proposed to find, manage, encourage, and improve it. Broadcasting as understood within the civic paradigm was not simply to be a one-way distribution of packaged entertainment and information, but a dialogue of a community with itself. Applicants to the FCC knew the language of localism well. Would the station in Fairmont, West Virginia, ever increase its proportion of network content? "No, we are very anxious to promote all the local activities that we possibly can, civic and also the finding of local talent and producing that."[181] What services did a new station in Troy, New York, propose to perform for its citizens?

> Keeping them abreast of the times, as far as the news is concerned; keeping them informed as to the civic questions that are ripe at the moment; and last but not least, giving an opportunity to the talent which is in Troy to gradually assimilate a radio education, and give them an opportunity to go further in the radio field, we hope beyond that of a local station.[182]

The existence of local talent was always a key issue at license hearings—how much was there, and how willing was it to broadcast? Successful applicants usually claimed to be familiar with the existing local talent, and committed to discovering and fostering more of it. What local talent was available in Rapid City, South Dakota?

> The Superintendent of Schools has arranged to supply the station with various musical groups. The municipal band of Rapid City, many soloists and dramatic artists have agreed to lend their services to the proposed station.... The Sheriff of Pennington County testified that the broadcasting service here proposed...would prove of material assistance in the apprehension of criminals....[183]

A successful applicant in San Luis Obispo, California, promised an even more comprehensive menu of civic programming:

> Amateur programs to develop local talent, a fifteen minute opening religious program daily, stock reports and weather reports, farm programs...news flashes, organ concerts, safety programs, educational programs by the high schools of San Luis Obispo County, Hawaiian programs by the Hawaiian trio of Santa Maria to be sponsored by the Travel Bureau, a Children's hour, Waltz Hour, popular music by local orchestras and local artists, hillbilly and cowboy music by local farmers,

---

181. Official Report of the Proceedings before the FCC at Washington DC, June 7, 1937, in the Matter of Monongahela Valley Broadcasting Co. Fairmont, West Virginia, Docket no. 4184, RG 173.5, NACP.

182. Official Report of the Proceedings before the FCC at Washington DC, March 16, 1937, in the Matter of Troy Broadcasting Co., Docket no. 4306, RG 173.5, NACP.

183. "In the Matter of Black Hills Broadcast Company, Docket no. 3066," *Federal Communications Commission Reports* 3 (Washington DC: U.S. Government Printing Office, 1937): 114.

electrical transcriptions, a Church Hour each Sunday, health programs to consist of talks given by local doctors and dentists, local civic and fraternal programs, sports programs of local interest....[184]

Successful applicants typically promised in this way not only to supply information needed by the local community, but also to foster its talent and allow its diversity of voices and its local and professional knowledges to be heard. That was the civic paradigm contract, which called forth at the very least an elaborate performance of concern about localism.

Conversely, unsuccessful applicants were often said to have displayed ignorance of both the needs and the talents of the local community. Even worse than lack of familiarity was a failure to appreciate existing local talent. An applicant for a license in Albany, Georgia (population 15,000), foolishly told the FCC that there was "none too much talent in any small town," and that he was for that reason looking forward to connecting his new station to the Columbia network. His application was unsuccessful.[185] If localism in program service was, as Kirkpatrick has observed of the pre-1934 period, "a game that both the FRC and the industry learned how to play," it was also clear that the game had real consequences.[186]

Local service was not just a yes-or-no business. It could be, and had to be within this system, assessed qualitatively. Where the granting of one license would impinge upon the operation of another, the FCC attempted to compare the levels of local service on offer. Applicants in Evanston in suburban Chicago were refused a license in part because their proposed station would have caused some interference with reception of a central Illinois station, WDZ in Tuscola, which was cited in the decision as an absolutely exemplary local station. WDZ broadcast such prosaically titled but imaginatively conceived local programs as *Man on the Train*, a daily broadcast of interviews with Chicago and Eastern Illinois Railroad passengers, *Farmer on His Farm*, which carried interviews with farmers "early in the morning direct from the field," and *At the Park*, a weekly Sunday broadcast from a large park near Tuscola.[187] Such distinctive local service could not, the commission decided, be put at risk to provide just one more radio outlet in metropolitan Chicago. [Companion website links 2.3, 2.4]

We can best see the invocation of the civic paradigm and its local focus in particular places. In 1938, the company that published both the *New York Times* and the *Chattanooga*

184. "In the Matter of Christina M. Jacobson Docket no.3827," *Federal Communications Commission Reports* 3 (Washington DC: U.S. Government Printing Office, 1937): 331–32.

185. "In the Matter of H. Wimpy, Docket no. 3995," *Federal Communications Commission Reports* 4 (Washington DC: U.S. Government Printing Office, 1938): 180.

186. Bill Kirkpatrick, "Localism in American Media 1920–1934," (PhD diss., University of Wisconsin–Madison, 2006): 209.

187. "In the Matter of Evanston Broadcasting Company, Docket no. 4609," *Federal Communications Commission Reports* 5 (Washington DC: U.S. Government Printing Office, 1939): 485. For a more detailed account of WDZ's innovative local programming strategies, and its commitment to hillbilly music, see Stephen D. Perry, "Securing Programming on Live Local Radio: WDZ Reaches Rural Illinois 1929–1939," *Journal of Radio Studies* 8 (2001): 347–71.

Times sought a license for a new radio station in Chattanooga, Tennessee. Had the license been granted, it would have been for the third radio station in that city. Although 1938 was a most dramatic year for news, the *Times* application said surprisingly little about the news service the station would offer, or about the ways in which the resources of the two newspapers would be an asset to it. The applicants did, however, present the FCC with a very detailed listing of the musical talent available in Chattanooga. There were 335 names of performers in all, including sopranos, altos, baritones, tenors, basses, blues singers, gospel singers, piano accompanists, vocal duets, trios, quartets, sextets, octets, glee clubs, madrigal groups, church choirs, string ensembles, piano duets, dancers, comedians, and even tap dancers. There was also a long list of civic organizations said to be enthusiastic about the prospect of a new radio station in town—fraternal, business, educational, political, charitable, religious, cultural, veterans, labor, women's, children's, and African American organizations.

The applicants had the task of demonstrating that the existing Chattanooga stations were not providing adequate service to the city. They contended that these stations played too much recorded music and advertising. It was shown that the smaller of the stations, WAPO, not yet affiliated with a network, played recordings 54% of the time, and that WDOD, a more powerful station affiliated with the CBS network, played recordings 24% of the time—although some of its live programming came through the network. The new applicants presented these figures as evidence of an excessive, even shameful, resort to the poor second best of recorded music, although we are likely to be more impressed today with how much, rather than how little, live and local music both these stations broadcast. Even WAPO listed live broadcasts of a jazz orchestra, a dance orchestra, a Hawaiian orchestra, as well as smaller groups. But the issue was quality, not just quantity. The *Chattanooga Times* applicants, hoping to trump the opposition, promised to employ a permanent staff orchestra, and undertook that 86% of their broadcasts would feature live performers. They also promised to present less "hillbilly" and more "good" music than the other stations.[188] Chattanooga in the 1930s was a major center for hillbilly music.[189] WDOD had numerous hillbilly programs from performers such as the String Dusters, the Three Pals, the Hawaiian Hillbillies, Grandpappy, the Busta Dawn Boys, and Uncle Herman's Hillbillies, as well as programs of banjo and fiddle music. Several of the witnesses at the license hearing asserted that there was too much hillbilly music on Chattanooga radio, and said that they hoped for something better from the new station. A spokesman for the Chattanooga Central Labor Union testified that the existing stations had "too much advertisement, too much canned music," and not enough "of what we would call good music for the betterment of the city." The union supported live music for industrial reasons, but its endorsement of the connection between "good" music and the betterment of the community is striking evidence of the shared language of the civic paradigm.

188. In Re the Application of the Times Printing Company, Chattanooga, FCC Docket File no. 4759, RG 173.5, NACP.

189. Charles K. Wolfe, *In Close Harmony: The Story of the Louvin Brothers* (Jackson: University Press of Mississippi, 1996): 27–28.

It was well known that hillbilly music appealed to poorer and less educated listeners. America's leading radio researcher, Paul Lazarsfeld, would note a couple of years later that whereas classical music selected out an audience at the "higher cultural levels," hillbilly strongly selected an audience among the lower income groups.[190] It was clearly a point of pride for many prominent Chattanoogans that the city's radio stations not be too obviously dominated by hillbilly. There was an assertive tone of civic betterment to the application. So many of those brought forward by the *Times* to testify in support of its proposed station had the idea that in various ways the new station could improve Chattanooga, and more adequately represent the achievements and aspirations of its most active and reform-minded citizens.

The *Times* also promised access to the proposed station for a great range of political, religious, ethnic, and racial groups. Here the claims were about the inclusive qualities of the proposed programming, but also about the way individual radio performers would be encouraged to emerge from the diverse groups within the city. The Chattanooga Central Labor Union expressed the hope that the new station would "participate from an unbiased view-point in the daily activities of our community." Principal W. J. Davenport of Howard High School—the historically black high school in Chattanooga—said he had not heard as much "colored" talent over the existing radio stations as he would have liked. He had asked for announcements to be made, and they had not been. He thought broadcasting musical performances from his school would be educational, because "many people, not knowing who was broadcasting the program, would appreciate the talent rendered, and when they said it was a colored broadcast, I believe it would be entirely educational in every respect." Asked repeatedly why he did not follow up on his request for announcements to be made over the existing stations, Davenport, an NAACP member, said, "I do not usually put myself in a position I would be embarrassed or humiliated, because I ask for something that was free and did not get it." His testimony was potentially important. The promise of a more truly inclusive radio station was clearly something that the applicants expected would sway the FCC. Their capacity to administer a station that allowed significant representative voices to be heard went to the heart of the civic paradigm. The terrain of argument before the FCC was always in this way the quality of local public service. Both sides accepted that the number of sopranos and banjo players in Chattanooga, and the desire of the city's high schools and hiking clubs and fraternal organizations to broadcast, was highly relevant to the case. Radio was intended to be civic and local and live.

Civic participation was the ground of the *Times* application, and it was also the reason for its failure. The FCC was not convinced "with respect to available talent that it would be able to render a high-class program service during the 86% of its time which it plans to devote to live talent."[191] The applicants' case was also weakened in that none of the representatives of community groups could say definitely that they had been denied time on the existing stations, although some, like Davenport, had clearly gained the impression that it was not worth asking. There may well have been a behind-the-scenes story to this

190. Lazarsfeld, *Radio and the Printed Page*: 22.
191. *Federal Communications Commission Reports* 40 (1938): 376.

case—of political influence or money or favors. But what is important here is not the "real" reason the FCC decided not to issue the license, but the dominance of the language of local public service in which broadcasting and its social consequences had to be discussed—the public debate at least was about sopranos and banjo players, and not only about money and markets.

It is important to see the historically contingent nature of this. Radio might have been understood mainly in national terms, connecting Chattanoogans to metropolitan American life and the national government. It might have been spoken of—as industry spokesmen often did—in purely market terms, as a means of giving the people what they wanted. The civic ideal and its language of local public service to an active community was a particular way of thinking about radio. It envisaged radio as a vital part of modern life, and specifically as a means of facilitating the self-expression and self-government of American citizens. Despite the actual dominance of network broadcasting, networks were not understood within the ideologically dominant civic paradigm to be the best form of radio; the networks had surprisingly few intellectual or governmental defenders. The ideal form of radio was almost always held to be local. The idealized moments in the 1930s were when the local performer got a national audience, and the local audience formed individual opinions on national issues, not—as we more commonly remember— when individuals could sit at home and hear their president.

Affirmative localism thus required that airtime be given to locally known but nationally undiscovered performers. The great popularity of amateur and talent discovery shows in the mid-1930s evidences the civic paradigm's emphasis on active audience participation, but also the genius of American radio for making entertainment out of what was required. The BBC's *Radio Times* in 1936 referred to the United States as "the land of coast-to-coast hook ups, six-tube sets, and amateur hours."[192] Major Bowes, the avuncular but precise host, had the most popular show on U.S. radio with his *Original Amateur Hour*: "no broadcast has led the popularity poll so long; no show ever evoked such a demand for studio tickets."[193] From 1937, spelling bees were also a major program feature. Jason Loviglio has argued that audience participation programs should be understood as evidence of the "self-consciousness with which network radio and its new mass audience came to think about the role that radio should play in national life."[194] So prevalent were the amateur and participation programs that some listeners began to tire of the format: "I think the amateur business is being done to death," commented one Worcester listener.[195] The earnest stress on improving local civic culture and fostering local talent was part of an idealized model of network broadcasting in which radio stimulated local cultural activity rather than replaced it. It rested on a vision of a network that could channel talent and culture up as well as down.

192. Camporesi, *Mass Culture and National Traditions*: 98.

193. Orrin Dunlap, "Tribunal of the Air," *New York Times*, September 27, 1936: X10.

194. Jason Loviglio, "Vox Pop: Network Radio and the Voice of the People," in Michele Hilmes and Jason Loviglio (eds.), *The Radio Reader: Essays in the Cultural History of Radio* (New York: Routledge, 2002): 89–112.

195. NBC Statistical Department, "Comments from Anderson, Nichols Survey in Worcester, Newark, Cleveland, South Bend and Kansas City August 1935," folder 12, box 34, NBC records, WHS.

Kirkpatrick has argued that the pre-1934 FRC used discourses of localism in a gate-keeping way, actually to suppress local diversity in broadcasting and to enforce a kind of broadcasting that reflected only the "tastes and sensibilities of white, cosmopolitan elites." Kirkpatrick is rightly critical of the way the FRC was "not especially interested in the needs and desires of diverse local groups of listeners." But diversity then was not understood solely as a property of (ethnic, racial, religious) groups. My argument is that, in the localism of the 1930s civic paradigm, the overriding commitment was to fostering individual opinion formation rather than group identities. Central to the national class, cosmopolitan orthodoxy that Kirkpatrick so accurately evokes, was a deeply modernist sense that the flexibility and rationality of individual opinion was more important and valuable than customary and inherited group identities. After 1934, Kirkpatrick observes, "the FCC did indeed begin to encourage affirmative localism"—and, I would argue, the connections between localist discourse and the formation of individual opinion grew even stronger.[196]

Of course the ideal of localism was not always achieved. In 1946 the FCC published its "Blue Book," *Public Service Responsibility of Broadcast Licensees*, a now familiar landmark of American broadcasting history, written in significant part by Charles Siepmann. It was the commission's first extended statement on programming responsibilities and it expressed strong concern about the yawning gulf between station promise and performance. KIEV in Glendale, California, had gained its license in 1932 on the basis of promises of cooperation with local "civic, educational, fraternal, and religious institutions," of programs aimed at the agricultural and the Spanish communities, of one-third of airtime being given over to educational programming. When the license came up for renewal in 1939, FCC inspectors found that the typical broadcast day was in fact largely filled with commercials, recorded popular music, and "announcements concerning lost and found pets." A search of the station's logs failed to disclose any of the "duets, quartets, excerpts from operas, cuttings from great poems" that had been promised.[197] This exemplified a more general pattern, the report noted, of stations undertaking at licensing time to perform local public service—local news; making air time available to local community, educational, and religious organizations; broadcasting local public forum programs, school programs, roundtable religious discussions, broadcasts of opera, and other local musical performances; and airing after-dinner speeches from fraternal organizations—but then failing to do so. The Blue Book expressed alarm at the limited quantity of "local live" programs actually broadcast, and at the way "few stations are staffed adequately to meet their responsibilities in serving the community."[198]

In part because of the Blue Book, radio history has better remembered the litany of broken promises than it has explained or interpreted the existence of the civic ideal in the

196. Bill Kirkpatrick, "Localism in American Media Policy, 1920–34: Reconsidering a 'Bedrock Concept,'" *The Radio Journal: International Studies in Broadcast and Audio Media* 4, nos. 1, 2, 3: 90, 99–100, 105.

197. Federal Communications Commission, *Public Service Responsibilities of Broadcast Licensees* (Washington DC: FCC, 1946): 3–4.

198. Federal Communications Commission, *Public Service Responsibilities of Broadcast Licensees*: 39.

first place.[199] The scandal of the Blue Book cases was generated in relation to an acknowledged civic ideal that had real effects. Of course, actual stations fell short of the ideal, sometimes spectacularly. But complete and open indifference to civic concerns was rarely possible for long. The Blue Book report bookends the period in which these civic concerns comprehensively dominated public discourse about U.S. radio. It was the fullest statement of the civic, local service paradigm, which appeared just at the moment of its waning. The dominance of American radio up until WWII by a historically particular set of civic ideals is the contention and the subject of this book.

199. Historians have generally followed Barnouw in regarding the Blue Book as ineffectual in altering the situation it lamented. Broadcasters, he said, "were soon proceeding as if it did not exist." Barnouw, *The Golden Web*: 227–36.

3

The Promise of Broadcast Classical Music

PROLOGUE: POSTWAR CLASSICAL MUSIC BROADCASTING

Something about American radio puzzled and even irritated me when I went to live in the United States as a graduate student in the mid-1980s. While there were two classical music stations in Chicago, they were both commercial. At peak listening times, they played shorter pieces—single movements rather than whole symphonies, so that more advertisements could be aired. That just did not fit my sense—newly arrived from Australia—of the way that classical broadcasting should have been carried out. The mixture of classical music and commercialism seemed transgressive to me, some kind of cultural mistake.[1] American friends were surprised at my surprise. They had grown up accustomed to just the kind of linking of classical music with upmarket consumerism that I was hearing.

There was a solemn, respectable advertising style favored on Chicago commercial classical station WFMT. Commercials were read only by the station announcers, who had impeccable pronunciation. There was evident in the advertising pitches a polished and practiced strategy of associating classical music with elite and discriminating consumption. WFMT manager Ray Nordstrand, the *Wall Street Journal* reported in 1985, had discovered "how much more likely classical-music radio listeners are than average adults to buy such tony goods as fur coats and BMWs." In consequence, WFMT was "able to charge twice as much as most stations for its fewer-than-normal ads."[2] Classical music broadcasters had successfully forged this connection with wealth and taste in consumption in the years after World War II—"fine music" interspersed with advertisements for jewelers, airlines, and luxury apparel—and it continues in attenuated form to the present. It was

---

1. A beneficiary of publicly funded broadcasting on the ABC (Australian Broadcasting Commission 1932–1983, then Australian Broadcasting Corporation 1983–), I took for granted an association of classical music with high culture and a sense of it as somehow above or opposed to commercialism. I was quite ignorant of the earlier history of classical music on Australian commercial radio—that there had been for a couple of decades after the creation of the ABC in 1932 a significant amount of classical music on commercial stations in Australia. See Colin Jones, *Something in the Air: A History of Radio in Australia* (Kenthurst, NSW: Kangaroo Press, 1995): 47; Bridget Griffen-Foley, *Changing Stations: The Story of Australian Commercial Radio* (Sydney: University of New South Wales Press, 2009): 247–48.

2. Meg Cox, "Chicago Radio Outlet Gets a Lot of Static," *Wall Street Journal*, September 17, 1985: 1.

announced in 2005 that the radio broadcasts of the Metropolitan Opera, on the air since 1931, would henceforth be sustained by Toll Brothers, "the nation's leading builder of luxury homes." "What more perfect marriage for a branding effort than to associate yourself with the Met Opera," Robert Toll was quoted as observing. "It's got to be one of the classiest products you could think of."[3]

This mingling of classical music with elite consumerism has a history. Those Chicago commercial classical stations were postwar creations—WFMT began broadcasting in 1951 and WNIB in 1955. They were products of the fragmentation of the radio audience into niche sectors in the television era. Specialist classical stations were founded just as classical music began to disappear from mainstream commercial radio. Radio underwent a cultural bifurcation in the television era, a rapid polarization into highbrow and lowbrow. The new classical commercial stations were founded as refuges for minority taste just as most radio stations were seeking larger audiences with increasingly specific kinds of popular music or talk. The postwar classical commercial stations, pursuing their small but affluent audience, forged a newly explicit association of classical music with wealth and taste and success. The memory of the very different ambitions and successes of prewar classical music broadcasting has been largely lost.

The cultural meaning of broadcast classical music changed quite remarkably over the later 20th century. This chapter explores the particular context and meanings of classical music on American radio in the 1930s and 1940s, when it was absolutely central to the legitimation and public presentation of radio, and before it shifted from the symbolic center of American broadcasting to its highbrow periphery. There is surprisingly little popular or academic history written about the importance of classical music to U.S. radio before WWII. Classical music carried some of the freight of expectations of the civic paradigm and offers an exemplary case study of the distinctive and productive tensions surrounding American radio.[4]

CLASSICAL MUSIC ON AMERICAN RADIO BEFORE WWII

That the American commercial broadcasters devoted so much airtime and so many resources to broadcast classical music even after their victory in 1934 is one of the most striking evidences of the influence of radio's civic paradigm. Prior to World War II, classical music found an important place in the schedules of most American radio stations. It was

3. "New Angel to Keep Met Opera on the Air," *New York Times*, September 8, 2005: B1.

4. I use the term *classical music*, despite the obvious problems with the term, because that was the category most commonly used by the broadcasting industry and the public in this period. It was then and is now a label with a fairly clear common meaning, although then as now those most knowledgeable about classical music tended to be the most uncomfortable with the term—because *classical* functions awkwardly both as a generic name for all Western art music and as the name for a period within it. In the 1930s, several classical music advocates argued that *serious music* was a better name—and NBC, for example, appointed Samuel Chotzinoff as its director of serious music. But *serious* had a rather forbidding air about it at the very time when popularization was understood as an important task, and *classical* remained the category overwhelmingly understood by the public at large to refer to the canon of European art music.

a crucial part of the well-rounded, something-for-everyone listening day to which most stations aspired, and which the regulatory system both encouraged and rewarded. This chapter explores the extent of the effort put in to broadcasting classical music, and to creating appreciation of and active engagement with it. Radio's ability to make classical music popular was widely held to be a measure of its persuasive efficacy. "If you can teach the people in this country to like classical music," observed a member of the House Committee on Interstate and Foreign Commerce, "why what couldn't you do with your radio if you just pounded out your philosophy all of the time at them?"[5] Broadcasters wanted and even needed classical music because it was so indisputably highbrow, sacralized, high status, and self-evidently in the public interest. Classical music was a crucial part of the civic paradigm, and its ambition to create modern citizens with a developed capacity to absorb information, empathize across cultural borders, experience and control emotion, and arrive at reasoned personal opinions. But American radio also changed classical music, even as it celebrated its timeless traditions and universal values, by juxtaposing high and low cultural idioms, and turning classical performers into stars, even making some perceptible progress for a time toward the announced goal of making classical the new popular music. There is considerable evidence that the generation of Americans that grew up with radio in the 1930s and 1940s developed and retained a love of classical music unmatched by those that followed them. For that generation, the almost constant availability of music of all kinds in their lives was often, just as music education professionals hoped it would be, a new, startling, and even life-changing experience.

Classical music, most of it broadcast live, was by all later standards astonishingly available to listeners to mainstream American commercial radio in the 1930s. The networks began very early to make significant commitments to the broadcasting of classical music, dramatically expanding the scope of what individual stations had been able to do. Heistad's reanalysis of Summers's figures on network programming shows an increase in concert music programming on the networks from 1928, reaching a peak in 1938, then dipping in 1939 and 1940, spiking during World War II, and then declining in the postwar years.[6] It was the more spectacular orchestral or operatic performances, rather than chamber music or solo recitals, that headlined radio's classical music programming, and it was to these large-scale performances that the networks referred most extensively in their publicity. Unlike putting a soprano and pianist in front of a microphone, broadcasting orchestral music was expensive, and needed network-scale profits to sustain it. Technically, too, it was more difficult to broadcast orchestral and operatic than chamber music. But the prestige and excitement and publicity were far greater. Theodor Adorno noted critically that, while chamber music was structurally best suited to radio transmission, for "socio-psychological reasons" it was rarely heard over the air.[7]

The major orchestras were for their part eager to broadcast, vying for a national audience and reputation and the phonograph sales that would follow. The New York

5. *Hearings Before the Committee on Interstate and Foreign Commerce, House of Representatives, 73rd Congress, 2nd session on HR 8301*: 357.

6. Heistad, "Radio without Sponsors": 167.

7. T. W. Adorno, "The Radio Symphony: An Experiment in Theory," in Paul F. Lazarsfeld and Frank N. Stanton (eds.), *Radio Research 1941* (New York: Duell, Sloan and Pearce, 1941): 111.

Philharmonic began broadcasting in 1922, the Boston Symphony in 1926, and the Philadelphia Orchestra in 1929. NBC through much of the 1930s carried concert series from the Boston, Cleveland, and Rochester orchestras and the Metropolitan and Chicago opera companies.[8] The New York Philharmonic, the Cincinnati Symphony, and the Philadelphia Symphony were regulars on CBS.[9] The networks carefully compiled statistics to demonstrate just how much costly and complex orchestral broadcasting they were undertaking. In 1936, NBC broadcast 346 concerts by American orchestras and 28 from Europe.[10] In the first 11 months of 1938, 32 U.S. orchestras broadcast 324 programs on NBC, while 18 European orchestras contributed 24 programs—"practically a symphony a day," the network's publicity noted.[11] In the month of January 1937, NBC broadcast 56 hours of classical music and 18 hours of opera.[12] CBS broadcast 613 hours of classical music in 1937, up from 386 in 1933.[13] When it is considered that this was almost entirely live and often orchestral music, these are significant figures. The smaller Mutual network was also very active in classical music broadcasting, including performances by Alfred Wallenstein's commercially sponsored Sinfonietta from 1933. As musical director at WOR, Wallenstein undertook some ambitious programming, including series of all 26 of the Mozart piano concertos, the seven Mozart operas, and an American Opera Festival.[14] Such high-profile orchestral and operatic broadcasts were absolutely central to the networks' presentation of themselves as commercial yet public service broadcasters. Classical programs were extensively referred to in network publicity and featured prominently when newspaper radio columnists around the country selected the highlights of the week's listening.

The networks' main interest was always in the most familiar works of the most familiar composers of the classical music canon—Bach, Beethoven, Brahms, Wagner. But, partly because there was so much classical music on the air, programmers had necessarily also to include many lesser known works. There was a more than symbolic effort at creating a new repertoire written especially for radio, and the networks gave surprising attention both to seeking out and to performing new compositions. The NBC Music Guild from 1934 offered regular chamber music performances and prizes for chamber works written especially for broadcasting. CBS commissioned new works by American composers, and sought out living composers to perform their own music on air—in 1937 including "Cadman, Blitzstein, Toch, Prokofieff, Tansman, Chaver, Gruenberg, Piston, Hindemith, Enesco, Ganz and Stravinsky." That year CBS commissioned Vittorio Giannini to compose a 29-minute radio opera.[15] CBS's Sunday afternoon *Music for*

8. See John Royal to Lenox Lohr, October 10, 1936, folder 4, box 108, NBC records, WHS.

9. Columbia Broadcasting System, *Serious Music for the Fall and Winter* (New York: CBS, 1936).

10. "Some NBC Firsts," folder 207, NBC history files, LOC.

11. "Broadcast Policies," January 27, 1939, folder 336, NBC history files, LOC.

12. H. M. Beville to C. W. Fitch, March 29, 1937, folder 62, box 92, NBC records, WHS.

13. Cited in Ray C. B. Brown, "Musical Audience Grows at an Astounding Rate," *Washington Post*, December 4, 1938: T55.

14. Michael Meckna, "Alfred Wallenstein: An American Composer at 100," *Sonneck Society for American Music Bulletin* 24, no. 3 (Fall 1998). Available: http://www.american-music.org/publications/bullarchive/Meckna.html. [January 27, 2007].

15. *New York Times*, October 24, 1937: 176.

Everybody commissioned 12 new works by American composers during 1937–38. CBS also broadcast 8 programs of contemporary American chamber music that season, and 10 programs surveying Russian piano music from Glinka to Shostakovitch.[16] By 1940, Wallenstein was said to have premiered 300 new works over the Mutual network.[17] Although it was never enough to satisfy living American composers, network radio did put what now seem quite extraordinary resources and creative energy into the presentation of new art music.[18]

Classical music appeared on network "sustaining" programs, but importantly also on commercial shows. For the sponsors, classical music was often seen as appropriate for institutional rather than product-based advertising. The General Motors concerts over NBC from 1929 to 1937 were performed by the General Motors Symphony Orchestra— the name itself a potent form of promotion, part of the attempt by large corporations to represent themselves as respectable public institutions.[19] GM also sponsored the Cadillac Concerts from 1933, described in the publicity as "the finest music in the world incomparably presented by a symphony orchestra especially selected for radio," all to form a "fitting background—a frame if you will, for the announcements which Cadillac wanted to make to the American public."[20] Large corporate sponsors were thus found for showcase classical broadcasts, creating programs such as the *Texaco Metropolitan Opera*, the *General Motors Symphony*, the *Cadillac Symphony Orchestra* (1933–35), and the *Ford Symphony Orchestra from Detroit*, which presented "familiar music in the majestic manner" on Sunday evenings.[21] Corporate sponsorship affirmed that orchestral concerts were among the most prestigious and desirable of radio's products. There were also several omnibus commercial shows that included classical music and were named for commercial sponsors—such as *The Atwater Kent Hour* (1926–1934), which featured stars from the Metropolitan Opera, the *Cities Service Concerts* (1927–1956), *The Carborundum Hour* (1929–38), *The Voice of Firestone* (1928–1949), *The Bell Telephone Hour* (1940–1958), and *The Magic Key of RCA* (1935–39).

Despite its intrinsic and desirable prestige, radio classical music before WWII was not generally marketed as an exclusive or elite product. Rather, classical programs were promoted as potentially for everybody, and their commercial sponsors included Lucky Strike and Chesterfield cigarettes, as well as RCA, General Motors, and Ford. The first products associated with commercial sponsorship of the Metropolitan Opera broadcasts were ordinary consumer items—Lucky Strike cigarettes and Listerine.[22] Classical music on radio

16. Columbia Broadcasting System, *A Resume of CBS Broadcasting Activities during 1937* (New York: CBS, 1938): 26–28; Davidson Taylor, "Long Range Policy for Radio," *Modern Music* 16, no. 2 (January/February 1939): 94–98.

17. "Last of the Wallensteins," *Time*, May 13, 1940.

18. See, e.g., Goddard Lieberson, "Over the Air," *Modern Music* 16, no. 2 (1939): 133–34.

19. On this point, see Roland Marchand, *Creating the Corporate Soul: The Rise of Public Relations and Corporate Imagery in American Big Business* (Berkeley: University of California Press, 1998): 193.

20. *Radio Enhances Two Distinguished Names* (New York: NBC, 1934): 3.

21. On the *Ford Hour*, see David L. Lewis, *The Public Image of Henry Ford* (Detroit: Wayne State University Press, 1976): 315–18.

22. Deborah S. Petersen-Perlman, "Opera for the People: The Metropolitan Opera Goes on the Air," *Journal of Radio Studies* 2, no. 1 (1993): 195.

was insistently pitched as something that all might one day appreciate. Announcing the 1935 Generals Motors concerts season, GM president Alfred Sloan identified the broad middle ground that the program sought to define: "The concerts will continue as in the past to present programs selected from the works of the great masters, but programs built and designed for the enjoyment of the majority of American music lovers rather than for any one particular group or taste." Guest conductors for the season were to include Toscanini, Beecham, Stravinsky, and Bruno Walter. The message was always that the greatest performers were being made available through the generosity of large corporations to the ordinary listener.[23] Particular efforts were made to render the program content interesting and comprehensible to those previously unfamiliar with classical music. Deems Taylor's narration of the Metropolitan broadcasts, for example, set the scene, told the story, and then interjected brief "word pictures" during the performance of the action on the stage, all designed to make the opera more accessible to a general public.[24]

Fortune magazine reported in 1938 that American broadcasters had discovered that "serious music is worth money as a builder of solid prestige with the masses."[25] "When national advertisers are willing to sponsor serious music," the NBC director of serious music, Samuel Chotzinoff, observed happily, "it can only mean that serious music has become a staple of the American public."[26] Corporate enthusiasm for classical music thus provided a key symbolic affirmation of the American system, a sign that the United States really could have both a commercial broadcasting system giving the people what they wanted, and a rapidly ascending level of popular taste—cultural uplift without paternalist state intervention. That was, of course, a persuasive and influential fiction, because the prevalence of classical music was in the end an artifact of the regulatory system and because, despite an impressive growth in audience, classical music was never really likely to have become the new popular music. But the idea that broadcast classical music was transforming American society was a crucial legitimating story for radio. That American broadcasters could bring the classics into the most remote and hitherto musically deprived American households was a highly important justification of their commercial occupation of the public airwaves.

Classical music was deployed strategically and extensively by radio as part of the Faustian bargain it had made with the federal government in 1934. It was Exhibit A whenever the networks were called upon to justify their profitable occupation of the public airwaves. When publicist William Hard was preparing NBC's case for the 1934 FCC inquiry into broadcasting, he wrote to an NBC executive, "I am especially interested in getting the data from Mr. Royal and his music manager, with the approbation of some independent music critic, of the percentage of 'cultural' in the NBC music performance. This is to my mind the first vital point in our case."[27] NBC called 10 witnesses to testify to the national importance of its musical programs. After 1934 the networks continued to

23. "General Motors Concerts Return to Air," *New York Times*, October 5, 1935: 9.

24. "Deems Taylor See for Listeners in Broadcasts from Metropolitan," *Wisconsin State Journal*, February 9, 1932: 5.

25. "Toscanini on the Air," *Fortune* 17, no. 1 (January 1938): 68.

26. Samuel Chotzinoff, "Music in Radio," in Gilbert Chase (ed.), *Music in Broadcasting* (New York: McGraw-Hill, 1947): 16.

27. William Hard to Henry Norton, September 2, 1934, folder 28, box 26, NBC records, WHS.

mention classical or "serious" music first among their public service contributions whenever they needed to describe them. The BBC's Felix Greene noted acerbically in 1936 that the American networks had "several good symphony concerts" that were "trotted out repeatedly like a stage army whenever the quality of programs is questioned."[28] There was a lot of classical music on prewar American radio, and it was there for some very strategic reasons.

THE MEANING OF BROADCAST CLASSICAL MUSIC

Acknowledgment of the pragmatic reasons for the proliferation of classical music on the air should not lead us, however, to discount the aspirations that the broadcasts expressed. Cultural history ought not to deal in either/or polarities, but in both/and complexities. The network commitment to classical music was always strategic and political in intent, but the personnel who worked to realize its potential were often buoyed and energized by loftier aspirations. A history of broadcast classical music needs both to describe the institutional and political context of the choices the broadcasters made, and also to try to understand and contextualize the almost utopian expectations that once surrounded it.

This means looking beyond the amount of classical music broadcast and the numbers who might have listened, to a more qualitative consideration of the reasons it was considered so important in the first place. Implausibly high hopes were once held for broadcast classical music, and a cultural history has to understand the social and cultural transformations that were expected to accompany it. Underpinning those great expectations were some audacious premises. One was a core belief that classical music was at least potentially, as the late-1930s CBS Sunday afternoon program had it, "*Music for Everybody*"—not just a niche or minority taste, but a genuinely popular music that could be liked and understood by all. There were insistent claims about classical music's "universal" value and appeal. Star conductor Leopold Stokowski began his 1943 book *Music for All of Us*, "Music is a universal language—it speaks to everyone—is the birthright of all of us."[29] Anthropologically and even sociologically absurd, these ideas were nevertheless of great importance in the history of classical broadcasting.

Ideas about popularity and universality were the platitudes of the early classical broadcasting era, and we are perhaps tempted to brush past them impatiently, looking for something more original or profound. But a cultural history of broadcast classical music must also acknowledge that many Americans really did believe what was so routinely claimed—that classical music represented universal values, that it thus at least potentially spoke to everyone. For all those who believed these things, the advent of the era of broadcast classical music could confidently be expected to bring in its wake some profound social and cultural transformations.

Part of the "universal" argument rested on a claim about "civilization." Classical music, it was confidently asserted, represented one of the pinnacles of civilization, understood as a singular and recognizable entity. Samuel Chotzinoff, NBC's director of "serious music", mused on "how astonished Beethoven would be to learn that his symphonies are

28. Felix Greene, Confidential Report "USA," January 22, 1936, BBC Written Archives Centre File E1/113/2.
29. Leopold Stokowski, *Music for All of Us* (New York: Simon and Schuster, 1943): 1.

now heard simultaneously by millions in every civilized corner of the globe," and he clearly meant that listening to Beethoven was itself a sign of civilization.[30] In the context of the threat of war in Europe in the later 1930s, such talk became more common. It appeared to many that civilization (only occasionally modified to "Western civilization") would have to be rescued in the United States, and that the broad dissemination of appreciation of the musical tradition was an important element in that rescue and defense. "America must preserve civilization if it is to be preserved at all," Hendrik Van Loon told a 1938 luncheon meeting of the Philharmonic-Symphony League of New York.[31] The civilizational imperative gave considerable added urgency and importance to the question of the diffusion of serious music in the United States in the later 1930s.

A further common ambitious hope was that classical music would develop the higher capacities of citizens and enhance their self-development and self-understanding. The social benefit of broadcast classical music was understood as the sum of the transformation and development of individuals. The characteristics that classical music was said to foster in individuals—cosmopolitanism, emotional control, articulated personal opinions—fitted well with the dominant civic paradigm of American radio. Expectations of the transformative power of broadcast classical music on individuals were extraordinarily high. Conductor and composer Howard Hanson proclaimed that "music is a kind of religion which works in strange and wonderful ways upon the lives of those who become impregnated with its beauty."[32] Boston Symphony conductor Serge Koussevitzky wrote in 1939 that music "reveals the truest and most intimate depths of the human soul, when it opens to man the knowledge and perception of new worlds, and arouses in him the feeling of ecstasy, or heroic aspirations to high deeds and ideals."[33] If these effects derived from the experience of classical music in general, it was clear that the broadcasting of classical music to huge new audiences must have world-historical significance. Leopold Stokowski thought that radio, with its capacity to broadcast music, was "one of the greatest mechanical means toward evolution of Mind and Spirit."[34] American defenses of classical music dwelt insistently on its capacity to transform individuals, and on the democratic availability of that capacity through broadcasting. It was impossible for those who believed these things to view the enterprise of broadcasting classical music with indifference. It clearly represented an epochal historical development. [Figure 3.1.]

COSMOPOLITANISM, PEACE, AND CLASSICAL MUSIC

Investigating the sociology of the "judgment of taste" in France in the 1960s and 1970s, Pierre Bourdieu argued that music was—sociologically—"the pure art par excellence. It says nothing and has nothing to say."[35] That was not how it was generally understood in 1930s America. In that time and place, broadcast classical music did carry values, and did

30. Chotzinoff, "Music in Radio": 5.

31. "Support for Music Urged by Speakers," *New York Times*, April 28, 1938: 26.

32. Howard Hanson, "The Democratization of Music," *Music Educators Journal* 27, no. 5 (March/April 1941): 14.

33. Serge Koussevitzky, "Soaring Music," *New York Times*, March 5, 1939: AS29.

34. Stokowski, *Music for All of Us*: 235.

35. Pierre Bourdieu, *Distinction: A Social Critique of the Judgment of Taste* (London: Routledge, 1998): 19.

AMBITIOUS music students draw inspiration from hearing the performance of the great maestros.

A few years ago only those in the largest cities could enjoy such experiences. Even then admission prices were often more than young students could afford.

How greatly radio has changed such conditions. No longer are music lovers, whether students or not, cut off from great performances, either by distance or lack of funds...The National Broadcasting Company sends out through the year a wealth of fine music performed by the world's leading artists. During 1938, 16% of all program hours broadcast by NBC, were devoted to opera, classical and semi-classical music.

This gift of music is a public service —just one contribution of NBC toward making this a better nation in which to live. It is the fixed intention of the National Broadcasting Company never to neglect its opportunities in this field.

NATIONAL
BROADCASTING
COMPANY

THE WORLD'S GREATEST
BROADCASTING SYSTEM
A RADIO CORPORATION
OF AMERICA SERVICE

Figure 3.1. Radio changed forever the sound world of ordinary Americans. Enthusiasts for the universal and humanizing powers of music were genuinely excited at the new possibilities. The networks constantly drew attention to their role in disseminating "serious music" to the millions, understood here as performers as well as listners.

represent a reformist intervention in American life. There were persistent hopes that broadcast classical music would transform individuals for the better, influence their thinking and feeling in specific ways. What was identified and understood as classical or "serious" music came from several European national traditions, and was often perceived within a nationalist context. But in the United States, classical works were more easily assimilated to the one seamless tradition of great music, which might be claimed to speak to all and express universal rather than narrowly national sentiments. To many American advocates of broadcast classical music, this was one of its most important characteristics—it transcended national antagonisms, spoke to all humanity, and thus both exemplified and advocated a cosmopolitan ideal. Those who expected great things from the broadcasting of classical music often expressed hopes for enhanced empathy and peace between peoples. "Radio has enriched the cultural life of almost everyone by making the music of many lands and many periods available all over the civilized world," exulted Leopold Stokowski. The celebrity conductor of the Philadelphia Orchestra advocated a universal rather than a "historical and national" standpoint in musical appreciation. Once this universal standpoint had been achieved, he enthused, the listener became "at home with all kinds of music—of all periods—all countries . . . . He is a citizen of the world."[36]

Crucially, this music-induced cosmopolitanism was to be emotional as well as rational. Glenn Frank, president of the University of Wisconsin, argued in 1933 that music *"can help men to cultivate the art of sensitiveness."* Music could be part of a sentimental education that would help them *"feel* a kinship with humanity . . . *feel* the tug of famine in China as keenly as they might feel the cry of hunger from a brother's child."[37] The hope that broadcast classical music would assist in transforming listeners into empathetic world citizens, keenly feeling the suffering of all humanity, is a poignant and now seldom-recalled expression of the high expectations that the broadcasting of classical music aroused in its heyday.

Of course the cosmopolitan message of the institution of classical music was not perceived by all. It was possible at any time, and perhaps particularly in the 1930s, for music to be heard as primarily national or nationalist in sentiment. The American advocates of musical cosmopolitanism vigorously contested this way of hearing. *Washington Post* critic Ray C. B. Brown wrote often against the persistence of nationalism in music, asserting that "contemporary music is so thoroughly internationalized that any attempt to disentangle the strands is hopeless."[38] Music was "quite capable of uniting most (eventually all) of the nations of the world." In any two antagonistic nations, the existence of a shared music "should be enough to convince the warlike citizens of both that some of their more important aspirations are held in common." World peace had not yet been achieved, he argued, only because "the men and women most sensitive to music do not hold the reins."[39]

Laid out so baldly, these might seem extraordinarily, naively, optimistic views. But Brown did in these remarks distill the common thinking of those in the 1930s who saw in broadcast classical music a powerful transformative force, something that might conceivably—in its mass address—bring peace to the world. Conductor Bruno Walter had just

36. Stokowski, *Music for All of Us*: 2–5.

37. Glenn Frank, "The Role of Music in the Life of the Time," *Music Supervisors Journal* 20, no. 1 (October 1933): 7.

38. Ray C. B. Brown, "European War Excludes Nationalism in Music," *Washington Post*, December 3, 1939: A4.

39. Ray C. B. Brown, "Music Explicable Only in Terms of Powers and Effects," *Washington Post*, January 17, 1937: E3.

left Nazi Germany to settle in the United States, when he told the *New York Times* in 1939 that "this radio machine is building up a new kind of community." "The people are being united in the spirit of Beethoven and Brahms by listening in," Walter assured Americans. "A new harmony is brought into the world."[40] This remarkably optimistic view had powerful resonance in the United States.

It was not only music professionals who held to such utopian views. Listeners quite outside that circle articulated the same audacious proposition: that classical music on the radio carried a transcendent and redemptive cosmopolitan appeal that just might bring peace to a troubled world. "The Miracle," a poem by Hannah D. Myrick published in the *Christian Century* in 1941 asked, in the context of engulfing war, about the peaceful influence of broadcast classical music:

> In the flick of a finger,
> In the turning of a dial
> Music flows
> Out of strange
> Nothingness.
> The symphonies of Mozart,
> Beethoven and Brahms
> Encircle all the earth
> In lyric stratospheres.
> How can this fragileness,
> This bright and holy breath
> Pierce the static
> Of human dissonance? [41]

The poet left the question unanswered, but the very asking of it is poignant testimony to the expectations that existed. It was a question that must have made sense to the very many Americans who had imbibed the interwar optimism about the mass diffusion of classical music. A mail clerk in Massachusetts was interviewed for the Federal Writers Project:

> "What do you like in the way of radio programs?" I asked.
> "Good news commentators and musical programs, mainly. Kaltenborn is my favorite commentator at present, and as for music, I think I've got a fairly good musical education from listening to good concerts. I still listen to Walter Damrosch's music appreciation hour, and I can identify most of the music he plays. Then there's Alfred Wallenstein and his good concerts on station WOR, but perhaps the philharmonic concerts on Sunday afternoons please me as much as anything."

40. Bruno Walter, "Seen from a Podium," *New York Times*, March 26, 1939: 144.
41. Hannah D. Myrick, "The Miracle," *Christian Century*, October 29, 1941: 1330. "The Miracle" by Hannah D. Myrick is reprinted by permission from the October 29, 1941, issue of the *Christian Century*. For more information about the *Century*, visit http://christiancentury.org.

"Is music your favorite form of art?"

"Possibly—yes, I suppose it is. And aside from the pure enjoyment I get listening to it, I'm very much interested in its social suggestions that, in spite of this era of nationalism and censorship are still allowed to go free. It seems to me that music is far more revolutionary than words are...."[42]

Broadcast music was surprisingly often perceived in the interwar period to have this capacity to counter nationalism, to introduce powerful cosmopolitan emotions, just as H. V. Kaltenborn's radio commentary on international affairs (discussed in the next chapter) allowed radio listeners to position themselves as possessors of a cosmopolitan wisdom about national ambitions and interests. In speaking to all, in standing for universal values, broadcast classical music might— its advocates speculated—bring peace to a troubled world. This was part of its sacred, unworldly status.

SACRALIZATION AND THE MISSIONARY PROJECT

Recent work on the cultural history of classical music in the United States has focused debate on the "sacralization" of art music in the later 19th century, on the taming and disciplining of the concert audience to sit in reverential silence before great performers of great works. But for all the attention to the process of sacralization, the subsequent complexities of maintaining sacralization in the era of broadcasting and mechanical reproduction, when classical music was available to all for the first time in history, and hence when audiences became able to listen to canonical classical music in the mundane surroundings of their homes, have been surprisingly little explored. Broadcast classical music provoked important and distinctive hopes and anxieties, but we know far less about them than we do about the early reception of, for example, jazz or rock.

Several historians have maintained that the sacralization of high culture in general, and classical music in particular, took a particularly intense form in the United States.[43] "More than Europeans," Joseph Horowitz argues, "Americans have worshipped musical masterpieces and deified their exponents."[44] Lawrence Levine, in his influential *Highbrow/Lowbrow: The Emergence of Cultural Hierarchy in America*, argued that while the lines between high and popular culture had been much less rigid in the 19th century, by the turn of the 20th century moves to sacralize high culture, to tame audiences and place them in submission to the expertise and judgment of trained arts professionals, had

42. Interview with Charles Monroe, New Marlborough, Massachusetts, February 15, 1939. Available: http://memory.loc.gov/cgi-bin/query/r?ammem/wpa:@field%28DOCID±@lit%28wpa 115050121%29%29)). [January 21, 2010].

43. R. Allen Lott, *From Paris to Peoria: How European Piano Virtuosos Brought Classical Music to the American Heartland* (New York: Oxford University Press, 2003); Joseph Horowitz, *Understanding Toscanini: How He Became an American Culture-God and Helped Create a New Audience for Old Music* (New York: A. A. Knopf, 1987).

44. Joseph Horowitz, *Classical Music in America: A History of Its Rise and Fall* (New York: W. W. Norton, 2005): 26.

largely succeeded in creating an elite culture that was firmly demarcated from the popular.[45] In symphonic music, this took the form of more "serious" programming, unleavened by the popular classics that had engaged socially mixed audiences in the mid-19th century. More and more, Levine reported, "it was asserted that only the highly trained professional had the knowledge, the skill, and the will to understand and carry out the intentions of the creators of the divine art."[46] The appreciation of serious music then became recognized as the mark of a serious and responsible person and as a marker of class.

Levine's book focused on the 19th and early 20th centuries, and does not extend its analysis far into the broadcast era. He had, partly for that reason, less to say about the significance of the cultural missionaries who set out to expand the audience for serious music, who saw it as a means of enlightening and civilizing the masses. Levine's critics, on the other hand, have sometimes taken the existence of an intention to enlarge the audience for classical music as itself a refutation of the sacralization thesis. Marcus, for example, argues that it "becomes difficult to uphold the notions of cultural hierarchy and 'sacralization' when we begin looking at the development of radio."[47] But of course sacralization and the democratizing impulse were neither logically nor historically incompatible. The stronger the belief in the redemptive or improving powers of classical music, the more compelling was the case for wanting larger numbers of people to share in them. The arguments of Levine and his critics have rarely engaged at the most critical point for thinking about radio—the intersection of sacralized classical music with a technology that allowed its dissemination to the masses and a missionary desire to awaken them to its life-changing worth.

Missionary activity was indeed a logical response to sacralization, and broadcasting was to be the means of grace. "Radio, as a winged missionary of a new art," wrote Orrin Dunlap in the *New York Times* in 1937, "has spread the gospel of good music; it has taught multitudes music appreciation."[48] For those who possessed a confident sense of cultural hierarchy, network radio was almost the perfect medium, for it allowed the simultaneous transmission of the very best music and musical performances to all. American musical evangelists sincerely believed that increasing the number of people who could appreciate classical music would improve American society, and transform individual Americans for the better.

The missionaries of classical music, with the aid of radio, did arguably achieve more conversions in this interwar period than ever before or since. Mary Anne Meehan, an Irish-American cook in her 70s, was one. She told a Federal Writers Project interviewer in 1937 that "kids is smarter nowadays then we was, lots smarter": "Look what children have nowadays—take th' radio—take what we're hearin' now...jes' look at th' fine music

45. Lawrence W. Levine, *Highbrow/Lowbrow: The Emergence of Cultural Hierarchy in America*, (Cambridge, MA: Harvard University Press, 1988).

46. Levine, *Highbrow/Lowbrow*: 85–146, 139.

47. Kenneth H. Marcus, *Musical Metropolis: Los Angeles and the Creation of a Music Culture 1880–1940* (New York: Palgrave Macmillan, 2004): 163.

48. Orrin E. Dunlap Jr., "Music in the Air," *New York Times*, March 7, 1937: 174.

alone. When we was kids we'd hear a couple o' sour noted souppranos in church an' maybe some lad who could play th' mouth organ or th' jews harp. Did we ever hear any good music? We did not."[49] Many Americans were, like Meehan, very optimistic about what this historically new access to music would do ("lots smarter") for the next generation. They had imbibed the high hopes that surrounded the early mass diffusion of classical music, and were quite willing to believe that the world might change for the better as a result of it.

Music in the early broadcast era thus had an acknowledged cultural power that considerably exceeded the category of entertainment. It was understood both to move and to transform people, to call forth and legitimize emotion, and to suggest modes of sublimating and communicating strong feeling. "The affinities and intersections of music and magic linger in our culture," argues music historian Gary Tomlinson, and the early broadcast era is a fascinating moment to observe the real excitement that first accompanied the possibility of the mass distribution of that magic.[50]

ACTIVE AUDIENCES

"There was a time when people played their own instruments and knew their music," writer Sinclair Lewis told a reporter in 1938. "Passive listening over the radio is a negation of music."[51] Lewis here succinctly expressed one recurrent concern about broadcast music. What if broadcasting Toscanini robbed the local orchestra of its audience, or caused dust to gather on the family piano? The public service of broadcast classical music might be negated if a consequence of making the best music available to all was that Americans gave up their own amateur musical activities or support of local professional musicians, and became merely passive consumers of great performances piped in from a few great metropolitan centers. The choice of Saturday nights as the time for the Toscanini *NBC Symphony Orchestra* broadcasts from late 1937 provoked protests from other symphony orchestras fearful of losing patrons, and from individuals who resented having to make a choice between their normal social events and the great broadcasts.[52] Nikolai Sokoloff, director of the WPA Music Project, warned that "the entire musical life of the country will atrophy if there is too much concentration on a few great musical broadcasts instead of forwarding community interest in cultural interests of their own making."[53]

One of the historically important things about broadcast classical music in the 1930s is the way that its organizers actually deliberately set out to counter this possibility of

49. Interview with Mary Anne Meehan, January 20, 1939. Available: http://memory.loc.gov/cgi-bin/query/r?ammem/wpa:@field(DOCID±@lit(wpa114021213)). [January 21, 2010].

50. Gary Tomlinson, *Music in Renaissance Magic: Toward a Historiography of Others* (Chicago: University of Chicago Press, 1993): 1.

51. Jane Voiles, "The Book Mark," *Placerville Mountain Democrat*, February 17, 1938: 2. Lewis prefaced his comments: "Now my wife talks over the radio (Sinclair Lewis' wife is Dorothy Thompson, radio commentator on world affairs) so I can't say much."

52. Larry Wolters, "Saturday Spot for Toscanini Evokes Protest," *Chicago Tribune*, October 23, 1937: 16.

53. "Radio Is Deplored, Protested and Praised," *Washington Post*, December 12, 1936: X17.

audience passivity. The *Chicago Tribune*'s critic Edward Barry expressed the hope that the reduction of most people to the status of audience for a talented few was only a "temporary result of an extremely rapid development of science and communication." He argued that anything that kept alive the musical activity of "the people themselves" had to be encouraged.[54] Music educators advised that radio music could be used to stimulate musical activity at home—Peter Dykema recommended that children be encouraged to play instruments, to sing and dance along with the radio.[55] Broadcasters, most importantly, were always conscious of the need to allay this persistent concern that radio induced passivity—including musical passivity—in listeners.

Rather than simply assuming that the broadcasting of music would of itself be enough to create serious and engaged listeners, those in charge of 1930s broadcast classical music often surrounded and reinforced it with a whole apparatus of pedagogical and institutional supports. At a time when skeptics were worrying that radio would render its audiences passive, that sitting by the radio would replace more active pursuits, including sporting, civic, musical, religious, and political activities, broadcasters and musicians notably attempted to retain and foster radio's links to an active musical culture. These links were what made classical music so important a part of radio's civic paradigm. Networks did this in their commitment to live rather than recorded music—even the music put to air when there were technical difficulties was performed by a live musician kept on standby for the purpose. Local stations necessarily played recorded music more often, but they too were obliged to minimize their resort to "canned music," and to demonstrate to the FCC that they had a deep commitment to live and local music.

In this regulatory climate, it is not surprising that the networks were permanently anxious about the possibility of being charged with discouraging musical activity, of replacing local talent with national and international performers. They were highly conscious of the need to encourage musical participation as well as forms of active listening and appreciation, lest radio be held responsible for destroying traditions of active music making in the home. Radio's classical music programming was thus constructed with dual objectives: first to introduce the audience to the best performances, with an emphasis on creating stars and recruiting name musicians, and second, to produce programs that would stimulate audience musical activity, that would instruct, facilitate, and encourage musical performance by listeners.

NBC was perhaps the most energetic in relation to this second ambition. The *NBC Home Symphony* program, begun in 1936, was "designed to stimulate individual music performance by presenting orchestral programs in which listeners who play musical instruments may participate," by playing along with a symphony orchestra broadcast.[56] Produced in consultation with the Music Educators National Conference, one of the aims of the program was to provide an opportunity for adults to continue to exercise the musical skills they had learned at school. In February 1938, for example, listeners were

54. Edward Barry, "Chicagoland Festival Features Public Music Making," *Chicago Tribune*, August 2, 1936: E3.

55. Peter W. Dykema, *Radio Music for Boys and Girls* (New York: Radio Institute for the Audible Arts, 1935).

56. John Royal to Lenox Lohr, October 7, 1936, folder 20, box 45, NBC records, WHS.

invited to accompany an orchestra performing the second movement of Haydn's "Military" symphony, and two selections from Grieg's Peer Gynt Suite.[57] Ernest La Prade, the conductor of the Home Symphony, reported that his fan mail showed that many keen amateur musicians played along to other orchestral broadcasts as well: "Toscanini and his colleagues would be surprised if they knew how many unofficial members their orchestra comprise."[58] La Prade described the kind of coordinated home activity that might be possible in the future: "10, 000 amateur musicians scattered throughout the continent, each invisible to the other, but all collaborating in a synchronized performance of a Mozart symphony."[59] He whimsically imagined "an audience three thousand miles wide, with fiddlers in Fargo, clarinets in Camden, and trombones in Tacoma, all playing their part in a Haydn symphony issuing simultaneously from ten thousand loudspeakers."[60] It was important for the networks to invoke this kind of vision of an active audience to counter possible criticism of the passivity that might be induced by star quality broadcast music. These amateur musicians, invisible and inaudible to each other, but linked in simultaneous time, listening and playing, created a rather paradoxical assemblage, and certainly a new kind of radio community. Paul Lazarsfeld expressed some reservations: "But if the man plays in his home with an invisible orchestra, if he carves wood according to the instructions of a radio course, might we not induce him to pseudo activities which make him drift still farther away from organized living with other people?"[61] Such elaborate audience participation shows were, however, evidence of the civic paradigm in operation, of the political need for broadcasters to encourage listening that culminated in local activity, whether spoken, written, or musical, whether heard by the radio audience or not.

There were numbers of these musical activity programs, some inviting audience participation, others offering a chance to hear fellow amateurs play or talk about their playing. NBC's *Fun in Music* offered home music lessons for aspiring band players from Dr. Joseph Maddy of the University of Michigan. The program was first broadcast in 1931 over Detroit station WJR, and supported by funding from the Carnegie Corporation. By 1933, Maddy was claiming to have taught 20,000 children by radio and to have made possible "hundreds of high school and grade school orchestras and bands in the rural schools."[62] Maddy also at different times offered Michigan state radio series in string playing, singing, and hymn singing. Also on NBC was *Music Is my Hobby* (1935–39), in which amateur musicians talked about their playing. NBC's *Music and American Youth*, sponsored by the Music Educators National Conference, featured performances from students in schools and colleges around the country, and talks from leading music

57. NBC press release, February 16, 1938.

58. "Home Music Is Preferred," *Washington Post*, December 29, 1938: XI.

59. "Listeners Play with Toscanini," *New York Times*, January 1, 1939: 106.

60. Ernest La Prade, "Audience Participation in Radio Programs," in *Proceedings of the Music Teachers National Association 1938*, quoted in Constance Sanders, "A History of Radio in Music Education in the United States" (PhD diss., University of Cincinnati, 1990): 154.

61. Institute for Education by Radio and Television, Ohio State University, *Education on the Air* 14 (Columbus, Ohio State University, 1938): 79.

62. Marian Welles Hornberger, "Teaching Music by Radio," *Christian Science Monitor*, October 31, 1933: 6.

educators. NBC's *Metropolitan Opera Auditions of the Air* was advertised as a chance to hear singers who were "aspiring to stardom" compete with one another. A Michigan Grand Piano Festival, broadcast over NBC, featured 175 pianists playing simultaneously in the Detroit coliseum.[63] From 1930, the *Chicago Tribune*'s Chicagoland Music Festival, broadcast over WGN and the Mutual network, culminated in a broadcast from Soldier Field of 6000 to 8000 musicians and singers leading an audience of up to 100,000 in communal singing. In 1935, the festival boasted performances by a massed band of 5000 players, and a "Negro chorus" of 1000 voices.[64] In Tucson in 1940, it was reported that 1200 radio-listening schoolchildren "dance weekly to the music of all nations, and join in group singing, even though groups may be separated by miles."[65] In all of this was a sense that radio must not kill amateur music by simply piping in the best performances—radio had to be reflective of, and help to promote, a broad culture of musical activity. Some of these programs assumed a considerable level of listener skill and active participation; others encouraged listening to, or appreciation of the skills of, keen amateurs. Programs at both local and network levels were thus deliberately constructed to foster local musical activity as well as active listening to great performances from faraway places. This active listening was to be taught by another kind of program—the radio music appreciation lesson.

MUSIC APPRECIATION ON THE AIR

While one branch of radio music education was concerned with musical activity, another focused on listening. American broadcasters before WWII understood that classical music listeners and appreciators were made as much as found. Broadcast classical music had its own pedagogy, teaching audiences how to listen, understand, and enjoy. Music educators were perhaps the group most concerned and excited about the possibilities of broadcast classical music. For those who taught music appreciation in the nation's schools, the arrival of radio was a watershed in their professional lives. It also, however, posed a number of fundamental challenges. Now their role was less likely to be one of introducing students to musics they had never heard before than it was teaching better ways of listening to music that was readily available. Questions abounded: Did the cultural and individual benefits of classical music flow simply from listening? Or was a particular kind of listening needed? Was the spontaneous response to music the most important? Or was that only the beginning of a process of learning and cultivation? Did radio broadcasts of great music themselves become the best education in musical appreciation, or was more focused cultural work necessary to realize the benefits of the revolution in the availability of music?

There was often a democratic, progressive, and Deweyan tone to the American discussion of these issues, which resulted in great emphasis being placed on the development of authentic personal experience of and personal opinion about music as opposed to the learning of conventional valuations. Progressive educational thought

63. "Sarnoff to Open Observance of Music Week," *Chicago Tribune*, May 1, 1938: N8.

64. "Music Festival to Be Broadcast Next Saturday," *Chicago Tribune*, August 11, 1935: SW4; "Music Festival on Mutual Net Coast to Coast," *Chicago Tribune*, August 14, 1938: SW4.

65. "What Goes On," *FREC Service Bulletin* 2, no. 2 (April 1940): 2.

derided the penumbra of conventional wisdom and received critical opinion that blocked or diminished the direct experience of music. In his 1916 *Democracy and Education*, John Dewey had observed that while an "individual may have learnt that certain characteristics are conventionally esteemed in music; he may be able to converse with some correctness about classic music; he may even honestly believe that these traits constitute his own musical standards," all of this would count for little if not supported by "his own past experience, what he has been most accustomed to."[66] For Dewey, the task of appreciation was to preserve the authentic experience of the art work from convention and traditions of "unquestioned admiration," to "restore continuity between the refined and intensified forms of experience that are works of art and the everyday events, doings and sufferings that are universally recognized to constitute experience."[67]

This broadly delineated the project of progressive music appreciation, an approach that remained influential, even orthodox, through the 1930s and 1940s.[68] At the heart of this project was the sovereign individual listener who would develop a personal and experientially based knowledge and valuation of music—modes of self-cultivation that were considered important to the project of producing democratic citizens.[69] When a group of musicians and critics got together to plan some lectures to celebrate the 50th anniversary of Carnegie Hall in 1941, they thus announced that they were determined to rescue the enjoyment of music from the "self-imposed shackles, the inhibitions, the fears, and the resulting insincerities and dishonesties" of formal music appreciation, to set about the task of "emancipating the American audience, of freeing it from its inhibitions."[70] Radio appeared to provide the material conditions for just this kind of individual and unmediated listening, to hold out the possibility of creating a nation of sovereign choice-making individuals with their fingers on the dial.

The less progressive wing of music appreciation focused on correct listening. But most music educators maintained that real progress in music appreciation would require something in addition to exposure to the broadcast of music. The creation of a mass audience for classical music could be realized, they argued, only through music education; otherwise all of the broadcasting effort would benefit only an existing cultural elite. Music educators thus generally held that although some discrimination was to be gained from "the universal use of radio," left to itself "the growth in discrimination is indubitably slow."[71]

The conviction that Americans needed instruction in how to listen found organized expression in the music appreciation movement, which was premised upon the belief

66. John Dewey, *Democracy and Education: An Introduction to the Philosophy of Education* (1916; reprint, New York: Macmillan, 1929): 275.

67. John Dewey, *Art as Experience* (London: George Allen and Unwin, 1934): 3.

68. See Thomas W. Miller, "The Influence of Progressivism on Music Education," *Journal of Research in Music Education* 14, no. 1 (Spring 1966): 3–16.

69. See Ruth Gustafson, *Race and Curriculum: Music in Childhood Education* (New York: Palgrave Macmillan, 2009), ch. 5.

70. Robert E. Simon Jr., "Introduction," in Robert E. Simon Jr. (ed.), *Be Your Own Music Critic: The Carnegie Hall Anniversary Lectures* (New York: Doubleday, Doran, 1941): ix.

71. Marion Flagg, "Music for the Forgotten Child," *Music Educators Journal* 23, no. 4 (February 1937): 25.

that "musicianly listeners are not born; they are made."[72] A great deal of discussion ensued about what would have to be added to the mere broadcast of classical music to make of it a culturally transforming force. The possibility of teaching music appreciation had been greatly expanded by the successive technological developments of player pianos, phonograph recordings, the school public address system, and then radio. By the 1920s, music appreciation was taught in many of the nation's public school systems, and the possibility of using radio to make the musical riches of the tradition available in even isolated rural areas was exciting much attention in the professional journals.

At first, music appreciation broadcasts were mainly short concerts with added commentary, talks, printed notes, or supplementary visual material and questions for classroom discussion. Every school in Rochester, New York, in the early 1930s was receiving typed announcements and slides to be shown in classrooms before Rochester Civic Orchestra broadcasts.[73] In Humboldt County in northern California, local station KIEM broadcast music instruction every afternoon at 1:30 p.m., enabling every school to follow the music education syllabus devised by the county music supervisor.[74] Many other local school boards and state universities all over the country broadcast local and regional music appreciation programs in the 1930s.

A more elaborate and national music appreciation program required network-sized resources. The CBS *American School of the Air* conducted music appreciation classes from its inception in 1930. The programs for lower grades involved much activity—clapping, singing, games. The upper-level broadcasts were mostly about listening, but each episode included one chance to sing. A 1939 folk music series was prepared by a team that included Alan Lomax.[75] On the West Coast, the *Standard School Broadcast* aired from 1926 after the Standard Oil Company of California contributed money to the San Francisco Symphony to keep it afloat—the *Standard Symphony Hour* was broadcast on a Wednesday evening, and the school music appreciation program broadcast would follow it on the Thursday morning.[76] The Mutual network broadcast *Music and You*, an evening music appreciation program partly funded by the Rockefeller Foundation, from 1937, and WLW the *Nation's School of the Air* from 1938.[77]

The NBC *Music Appreciation Hour* was first broadcast in 1928.[78] Its presenter was former New York Symphony conductor Walter Damrosch, who was to become the most nationally known radio musical missionary and exponent of radio musical appreciation.

72. Lillian Baldwin, "Music Appreciation," *Music Educators Journal* 25, no. 2 (October 1938): 30.

73. Alice Keith, "Radio Programs: Their Educational Value," *Music Supervisors Journal* 17, no. 4 (March 1931): 60.

74. Marie Clarke Ostrander, "Music Education by Radio," *Music Educators Journal* 25, no. 3 (December 1938): 28.

75. Constance Sanders, "A History of Radio in Music Education in the United States," (PhD diss., University of Cincinnati, 1990): 83–87.

76. Sanders, "A History of Radio in Music Education in the United States": 118–19.

77. Sanders, "A History of Radio in Music Education in the United States": 144–45; Frank Ernest Hill, *Listen and Learn: Fifteen Years of Adult Education on Radio* (New York: American Association for Adult Education, 1937): 117–18.

78. The first season sponsored by RCA as the *RCA Educational Hour*, thereafter as the *NBC Music Appreciation Hour*.

Damrosch thought that radio could do invaluable work in democratizing access to good music. Appointed NBC music counsel, he had written to John Royal in 1931 complaining that most of the music on the network was "trash—an overwhelming amount of jazz, dance tunes, and crooning"—and asking for more sustaining fare of "lovely, interesting musical programs."[79] He exulted in the number of people his proselytizing music appreciation broadcasts reached. In the United States, he said, "a cultured upper class has supported the higher forms of music," but this was "all wrong." America would become a truly musical country only when the "so-called common people take it into their hearts to regard it as their common heritage."[80] At the height of its commitment to music appreciation in the late 1930s, NBC broadcast other related series—*Music for Young Children* offered music appreciation for younger children from 1938.[81]

The *Music Appreciation Hour* was broadcast from 1928 until 1942, when it was dropped after the forced separation of NBC's Red and Blue networks. The *Hour* was aimed in the first instance at schools and was organized in four-week series for different age groups. It evoked a strong response. During the 1929–30 series, NBC reported receiving 16,929 letters and distributing 47,999 manuals to schools.[82] The *Music Appreciation Hour* was a crucial part of the NBC public service image, and it was referred to extensively in network publicity. In 1934, NBC sent copies of the Instructor's Manual and Student Notebooks to members of Congress, as evidence of its concern for the public interest.[83] NBC estimated Damrosch's audience at over 7 million children by the mid-1930s, with a "vast" audience of adults also listening in. Damrosch thought the program might "lead directly to a revolution, culturally, among the American people."[84] But would this be a revolution in taste based only on passive listening, or would it lead out into musical activity? Damrosch once perhaps unwisely dismissed as misplaced any nostalgia for the era of the living-room piano—it had in most cases, he said, "only been opened to play sentimental trash." Good music over the radio was in contrast "doing much to revivify home life, which but a few years ago was seriously threatened."[85] But generally Damrosch remembered to espouse the official line, that broadcast music would stimulate rather than dampen enthusiasm for local music making, that the *Music Appreciation Hour* would "lead to the formation of amateur town bands and orchestras all over the United States" and thus solve the Depression problem of what to do with increased leisure time.[86]

The democratic mission of the *Music Appreciation Hour* was not just about stimulating musical activity or learning to listen. The program also provided instruction in how to talk about classical music. The lessons the *Hour* offered in discussing music were

79. Walter Damrosch to John Royal, November 12, 1931, folder 208, NBC history files, LOC.

80. "Damrosch, 72, Finds City Is Musical," *New York Times*, January 30, 1934: 21.

81. Sanders, "A History of Radio in Music Education in the United States": 125.

82. "Report on the Music Appreciation Hour 1930 to Mr. Elwood," folder 208, NBC history files, LOC.

83. "Report on the Music Appreciation Hour 1934," folder 208, NBC history files, LOC.

84. "The First Fifty Years," *New York Times*, April 7, 1935: X11; Orrin E. Dunlap Jr., "Music in the Air," *New York Times*, March 7, 1937: 174.

85. "Damrosch Gauges Our Musical Growth," *New York Times*, April 7, 1935: SM4.

86. Orrin E. Dunlap Jr., "In the Days of Recovery," *New York Times*, April 29, 1934: X9.

insistent and extensive. They ranged from guidance on pronouncing the names of the canonic European composers to learning something of the composer "as a man: his time, place, position, friends, habits, disposition, tastes," to assisting students to hear, and thus to be able to discuss, the "charm" of this or that aspect of the music.[87] Students were asked to complete sentences in their workbooks such as, "Debussy was predisposed to a...Life." Or to choose from options: Mendelssohn's "music in general reflects the happy/discouraging/tragic circumstances of his life."[88] These were the ingredients of conventional educated conversation about music, rather than the elements of a systematic study of music history or aesthetics. All of this drew the ire of Theodor Adorno, who noted the emphasis on the pronunciation of names—"Sanh Sawnhss, Bahkh, and Beezay"—which was, he noted scornfully, "intended to make the student capable of discussing music in drawing rooms."[89]

Underlying all this was still a belief in a ladder of musical worth, and a confidence that a mix of individual listening and guidance would lead toward it. Educators were convinced that absence of supply, rather than conscious and informed preference for inferior popular forms, was responsible for the minority status of classical music. The cause of musical appreciation was thus understood as democratic, as creating the conditions in which more of the people could share in the best available music. It was the kind of democratic cause that had strong resonances within American culture. If there was a best, why should it not be available to all? The broadcasting of classical music would awaken interest in serious and worthwhile music amongst people who had not previously had a chance to develop such an appreciation. Radio would overcome the disadvantages of distance, education, wealth, and health to provide everyone with access to the world's great music. This was a conception of a more equal, participatory, and culturally enriched, if more culturally homogenous, world. It aspired to help all up the ladder of cultural appreciation and knowledge, even as it sought to concentrate the gaze of all on the one ladder—which also incidentally created the possibility of appreciative, network-sized audiences for classical performances.

Radio music appreciation generally sought to humanize the great composers, and to relate their music to their individual personalities, and thus—importantly—to open up the possibility of the listener engaging empathetically and emotionally with the music. The NBC *Music Appreciation Hour* student notebooks encouraged students to respond individually to the music played, beyond providing answers to the set questions. A blank page was provided for students to write down what they wished to remember about the concert or to paste in "any pictures or poems that seem to you to fit the music"—or "better still, draw your own pictures or write your own poems."[90] This injunction to self-expressive empathetic response was a common trope in radio music appreciation pedagogy. After hearing the Largo from Dvorak's New World Symphony, students in

87. *Instructor's Manual—NBC Music Appreciation Hour, Eighth Season 1935/36.*

88. *Student Notebook—NBC Music Appreciation Hour 1932–33, Series D*: 24, 14.

89. Theodor Adorno, "Analytical Study of the NBC Music Appreciation Hour," in Robert Hullot-Kentor (ed.), *Theodor Adorno: Current of Music: Elements of a Radio Theory* (Cambridge: Polity, 2009): 210.

90. *Student Notebook—NBC Music Appreciation Hour 1932–33, Series B*: 5.

Rochester, New York, were asked, "Can you imagine how you would you feel if you were to leave home, your friends, your family and live in a foreign country? If you can, then you know how an immigrant may feel when he comes to America."[91]

If music appreciation was really to have a demonstrably democratic outcome, the result had to show in public conversation, not merely in private satisfactions. The point of listening was not some silent reverie or purely personal and individualized pleasure—it was in the discussion that followed, both in the self-expressive empathetic response and in the gradually improving exercise of discrimination and the formation of opinion. Such emphasis on individual discursive capacity was consistent with the aims of the civic paradigm to develop individualism and personal opinions. Prominent music educator James Mursell argued that all music education should be about "self-expression, emotional release, and the creative impulse." Individual appreciation of music lay at the heart of the progressive program, and music educators became quite prescriptive about the necessity for this. "Music education *must* be founded on appreciation," Mursell insisted, "and the goal of music education can only be better and deeper appreciation."[92] The reiterated imperatives revealed the nonnegotiability of the demand for individualization that ran through the discourse of progressive music education. Mursell told the New York Music Educators Club that "what a person learns to love and hate is more important than what he learns to do."[93] Listening was to be spontaneous and individual, and it was to culminate in opinion-centered discussion with others—in this way, radio's civic paradigm articulated neatly with progressive music education goals.

As the demand for individual opinion became more insistent, the institution of broadcast classical music became disciplining even as it was enlightening. In the programs of musical appreciation, there was so often this exhortation to individuate, to develop opinion and discrimination. This could be described as a liberation—music critic Olin Downes celebrated the possibility that "everyone can be familiar with masterpieces and choose from among them those that he prefers for his private enjoyment."[94] But the development of opinions and preferences, the entry into critical and discriminatory discourses, was also to be understood as a civic duty. The desire for individuation, for individual preferences and tastes to be developed and articulated, became an imperative, a demand for differentiation and demonstration of the capacity to make and elaborate distinctions in response to music listening. The civic paradigm was thus about self-improvement in its public setting, not just isolated cultivation.

One of the biggest stars of broadcast classical music was also one of the greatest advocates of individual opinion formation. Leopold Stokowski, whose Philadelphia Orchestra broadcast regularly over CBS, wrote insistently in his democratic manual *Music for All of*

91. Rochester Civic Orchestra, *Music Notebook* 1935, Lesson 1, reproduced in Sanders, "A History of Radio in Music Education": 325.

92. Mursell quoted in Frances Elliott Clark, "Music Appreciation and the New Day," *Music Supervisors Journal* 19, no. 3 (February 1933): 13–14.

93. Mursell quoted in Ernest G. Hesser, "Music in the New Social Order," *Music Educators Journal* 22, no. 5 (March 1936): 21–22.

94. Olin Downes, "Be Your Own Music Critic," in Simon (ed.), *Be Your Own Music Critic*: 7.

Us that it was "of vital importance that we all respond to music in our own way." He too turned to further imperatives: "We must be free to enjoy that kind of music which appeals to us."[95] Stokowski told the press that he always personally read the letters he received in response to the Philadelphia broadcasts, "for I am curious to see whether the preferences expressed for various composers or types of music seemed to reflect the influence of climate, or geographical factors, or of particular environment." He reported with some satisfaction that there was no evidence to support any such environmental theories. What the letters really showed, he concluded, was that "listeners all over the country, regardless of local environment, reflect intensely individual preferences and musical tastes" and that "this is as it really should be." Music remained, he affirmed, "above all an intensely personal emotional and spiritual expression and experience."[96]

When Lyman Bryson gave a lecture to the Radio Institute of Audible Arts in 1935, he stressed that the cultural advancement that broadcasting brought through the "musical education of everybody" occurred at the moment when listeners to radio music began to discuss their "likes and dislikes" with others.[97] The element that was nonnegotiable in music appreciation was taste formation, and entry into the pluralist world of opinion sharing and comparing. To help promote such individual critical discourse, NBC first sponsored and broadcast the National Music Discrimination Contest in 1932. Contestants were tested on their ability to identify some broadly defined musical styles, forms, periods—to distinguish, for example, classical from Romantic and modern, folk songs from operatic arias—and to be able to recognize some of the canonical composers. Entrants could still be given a high grade if they confused Mozart and Haydn, but if, for example, a student identified a piece as from the classical era and named Tchaikovsky as the composer, "it showed plainly that he had had no experience in discriminating listening."[98] Much of the competition was thus about demonstrating an ability to reproduce conventional categorizations, and to recognize familiar pieces and styles. But importantly, space was also to be allowed for individual difference: "In order to give an opportunity for individual expression, one unfamiliar composition will be played and students permitted to write their reactions."[99] In music appreciation more broadly, that permission was more like an obligation. The ideal subject of music appreciation constantly faced the challenging dual task of reproducing accepted judgments and yet showing some evidence of fresh individual response and personal opinion.

The insistence on the need for articulable individual opinion was to some extent at odds with the standardizing of judgment about musical greatness that radio also encouraged. The broadcasting of classical music helped everyone learn that Beethoven and Toscanini were the greatest, but it also allowed and encouraged, even insisted, that they form their own opinions and judgments. The education was to be in the development of an individual sensibility, about the capacity to generate personal opinions that still more

---

95. Stokowski, *Music for All of Us*: 43.

96. "New Interest in Classical Music Seen," *Syracuse Herald*, October 28, 1934: X.

97. Lyman Bryson, "Listening Groups" 1935, box 20, Lyman Bryson papers, LOC: 2–3.

98. Mabelle Glenn, "National Music Discrimination Contest," *Music Supervisors Journal* 18, no. 5 (May 1932): 34.

99. "National Music Discrimination Contest," *Music Supervisors Journal* 18, no. 3 (February 1932): 3.

or less (with some allowance for personal idiosyncrasy and divergent fresh responses) reproduced the conventional hierarchies. To become an insider, there was a body of knowledge that needed to be acquired, but also a set of aesthetic preferences and judgments that had in the first instance to be learned, much as they might become habitual or instinctive over time.

People of high cultural capital and individual learning often of course had a sense of cultural and musical worth that was quite different from the ranked order of Western art music now championed on the radio. Just as popular songs were plugged, so was a canon of classical great works, and—as importantly for diffusing the ability to discuss serious music—a roster of stories and facts about the musical canon. Knowledge previously available only to those with some wealth or education was now being broadcast to the masses. This attempt to elevate the taste of all was quickly met with scorn from a self-conscious cultural elite, which needed to distinguish its own inherited taste and discernment from those of the recently instructed masses. There were numerous complaints from music lovers about the banality of musical commentary heard on radio. One disdainful critic wrote of the announcers who "tell me that [da da da daaa] is fate knocking at the door. That Bach had innumerable children. . . . Where Saint Saens travelled in his busy life. And finally, the purveyors of the phrases: 'the great German master,' 'sublime in its . . . etc.,' 'the great Finnish master,' 'that rare genius for work,' etc."[100] Taken too far, such instruction in how to engage in conventional conversation about classical music could impede progress toward the other goal of individual opinion formation. The demand for individual opinion formation about classical music was one of the crucial links between the institution of broadcast classical music and the civic paradigm. As in other areas, in classical music programming American broadcasters before World War II did not assume that broadcasting elevated content was enough on its own. The addition of supplementary measures, including formal music appreciation instruction and stimuli to musical practice and local performance, was indicative of the general commitment to the production of active audiences and the individuation of opinion. Being a modern citizen entailed taking responsibility for one's own listening, learning how to listen effectively and critically.

BROADCAST CLASSICAL MUSIC AND DEMOCRACY

Broadcast classical music was always under suspicion of elitism. Leon Botstein goes so far as to assert that classical music "has never had a comfortable place in democratic culture."[101] But on 1930s radio, it came closer to a democratic context and presentation than we have remembered. Robert Hullot-Kentor has recently observed in passing that "in the early and genuinely class-conscious decades of American radio . . . the broadcast of European art music was a model of possible democratization."[102] The networks

---

100. Goddard Lieberson, "Over the Air," *Modern Music* 15, no. 3 (March–April 1938): 190.

101. Leon Botstein, "Music of a Century: Museum Culture and the Politics of Subsidy," in Nicholas Cook and Anthony Pople (eds.), *The Cambridge History of Twentieth-Century Music* (Cambridge: Cambridge University Press, 2004): 44.

102. Robert Hullot-Kentor, "Second Salvage: Prolegomenon to a Reconstruction of 'Current of Music,'" *Cultural Critique* 60 (Spring 2005): 139.

maintained a strong commitment to classical music with at least some hope that the audience for it would grow sufficiently to make it a solid commercial proposition.[103] Jazz and swing were often understood as invasive and addictive—things that might take over all musical life if the upholders of traditional standards were not vigilant. It was important for upholders of the civic paradigm to know that the existing audience for classical music was holding out against the tides of mass culture and retaining its ability to discriminate.

One of the great challenges that the American radio networks faced in the 1930s was to find ways to incorporate the indubitable and marketable prestige of classical music into a democratic and American cultural context. It was vital for commercial and political reasons that broadcast classical music become part of a democratic program of uplift and more equal provision of access to esteemed culture for all, that it not simply remain a form of entertainment for an already privileged minority. Particular attention was paid to college students. Here, certainly, if the civic paradigm was succeeding, there ought to be increases in interest in classical music. A survey of students at Cornell University in 1934 found reassuringly that three times as many claimed that they preferred classical music as popular. The five most popular composers were Wagner, Beethoven, Victor Herbert, Irving Berlin, and George Gershwin.[104] At Hobart College in 1937, the enrollments in music appreciation increased 200% and 44 men joined the glee club—in part, it was said, because of its enhanced profile through broadcasting over local station WMBO.[105] There were then some genuinely hopeful signs that simply by broadcasting classical music, radio could increase its popularity. In a 1938 *Fortune* poll, 62.5% of those surveyed said they liked to listen to classical music on the radio.[106] The Saturday afternoon Metropolitan Opera broadcast audience was estimated in the late 1930s to be as high as 12 million.[107] Music publisher Hans Heinsheimer claimed in 1938 that, in part because of radio, there was an audience for classical music in the United States larger than that available in Europe.[108] It was easy to demonstrate that the American classical music audience was growing in size, and plain to most observers that radio was the most likely explanation. Conductor Fritz Reiner asked a reporter in 1937, "Can you imagine 20,000 people turning out for a Wagnerian concert before the advent of radio? Yet that is what happened in the Hollywood Bowl."[109]

Young people growing up in the 1930s were exposed to mainstream classical music on radio. As a consequence, the U.S. military discovered during World War II that it had recruited and conscripted men with a taste for classical music. A 1942 survey of enlisted men found 32% who said they enjoyed listening to classical music—making it a significant minority taste.[110] The USO set up a separate division to provide classical concerts to the

103. FCC survey cited in John Gray Peatman, "Radio and Popular Music," in Paul F. Lazarsfeld and Frank N. Stanton (eds.), *Radio Research 1942–1943* (New York: Duell, Sloan and Pearce, 1944): 335.

104. "Taste for Jazz Nil at Cornell, Survey Shows," *Chicago Tribune*, February 18, 1934: 16.

105. "Music Appreciation Growing at Hobart," *New York Times*, November 6, 1938: 58.

106. "Toscanini on the Air," *Fortune* 27, no. 1 (January 1938): 62–64.

107. Philip Kerby, "Radio's Music," *North American Review* 245, no. 2 (Summer 1938): 300.

108. Hans Heinsheimer, "Challenge of the New Audience," *Modern Music* 16, no. 1 (1938): 31.

109. "Radio's 'True Tempo,'" *New York Times*, August 1, 1937: 146.

110. "Enlisted Men Prefer Music, News, Comedy," *Broadcasting* 23, no. 14 (October 5, 1942): 8.

Figure 3.2. A wartime mass audience for classical music—soldiers listening to Leopold Stokowski conducting the Los Angeles Symphony in a performance of Shostakovich's Seventh Symphony, "Leningrad," at the recently created Camp Young, Indio, California, in October 1942. (Photo by Peter Stackpole/Time Life Pictures/Getty Images.) Ed Ainsworth described the scene for the *Los Angeles Times*: "It was universal war music, the language of a warrior overleaping race and language and boundaries.... The lights shone on the packed masses standing there listening to the martial summons that so many will answer soon as they join the battle at the front." Ed Ainsworth, "Soldiers Hear Shostakovich," *Los Angeles Times*, Oct. 12, 1942: 1.

camps—classical performers such as Menuhin, Heifetz, and Szigeti drew audiences of up to 4000 men.[111] Soldiers and shipyard workers at Panama City, Florida, in 1943 demanded classical concerts from the USO. "They don't want jive and jitterbug tunes," reported the local USO director. "The majority of our requests have been for programs of classical music."[112] One war correspondent reported that U.S. Army radio in North Africa had a lot of request shows and "they got so many requests for classical music, from the G.I.'s mind you, that they now have a solid hour daily of highbrow music."[113] [Figure 3.2.]

Radio had thus quite apparently dramatically and rapidly expanded the audience for classical music, and the networks made a great deal of this in their publicity. "Today," crowed an NBC publicity brochure, "the Maine fisherman, the Texas rancher, the Montana miner, the Louisiana cotton-picker, farmers, villagers and townsmen living far removed

111. "The World of Music," *San Mateo Times and Daily News Leader*, September 15, 1942: 8.
112. "Classical Music Asked for USO Sunday Program," *Panama City News-Herald*, April 6, 1943: 3.
113. "Quentin Reynolds Talks," *Billboard*, October 30, 1943: 4.

from music centers can and do enjoy as much symphonic music as the most ardent music patrons can hear in the concert halls of New York, Berlin, Vienna, Paris, London or Rome." The nation had acquired a "growing appetite for the great tonal masterworks."[114] The broadcasters also took every opportunity to claim credit not just for the expansion of the size of the classical music audience, but for the enhancement of its critical capacities. In 1937, NBC broadcast a scripted series, *The ABC of NBC*, which took listeners on a tour of the various departments of the network. Episode 9 featured a "GIRL" visiting the music department and speaking to resident conductor Frank Black:

Girl: "Mr. Black, do you think that classical music is becoming more popular through the medium of radio?"

Black: "Very definitely—yes! Through radio the music of the classics—opera—the symphony—and the works of all the great composers have been brought right into the homes of everyone. And through this—more people are becoming acquainted with this type of music and enjoying it too."

Girl: "Well—what effect does this increased audience have?"

Black: "It betters the performances. By that I mean that audiences are becoming more discriminating...because through radio they have come to know good performances. This necessitates a higher standard in all performances which incidentally does not only include symphonic and operatic works but also takes in the modern popular type of music."[115]

This was a key part of the legitimating claims made for broadcast classical music. Radio was not just providing entertainment to an already privileged cultural elite, it was creating a mass audience for good music, helping it exercise discrimination in all its music listening, and thus fostering a demand for better and better music. "In its own brief experience," summarized an NBC publicity brochure, "the Company has seen the musical tastes of the few become the tastes of the many."[116]

Classical music optimists thus imagined an imminent future in which there was no cultural divide between the classes, in which the uplifting and civilizing benefits of the classical tradition belonged to all. The somewhat paradoxical promise was of a democratic high culture, one that affirmed the intelligence and discrimination of the many not the few, and that improved and uplifted all. This broader missionary project was in many ways sociologically naïve. The high cultural status of classical music, one might argue, arose precisely from its minority status, from the inescapable fact that classical music appreciation was often associated with wealth and education and leisure. Music appreciation had been an elite skill, and conspicuous consumption of classical music served effectively to distinguish those with the "right" education and upbringing from outsiders.

114. *The NBC Symphony Orchestra* (New York: National Broadcasting Company, 1938): 9–10.

115. "The ABC of NBC," Episode 9 by James Costello: 8, broadcast May 8, 1937, folder 1, box 408, NBC records, WHS.

116. *Broadcasting in the Public Interest* (New York: National Broadcasting Company, 1939): 68.

Those who imagined a truly democratic culture in which all had the skills of classical music appreciation valiantly sought to separate out authentic enjoyment of music from the social pleasures of the conspicuous consumption of a scarce and expensive entertainment commodity. But in a world in which all could whistle tunes from Wagner, would attending the opera retain its status? Just as the economic version of the American dream offered the implausible possibility of a society consisting only of winners, so the democratic cultural narrative espoused by radio's musical missionaries evoked a world in which high cultural capital belonged to everyone, as though the erasure of the marks of social distinction could be achieved simply by teaching the current orthodoxies of discrimination to all. But for the democratic project to succeed, the mode of musical discrimination that confirmed the high worth and universal status of the classical tradition had to be internalized, adopted as one's own—a personal response was required. Leading music educator Frances Clark insisted, "Culture comes from within; musical culture in this country is measured only by the growth of appreciation and understanding of a vast deal of music by a large percent of the population, a national consciousness, of more and more, finer and finer, music."[117] Broadcast classical music was targeted at individual appreciation, and embedded in an optimistic democratic narrative about steadily increasing popularity. One strategy for achieving this was to drop morsels of classical music into programs of more popular fare, or to make jazz arrangements of classical pieces.

COMMERCIAL PROGRAMS MIX UP THE CLASSICAL

Early radio had provoked a debate about the merits of classical as against popular music. By the later 1930s, the arguments were about the mixing and mingling of forms—which was possible only because radio had mainstreamed classical music, and introduced it into homes where it had never been heard before. In 1938 the president of the Bach Society of New Jersey, a stockbroker, asked the FCC to intervene to stop radio stations from broadcasting swing versions of the classics—he suggested suspension of license for a first offence and cancellation for a second.[118] The FCC, as it always did in such circumstances, reminded the public that it was expressly prohibited by the 1934 Communications Act from exercising censorship. But the Bach Society's intervention did trigger some public discussion not only of whether state regulation was the appropriate means of protecting the classical tradition, but more broadly of its sacralized status. Only a small minority wanted state intervention to protect the sacred tradition from radio's promiscuous mixing, but many more felt that the practice of swinging the classics was wrong and ought to be discouraged. A survey of Barnard College women found them to be generally opposed to swinging classics—it "lowers the dignity of one of the sublimest arts"; "it's sacrilegious."[119]

117. Frances Clark, "The Development of Musical Culture in America" (1931), folder 1.2.7, box 2, Frances Clark papers, Music Educators National Conference Historical Center, University of Maryland, College Park.

118. See Olin Downes's erudite discussion of the proposal: "'Swinging' Bach," *New York Times*, October 30, 1938: 167.

119. "Query," *Barnard Bulletin*, November 11, 1938: 2.

While most Americans would have rejected state intervention to preserve the purity of Bach, probably few of them would have reflected on the extent to which indirect government intervention through the licensing system was responsible for the presence of so much classical music on the air in the first place. With its distinctive commercial but publicly licensed and obligated system, American radio was juxtaposing classical and popular music in interesting but unsettling ways. Radio thus worked both sides of the classical musical street—in its mixed programs effectively reviving older traditions from before the sacralization and rigid segregation of highbrow from lowbrow culture, while at the same time ostentatiously proclaiming and surrounding itself with the sacred aura of the classical musical tradition and its great performers. Radio's commercial but civically responsible public sphere was being filled with an often self-conscious juxtaposition of high and low, classical and popular.

The result was that if the most ambitious democratic cultural mission—making classical music the new popular—inevitably failed, something else unexpectedly succeeded. Classical music entered rather than displaced popular culture. Classical music on American radio became part of the variety format, simply one form among many. It took its place in an aural fairground of competing entertainments. Moreover, radio subjected the higher claims of classical musicians and critics—that the music had universal meaning and world-straddling significance—to sustained comic ridicule. American radio has sometimes been written about as a producer of middlebrow culture—the radio symphony as the equivalent of the Book of the Month Club.[120] It is true that the middlebrow has suffered in American culture from being attacked from both sides, being perceived, as James Gilbert puts it, as "pretentious as well as excessively democratic."[121] Classical music on American radio suffered some of that fate. But the networks' determination to present and defend and compete with their classical music offerings, while striving to retain a popular audience, suggests something more innovative than middlebrow gentility was being produced here. Indeed what was striking about broadcast classical music in the 1930s, taken as a whole, was not its bland middle-of-the-road qualities, but rather its persistent carnivalesque mixing of high and low. The president of the National Piano Manufacturers Association reported in 1940 that even swing and jazz musicians were coming under the sway of classical music: "Most of our maestros of popular music are…taking their cue from symphonic works," he observed, just as symphonic music was borrowing from jazz and swing.[122]

Classical music found its way into variety shows as part of the mix of entertainment. It was not segregated on highbrow, low-audience shows or stations, and was not so sacred that it had to be kept apart from more popular forms of entertainment. The evidence of

120. See, e.g., Joseph Horowitz, "'Sermons in Tones': Sacralization as a Theme in American Classical Music," *American Music* 16, no. 3 (Fall 1998): 328–29; Louis Carlat, "Sound Values: Radio Broadcasts of Symphonic Music and American Culture 1922–1939" (PhD diss., Johns Hopkins University, 1995): chs. 4 and 5; Philip Napoli, "Empire of the Middle: Radio and the Emergence of an Electronic Society" (PhD diss., Columbia University, 1998).

121. James Gilbert, "Midcult, Middlebrow, Middle Class," *Reviews in American History* 20, no. 4 (December 1992): 343.

122. "Swing Swinging to Symphony, Is Leaders Verdict," *Freeport Journal-Standard*, August 3, 1940: 3.

mixing was all around. The *Magic Key of RCA* on November 27, 1938, contained a typical mixture of high and low, popular and classical: the show featured a 40-piece orchestra, a tenor from the Metropolitan Opera, a blackface minstrel act, and Gertrude Lawrence. The music included pieces from Dvorak, Enesco, Wolf, and Lalo.[123] Classical music and musicians appeared in many other surprising places on the schedule. The *National Barn Dance* is remembered for its airing of country music, but the program also featured classical musicians—in November 1938, for example, the Vienna Boys Choir sang Schubert and Haydn.[124] Musical variety programs regularly featured classical performers. Bing Crosby's very popular *Kraft Music Hall* replaced its musical director Jimmy Dorsey in 1937 with John Scott Trotter, when the sponsor was insisting that more classical performers appear on the show.[125] One not atypical *Kraft* show in 1938 featured both jazz drummer Gene Krupa and star soprano Mafalda Favero, who was about to make her Met debut in *La Boheme*.[126] This mixing placed considerable demands on studio musicians. NBC's central division director of music pointed out that the musicians on his own *Revue* program needed great versatility: "On a given program, the men in the band are confronted with a variety of music that fills half a dozen categories. The latest piece of brass business by Rodgers and Hart might very well follow an obscure tune turned out by some Florentine composer for rendition on a clavo-cembello, or something straight out of Verdi's *Aida*." The "symphony to swing" transition was nothing to these musicians, he observed.[127] Alongside all the solemn reverence for the musical tradition and its interpretation by performers of genius, then, the networks injected a distinct note of showmanship. *Billboard* enthused in 1943 that "the longhair maestri have developed a flair of showmanship and are eager for that big publicity break."[128]

Music educator Floyd Hart thought radio and movies had sparked a revolt against placing art on a pedestal: "When Yehudi Menuhin and Lauritz Melchior appear with the Saturday night swing club, when Giovanni Martinelli not only sings on Eddie Cantor's program but sings 'Dinah' as one of his numbers, when the other Metropolitan artists willingly play in our movies...what other conclusion can one draw?"[129] One of the longest-running gags on Bob Hope's radio show, during and long after a guest appearance from celebrity violinist Yehudi Menuhin in 1939, was comedian Jerry Colonna's repeated question: "Who's Yehudi?" NBC, it was reported, received hundreds of serious and silly answers to the riddle every day.[130] The question acquired a broader significance when the gag entered U.S. Army slang as a reference to the "man who wasn't there," the scapegoat for any newly discovered problem. Both references were then obliquely picked up in a 1940 song "Who's

123. NBC press release, November 22, 1938.
124. NBC press release, November 14, 1938.
125. John Dunning, *On the Air: An Encyclopedia of Old-Time Radio* (New York: Oxford University Press, 1998): 91.
126. NBC press release, November 7, 1938.
127. NBC press release, November 8, 1938.
128. "Symphs Using Showmanship," *Billboard*, December 4, 1943: 13.
129. Floyd T. Hart, "The Relation of Jazz Music to Art," *Music Educators Journal* 26, no.1 (September 1939): 25.
130. *Life*, September 23, 1940: 8.

Yehudi?" recorded by Cab Calloway and also by Lane Truesdale with Kay Kyser's band.[131] Yehudi Menuhin was enough of a celebrity that one of the most popular jokes of the era could revolve around the absurdity of not knowing who he was.

All this jostling and mixing upset the purists, like the New Jersey Bach Society, concerned with maintaining the sacralization of classical music. The *Magic Key of RCA* was too "clambaky," one critic sniffed in 1938—complaining of the juxtaposition of the sublime singing of the Flagstad sisters with a jazz song: "Some other item should have been inserted between."[132] A Syracuse man wrote to the *New York Times* to say that he and his wife regarded the mixing of classical music with jazz as "inexcusable and in very bad taste."[133] Former Metropolitan Opera soprano Marion Talley, who had her own show sponsored by Ry-Krisp on NBC from 1936 to 1938, singing "the music all America loves to hear," condemned radio's "growing tendency to mix extremes in music": "An opera or concert star doesn't do himself much good by appearing on a variety show in which swing music and comedy routines are mixed with the classics. And I think the listeners have grown tired of hodge-podges."[134] [Companion website link 3.1.] Such mixed programs were bad enough for the purists, but a further issue was the consequent fear that popular styles were contaminating classical performances. On the *General Motors Symphony Concert* broadcasts, one music critic alleged, the conductor had "one leg in Radio City Music Hall, and the other in Carnegie Hall."[135]

Even more popular than variety shows were the big comedy programs, which consistently rated among radio's most popular productions right through the 1930s. As a direct result of the jostling of high and popular cultural forms in the schedules of American broadcasters, American radio comedians were particularly preoccupied with and adept at sending up the pretensions of high culture. As Michele Hilmes and others have noted, the distinctions between highbrow and lowbrow culture provided rich material for radio comedy.[136] Classical music in particular provided an obvious reference point for radio, and was the subject of much comic attention. Jack Benny's violin playing is one prominent example—classical musical pretension was one of the key character foibles of the nation's most popular radio comedian. While the musical interludes on the Benny shows featured bright popular swing or crooning tenor songs, the Jack Benny character was an aspiring classical violinist with delusions about his own talent and inappropriate aspirations to art music seriousness. The audience was invited to laugh knowingly at his efforts, conscious that they could distinguish real classical seriousness from the comic burlesque of it—as when in 1938 NBC announced that Benny would be performing Finkelburg's "Opus for Cello and Fiddle Being Beaten Together," composed "in a dark room in Venice in the

131. Arthur Frank Wertheim, *Radio Comedy* (New York: Oxford University Press, 1979): 297. The song, written by Bill Seckler and Matt Dennis, and performed by Lane Truesdale is available at http://www.youtube.com/watch?v=eu7KL710F70. [January 27, 2010].

132. "Radio Swing Feast Promised," *Christian Science Monitor*, January 11, 1938: 12.

133. Byron E. White, letter to editor, *New York Times*, November 14, 1937: 194.

134. Carroll Nye, "Radio Variety Bills Shunned by Singer," *Los Angeles Times*, August 30, 1936: C8.

135. Goddard Lieberson, "Over the Air," *Modern Music* 15, no. 2 (January/February 1938): 115.

136. Hilmes, *Radio Voices*: 187.

summer of 1733."[137] NBC's *Bughouse Rhythm*, first broadcast in 1936, was a swing program that satirized classical music. A 1938 episode presented swing versions of Liszt and Schubert, and a "brief but alert discussion on modern music through the ages" by Miss Martha Murgatroyd.[138] This show led to the 1940 NBC creation of the *Chamber Music Society of Lower Basin Street*, another weekly mixture of satire of classical music and performance of swing. The mock solemn announcer, who introduced all the performers as "Dr." or "Professor," was Milton Cross, the regular announcer on the Metropolitan Opera broadcasts.[139] As with the Benny skits, the humor worked only because the language of classical music appreciation and performance was in some degree familiar to radio listeners. So much radio comedy was about radio, referring cleverly to the shared knowledge that attentive listeners had built up, and a rich part of that shared knowledge for comedians had to do with the trappings of the presentation of classical music.

Knowledge of current classical radio stars was also assumed on the small-town Midwestern comedy *Fibber McGee and Molly*. On one episode in 1938, Mrs. Uppington, president of the Ladies Wednesday Evening Shakespeare, Literary and Drama Club, is presenting a concert by the Wistful Vista Silver Cornet Business Man's Band. Fibber tells her, "Ye know...what this band really needs, Mrs. Uppington, is an outstanding personality to direct it. Like Toscanini of New York...Stokowski of Garbo...er...Philadelphia...or McGee of Peoria...." Toscanini and Stokowski were, of course, network stars, and Stokowski's relationship with Greta Garbo had preoccupied gossip columnists in 1938. Mrs. Uppington agrees that Fibber can conduct the band. He then tries to impress her with his musical expertise: "I says," he lectures her, "as Beethoven pointed out in his later works, the goldjerk rarely incudates the snug, unless you can find a halfsquirt to fill out the squimpet of a 2-tone zorddle."[140] The audience laughs at Fibber's clumsy impersonations of a high culturally literate person, but the humor of course presumes some knowledge of high cultural texts and terms, in order that the audience can hear the satire. In another *Fibber McGee* sketch from 1938, a department store employee addresses a Chinese customer (Gooey Fooey, identified in the written script as a "Chink"), who asks whether this is the shirt counter: "Oh rawtheh, sir. Here is our latest number. We call it the shirto conshirto. A symphonic color combination, you see?"[141] Here the racist humor also presupposes an audience that knew what a concerto was, and were ready to laugh both at the Chinese customer's taste and at the effete store attendant.

Because the radio comedies were always in part about radio itself, they reflected an accurate picture of its characteristic tensions. In their play with the pretensions of high culture and its self-important, foreign, effete patrons, the comedians sided with everyman against the elites. But in also often suggesting that these elites had falsely captured a kind of music that could and should belong to real and ordinary Americans, they were complicit with the networks' own strategy of holding out the utopian promise of a high

---

137. NBC press release, February 7, 1938.
138. NBC press release, February 7, 1938.
139. See Dunning, *On the Air: An Encyclopedia of Old-Time Radio*: 147.
140. *Fibber McGee and Molly* script for October 11, 1938, WHS.
141. *Fibber McGee and Molly* script for April 5, 1938, WHS.

culture available to all.[142] The preoccupation of the most popular American radio comedies with cultural hierarchies needs to be seen as another artifact of a distinctive American system—a system that constantly and uneasily juxtaposed public service and apparently irreverent commercial popular entertainment.

TOSCANINI AS MUSIC GOD AND AS RADIO STAR

One of the most significant results of radio's mixing of high and low was its creation of a whole new level of classical music stars. NBC's 1937 formation of the NBC symphony for the star Italian conductor Arturo Toscanini epitomized the way network radio both built upon but also fundamentally changed the sacred status of classical music. Toscanini was well known in the United States as conductor of the New York Philharmonic-Symphony, which broadcast regularly over CBS. On RCA president David Sarnoff's initiative, NBC brought Toscanini back to the United States in 1937, and formed the NBC orchestra for him. "If great and famous conductors, why not the greatest and most famous of all?" asked Sarnoff, in an NBC press release.[143] It was to be a new beginning for the only recently departed Toscanini in the United States. Superlatives abounded in the NBC publicity and consequent press coverage. Sarnoff named Toscanini "the world's greatest conductor"; Samuel Chotzinoff called him "the greatest musical interpreter of our time—perhaps of any time."[144] It was made clear that it was radio that had lured the 70-year-old Toscanini out of retirement: "The main force encouraging Mr. Toscanini to accept is that radio enables him to reach such an infinitely larger audience in one broadcast than during an extended concert tour."[145] This specially created radio orchestra was to be the supreme demonstration of what American commercial radio could do in the public interest—no matter that Toscanini had been broadcasting on CBS with the New York Philharmonic-Symphony up until 1936; the NBC orchestra was launched in a blaze of publicity that suggested that nothing of this kind had ever been attempted before. The NBC orchestra broadcasts would build on an established reputation, but bring it to a new level of public exposure and acclaim.

To some critics, at the time and since, the creation of the NBC Symphony for Toscanini represented the ultimate commodification of the classical musical tradition. Music historian Joseph Horowitz has argued that Toscanini represented the high point of the American tendency to make of conductors not just priests but gods.[146] Horowitz laments the effects of Toscanini's celebrity—his limited and European repertoire anchored in Beethoven, Brahms, and Wagner, his lack of interest in modern or American works.[147] But all that Horowitz regrets—Toscanini's standing for tradition, for Europe, for a sacred and certifiable body of works that he interpreted with special authority—was of course

142. This line of argument was brilliantly developed by Margaret McFadden, in a 2001 AHA paper.

143. NBC press release, November 23, 1938, folder 1241, NBC history files, LOC.

144. Horowitz, *Understanding Toscanini*: 165–67.

145. Orrin E. Dunlap, "Music in the Air," *New York Times*, March 7, 1937: 174.

146. Joseph Horowitz, "Sermons in Tones": 311–40.

147. See Horowitz, *Understanding Toscanini*.

precisely what made him valuable to NBC. The network wanted an already revered conductor with unquestionable status, and in Toscanini they had one ready made.

The argument about the sacralization of classical music deals with metaphors, but they were persistent and influential ones. *Modern Music's* Goddard Lieberson commented somewhat archly, "The National Broadcasting Company is setting out to prove that the only true God is Music and Toscanini is His messenger."[148] A medical columnist in the *Los Angeles Times* noted that Toscanini had become "almost an object of worship to American music lovers."[149] Toscanini toyed with sacred metaphor himself, warning a correspondent in 1937 not to refer to Toscanini's fifth or ninth, but rather to his interpretations of them—"I hate to see the names of miserable mortals put on a par with those of the Gods."[150] Toscanini was portrayed as a conductor who had a "horror for personal publicity and showmanship."[151] And yet, when he reached New York, he did seem to take some pleasure in the excesses of the treatment he received, noting, "The entire personnel of the NBC, from President Sarnoff (a truly exceptional man) and the board of directors down to the doorman, are enchanted with me and treat me like their God."[152] NBC programmed the first Toscanini broadcast with the new NBC orchestra for Christmas night 1937, enhancing suggestions of a sacred aura. Toscanini's fastidious renunciation of show was its own kind of showmanship, and he remained somewhat coyly aware of the talk about sacred music and his own divinity that was swirling all around him. [Figure 3.3.]

The sacralization of Toscanini and of the music he conducted was what made him such a great investment in public relations and political legitimation. NBC boasted in 1938, "Great plays... great music... spectacular special events programs... are now almost daily fare for the millions who listen regularly to NBC. Such consummate artists as Arturo Toscanini lend the touch of genius to NBC programs of service." In accompanying text, "Arturo Toscanini and the NBC Symphony Orchestra—The world's finest music performed by a great symphony orchestra" is listed first among NBC's accomplishments. The investment in Toscanini brought gratifying results in publicity. In June 1939, the National Federation of Press Women announced the results of its 1939–40 nationwide poll on radio programs. David Sarnoff was given an award for "disregarding the popular fallacy that radio listeners have the average mentality of children" for NBC's decision to employ Toscanini.[153] The networks confided to radio columnists that "the symphony audience is one of radio's most intelligent."[154] The intelligence of the radio audience was becoming a matter of national concern by the late 1930s, and radio programming that recognized and enhanced audience intelligence sustained the claims of the networks to be performing nationally important public service work.

148. Goddard Lieberson, "Over the Air," *Modern Music* 15, no. 2 (1938): 115.

149. Ira S. Wile, MD, "Here's Why We 'Feel' Music," *Los Angeles Times*, February 20, 1938: J15.

150. Arturo Toscanini to Ada Mainardi, November 17, 1937, in Harvey Sachs (ed.), *The Letters of Arturo Toscanini* (New York: Alfred A. Knopf, 2002): 313.

151. Orrin E. Dunlap Jr., "The Maestro's Magic," *New York Times*, January 9, 1938: X 12.

152. Arturo Toscanini to Ada Mainardi, December 23, 1937, in Sachs (ed.), *Letters of Arturo Toscanini*: 318.

153. Press release, June 26, 1939, folder 1241, NBC history files, LOC.

154. "Toscanini's 7000 Letters," *New York Times,* March 6, 1938: 160.

Figure 3.3. Arturo Toscanini conducting the NBC Symphony Orchestra in its first broadcast concert, Christmas night 1937, from Studio 8H. Copyright © NBC Universal, Inc., All Rights Reserved.

The networks transformed classical music as they embraced it, skillfully injecting a considerable dose of showmanship into the solemn reverence for the musical tradition and its interpretation by performers of genius. NBC created around Toscanini a cult of the difficult but brilliant "maestro." John Royal years later recalled fondly that Toscanini was "not only a great musician and a great man but he was probably the greatest trouper I have ever known and I say 'trouper' that is the highest compliment that I can pay anybody."[155] Royal's ability to spot the utility of Toscanini for NBC radio stemmed in part from his career experience of making radio capital out of earlier stage careers. Royal had always understood vaudeville to be the natural talent pool for radio. He wrote to Ed Sullivan's newspaper column once to say that vaudevillians "were great per-formers...troupers who knew every angle of show business and whose talents have saved shows, on the radio, in pictures, and on the stage."[156] Toscanini fitted this mold, as a sea-soned stage performer ready to become a major radio star. [Figure 3.4.]

Radio's publicity for its classical music stars emphasized their surprisingly ordinary qualities. An article in *Radio Stars* described Frank Black, NBC's musical director, as "a sports fan and regular guy," and thus "a contradiction of the popular conception of conductors."[157] The publicity developed about Arturo Toscanini similarly worked both to

155. John Royal interview (1964): 11, folder 3, box 3, William Hedges papers, WHS.
156. Ed Sullivan, "Looking at Hollywood," *Chicago Tribune*, December 9, 1938: 27.
157. "Black Is White," *Radio Stars*, October 1937: 32.

Figure 3.4. Toscanini conducting, January 25, 1938. *New York Daily News* photo archive.

maintain the cult of the genius and to supplement and enhance it with stories about the ordinary humanity of the off-duty maestro, stories that usefully also served to Americanize Toscanini. It became important to publicize the fact that he was a radio fan as well as a radio star. When NBC's John Royal visited Toscanini in Palestine in 1938, he was pleased to share with the press his discovery that the maestro "listens to radio several hours a day and enjoys popular music as well as the classics."[158] Toscanini was a radio "star" of the stature of Jack Benny, and everything about him was of interest to magazine readers. When the *Ladies Home Journal* wrote about "Mr. and Mrs. Toscanini" in April 1940, it promised insights into "the world's most famous conductor as you have never seen him before—when he lays aside his baton and goes home." The article concentrated on the maestro's eating habits, which turned out to be comfortingly mundane:

> A friend once invited him home to share a potluck dinner. Wives will understand the confusion of the suddenly appointed hostess to Arturo Toscanini. It was too late to prepare anything elaborate, and yet—there was the world's greatest conductor waiting for his dinner. With a prayer on her lips, she opened a can of tomato soup for a first course. Toscanini was delighted, asked for an encore, and wanted nothing more.[159]

158. Orrin Dunlap, "On a Holiday Overseas," *New York Times*, May 29, 1938: 120.
159. Gama Gilbert, "Mr. and Mrs. Toscanini," *Ladies Home Journal* April, 1940: 14.

The article, and much other Toscanini publicity, worked to identify the Italianness of Toscanini as lovable eccentricity and childish simplicity rather than puzzling or threatening foreignness, and to absorb his high cultural aura into the everyday world of consumer mass culture that was most familiar to the magazine's readers. Horowitz refers to this as the media creation of "the 'other' Toscanini," an "unusually warmhearted version of the self-made American."[160]

Something of the same strategy can be seen in the musical commentary that accompanied the Toscanini concerts. In September 1939, NBC appointed Samuel Chotzinoff to the position of director of "serious music". Chotzinoff had been instrumental in signing the conductor to NBC. He provided commentary during the intervals of the Toscanini broadcasts from the second series (1938–39), attempting to "humanize the lives of the great composers." Chotzinoff's practice was to concentrate on "finding the common denominator which will serve to reveal the musical genius as a man closely associated with the average person…trying to find out more about the composer's day-to-day life, how he reacted to the trials and tribulations of the struggle for existence, who his friends were, and what part he played in the affairs of his community and nation."[161] In 1936 Deems Taylor had begun his New York Philharmonic intermission talks for CBS with much the same idea. One critic praised the way Taylor talked about composers "as though they were actual men with human frailties."[162] All of this publicity effort to humanize the composer of genius as well as the god conductor was directed toward creating a mass and popular audience for classical music. Serious music devotees were liable to be offended by biographies and the mass marketing of the maestro.[163] One wrote to New York Times music critic Olin Downes:

> As a music lover, I deplore the whole situation. I believe the final outcome of the awful build-up Mr. Toscanini has received at the expense of all other conductors and orchestras (and when the truth dawns upon music lovers that there are other orchestras and other conductors worth listening to) will result in an incalculable loss to symphonic music. Further it will amount to a major scandal in music—as much so as was the White Sox sell-out years ago in baseball, and just about as cheap.[164]

The Toscanini phenomenon did, however, lift the bar for broadcast classical music publicity. After Toscanini's first season at NBC, the New York Philharmonic had public relations firm Ivy Lee and T. J. Ross make suggestions about how to lift the profile of new conductor John Barbirolli—suggesting, for example, that Barbirolli appear on other CBS

160. Horowitz, *Understanding Toscanini*: 257.

161. Press release, November 25, 1938, folder 1241, NBC history files, LOC.

162. James A. Pegolotti, *Deems Taylor: A Biography* (Boston: Northeastern University Press, 2003): 220.

163. Indeed, many established NY New York Philharmonic devotees found Taylor's commentary insufferable—see protest letters in folder 27, box 27, New York Philharmonic Archives.

164. Letter to Olin Downes, April 11, 1938, folder 18, box 27, New York Philharmonic Archive.

Figure 3.5. CBS advertisement for its post–Toscanini New York Philharmonic broadcasts, "On Sunday Carnegie Hall Holds Ten Million Listeners," *Broadcasting* 16, no. 3A (1939): 44–45.

programs, that "Mr. Barbirolli do something a little quixotic and spectacular. Suggest devoting one of his concerts to, say, 'Praise of Peace,' or insisting on playing one of his pieces in the dark."[165] A meeting in William Paley's office at CBS agreed on the objective of having Barbirolli "publicized to the point where his name and personality are nationally known and loved."[166] [Figure 3.5.] But they could not compete with the established aura of Toscanini. The creation of the Toscanini phenomenon was a clear expression of the distinctive tensions and contradictions of the American system of broadcasting—both in the trumpeting of a commitment to high cultural dissemination as the first and most important legitimation of commercial broadcasting, and in the introduction of distinct elements of a more popular showmanship to that high cultural public service broadcasting.

COMMERCIAL TENSIONS

Orchestral music was expensive. Behind the scenes, inevitably, there were discussions about money. Always within NBC there was the tension between wanting to find a commercial or philanthropic sponsor to help pay the costs of an expensive program and

165. "Publicity suggestions from Ivy Lee and T. J. Ross," March 4, 1938, folder 18, box 27, New York Philharmonic Archive.
166. Dorle Jarmel memo, March 10, 1938, folder 18, box 27, New York Philharmonic Archive.

needing to maintain a showpiece of public service broadcasting as something that the network itself provided for the public good. NBC reduced Walter Damrosch's pay in 1932 and wanted to do it again in 1935.[167] There was talk about finding a commercial sponsor for the *Music Appreciation Hour* in 1934 and at other points in the program's history. The company had also been engaged in protracted disputes with Damrosch about the number and remuneration of the musicians employed on the *Hour* since its inception.[168] In 1937, NBC Artists Services tried to interest Damrosch in endorsing a "highly thought of breakfast food," in a campaign they expected would involve "several magazine or newspaper pictures of you at breakfast." Damrosch refused, noting that he had always "ridiculed and sometimes despised" prominent people who sold their names to endorse a commercial product: "I know it is constantly being done but I just can't do it at this late stage of my life."[169] Walter Damrosch was sure that the musical education he provided needed to be kept quite separate from and untainted by the commercial business that supported it.

The NBC Symphony and Toscanini were expensive programming for NBC. "We were asked to pay unheard-of salaries to first-desk men," Samuel Chotzinoff recalled, "and we agreed to pay them."[170] [Companion website link 3.2.] Horowitz points out, however, that at least some of the expenditure would have been forced on NBC anyway by new labor agreements that limited musicians to a five-day week. For the 1937–38 season, NBC was paying Toscanini $40,000 for 10 symphonic performances and an agreement that he perform no other engagements in the United States during that period. From February 1938, there was a new three-year contract that gave Toscanini $48,000 and traveling expenses each year to Europe in return for 12 radio concerts a season.[171] This was far above anything paid to the other staff or guest conductors broadcast on NBC. In 1938, Toscanini was being paid about five times more per concert than any of the other NBC guest conductors, such as Boult, Monteux, or Mitropoulos.[172]

NBC bore these expenses as an investment in the viability of the whole American system of broadcasting. Chotzinoff calculated that the cost of maintaining the NBC Symphony was $82,260 a year. "It seems to me," he concluded, in a frank report to the NBC president, "that the prestige, the cultural value and the effect on the FCC more than justifies an expenditure of $82,260 per year."[173] It was important in this context to stress at the beginning that this was to be NBC's orchestra, and that the network was not seeking commercial sponsorship for it. As early as February 1937, Olin Downes reported in the *New York Times* that the concerts would be heard "free of any advertising consideration, for the benefit of the great public of the air," and would be given "on a purely artistic basis."[174] Radio had become, Downes wrote later in the year, "a protagonist, in its own right, of the symphony."[175]

167. Heistad, "Radio without Sponsors": 258–60.

168. Alfred Morton to R. C. Patterson Jr., January 19, 1935, folder 4, box 36, NBC records, WHS. On the earlier history of Damrosch's financial disputes with NBC, see Carlat, "Sound Values": chs. 4 and 5.

169. George Engles to Walter Damrosch, July 20, 1937, and reply, folder 7, box 53, NBC records, WHS.

170. Samuel Chotzinoff, *Toscanini: An Intimate Portrait* (New York: Alfred A. Knopf, 1956): 85.

171. Folder 1242, NBC history files, LOC.

172. Figures in John Royal memo to Lenox Lohr, January 16, 1939, folder 207, NBC history files, LOC.

173. Samuel Chotzinoff, Report to Lenox Lohr, December 7, 1938: 8, folder 207, NBC history files, LOC.

174. Olin Downes, "Return of Toscanini," *New York Times*, February 14, 1937: 167.

175. Olin Downes, "Toscanini's Return," *New York Times*, September 19, 1937: 181.

On commercial radio, time was money. One of the reputed problems with radio and serious music was known to be the networks' attachment to punctuality, which resulted in playing times being adjusted. "We play everything faster now—have to," the conductor of the Philco radio orchestra was reported to have said. "It's the new expression that's all. The faster tempo doesn't distort the music. It sounds just as well faster. The quick nervousness of our current interpretation of the master scores puts a new vitality into them."[176] But Toscanini was to be shielded from this industrial time pressure—NBC, signaling his unworldly and even sacred status, let it be known that during his broadcasts, not only were there to be no commercials, but the studio clock was to be covered up, thus removing the broadcast even further from the normal commercial context of sale of, and precise adherence to, time: "The maestro was never seen to glance toward the control room for instructions as do other conductors; no production man rushed out to notify him to cut or hurry the program."[177] Barbirolli's Sunday concerts on CBS, on the other hand, had to adhere strictly to time—he had to be off air by 4:27 to make way for a commercial program at 4:30. In 1940, there was some conflict about Barbirolli's slow entrances for broadcast concerts. A CBS official reported overhearing him asking "if 'this is a factory,'" and offering to take the blame if the broadcast ran over.[178]

NBC's Roy Witmer said at the FCC monopoly inquiry in December 1938 that the Toscanini broadcasts were not for sale because NBC "feels that that is something that they, themselves, would like to serve the radio audience with." FCC commissioner Paul Walker interjected helpfully: "You have a feeling of service in giving this fine program to the public?" "Yes," replied Witmer, "We are, I might say, only human, we like to do a lot of things ourselves, over our own name."[179] The tension between the public service and commercial functions of the network were, however, not long in surfacing. By the beginning of 1939, John Royal was suggesting a reduction in Toscanini's pay, and was arguing more generally that NBC had overinvested in serious music. "We could save $200,000 out-of-pocket cost and improve our over-all program structure 30%, if we were to abandon the symphony orchestra next year," he wrote to NBC president Lenox Lohr. Royal worried that NBC had become too focused on "highbrow" music, while CBS "have made great strides in their appeal with popular programs." NBC local stations, he reported, "have definite feelings about us going too 'arty.'"[180] Two months later, Royal was still worried about Toscanini. "The show is costing us too much for a 4.8 rating," he wrote to Lohr.[181]

Inevitably, in this context, the question of commercial sponsorship arose. In 1939, NBC executives were nervously discussing the possibility. Toscanini was at first resistant. In September 1940, he said "definitely no" to the idea.[182] But eventually the 1943–44 season

176. B. H. Haggin, "The Music That Is Broadcast in America: A Study of the American Wireless Mind," *The Musical Times* 73, no. 1070 (April 1932): 306.

177. "Toscanini's 7000 Letters," *New York Times*, March 6, 1938: 160.

178. Douglas Coulter to Arthur Judson, December 10, 1940, folder 9, box 27, New York Philharmonic archive.

179. Docket 5060: 2408, box 1403, RG 173, NACP.

180. John Royal to Lenox Lohr, January 16, 1939, folder 207, NBC history files, LOC.

181. Royal to Lohr, March 13, 1939, folder 9, box 77, NBC records, WHS.

182. Chotzinoff to Royal, September 27, 1940, folder 100, box 80, NBC records, WHS.

was sold to General Motors. There were suggestions the name of the program be changed from *NBC Symphony of the Air* to *General Motors Symphony of the Air*. Samuel Chotzinoff was indignant: "General Motors might just as well change Mr. Toscanini's name to 'Mr. General Motors.'"[183] But the program was nonetheless renamed the *General Motors Symphony of the Air*, and began featuring intermission talks on science and invention from General Motors vice president Charles F. Kettering.[184]

NBC extended Toscanini's contracts through the war; he was to continue conducting the NBC orchestra until 1954, making the transition into the television era. Before and especially during the war, Toscanini was widely publicized as an antifascist hero, which only added to his symbolic value to the network. He had been attacked and beaten by a fascist gang in Italy, and had refused to conduct at Bayreuth from 1933, in protest at the Nazi government's treatment of Jewish musicians. In 1936, he refused to have his Salzburg festival performances broadcast into Germany. He began more frequently playing the music of Mendelssohn, in response to Nazi bans on works by Jewish composers. Toscanini selected other music with antifascist resonance—for example, a broadcast in 1943 of Verdi's hitherto little-known "Hymn of the Nations" into which he interpolated the "Star Spangled Banner" and the "Internationale."[185] NBC international commentator Dorothy Thompson published a book in 1943 entitled *Arturo Toscanini: A Photobiography*. She was quoted in a press release as arguing that Toscanini was antifascist even in personality: "'Toscanini,' Miss Thompson continues, 'has been called a tyrant, as a conductor. Nothing is farther from the truth. A tyrant is a man of whims, who governs arbitrarily, and out of the sum of his arbitrary whims creates an enforced "order." Such a man is Mussolini.'"[186] But the rise of fascism in Europe was actually to be one of the factors that gradually eroded the claims of broadcast classical music to transcendent and universal status.

RACE MUSIC

Classical music in the 1930s was always potentially also national and nationalist. One of the virtues of popular music to Americans was indeed that it was so often indisputably American in origin and form. Inescapably through the later 1930s, the fact that classical music's most eminent nations of origin had turned to fascism had implications for claims about its universal status and peacemaking, cosmopolitanizing effects. The canonic ranking of classical music was not geographically or racially random. It systematically elevated the cultural productions of western and northern Europe, and Germany and Austria in particular, over those of other parts of the world.[187] Mueller and Heynes counted the number of performances of works by each composer for the eight leading American orchestras from 1875 to 1941, and found that, even with the dramatic dip in

183. Samuel Chotzinoff to Wynn Wright, August 27, 1943, folder 3, box 373, NBC records, WHS.

184. Mortimer Frank, *Arturo Toscanini: The NBC Years* (Portland: Amadeus Press, 2002): 71.

185. Press releases, folder 1241, NBC history files, LOC.

186. Press release, folder 1241, NBC history files, LOC.

187. Jessica C. E. Gienow-Hecht, "Trumpeting Down the Walls of Jericho: The Politics of Art, Music and Emotion in German–American Relations, 1870–1920," *Journal of Social History* 36, no. 3 (Spring 2003): 585–613.

performance of German works during WWI, German and Austrian works were still by far the most performed in the interwar years, followed a long way back by British, French, Russian, Italian, and Scandinavian pieces.[188] Despite its cosmopolitan reputation, classical music was inevitably and inescapably embedded within the racial understandings of the time. Within the United States, the question of the relative musical capacities of the races was an anxious one. Social science research attempted to subject the general cultural sense that the African Americans were an unusually musical people to empirical scrutiny. Much of the research purported to show that whites were in fact more musical—"scores earned by the whites show them to be superior to the Negroes in Melodic and Harmonic Sensitivity," reported one study.[189]

Anxiety about the racing of classical music surfaced through the 1930s in different ways, one of them being the difficulty of firmly dissociating the German and Italian musical traditions from the fascist present. The democratic program of the classical music missionaries in the United States headed in the 1930s into an almost inevitable confrontation with fascism, because of the great importance of German, and to a lesser extent Italian, music in the classical canon. There was an emerging cognitive dissonance for many Americans between Germany as the home of classical music and Germany as fascist nation. One historian reported of her interviews with American World War II veterans that they "hated the Germans for having drawn them into this war, for forcing them to leave their homes and fight abroad and, worst of all, for what they had done to the Jews. 'But you know,' they would often add after a brief pause, 'the Germans, they also gave us Beethoven.'"[190] The German and Austrian classical and Romantic traditions exemplified classical music for most Americans—Beethoven, Brahms, Mozart, and Wagner were in that order the four most often played composers by the seven leading U.S. orchestras in the years 1936–41, and radio followed the pattern.[191]

Broadcasts from Europe of German, Austrian, and Italian music were very important to the radio networks. NBC first broadcast music from Europe at Christmas in 1929, and by 1931 there was a significant number of such prestigious broadcasts in the calendar—symphony, choral, and chamber concerts from numbers of sites in Europe, opera from Covent Garden and Salzburg. In 1936, NBC broadcast 35 European symphony concerts, as the competition between the networks for publicity about their close association with European classical music festivals and performers intensified. The networks were seeking competitive advantage in access to Europe's auditory cultural riches just at the time when those musical and performance traditions were threatened by fascism and war. NBC vice president John Royal traveled to Europe most summers. Royal wrote to NBC president Lenox Lohr in April 1937 to ask whether RCA president David Sarnoff was going to Europe that summer: "Just to remind you that [CBS president] Mr. Paley told you he was going to Europe in June. He may go to Salzburg. He usually does. What are Mr. Sarnoff's plans?"[192]

188. John H. Mueller and Kate Heynes, *Trends in Musical Taste* (Bloomington: Indiana University Press, 1941): 86.

189. Mary Emma Allen, "A Comparative Study of Negro and White Children on Melodic and Harmonic Sensitivity," *Journal of Negro Education* 11, no. 2 (April 1942): 164.

190. Gienow-Hecht, "Trumpeting Down the Walls of Jericho": 585.

191. Mueller and Heynes, *Trends in Musical Taste*: 59.

192. John Royal to Lenox Lohr, April 28, 1937, folder 10, box 108, NBC records, WHS.

NBC had in 1929 entered into a relationship with the German national broadcaster, which called for exchange of programs of typically American or German character.[193] NBC carefully guarded this exclusive relationship well into the Nazi era. It had "first refusal" on all programs originating from Germany.[194] This was in 1935 NBC's only contractual arrangement with a foreign broadcaster.[195] In August 1935, John Royal traveled to Germany and at a reception held by the directors of the Reichsrundfunk was quoted as saying that "NBC hopes in the future to make its cooperation with the Reich in radio even more intimate."[196] In September 1937, Royal wrote to Kurt von Boeckmann at the Reichs Rundfunk Gesellschaft, thanking him for the "delightful" hospitality, and stating that he thought the Rundfunk was "doing the greatest job in short-wave in the world."[197] In March 1941, Boston radio commentator Marion Hertha Clarke told an audience of clubwomen that "one broadcasting company" paid the German government $1000 a day "to bring you broadcasts from Hitler's controlled countries." Clarke justified this payment in civic paradigm terms: "We're paying him $1000 a day, not because we want to do it, but because of the tremendous foreign population here, and because the radio must bring you all sides of a question."[198]

It was difficult to separate relations with state-controlled European broadcasters from relations with their governments. At about the same time as John Royal's 1935 visit to Germany, the New York Times noted, the business manager of the Reich radio was giving an address in which he stated that in Germany the radio "existed primarily to aid in inculcating the Nazi viewpoint and Nazi doctrine."[199] American radio was supposed to work in the opposite way, inciting individualism—but it needed the classical music and hence the goodwill of the fascist broadcasters. We get a sense of the importance that the networks attached to their European musical connections from the lengths that NBC went to maintain its exclusive relationship with the German broadcaster right up until 1939.[200] NBC European representative Max Jordan was urging the network to foster its good relations with the Rundfunk, in part to ward off the advances of CBS (in the person of its European representative Edward R. Murrow) and Mutual. Jordan reported that Murrow was trying to get a personal audience with Goebbels, but that he was using his influence to prevent this—"Murrow was unable to see Goebbels so far, and will probably *not* see him! Everything has been done to make sure of this, with perfectly straight means."[201] Jordan wanted NBC to invite the Rundfunk's general manager, Dr. Heinrich Glasmeier, to visit NBC in New York at their expense when he was in the United States— "Murrow will be busy behind the scenes. That's why I think fast work is required."[202] NBC

193. "German-American Air Programs Soon," New York Times, November 3, 1929: A5.
194. "NBC Has an Option on Reich Programs," New York Times, November 23, 1938: 12.
195. Max Jordan memo to A. L. Ashby, November 26, 1935, folder 44, box 91, NBC records, WHS.
196. "Urges Radio Exchanges," New York Times, August 9, 1935: 10.
197. John Royal to Kurt von Boeckmann, September 8, 1937, folder 14, box 108, NBC records, WHS.
198. "Clubwomen Are Told Public at Fault for Poor Radio Programs," Lowell Sun, March 4, 1941: 4.
199. "Urges Radio Exchanges," New York Times, August 9, 1935: 10.
200. NBC had a 5-year contract with German radio that expired in 1934, but retained first right of refusal on all German programs.
201. Max Jordan to John Royal, February 15, 1938, folder 23, box 61, NBC records, WHS.
202. Max Jordan to John Royal, folder 23, box 61, NBC records, WHS.

president Lenox Lohr did send a telegram: "Delighted at prospect of meeting you and hope you will be guest of NBC while in New York."[203] Glasmeier wrote back to say that he had been busy "during the historically memorable days of the return home of Austria into the German Reich," and so would probably not be able to make the visit.[204]

Edward R. Murrow's starring role in the remembered history of American radio has somewhat obscured understanding of the importance of classical music to radio at the time. In Stanley Cloud and Lynne Olson's *The Murrow Boys*, for example, the classical music that dominated CBS's conception of the tasks of Murrow and William L. Shirer in Europe appears as something of a ludicrous distraction. The "boy" heroes of the book are itching to get into some real journalism, but CBS, having sent Shirer to Vienna in 1938, was determined that he continue his work on a series of broadcasts of the children's choirs of Europe, rather than move into news gathering.[205] But there was indeed a high-stakes struggle for access to the most prestigious sources of European classical music; the networks were slow to understand that European news was about to become an even hotter commodity than European music.

CBS and Mutual worked determinedly to try to break NBC's exclusive relationship with the Rundfunk, and it became Max Jordan's mission to keep them out. The prize CBS (and Mutual) sought was access not only to news and political broadcasts, but also to the treasured musical broadcasts from Germany, which continued through the late 1930s. Two or three programs a month live from Germany were heard on NBC. In 1937, for example, NBC listeners heard the Berlin Philharmonic, *Lohengrin* live from Bayreuth, a military band concert from Berlin, and a discussion from the International Chamber of Commerce meeting in Berlin of "World Peace through World Trade."[206] In February 1938 listeners heard the Dresden Philharmonic playing Beethoven, Weber, and excerpts from the *Valkyrie*.[207]

Max Jordan's perceived closeness to the Nazi broadcaster, and his tireless efforts to ensure that NBC did nothing to offend it, made him vulnerable to suggestions that he was a Nazi sympathizer. The Rundfunk's U.S. representative, Kurt Sell, went out of his way to praise Jordan's "splendid objective" coverage of the Austrian *Anschluss*. Sell sent a long telegram to the German News Bureau lauding Jordan's efforts at reporting that "the German soldiers were heartily welcomed and given gifts by the Viennese."[208] Jordan had a scoop over CBS on coverage from Vienna because NBC initially invoked its agreement with Austrian broadcaster Ravag to keep CBS out. When William Paley complained personally to Lenox Lohr, NBC agreed to allow CBS in for a week. Murrow arrived in Vienna

203. Telegram, Lenox Lohr to Glasmeier, March 4, 1938, folder 23, box 61, NBC records, WHS.

204. ("der geschichtlich denkwurdigen Tage der Heimkehr Oesterreichs in das Deutsche Reich"): Glasmeier to Lenox Lohr, May 30, 1938, folder 18, box 61, NBC records, WHS.

205. Stanley Cloud and Lynne Olson, *The Murrow Boys: Pioneers on the Frontlines of Broadcast Journalism* (Boston: Houghton Mifflin, 1996): 32–33.

206. Detailed listing of programs to and from Germany to 1937 is in folder 18, box 61, NBC records, WHS.

207. NBC press release, February 2, 1938.

208. Kurt Sell to John Royal, March 15, 1938, and Kurt Sell to German News Bureau, March 13, 1938, folder 19, box 61, NBC records, WHS.

angry, and said that liberals and radicals in the United States had objected to "Fascist influences in the NBC program department."[209] There was concerned correspondence between NBC executives after an article by Robert Landry in *Scribner's Magazine* explained why Murrow rather than Jordan had been given an award for coverage of the Austrian *Anschluss*. NBC had had the scoop because of its relationship with the Austrian broadcaster Ravag, but the award from the Headliners Club in Atlantic City had gone to Murrow, Landry wrote, because "the anti-Nazi committee had turned Jordan down."[210] John Royal phoned from Miami to say he thought the statement "insinuating that Jordan was a Nazi...should be investigated."[211] But even to NBC enthusiasts for the German connection, it was clear that closeness to the Nazi broadcaster was rapidly becoming a liability.

By the mid-1930s the Nazi regime was making the relationship with NBC both morally and practically difficult. Jordan reported in 1935 that alternative arrangements had had to be made through the German post office when the broadcasting authorities refused to allow a Bruno Walter concert from Budapest to be broadcast to the United States through German shortwave facilities. The German authorities felt, Jordan reported, that "it was too much of a risk to turn music conducted by a Jewish conductor over to America, even if the program was not rebroadcast in Germany."[212] Also in 1935, Jordan had to explain to NBC headquarters in New York why the German broadcaster would no longer accept broadcasts of jazz music: "Jazz is being described...as 'an unrefined form of dance music which has had a demoralizing effect....Jazz music is a manifestation of the culture of semi-wild people, and therefore belongs in a museum of racial history rather than in an art institute.'"[213]

In 1938, Jordan assured John Royal that the German broadcaster remained committed to its exclusive NBC connection: "The Rundfunk has spent about 18,000 Marks this year for talent, announcers and land-lines in connection with the special broadcasts they arranged for NBC exclusively."[214] A series of fortnightly musical programs from the Rundfunk began in January 1938. The first broadcast featured the Berlin State Orchestra in a program that included two selections from Wagner.[215] At the same time, Jordan had much correspondence with NBC executives in New York about finding work in the United States or with NBC for musicians and radio people who had to leave Germany. By 1939, even Jordan was beginning to feel uncomfortable. He wrote to Royal that "Dr. Glasmeier, the German broadcasting chief had a long talk with me the other day and was trying to make me agree to a special series of broadcasts originating from various spots in Germany where activities of the new regime could be described. This again goes

209. Max Jordan to John Royal, March 18, 1938, folder 74, box 59, NBC records, WHS.

210. Robert J. Landry, "Edward R. Murrow," *Scribner's Magazine* 104, no. 6 (December 1938): 11.

211. William Burke Miller to Lenox Lohr, December 1, 1938, folder 74, box 59, NBC records, WHS.

212. Max Jordan Monthly Report for March, 1935, folder 45, box 91, NBC records, WHS.

213. Max Jordan Report for September, October, and November 1935, folder 45, box 91, NBC records, WHS.

214. Max Jordan to John Royal August 16, 1938, box 94, folder 39, NBC records, WHS.

215. "New Series from Germany," NBC press release, January 7, 1938, NBC history files, LOC.

to show how delicate the situation is."[216] But in 1939, NBC still took broadcasts from Rome, Berlin, Salzburg, and Vienna. Only the outbreak of war in Europe in September finally ended these musical broadcasts.

NBC, for its part, regularly sent broadcasts to Germany, usually two or three each month. From 1933, these programs included each year a series by Rundfunk correspondent Kurt Sell, who broadcast regular commentaries on American affairs back to Germany. NBC also sent musical, news, and sporting programs to Germany. By the later 1930s, however, the network was struggling to find musical programs to satisfy the increasingly stringent Nazi aesthetic requirements: no commercial shows, no jazz, no Broadway melodies, no Jewish music.

In October 1938, Max Jordan urged NBC to "display an active interest in promoting the program exchange" with the German broadcaster.[217] Later that month, there was a request from the Rundfunk to NBC for some musical programs. The German broadcaster wanted some of the regional and folk musics of the United States—including "typical folk music from Alaska," Hawaiian songs ("of course only native music is wanted"), typical cowboy music, typical American Indian music ("the German listeners would go for this very rare type of musical programs"), and some "folk songs and dances of the fishermen on the Great Lakes."[218] Although NBC executives were bemused at this expression of the Nazi *völkisch* aesthetic, they did their best to fill the order. They had no idea about Native American music. "Where the heck do you find the vanishing race—no suggestion," someone at NBC scrawled on the sheet. Neither was there any Alaskan or Great Lakes fishermen's music available at the National Broadcasting Company. Someone suggested a special program conducted by Phil Spitalny and his all-girl orchestra (as featured on the General Electric *Hour of Charm*), but someone else thought better of it: "He announces numbers in his very best Jewish accent. Therefore this *is out*."[219] NBC was still in late 1938 willing to put considerable effort into pleasing the Nazi broadcaster. The claims for classical music as universal and transcendent were becoming more difficult to sustain in a world in which music was rapidly becoming reracialized and renationalized. First the rise of fascism and then the war seriously dented the claims of classical music to universal and pacific status. As it took its place in a more nationalist and militarized cultural context, classical music lost some of its claims to transcendent value. Meanwhile, out of the spotlight, an ardent defender of the worth of classical music was developing an elaborate critique of radio's capacity to bring great music to the masses.

ADORNO ON RADIO AND CLASSICAL MUSIC IN THE UNITED STATES

NBC took out a full-page newspaper advertisement in 1940 that referred to the 50 million radio receiving sets in the United States: "NBC provides these listeners with serious and popular music, news and information, drama and education, public forums and

216. Max Jordan to John Royal, May 2, 1939, folder 58, box 94, NBC records, WHS.
217. Max Jordan to Phillips Carlin, October 4, 1938, folder 15, box 61, NBC records, WHS.
218. Kurt Sell to John Royal, October 31, 1938, folder 1, box 69, NBC records, WHS.
219. Folder 1, box 69, NBC records, WHS.

religious services." Under the American system of broadcasting, the advertisement explained, "the finest and most extensive variety of programs to be found anywhere in the world is free to the listening public. *The richest man cannot buy what the poorest man gets free by radio.*"[220] This was the kind of self-justification that so provoked social theorist Theodor Adorno when he arrived in the United States in 1938. He regarded radio music as one of the things that served to "keep dormant critical analyses by listeners of their material social realities." Radio fostered the happy illusion, he wrote, that "the best is just good enough for the man in the street": "the 'broke' farmer is consoled by the radio-instilled belief that Toscanini is playing for him and for him alone, and that an order of things which allows him to hear Toscanini compensates for low market prices for farm products, or that even though he is ploughing under cotton, radio is giving him culture."[221] Adorno had little experience of actual American farmers, but here he astutely identified one of the key legitimating claims of the American broadcasters.

Adorno came to New York in February 1938, to work half-time for both the Princeton Radio Research Project and the transplanted Frankfurt Institut für Sozialforschung. [Figure 3.6.] His work on radio music in the United States in the late 1930s put forward self-consciously heterodox opinions. While much cultural criticism has grown up around Adorno's writings on music, particularly his views of jazz, little of it sets his arguments against the late 1930s American orthodoxies about broadcast classical music and its expected social effects. Adorno's often brilliant, often perverse, readings of American radio's attempts to bring classical music to the masses have long remained partially hidden from view because much of the work was never published. Recent publication has drawn some appropriate attention to this fascinating material, but so far little attempt has been made to contextualize Adorno's radio research within the peculiarities of and tensions within the American system of broadcasting.[222] This is necessary because his waspish attacks centered with some precision on the key legitimatory claims of the American system to be making classical music available to all of the people.

While critics have debated the extent to which Adorno really knew or understood jazz, there can be no doubt that he clearly understood the central elements of radio's civic paradigm. His sharp critiques were targeted accurately at the heart of the self-legitimation of the American broadcasting system—its attempts to create active and opinion-forming individual listeners—and he understood clearly the central role that classical music played in this legitimation. Encountering publicity for NBC's *Music Is My Hobby* that talked of its purpose as "encouraging others to discover the pleasures of self-expression in terms of music," Adorno ridiculed the idea that amateurs could possibly be expressing themselves when "they are only obeying orders that they get from somewhere else." He observed a larger paradox embedded in this program: "The more completely the

220. RCA advertisement, "Radio Answers the Call of Total Defense," *Los Angeles Times*, December 30, 1940: 8.

221. Theodor Adorno, "On a Social Critique of Radio Music," Bureau of Applied Social Research files, paper no. 0076, CRBM: 8.

222. Robert Hullot-Kentor (ed.), *Theodor Adorno: Current of Music—Elements of a Radio Theory* (Cambridge: Polity, 2009).

Figure 3.6. Theodor Adorno in Oxford in 1935. In 1938 he moved to New York to begin work with the Princeton Office of Radio Research. Theodor W. Adorno Archiv, Frankfurt am Main.

listener is subordinated to the arbitrariness of radio institutions, the more they try to make him believe that he expresses himself when he switches on his radio or even when he has got the opportunity of playing before the microphone." Adorno evinced characteristic scorn for the show's attempt to persuade people that classical music "is not so serious as it is supposed to be, but that it is a kind of fun which everyone can have."[223]

Adorno's work with the Princeton Radio Research Project, and his clash of temperament and belief with the project's director Paul Lazarsfeld, have become part of the folklore and tradition of the field of communications research in the United States.[224] Adorno

223. Theodor Adorno, "Some Remarks on a Propaganda Publication of NBC," in Hullot-Kentor (ed.), *Theodor Adorno: Current of Music: Elements of a Radio Theory* (Cambridge: Polity, 2009): 470–72.

224. On the clash, see Rolf Wiggershaus, *The Frankfurt School: Its History, Theories and Political Significance* (Cambridge, MA: MIT Press, 1994): 236–46; David E. Morrison, "*Kultur* and Culture: The Case of Theodor W. Adorno and Paul F. Lazarsfeld," *Social Research* 45, no. 2 (Summer 1978): 331–55; David Jenemann, *Adorno in America* (Minneapolis: University of Minnesota Press, 2007): ch. 2.

insisted that there were close connections between his theoretical work with the Institut für Sozialforschung and his Princeton radio work: "In the theoretical texts that I then wrote for the Institut, I formulated the points of view and experiences which I then wanted to employ in the Radio Project."[225] Lazarsfeld had explicitly invited Adorno to take up a more pessimistic position in relation to radio than other sections of the Princeton project would adopt. He wrote to Adorno in 1937, "I intend to make the musical section the hunting ground for the 'European approach.' By that I mean two things: A more theoretical attitude toward the research problem, and a more pessimistic attitude toward an instrument of technical progress." Adorno took up both these challenges with some alacrity. His most relevant pessimism here was about the survival of individualism—he understood that he lived "in a period where individuals, thoroughly subjected to standardizing influences, seem virtually to become more and more similar to each other."[226] He was clearly less certain how to respond to Lazarsfeld's other request, that he work toward an "empirical research problem" and an "actual execution of the fieldwork."[227]

Paul Lazarsfeld explained in a 1939 funding renewal application to the Rockefeller Foundation why he had chosen music as a special area of study, and why he had sought Adorno's critical perspective for the task. He wrote, "It is obviously undesirable to omit entirely from a study of a privately-owned medium of communication in a democracy the pervasive factor of what such private control does to radio broadcasting and listening." Since "this is a delicate matter," music had been chosen as "the mildest and least explosive area of broadcasting."[228] The broadcasting of music was to serve as a proxy for a study that asked about the compatibility of commercial broadcasting and democracy. This was, as Lazarsfeld correctly observed, an explosive topic in the United States in the 1930s, and a dangerous one for radio researchers likely to be dependent at some point upon industry goodwill for research funds and commissions. Adorno too always insisted on this as the larger context for the music project—that "we live in a society of commodities . . . a society in which production of goods is taking place, not primarily to satisfy human wants and needs, but for profit." Music became a commodity in such a society, susceptible to the general trend toward monopolized mass production of standardized goods.[229]

Adorno felt that much was at stake in his clashes with Lazarsfeld and the empirically based research of the Radio Project. He wanted to produce analyses that described the

225. Theodor W. Adorno, "Scientific Experiences of a European Scholar in America," in Donald Fleming and Bernard Bailyn (eds.), *The Intellectual Migration: Europe and America, 1930–1960* (Cambridge, MA: Harvard University Press, 1969): 341.

226. Theodor Adorno, "Radio Physiognomics," in Hullot-Kentor (ed.), *Theodor Adorno: Current of Music*: 66.

227. Lazarsfeld letter to Adorno, November 29, 1937, cited in Thomas Y. Levin with Michael von der Linn, "Elements of a Radio Theory: Adorno and the Princeton Radio Research Project," *Music Quarterly* 78, no. 2 (Summer 1994): 320.

228. "Proposal for Continuation of Radio Research Project for a Final Three Years at Columbia University", Paul Lazarsfeld papers, box 26, CRBM: 25.

229. Theodor Adorno, "A Social Critique of Radio Music," in Hullot-Kentor (ed.), *Theodor Adorno: Current of Music*: 135.

essence of the experience of music, and how distorted that essence became when radio intervened. But he found at the Project only elaborate investigations into the opinions of listeners. This was in part because the origins of what became the Princeton Radio Research Project lay with psychologists. Hadley Cantril (whose idea the project had been in the first place) and his fellow project directors Frank Stanton and Paul Lazarsfeld had PhDs in psychology and they were interested above all in the subjectivity of radio listeners. Adorno was increasingly dismayed by this emphasis on listener perception and opinion. He found his own analyses simply categorized as "expert opinion": "Obviously it is very difficult in America…to comprehend the notion of the objectivity of anything intellectual. The intellect is unconditionally equated with the subject who bears it."[230] Here Adorno was directly confronting a central tenet of the civic paradigm—that producing listeners with individual and discussable opinions was one of the important goals of radio broadcasting. For Adorno, the corrupting pluralism of American radio's world of opinion and counteropinion had to be kept, at all costs, away from the field of serious music.

One early product of Adorno's radio work was a paper, "On a Social Critique of Radio Music," which he delivered to the Princeton Radio Research Project on October 26, 1939. In it, he tried to explain what a *critical* approach to the study of radio music would look like. He rejected the approach of *administrative* research (as he characterized Lazarsfeld's empirical and audience-focused sociology) as being "moulded according to the ideal of a skilled manipulation of masses."[231] Where administrative research might take as unproblematic the research question of how to bring good music to the masses, a critical approach required the questioning of just what constituted good music and of how the masses actually listened to broadcast music. How did the radio listeners hear a Beethoven symphony? "Is there not a strong likelihood that they listen to it as they would to a Tchaikovsky symphony, that is to say, simply listening to some neat tunes or exciting harmonic stimuli? or do they listen to it as they do to jazz…? Would not such a type of listening make the high cultural ideal of bringing good music to large numbers altogether illusionary?"[232] Adorno was convinced that the democratic program of American broadcast musical appreciation was aesthetically naïve, and that it was inevitably undermined by radio's commercial structure. He doubted that real musical appreciation could be learned over the radio, and he developed an elaborate and ingenious series of arguments to prove it. His extended and excessive critique of NBC's *Music Appreciation Hour* pointedly contrasted "actual musical understanding" with the "mere dissemination of information about music." The *Hour*, he argued, promoted a musical "pseudo-culture" that was barbaric, maudlin, and fetishistic, and encouraged enjoyment "not of the music itself, but *of the awareness that one knows music.*"[233] The program, he complained, promoted "musical Babbittry," and even here "radio, at its 'benevolent' best, in a nation-wide, sustaining program of purely educational character, fails to achieve its aim—namely to

230. Adorno, "Scientific Experiences of a European Scholar in America": 349–50.
231. Adorno, "A Social Critique of Radio Music": 134.
232. Adorno, "A Social Critique of Radio Music": 135.
233. Theodor W. Adorno, "Analytical Study of the NBC Music Appreciation Hour," *Musical Quarterly* 78, no. 2 (Summer 1994): 328, 358.

bring people into an actual life relation with music."[234] Damrosch's program attempted to interest children in music through the "personalities" of the instruments or the mimetic capacities of music or the lives of the composers. "It may suffice to mention," Adorno observed loftily, "that a person who is in a real life relation with music does not like music because as a child he liked to see a flute, then later because music imitated a thunder storm, and finally because he learned to listen to music as music."[235] Adorno had the modernist insistence that it was the "essential structure" of music that mattered, not surface color or effects, or the sound of particular instruments. He regarded the concentration on the sound of particular instruments or on individual themes as part of a fetishizing process, symptom of a "jitterbug attitude" that made music a commodity.[236] Indeed, for Adorno, one of the goals of musical education by radio had to be to explain to children how structurally impoverished popular music was, to demonstrate "step by step, in what sense present-day market music is primitive and undeveloped as against serious music."[237]

The discussion in the workbooks of the *Music Appreciation Hour*, Adorno argued, had a "shrewd propagandistic purpose: the sponsors of the Hour are more interested in convincing the public of the brilliant job they are doing, than they are in the job itself."[238] This pessimistic critique was extended empirically by another Office of Radio Research investigator, Edward Suchman, who in a 1941 article reported that listeners who had been introduced to classical music by radio had a "relative lack of a serious approach toward understanding music." Such listeners tended to be "romantic or emotional," to use music merely "to dream and to forget."[239] Those introduced to serious music by radio, that is, appropriated it into their lives and emotions rather than attempted to respond to it structurally or on its own terms. These arguments, like Adorno's, went to the heart of radio's use of classical music as legitimation and attempts to make of it a popular form of entertainment.

Adorno's views on radio classical music were the obverse of his theories about popular music, which he regarded as, on the contrary, perfectly suited to radio. The force of Adorno's critical case that radio listeners would listen to Beethoven in the same way that they listened to jazz rested on his assertion of the affinities between radio and popular music. The fundamental characteristic of popular music was standardization—because the structure of the whole is "pre-given and pre-accepted," the listener focuses on the detail rather than the structure.[240] But the extent of standardization has to be hidden from listeners, for "unhidden they would provoke resistance." A process of "pseudo-indi-

234. Adorno, "Analytical Study of the NBC Music Appreciation Hour": 326–27.
235. Adorno, "Analytical Study of the NBC Music Appreciation Hour": 328.
236. Adorno, "Analytical Study of the NBC Music Appreciation Hour": 330–31.
237. Adorno, "Analytical Study of the NBC Music Appreciation Hour": 342.
238. Adorno, "Analytical Study of the NBC Music Appreciation Hour": 363.
239. Edward A. Suchman, "Invitation to Music: A Study of the Creation of New Music Listeners by the Radio," in Paul F. Lazarsfeld and Frank N. Stanton (eds.), *Radio Research 1941* (New York: Duell, Sloan and Pearce, 1941): 176.
240. T. W. Adorno with George Simpson, "On Popular Music," *Studies in Philosophy and Social Science* 9 (1941): 17–18.

vidualization" persuades listeners that they have free choice, makes them forget that their music is predigested. So a song needs to be alike enough to other song hits to be recognizable as a type, but to have one distinguishing feature of its own in order to be able to be made into a hit.[241] "Plugging"—the repeated playing of a song on the radio—creates the desire for particular songs, and "leads the listener to become enraptured with the inescapable."[242]

The study of plugging was quite central to Adorno's understanding of the way that popular music worked on radio, for it was his contention that the songs played were so standardized and industrially produced that listeners would find them indistinguishable and quite unmemorable were it not for their "ceaseless repetition" on the air—radio's power as a medium was that it could create intense desire for quite ordinary material. The qualities of the music itself, Adorno insisted, were almost irrelevant: "Provided the music fulfills certain minimum requirements, any given song can be plugged and made a success."[243]

The records of the Princeton Radio Research Project contain discussions of elaborate proposed studies aimed at proving the plugging hypotheses. The typed record of meetings in 1938 of Lazarsfeld with Adorno and G. B. Wiebe includes details of plans for a variety of studies to test the relationship between song quality and success—plugging "bad" songs, testing "good" but unplugged songs on listener panels, testing the predictions of panels of industry experts, and so on. "I think that it would work properly if we could find that something regarded by everyone as very poor can become a success; and that something regarded as very good does not become a success if it is not plugged."[244] Through the discussion came Adorno's blunt assertion, against Lazarsfeld's empirical interest in listener psychology and likes and dislikes, that "this is a matter of recognition and recollection and not dislike and like." There was for Adorno a circular logic compromising the social psychological attempt to understand individual preferences: "The problem is what makes a song a success. A song hit should be defined, for our purposes, as one which the public cannot escape."[245] All hits, Adorno argued, had both an aesthetic component (understood as likes and dislikes) and an advertising component (understood as recognizing and recollection). "One of the new effects of advertisement and propaganda is the fact that one yields to something which is so much stronger than he, not because he likes it, but because he can't escape it."[246]

This argument grew from a theory of fetishization and commodification. Once the plugged song became familiar, its familiarity became a possession for the audience: "The basic principle behind it is that one need only repeat something until it is recognized in order to make it accepted."[247] So the pleasure is derived from both recognition and possession: "The listeners are executing the order to transfer to the music itself their

241. Adorno with Simpson, "On Popular Music": 24.
242. Adorno with Simpson, "On Popular Music": 27.
243. Adorno with Simpson, "On Popular Music": 27.
244. "Results of a Meeting with T. W. A. and G. B. Wiebe," Bureau of Applied Social Research records, B0070 CRBM: 25.
245. "Results of a Meeting with T. W. A. and G. B. Wiebe": 21.
246. "Results of a Meeting with T. W. A. and G. B. Wiebe": 22.
247. Adorno with Simpson, "On Popular Music": 32.

self-congratulation on their ownership."[248] The fetishism inherent in radio music listening meant that in radio there was no direct relationship between the listener and the music, but only "between the listener and some sort of social or economic value which has been attributed either to the music or to its performers."[249]

It was clear that Adorno thought it was "the masses" who were most likely to find in the standardized musical products plugged on the radio a satisfying recreation. The whole sphere of cheap commercial entertainment appealed only to those who needed an escape from mechanized labor, and its very standardization and mechanization "is molded after those psychological attitudes to which their workaday world exclusively habituates them. Popular music is for the masses a perpetual busman's holiday." Popular music induced two kinds of conformity, as it became a "social cement." The first was "rhythmical obedience." Here Adorno noted the similarities between the standardized beat of dance music and that of military marching music. Both suggested "the coordinated battalions of a mechanical collectivity." Adorno indeed constantly suspected connections between radio programming and the military. He noted that in England, program makers were often ex-army officers: "This fact is certainly indicative of their whole attitude. It would be rather interesting to know if similar tendencies can be found in this country." The second mode of conformity he detected was that of emotional release, which he explicitly linked to women's experience of the "pleasure obtained from emotional, erotic music." This release of emotion offered catharsis for the masses, Adorno argued, and was also a way of reconciling listeners to the social order: "Music that permits its listeners the confession of their unhappiness reconciles them, by means of this 'release,' to their social dependence."[250] This gloomy depiction of the audience reception of popular music on the radio provided the building blocks for Adorno's case about what radio did to classical music.

Adorno's radio work-in-progress, his emerging thought on broadcast classical music, was outlined in a 160-page memorandum submitted to the Princeton Radio Research Project in June 1938. Lazarsfeld had asked Adorno to "summarize his ideas" in such a memorandum after criticisms had been made by the other directors of the project of what they had learned of Adorno's work, and by broadcasting industry figures who had encountered Adorno or been interviewed by him.[251] Adorno began by saying that the work was still evolving, that as he learned more about American conditions he was led to reformulate his theoretical approaches—while pointing out that he did not accept that there was a division between theoretical and empirical work.[252] This memo led to open, if cordial, conflict between Adorno and Lazarsfeld.[253]

248. Adorno with Simpson, "On Popular Music": 36.

249. Theodore Wiesengrund-Adorno, "Memorandum: Music in Radio", microfilm copy in Paul Lazarsfeld papers, CRBM: 93.

250. Adorno with Simpson, "On Popular Music": 38–41; Wiesengrund-Adorno, "Memorandum: Music in Radio": 108.

251. Lazarsfeld, "An Episode in the History of Social Research: A Memoir": 323.

252. Wiesengrund-Adorno, "Memorandum: Music in Radio": i.

253. Neither Adorno nor Lazarsfeld was primarily interested in radio for itself. Lazarsfeld saw radio mostly as a convenient (and fundable) subject upon which to develop his interest in research methodologies. On this point, see David Morrison, "The Beginning of Mass Communication Research," *Archives Europeennes de Sociologie* 19, no. 2 (1978): 347.

Adorno was interested in the effects of the capitalist structure of American broadcasting upon radio and saw in radio "a sort of pattern or microcosm containing all the problems, antagonisms, tensions and tendencies which are to be found in the whole of modern society."[254] Little commentary on this subject, he observed, had gone "very much beyond a general statement of the fact that the companies are dependent upon business interests and 'educational tendencies' are considered opposed to these interests." Adorno had a far more socialized view of the matter. He wanted to show, he said, "that the very economic mechanism penetrates radio and, in the last analysis, the listener as well."[255] This was one of the issues that Lazarsfeld took up. In the margin alongside where Adorno wrote of how radio was "full of contradictions and antagonistic tendencies which probably truly reflect contradiction in the social structure as a whole," as the individual members of society became more and more alienated from each other and yet more similar to each other, Lazarsfeld wrote "!!??."[256] Not only was this grander pessimistic social speculation quite outside Lazarsfeld's conception of what radio research ought to be, but it would also certainly have been unwise for him to have associated himself with a mass culture critique so contrary to the individualizing core premise of U.S. radio's civic paradigm.

The research project outlined in Adorno's memorandum was an ambitious one— nothing less than a "social theory of radio music." Most important, Adorno distinguished his interests from those of an empirical sociology that would seek only to discover, for example, who listened to the radio: "It is necessary to discover the extent to which a relation is maintained between the isolated atoms who are the recipients of radio's content on the one hand, and on the other hand, one centralizing principle which directs them even though they are not aware of it."[257] This search for the "one centralizing principle" was at once the most elusive and the most creative aspect to Adorno's radio work, but it also had most to do with placing him at uncomprehending odds with the research-institution building Lazarsfeld. Adorno insisted, for example, that the consciousness of listeners had to be subjected to interpretation, and could not possibly be left as the end point of an investigation into radio—"we must avoid the naive assumption that it is necessary only to examine the listeners in order to get the insight which we hope to gain by our entire study." Listener responses should not be understood as being marked by anything like "spontaneity, freedom and independence." The individual listener had to be understood as "the product of social mechanisms," not as a sovereign individual "influenced" by social factors.[258] When, a little later in the memo, Adorno reiterated that "listeners' reactions cannot be regarded as final sources," Lazarsfeld scribbled in the margin of his copy, "for what?"[259] The question neatly expressed the mutual incomprehension that marked this encounter. What was the something else, Lazarsfeld demanded, of which listener reactions were only an expression? He doubted, I think, that there was any such

254. Wiesengrund-Adorno, "Memorandum: Music in Radio": 2.
255. Wiesengrund-Adorno, "Memorandum: Music in Radio": 6–8.
256. Wiesengrund-Adorno, "Memorandum: Music in Radio": 30.
257. Wiesengrund-Adorno, "Memorandum: Music in Radio": 1.
258. Wiesengrund-Adorno, "Memorandum: Music in Radio": 4.
259. Wiesengrund-Adorno, "Memorandum: Music in Radio": 22.

thing. Looking back, Adorno reiterated this fundamental difference of theoretical orientation: "What was axiomatic according to the prevalent rules of social research, namely, to proceed from the subject's reactions as if they were a primary and final source of sociological knowledge, seemed to me thoroughly superficial and misguided." It remained unproven, Adorno felt, that "one can really proceed from the opinions and reactions of individuals to the social structure and the social essence."[260] This empiricist delusion and its reified methods were for Adorno embodied in "that machine," the Lazarsfeld–Stanton Program Analyzer, which measured the reactions of listeners to radio programs.[261] But Lazarsfeld, dependent upon industry and foundation funding, had to believe—in line with the dominant civic paradigm—that listener opinions were foundational to, if not sovereign in, the broadcasting enterprise. Radio was supposed to help shape articulate, opinionated listeners. The process by which people formed opinions in response to broadcasting was of vital commercial interest to advertisers, and of crucial civic interest to all those concerned about the possibility of a mass-mediated democracy. Lazarsfeld had to treat opinions and opinion formation as important topics in radio research, while for Adorno such opinions were merely epiphenomenal and hence of little interest.

This conflict played out particularly in relation to music. As we have seen, much of radio music appreciation was about opinion formation, and it was reviled by Adorno for just that reason. Music actually had no "content," he argued, and that was why it revealed more clearly the "social and technical mechanisms" of radio when broadcast.[262] Adorno's modernist insistence that the only content of music was its structure, and that ideal listening to broadcast music would consist of following unfolding structure, led him to propose some very prescriptive—and in the context of American radio's mainstream treatment of classical music, subversive—research projects. For example, he imagined a study in which an interviewer would follow a listener's reactions to a whole broadcast symphony. The interviewer would "try to determine how long they are able to concentrate fully; when they get tired; when they begin to produce vague associations instead of following the stream of the music; when they begin to show emotional reactions, when these emotional reactions are confined to the very structure of the music."[263]

The memorandum articulated Adorno's pessimism about the cultural mission of radio music. He argued that although radio had increased the number of people listening to music, it had also brought about a "qualitative decrease of musical taste." It created "depraved music," which was listened to in "'infantile,' sport-like, merely sensual and alienated" fashion.[264] Radio, Adorno insisted, had "completely destroyed" the aura around music as a work of art, completing the work begun by the phonograph. So music on radio sounded not like music itself, but like "information about music."[265] The repetition of great works on radio

260. Adorno, "Scientific Experiences of a European Scholar in America": 343, 345.
261. Adorno, "Scientific Experiences of a European Scholar in America": 347.
262. Wiesengrund-Adorno, "Memorandum—Music in Radio": 3.
263. Wiesengrund-Adorno, "Memorandum: Music in Radio": 6.
264. Wiesengrund-Adorno, "Memorandum: Music in Radio": 12–13.
265. Wiesengrund-Adorno, "Memorandum: Music in Radio": 35.

also had a deteriorating effect—certain works were recorded and broadcast so often "for the sake of profit-making," that they have "definitely lost their meaning."[266]

The loss of aura was compounded by the fact that radio allowed people to listen to music in the mundane surrounds of their homes, perhaps "as a background to console them for their trivial lives."[267] Adorno thought research into the relationship between radio music listening and digestion "deserves special attention": "Do they listen before meals, during meals, or after meals?" Even Lazarsfeld was moved to write "good" against the suggestion that if they listened after meals "this would prove the easing, distracting effect which music attains today."[268] In modern America, "the listener can hear a Beethoven symphony while he shaves or takes a nap."[269] The domestication of great music, and the loss of its concert-hall aura, was for Adorno a serious problem. He blamed radio's repetition of standard works and its ubiquity. Musical works "no longer keep their distance from listeners," they "show instead a tendency to mingle in his everyday life because they can appear at practically any moment, and because he can accompany brushing his teeth with the Allegretto of the Seventh."[270]

Adorno compared radio with the public utilities of gas, water, and electricity, in that the consumer had little control over the production of the service—he had only the power to turn it off. Hence, the "individual is at the mercy of society even within the sphere of his extreme privacy; and that subjectively this dependence causes a perpetual state of fear within him."[271] This isolation and fear was increased by the fact that radio music encouraged people to listen to music alone. While live music was socially integrating, this "power of creating a community is definitely lost by radio transmission." Radio listeners were joined in time but not in space: "The jubilation of the Ninth Symphony is no longer jubilation when men who are declared to be brethren can no longer face each other."[272]

Adorno also articulated a series of technical speculations, about the ways in which radio transmission affected music broadcasting. Radio, he argued, imbued even serious music with the sound qualities ("fundamentally mechanical") of jazz. This new sound quality, common to both radio music and jazz, was responsible for what Adorno called the "regression of listening."[273] Radio stood, he maintained, in the same relation to natural sound as canned food did to fresh food: "People react to jazz and to radio music in approximately the same ways."[274] He remarked in another Project paper that the "astonishing fact about radio is that this fundamental character of triviality appears as a phenomenological characteristic of the technical instrument itself and is not aboriginally connected with any profit-making process."[275] So jazz and radio for Adorno had "a deep

266. Wiesengrund-Adorno, "Memorandum: Music in Radio": 47.

267. Wiesengrund-Adorno, "Memorandum: Music in Radio": 127.

268. Wiesengrund-Adorno, "Memorandum: Music in Radio": 132.

269. Wiesengrund-Adorno, "Memorandum: Music in Radio": 52.

270. Theodor Adorno, "Radio Physiognomies": 91.

271. Wiesengrund-Adorno, "Memorandum: Music in Radio": 17.

272. Wiesengrund-Adorno, "Memorandum: Music in Radio": 28.

273. Wiesengrund-Adorno, "Memorandum: Music in Radio": 25–26.

274. Wiesengrund-Adorno, "Memorandum: Music in Radio": 24.

275. Adorno, "Social and Psychological Aspects of 'The Radio Voice,'" file B0076, Bureau of Applied Social Research collection, CRBM: 2.

affinity." He found some people who preferred hearing their jazz over the radio, while not liking to hear classical music broadcast: "The normal inadequacy of the radio machine, so to speak, comes to the aid of the more mechanical features of jazz."[276] Adorno was careful to distinguish his criticisms of jazz from those of the Nazis—"the argument is not directed against its being discordant or noisy, or vicious or 'negroid,' but only against its being backward, boring, outworn and commodity-like itself."[277]

It was chapter 3 of Adorno's memo on "Reception," that most raised the ire of Lazarsfeld, for it was in this section that Adorno tried to turn his theories into research proposals. Again, it was in part Adorno's determination to read listener reactions as merely symptoms, and symptoms of something to do with the structure of radio itself, and behind that the structure of society, which caused the trouble. He wrote, "Our viewpoint has the principal purpose of trying to trace the attitude of the recipients of radio programs back to the actual radio mechanism to which they are subjected."[278] Adorno talked a good deal about conducting interviews ("About what!" Lazarsfeld scrawled in the margin), despite repeatedly noting his conviction of "the fallaciousness of what people say about music." He noted, "It is very likely that a number of our respondents will be unable to give adequate reasons for liking one thing and disliking another."[279]

In the fourth section of the memo, Adorno displayed most clearly the "more pessimistic attitude" that Lazarsfeld had invited him to develop, arguing bluntly about the "inadequacy of radio reform." Every attempt to change the mechanical nature of radio "would be contradictory to radio itself": "It is fallacious to believe, for example, that a mechanical tool such as radio is at the disposal of human immediacy and spontaneity." Yet this, he wrote, was the basic premise of all the reformist tendencies, this was what made of reform a "pseudo-activity." It was foolish to blame the businessmen who ran the radio industry—it was not their shortcomings but "the character of our society itself" that prevented radio from becoming better. Reform was impossible. Control of broadcasting by the state as in Europe would not help, and "would most probably merely oppress the few elements of productive initiative which are still to be found in America." This bleak assessment ran quite counter to the optimism of the civic paradigm and the hope of funders such as the Rockefeller Foundation that radio's civic function might actually be enhanced and improved—and also to Adorno's own practice, for he was in 1940 working enthusiastically on plans (never realized) for a Sunday afternoon music appreciation program, and on introductory talks for concerts of 20th-century music over New York municipal station WNYC.[280]

The only positive suggestions Adorno had to offer had to do with taking radio completely out of the context in which radio reformers put it. He suggested emancipating radio from the imitation of natural sound.[281] Broadcasting rehearsals rather than concert musical performances would better bring out the construction of the works and "enable

276. Wiesengrund-Adorno, "Memorandum: Music in Radio": 85.
277. Wiesengrund-Adorno, "Memorandum: Music in Radio": 148–49.
278. Wiesengrund-Adorno, "Memorandum: Music in Radio": 99.
279. Wiesengrund-Adorno, "Memorandum: Music in Radio": 101–103.
280. See mentions of this radio work in Christoph Godde and Henri Lonitz (eds.), *Theodor Adorno: Letters to His Parents* (Cambridge: Polity, 2006): 38, 43, 47, 51.
281. Wiesengrund-Adorno, "Memorandum: Music in Radio": 135–36.

the listener to avoid the reified final performance."[282] Or perhaps a new kind of electrically produced music would solve the problem of reproducing sounds on radio, so that music would no longer be broadcast but rather played on the radio "in the same sense that one plays on a violin." This would put an end to the fetish of the original sound or the original work.[283] Adorno thought in fact that listeners had already begun to play their radios in this way, as they twirled the dial in search of novel sounds. Having radio stations broadcast only recordings of music rather than live performances, as Berlin radio had done earlier in the 1930s, could also help. All of this interest in listening as an abstract art was absolutely opposed to the fundamental tenets of American radio's civic paradigm, with its demand for live performance rooted in community.

While Adorno rejected the earnest reformism of the educators, he did, as these examples suggest, have his own almost parodic set of reform plans to rid radio music of some of its commodification and reification. He imagined a program called "They Can Do It As Well," which would feature comparatively unknown players whose performances would prove to be just as capable as those of popular artists. Another program, he thought, might have as its aim to point out "how few great works actually exist" and "that even great artists have worked along a certain pattern, rarely achieving anything really significant."[284] Yet another program might be called "It's All Rubbish" and would aim to demonstrate to listeners that "all 'raised' entertainment music, pseudo-folk music, and jazz is completely standardized and mechanical and is, therefore, ludicrous." The aim would be to make people "ashamed" of listening to jazz. It was important to make clear to people that jazz was not harmless, and to trace the "clearly defined lines leading from the psychology of jazz to the psychology of the pogrom," and similarly the affinity between pseudo-folk music and nationalist ideas, and between "raised" music and "the bad interiorization of the individual."[285] Taking away these kinds of radio entertainment from the people might appear to make them unhappy. But really it would "deprive them of a substitute for that real joy which they may perhaps achieve some day when they have become strong enough to confront their weakness." Indeed, in a world "in which everyone has every reason to be afraid, it is better and more in keeping with reality to have the courage of one's fear and to face them rather than drown them by entertainment of that type."[286]

Previous accounts have stressed the confrontation between Lazarsfeld and Adorno as one between critical theory and empiricism, and the contrasting personalities involved.[287] But as important was Adorno's almost complete inversion of the ideas of the civic paradigm, his extended, elaborate, perverse denial of each of the fundamental ideas that dominated American radio in the 1930s. The more he scorned the possibility of radio as an individualizing technology that aided the development of individual personal opinions,

282. Wiesengrund-Adorno, "Memorandum: Music in Radio": 142.
283. Wiesengrund-Adorno, "Memorandum: Music in Radio": 151.
284. Wiesengrund-Adorno, "Memorandum: Music in Radio": 144.
285. Wiesengrund-Adorno, "Memorandum: Music in Radio": 145–46.
286. Wiesengrund-Adorno, "Memorandum: Music in Radio": 148.
287. Everett M. Rogers, *A History of Communication Study: A Biographical Approach* (New York: Free Press, 1994): 280–83; Morrison, "*Kultur* and Culture": 331–55.

or ridiculed the attempts to bring the experience of classical music listening to the masses, the more he put himself outside the social and political and discursive realm in which American radio then existed.

On April 27, 1938, Lazarsfeld, in a memo to fellow Project directors Hadley Cantril and Frank Stanton, stated that he wished to keep Adorno employed "as long as possible," and asked for "any final discussion" and the "psychological handling" of the matter to "be reserved for me."[288] Lazarsfeld sent a five-page letter to Adorno outlining the reasons for dissatisfaction with his work—while reassuring Adorno that he had "an unchanging respect" for his ideas. The letter, he wrote, had cost him "two solid working days." At first he had thought that the "grave shortcomings" of Adorno's "Memorandum Music in Radio" were to be explained by his "difficulties of initial adaptation." But, Lazarsfeld wrote, he had come to perceive in Adorno a kind of intellectual arrogance: "You think," he wrote, "because you are basically right somewhere you are right everywhere." The music memo, Lazarsfeld stated, was "definitely below the standards of intellectual clean-liness, discipline and responsibility which have to be requested from any one active in academic work." He was particularly offended by references to "the usual" experimental methods. "It happens," he wrote, "that the word 'usual' cannot possibly have any sense," because the experimental methods used by different psychologists and sociologists are so utterly different. The offence was to Lazarsfeld's sense of himself as a pioneer in relatively uncharted territory, in a field in which methods had not yet hardened into orthodoxy. Lazarsfeld accused Adorno of being too easily satisfied with an insulting remark "without considering other insulting possibilities": "You express a theory that the broadcasting officials who decide on programs pick out so low-grade programs because they are as bad taste as the broad markets have. Could it not be that those officials are not morons but scoundrels who corrupt the masses against their better knowledge? (How many radio officials listen to their own programs in private life?)" But most insistently, Lazarsfeld pointed to passages in Adorno's memo in which it was clear that he had not formulated any empirical procedure for checking his assumptions, in which he spoke of a theory to be "ascertained" rather than "ascertained or disproved," passages indeed that, Lazarsfeld wrote, lead "to the suspicion that you don't even know how an empirical check upon a hypothetical assumption is to be made." It was not enough to propose a study without stating how it might be carried out—it almost seemed that "you would consider it empirical research if someone would say: 'Let's make a study whether there are human beings living on other planets.'" Lazarsfeld concluded by assuring Adorno of his "unwavering respect, friendship and loyalty."[289]

In January 1940, John Marshall of the Rockefeller Foundation recommended during a foundation meeting that no further funding provision be made for Adorno's music study. Lazarsfeld protested, and Marshall reconsidered but confirmed his conclusion. He recognized, he said, the originality of the work, but the real issue was utility. Adorno's critique would need to be supplemented by a "positive statement of what Adorno believes can be done for music through broadcasting." Yet the tone of Adorno's work to date cast

288. Memo Lazarsfeld to Cantril and Stanton April 27, 1938, box 25, Lazarsfeld papers, CRBM.
289. Letter from Lazarsfeld to Adorno, n.d., folder 19, box 25, Lazarsfeld papers, CRBM.

doubt on whether he would be able to provide such a positive statement or collaborate with someone who could: "He seems psychologically engaged at the moment by his ability to recognize deficiencies in the broadcasting of music to an extent that makes questionable his own drive to find ways of remedying them."[290]

In the summer of 1940, Adorno left the Radio Project, and in 1941 he moved to Los Angeles, where he spent the next four years collaborating with Max Horkheimer on the work that would become *The Dialectic of Enlightenment*. His fall from grace at the Radio Research Project was evidence that articulate dissent from the civic paradigm was not easily publicly spoken. The whole institution of broadcasting was premised upon the truth of the tenets of the civic paradigm, preeminent amongst them that broadcast classical music was a socially transcendent and individualizing and morally improving entity. Adorno's brilliant, stubborn contestation of each of those assumptions was to be largely hidden from view for another generation. The awkwardness and hostility that surrounded his attempted intervention in American public discussion of the social and cultural effects of broadcast classical music was symptomatic of the fragility of the whole apparatus of commercial public service broadcasting in the United States.

ELITE MUSIC AFTER ALL

The proportion of popular music on American radio increased "fairly steadily" from 1933. Popular music was 60% of all music broadcast on NBC in 1932 but about 75% by 1941.[291] The broadcasters were both responding to and creating popular taste. When Robert and Helen Lynd returned to Muncie, Indiana, in the mid-1930s, they found that the inhabitants overwhelmingly preferred popular music on their radios.[292] By 1932, sales of classical sheet music and registration of classical music copyrights were at a low ebb, and composer and publisher William Arms Fisher attributed the decline to both the Depression and radio.[293] Popular music was also increasing as a proportion of the broadcast day—the 1938 FCC monopoly study found that nationally about 40% of airtime was devoted to it. The beginnings of the retreat of classical music to being simply a product for a niche audience were evident by the late 1930s.

Signs of decline appeared even at the height of the golden age of mainstream classical music broadcasting. There were many listeners, but in the end not enough to make classical music broadcasting competitive in the marketplace. Its privileged position remained vulnerable, because it was so clearly an artifact of the regulatory regime. Worse news was that the classical audience continued to be found mostly amongst an already privileged minority. It remained evident to all who investigated the question that the audience for classical music was significantly wealthier and better educated than average. The defeat of the highest ambitions of the advocates of broadcast classical music was

290. "Discussion of the Columbia University Request," January 5, 1940, folder 3243, box 272, Series 200R Record Group 1.1. Rockefeller Foundation Archives, RAC.

291. Peatman, "Radio and Popular Music": 337.

292. Robert S. Lynd and Helen Merrell Lynd, *Middletown in Transition* (New York: Harcourt, Brace, 1937).

293. "Denies Interest in Music Is Lagging," *New York Times*, June 8, 1932: 22.

evident in arguments that classical music deserved its place in the station schedule because it delivered a wealthy and attentive audience to advertisers. Walter Damrosch argued, "The class of listener devoted to music of the higher order listens to a program from beginning to end."[294] While the networks talked the civic and democratic language of the musical missionaries, individual stations courting advertisers were more likely to emphasize the elite social demographics of the classical music audience. *Variety* noted frankly that the turn to classical music programming in 1934 was part of an attempt to "find an audience among those richer listeners who for two years had evidenced a diminished interest in radio."[295] Los Angeles station KECA stated in publicity in 1936 that its classical broadcasts attracted an audience of "the most solid and responsible elements of the community" who would be "whole-heartedly in favor of dignified, intelligent broadcasting of fine things."[296]

The seeds of the dominant postwar association of classical radio and affluence, the love of "fine things," were thus already being sown. Evidence was also mounting that broadcast classical music was not reaching the masses in the numbers for which the optimists had hoped. NBC vice president John Royal had assured the FCC monopoly inquiry in 1938 that "a man's appreciation of music isn't based on his economic income or intellectual capacity."[297] But the networks' own research told them that the democratic cultural aspiration of the broadcast classical music enthusiasts was very far from being realized in the United States. It was becoming more and more difficult to uphold the view that radio classical music was to be an agent of social and cultural transformation on a historically significant scale. The heartland of classical music appreciation remained in the homes of the wealthy and the educated.

Subsequent research pointed out quite bluntly that classical was consistently the least popular category of music when Americans were asked what they liked, and that popular music was steadily becoming more popular. Paul Lazarsfeld reported on figures in 1939 which showed professed interest in broadcast classical music falling significantly with each step down a three-tiered measure of economic status.[298] A large 1945 survey by the National Opinion Research Center found that while 62% of college-educated people who lived in cities of over 100,000 liked to hear classical music on the radio, that figure dropped to 12% for people who were both rural and less-educated.[299] Even *Fortune*'s very positive 1939 survey had found that the audience for classical music clustered on the coasts, in cities of over a million, and amongst the wealthy.[300] In 1939, published work from NBC's research manager Hugh Beville confirmed that actually, as Lazarsfeld summarized it, "good music was the monopoly of the upper income classes."[301]

294. "Damrosch Defends Classics," *New York Times,* October 10, 1934: 23.

295. Edgar A. Grunwald, "Program Production History 1929–1937," *Variety Radio Directory 1937–1938*: 24.

296. KECA program 1, no. 9 (January 1936), quoted in Marcus, *Musical Metropolis*: 153.

297. FCC Chain Broadcasting inquiry, docket 5060: 477, box 1400, Series 120A, RG 173, NACP.

298. Paul Lazarsfeld, "Interchangeability of Indices in the Measurement of Economic Influences," *Journal of Applied Psychology* 23, no.1 (1939): 40.

299. Lazarsfeld, *The People Look at Radio*: 47.

300. "Toscanini on the Air," *Fortune* 27, no. 1 (January 1938): 63.

301. Paul Lazarsfeld, "Foreword," in H. M. Beville, *Social Stratification of the Radio Audience* (Princeton: Office of Radio Research, 1939): v.

Even more gloomily, NBC research showed that internationally, the more classical music that was broadcast in a nation, the fewer people even bothered to acquire a radio set. Beville produced some charts for the FCC's 1938 monopoly inquiry that correlated the percentage of time devoted to dance music and serious music with levels of radio ownership in six European countries and the United States. He explained that he had found a "very close correlation": "As the percentage of ownership of radios decreases, there is a decrease in the percent of dance music," and, conversely, there was "a general pattern of increase in serious music with the decrease in the percentage of radio set ownership."[302] It is testament to the magic legitimatory power that the networks saw in classical music that, knowing this, they still invested so heavily in it.

POSTLUDE

Even with the postwar formula of associating broadcast classical music with affluent consumption, it has not been easy to make a commercial success of classical music radio in the United States. One study dates the beginning of the steep decline in classical music broadcasting to 1942—thereafter the total number of classical programs was declining, as was the proportion that were commercially sponsored.[303] In 1951, David Randolph from New York municipal station WNYC lamented the decline of serious music on American radio: "We are going down hill quite rapidly":

> Do you remember the CBS symphony orchestra? And do you recall the series of programs called "Invitation to Music" that CBS used to broadcast on Wednesday evenings? And do you remember the Thursday night symphonic programs that NBC used to have? And do you remember the ABC symphony orchestra programs, that took place on Saturday afternoons...and the Boston symphony broadcasts on Tuesday evenings? Well, as you think of those programs may I suggest that you doff your hat, and observe a respectful silence, because you are thinking of ghosts. Not one of them exists any more!

Randolph complained that radio provided its listeners with "practically nothing but hillbilly music." He regarded the decline as inevitable, an irreversible response to the small audience and high cost of broadcast classical music.[304] Already, by the beginning of the 1950s, the recent extensive presence of classical music on the American commercial radio networks was seeming a puzzle. How could commercially astute, market-sensitive broadcasters have given so much airtime and prominence to what was so clearly a minority form of entertainment? The strength of radio's civic paradigm was already a fading memory.

The formation of National Public Radio in 1970 was one of the factors diminishing the likelihood that classical music would be found on commercial stations. By the end of the 20th century, it was estimated that only 1.5% of the radio audience listened to any

---

302. FCC Chain Broadcasting inquiry, docket 5060: 380, box 1400, Series 120A, RG 173, NACP.
303. Heistad, "Radio without Sponsors": 180.
304. David Randolph, "Lewisohn Intermission Talk," *Music Educators Journal* 38, no. 2 (1951): 48.

classical music at all.[305] The number of commercial classical stations in the United States slowly declined—by 2003, there were 32, down from 50 in 1990.[306] Then, even these remaining commercial classical stations began to go—shedding either their classical music format or their commercial status. Washington DC's WGMS, Classical 104.1, closed down in 2007; that year Los Angeles commercial classical station K-Mozart switched format to become "Go Country 105"; WQXR in New York was taken over by municipal station WNYC in 2009. Some of the remaining commercial classical stations survived by switching to a listener-supported, public radio model, but by the 1990s classical programming was declining even on public radio. Mindful of station revenues, conscious of their civic role in times of national and international crisis, public radio stations shifted time toward the popular talk and news programs produced by NPR, at the expense of local classical programming. The classical music radio audience was found to be both aging and declining in size, and NPR stations needed to attract new generations of listeners.

Once classical music became defined as a minority entertainment with a particular demographic, the logic behind its shrinking share of the airwaves was inexorable. "Classical owners have to consider how much money this format, with its bias, will be worth in a given market," warned the owner of a successful Seattle classical station in 1996.[307] Classical music on commercial radio now represented simply a small niche market, viable in only a few of the more culturally diverse American cities. The classical audience was understood to be older, wealthy, and white, and the possibilities of audience growth among young people minimal. So toxic has classical music been perceived to have become to many young people, that it has been used in several cities internationally in recent years to deter loitering in public parks and rail stations.[308] In West Palm Beach in 2005, in an area notorious for drug dealing, police began blasting classical music from the roof of a building: "The officers were amazed when at 10 o'clock at night there was not a soul on the corner. We talked to people on the street, and they said, 'We don't like that kind of music.'"[309]

It is important to realize how recent a development is this pervasive sense not only that classical music belongs to older, wealthier, white people, but that it would be obnoxious to others—a further reminder of how surprisingly discontinuous the recent history of classical music has been. A search for newspaper articles using the words "classical

305. Leon Botstein, "Music of a Century: Museum Culture and the Politics of Subsidy," in Nicholas Cook and Anthony Pople (eds.), *The Cambridge History of Twentieth Century Music* (Cambridge: Cambridge University Press, 2004): 41.

306. Michael Markowitz, "The Slow Death of Classical Music," *Media Life*, June 21, 2002. Available: http://www.medialifemagazine.com/news2002/jun02/jun17/5_fri/news3friday.html. [January 27, 2010]; Daniel J. Wakin, "In Shadow of Texas Oil Derricks, Fighting to Keep Brahms on the Air," *New York Times*, June 26, 2006: A1; Pierre Ruhe, "Classical Stations Face the Music," *Atlanta Journal-Constitution*, September 7, 2003: M1.

307. Stacy Lu, "Roll Over, Pearl Jam, Classical Radio Lives," *New York Times*, May 6, 1996: D7.

308. "Roll Over Beethoven," *Hartford Courant*, June 4, 2006: 1.

309. Scott Timberg, "Classical Music as Crime Stopper," *Free New Mexican*, February 16, 2005. Available: http://www.freenewmexican.com/artsfeatures/10701.html. [August 7, 2008].

music" and "demographic" reveals nothing before the 1970s, but thereafter a rising tide of gloomy commentary on the ways in which classical music was coming to be understood as the music of age and privilege and cultural status. Classical music increasingly became in the decades after World War II a clear marker of class and taste—the "only regularly recognizable class distinction," Allan Bloom asserted in the 1980s, "between educated and uneducated in America."[310]

By the end of the 20th century, even that apparently stable equation had begun to crack. Sociologists pointed to a profound generational shift in the attribution of cultural value. "The Depression and World War II babies have always been and remain enthusiastic about the arts," noted sociologist Richard A. Peterson, but younger generations prize cultural omnivores more than close-minded high culture devotees.[311] It was partly radio that had produced a different orientation to high culture in general and classical music in particular in the earlier generation. The perceived social role of broadcast classical music as a free cultural good, a kind of cultural capital give away, was diminishing.

The overall reduction in radio airtime devoted to classical music is one cause of what is so often now perceived to be a general decline in the institutions of and audiences for classical music in America. This perception is reflected in book titles such as *Classical Music in America: A History of Its Rise and Fall* and *No Vivaldi in the Garage: A Requiem for Classical Music in North America*.[312] In these jeremiads, the beginning of the decline in the audience for classical music is most often dated to the late 1950s and early 1960s.[313] The evidence for decline since that period is impressive—diminishing sales of classical recordings, aging concert audiences, shrinking radio presence. Botstein neatly sums up the historical paradox: "Despite striking developments in the transmission of music by electronic means throughout the twentieth century (thereby ensuring music's wide accessibility), classical music moved to the periphery of culture and politics."[314] Few Americans now would believe that world peace, or significantly greater tolerance and understanding, would result from increased levels of classical music appreciation in the population.

One sign of the loss of aura surrounding broadcast classical music is its marketing as background rather than foreground listening, something to accompany other activities, mood music—the very kind of listening that was anathema to 1930s broadcast music enthusiasts and, of course, to Adorno. The few remaining classical commercial stations in the United States today sometimes adopt a lifestyle focus, promoting the ways in which their music can helpfully or restfully accompany other important activities. Until it closed in 2007, WGMS in Washington DC played "the great music that helps your day go better." San Francisco's Classical 102.1 ("casual—comfortable—classical") marketed itself as a mood-matching soundtrack to busy lives—"KDFC is the perfect companion." At

310. Allan Bloom, *The Closing of the American Mind* (New York: Simon and Schuster, 1987): 69.

311. Judith Miller, "As Patrons Age, Future of Arts Is Uncertain," *New York Times,* February 12, 1996: A1.

312. Horowitz, *Classical Music in America*; Sheldon Morgenstern, *No Vivaldi in the Garage: A Requiem for Classical Music in North America* (Boston: Northeastern University Press, 2001).

313. Botstein, "Music of a Century": 41.

314. Botstein, "Music of a Century": 40.

drive time, the music's role was to soothe and distract: "Music that moves you—even when you're stuck in traffic." Plenty of classical music purists objected to such programming strategies, the reduction of what they regarded as serious music to mood enhancement. When music is everywhere, Daniel Barenboim complained, "You create the conditions for being oblivious to music. If you are oblivious to a Beethoven symphony in an airport or in a store, you will also be oblivious to it when you go to the concert hall."[315] Such complaints belong to a long tradition. Broadcast radio had also brought with it the possibility that people would listen inattentively or disrespectfully. It was in 1936 that Muzak introduced its standardized formatted music, targeted to moods appropriate at each time of the day.[316] Mixed with the euphoria about great music at last being available to everyone were always fears—such as Adorno's—about its degradation in the process.

Radio's civic paradigm was never more clearly visible than in the sphere of classical music broadcasting. But we have almost forgotten why it was that talk of classical music was intrinsic to almost all attempts to define broadcasting "in the public interest" before World War II. The democratic and cosmopolitan high hopes that surrounded the advent of broadcasting of the classical tradition have not been well recalled, nor the relationship of state regulation to the often-impressive classical broadcasting activity of the era.

315. "Stuart Wavell Talks to Daniel Barenboim," *Sunday Times*, April 9, 2006. Available: http://www.timesonline.co.uk/tol/news/article703370.ece. [January 27, 2010].

316. Joseph Lanza, *Elevator Music* (New York: St. Martins Press, 1994): 41–42.

4

Democratic Radio

Before the advent of the broadcaster, parts of the South, it is said, never heard a Republican speech and remote counties in the West never heard a Democrat. Adherents of one creed never listened to the preachers of another nor the creedless to any sort of religious teaching. Farmers had no daily market reports and neither they nor city folk had overheard discussions on the problems of the others. Do these exchanges make for partisanship, for religious tolerance, for community of interest, or the reverse?

Anne O'Hare McCormick, *New York Times April 3, 1932*[1]

Journalist Anne O'Hare McCormick formulated this perceptive and prescient question about radio and civic life in 1932. When educated Americans worried about radio and democracy in the 1930s, this was so often the question that concerned them—would exposure via radio to multiple opinions enhance tolerance or simply reinforce existing partisan views? Much optimism about radio had to do with civic paradigm expectations that enhanced understandings and empathies would arise from new exposure to other points of view. Many Americans read newspapers that had a clear point of view.[2] The regulation of U.S. radio was, as we have seen, built upon expectations that it would provide the opposite, "ample play for the free and fair competition of opposing views."[3] This pluralist promise was one of the things that most excited democratic reformers about radio. Today the Internet has again created the possibility that many Americans will be getting their public affairs "filtered" in such a way that they will rarely be exposed to disagreeable views. Sunstein has recently reasserted optimism about exposure to diversity. "People should be exposed to materials they would not have chosen in advance," he insists, with 1930s civic paradigm like certainty. "Unanticipated encounters, involving topics and points of view we have not sought out and perhaps find irritating, are central to democracy and even to freedom itself."[4] Offering a new critique of the newest

1. Anne O'Hare McCormick, "Radio's Audience: Huge, Unprecedented," *New York Times*, April 3, 1932: SM4.

2. Michael Schudson, *Discovering the News: A Social History of American Newspapers* (New York: Basic Books, 1978).

3. *Third Annual Report of the Federal Radio Commission* (Washington DC: United States Government Printing Office, 1929): 32–34; "In Re Docket 4758," *Federal Communications Commission Reports* 6 (Washington DC: U.S. Government Printing Office, 1940): 372.

4. Cass Sunstein, "Democracy and Filtering," *Communications of the ACM* 47, no. 12 (December 2004): 57.

medium, Sunstein was also reiterating with uncanny fidelity the message of those 1930s civic paradigm reformers who saw in the narrow input pipe of broadcasting—that only a small representative selection of voices could speak on the air and so any given individual would necessarily hear things with which they did not agree—an instrument of mass socialization into cosmopolitan tolerance.

One of the characteristic recurring tensions of American radio was between the commercial imperative to offend no one and this civic paradigm emphasis on exposing people to multiple perspectives. After comedian Ben Bernie upset many listeners in 1935 with a parody of the Gettysburg Address, *Advertising Age* reminded advertisers and broadcasters that "program material should be prepared so that it will be absolutely certain not to run counter to the prejudices and predilections of various groups in the audience."[5] The civic paradigm tugged broadcasters in exactly the opposite direction—positively to seek out diverse perspectives that would almost certainly be alien and disagreeable to some part of their audience. But more fundamentally, the restless, critical, and self-critical ethos of the civic paradigm could itself be offensive to some listeners. One North Dakota listener heard the Bernie parody as but further confirmation of Jewish control of radio: "Men like this should be barred from the air.... Such things never emanate from anyone but a Jew."[6] Those Americans who distrusted cosmopolitanism and cultural pluralism all too commonly found in populist anti-Semitism a ready-made explanation for what troubled them.

Radio came along in the 1920s at a time of considerable debate in the United States about the very possibility of modern mass democracy. Mass communication stimulated a new set of democratic hopes, dreams of the new technology provoking historically unprecedented levels of civic awareness and engagement. When radio histories note the utopian hopes that early radio briefly sustained, however, they usually move rapidly on to an account of golden age radio's domination by commercial entertainment; we have little detailed history of the democratic aspirations and programs of American radio in its golden age.

One of radio's democratic promises was that it might help solve the problem of political ignorance and disengagement and consequent low voter turnout.[7] Optimists expressed the hope that politics in the broadcast era might become more rational, because while live demagogues could sway a crowd, a calm listener at home would be less susceptible to emotional suasion. "Even the most average of average Americans is a more critical listener when he is not part of a mass meeting," maintained University of Wisconsin president Glenn Frank.[8] Radio listeners were "not affected by the contagion of the gathered mob," asserted the ACLU's Arthur Garfield Hays.[9]

Roosevelt's fireside chats were exemplars of the new form of intimate, calm public address that radio had made possible. But were they evidence that radio was fostering a

---

5. "Don't Monkey with the Buzz-Saw," *Advertising Age* 6, no. 26 (July 1, 1935): 10.

6. Letter to James G. Harbord, June 4, 1935, folder 35, box 34, NBC records, WHS.

7. On concerns about civic disengagement and low voter turnout, see Michael McGerr, *The Decline of Popular Politics: The American North 1865–1928* (New York: Oxford University Press, 1986).

8. Glenn Frank, "Radio as an Educational Force," *Annals of the American Academy of Political and Social Science* 177 (January 1935): 120.

9. Arthur Garfield Hays, "Civic Discussion over the Air," *Annals of the American Academy of Political and Social Science* 213, no. 1 (January 1941): 39.

more rational public discourse, or more insidiously a new form of avuncular propaganda that skillfully used radio's intimacy to political advantage? Loviglio sees the audience for the chats as a self-conscious public, one that "sought to participate in a new sense of public life by working to define who and what that public encompassed."[10] Lenthall more pessimistically argues that the radio chat was a one-way form of communication that enabled ordinary people to "imagine" that they "belonged to a shared and familiar political community," but that actually made political participation a "more private and passive matter."[11]

This is an important debate. But today the fireside chats are almost all that has been remembered of what was a much broader set of thoughtful and sustained 1930s attempts to use radio in a democratic manner. Arguing about the chats in isolation can divert attention from the great variety of other 1930s efforts to use radio to foster active democratic citizenship. None of those who thought seriously about radio and democracy in the 1930s concluded that radio addresses by elected leaders constituted the only or even the most important, democratic role of the medium. Whatever else we can say about 1930s radio and democracy activists, they cannot be accused of resting content with the creation of audiences rather than publics for broadcast discussions of public affairs. What we *should* remember are their strenuous attempts to use radio to make critical, opinionated, rational, and tolerant citizens in a newly permeable public sphere. Inevitably, golden age radio's democratic aspirations were not fully realized, but too quick or summary a judgment along those lines can obscure some of the things we can still learn from this past. In many ways the reflective practice of those who led the democratic radio movement remains a corrective to some of the simpler technology-inspired hopes for electronic democracy of more recent decades.

THE DEWEYAN MOMENT

The 1930s advocates of democratic radio were influenced by the contemporary ideals of progressive education. For the Deweyans, there was no clear line between educational and democratic work—one of the functions of education was to prepare for life in a democracy, while participation in the public life of a democracy was itself understood to be educational. A distinctive Deweyan legacy was passed down to radio and democracy activists through a chain of personal influence—one consequence of the fact that, in the United States, radio reformers united under the banner of radio and education, and conceived of radio's democratic task as primarily educational in nature. A strong belief in the educational value of the kind of public discussion that exposed individuals to different points of view, and exhortations to form individual opinions and discuss them with others, were absolutely central to these educative efforts. Radio was to teach by example, modeling reasoned, tolerant, pluralist discussion of public affairs.

The now classic 1920s debate between John Dewey and Walter Lippmann about the very possibility of modern mass democracy lies in the background of the story of radio's

10. Jason Loviglio, *Radio's Intimate Public: Network Broadcasting and Mass-Mediated Democracy* (Minneapolis: University of Minnesota Press, 2005): 27.

11. Bruce Lenthall, *Radio's America: The Great Depression and the Rise of Modern Mass Culture* (Chicago: University of Chicago Press, 2007): 85–87.

democratic experiments in the 1930s. Lippmann in his 1922 *Public Opinion* set high the bar of knowledge and expertise needed to govern a modern society, and concluded that the public could not possibly possess the necessary ranges of skills and competences: "Every one of us is an outsider to all but a few aspects of modern life, has neither time, nor attention, nor interest, nor the equipment for specific judgment. It is on the men inside, working under conditions that are sound, that the daily administrations of society must rest."[12] Democratic self-government had arisen, he argued, in simple self-contained communities, in which citizens were interchangeably competent. There were now serious questions, Lippmann contended, about how such a system of government could work in an ethically diverse, mass-mediated society in which "the common interests very largely elude public opinion entirely, and can be managed only by a specialized class whose personal interests reach beyond the locality."[13]

In *The Phantom Public* (1925), Lippmann argued that the root of the problem was a wrong way of thinking about citizens and their capacities. The civics textbooks provided no guidance to the citizen on just how, "while he is earning a living, rearing children and enjoying his life, he is to keep himself informed about this swarming confusion of problems."[14] Writing so early in the radio era, Lippmann already perceived radio as a contributor to civic helplessness:

> And if by some development of the radio every man could see and hear all that was happening everywhere, if publicity in other words became absolute, how much time could or would he spend watching the Sinking Fund Commission and the Geological Survey? He would probably tune in on the Prince of Wales, or, in desperation, throw off the switch and seek peace in ignorance.

Radio, Lippmann thus predicted, would simply compound existing information overload, creating conditions in which people were "condemned to live under a barrage of eclectic information," their minds the "receptacle for a hullabaloo of speeches, arguments and unrelated episodes."[15]

John Dewey replied in his 1927 *The Public and Its Problems*, reasserting the possibility of a participatory and deliberative democracy.[16] Dewey denied that the expertise of individuals would now have to replace the opinions of the public because "in fact"—here is the central and radical claim—"knowledge is a function of association and communication."[17] The essential need of modern democratic life was for "the improvement of the conditions of debate, discussion and persuasion."[18] Most famously, democracy

---

12. Walter Lippmann, *Public Opinion* (New York: Harcourt, Brace, 1922): 400.
13. Lippmann, *Public Opinion*: 310.
14. Walter Lippmann, *The Phantom Public* (New York: Macmillan, 1927): 14.
15. Lippmann, *The Phantom Public*: 33–34.
16. Westbrook contends that Dewey chose to address the "democratic realist with whom he had the greatest affinity." Robert B. Westbrook, *John Dewey and American Democracy* (Ithaca: Cornell University Press, 1991): 294.
17. Dewey, *The Public and Its Problems*: 158.
18. Dewey, *The Public and Its Problems*: 208.

"will have its consummation when free social inquiry is indissolubly wedded to the art of full and moving communication."[19] Dewey thus expressed his considerable optimism about communications technologies, arguing that the "physical tools of communication" could enable the transformation of the Great Society into the Great Community.[20] There was, of course, a great challenge ahead—"a subtle, delicate, vivid and responsive art of communication must take possession of the physical machinery of transmission and circulation and breathe life into it."[21] Only then would it be possible for "remote and indirect" associations to revivify local community. For Dewey, communal life needed to be local (as in his affirmation that "the local is the ultimate universal, and as near an absolute as exists") but not isolated—and radio could be one of the means for achieving that desirable equilibrium.[22]

Dewey's other writings on mass media and the public sphere have been less noticed than *The Public and Its Problems*. In his 1930 *Individualism Old and New*, Dewey surveyed the ways that "radio, the movies, the motor car, all make for a common and aggregate mental and emotional life."[23] He wrote at length of the standardizing threats posed to individualism by the new corporate forms of life, the mass media, and propaganda: "We live exposed to the greatest flood of mass suggestion that any people has ever experienced."[24] Like many of his contemporaries, Dewey worried that propaganda might destroy democracy: "Democracy will be a farce unless individuals are trained to think for themselves, to judge independently, to be critical, to be able to detect subtle propaganda and the motives which inspire it."[25] But in the 1930 book too, Dewey answered his own concerns with the reassurance that media-induced conformity would be both shallow and temporary: "All agreement of thought obtained by external means, by repression and intimidation, however subtle, and by calculated propaganda and publicity, is of necessity superficial; and whatever is superficial is in continual flux." He reflected that perhaps his own irritation at such terms as "radio-conscious" and "air-minded" testified to a "half-conscious sense of the external ways in which our minds are formed and swayed and of the superficiality and inconsistency of the result."[26] But could radio also help produce something more deeply grounded, a new and stronger form of individualism?

In *Individualism Old and New*, Dewey again defined modern individualism as the product of association and communication, not as its victim: "The particular interactions that compose a human society include the give and take of participation, of a sharing that increases, that expands and deepens, the capacity and significance of the interacting factors. In contrast, "Conformity is a name for the absence of vital interplay;

19. Dewey, *The Public and Its Problems*: 184.
20. Dewey, *The Public and Its Problems*: 142.
21. Dewey, *The Public and Its Problems*: 184.
22. Dewey, *The Public and Its Problems*: 213–16.
23. John Dewey, "Individualism Old and New," in Jo Ann Boydston (ed.), *The Later Works of John Dewey 1925–1953* Volume 5, *Essays 1929–30* (Carbondale: Southern Illinois University Press, 1990): 61.
24. Dewey, *Individualism Old and New*: 61.
25. John Dewey, "American Education Past and Future," in Jo Ann Boydston (ed.), *The Later Works of John Dewey 1925–1953 Volume 6* (Carbondale: Southern Illinois University Press, 1990): 97–98.
26. John Dewey, *Individualism Old and New*: 82.

the arrest and benumbing of communication."[27] The new individualism would be "achieved only through the controlled use of all the resources of the science and technology that have mastered the physical forces of nature."[28] The language here is significant—the new individualism will be "achieved" with technological assistance; it will have to be produced and will not be a naturally occurring phenomenon. It was on Dewey's account possible for radio to be one of the means of producing this "new individualism, consonant with the realities of the present age," but it would take effort and activity on the part of each member of the audience.[29] Dewey insisted, "The radio will make for standardization and regimentation only as long as individuals refuse to exercise the selective reaction that is theirs."[30] The implication was clear—self-conscious "selective reaction" to broadcast opinion, the formation of an opinionated self, was a civic responsibility shared by all.

Dewey hailed radio in 1934 as "the most powerful instrument of social education the world has ever seen," a "means for exchange of knowledge and ideas" that held the prospect of a contribution to "the formation of that enlightened and fair-minded public opinion and sentiment that are necessary for the success of democracy."[31] These specific Deweyan hopes for radio's public sphere were highly influential in the United States, amongst radio reformers and "educational" broadcasters alike. Dewey continued through the 1930s his insistence on public discussion as the enabler of democracy, which was one of the things that made his social thought so particularly relevant to those charged with thinking about radio's civic and educational roles. He reiterated that "the open air of public discussion and communication" was an "indispensable condition of the birth of ideas and knowledge," and that genuine tolerance could only arise in discussion.[32] His *Ethics* asserted that "toleration is thus not just an attitude of good-humored indifference. It is positive willingness to permit reflection and inquiry to go on in the faith that the truly right will be rendered more secure through questioning and discussion, while things which have endured merely from custom will be amended or done away with."[33] This principle of active, critical tolerance needs to be understood in the context of Dewey's belief that the modern world was in a condition of continual change, in which no fixed or transcendent values could endure, and "social and moral existences are, like physical existences, in a state of continuous if obscure change." A true philosophy of experience, he argued, "will make no attempt to set fixed limits to the extent of changes that are to occur. For the futile effort to achieve security and anchorage in something fixed, it will substitute the effort to determine the character of changes that are going on and to give

27. John Dewey, *Individualism Old and New*: 82.

28. John Dewey, *Individualism Old and New*: 86.

29. John Dewey, *Individualism Old and New*: 88.

30. John Dewey, *Individualism Old and New*: 116.

31. John Dewey, "Radio's Influence on the Mind" (1934), in Jo Ann Boydston (ed.), *The Later Works of John Dewey 1925–1953 Volume 9* (Carbondale: Southern Illinois University Press, 1990): 309.

32. John Dewey, "Philosophies of Freedom," in Jo Ann Boydston (ed.), *The Later Works of John Dewey. 1927–1928 Volume 3* (Carbondale: Southern Illinois University Press, 1990): 113.

33. John Dewey, "re *Ethics*," in Jo Ann Boydston (ed.), *The Later Works of John Dewey 1925–1953 Volume 3* (Carbondale: Southern Illinois University Press, 1990): 231.

them in the affairs that concern us most some measure of intelligent direction."[34] In a world of change, individuals were thus necessarily works in progress, subject to constant adaptation. In his important 1935 book *Liberalism and Social Action*, Dewey argued that for this reason a new understanding of individualism as something constructed or produced was needed: "The underlying philosophy and psychology of earlier liberalism led to a conception of individuality as something ready-made, already possessed, and needing only the removal of certain legal restrictions to come into full play. It was not conceived as a moving thing, something that is attained only by continuous growth."[35] American progressive educators adopted this idea that individuals were in flux, constantly growing, changing and adapting, and that the fostering of individual difference was fundamental to democracy. The Educational Policies Commission of the National Education Association noted that the "members of a successful democracy are ... eager to recognize, develop, and protect the unique and valuable traits of each individual child and adult."[36] The opinions of others had to be respected because "differences in opinion on social issues arise not alone from the lack of knowledge ... but even more from the differing sets of values which ... each student brings to the study of social problems."[37] Young people needed to be "taught to reach their own opinions and within reason to hold to them, at the same time accepting the fact that others are entitled to different opinions honestly reached and similarly defended."[38]

Dewey's belief in the importance of public discussion was arguably the most pervasive influence on those who sought to create a more democratic radio, and little about American radio's civic ambitions in the 1930s makes sense unless we recognize this thread. Philosopher S. E. Frost wrote his 1937 study *Is American Radio Democratic?* at Teachers College under the guidance of William H. Kirkpatrick, a follower of Dewey and a leading figure in progressive education in his own right. Frost, as we have seen, defined democratic radio in strikingly Deweyan fashion; radio was, he wrote, democratic "to the degree that it is regulated, controlled, and operated so that all listeners are guaranteed broad, wide, varied, and rich shared contacts with others and with their physical environment, open-mindedness, and increased flexibility of thought and action."[39] The adjectives are carefully chosen—democratic radio is to be broad, wide, open, flexible, and opposed to all that is narrow, local, closed, fixed. Those oppositions, at least as much as the more obvious divisions between highbrow and lowbrow programming, underlay debate about the democratic capacities of American radio. Frost argued that if radio allowed the listener to continue to live a life limited by prejudices and "'principles' which are not open to question or evaluation," it would have failed to contribute to making possible

34. John Dewey, "What I Believe," in Jo Ann Boydston (ed.), *The Later Works of John Dewey 1925–1953 Volume 5* (Carbondale: Southern Illinois University Press, 1990): 271.

35. John Dewey, *Liberalism and Social Action* in Jo Ann Boydston (ed.), *The Later Works of John Dewey 1925–1953 Volume 11* (Carbondale: Southern Illinois University Press, 1990): 30.

36. Educational Policies Commission, *The Purposes of Education in American Democracy* (Washington, DC: Educational Policies Commission, 1938): 21.

37. Educational Policies Commission, *The Purposes of Education in American Democracy*: 111.

38. Educational Policies Commission, *The Purposes of Education in American Democracy*: 112.

39. Frost, *Is American Radio Democratic?*: viii.

"intelligent action" in a democratic society. Frost was indeed quite dogmatic about the necessity for creating open-minded citizens—he labeled as simply "bad" any broadcast that sought to indoctrinate individuals, or to produce a "closed mind."[40]

Frost was a theorist of democratic radio, but many active educational broadcasters shared these Deweyan ideas. James Rowland Angell, although no progressive, was very familiar with this thought—he had been a student of Dewey's at the University of Michigan, and was then recruited by Dewey to teach at the University of Chicago—the two men shared a functionalist psychology and their careers intersected at several points. At NBC, Walter Preston, also certainly no radical, explained in a 1941 letter that his definition of educational radio had to do with radio's "ability to 'expose' the listener to certain experiences which otherwise he probably would not have, and in this way, in some degree modify his attitudes and his range of interest"—"I believe that all experience of whatever type is educational."[41] Of course the commercial broadcasters had an interest in defining almost anything they broadcast as "educational." But there was something more broadly representative in Preston's definition of education as personal change—not growth toward an ultimate truth, but simply attitude change as an unending but valuable process.

Possessed of this insight, that broadcasting could be a means of exposing the masses to difference, lifting them out of their parochial certainty into cosmopolitan flux and change, many of those concerned with radio and democracy began to see exciting possibilities in the same communications technologies that had led pessimists such as Lippmann to conclude that henceforth citizens' opinions would reflect only the views of the skilled propagandist who had gotten to them most recently. In focusing on the canonical Lippmann/Dewey debate and thus on the moment of intellectual anxiety or despair about mass democracy, historians have fixated on the threat that the mass media posed to democracy rather than on the creative response to that threat. What has been lost sight of is a practical tradition—a belief that while radio would not of itself create democracy, it could with work, with added human intervention, produce socially transformative and democratic effects. The key individuals in this tradition—including John W. Studebaker, Chester S. Williams, Lyman Bryson, and George V. Denny Jr.—were each in their way practical theorists of the techniques of democracy, tireless workers in the field of public discussion. They saw in radio a means for the mass production of individual opinion. While it is important to document and analyze the limitations and failures of the radio and democracy reformers, and to note their pedagogic dogmatism, it is also important to recall their ambitions.

FORUMS AND DEMOCRACY

Perhaps the most important genre of self-consciously democratic radio was the forum discussion program, which exposed listeners in its very design to multiple opinions. When U.S. commissioner of education John Studebaker asserted in 1935 that "the people

40. Frost, *Is American Radio Democratic?*: x.

41. Walter G. Preston Jr. to William Benton April 10, 1941, folder 11, box 18, University of Chicago, Office of the Vice President Records 1937–46, UCSC.

have an inalienable right to hear every important point of view," it was the radio forum that best exemplified what he had in mind: "I want to see the ablest proponents of conflicting ideas and philosophies freely argue their cases before the bar of public opinion." For Studebaker, "the essence of democracy" was "freedom of choice," being aware of multiple perspectives and consciously choosing between them.[42] For the broadcasters, the radio forum was also of course in some ways a useful safety valve—a way of quarantining controversial material to a safer space where every opinion met its balancing opposite. But the radio forum was rarely in practice an entirely safe or uncontroversial form.

The idea of the radio forum grew from the Progressive interest in community forums as a means of enhancing democratic skills. There had been a strong emphasis in Progressivism on improving local public life and producing a new kind of unity out of the chaotic diversity of immigrant America. Social or community centers were key tools in these reformers' quest to create (or, as they more often said, to re-create) genuine community in American cities. Using school buildings for community purposes after hours was a favorite theme of Progressive reformers, but the project was also driven from below, by a variety of groups who wanted a neutral public space for meeting and discussion.[43] A forum movement grew in the United States in the years before World War I, both advocating and assisting forum organization.[44] These forums usually combined a knowledgeable speaker with audience questions. Although question time could be a constrained kind of public discussion, the core idea of the forum organizers was to turn an audience for debate into a genuine public because, as Glenn Frank explained it in 1919, "the audience habit is death to the political creativeness of a people."[45]

One of the aims of Progressive reformers was to create public spaces that would replicate the convivial discussion and exchange characteristic of the saloon, without the drinking.[46] Massachusetts Congregational minister Raymond Calkins noted astutely that any substitute for the saloon had to match its ability to provide "some stimulus to self-expression and a kind of personal feeling towards those into whose company one is thrown."[47] But social centers carried the burden of too many reform hopes, and they were at times weighed down with expectations. Mattson argues that collaboration by social centers activists with the effort to gain public support for U.S. involvement in WWI led

42. John Studebaker, "Educational Broadcasting in a Democracy," speech given May 15, 1935, folder 36, box 36, NBC records, WHS.

43. See Paul S. Boyer, *Urban Masses and Moral Order in America 1820–1920* (Cambridge: Harvard University Press, 1978); William J. Reese, *Power and the Promise of School Reform* (New York: Teachers College Press, 2002), ch. 7.

44. Kevin Mattson, *Creating a Democratic Public: The Struggle for Urban Participatory Democracy during the Progressive Era* (University Park, PA: Pennsylvania State University Press, 1998): 44.

45. Quoted in Mattson, *Creating a Democratic Public*: 45.

46. On the Progressive democratic reformers, see Mattson, *Creating a democratic public*; Allen Freeman Davis, *Spearheads for Reform* (New Brunswick: Rutgers University Press, 1984): 79–83.

47. Raymond Calkins, *Substitutes for the Saloon* (Boston: Houghton Mifflin, 1901): 2, 8.

to "a long-term defeat of both democratic institutions and ideas," and that the vibrant Progressive tradition of public discussion was dead by the 1920s.[48]

In the 1930s, however, partly in response to the Depression, community forums and discussion groups were once again established all over the United States. A 1938 book contended that the "growth of the discussion movement, particularly since the beginning of the present decade, can only be expressed as extraordinary."[49] The *New York Times* referred in 1937 to "a spectacular boom in public discussion, dwarfing even the lyceum movement a century ago."[50] But the emphasis had shifted significantly from the Progressive attempt to create new unity through discussion to a more pluralist emphasis on the *process* of democratic discussion. The (Deweyan) goal was the formation of open-minded individuals, who understood that constant adaptive change was the inescapable condition of modern life. Chester S. Williams, who worked alongside John Studebaker at the U.S. Office of Education, and was himself an important figure in the 1930s forum movement, argued that in the "real modern world the status quo is a thing to be dated.…What we are after is an education which will help us create new social orders as we need them."[51]

Studebaker was one of the central actors in the 1930s history of forums in the United States. He studied for a master's degree in 1917 at Teachers College, where he was taught by William H. Kirkpatrick and came under the influence of John Dewey. Although not generally regarded as a progressive in educational philosophy, Studebaker was very familiar with progressive educational ideas.[52] As superintendent of the Des Moines school system during the Depression, he was most struck by the adult education needs of the community: "Education for citizenship, surely, must follow students beyond the school doors into life if popular government was to work."[53] He gained funds from the Carnegie Corporation for a five-year demonstration program of public forums to be run through the Des Moines public school system from 1933.[54]

Lyman Bryson, who was at that stage director of the California Association for Adult Education, and Chicago political scientist Carroll Wooddy were appointed as forum leaders in Des Moines. It has been suggested that it was Bryson who supplied Studebaker with the idea of the forums for Des Moines.[55] Certainly Bryson had already had experience running a comparable scheme, as director of the California Association for Adult

48. Mattson, *Creating a Democratic Public*: 106, 112.

49. Lyman Judson and Ellen Judson, *Modern Group Discussion, Public and Private* (New York: H. W. Wilson, 1938): 3.

50. Catherine Mackenzie, "Forums Booming All Over Nation," *New York Times,* January 3, 1937: N7.

51. Chester S. Williams, draft of incomplete book, *The Crisis of Education* (1938): 64, folder 4, box 2, Chester S. Williams papers, University of Oregon Library.

52. Alfonso Narvaez, "John W. Studebaker Dies at 102," *New York Times,* July 28, 1989; William M. Keith, *Democracy as Discussion: Civic Education and the American Forum Movement* (Lanham, MD: Lexington Books, 2007): 100; Paul C. Pickett, "Contributions of John Ward Studebaker to American Education" (PhD diss., State University of Iowa, 1967): 40.

53. Frank Ernest Hill, "Back to 'Town Meetings,'" *New York Times,* September 15, 1935: SM9.

54. See Robert Kunzman and David Tyack, "Educational Forums of the 1930s: An Experiment in Adult Civic Education," *American Journal of Education* 111, no. 3 (May 2005): 320–40.

55. Pickett, "Contributions of John Ward Studebaker to American Education."

Education from 1929. In 1929–30, Bryson was working in San Diego, giving a summary of world affairs every fourth Sunday to the city's forum, to audiences as large as 750 people. He was also presiding over a scheme of holding forums in public schools, in San Diego, Long Beach, Pasadena, Bakersfield, Los Angeles, and other cities. He developed a method for encouraging the articulation of different opinions: "As soon as some polarization around contrary opinions became evident, the group split up into as many smaller units as there were points of view, each represented by a spokesman with a noticeably definite opinion." Each separate group was then encouraged to clarify and articulate its opinion before the larger group reconvened after this "interval of polarization."[56] From early in his career, Bryson was thus becoming a technician of opinion formation, skilled at helping individuals to differentiate and articulate their opinions.

The Des Moines forums operated after hours in public schools, under the direct administration of the public school system. The Carnegie funds paid for qualified speakers ("authorities in their fields") and forum leaders. Discussion focused on national and international rather than state or local issues.[57] A discussion leader talked for the first half of the meeting and then "members of the audience take part in the discussion, asking questions and expressing their personal opinions."[58] The speaker could give his opinion, Studebaker explained, "but he will give it in a way to indicate that another opinion is possible, and that each of his hearers has a right to his own." Soon "the audience will acquire the wish to know the facts on both sides."[59] By 1934, it was reported, 70,000 adults in Des Moines out of a population of 144,000 had attended forums.[60] This striking success of the Des Moines scheme attracted national attention.

Lyman Bryson, now appointed to Teachers College at Columbia University, told an audience in 1934 that Des Moines had proven that citizens of a typical American community "will listen to a fair presentation of all points of view on the most exciting and controversial of questions, will learn to express their own opinions calmly and reasonably."[61] A couple of months later, Bryson "admitted" to a Pittsburgh reporter that forums were a safety valve for emotion and that he believed it was only through discussion that people could cope with the "sinister and destructive factors" in contemporary industrial society.[62] But those educators who were optimistic about Des Moines liked the public forum not just as a guard against radicalism, but also because it at least appeared to prove that the Deweyan program—of continual discussion and change—could be popular, that the people wanted to be inducted into a more fluid, contingent, evolving kind of public discussion.

56. Lyman Bryson, *A State Plan for Adult Education* (New York: American Association for Adult Education, 1934): 20–23.

57. Frank Ernest Hill, "Back to 'Town Meetings,'" *New York Times,* September 15, 1935: SM9.

58. Wayne Gard, "Adults Learn by Talking," *New York Times,* March 26, 1933: XX5.

59. Hill, "Back to 'Town Meetings,'": SM9.

60. J.W. Stubebaker, *Education for Democracy* (Washington DC: U.S. Office of Education, 1936): 18; Hill, "Back to 'Town Meetings,'" SM9.

61. Lyman Bryson, "Community Forums," box 20, Lyman Bryson papers, Manuscript Division, LOC.

62. "Columbia Professor to Air His Views to Local Groups," *Pittsburgh Post-Gazette,* October 8, 1934: 17.

John Studebaker took the forum idea with him to Washington when he was appointed U.S. commissioner of education in 1934. He told reporters that the country needed "better machinery than now exists for the rational development of public opinion."[63] In Washington in 1935, he argued for the importance of forums as continuing education: "At no other point in our whole system of human influences, whether public or private, is there to be found a setting which is so conducive of genuine education as in a *public forum*."[64] Studebaker won the funding to begin the Federal Forum Project—a remarkable and little-remembered New Deal program that operated between 1936 and 1941. Over 2.5 million citizens attended its "modern American town meetings" in 600 communities at a total cost of $1.5 million.[65] Hundreds of WPA relief workers were employed as "artists, assistant librarians, accountants, stenographers, correspondents, messengers, typists, and publicity workers."[66] Both Lyman Bryson and Carroll Woody came to Washington to work on the program. Studebaker claimed that his forums would increase tolerance and reduce misunderstanding, that they would foster "confidence and hope" as well as open-mindedness and courtesy.

Some Federal Forum project organizers turned to radio—although a 1939 survey found that only 44 of 557 forums used radio either to publicize regular forums or to broadcast special radio forums.[67] In Chattanooga, stations WDOD and WAPO gave two 15-minute evening periods each week for forum-related talk among "several civic-minded local citizens, newspapermen, forum officials, and members of the forum staff."[68] Emily Woodward, newspaper owner and editor, and leader of the Atlanta Public Forum and the Georgia State Forums, ran a Sunday radio forum on WSB Atlanta. Forum leaders and organizers had skills that could be of direct use to broadcasters.

The 1930s forums had different goals to the Progressive era ones. They were more about process—discussion and opinion formation and change understood as the permanent and unavoidable elements of life in a modern democracy. The forums were to enable democratic government by converting the mass into articulate and reflexive citizens, responsible custodians of their own always provisional opinions. "Public discussions are useful," Lyman Bryson wrote in 1937, "because they can disturb complacency and lead to restless uncertainty about one's self that has long been known as the beginning

63. Webster Peterson, "A National Forum Plan," *New York Times*, September 30, 1934: XX5.

64. Radio address by John W. Studebaker, "Democracy's Demands upon Education," folder 12, box 1, Chester S. Williams Papers, Special Collections, University of Oregon Library. The presence of the speech in Williams's papers suggests that he may have written it.

65. Memorandum to Dr. Studebaker, May 21, 1940, Entry 189, box 5, Office of Education records, RG 12, NACP. On the New Deal forum movement and Federal Forum project, see David Goodman, "Democracy and Public Discussion in the Progressive and New Deal Eras: From Civic Competence to the Expression of Opinion," *Studies in American Political Development* 18, no. 2 (Fall 2004): 81–111, and Kunzman and Tyack, "Educational Forums of the 1930s": 320–40.

66. J. W. Studebaker, "'Let There Be Light': Federal Emergency Funds Advance Education," *Work* 3 (1936).

67. Office of Education, "Summary of a Survey on Public Forums under Various Sponsorships" (July 1939): 8.

68. Chattanooga-Hamilton County Public Forum, *Final Report of the Chattanooga–Hamilton County Public Forum April 1936–June 30, 1937*: 126. Copy in Chattanooga-Hamilton County Bicentennial Library.

of wisdom."[69] It was amidst this set of ideas and practices that radio emerged as a significant new factor, as reformers began to imagine the civic benefits of the forum conveyed through broadcasting to audiences almost unimaginably larger. The radio forum, conceived within this milieu of 1930s Progressive educational thought, was to become one of the central programming pillars of civic paradigm radio.

THE RADIO FORUMS

There were in the 1930s a few who thought that radio might facilitate a mass direct democracy, in which important issues could be decided by plebiscite. Norman Thomas, the Socialist leader, was a great believer in radio forums and radio's capacity to make American democracy more directly responsive to the people's will. In 1939, the year after the defeat of Representative Louis Ludlow's proposed constitutional amendment that would have required a referendum before Congress could declare war, Thomas again took up the referendum idea and suggested that radio town meetings could enable rapid national debate and deliberation about the gravest of national decisions. He quipped, "A whole series of town meetings on the air could be held in less time than it takes a Southern Senator to explain why a federal anti-lynching law is undemocratic."[70]

More often, however, 1930s democratic reformers imagined not a direct radio democracy, but democratic broadcasting playing its part in enlivening and activating citizens, training them in civic competence. Liberal enthusiasts for democracy thought about what would have to be added to make of Americans in the radio age not just simultaneous listeners, but fellow citizens. They imagined a new kind of porous democratic society in which such discussions would render all Americans open to rational persuasion on matters of public importance. In an era of political dogma, the abilities to listen, empathize, and understand the point of view of the other seemed among the most precious of social qualities, and radio held out the promise of being able to mass produce them. Lyman Bryson defined the purpose of a public forum as to "encourage tolerant exchange of opinion in the hope of making political and social processes more rational."[71]

The radio forum was one of the most visible, lauded, and discussed innovations of the radio era. "Although radio has made a general contribution to the cultural life of our people," President Roosevelt said in November 1936, "it is the maintenance of the open forum for friendly and open debate and discussion that gives the American system of broadcasting pre-eminence."[72] The democratic aspirations of American radio in the 1930s were informed by the liberal imagination of the New Deal era, and inspired by its Depression-generated sense that it was class rather than race or gender divisions that

69. Lyman Bryson, "The Limits of Discussion," April 1937, typescript, box 20, Lyman Bryson Papers, LOC.

70. *Town Meeting: Bulletin of America's Town Meeting of the Air* 4, no. 25 (May 1, 1939): 5.

71. Lyman Bryson, "Public Forums," [speech from October 1936], box 20, Lyman Bryson papers, LOC.

72. FCC press release, November 10, 1936, box 399, RG 173, FCC, Office of the Executive Director, General Correspondence 1927–46, 44–3, NACP.

posed the greatest threats to American democracy. The technology of radio seemed to offer a new means to bring Americans from both sides of the tracks into a common conversation.

The multiperspective radio forum programs grew directly from the stimulus and examples of the public forum movement. While Progressive forums had emphasized local affairs, by the 1930s the purpose of the forum was held to be above all else to help citizens understand national and international affairs—and this made it particularly suited to adaptation to network radio. John Studebaker argued in 1935 that "the voter can understand his local problems much more easily than he can the national or international ones. It is these which puzzle him today."[73] In May 1935, Studebaker talked of the "importance of the radio as a means of extending the public forum to the air," with minority groups being given fair representation.[74] The radio industry, as we saw in chapter 1, watched Studebaker's activities in the U.S. Office of Education very closely. John Royal warned another NBC executive, "We must be careful that this man, who we realize can be dangerous if not handled properly, does not get too deeply entrenched in his contacts with radio."[75] But the networks also saw opportunity in the government interest in forums.

For forum activists, the optimism about the results of bringing forum programs to the millions by radio was tempered only by their sense of the enormity of the project. "We should have no illusions as to the size of the job," warned Paul Sheats of the Office of Education. "The sheer magnitude of the task of educating some 76 million adults to a level of political and economic literacy where they can tackle their civic chores with even a minimum of competency is enough to overwhelm all but the most confirmed optimists and Pollyannas...." Nevertheless, he insisted, radio could provide the technical means to tackle the problem: "The fact remains that well-planned and well-managed programs of public affairs discussion broadcast into homes which before radio were without recourse to the facts, data and leadership needed in intelligent choice-making can be a tremendous influence toward raising the level of individual participation in the self-governing process."[76] Sheats articulated the civic paradigm in pitch-perfect fashion, confident that the mass medium could become a manufacturer of individualism and self-conscious decision making.

THE NETWORK FORUMS EXPOSE LISTENERS TO MULTIPLE PERSPECTIVES

By the mid-1930s, each of the major radio networks had its own national forum program. The *University of Chicago Round Table (UCRT)* was an innovative and important show that consisted of unscripted studio discussion between university teachers and public

73. Hill, "Back to 'Town Meetings,'": SM9.

74. John Studebaker, "Educational Broadcasting in a Democracy," speech given May 15, 1935, folder 36, box 36, NBC records, WHS.

75. John Royal to Richard Patterson, May 3, 1935, box 108, Royal correspondence, NBC records, WHS.

76. Paul H. Sheats, *Forums on the Air* (Washington DC: FREC, 1939): 6.

figures—"point for point discussion among qualified authorities," as University of Chicago president Robert Hutchins described it.[77] It began on Chicago station WMAQ in 1931 and was an NBC network program from October 1933 to 1955. The *Round Table* was designed to model opinion articulation and comparison in conversation about public affairs. Three was the favored number of participants, to demonstrate that there were more than two sides to most issues.[78]

The University of Chicago had emerged very early as a proponent of cooperation in educational broadcasting, and it sustained a long collaboration with NBC station WMAQ and its cultural and educational manager, Judith Waller. Robert Hutchins wrote to Waller in 1931 that the university's then nine-year cooperation with WMAQ had "confirmed our original decision that a larger audience could be reached through a high powered station with a well-rounded program than through a station carrying nothing but educational material."[79] Although there were subsequently many moments of tension and frustration between the university and NBC, primarily over changes to the scheduled times of programs, Chicago continued to broadcast over NBC and to cultivate its relationships with the leadership of both networks.

The idea behind *UCRT*, a 1932 university radio program guide explained, was that "perhaps the only way" to secure impartiality was "to put partial views against each other and trust to the creative capacity of the listener to make from partial views an impartial judgment."[80] Allen Miller, the director of the cooperative University Broadcasting Council in Chicago, described the program's purpose as being to demonstrate that "intelligent people who hold differences of opinion can engage in friendly discussion and, through it, can come to a closer understanding."[81] When Chet Bowles, University of Chicago vice president William Benton's former partner in the Benton and Bowles advertising agency, recommended turning *UCRT* into something more like a conventional debate, there was a sharp response from Miller: "The Round Tablers have no desire to present current economic, political and social situations as all black or all white."[82]

Sometimes that worked against communication. There were always concerns about keeping the language accessible and the professors from being too academic, as the program director reported in 1938: "Every post-mortem we have had on a program has brought the almost universal comment that the professors fool around and quibble all through the show and never get down to cases."[83] The show worked best with a relatively

77. See, e.g., Robert Hutchins to Niles Trammell, November 6, 1944, folder 11, box 175, University of Chicago, Office of the President—Hutchins Administration files, UCSC.

78. Hugh Slotten, "Commercial Radio, Public Affairs Discourse and the Manipulation of Sound Scholarship: Isolationism, Wartime Civil Rights and the Collapse of the Attractiveness of Communism in America, 1933–1945," *Historical Journal of Film, Radio and Television* 25, no. 3 (August 2005): 374–75.

79. Robert Hutchins to Judith Waller, June 23, 1931, folder 38, box 26, NBC records, WHS.

80. *The University of Chicago Radio Program*, Spring 1932: 2.

81. Allen Miller to William Benton, February 22, 1938, folder 1, box 2, University of Chicago, Office of the Vice President Records 1937–46, UCSC.

82. Allen Miller to William Benton, February 22, 1938, folder 1, box 2, University of Chicago, Office of the Vice President Records 1937–46, UCSC.

83. Charles Newton to William Benton, April 18, 1938, folder 3, box 2, University of Chicago, Office of the Vice President Records 1937–46, UCSC.

stable cast of speakers who were known to each other and could argue in a way that was both accessible and entertaining—James Rowland Angell thought it most successful when confined to Chicago faculty, already familiar with one another.[84] William Benton pointed out that the Chicago professors who appeared regularly on the program "come closer to being trained in broadcasting technique than any other academic group."[85]

An issue with 1930s radio forums was always the balance of spontaneity or planning. One thing that distinguished these forums from later opinionated talk programs was the element of prior research and planning. In California, Bryson had taken his technique of polarization and articulation of opinion onto the radio. Wanting something with "some of the vitality of a real give-and-take of ideas," but needing a prepared script for the broadcasting stations, Bryson would invite three participants to lunch and a free-flowing conversation on the topic. His associate director would sit and make notes of the "most striking comments and the pattern of differing opinions." Then a script was prepared, "assigning to each member of the trio his own opinions, but arranging and editing the spontaneous remarks into a more coherent and dramatic sequence."[86] Similarly, the conversations on *UCRT* were unscripted but well prepared—from early in the show's history, a Saturday night dinner allowed the speakers to rehearse their ideas before the Sunday broadcast. Allen Miller later described his method of preparing for the show. On Tuesday at lunchtime, the speakers would meet with the director "to determine the sequence of the discussion and to delimit it." But, Miller recalled, "if contestants began to knock heads in the discussion I would pull them out of any real meeting on the sub-issue. The purpose was to retain spontaneity in argument while achieving structure." Later, as the show became more nationally prominent, the preparation became more elaborate. The University Radio Office would supply each participant with a research memorandum a week in advance, which would contain both background research and articles on the topic, and 50 replies to a listener questionnaire asking what they already knew about the topic.[87] An NBC publication in 1941 outlined the sequence from there:

Eight days before—Research department goes into action, querying participants on their points of view and servicing them with factual information obtained from many sources.

Six days before—Research staff draws up a two-page outline which is sent to each participant.

Five days before—Participants (those in Chicago) meet for lunch and make changes in the outline during a session usually lasting about three hours....

One day before—All participants meet for dinner on Saturday night for a general discussion of the outline and subject.

84. James Rowland Angell to William Benton, May 17, 1938, folder 1, box 1, University of Chicago, Office of the Vice President Records 1937–46, UCSC.

85. William Benton to James Rowland Angell, December 8, 1937, folder 1, box 1, University of Chicago, Office of the Vice President Records 1937–46, UCSC.

86. Lyman Bryson, *A State Plan for Adult Education* (New York: American Association for Adult Education, 1934): 50–52.

87. Allen Miller to Charter Heslep, 15 July 1963. Allen Miller papers, WHS; Sherman Dryer, *Radio in Wartime* (New York: Greenberg, 1942): 184.

Day of broadcast—Speakers gather in the Mitchell Tower studios on the University campus. An informal run-through is "waxed" (put on a record which is played back to the speakers so faults can be checked before broadcast). Coffee and sandwiches are served between run-through and broadcast to relax tension.[88]

The *Round Table* was thus by 1941 highly prepared and rehearsed, although formally "unscripted." But the careful preparation of this successful show tells us something about the belief of the time that broadcast multi-opinion conversation needed careful curating. "Spontaneity is best achieved by adequate preparation," Sherman Dryer concluded from his experience on the *Round Table*.[89]

Despite the preparation, NBC frequently had qualms about the spontaneity of the *Round Table*; John Royal observed in 1935 that "in many ways it is dangerous. The men speak without scripts and it is the very ultimate in free speech on radio."[90] NBC's anxiety was evidenced in May 1939, when the *Round Table* planned a discussion on the topic "Is the Negro Oppressed?" The participants were to be Chicago professors Paul Douglas and Louis Wirth, and Walter White, secretary of the NAACP. Judith Waller in Chicago sent a concerned telegram to John Royal: "I question desirability [on] this subject when only one side [is] adequately represented....If you agree[, I] suggest you wire Sherman Dryer University of Chicago that [the] subject [is] so controversial in the South that it appears particularly essential that we have well balanced discussion...."[91] The proposed program was cancelled and replaced with a discussion of a coal strike. There was some pressure to reschedule, but John Royal advised NBC president Trammell in a blunt letter that the program should not go ahead: "They would *like* to have a Southerner on, but you, as a Southerner, know more than anyone else that you cannot *discuss* the nigger question."[92] Royal perhaps intuitively understood something about the inadequacy of the New Deal era forum when confronted with the obduracy of race and racialized power. Hearing both sides, changing one's mind, and remaining open to persuasion seemed rather academic preoccupations in the face of institutionalized white supremacy.

For all its donnishness, the *Round Table* became a relatively popular program. It moved in 1938 from Sunday morning with 42 stations, to an evening time with 24, in the hope of finding a larger audience—Benton was sure that the *Round Table* audience "is in large part a church-going audience."[93] He may well have been right—the *Round Table* audience increased 55% between 1939 and 1941, and by 1940, *UCRT* had become the most popular forum on network radio.[94] This increase in audience through the years of crisis about U.S. entry into

88. *NBC Presents: Programs in the Public Interest* 3, no. 6 (February 1941): 4.

89. Sherman Dryer, *Radio in Wartime*: 179. [Companion website link 4.1.]

90. John Royal to Richard Patterson, March 22, 1935, folder 24, box 35, NBC records, WHS.

91. Telegram Waller to Royal, May 12, 1939, folder 32, box 73, NBC records, WHS.

92. John Royal to Niles Trammell, July 6, 1939, folder 32, box 73, NBC records, WHS. This exchange is also discussed in Barbara Dianne Savage, *Broadcasting Freedom: Radio, War and the Politics of Race 1938–1948* (Chapel Hill: University of North Carolina Press, 1999): 195–97, and Slotten, "Commercial Radio, Public Affairs Discourse and the Manipulation of Sound Scholarship": 383–84.

93. William Benton to James Rowland Angell, February 25, 1938, and May 16, 1938, folder 1, box 1, University of Chicago, Office of the Vice President Records 1937–46, UCSC.

94. Ratings data is in the correspondence between Lucy Perry and William Benton through 1940 and 1941, folder 9, box 18, University of Chicago Office of the Vice President Records 1937–46, UCSC.

WWII may also have had something to do with the show's coverage of the war issues. The University of Chicago—because of the public stands of President Robert Hutchins and Vice President William Benton—was associated in the public mind with isolationism, although *UCRT* was studiously nonpartisan. Studying the mail received by Hutchins after his April 1941 national radio address on the war issue, Benton concluded that it was "the poor and the great inarticulate mass of people who are against intervention."[95] The war debate was for *UCRT* a moment of connection between academic and popular concerns.

William Benton took the vice president position at the University of Chicago in 1937 partly because he was interested in developing the educational use of radio and motion pictures. Seeking to build on the undeniable success of the *Round Table*, he was actively developing new program ideas for what he—with his background in advertising and entertainment radio—could identify as "both good education and good broadcasting."[96] He proposed another forum program to CBS in 1938, to be called "America Votes," and billed as "an experiment in democracy." Matters of "crucial public interest" would be discussed by "nationally known partisan spokesmen." Then "specially qualified university authorities" would analyze the conflicting points of view, and finally the results of a commissioned opinion poll would be announced. Benton enthused that the program would have a "lot of showmanship plus the element of an effort at unbiased analysis plus a weekly opportunity to hear what the public thinks."[97] The show was never made, but Benton's elaborate tinkering with the various components of the radio forum format clearly displays civic paradigm era creativity about how to combine—in the terms of the day—academic expertise, public opinion, and showmanship.

Lyman Bryson's *People's Platform*, a later variant on the *Round Table* model was, as discussed in chapter 2, an archetypal civic paradigm forum program. An early pitch for the idea of the show stressed the ultimate goal of listeners forming their own opinions—it was this that made the program recognizably an exercise in adult education. The plan was for a program to be titled "What Do You Think?": "A group of persons from all walks of life, furnishing a cross-section of public opinion and led by an expert, meeting at an actual dinner table, would discuss informally and conversationally questions of national interest. Each broadcast would conclude with the question—'What do YOU think?'"[98] The basic idea of the *People's Forum* is evident in this early formulation, although with even more insistence on the trajectory toward audience opinion formation.

These studio-based forum programs were innovative and important. But by the mid-1930s, with the forum movement and Federal Forum program developing nationally, there was a demand for something even more ambitious—a radio forum discussion in front of a live audience that could ask questions on air. From the broadcasters' point

95. Quoted in James C. Schneider, *Should America Go to War? The Debate over Foreign Policy in Chicago, 1939–1941* (Chapel Hill, NC: University of North Carolina Press, 1989): 191.

96. William Benton to James Rowland Angell, December 8, 1937, folder 18, box 1, University of Chicago, Office of the Vice President Records 1937–46, UCSC.

97. Telegram William Benton to William Lewis, June 6, 1938, folder 1, box 1, University of Chicago, Office of the Vice President Records 1937–46, UCSC.

98. Stirling Fisher to William Benton February 8, 1938, folder 1, box 1, University of Chicago, Office of the Vice President Records 1937–46, UCSC.

of view, this was considerably more dangerous than unscripted studio discussion, but nevertheless two of the networks did commit to such live audience forums.

The *American Forum of the Air*, on the Mutual network from 1937 to 1949, featured opening statements, panel discussion, and audience questions. The show was broadcast from various hotels in Washington DC, or from the Department of the Interior's studio auditorium. The moderator was lawyer Theodore Granik, who, it was reported in 1945, "knows just about everybody—legislators; government officials, high and low; newspapermen, diplomats, military leaders."[99] Speakers on the *American Forum* were mainly members of Congress and spokespeople for national, Washington-based organizations. Congressmen "have made up the greater part of the guest list," Granik explained, "mainly because their opinions were of greater importance on the topics selected." Transcripts of the program were read into the *Congressional Record*.[100] This Mutual network show had a smaller national audience than the forums on NBC and CBS, but its reach was extended through a newspaper column, in which the speakers briefly stated their views, and readers were invited to vote by mail—ticking a box to agree with one point of view or the other, or selecting a third box: "I enclose letter stating my views." "You the American public," the column reminded readers, "must make the final decision on this and every other public question."[101]

AMERICA'S TOWN MEETING OF THE AIR

The most well known and best resourced radio forum was *America's Town Meeting of the Air*, broadcast on NBC from 1935 and then, from the separation of NBC's networks, on ABC from 1943 to 1956. After the announcement of the Federal Forum project, radio was pitched many ideas for forum programs. John Royal wrote in April 1935 that NBC had been "besieged from various sides with Town Hall suggestions." It was George V. Denny Jr. of the League for Political Education who succeeded in convincing Royal to enter a partnership with his organization. Civically worthy controversy that was also entertaining appealed strongly to the broadcasters. John Royal regarded *ATMA* as his "pet project," and appreciated the theatrical air that Denny gave the show from the beginning. Denny often described himself as part educator and part entertainer, and that was always an attractive mix to NBC. But he retained a seriousness of purpose about the task of his radio forum. "Just to live today as a citizen of a democracy is not easy," he observed in 1936. There was an "urgent necessity for the spread of non-partisan political education throughout the world."[102]

The League for Political Education had been founded in 1894 by a group of New York women in the wake of the defeat of a women's suffrage amendment in New York State.

99. *St. Petersburg Times*, August 19, 1945: 37; David Goodman, "Programming in the Public Interest: *America's Town Meeting of the Air*," in Michele Hilmes (ed.), *NBC: America's Network* (Berkeley: University of California Press, 2007): 44–60.

100. R. W. Stewart, "Where Free Speech Prevails," *New York Times*, September 15, 1940: 142.

101. "The American Forum," *Capital Times*, October 20, 1940: 28.

102. Richard Patterson to David Lawrence, 27 April 193, and John Royal to David Rosenblum 23 April 1935, folder 8, box 34, NBC records, WHS. Speech by Denny, April 3, 1936, at League for Political Education luncheon, box 24, Series 1, Denny papers, LOC.

Confidently concluding that the main cause of the defeat was political ignorance among both men and women, the aim of the new organization was to advance the campaign for women's rights indirectly: "to arouse among women practical interest in public affairs, in civic institutions and in good government, by means of a broad and systematic study of the same."[103] In January 1921 the league opened the Town Hall on 43rd Street. In 1935, it signed a contract that committed it to the organizational work of a national radio forum while NBC was to pay the running expenses of the show. Denny himself was to become the moderator of the radio program.[104] He recalled the excitement of the idea: "Here was something new in radio: ten-minute speeches by four speakers holding widely diversified points of view, speaking from the same platform on the same evening, and being questioned by an audience of fifteen hundred people."[105] *America's Town Meeting of the Air* greatly expanded the scope of the league's civic work and rapidly became its highest profile activity, so that when George Denny became director of the league in 1937, there was little resistance to his proposal to change the name of the organization to Town Hall Inc.

It was clear by the mid-1930s that forums were now ranked very high—in Washington and elsewhere—among the possible civic and educational contributions that radio could be and ought to be making. In a brief moment of enthusiasm in 1936, John Royal at NBC was even contemplating further commitment to forums, writing to Frank Russell that "Studebaker will feel very flattered and happy over the President's comment last night about wishing to have forums spread all over the country....What do you think of the NBC's grabbing off this idea, and in addition to our Town Hall of the Air, which starts immediately after the election, have all the local stations do it?"[106] Indeed, having accepted the forum program with all its attendant risks for strategic and defensive reasons, the broadcasters soon found that the multi-opinion format could be a useful way of dealing with controversial material. Wrestling in 1939 with the question of whether NBC should broadcast a Dorothy Thompson speech from Detroit against the German-American Bund and similar organizations, John Royal wrote to RCA president David Sarnoff, "I didn't think that this was a thing we wanted to get into, on the basis that it might get out of control." But, he added, *ATMA* could provide a solution:

> We are trying to keep as many as possible of this kind of talks on the Town Hall, and we have arranged with George Denny for a program scheduled Thursday, March 23rd, on how America should handle the Bund and similar organizations. If we start taking the public anti-Bund meeting in one city we will probably have to take them all over the country. That is something that would be very difficult to handle.[107]

103. Helen Norton Stevens, *Memorial Biography of Adele M. Fielde, Humanitarian* (New York: Fielde Memorial Committee, 1918): 238–40.

104. John Royal to David Lawrence, April 27, 1935; John Royal to David Rosenblum, April 23, 1935, folder 8, box 34, NBC records, WHS.

105. George V. Denny Jr., "Radio Builds Democracy," *Journal of Educational Sociology* 14, no. 6 (February 1941): 373.

106. John Royal to Frank Russell, September 24, 1936, folder 31, box 92, NBC records, WHS.

107. John Royal to David Sarnoff, March 11, 1939, folder 4, box 73, NBC records, WHS.

The forum format thus allowed the framing of controversial material as controversial, and hence a distancing of the broadcaster from it.

Each *ATMA* broadcast began with a costumed town crier ringing a bell and calling out "Town meetin' tonight!" and announcing the topic for the evening. The speakers read from prepared scripts. *ATMA*, like the other important forum programs, rested upon a considerable amount of preparation—speakers met on the morning of the broadcast and then had the afternoon to revise their scripts. The transcripts of each broadcast—questions and answers as well as speeches—were published by Columbia University Press as *Bulletin of America's Town Meeting of the Air* and sold for 10 cents each.

In the final 20 minutes of each program, the Town Hall audience asked short questions (no more than 25 words) of the speakers. In the early years of the program, while some prepared questions were planted in the audience to avoid embarrassing pauses, most questions were asked by audience members unscripted and unplanned. No "personal" questions were allowed—only ideas were to be discussed, and Denny as moderator would rule out of order questions he deemed to be too personal.[108] The live audience introduced an unpredictable element, giving the show much of its drama and an air of danger that the studio discussion programs sometimes lacked. Denny recalled how anxious he had been before the first *ATMA* broadcast in 1935: "Only I knew how utterly unprepared I was to cope with any irregular or unpredictable action on the part of our audience. Suppose no one should ask a question! Suppose several people should try to talk at once! Suppose the Commies should try to take over the meeting! Suppose the speakers should start calling each other names."[109] The rowdiness of the Town Hall audience, however, soon became a key ingredient of the entertainment offered by *ATMA*, and something that was always mentioned in publicity. *Movie-Radio Guide* described audience members as "spectator-hecklers."[110] George Denny, one admiring magazine article observed, "didn't invent heckling, but he is the first man to organize it and sell it as headline entertainment."[111] Before the broadcast, there was a 45-minute preliminary discussion, led in the early years by Arthur Bestor or Lyman Bryson, to warm up the audience. Bryson recalled that his task was to get the "audience whipped up and excited about the issues," so that the speakers "came into an already dramatic situation." In Bryson's view, *ATMA* had "the most perfect format for discussion on air there is. I think you get a degree of excitement with a degree of rationality and inter-change that you can't get with any other format."[112]

A 1941 book observed of *ATMA*, "Heckling to the listener is the highest kind of excitement and entertainment."[113] Denny described the program as "a dramatic contest about something that concerns us all," full of suspense because "anything may happen at these

108. Harry A. Overstreet and Bonaro W. Overstreet, *Town Meeting Comes to Town* (New York: Harper and Brothers, 1938): 37–40.

109. George V. Denny Jr., "The First 500 Hours," in *A Short Story of "America's Town Meeting of the Air"* (New York: Town Hall, 1948): 1.

110. "America's Town Meeting of the Air," *Movie–Radio Guide*, December 13–19, 1941: 38.

111. Frederick L. Collins, "He Makes Democracy Think!," *Liberty*, December 9, 1939: 44.

112. "Reminiscences of Lyman Bryson," Columbia Oral History Research Unit: 111–12, 156, in Lyman Bryson papers, box 40, LOC.

113. Robert West, *The Rape of Radio* (New York: Rodin, 1941): 436.

meetings."[114] A 15-year-old high school student from Chicago confirmed that there was entertainment in conflict: "Bitter controversies are always more welcome than long, boring explanations of the Constitution or the political situation."[115] The "freedom and informality" of *ATMA* reminded a *New York Times* critic of "the amateur hour, another of 1935's popular radio events."[116] *ATMA* provides another example of the fascination of the time with radio's capacity to broadcast the voices of ordinary people.[117] In 1939, 16.7% of commercial network evening programs involved audience participation; by 1940, the proportion had risen to 20.1%.[118] *ATMA* was thus an important civic paradigm program that attempted to combine its work of fostering opinion formation and tolerance in its audience with entertainment.

George Denny, as president of Town Hall Inc. and moderator of *ATMA*, was always the guiding figure behind the program. Born in 1899 in Washington, North Carolina, he spent six years in military school before studying commerce at the University of North Carolina. He paid his way as a student by "by selling clothes on a commission basis and teaching dancing to his fellow-students."[119] At the university, he also acted with, and from 1924 to 1926 managed, the Carolina Playmakers, no doubt absorbing some of the spirit of drama professor Frederick H. Koch's mission to create a regional folk drama "earth-rooted in the life of our common humanity," but also gaining valuable entrepreneurial and managerial skills.[120] Denny then briefly acted on the New York stage, directed the extension program at Columbia University, and was appointed associate director of the League for Political Education in 1930.

With his theatrical training, Denny was in the forefront of those asserting the necessity of "showmanship" in educational and civic radio. The three things that went to make up the *Town Meeting of the Air*, he once wrote, were "educational integrity, showmanship, and fair play"—or in another version, conflict, suspense, and fair play.[121] There was considerable theatricality to the *ATMA* broadcasts—from the opening town crier to Denny's quick repartee as he managed questioners. Denny's initial pitch to NBC had even suggested that the questioners and hecklers who spoke during the forum period of the show might be "professional actors."[122]

114. George V. Denny Jr., *Town Meeting Discussion Leader's Handbook* (New York: Town Hall, 1940): 9–10.

115. "Symposium of Listeners," C. S. Marsh (ed.), *Educational Broadcasting 1937—Proceedings of the Second National Conference on Educational Broadcasting* (Chicago: University of Chicago Press, 1938): 363.

116. *New York Times*, June 30, 1935.

117. On this phenomenon, see Jason Loviglio, "Vox Pop: Network Radio and the Voice of the People," in Michele Hilmes and Jason Loviglio (eds.), *Radio Reader: Essays in the Cultural History of Radio* (New York: Routledge, 2002): 89–111, and Wayne Munson, *All the Talk: The Talk Show in Media Culture* (Philadelphia: Temple University Press, 1993): 30–34.

118. *Broadcasting* 18, no. 2 (January 15, 1940): 21; *Broadcasting* 20, no. 1 (January 13, 1941): 19.

119. S. J. Woolf, "Umpire of the Town Meeting," *New York Times*, June 6, 1943: SM16.

120. Frederick H. Koch, "Drama in the South," in Archibald Henderson (ed.), *Pioneering A People's Theatre* (Chapel Hill: University of North Carolina Press, 1945): 11.

121. "Freedom of Discussion," *United Business Men's Review* (December 1943): 4; George V. Denny Jr., *A Handbook for Discussion Leaders* (New York: Town Hall, 1938): 9–10.

122. Margaret Cuthbert to Richard Patterson, April 8, 1935, folder 8, box 34, NBC records, WHS. [Companion website link 4.2]

Like the Iowan John Studebaker and the Nebraskan Lyman Bryson, George Denny the North Carolinian came from outside the major metropolitan centers of the United States, bringing a message about restoring democracy: "It may seem rather presumptuous at first," he remarked in a speech at Harvard University, "for a Southerner to come to the birthplace of the American town meeting to urge its revival."[123] While Studebaker and Bryson as Midwesterners were drawn first of all to the public school as a site for public discussion, for Denny as a Southerner it was the disembodied medium of radio that seemed to hold the greatest democratic potential. Broadcasting, after all, could bring the same discussion to all, even in a nation in many parts of which blacks and whites were unable to engage openly in public conversation and the public school was not a symbol of shared and democratic space.

Denny was a tireless promoter of the central civic paradigm idea that there were both civic and personal benefits to exposure to diverse points of view: "If Democrats go only to hear Democrats and Republicans go out only to hear Republicans and Isolationists to hear Isolationists, can we possibly call this an honest or intelligent system of political education? The morons could do as much if they were properly labeled."[124] The story Denny always told about the invention of *ATMA* was that the idea came to him walking home one evening, when one of his neighbors said to him of another that he "would rather be shot than caught listening to Roosevelt on the radio." Denny thought to himself:

> But here's a man who just won't listen. Even with the radio right there in his room and a chance to hear what the other side has to say for itself, he deliberately closes his mind. And, if he is like the rest of us, he reads the newspapers he approves and doesn't read the others; he listens to his friends who believe as he does and doesn't listen to others. Talk about dangers to democracy—There's the real danger!

"I determined then," he recalled, "to try to develop a radio program where he would have to listen to the other side in order to hear his own side presented."[125] Denny believed that democracy could work only if "people of diverse views learned to think together."[126] Empathetic listening was the ideal, but any listening to contrary opinions was an advance: "If we are even to approach an understanding of each other's problems, we must surely be willing to hear each other's point of view stated."[127] Figure 4.1.

ATMA listeners in the early years readily understood the need for the program and responded to it warmly in terms similar to those of its makers.[128] "We couldn't believe

123. George V. Denny Jr., "Bring Back the Town Meeting!," in Warren C. Seyfert (ed.), *Capitalizing Intelligence: Eight Essays on Adult Education* (Cambridge: Graduate School of Education, Harvard University, 1937): 101.

124. Speech by Denny April 3, 1936 at League for Political Education luncheon, box 24, Series 1, Denny papers, LOC.

125. Frederick L. Collins, "He Makes Democracy Think!," *Liberty*, December 9, 1939: 42.

126. Overstreet and Overstreet, *Town Meeting Comes to Town*: 3–4.

127. Denny, "Bring Back the Town Meeting!": 117.

128. For a study of the fan mail received by ATMA for the 1937/38 season, see Jeanette Sayre, "Progress in Radio Fan-Mail Analysis," *Public Opinion Quarterly* 3, no. 2 (January 1939): 272–78.

it," wrote a listener. "Actually to hear an intelligent and untrammeled discussion of things that matter by qualified spokesmen for the points of view."[129] *ATMA* fans understood and endorsed the program's sense of the social significance and urgency of its work. A retired naval officer wrote, expounding his sense of the importance of the program in accustoming the American population to change and modernity: "We must dispense with limitations in our thinking of time and space and change....We are dealing today with the perils of an aircraft age. We also have need for some aircraft minds at the same time, that can fly higher and fly over the dangers of prejudice, provincialism, ignorance and indifference."[130] Another common theme in the listener mail was gratitude for a radio program suitable for the intelligent listener. One listener commented that "in my opinion there has never been a time when it was more important for intelligent people to use every means at hand to strengthen democracy."[131]

ATMA's most enthusiastic and civic-minded listeners then understood and endorsed the program's rhetoric about the social importance and urgency of its work, and warmed to its interpellation of them as intelligent and public-minded listeners. A Los Angeles doctor observed, "Politics has always assumed that the human being is unable to rise above its own selfishness and therefore must be appealed to as a person who is selfish, intolerant and ignorant." But through *ATMA*'s analytical discussions, he reported, "one is brought out of his own conceit, and becomes a thinking human being."[132] These self-identified "intelligent listeners," as conscientious listeners to the *Town Meeting* program, were proud of their openness. They understood themselves as receptive to new information and open to reasoned persuasion. In October 1936, Hadley Cantril's survey of 500 listeners to *ATMA* and 500 who attended at the Town Hall found the following:

Of radio audience:

72% feel thwarted because they cannot speak out
Of Town Hall audience:
96% think it more exciting in Town Hall than over air
79% are swayed by speakers more in Town Hall than on radio
Of both audiences (i.e., total of 1000):
28% always continue discussion after broadcast
50% usually continue discussion after broadcast
90% usually follow up discussion with relevant reading
34% believe opinions have been changed
77% have telephones

129. Overstreet and Overstreet, *Town Meeting Comes to Town*: 11.

130. Memo for *America's Town Meeting of the Air* from retired Lt. Commander Stewart F. Bryant, U.S. Navy, n.d. California correspondence file for Frank Hill's study of radio listening groups, box 1, American Association for Adult Education Collection, NYPL.

131. Report of Advisory Service, in Annual Report of the Town Hall Inc. Season 1939–40, Town Hall Inc. papers, NYPL.

132. Letter to Town Hall, November 12, 1937, in folder 61, box 51, NBC records, WHS.

72% have automobiles

50% prefer no definite solution to subjects

59% do not mind big words used by speakers

82% would not like commercial sponsors

84% believe a commercial sponsor would make program one sided.

"HOW CAN I MAKE AMERICA SEE BOTH SIDES?"

IT WAS DECEMBER OF '31. As he watched the throngs stamping through the snow that lay moist and fresh on the sidewalks, a sentence ran again and again through the mind of George V. Denny, Jr.

"I'd rather be shot than listen to ———."

The words were those of a friend of Denny's—a man with a closed mind—a man who, although claiming to have a liberal viewpoint, nevertheless vehemently refused to listen to the exciting coast-to-coast broadcasts of a political bigwig, because the latter epitomized the opposite political faith. Immediately after listening to one of these broadcasts, Denny returned to his office in America's Town Hall, and as he gazed out of the window at the hurrying crowds below, the thought came to him: "How can I make America see both sides?"

The answer was America's Town Meeting of the Air.

The amazing success of this outstanding radio program is summed up in one sentence: *On October 5th it begins its fifth consecutive year as an hour-long Thursday night NBC Blue Network feature!*

And on Thursday, October 5th, more than 6,000,000 Americans will eagerly await it. For this NBC program gives them the opportunity to hear prominent industrial, political and professional leaders discuss the pros and cons of timely controversial issues of national and international significance. It enables listeners to conduct their own forums. It promotes the American heritage of free thought and free speech.

The NBC Town Meeting of the Air is the old New England Town Hall on a national scale. In cities, towns and hamlets from Atlantic to Pacific, it has stimulated the creation of thousands of town hall groups—comprising citizens in all walks of life—who listen avidly to the radio discussions and who then, for hours after the program is over, give voice to their own opinions and ideas. It is a program that educates by stimulation—a program that champions democracy and is the mortal foe of dictatorship. In broadcasting this program, NBC believes it is performing the type of public service which this company regards as an important duty.

World's Greatest Broadcasting System

NATIONAL BROADCASTING COMPANY

A RADIO CORPORATION OF AMERICA SERVICE

Figure 4.1. ATMA was a flagship public service program for NBC because it so well exemplified civic paradigm virtues—the fostering of tolerance and empathy for other points of view, as well as critical intelligence. "How Can I Make America See Both Sides?" *Broadcasting* 17, no. 7 (Oct. 1, 1939): 29. © 2009, NBC Universal Inc., All Rights Reserved.

George Denny wrote to John Marshall of the Rockefeller Foundation, "There are some mighty important revelations here, particularly the 34% changed opinions."[133] That was the highest legitimation of a program under the civic paradigm. An Ohio State University study found on the contrary that few school-age *ATMA* listeners changed their opinions after listening to the program, and that those that did mostly remained within the attitude group ("radical," "liberal," or "reactionary") in which they had begun.[134] The Office of Radio Research at Columbia University found that "most of the fan mail to this program comes from persons in a high socio-economic status" and from larger cities, and hence that the program was "not reaching the group for which it is intended."[135] Through all the conflicting evidence, however, it was clear that changing the opinions of listeners was in the 1930s the agreed measure of success of a radio forum.

An educational doubt about the radio forum was always that the benefits would come to the active participants in the live audience but not to the passive listeners at home—that while there might be a public in Town Hall, there was only an audience for the radio program. One response to this was the organization of *ATMA* listening groups, to continue discussions after the broadcast. Nevertheless Harvard's Carl Friedrich wrote to James Rowland Angell in 1940 with some friendly criticisms, arguing that despite *ATMA*'s repeated claims to revive the New England town meeting, it actually failed to re-create that form of "democratic discussion of important governmental problems by the citizens of a community." Instead, "authorities present their point of view and are questioned by an otherwise passive audience.... One does not feel that the group itself is participating in the solution of the problems presented." In reply, Angell reminded Friedrich of the commercial constraints, that stations taking the broadcast needed some guarantee that "the personalities on it will attract appreciable public interest." "In effect one therefore has to choose between a bona fide Town Meeting situation and one like the present set-up, in which set speeches are delivered and the speaker then is exposed to cross questioning."[136]

Adult educators Harry and Bonaro Overstreet, evangelists for the radio forum, had an answer for this kind of criticism. In the book that was a kind of authorized biography of *ATMA*, they explained the national educational benefit of *ATMA*'s question time in this way: it put millions into a "mood to ask questions," and gave listeners "the chance to hold their own puzzlements out at arms length and see them a little more clearly." The listeners at home were at least formulating questions for themselves, and "a question asked but not answered is at an infinite remove from a question not even asked."[137] If the task of the listener was to nurture and update their own opinions, the radio forum at least provided a valuable stimulus. The question period, live on national radio, modeled the

133. George Denny to John Marshall, October 30, 1936, folder 3233, box 271, Rockefeller Foundation Archives, RAC.

134. Ronald R. Lowdermilk, *A Study of America's Town Meeting of the Air*, Bulletin no. 46, Evaluation of School Broadcasts (Columbus: Ohio State University, 1942).

135. Jeanette Sayre, *The Audience of an Educational Program* (New York: Columbia University Office of Radio Research, 1940): xxxi, xli.

136. C. J. Friedrich to James Angell, November 22, 1940; James Angell to C. J. Friedrich, November 29, 1940, folder 27, box 74, NBC records, WHS. [Companion website 4.3.]

137. Overstreet and Overstreet, *Town Meeting Comes to Town*: 49.

way an active audience could become a public, set its engaged listeners firmly down the path of self-reflexivity and openness to new ideas. During one 1936 broadcast, an audience member told discussion chair Lyman Bryson, "We all want the opportunity for the fullest expression of our spirit....Each individual is here to express his unique spirit." Bryson affirmed, "We all want a chance to be ourselves," and "We all want our personalities to count for something in the world."[138] In June 1940, Temple University gave Denny an honorary doctorate and observed in the citation that *ATMA* was "living proof that in the United States democracy is vital and vibrant, that here a man may speak his mind."[139] *ATMA*, like the other radio forums, was thus understood to have an educational role, which was all about the formation of listener opinion. The radio forum was to be a means of mass-producing individual difference among opinionated but reasonable individuals.

Opinion formation and assertion, however, was only part of the forum program's mission. The other crucial part was empathy for and tolerance of the views of others. On the stage of the Town Hall, a banner proclaimed, "Tolerance, Reason, Justice." Each was important, but the chosen order was significant—tolerance of and engagement with the views of others was the cardinal virtue in Denny's radio democracy. He began each show with the greeting "Good evening neighbors." His ideal public sphere was not only a site for rational discussion, but also a place of empathy and connection where—in Deweyan fashion—the process of discussion and relationship maintenance was more important than any particular conclusions reached. A 1940 Women's National Radio Committee survey confirmed that radio forum programs appealed particularly to women listeners.[140]

The League for Political Education had grown from the movement for women's suffrage, and there was in Town Hall rhetoric some residual trace of the grand promise of civic renewal originally held out by that movement. Denny often spoke of the power that the civically aware and educated minority of "independent voters...trained to the responsibilities of intelligent citizenship" could have in American democracy. "This is what the feminist element should have done when they were granted the franchise," he told a reporter in 1937.[141] Denny was an advocate of the kind of rational and discursive public sphere that was later so influentially described by Habermas, but that in his own time was an expression of the Deweyan principles of conscious tolerance, openness to change, and constructive individual engagement with public conversation.[142]

The Overstreets explicated *ATMA*'s perspectivalist ethos: "Men sometimes act as if they had answers...but...their views are, in reality, their opinions, shaped out of such

138. "What Is America's Platform?," *Bulletin of America's Town Meeting of the Air*, February 13, 1936 (New York: American Book Company, 1936): 17.

139. Box 30, Series 1, Denny papers, LOC.

140. "Forum Programs Preferred by Women,"*Broadcasting* 18, no. 11 (June 1, 1940): 66. Although ATMA did feature significant numbers of women speakers, in the first eight seasons they amounted to only between a fifth and a fourteenth the number of male speakers.

141. *Birmingham News-Age-Herald*, March 21, 1937.

142. Jürgen Habermas, *The Structural Transformation of the Public Sphere: An Inquiry into a Category of Bourgeois Society*, trans. Thomas Burger with Frederick Lawrence (Cambridge, MA: MIT Press, 1991).

experience and observation as they have been able to achieve." Naïve certainty offered only false comfort, they concluded: "We have to work at our social problems under the precarious condition of never being quite sure whether or not what we think is true."[143] Here in an authorized statement of *ATMA*'s philosophy was a succinct summary of the tensions that underlay it. Social knowledge was opinion, relative to experience. But this was a nonnegotiable truth—we "have to" accept this "precarious" epistemological status; it is "a matter of fact" that social knowledge is not fact. The goal of the program was a remaking of the self—a refashioning, as the Overstreets described it, "along more democratic lines." We need to expose ourselves to "more and more types of mental and social situations until we feel enough at home in them to be less naïve, irritable, and dogmatically bad-mannered than we are at present." We are, the Overstreets concluded, "unskilled in changing our minds."[144] Here was the Deweyan program of *ATMA*, with its characteristic expression of certainty about uncertainty and change, laid out in striking fashion.

One of the primary objectives of *ATMA*, Denny wrote, was "to make people think for themselves," to persuade them that truth was complex and might not be grasped immediately.[145] In setting out instructions for those running discussion groups after *ATMA* broadcasts, Denny stated that "it is rarely possible and often undesirable to attempt to arrive immediately at conclusions about the subjects discussed on the Town Meeting program.... Judgment should be reserved on a great many proposals until more mature consideration has been given the subject."[146] The program attempted to create an ideal public forum, which would be open, provisional, discursive, and disinterested—and quite unlike the actual world of politics in which money and power and pragmatic deal making rather than rational argument determined outcomes.

The challenge to democracy was, Denny thought, whether it was possible "for a highly complicated, industrialized, citified civilization to conduct its affairs by those modes of common discussion and mutual understanding that were successful in a village society?"[147] It was Lippmann's question. And in the practice of *ATMA*, Denny returned a Deweyan answer. But he never stopped posing the Lippmann question, and it remained an open question for him. "Are We Ready for Democracy?" he asked in a 1935 speech, asserting that, in order to have a sound democracy, "we must have citizens who are capable of meeting the challenge of self-government."[148] "Can we discover a method of making our democracy responsive to the will of the *best* rather than the *worst* elements in our society?" he asked in 1937: "Are capacity tests possible or desirable? What about universal suffrage? Should or can we abandon it?"[149] These were in some ways shocking questions for an American advocate of democracy to be contemplating. But in other ways, the success of

143. Overstreet, *Town Meeting Comes to Town*: 12.

144. Overstreet, *Town Meeting Comes to Town*: 256–57.

145. Denny, *Town Meeting Discussion Leader's Handbook*: 10–11.

146. Denny, *Town Meeting Discussion Leader's Handbook*: 23–24.

147. Overstreet and Overstreet, *Town Meeting Comes to Town*: 6.

148. George V. Denny Jr., "Are We Ready for Democracy?," address before NY Federation of Women's Clubs, Syracuse, NY: 2, Box 3, Series 2, Denny papers, LOC.

149. Denny, "Bring Back the Town Meeting!": 110.

ATMA rested on Denny's willingness to air this kind of root and branch questioning of American liberal democratic fundamentals, whether from the left or the right. Georgia Congressman Eugene Cox, at times elected unanimously because of the racially restricted suffrage in Georgia, observed in an *ATMA* discussion of the poll tax in 1942, "I do not believe…that good results would follow a universal suffrage. In other words I do not believe…that everybody, irrespective of all qualifications, should come in and express his views."[150] *ATMA* allowed its speakers to ask these basic, even disturbing, questions about the scope and functioning of democracy, despite its constant affirmation that fostering democracy was its role and purpose.

Further, *ATMA* never allowed listeners to think of existing social, political, and economic arrangements as natural or inevitable, and it consistently provided space for advocates of alternative social, political, and economic systems. Remarkably, *ATMA* did place the free market capitalist democratic system under scrutiny, as but one of a range of possible options for American society. The opening program in 1935 presented a communist, socialist, fascist, and a democrat. A January 1936 program asked "Which Way Capitalism—Competition or Cooperatives?" and featured one speaker arguing for "competitive capitalism" and another speaking for cooperatives.[151] *ATMA* in the mid-1930s was allowed to ask fundamental social and political questions and to present a range of genuinely differing views. Topics covered in the early years included social security, economic cooperatives, the Townsend Plan, unions, world peace, unemployment, propaganda, foreign policy, and democracy.

Some listeners, however, responded with hostility to this kind of openness. If Town Hall enthusiasts tended to reproduce the liberal rhetoric of the program's planners, to praise its openness and responsiveness to change, critics of the show often found a disguised radicalism in the questioning of the American status quo that the program seemed to enable and encourage. NBC received a letter of complaint from a Philadelphia advertising agency owner, who wrote that the League for Political Education "seems obviously to be a creature of communism, not only because of the nature of their discussions but judging by the speakers' views and the enthusiastic reception given their subversive platforms by the audience."[152]

As this letter suggests, the audience at Town Hall often differed in response from the radio audience. Listeners to the broadcast were aware of the reactions of the live audience and would comment in letters on what they heard and surmised about it. Those respectable New Yorkers who were Town Hall members were from very different backgrounds from much of the rest of the audience that *ATMA* broadcasts attracted. During a controversy in 1940 about audience bias in a debate between Republican presidential candidate Wendell Willkie and Attorney General Jackson, Denny explained that 1200 of the 2000 tickets for the broadcast were for members of Town Hall, who were "undoubtedly conservative and probably favored the ideas of Mr. Willkie."[153] These Town Hall members

150. "Should the Poll Tax Be Abolished?," *Bulletin of America's Town Meeting of the Air* 8, no. 26 (October 26, 1942): 14.

151. George Denny to John Royal, December 30, 1935, folder 7, box 34, NBC records, WHS.

152. Letter to M. H. Aylesworth, November 15, 1935, folder 2, box 34, NBC records, WHS.

153. "Denny Recalls 100-Ticket Error," *New York Times,* October 25, 1940: 10.

were often outraged by the heterogeneity of the audience that the broadcast town meet-ings attracted. One woman reported in 1935 that she and four of her friends had decided not to come to the town meetings in the future because of the audience: "Such a mob of booing, baaing, hissing creatures I never saw—most of them east side Jews. Their ques-tions were not to the point and were put in a very rude way."[154] *ATMA* radio listeners also commented on what they could deduce about the New York audience from hearing audi-ence noise during the broadcast. One anonymous listener detected foreign and undemo-cratic qualities in the "Jewish Socialist" Town Hall audience: "Most of your questioners are Jews and from the manner they have of booing they appear to act like any pack of wolves in ganging a speaker who disagrees with them."[155] There had been correspondence from the inception of *ATMA*, charging that the speakers and/or audience of the program presented foreign views. In 1935 a man from New Jersey reported that he had heard in the "background of noise" during one program "continuously broken English of Italian, English, German or Jewish flavors." He proposed that "at least three generations of American citizenship" be required of people who spoke on the radio.[156]

ATMA in its early years had boldly proclaimed its openness to all views. The first broadcast asked, "Which Way America? Fascism, Communism, Socialism, Democracy?" and included communist speaker A. J. Muste, chair of the Workers Party of the United States. In a 1938 interview, Denny reported proudly that "Communists frequently are in our audience on Thursday evenings airing their views and asking questions."[157] Other communists spoke on the show—Clarence Hathaway, editor of the *Daily Worker* and member of the central committee of the Communist Party spoke in 1938, and Earl Browder spoke in January 1939. After the Nazi-Soviet pact of August 1939, however, and in the context of Martin Dies' House Un-American Activities Committee's investigations into communism and fascism in the United States, Denny and Town Hall changed their minds about allowing communists in front of the *ATMA* microphone. Town Hall's exec-utive committee agreed in December 1939 (4 votes to 2) that neither Earl Browder nor German American Bund leader Fritz Kuhn would be invited onto the program in future.[158] A Town Hall press release under Denny's name was sent to the Dies Committee, stating that because of the external loyalties they served, neither Browder nor Kuhn was "entitled to the privileges of fair competition in debate where honesty and integrity are essential."[159] By 1939, Denny's ideal for *ATMA* had to this extent been significantly compromised.

ATMA rapidly gained critical acclaim for its practical demonstration of what radio could do for American democracy. NBC needed the public praise—Margaret Cuthbert

154. Letter to George Denny, December 17, 1935, box 77, Town Hall Inc. papers, NYPL.

155. Anonymous letter, n.d., Radio Department Correspondence late 1930s, box 77, Town Hall Inc., papers, NYPL.

156. Letter to Town Hall, November 23, 1935, box 77, Town Hall Inc papers, NYPL.

157. *Bulletin of America's Town Meeting of the Air* 3, no. 12 (January 24, 1938): 32.

158. Minutes of Town Hall Executive Committee Meeting, December 18, 1939, Town Hall Inc. papers, NYPL.

159. "Statement by George V. Denny, Jr., President, The Town Hall, Inc." n.d., box 20, series 1, Denny Papers, LOC.

had predicted in 1935 during preliminary discussions that *ATMA* would "no doubt" get a prize from the Women's National Radio Committee.[160] The program did regularly win awards. "Because this series has best typified the spirit of justice, freedom and democracy," reported the *Radio Guide* in 1938, "it has repeatedly been selected as the finest program of its kind."[161] The reception of the program outside the United States was important to NBC as well—in 1936, John Royal organized for distribution of *ATMA* bulletins to delegates of the International Broadcasting Union and to NBC's British and European representatives.[162]

Despite its symbolic and political importance, NBC as a business could not guarantee the national reach of the program on local affiliate stations. The first *ATMA* broadcast went out over 14 NBC stations; by 1939, it was being carried by 78 stations of the 88 on the Blue network, but with limited coverage in the South—as always, local station acceptance, not just network broadcast, was needed to gain a genuinely national audience.[163] The Blue was the smaller and less popular NBC network, and *ATMA* by the late 1930s faced tough competition on Thursday evenings. John Royal admitted in 1939 that, pitted against Maxwell House and Bing Crosby on NBC Red, and Major Bowes's amateur hour on CBS, *ATMA* had "the strongest opposition of any show on the air."[164]

At various times, NBC complained about the cost of sustaining *ATMA* and talked about selling it to a sponsor. Denny had then to mobilize opinion in support of retaining *ATMA*'s sustaining, advertisement-free, status. "It seems to me the more I think of it," he wrote to Royal in 1939, "that the interests of NBC and Town Hall and American democracy will best be served by continuing on the present basis....We have a tremendous responsibility to the nation."[165] There was strong opposition to selling *ATMA* and the other forum programs from forum advocates such as Socialist leader Norman Thomas. But other friends of the radio forums were concluding that sponsorship might be the only way to guarantee good and stable broadcast times. In 1941, *ATMA* was shifted to 10 p.m. on the West Coast. There was protest from *ATMA* discussion groups that 11 p.m. was simply too late to begin a postbroadcast discussion. Some detected a class bias in the shift, arguing that working people could not stay up so late—a California listener complained that *ATMA* did not come on "until the shameful hour of 10 P.M. An hour when all working people are in bed."[166] Town Hall's Byron Williams reported from the West that "this thought has been broached by nearly every person I have spoken with," and that many now understood that only a sponsor buying the time "guarantees the listener the right to her programs at a decent hour."[167] NBC did keep *ATMA* as a sustaining program through until the splitting of its networks. It

160. Margaret Cuthbert to Alfred H. Morton, July 29, 1935, folder 6, box 34, NBC records, WHS.

161. *Radio Guide*, November 12, 1938: 14.

162. John Royal to Franklin Dunham, November 11, 1936, folder 31, box 92, NBC records, WHS.

163. Marian S. Carter, "Town Hall—Radio Forum Division Report 1938–39": 22, folder 12, box 66, NBC records, WHS.

164. John Royal to Lenox Lohr, May 2, 1939, folder 10, box 66, NBC records, WHS.

165. George V. Denny to John Royal, October 18, 1939, folder 12, box 66, NBC records, WHS.

166. Letter to Denny, November 9, 1941, box 18, Town Hall Inc. papers, NYPL.

167. Byron Williams to Chester Snell, February 26, 1941, box 14, Town Hall Inc. papers, NYPL.

was ABC in 1943 that commercialized the *Town Meeting*, taking *Readers Digest* as a sponsor in 1944, and thereafter selling the program as a "cooperative" with several sponsors.

BEYOND THE BROADCAST: LISTENING AND DISCUSSION GROUPS

The innovations in democratic radio of this era were not limited to forum programs. There was consensus among radio and democracy activists that the broadcast was only a part of the process of using radio to foster democracy. The follow-up was as important, because it was opinion formation that mattered most—people had not only to receive the stimulus of listening to multi-opinion radio, they had then to exercise their skills at opinion forming and articulate their own opinions.

The conversation was the thing for Denny, as for Dewey, not the conclusions reached. In this he anticipated the two-step argument of Lazarsfeld and others in the postwar period, understanding the buffering of media messages in local conversation as an essential defense against propaganda. "When they talk things over they get an interchange of ideas," he explained to the *New York Times* in 1943, quoting Hitler on the way a mass audience could be addressed so that the words were "received under a hypnotic influence, ineradicable and impervious to every reasonable explanation."[168] Town Hall, along with the other advocates of democratic radio, always insisted that broadcasting multi-opinion programs was only half the job—people had also to be taught to listen attentively and then to discuss what they had heard. One of the questions addressed in the Forum Project's 1939 *Forum Planning Handbook* was, "Why plan forums when we can listen to all sorts of discussions on the radio?" The answer emphasized the importance of participating in discussion as well as hearing it: "We do not ourselves grow in understanding and articulate ability as much as we should when we merely consume prepared presentations.…If they are to mean much to us, we must digest them, challenge them, and talk them over in groups.…The radio increases rather than diminishes the need for face-to-face discussion."[169] Denny gave an address at Harvard on the town meeting as adult education, in which he observed that "we are functioning now in only one area of education, namely, stimulation." Lyman Bryson commented on the speech in a letter to Denny: "We both know that discussion is most important as a stimulus, that is, it is part of a process and the other parts, thoughtful study and social experiment, are equally necessary. Studebaker seems to think that discussion will do the work all by itself.…I think he is wrong."[170] Bryson, in this private jibe at his former colleague's forum enthusiasm, was in fact articulating the orthodox wisdom of educators at the time—that forum discussion (live or broadcast) did not produce civic or educational effects on its own. The organized listening group was part of the answer to this problem.

168. S. J. Woolf, "Umpire of the Town Meeting," *New York Times*, June 6, 1943: SM 16.

169. J. W. Studebaker, *Forum Planning Handbook* (Washington, DC: U.S. Office of Education, 1939): 59.

170. Lyman Bryson to Denny, August 6, 1937, box 24, series 1, Denny papers, LOC.

In the Harvard speech, Denny described plans for an ambitious five-story addition to the Town Hall building that would have included space for the extension division to service "listening groups and other town hall centers" all over the country.[171] He formulated this strategy for a national Town Hall movement—to ensure the "perpetuation of democratic institutions through education" and to stem the "rising tide of dictatorship"— during the successful second season of *ATMA*. The main aim was to encourage and support the formation of listening groups:

> In these community forums for the discussion of common public problems, there may be developed a constantly growing group of politically independent citizens, self-trained to consider both sides, or many sides, of civic issues, and self-prepared in consequence to demand of their political representatives decisions which commend themselves to intelligence rather than to prejudice or passion.[172]

Town Hall sought donations to sustain the work, and the Town Hall Advisory Service, which serviced the discussion groups, also gained some public assistance in the form of National Youth Administration workers (28 of them in 1939).[173] Chester D. Snell, the former dean of the highly regarded Extension Division at the University of Wisconsin, was hired to run the national advisory service. Snell reported to a former Wisconsin colleague that "'it is easy to organize the forum groups for they organize themselves and then write in asking for service. The demand is simply terrific, amounting some days to over 7000 letters."[174] The material sent to groups included a copy of the Overstreets' book, the *Town Meeting Discussion Leader's Handbook*, a booklet for each person in the group titled *How to Discuss—Suggestions to Group Members*, access to a correspondence advisory service, reading lists, and the *Town Meeting* bulletin, which contained the transcript of last week's broadcast and a selected bibliography for further reading.[175] A member of one listening group in Ransom, Kansas (population 600), wrote to Town Hall in 1939 to describe the operation of his group:

> We start our meetings at 7:30 pm, one hour before your broadcast starts. We discuss the same subjects as you discuss. Usually have about three speakers. Then when the broadcast starts we listen to it, and have a question period after....Those that attend regularly are: High School professor, Doctor, two bakers, merchants, Catholic Priest, Methodist Minister, High School boys, County Attorney, Editor of Ness County News, two ex-representatives in State Legislature, farmers and laborers .....[176]

171. Denny Jr., "Bring Back the Town Meeting!": 119–20.

172. "Plan of the League for Political Education for Making Its Facilities Available to Cooperative Groups in All Sections of the Country," box 20, series 1, Denny Papers, LOC.

173. Chester Snell, "Town Hall Advisory Service Report": 27, folder 12, box 66, NBC records, WHS.

174. Chester Snell to Prof. R. J. Gilbert, Madison, Wisconsin, January 14, 1938, box 13, Town Hall Inc. papers, NYPL.

175. Hill and Williams, *Radio's Listening Groups*: 45, 88.

176. Letter, January 13, 1939, box 13, Town Hall Inc. papers, NYPL.

ATMA discussion groups met to discuss the national and international issues heard over the NBC broadcast, but "frequently," as was reported from Wilkes-Barre, "such discussions lead to expressions of views on local issues and, in a number of cases, have brought about the establishment of permanent weekly forums."[177] This vindicated Denny's internationalist belief that the discussion of world affairs served as training for local citizenship: "They become much more skilled in discussing local civic affairs through first trying out their voices on national and international issues."[178] Advocates of radio forums and listening groups hoped that in just this way, the combination of radio forums and listening groups might have the reach and power to do something about the problem of civic competence. By 1940, it was estimated that there were more than 3000 *ATMA* discussion groups in the United States, one-third of which paid for affiliation with Town Hall and received its publications and assistance. Denny proposed a target of 1000 Town Hall centers and 50,000 discussion groups meeting throughout the nation each Thursday evening.[179] Radio forum advocates never doubted that the leadership of trained discussion experts would be necessary to forge useful local forums. Radio would provide the occasion, the high-level stimulus piped in from elsewhere; the discussion group was needed to localize and actualize the potential of the forum. The Overstreets, reading *ATMA*'s mail, enthused: "Letter after letter from all over America tells of this almost inevitable falling into groups."[180]

Local town meeting radio programs were also part of Denny's grand plan—by 1939, they existed in Chicago, Columbus, Boston, Buffalo, Lawrence, Albuquerque, El Paso, Memphis, Philadelphia, and several other centers.[181] In Ohio, the *Columbus Town Meeting of the Air* had its first broadcast in March 1939 on WCOL on the topic "What is the meaning of 'un-American'?" The Columbus meeting also addressed a range of local problems: "What is the Answer to Columbus Unemployment?"; "What is Columbus Doing for the Health of its People?" "Is Columbus Solving its Traffic Problem?"; "Do Our Schools Prepare for Democracy?"[182] This complied with the stated wish of Town Hall in New York that local radio forums restrict themselves to local issues—Denny wrote to Columbus to say that Town Hall was glad to render any assistance but trusted that "in return" they would "deal principally with local and regional problems."[183] Dr. Samuel Shellabarger, headmaster of the Columbus School for Girls and a member of the Columbus *Town Meeting* advisory committee, disagreed—in his opinion, it was necessary

177. "Radio Club to Meet at 'Y.M.' on Thursdays," *Wilkes-Barre Times*, November 10, 1937.

178. Denny, *Town Meeting Discussion Leader's Handbook*: 18.

179. "Town Hall President's Report 1940," in Volume of Minutes of Meetings of Executive Committee May 1939–April 1941, Town Hall Inc. papers, NYPL; "Appraisal of the Plan for Town Hall's Proposed Relationships with Affiliated Town Halls and Discussion Groups," October 1947, in box 20, Series 1, Denny papers, LOC. The money for the Advisory Service ran out however after three and a half years, and it was closed down.

180. Overstreet and Overstreet, *Town Meeting Comes to Town*: 57.

181. Marian S. Carter, "Town Hall—Radio Forum Division Report 1938–39": 23, folder 12, box 66, NBC records, WHS.

182. Folder 7, box 1, Columbus Town Meeting Association Records, MSS 522, OHS.

183. Letter from George Denny to Ed Bronson, Program Director, WCOL, February 13, 1939, folder 7, box 1, Columbus Town Meeting Association Records, MSS 522, OHS.

to widen the range of subjects from local and state to national and international questions because "statesmen want to know opinions of communities, even to the smallest hamlet."[184] There was some discussion in Columbus about whether a vote should be taken at the conclusion of each town meeting, but there was among the organizers "a somewhat general feeling that the attempt to crystallize feelings by means of a ballot was directly opposed to the principle of Town Meeting, the central core of which is open and free discussion without any final attempt to arrive at a majority conclusion."[185] Committee member Herschel W. Nisonger, professor of adult education at Ohio State University, wrote an information sheet to explain their position: "We do not expect our discussions to settle questions or to provide all the answers. For some, the discussions will merely sharpen areas of conflict. But for all who listen, opinion will become more informed, and thinking will be stimulated, and freedom against the sway of mass emotion will be strengthened."[186]

Lyman Bryson described the radio listening group as an attempt to compensate for one of radio's disabilities, the fact that "listening is no longer necessarily a social function." Mature men and women, Bryson asserted, "quicken their own mental lives and refresh themselves by the tolerant comparison of what they themselves think with what is advanced by others." But the civic advantages were even more important. Bryson defined "genuinely productive" listening to "the best radio speakers" as often involving challenge and discomfort—"they make us uncomfortable in our complacent assurance that we must be right about everything." It was clear that for Bryson, discussion groups were "for people who live on a higher intellectual plane and who find the play of ideas interesting in itself, people who have enough of the philosophic temper to know that others may differ with them and still be reasonable."[187] Bryson understood that not all Americans had "enough of the philosophic temper" to enjoy the play of ideas, the constant openness to new perspectives, that was at the heart of the forum idea. The remaining chapters explore the consequences of that insight.

184. Minutes of Meeting of Advisory Committee, April 4, 1939, folder 4, box 1, Columbus Town Meeting Association Records, MSS 522, OHS.

185. Minutes of Annual Meeting, April 1, 1940, folder 4, box 1, Columbus Town Meeting Association Records, MSS 522, OHS.

186. Typed sheet: Herschel W. Nisonger, "The Columbus Town Meeting: A Community Radio Forum," October 1940, folder 5, box 1, Columbus Town Meeting Association Records, MSS 522, OHS.

187. Lyman Bryson, "Listening Groups" (address to the Radio Institute of Audible Arts, August 1935), box 20, Lyman Bryson papers, LOC.

Part II
Division

5

Class, Cosmopolitanism, and Division

The most contested line of division among radio listeners in the 1930s was not that between highbrow and lowbrow, to which historians have given much attention, but between open and closed, change and stability. My argument in this chapter is that, as a direct consequence of its domination by a set of civic values that were also cosmopolitan and pluralist, radio had a class-divided audience. Civic paradigm influenced programming embraced diversity and inclusion, stood for pluralism and tolerance. That this kind of broadcasting divided as much as it united was one of the slowly dawning and almost tragic discoveries about broadcasting in the later 1930s.

Elite listeners brought to debates about radio in the late 1930s, and to their own listening to radio, shared civic paradigm ideas—a sense of the constructedness and the constantly changing nature of identity, a culturally pluralist perception that our normal is someone else's strange, and that it is good for us to experience what we must look like to them. Some listeners enthusiastically embraced these particular hopes for radio and the kind of education it might provide. They expected a better society and a better world to result from this kind of exposure to difference. Other listeners both recognized and rejected these ideas.

Radio under the civic paradigm was expected to transform listeners into more civically competent citizens, more active, flexible, and self-reflexive. Philosopher Sidney Hook argued in 1938 that the crucial educational function of radio was "the training of the radio audience in the powers of independent and critical reflection." More important than either information or entertainment, he maintained, was "the development of the listener's intelligence to a point where he can find entertainment in the play of ideas, the confrontation of argument with argument, and the quest for truth."[1] Hook articulated clearly the transformative hopes of radio's democratic reformers and isolated the very thing that other radio listeners would recognize and resist—the prizing of the "play of ideas" above the living out of any particular fixed or inherited identity.

Defenders of the American system, as we have seen, described European radio as putting only the point of view of the government of the day, and American radio as committed to representing all points of view. When William Hard argued in 1935 that "the highest duty" of the American broadcaster was "to admit all schools of thought to his

---

1. Sidney Hook broadcast on WEVD, New York, November 11, 1938, quoted in Paul H. Sheats, *Forums on the Air* (Washington DC: FREC, 1939): 6.

studios," he added that it was "necessary that we require each and every radio station...to become, in and of itself, a reasonably complete epitome of the whole battle of social contentions in the audience that it serves."[2] Hard was a Republican; this commitment to broadcasting representative diversity was, as discussed above, the more conservative option available to broadcasters in the 1930s. But this should not blind us to the unsettlingly liberal and progressive quality of the idea that citizens should be exposed to the "whole battle of social contentions." This idea proved socially divisive in the 1930s, as the commitment to pluralism and multiple perspectives offended those Americans who knew there to be truths beyond opinion. The civic paradigm contained an ethical and prescriptive view that Americans ought to be, had to be, taken out of their think-alike communities and exposed to difference.

HANS KALTENBORN'S TWO AUDIENCES

The Czechoslovakian crisis of September 1938, culminating in the Munich Agreement, was a defining moment for very many American radio listeners. Radio's coverage of the crisis was recognized at the time—and has been named by historians ever since—as one of the moments when American radio "came of age" as a provider of instantaneous international news. Newspapers simply could not match radio's capacity to provide constant updates to a rapidly changing situation. Radio allowed American listeners to hear speeches from European leaders live, with commentary from American reporters on the spot. The BBC's Felix Greene was impressed and concerned—he reported to London his experience of listening in Canada to "the excellent hour by hour American news reports from the capitals of Europe and hearing nothing comparable from the BBC."[3] During the Czechoslovakian crisis, American radio self-consciously set out to demonstrate its capacity to respond to an international crisis in the same way it attempted to cover social and political issues at home—by exposing listeners to all sides of the argument and encouraging them to form their own opinions. NBC advertised that its coverage of the Czech crisis demonstrated its commitment "to serve the public interest, covering with complete neutrality all phases and viewpoints of the situation."[4] To the civic paradigm imagination, this was an opportunity to demonstrate the difference radio could make to dealing with conflict at the most serious and consequential level. John Studebaker enthused in October about the educational functions of radio's international crisis coverage: 'What is happening today is grist for the mill of the teachers of psychology, sociology, civics and history. There is nothing in the textbooks to compare with it.'[5]

At CBS, veteran radio commentator H. V. Kaltenborn—who had been broadcasting since 1926, and was now 58 years of age—staged a marathon performance. He "kept vigil

---

2. William Hard, "Radio and Public Opinion," *Annals of the American Academy of Political and Social Science* 177, no. 1 (January 1935): 106, 111.

3. Felix Greene report, November 14, 1938, BBC Written Archives File E1/113/3.

4. *Broadcasting* 15, no. 7 (October 1, 1938): 7.

5. "War Service Radio a High Spot," *Broadcasting* 15, no. 8 (October 15, 1938): 62.

Figure 5.1. H. V. Kaltenborn, CBS radio news commentator, in September 1934. CBS/Landov.

by the microphone night and day from Hitler's Nuremberg speech on September 12th until the day after the signing of the four-power agreement in Munich on the 29th," sleeping only briefly on a cot brought into the studio. During those days, Kaltenborn made 85 broadcasts—each unscripted, "being an analysis of the news as it was occurring."[6] If an important new piece of information came in over the wire service tickers, a special white button on his desk allowed a news "flash" to cut in on network programs: "Immediately, all other programs are cut off the air, and all stations are connected with my microphone."[7] Figure 5.1. [Companion website link 5.1.]

When Kaltenborn published *I Broadcast the Crisis* in late October 1938, he was confident that war had been averted. "We were saved from war, I am convinced," he wrote, "by the mobilization of world opinion for peace." This had happened because of radio: "The people heard not merely from their own leaders, but…from the leaders of all nations involved in the crisis." In turn, "the people carried back to their leaders their response to every move…a demand for peace which even the most hardened dictator could not but obey." In the future, Kaltenborn proclaimed, "the ultimate issue of peace or war is to be decided by all mankind in the great forum of the air." Kaltenborn believed at that moment that radio had inaugurated a new era of global discursive democracy. As a loyal employee

6. H. V. Kaltenborn, *I Broadcast the Crisis* (New York: Random House, 1938): 8–9.
7. Kaltenborn, *I Broadcast the Crisis*: 11.

of CBS, Kaltenborn added that, of course, "America, with the only free radio system in the world today, led the way." [8]

The fan mail received about the war crisis broadcasts heaped praise on Kaltenborn for his efforts. Listeners told of how their normal lives had been put on hold for the duration. "Every spare moment," wrote one New York listener, "I, my friends and my family, have had our ears glued to the radio, your comments, and the work of your associates."[9] A Coney Island pharmacist wrote, "You were marvelous. I refused to wait on people in my drugstore till you were through speaking."[10] A New York man reported, "In the past few days we have been keeping the radio open practically all day and half of the night so we may not miss any of the news dispatches as well as your commentaries."[11] Out in Santa Monica, another man confessed, "I can't do any work at all. I sit here by the radio from morning to night waiting for more news."[12] For those whose work allowed them some flexibility, the crisis took over most of their lives for those days. One Connecticut doctor reported, "So urgent was our desire not to miss a single comment that we were ultimately reduced to sleeping in shifts so that the one awake might waken the others for each new announcement. The crisis became the most important matter in the household, not excluding my own professional work."[13]

This is the familiar story of the 1938 crisis—it was a time when Americans of all kinds stayed close by their radios, as the networks provided unprecedented coverage of the events in Europe around the clock. Kaltenborn had become in those weeks, at the age of 58, a major radio star and a serious international commentator. Even so skeptical a listener as Theodor Adorno informed his parents in September 1939 that CBS had "better commentators (Kaltenborn)" than NBC.[14] What is less often analyzed is the divided response to the news. One class of listeners took Kaltenborn at his word when he said his aim was the production of a kind of objective knowledge, assembled from all the various conflicting propagandas and interested accounts, by the exercise of his educated and critical skills. "I notice that many of you are grateful to me for what you call my 'expression of my opinion.' Well, now, I only hope that I didn't express my opinion too often.... What one individual thinks or believes is of absolutely no importance in a crisis of this kind."[15] Many listeners responded to this, acknowledging that the construction of objective knowledge was an arduous and demanding task. One woman expressed her "admiration for the restraint, fairness and objectivity which you are displaying under exceedingly difficult conditions. To appraise the situation coolly, to listen to both sides with as little prejudice as is humanly possible, and to give all available facts to the public...is a task requiring great tact, steady nerves, and a very broad outlook."[16] Some of

8. Kaltenborn, *I Broadcast the Crisis*: 3.

9. Letter to H. V. Kaltenborn, September 26, 1938, folder 2, box 31, Kaltenborn papers, WHS.

10. Letter to H. V. Kaltenborn, September 5, 1938, folder 3, box 31, Kaltenborn papers, WHS.

11. Letter to H. V. Kaltenborn, September 28, 1938, folder 4, box 31, Kaltenborn papers, WHS.

12. Letter to H. V. Kaltenborn, September 27, 1938, folder 3, box 31, Kaltenborn papers, WHS.

13. Letter to H. V. Kaltenborn, October 9, 1938, folder 1, box 33, Kaltenborn papers, WHS.

14. Theodor Adorno to parents, September 8, 1939, in Christoph Godde and Henri Lonitz (eds.), *Theodor Adorno: Letters to His Parents* (Cambridge: Polity, 2006): 17.

15. Kaltenborn, *I Broadcast the Crisis*: 254.

16. Letter, New York City, September 27, 1938, box 31, Kaltenborn papers, WHS.

these listeners who recognized and praised the work that was involved in Kaltenborn's broadcasts were themselves involved in the production of professional knowledge. A doctor from Akron found Kaltenborn's broadcasts "so clear and your opinions so concise and unbiased." "As a professional man," he wrote, "I can understand the terrific strain and ordeal you are encountering."[17] A New York man confided that he thought "few of the many thousands who listen to your analyses of the crisis overseas have any conception of the uncanny balance, and point of view finesse, which flavor your frequent comments."[18]

These listeners recognized and applauded Kaltenborn's skill. They could view his broadcasts as a kind of performance, and they praised him as a missionary of the civic paradigm virtues of rationality, tolerance, and critical analysis. They were convinced of the universal appeal of such values and virtues, and dwelt lovingly on the influence that they felt sure Kaltenborn's broadcasts were already having on the world. "My husband and I," wrote a woman from Newburgh, New York, "feel such a deep sense of gratitude to you and admiration for your fairness, clarity and intelligent interpretation of the fateful news of these days.... If only—oh, if only all the men and women in Germany might hear you!"[19] There was for some a quite visceral pleasure in hearing such a performance of calm and rationality in the face of mounting chaos and unreason: "Only this morning, a woman spoke to me of the way in which you translated Hitler's harangue—of your calm, cultivated voice coming so gravely and steadily between the hysterical outbursts of the Fuhrer. 'It was so beautiful,' she said, 'It thrilled me.'"[20] Listeners praised Kaltenborn's manner of speech: "There is a 'something' about your crisp utterance which adds to the items of foreign news an element lacking in most commentators," wrote a Florida woman. "To explain the developments so clearly and concisely and in English so simple that even a child may understand is indeed a gift from God," wrote another woman.[21]

Such listeners acknowledged that they themselves lacked the expertise correctly to interpret the flow of information from Europe. "We are able, in our own way, to analyze them," said a Hollywood man, "but when we have listened to you we realize how little we would know of their real significance without your help."[22] These listeners also endorsed Kaltenborn's hope that radio in general, and Kaltenborn's enlightened commentaries in particular, might bring peace. Such listeners wanted to remind Kaltenborn of the extent to which the fate of the world rested on the successful conduct of his broadcasts. "If sober thinking based on firm conviction, like your own, can arouse enthusiasm in me, the chances of its doing the same in others is excellent, and the likelihood of an equitable solution to world ills is no longer inconceivable," wrote one resident of New York's Fifth Avenue. "The decline of the fanatic may well be at hand. My own life in the meantime hanging in the balance, my admiration is not wholly unselfish. It is upon the continued

17. Letter, Akron, OH, September 28, 1938, folder 4, box 31, Kaltenborn papers, WHS.
18. Letter, New York City, September, 1938, folder 2, box 32, Kaltenborn papers, WHS.
19. Letter, Newburgh, NY, September 27, 1938, box 31, Kaltenborn papers, WHS.
20. Letter, New Orleans, October 5, 1938, folder 1, box 33, Kaltenborn papers, WHS.
21. Letter, Albany, NY, September 26, 1938, box 31, Kaltenborn papers, WHS.
22. Letter, Hollywood, CA, September 25, 1938, box 31, Kaltenborn papers, WHS.

sanity of men like your self that peace, for America at least, now rests."[23] One New York State woman exhorted Kaltenborn to teach: "There must be some other way beside wholesale murder to settle the nation's ills, and I think this is your opportunity to train your listeners accordingly."[24] A man from Troy, New York, was so moved that he sent a telegram: "Men like you are indeed indispensable to the freedom of thought and integrity of press and to the rescue of public opinion from the menace of deliberately misguided propaganda."[25] From recognizing Kaltenborn's contributions to international peace, it was only a small step to seeing him as a future leader of the nation. One Los Angeles man hoped "that some time in the not too distant future you will occupy a post in our country to assist in the guiding of its destinies."[26]

For many listeners, it was Kaltenborn's rationality that would provide the cure for the world's strife. A New York man wrote, "To keep the citizens of the United States on an even keel and thinking straight when emotion and sentiment run high is a gargantuan task but your untiring efforts have done much toward that end."[27] "Congratulations on your analysis this morning at 11:20," wrote a Pennsylvania listener. "I think that if the German population had the opportunity of hearing it, it would be more effective than all the diplomatic negotiations."[28] From Minnesota: "We appreciate your excellent reporting and venture to say that you are in yourself contributing to world peace + progress."[29]

More specifically, there was the hope that radio might provide a new forum for the settling of international quarrels. A Florida man was full of hope for a new era of internal peace and understanding: "After all the plans in the past for setting up agencies, leagues, combines etc., to prevent war…we find that the world through the medium of radio broadcasting has developed the greatest preventative of war in the history of the world. I think that a real first class war amongst the big powers will be a difficult thing to ever again become a reality."[30] A Spokane listener wrote, "I wish the next world war would be fought over radio by men like you who give up personal ambition, so that selfishness, envy and intolerance will be entirely settled by radio conversations rather than on battle fields."[31] A Hollywood man anticipated radio making neighbors of all the citizens of the world: "It means that the whole world has had a seat at the very table where policies are deliberated and formulated. I am aware that no one is so entrenched or insulated from 'Public Opinion,' as not to feel the effects of the accumulation of this force. And this force is always on the side of Justice, Intelligence, Toleration, and Neighborliness."[32] For these civic paradigm enthusiasts, the only possible explanation for the rise of fascism was lack of intelligence. A Pennsylvania woman wrote that Hitler's followers "remind

23. Letter, New York City, September 26, 1938, box 31, Kaltenborn papers, WHS.
24. Letter, Utica, NY, September 19, 1938, box 30, Kaltenborn papers, WHS.
25. Letter, Troy, NY, September 23, 1938, box 31, Kaltenborn papers, WHS.
26. Letter, Los Angeles, September 28, 1938, folder 4, box 31, Kaltenborn papers, WHS.
27. Letter, Tonawanda, NY, September 23, 1938, box 31, Kaltenborn papers, WHS.
28. Letter, Wilkes Barre, PA, September 27, 1938, box 31, Kaltenborn papers, WHS.
29. Letter, Duluth, MN, September 29, 1938, box 31, Kaltenborn papers, WHS.
30. Letter, West Palm Beach, FL, September 28, 1938, Kaltenborn papers, box 31, WHS.
31. Letter, Spokane, WA, September 26, 1938, box 31, Kaltenborn papers, WHS.
32. Letter, Hollywood, CA, September 28, 1938, box 31, Kaltenborn papers, WHS.

me of a herd of sheep who follow their leader even unto destruction," and wondered, "are they capable of reasoning or have they sunk so low as to have gone back to animal life?"[33]

But not all listeners shared this confident and optimistic consensus. Other listeners had no time for Kaltenborn's claim to be producing an unbiased account of current history. They regarded the claims of "objectivity" as an artifice that had to be ripped aside to reveal the real identity of the speaker and the real intentions of the broadcasts. Their letters—or more often cards—were blunt and rude. They told Kaltenborn quite directly that they knew who he was, and that they were not fooled: "Its people like you that make trouble and stir up things. We all heard what those fellows said we didn't need you to turn things around. Are you by any chance a Czech or Jew?"[34] From Detroit: "You should not talk on the radio,—you and all the Columbia commentators of Europe are Jews, you are not talking the truth.... People should protest against the Col. Broadcasting Station. You hear only Jewish propaganda."[35] From Chicago: "Dear Jew: despite your dirty work truth, justice and sanity has won another battle over the sinister forces of the International Jewish gangsters and banksters."[36] Kaltenborn's cosmopolitan reputation and his foreign-sounding name were clearly enough to position him as a Jew for these listeners. Some of these hostile, populist listeners understood Kaltenborn's comments as elaborately disguised support for American military intervention in Europe and concluded that Kaltenborn must be in the pay of the warmongers. "So easy to talk for pay, so hard to die," wrote a man from Detroit. "Let us at last be firm and brave and resist the war capitalists over here. Believe me it will be war 'over here' next time. Your type is not going to propagandize the people to sheep-like docility this time. My type will fight you."[37] Such listeners knew that a vast conspiracy controlled the media. A New York woman wrote, "I realize that if you gave an expression of opinion which did not reflect the Semitic Communistic propaganda ... you could not possibly continue to hold a public position."[38] Another listener, "Americans should start thinking about taking radio control away from the Jews and place it in purely American hands."[39] An Oak Park woman reported, "For many months your broadcasts have been coming into our home and each time I listened to your comments the thought would invariably come to me that you were far more International minded than you were a true American, but this present crisis has enabled me to place you in your correct sphere. You are one hundred per cent communist most likely in the employ of Moscow."[40]

All of this was remarkable in that there was so little in the content of the broadcasts for such critical listeners to work with. Culbert comments of Kaltenborn, "There is so little solid content in his extemporaneous newscasts that they can scarcely be considered serious

33. Letter, Beaver Falls, PA, September 23, 1938, box 31, Kaltenborn papers, WHS.
34. Letter, Latham, NY, September 28, 1938, box 31, Kaltenborn papers, WHS.
35. Letter, Detroit, September 25, 1938, box 31, Kaltenborn papers, WHS.
36. Letter, Chicago, September 30, 1938, box 31, Kaltenborn papers, WHS.
37. Letter, Detroit, September 18, 1938, box 30, Kaltenborn papers, WHS.
38. Letter, New York City, September, 1938, box 32, Kaltenborn papers, WHS.
39. Letter, September 3, 1938, box 32, Kaltenborn papers, WHS.
40. Letter, Oak Park, IL, September 30, 1938, box 32, Kaltenborn papers, WHS.

commentary."[41] Most of the hostile letters are clearly from less wealthy listeners. There are many more hand-scrawled postcards—often in pencil, not pen—and far fewer printed letterheads, in the hostile correspondence. For such listeners, Kaltenborn's interpretive comments were a problem, not something to be praised. From San Diego: "Please will you stop commenting on speeches from Europe. Nearly every American can understand English, and as it seems even better than you do for your comments twist and stretch the words of the speakers in such a way as only war-mongers would do."[42] These listeners heard isolated comments from Kaltenborn and jumped to conclusions about his overall motives. "You say that Hitler has every right to parts of any country where there is 70% of German speaking people at least that is your stand on the Slovak question. I suppose you would advocate Hoboken being ceded to Hitler because 70% speak German."[43] Beneath the wildly contradictory conclusions these listeners reached, they each thought that in one way or another they could see through Kaltenborn's performance to his true identity. They understood themselves as skilled listeners who could cut through the webs of artifice and reveal the true identity of those who spoke to them over the air—that was their interpretive work, and it stood in declared opposition to civic paradigm values of empathy, tolerance, and openness to change. These listeners had, in contrast, a fixed and essentialist understanding of identity—people were who they were, with opinions to match.

STUDYING CLASS, COSMOPOLITANISM, AND DIVISION

That radio amplified cultural divisions is not at all the way that it has most often been remembered. The dominant narrative employed by popular historians and celebrants of old-time radio is that radio had a culturally leveling effect—that it was a great aggregator and homogenizer. Celebratory accounts of the rise of network radio assert that it created a new sense of the one-ness of the nation as it was addressed simultaneously, with common cultural reference points—Amos 'n Andy, the fireside chats. This simply echoes the view so often advanced in the heady enthusiasm of the early network era itself. University of Wisconsin president Glenn Frank wrote in 1935 that "radio is an agency of national unification whose development and freedom we must guard with jealous care."[44] Cantril and Allport believed it was "the nature of radio to encourage people to think and feel alike."[45] The repetition of this claim has remained the staple ingredient of popular radio history. "Radio played a strong role in drawing the country closer together and making it more homogeneous," argued Robert J. Brown. It "created a mass audience with a more or less unified disposition."[46] Leonard Maltin wrote of the success of Amos 'n Andy, "This was

41. David Holbrook Culbert, *News for Everyman: Radio and Foreign Affairs in Thirties America* (Westport, CT: Greenwood 1976): 67.

42. Letter, San Diego, September 25, 1938, box 31, Kaltenborn papers, WHS.

43. Letter, September 27, 1938, box 31, Kaltenborn papers, WHS.

44. Glenn Frank, "Radio as an Educational Force," *Annals of the American Academy* 177, no. 1 (January 1935): 121.

45. Cantril and Allport, *The Psychology of Radio*: 20.

46. Robert J. Brown, *Manipulating the Ether: The Power of Broadcast Radio in Thirties America* (Jefferson, N.C.: McFarland & Co., 1998): 4–5.

something new in our country: a shared, common experience that came right into one's living room, night after night."[47] This received popular history sees the crowning moment of national acceptance and importance of "golden age" radio as occurring during the World War II. The heroic image of Edward R. Murrow broadcasting from the roof of the BBC building during the Battle of Britain provides the unifying motif for this dominant narrative of the history of American radio. In this story, the commercial basis of American broadcasting, and any divisions or antagonisms among listeners, were progressively forgotten as the network broadcasters became more and more closely entwined in popular imagination with the nation itself. Laurence Bergreen, in his history of network broadcasting, wrote, "Murrow functioned as the eyes and ears of the nation."[48]

Radio, however, was also a site of great cultural conflict. Susan Douglas acknowledges the "enormous tensions surrounding network radio's role as a culturally nationalizing force."[49] Paradoxically, in exposing many to an identical aural experience, radio drew attention to the very different ways that people could respond to the same thing. Roger Chartier has argued that one of the important tasks of cultural history is to understand how "the same texts could be diversely apprehended, handled and understood."[50] Networked radio provided the same sounds to many people in many parts of the country, but they were heard and understood in very different ways. In addressing great national audiences, radio insistently drew attention to differences in beliefs, tastes, and ways of listening.

Within the civic paradigm, that was a good thing—the concern was only how few Americans seemed to be benefiting from exposure to difference. Radio's public affairs discussion programs generally had respectable audiences—a few million nationally, and skewed to the upper income groups. These audiences were dwarfed by the tens of millions who listened to the most popular comedy and variety shows of the era. Educational broadcaster Parker Wheatley asked somewhat forlornly in 1941, "Are radio jokes more important to the American people than discussion of issues which deeply concern them?" He worried that most lower income voters listened not to balanced discussion that represented many points of view, but to "direct, uncontroverted propaganda" that simply reinforced preexisting attitudes.[51]

One of the fundamental class issues in radio then had to do with openness to the world and its difference. To an elite, one of radio greatest gifts was its ability to expose listeners to diverse ways of thinking and feeling. Journalist Ann O'Hare McCormick intuited this early, and applauded it. Broadcasting was, she wrote in 1932, creating the conditions for cosmopolitanism, making nations and their boundaries less meaningful: "Up to

47. Leonard Maltin, *The Great American Broadcast: A Celebration of Radio's Golden Age* (New York: Dutton, 1997): 16, 25.

48. Laurence Bergreen, *Look Now, Pay Later: The Rise of Network Broadcasting* (New York: Doubleday, 1980): 102.

49. Susan J. Douglas, *Listening In: Radio and the American Imagination* (New York: Times Books, 1999): 57.

50. Roger Chartier, "Labourers and Voyagers: From the Text to the Reader," in David Finkelstein and Alistair McCleery (eds.), *The Book History Reader* (London: Routledge, 2002): 50.

51. Parker Wheatley, "Adult Education by Radio: Too Little? Too Late?," *Journal of Educational Sociology* 14, no. 9 (May 1941): 547, 550.

now we have lived on the ground, separate, with space between continents and walls between houses. Now we live in one room, the open terrace of the air…where there can be no silence, no secrets, no really aloof or primitive people."[52] McCormick, long a foreign correspondent, no doubt had international developments in mind. But within the United States there was also increasing understanding and promotion of radio's cosmopolitan capacities. Listeners to network radio, as well as those venturing into shortwave, could expect to hear programs from around the world—"Radio Brings World to Your Own Fireside."[53] Rural electrification extended this cosmopolitan experience to those Americans whose lives had been the most locally circumscribed. The Piqua, Ohio Municipal Light Department, describing in 1939 the benefits of rural electrification, celebrated the new comforts as well as the new openness to the world:

> The farm wife keeps house electrically. An electric range cooks her food, an electric refrigerator protects it. Plenty of electrically heated hot water makes cleaning tasks easy. A washing machine makes even heavy overalls easy to keep clean. Drudgery is gone from house and barn, and in the evening, the family gathers in the well-lighted living room while radio brings the world and its entertainment into the home.[54]

Some of the radio audience shared this delight at the prospect of a more cosmopolitan world entering American homes, and the appreciation of radio as a socially transformative technology. Others understood but turned away from it, wanting radio rather to project a familiar world, to speak truths rather than provide a stream of unsettling new perspectives. Radio researcher Paul Lazarsfeld observed in 1940 that one of the central reasons for the weakness of "serious, informative radio programs" was the "tendency to listen only to those things one is 'for' in advance." This, he warned, imposed a handicap on the "central purpose of serious broadcasting," which was—note both the audacity and the taken-for-granted tone of the remark—"to *change* habits of thought and action, rather than simply to confirm existing ones."[55] Between McCormick's enthusiasm and Lazarsfeld's disappointment, between the attempts to change Americans by radio and the concerted popular resistance to such attempts, lies much of the history of golden age American radio.

It is only recently that the class divide in radio audiences has begun to be explored by historians, in a new wave of studies that situate the nationalizing aspirations of network radio in increasingly sharp relief against its local and parochial competitors. This work begins to point to the ways in which the high culture and cosmopolitanism of national radio alienated listeners who had already, by the early 1930s, become used to something else in radio—the provision of a local, opinionated, parochial radio service—creating what

52. Anne O'Hare McCormick, "The Radio: A Great Unknown Force," *New York Times,* March 27, 1932: SM1.

53. *Syracuse Herald,* October 2, 1931: 6.

54. Advertisement in the Piqua, Ohio, *Piqua Daily Call,* February 20, 1939: 7.

55. "Proposal for Continuation of Radio Research Project for a Final Three Years at Columbia University", Box 18, Lyman Bryson papers, LOC: 1.

Doerksen calls "segregated listening publics."[56] Kirkpatrick observed of the 1920s that "even the staunchest supporters of cosmopolitan radio had to recognize that non-cosmopolitan audiences were stubbornly, mysteriously, clinging to their cultural tastes and preferences."[57] Most of this new scholarship has so far, however, focused on the 1920s and early 1930s.[58] I argue in this chapter that the high pluralist and cosmopolitan civic ambitions for U.S. radio continued to be contested by listeners through the 1930s. Far from creating a bland "empire of the middle," radio was a site of a constant cultural struggle that pitted cosmopolitan civic paradigm aspirations against populist claims to be speaking for the real or actual American people, even as they drew racial and religious lines of exclusion around that body.[59]

RADIO RESEARCHERS ON CLASS AND THE CIVIC PARADIGM

We know about this struggle in part because radio researchers in the 1930s—those social scientists who, often with foundation funding, were investigating radio's social and cultural impact as it was happening—put the radio listener rather than the program maker at the center of the emerging discipline of communication studies. Early radio research focused on a cluster of questions thrown up by the civic paradigm, including how radio's civic potential related to class—whether radio could dissolve established cultural divisions, or was condemned simply to reflect them. The intellectual and institutional history of radio research in the United States has been narrated before, but I need briefly to retell some of the story here in order to show how the relationship of class to the civic paradigm emerged as a central question.[60]

56. Clifford Doerksen, *American Babel: Rogue Radio Broadcasters of the Jazz Age* (Philadelphia: University of Pennsylvania Press, 2005): 10.

57. Bill Kirkpatrick, "Localism in American Media 1920–1934" (PhD diss., University of Wisconsin–Madison, 2006), 282.

58. See Derek Vaillant, "'Your Voice Came in Last Night...But I Thought It Sounded a Little Scared': Rural Radio Listening and 'Talking Back' during the Progressive Era in Wisconsin, 1920–1932," in Hilmes and Loviglio (eds.), *The Radio Reader*: 63–88; Derek Vaillant, "Bare-Knuckled Broadcasting: Enlisting Manly Respectability and Racial Paternalism in the Battle against Chain Stores, Chain Stations, and the Federal Radio Commission on Louisiana's KWKH, 1924–33," *Radio Journal* 1, no. 3 (2004): 193–211; Elena Razlogova, "The Voice of the Listener: Americans and the Radio Industry 1920–1950" (PhD diss., George Mason University, 2003); Bill Kirkpatrick, "Localism in American Media 1920–1934," (PhD diss., University of Wisconsin-Madison, 2006); Doerksen, *American Babel*.

59. See, e.g., Philip Napoli, "Empire of the Middle: Radio and the Emergence of an Electronic Society" (PhD diss., Columbia University, 1998).

60. See, e.g., Timothy Glander, *Origins of Mass Communications Research during the American Cold War* (Mahwah, NJ: L. Erlbaum, 2000); Herbert Hiram Hyman, *Taking Society's Measure: A Personal History of Survey Research* (New York: Russell Sage Foundation, 1991), ch. 6; Everette E. Dennis and Ellen Wartella (eds.), *American Communication Research: The Remembered History* (Mahwah, NJ: Erlbaum, 1996), chs. 8 and 9; Douglas, *Listening In*, ch. 6; Bruce Lenthall, *Radio's America: The Great Depression and the Rise of Modern Mass Culture* (Chicago: University of Chicago Press, 2007): ch. 5; William J. Buxton, "Reaching Human Minds: Rockefeller Philanthropy and Communications, 1935–1939," in Theresa Richardson and Donald Fisher (eds.), *The Development of the Social Sciences in the United States and Canada: The Role of Philanthropy* (Stamford, CT: Ablex, 1999): 177–92; Everett M. Rogers, *A History of Communication Study: A Biographical Approach* (New York: Free Press, 1994), ch. 7.

Institutionally, radio research grew from the settlement of 1934, in that the FREC was charged with conducting research on radio's civic and educational roles. FREC came up with nine research problems—four of them to be financed by the broadcasting industry and the rest from foundations and other sources.[61] John Marshall at the Rockefeller Foundation, familiar with psychologist Hadley Cantril's earlier radio work, turned to him for guidance. Social psychology was to contribute a great deal to the distinctive concerns of 1930s radio research.[62] In May 1936, Cantril drew up a research grant application centered on radio listeners and education and proposing experiments on children to investigate topics such as the effects of programs on attitudes, the role of fantasy and imagery, and the differences in program preferences of girls and boys. After further discussion with Marshall, Cantril revised the project to make it less about how to make educational programming, and more focused on civic paradigm questions about all radio's social and civic effects. The main goal now was to understand how people altered their opinions and beliefs in response to their listening.[63] The research emphasis was thus on radio's ability to transform and improve persons, to change thinking and opinion. [Companion website link 5.2.]

In May 1937, the Rockefeller Foundation agreed to grant $67,000 over two years for a study of "the value of radio to listeners." Cantril, by now at Princeton University, had begun to doubt that he could take on leadership of the project himself. He tried to persuade Frank Stanton, who had a PhD in psychology from Ohio State University and headed the research department at CBS, to accept the directorship. Stanton, however, wrote to Marshall that he had decided to stay with CBS "for the present," adding, "you have my word that I will continue to cooperate on the project."[64] Cantril then began considering émigré Austrian scholar Paul Lazarsfeld for the job. Lazarsfeld had come to the United States in September 1933 on a Rockefeller fellowship, and by the autumn of 1935 had decided he wanted to stay. In 1935, with the help of Columbia sociologist Robert Lynd, Lazarsfeld obtained a position supervising student relief workers for the National Youth Administration at the University of Newark. By 1936, Lazarsfeld was director of a research center at Newark, at which he had to raise half his salary from contract research. Max Horkheimer's Frankfurt Institute for Social Research located some of its work at the Newark center.[65]

61. "Hot List—April 28, 1937. Humanities. Princeton," folder 3234, box 271, Series 200 R, Record Group 1.1, Rockefeller Foundation Archives, RAC.

62. See the discussion of the socially critical aspects of 1930s social psychology in Katherine Pandora, *Rebels within the Ranks: Psychologists' Critique of Scientific Authority and Democratic Realities in New Deal America* (New York: Cambridge University Press, 1997); Kathleen Pandora, "'Mapping the New Mental World Created by Radio': Media Messages, Cultural Politics, and Cantril and Allport's *The Psychology of Radio*," *Journal of Social Issues* 54, no. 1 (1998): 7–27; Michael J. Socolow, "Psyche and Society: Radio Advertising and Social Psychology in America, 1923–1936," *Historical Journal of Film, Radio and Television* 24, no. 4 (2004): 517–34.

63. Letter Cantril to Marshall, December 31, 1936, folder 3233, box 271, "Princeton University—Radio Study," Series 200 R, Record Group 1.1, Rockefeller Foundation Archives, RAC.

64. Letter to Marshall from Stanton, July 12, 1937, folder 3234, box 271, Series 200 R, Record Group 1.1, Rockefeller Foundation Archives, RAC.

65. Robert Lynd helped forge the connection between Horkheimer and Lazarsfeld—see Thomas Wheatland, "Critical Theory on Morningside Heights," *German Politics and Society* 22, no. 4 (Winter 2004): 62.

Cantril wrote to Marshall in August 1937 that Lazarsfeld had accepted the directorship of the Princeton Radio Project: "He is an old friend of mine and next to Stanton the best man in the field."[66] Cantril and Stanton were appointed as associate directors. There are hints in the record that Lazarsfeld's Jewishness was an issue at Princeton.[67] In March 1939, Cantril explained to John Marshall—in the context of discussions about whether the Radio Project should be moved from Princeton to New York—that "he doubts if it would be advantageous to Lazarsfeld or to the Project to have Lazarsfeld working in Princeton, particularly on the grounds that Lazarsfeld would not be personally very acceptable to the members of the Princeton faculty he would come in contact with."[68] Frank Stanton recalled decades later that "Paul did not hit it off in Princeton. He was head and shoulders above many of the people there but because of his Jewishness, his Viennese accent, his behavior patterns generally just didn't mix with the white Anglo-Saxon community."[69] Lazarsfeld did manage to do most of the work of the Princeton project from Newark until 1938, when the project moved to a building in Union Square, New York.

Lazarsfeld always insisted that his interest was not in radio as such, but in social research methodology. Yet he clearly had some feeling for American radio and for what it might mean to listeners. "When I came to this country several years ago," he recalled in 1937:

> one of the most outstanding experiences was the American radio, and for a very simple reason. I came here and found myself pretty much alone on the whole continent, and however exciting it is, that is sometimes rather difficult to stand. Then coming home and being able to turn on the radio and having such an amount of consolation as it could give me meant enormously much, and no one who didn't live through that experience can quite appreciate it.... As a result I knew everything about the radio....[70]

Perhaps recalling his own emotional responses, Lazarsfeld consulted both psychologists and sociologists for insights into the subjective experience of radio listening. To

66. Letter to Marshall from Cantril, August 27, 1937, folder 3234, box 271, Series 200 R, Record Group 1.1, Rockefeller Foundation Archives, RAC.

67. On Princeton's "pervasive anti-Semitism" in this period, see James Axtell, *The Making of Princeton University: From Woodrow Wilson to the Present* (Princeton: Princeton University Press, 2006): 127–42.

68. Interview: J. M. and Hadley Cantril and Frank Stanton, March 2, 1939, folder 3239, box 272, Series 200R, Record Group 1.1. Rockefeller Foundation Archives, RAC.

69. Interview with Frank Stanton, Columbia University Oral History Office. Available: http://www. columbia.edu/cu/lweb/digital/collections/nny/stantonf/transcripts/stantonf_1_3_109.html. [January 27, 2010].

70. Typed transcript of the Second National Conference on Educational Broadcasting, Chicago Nov./Dec. 1937, box 2, RG 12 Radio Education Project, Entry 181, Records Relating to National Conferences on Educational Broadcasting, 1936–37. I assume this is closer to what Lazarsfeld actually said on the day than the edited version which appears in C. S. Marsh (ed.), *Educational Broadcasting 1937: Proceedings of the Second National Conference on Educational Broadcasting* (Chicago: University of Chicago Press, 1938): 227, in which Lazarsfeld says more modestly that he and another European émigré "thought we knew everything about what radio did to people."

psychoanalysts such as Karen Horney, Harry Stack Sullivan, John Dollard, and Erich Fromm, he forwarded a list of questions about the psychoanalytic dynamics of entertainment—how would they account for the success of particular programs, and analyze the experience of listening to the radio?[71] At the more empirical and civic end, the Radio Project conducted a survey in New Jersey aimed at gauging the extent to which radio was influencing political opinion during the gubernatorial campaign.

There was considerable excitement at the outset that, tackling the big questions about how radio changed people's ideas on many fronts, it really might be possible to make some significant discoveries about radio as a civic and persuasive instrument. Lazarsfeld met with Marshall in November 1937 and reported that he expected to have a 60-page memo on the motivation of radio listening completed by the end of the year to "serve as a theoretical framework for the Princeton Study." Marshall, always nudging the project back toward civic paradigm questions, asked whether it might not be wise "to attempt some theoretical formulation of what radio might do to serve the public interest."[72] At the end of the first year, Lazarsfeld reported on what looked like extraordinary progress. "Plans for Publication" listed 10 mostly book-length projects—Stanton on measurement techniques, Lazarsfeld on psychological theories of motivation as applied to radio, Cantril and James Rorty on radio commentators, Adorno on radio music, books on reading and listening and on educational broadcasting, a study contrasting rural and urban radio listening, a book on listener panels in research, one on statistical methods in radio research, and a handbook on listener research.[73] Despite, or perhaps because of, this flurry of promises, Lazarsfeld recalled that by the fall of 1938 he had become aware that the reputation of the office was suffering under his policy of "research improvisation guided by available material and personal interests and contacts."[74] In early 1939 the Rockefeller Foundation arranged an external review of the project.[75] The resulting review was favorable and largely endorsed the views of the project directors about the future. The foundation, however, decided "not to recommend further support of the project at this time" until it could see some formulation of the results of the first two years' work. Marshall warned Lazarsfeld that much was at stake: "JM naturally believed with Lazarsfeld that the project can and does offer much information of significance for bettering broadcasting; but others do not share this belief."[76] This pressure from the foundation led Lazarsfeld to "review the available material and to select a theme around which a good part of it could be organized." The

71. Folder 3234, box 271, Series 200 R, Record Group 1.1, Rockefeller Foundation Archives, RAC; Lazarsfeld, "An Episode in the History of Social Research: A Memoir": 319.

72. Interview: J. M. and Lazarsfeld, November 17, 1937, folder 3234, box 271, Series 200 R, Record Group 1.1, Rockefeller Foundation Archives, RAC.

73. Report to the Committee of Six, folder 3236, box 271, Series 200 R, Record Group 1.1, Rockefeller Foundation Archives, RAC.

74. Lazarsfeld, "An Episode in the History of Social Research: A Memoir": 317.

75. "Princeton University—Radio Study," folder 3233, box 271, Series 200 R, Record Group 1.1, Rockefeller Foundation Archives, RAC.

76. "Talk with Dr. Paul Lazarsfeld," March 21, 1939, folder 3239, box 272, Series 200R, Rockefeller Foundation Archives, RAC.

result was the 1940 book *Radio and the Printed Page*.[77] [Companion website 5.3.] Rockefeller renewed the grant, and it was agreed—in part because of increasing tension between Lazarsfeld and Cantril—that the Office of Radio Research would move to Columbia University.[78]

As the results of the first phase of research were assembled and reviewed, radio's civic promise seemed to be proving elusive. Lazarsfeld now identified the key problem facing communications research as the gaining of popular acceptance: "Our chief national hazard is not the application of intelligence to our problems but the dragging lag in popular knowledge and acceptance that shackles the application of intelligence."[79] There were two main reasons for the weakness of "serious, informative radio programs." The first was, as we have seen, the "element of self-selection in listening," the "tendency to listen only to those things one is 'for' in advance." This, Lazarsfeld warned, imposed a handicap on the "central purpose of serious broadcasting," which was "to *change* habits of thought and action, rather than simply to confirm existing ones." The second weakness he identified was the failure of serious broadcasting to learn "adequate skills as to format and level of psychological appeal" from popular commercial programs.[80]

One of the new projects proposed was a study of individuals who did change their minds or habits in response to a continuous sequence of broadcasts—the programs made by the U.S. Department of Agriculture were to be used for this purpose. Looking back, Lazarsfeld regarded the intention to locate and study those individuals who changed their minds in response to radio as the "crucial part of the proposal"—which perhaps explains why the Department of Agriculture study, as he recalled, became ("I do not remember how") a study of the 1940 election, and the book *The People's Choice*.[81] That book famously argued that radio was less successful at changing minds than had been thought, and that personal influences were at least as powerful. In a classic 1948 essay, Lazarsfeld and Merton argued that mass media propaganda needed ideal conditions to work, and one of those conditions was "face to face contact in local organizations as an adjunct to the mass media."[82] Without reinforcement, the prospects for propaganda— even benign propaganda—were not good. As Jefferson Pooley has observed, in the 1940s "the quantitative study of short-term, media-induced attitude or behavior change was, time and again, to produce only minimal evidence for conversion."[83] Lazarsfeld made this

77. Lazarsfeld, "An Episode in the History of Social Research: A Memoir": 328.

78. Lazarsfeld, "An Episode in the History of Social Research: A Memoir": 329.

79. "Proposal for Continuation of Radio Research Project for a Final Three Years at Columbia University."

80. "Proposal for Continuation of Radio Research Project for a Final Three Years at Columbia University."

81. Lazarsfeld, "An Episode in the History of Social Research: A Memoir": 330.

82. See Raymond Boudon, "Introduction" to Paul Lazarsfeld, *On Social Research and Its Language* (Chicago: University of Chicago Press, 1993): 19; Paul Lazarsfeld and Robert Merton, "Mass Communication, Popular Taste, and Organized Social Action," in Lyman Bryson (ed.), *The Communication of Ideas: A Series of Addresses* (New York: Harper and Brothers, 1948): 95–118.

83. Jefferson Pooley, "Fifteen Pages that Shook the Field: Personal Influence, Edward Shils, and the Remembered History of Mass Communication Research," *Annals of the American Academy of Political and Social Science* 608, no. 1 (2006): 143.

point bluntly in a postwar article on "tolerance propaganda"—"tendencies toward discrimination against other racial groups are deeply imbedded in people's personality development" and they will "evade" tolerance propaganda by a variety of psychological devices in order to "keep their discriminatory attitude intact." By 1947, Lazarsfeld was thus asserting as a general truth that "most people read and listen only to those materials with which they are likely to agree."[84]

The major radio research program in the United States was thus built around the civic paradigm idea—that radio's highest mission was to change opinions, to develop attentive listeners who were alert, critical, and active citizens. The insistent posing of that question was part of what generated—in response to empirical data—the now classic *limited effects* answer. This moment of disillusion, and the general conclusion that media had limited effects, became canonical American social science. But the civic paradigm that posed the question, that generated the hopes of positive change in the first place, has been less well remembered, as has the conclusion—well grounded in radio research— that the response to the civic paradigm was deeply classed. As a part of the research into opinion change, radio researchers studied class differences in listening practices. They were well placed by training and temperament to investigate these patterns. What they discovered threatened to undermine faith in the civic paradigm, by locating it as a class rather than a universal ideal.

American radio research began with a strong interest in social class, an intention to inquire into the different ways that rich and poor Americans heard their radio. The class analysis led to discoveries about the intractable aspects of American society, the ways things stayed the same despite all efforts to change them. When the Princeton Radio Research Project published its first volume, it sounded, not a welcome hosanna to the new democratic citizenship of the radio age, but a pessimistic warning. The idea, Lazarsfeld declared, "that radio is at this moment a tool for mass education, for considerably increasing serious responses in the community, is groundless."[85] And the main problem, he wrote to Lyman Bryson, was "the sheer stubborn resistance of persons of low socio-economic rating to listening to serious discussions of public problems over the air."[86]

That important first volume set out to compare radio to print in civic paradigm terms. Emotion, "so likely to color judgment, can best be overcome if one returns repeatedly to the cold explicitness with which the printed page can present all arguments on both sides." Could radio ever approach this condition of print? Had radio, so far, increased "the scope of serious responses" beyond those achieved historically by print?[87] Central to the book's analysis was the definition of "serious" responses and serious radio listening. Lazarsfeld began by defining *serious* as an interest in public and civic affairs rather than personal development or self-improvement. Serious radio programs were marked by a

84. Paul F. Lazarsfeld, "Some Remarks on the Role of Mass Media in So-Called Tolerance Propaganda," *Journal of Social Issues* 3, no. 3 (Summer 1947): 18–19.

85. Lazarsfeld, *Radio and the Printed Page*: 48.

86. Letter from Lazarsfeld to Bryson, May 19, 1941, Lyman Bryson papers, LOC.

87. Lazarsfeld, *Radio and the Printed Page*: 4–5.

"detached, objective" quality, as opposed to emotional propaganda.[88] One had then to listen to a serious program seriously—it would not be enough just to tune in.

There was already data on the relations of social class and radio listening, because advertisers cared a lot about who listened to particular programs and how much money they had to spend. Hugh Beville, research manager at NBC, published in 1940 his analysis of radio ratings surveys by socioeconomic status. Using a four-part classification based on income, Beville reported that the wealthiest, A households, listened less than average, C households listened significantly more than average, while the poorest, or D households, were a little below average—the rich, he speculated, had many other ways to spend their leisure time, while the very poor lacked the living rooms that were the scene of so much middle-class listening.[89] A survey of the listening preferences of 10,000 Minnesotans published in 1937 found that the "average amount of time the radio is in use each day is greater in the homes of lower socio-economic status." This survey also demonstrated that listening preferences were related to socioeconomic status. Professional and semiprofessional groups liked "opera, symphonies, and classical music, news commentators…and educational broadcasts," while slightly skilled and unskilled groups preferred programs "characterized by a high degree of excitement and dramatic appeal, comedy, amateur performances, and serial dramatizations."[90] This confirmed what broadcasters already knew—that the appeal of different program types correlated strongly with class. There is a familiar highbrow/lowbrow story here.

Beville's categories had been economic—A homes had incomes of more than $5000, B homes between $3000 and $5000, and C homes between $2000 and $3000—but he also declared a "direct relationship between economic status and cultural level."[91] Lazarsfeld went somewhat further by asserting that these two things could be regarded as functionally the same, so that income categories could simply stand as proxies for "cultural level." He defined *cultural level* as "any index which has a reasonable, positive relation to the ability and inclination of a group to pay attention to serious subject matter," in print or on the radio.[92] In later critiques—most famously from his former junior colleague C. Wright Mills, Lazarsfeld came to be regarded as an accommodationist, even conservative, figure in American sociology.[93] But underlying the assertion of the equivalence of wealth and cultural level was a highly critical understanding of life in a capitalist society. In this simple, elegant, substitution of cultural level for household income, lay a sweeping aside of all the traditions of belief in social mobility and self-improvement that lay at the heart of American social thought. High cultural level, Lazarsfeld was saying, might be a product of

88. Lazarsfeld, *Radio and the Printed Page*: 5.

89. H. M. Beville, "The ABCDs of Radio," *Public Opinion Quarterly* 4, no. 2 (Jun. 1940): 195–206.

90. Kenneth H. Baker, "Radio Listening and Socio-economic Status," *Psychological Record* 1, no. 9 (Aug. 1937): 115.

91. Beville, "The ABCDs of Radio Audiences": 196.

92. Lazarsfeld, *Radio and the Printed Page*: 14.

93. C. Wright Mills, *The Sociological Imagination* (New York: Oxford University Press, 1959), ch. 3. On Mills and Lazarsfeld, see Jonathan Sterne, "C. Wright Mills, the Bureau for Applied Social Research, and the Meaning of Critical Scholarship," *Cultural Studies ↔ Critical Methodologies*, 5, no. 1 (2005): 65–94.

hard work or personal virtue or innate taste—but taken as a whole, it could be regarded simply as a proxy for wealth. Money bought time for serious attention to public affairs and high culture, and so "people actually do less serious listening as the cultural level descends." The message was clear and disturbing—high cultural level was in general simply a by-product of wealth.[94]

Lazarsfeld had been a socialist in his native Vienna, but relatively little attention has been paid to the ways in which he brought some of the assumptions and habits of his Viennese work to his American research career.[95] The other staff at his Radio Project shared his critical outlook. Herta Herzog had been a student of Lazarsfeld's in Vienna, and then joined him in the United States in 1935, when they married. Her studies were also marked by a confident, almost off-hand, form of class analysis.[96] She remarked in passing in a report on children's radio listening that "intelligence and socio-economic background are in our culture fairly interchangeable indices."[97]

There were other reasons that class was central to early radio research. The Depression had exacerbated class divisions in the United States, and it must have seemed only commonsensical that radio listening too would be class differentiated. There was, finally, an easy synergy between the broadcasting and advertising industries' desire to know the economic status of their listeners, and the researchers' class interests—Lazarsfeld used his entrepreneurial skill to persuade commercial broadcasters and advertisers to share their data for reanalysis by the Radio Project's researchers. Early project studies confirmed existing industry knowledge that both amount and type of radio listening varied considerably by economic level—rich and poor listened to different programs and in different ways.

Douglas astutely notes an "elitist bias" to Radio Project research, in that it scrutinized listening on the "lower" cultural levels but left "higher" cultural practices unanalyzed and unproblematized.[98] To put it another way, the civic paradigm generated the questions but was not itself an object of analysis. This was true of modes of listening as well as of program content. It was always for Project researchers not just what people listened to—symphonies or soaps—but how they listened, that mattered. People on lower cultural levels (poorer people) listened to the radio longer but less attentively than people on higher cultural levels (richer people). The correlation was neat and clear: the poorer the household, the more likely it was that the radio was on for long periods of time. Almost 20% of the poorest category of household reported radios on for more

94. Lazarsfeld, *Radio and the Printed Page*: 21.

95. An important recent exception is Douglas, *Listening In*: 126–28. See also John Dryzek's speculation that a certain socioeconomic determinism continued to pervade Lazarsfeld's Bureau of Applied Social Research voting studies, and that this perhaps formed at least part of the reason why Michigan rather than Columbia came to dominate U.S. voting studies during the Cold War period: John S. Dryzek, "Opinion Research and the Counter-Revolution in American Political Science," *Political Studies* 40 (1992): 679–94.

96. See Elizabeth Perse, "Herta Herzog," in Nancy Signorielli (ed.), *Women in Communication: A Biographical Sourcebook* (Westport, CT: Greenwood, 1996): 202–11.

97. Herta Herzog, "Children and Their Leisure Time Listening to the Radio" (New York: Office of Radio Research, 1941): 24—although, as Douglas points out, race was ignored and gender dealt with in more "ancillary fashion": Douglas, *Listening In*: 142.

98. Douglas, *Listening In*: 143.

than 10 hours a day.[99] If the radio was on in a household for that long, the listening was almost certainly for much of the time distracted rather than attentive—and hence those people, understood as being on the lower economic and cultural levels, were much less likely to be listening in the active and critical manner the civic paradigm demanded.[100]

The optimistic strand of *Radio and the Printed Page* was its argument that the commercial techniques of some popular programs could be adapted by educators to bring "serious" content to larger audiences. The women Herta Herzog interviewed said they learned things relevant to the everyday conduct of their lives from soap operas. Similarly, high school students reported that they learned from quiz shows, and from crime and historical drama programs.[101] Lazarsfeld admitted that quiz shows generally purveyed knowledge rather than information, and that they appealed to people who wanted to know a little about everything rather than develop specialized knowledges. Nevertheless, he concluded, "the programs from which people claim to learn most are put on the air by advertisers and not by educators."[102] *Radio and the Printed Page* was thus at best a rather cautious, muted manifesto for the civic paradigm. The book's really important insight was that radio listening was socially embedded and that people's desire to listen grew directly from the rest of their lives.

Radio researchers were beginning to report that there were actually two fundamentally different ways of listening to radio, one open to change and new ideas, the other firmly ensconced in existing ways of thinking. The least wealthy and educated radio listeners preferred local rather than network stations, and programs on which they could hear known and local people. Lazarsfeld and his researchers concluded that "the psychological universe of people in the lower-income groups is limited socially and geographically."[103] Early radio research described a clearly classed response to radio and even speculated that there were "psychological distances" between socioeconomic groups, "beyond which the processes of imagination, identification or escape cannot function."[104]

This discovery was made in many research locations. In a contrasting study of two rural counties—a more prosperous one in Nebraska and a poorer one in Illinois— Lazarsfeld's researchers found significant differences in radio listening. In the Nebraska county, there were much higher levels of involvement in clubs and organizations—group participation was "at least three times as frequent"—and there were significantly higher levels of reading. This was reflected in radio preferences; the Nebraskans were much more likely to listen to what Lazarsfeld defined as "serious" radio programs. People with a greater range of personal interests and associations were attracted to "serious" programs because they had more points of connection with the topics likely to be discussed. When people on

99. Lazarsfeld, *Radio and the Printed Page*: 18.

100. For further explication of this argument, see David Goodman, "Distracted Listening," in David Suisman and Susan Strasser (eds.) *Sound in the Era of Mechanical Reproduction* (Philadelphia: University of Pennsylvania Press, 2010): 15–46.

101. Lazarsfeld, *Radio and the Printed Page*: 52–54.

102. Lazarsfeld, *Radio and the Printed Page*: 92–93.

103. Lazarsfeld, *Radio and the Printed Page*: 102–3.

104. Alvin Meyrowitz and Marjorie Fiske, "The Relative Preference of Low Income Groups for Small Stations," *Journal of Applied Psychology* 23, no. 1 (Feb. 1939): 162.

lower cultural levels did listen to "serious" programs, it was often because of strong partisan affiliation with a cause—Townsendites, labor union members, and "adherents of other pressure groups" listened and tried to persuade their friends to listen, not out of a broad interest in hearing many points of view, but to check on the treatment of their own cause. In contrast, people with broad social and cultural engagements, the researchers found, could listen in a more disinterested, more open fashion.[105] Lenthall sees Lazarsfeld and his group as concerned with "finding a way for experts to gain effective voices in their mass society," with how to "make the reality of a centralized culture a positive."[106] It is true that local culture and associations were often understood in Radio Project writings as limiting and confined. But it was also true that the civic paradigm belief shared by project researchers was always that the national and international issues that radio raised had to be discussed locally—so the Nebraskans' active face-to-face community life made them better civic paradigm listeners, able to gain pleasure and accrue wisdom and perspective from hearing diverse points of view. The conclusion of many Radio Project studies was that it was local engagements and associations—knowing a Japanese person rather than reading about Japan—that led to interest in discussion of more distant issues.

The definition of "serious" listening described a class habit rather than a universally valued practice. Lazarsfeld simply defined the more open and cosmopolitan listening of the elite as "serious," and in comparison cast the radio listening of the majority as at once less serious and more personal, more self-preoccupied. Seriousness was defined by a concern for public and civic affairs rather than personal development or self-improvement and practical advice programs; serious programs had a "detached, objective" quality, rather than an emotional tone.[107] *ATMA* was a serious program for Lazarsfeld, but home economics advice fell into the category of "service programs." These "service programs" appealed to people on the "lower" cultural levels, presumably because they were interested in practical forms of self-improvement and advancement more than in "detached" consideration of public affairs. For Lazarsfeld, radio's ideal public sphere—like Habermas's decades later—was to be devoted to the detached and objective discussion of public affairs, not littered with personal and emotional issues and mere self-improvement.

What this suggests, bluntly, is that the civic paradigm was a class-specific ideal. It appealed to one class of listeners, but its pluralism offended others, who wanted to be able to listen to voices they agreed with. There was continuing listener resistance to the ideals underpinning the civic paradigm, which showed up in research whenever listeners were studied qualitatively. William S. Robinson found in Pike County, Illinois, that rural listeners did not have a "well-established interest in the news" and hence had little interest in "opinions and comment." While 75% of men and 65% of women in his survey regularly tuned in to the news, only 36% of men and 38% of women regularly chose to hear commentators. The rural listener, Robinson decided, will "listen to news bulletins because this is easier than reading, but in general he does not care sufficiently about the news to

105. Lazarsfeld, *Radio and the Printed Page*: 100–11.
106. Lenthall, *Radio's America*: 153.
107. Lazarsfeld, *Radio and the Printed Page*: 5.

put himself out to get more information or interpretive comment."[108] Robinson also found that radio was not influential in forming new opinions among rural people. Startlingly, he recalled that his rural subjects appeared not to have any recognizable opinions on "important and controversial questions":

> Because of their low economic status, these people had been isolated from propaganda and controversy on these topics.... Their attitudes, in fact, dealt mainly with matters where direct experience underlay opinion, and not with topics of national but not necessarily local or personal importance. The radio thus introduced them to a new world of controversy and persuasion and emphasized problems of which they had not heard much before.[109]

Robinson reported that in three-quarters of cases, when someone heard an opinion they disagreed with over the radio, they turned the program off: "Radio is ineffective in changing rural opinions, it appears, because rural people generally will not listen to opinions with which they seriously disagree."[110] Robinson's research questions, formulated entirely and somewhat unreflectively within the civic paradigm, led him to a condescending portrait of rural radio listeners, but one that probably did accurately identify something about their lack of interest in being inducted into a world of endless debate and interpretation of remote events and issues. Forming opinions on new topics about which they knew little, or changing opinions about matters they knew well, were not in their world culturally valued activities; the constant self-remaking and opinion updating of modernity had little appeal.

The radio researchers discovered that the audience for interpretive news commentators was "stratified towards the higher economic groups." A study of Newark high school students found that interest in commentary programs decreased sharply with declining levels of "scholarship and intelligence."[111] Frederick J. Meine studied how 1200 Trenton high school students were getting their news from radio and newspapers.[112] He obtained the "intelligence score" of every student in the sample from the school system and discovered—quite unsurprisingly given the assumptions embedded in the question—that "the more intelligent have better news-consumption habits than have the less intelligent."[113] Students of "high intelligence" usually got more of their news from newspapers, while those of "low intelligence" favored radio.[114] The "less intelligent" were less likely to discuss the news at home, more likely to treat radio as a source of information than as stimulus for discussion. Elite listeners again were discovered to be those who looked to radio for

---

108. William S. Robinson, "Radio Comes to the Farmer," in Paul F. Lazarsfeld and Frank N. Stanton (eds.), *Radio Research 1941* (New York: Duell, Sloan and Pearce, 1941): 242.

109. Robinson, "Radio Comes to the Farmer": 259–60.

110. Robinson, "Radio Comes to the Farmer": 266–67.

111. Lazarsfeld, *Radio and the Printed Page*: 241–44.

112. Frederick J. Meine, "Radio and the Press among Young People," in Lazarsfeld and Stanton (eds.), *Radio Research 1941*: 313.

113. Meine, "Radio and the Press among Young People": 312.

114. Meine, "Radio and the Press among Young People": 310.

opinion and interpretation, for prompts for conversation that they could take up in their own local contexts. This all mattered, Lazarsfeld pointed out, because interest in critical and interpretive discussion on the radio was linked to the ability to be critical of what one heard. He concluded, pessimistically, that "people on the lower cultural levels are apparently more suggestible than those on the higher cultural levels." That was a serious conclusion in the age of propaganda: "Radio is the preferred medium of the more suggestible man."[115]

From the evidence collected by the radio researchers, it is possible to abstract ideal types of two different kinds of radio listeners. One audience consisted of relative cultural elites, people who felt themselves addressed by civic programming and its call for a more individuated, conscientized, discursive, relativist, rational, argumentative, critical, civic, listening, and who identified with the national and cosmopolitan outlook of the network broadcasters. These listeners were actively engaged with the content of the broadcasts they heard—they wrote letters and discussed programs in familial, organizational, and neighborhood settings. While critical of many of the more sensational and sentimental dramatic programs, they found radio richly rewarding and affirming. It broadened their world immeasurably, gave them access to more of the things they valued—more music, discussion, news, drama, firsthand experience of public life—than they had ever had before. Such people often had a fiercely protective attitude to radio, and they did not want to lose these things, or their ability to choose their own listening. They were modern listeners, who had taken on the tasks and risks of self-management.[116] They understood that knowledge was in some sense relative to the knower, that debate and discussion had value in themselves as process as much as for the conclusions reached.

These elite, educated, urban listeners embraced radio's practical cosmopolitanism and wondered at the marvels of technology that allowed them to hear voices from all over the world live in their living rooms. They liked the flow of opinion and information radio provided, and sought out those programs that began from the premise that there were different possible points of view. Sociologist Robert K. Merton argued in the 1940s that cosmopolitanism was a relatively elite characteristic. While this might seem surprising in an immigrant society in which the working class lived and worked in demonstrably more diverse social environments than the middle class, Merton argued that it was not solely interest in a wider world that distinguished cosmopolitans from locals. Rather, it was the level of interest in engaging with the process of cultural interpretation, and hence the degree of interpretive overlay they desired or tolerated—so on radio, "cosmopolitans prefer the more analytical commentators (Swing, Hughes) while the locals are more interested in those who forego analysis and are virtually newscasters (Thomas, Goddard, etc.)."[117]

115. Lazarsfeld, *Radio and the Printed Page*: 256–57.

116. In contemporary modernity, Beck argues, "Biographies are removed from the traditional precepts and certainties, from external control and general moral laws, becoming open and dependent on decision-making, and are assigned as a task for each individual." Ulrich Beck and Elisabeth Beck-Gernsheim, *The Normal Chaos of Love* (Cambridge: Polity, 1995): 5.

117. Merton, *Social Theory and Social Structure*: 463.

Ernest Dichter, reporting on "detailed and intensive" interviews with 100 radio listeners "in all walks of life," found some typical elite listeners excited by the way radio brought the world to them.[118] One reported breathlessly,

> I feel so completely in touch with what's going on all over the world.... I can almost recall a description of the battle of the Graf Spee, Kaltenborn's report from a dugout in Spain, and another broadcast I recall so vividly was during the Munich crisis, Maurice Hindus broadcasting from Prague, the hopelessness of the world situation, and the next day hearing Hitler speak himself.

This listener came to a significant conclusion: "We don't need historians nowadays; we can make our own analysis."[119] This listener was the exemplary subject of the civic paradigm. Taking responsibility for his own listening and opinion formation, he was excited and enlivened by the horizon-expanding power of radio, by the possibility of joining a world of debate and interpretation and constantly updated information.

Merton's attempt to distinguish "cosmopolitan" from "local" interests and loyalties in American society was taken up enthusiastically by American sociologists in the 1950s, seeking some interpretive purchase on a society that seemed to them characterized by a "tolerant elite" and an "intolerant majority."[120] One of the assumptions (and conclusions) of such work was that—in Merton's words—"education is everywhere associated with tolerance."[121] These ideas informed Richard Hofstadter's influential histories.[122] Historian Robert Wiebe argued more recently that the two-class structure that dominated 19th-century American society was by the 1920s transforming into a three-class structure, as a new "national class" formed over the top—national, he argued, "both in the sense of transcending local attachments or boundaries and in the sense of holding central, strategic positions in American society," legitimated by their production of and utilization of expert knowledge.[123] Those left out were resentful: "Competing with a blare of national-class publicity for efficiency at work and live-and-let-live tolerance at leisure, those traditional values tended to acquire a defensive, suspicious tone from people who sensed that they were losing authority to a distant, powerful enemy."[124]

The model is suggestive, but a danger of writing about radio audiences in this frame is that of simply reproducing existing intellectual traditions of disparaging popular prejudice and celebrating urban and educated tolerance. While I certainly share many of the values of the elite proponents of civic paradigm radio, I am trying here to illuminate

118. Ernest Dichter, "On the Psychology of Radio Commercials," in Paul F. Lazarsfeld and Frank N. Stanton (eds.), *Radio Research 1942–1943* (New York: Duell, Sloan and Pearce, 1944): 466.

119. Dichter, "On the Psychology of Radio Commercials": 469.

120. Merton, *Social Theory and Social Structure*: 454.

121. Merton, *Social Theory and Social Structure*: 459–60.

122. Richard Hofstadter, *The Age of Reform: From Bryan to FDR* (New York: Knopf, 1955); *The Paranoid Style in American Politics and Other Essays* (New York: Knopf, 1965).

123. Robert H. Wiebe, *Self-Rule: A Cultural History of American Democracy* (Chicago: University of Chicago Press, 1995): 141–42.

124. Wiebe, *Self-Rule*: 144.

historically the way these admirable beliefs of the educated, cosmopolitan, national-class elite could themselves operate as a form of prejudice and intolerance. An adequate cultural history of radio needs to understand the way radio's relentless emphasis on the difficult but worth-striving-for goal of "balanced" and "objective" knowledge, on the need to empathize and understand the viewpoint of others in order to transcend one's own limited perspective, and on processes of growth and inquiry, rather than fixed truths or identities, was clearly perceived and rejected by many ordinary radio listeners, who understood themselves and others in terms of relatively fixed and stable identities and interests.

Less elite listeners also loved their radio. They enjoyed the many popular programs the American commercial network system provided them—the popular music, the comedians, the sports, the general pace and bustle and liveliness of American radio. They were actively engaged and highly skilled as listeners, but they listened sure of their own beliefs and identities, not in a quest for change or self-improvement. Some of the best radio comedy was self-referential—about radio and other shows; it appealed to the kind of knowledge that dedicated listeners had built up. Much radio comedy was about identity—ethnic, gender, class identity—and played upon and rewarded listeners' skill in recognizing and understanding the various types and their characteristics. The most popular programs on radio played with fixed identities rather than imagined their transcendence.

The intrusion of distastefully different or self-evidently wrong opinions into the home troubled many Americans, perhaps particularly those who still lived in relatively homogenous communities, which shared religion, ethnicity, race, class, locality—not only in rural "island communities," but also in the residential areas of larger cities that had high levels of segregation by class or race or ethnicity.[125] Radio interrupted this homogeneity with reminders that somewhere else there were people who thought and sounded quite different. The very profusion of voices on the air drew attention to the existence of a world of endlessly conflicting points of view. Radio developed program structures designed to dramatize the existence of this diversity and to manage it—it was a relativizing instrument as well as a unifying one.

There were then two contrasting visions of radio's public sphere—one an officially sanctioned imagining of a discursive, open, and critical sphere, and the more popular view, which understood the public sphere as a place of stable identities and truth telling. The civic paradigm elaborated the modern, pluralist, culturally elite vision of self making. Because radio could carry dangerous messages, because its public/private ambiguity was understood to be dangerous, it was crucial that the radio listener become self-regulating and self-monitoring. In an age of propaganda, proper listening became a civic responsibility. Dispersed and unsupervised, radio listening was known only by its effects. Citizens had to take responsibility for their own opinions, to listen responsibly to both sides, remain open to new evidence, behave civilly toward those with whom they disagreed. But those arguably admirable goals were also socially and culturally divisive for radio because they also brought an often-unwelcome reminder that

125. Robert H. Wiebe, *The Search for Order, 1877–1920* (New York: Hill and Wang, 1967).

in a large, diverse, and pluralist society, there were many points of view, and—importantly—no final arbiter of truth.

Of course all such generalizations are dangerous, even potentially offensive. But the classed patterns noted repeatedly by contemporary researchers were based on evidence to some extent still available for our scrutiny, and the patterns remain legible. I do attempt here to sketch a substantive class analysis while filtering out the unsympathetic class prejudice that is all too clearly evident in some of the contemporary research. Paul Lazarsfeld was quite confident that the programs "which are definitely preferred by people lower in the cultural scale, are those which can be characterized as of definitely bad taste."[126] The judgment highlights the class basis of the civic paradigm—something discovered empirically by contemporary radio researchers but so often interpreted by them unreflectively.

Modern liberal government, it has plausibly been argued, is about choice—but with no escape from the necessity of choosing. Rose has argued influentially that "the forms of freedom we inhabit today are intrinsically bound to a regime of subjectification in which subjects are not merely 'free to choose' but are *obliged to be free*."[127] The civic paradigm of American radio in the 1930s contained precisely this kind of compulsion—to remain open to new information, to hold on to the possibility of changing your mind. It imagined listeners as choice makers, always in the process of arriving at provisional new opinions, not settled in comfortable prejudice. This made radio an archetypically modern technology. "What is characteristic of modernity," argues Anthony Giddens, "is not an embracing of the new for its own sake, but the presumption of wholesale reflexivity."[128] But while social theorists such as Giddens and Beck see the fundamental shifts toward a more reflexive modernity as occurring only after the 1950s, it seems clear that key elements of this more reflexive sense of self were in place in the 1930s in the United States, and that radio was an important technology for propagating it.[129] Radio was constantly asking Americans to consider their own opinions against the backdrop of the range of other possible points of view, inviting them to reflect, change their minds, and assimilate new information, at an increasing pace. This promoted a highly reflexive sense of self—taking responsibility for one's own opinion and choices.

Less elite listeners resisted this relativizing message. They looked to radio for truth, not confusion and endless choice. The 1930s radio researchers defined intelligence as reflexivity, confusing modern, cosmopolitan pluralism with a higher mental capacity. Many ordinary Americans, who did not have this relationship to social knowledge, found themselves defined by their radio preferences as not only not "serious" listeners and citizens, but as less intelligent. These Americans also had a patterned response to

126. Lazarsfeld, *Radio and the Printed Page*: 23.

127. Nikolas Rose, *Inventing Our Selves: Psychology, Power, and Personhood* (Cambridge: Cambridge University Press, 1996): 17; see also Nikolas Rose, *Powers of Freedom: Reframing Political Thought* (Cambridge: Cambridge University Press, 1999): 87.

128. Anthony Giddens, *The Consequences of Modernity* (Stanford, CA: Stanford University Press, 1990): 39.

129. See, e.g., Ulrich Beck and Elisabeth Beck-Gernsheim, *Individualization: Institutionalized Individualism and Its Social and Political Consequences* (London: Sage, 2001).

what they heard on radio. They understood there to be truths, and they wanted to know them. They took the knowledge of their own social world into their listening to the new medium of radio. They sometimes actively resisted the ideals of those who hoped for a new and more open public sphere seated around the radio. They wrote back to broadcasters in curt, abusive, angry terms, often sure that they had detected the real agenda behind radio's open-ended talk. They found that their sense of what the medium should be for, while it may have been the majority view, was not the dominant one. The official view was that radio would aid citizenship by exposing Americans to many points of view. Radio forced Americans to choose in the marketplace of ideas, to exercise the freedom to make their identity and convictions a matter of self-conscious selection rather than inheritance or assumption. The dominant civic ideal, and hence radio itself, divided as well as unified Americans. That division provides one of the tragic dimensions to the romance of radio in its golden age.

6

Radio and the Intelligent Listener
The War of the Worlds Panic

But in precisely the same way that modern science gives us new and deadly weapons of destruction—battleships, airplanes, gas, and the whole equipment of mass slaughter—so also modern science gives our opinion leaders weapons of mass impression which can slay our minds quite as effectively as machine guns deaden our bodies.[1]
Edward Bernays, 1937

The individual citizen is subjected daily to such a barrage of propaganda and miscellaneous information from every source that often even the best human organisms break under the strain.[2]
George V. Denny Jr., 1938

Every intellectual and economic stratum of society is represented in the radio audience. Intelligent persons listen as well as those less fortunately endowed in mentality or education. Radio must weigh carefully what it carries over the air, for it must serve them all to good purpose.[3]
NBC *Broadcasting in the Public Interest*, 1939

The ethos of the civic paradigm, that radio listening should be an active, civic, self-aware activity, and that individuals were responsible for their own listening, was exposed and subjected to public debate in one dramatic incident: the October 1938 CBS *Mercury Theater on the Air* dramatization of H. G. Wells's *War of the Worlds*, which famously caused a panic among some listeners who thought that Martians really had invaded New Jersey. That event, more than any other, seemed to prove the power of radio and the dangerous susceptibility of much of the American population to propaganda. The obverse of the civic paradigm, of the belief that radio could shape behavior and render great good in the world, was the fear that if broadcasting really was so influential, it could also be an instrument for evil. The "War of the Worlds" panic of 1938 appeared to offer direct evidence of the susceptibility of Americans to irrational behavior under the influence of radio, and hence of the dangerousness of radio. Lyman Bryson observed shortly after the Mars invasion broadcast that radio was "one of the most dangerous elements in modern

1. *America's Town Meeting of the Air: Propaganda: Asset or Liability in a Democracy?* (New York: American Book Company, 1937): 20–21.
2. *America's Town Meeting of the Air: Democracy and American Ideals* (New York: Town Hall, 1938): 8.
3. *Broadcasting in the Public Interest* (New York: National Broadcasting Company, 1939): 21–22.

culture" and that the incident had shown that the United States was "not immune to the kind of terror the radio can give."[4] [Companion website link 6.1.]

Less remembered has been the way the panic broadcast seemed to many Americans to be evidence of a massive failure of listening and hence of civic responsibility among a part of the radio audience. The Welles/Wells broadcast was the occasion for a fundamental debate about the place of intelligence, rationality, and emotion in American public life, about the very possibility of democracy coexisting with mass media and propaganda. It was a moment when the cultural divide in the radio audience became starkly apparent, when the civic paradigm façade of American radio revealed its divisive and intolerant aspect.

It has often been said since, by way of explanation of the panic, that the war scare in Europe and the longer term experience of the Depression had left the American population in a nervous state. The recent crises in Europe, and radio's breathless reporting of them, contributed to anxiety. Hurricane and floods in New York and New England in September 1938 killed over a hundred people. There were certainly reasons for Americans to feel less secure than usual in 1938. But these are naturalizing, commonsense explanations, which explain away rather than closely examine the panic broadcast as an event. The dominant explanations in 1938 were not of this liberal, commonsense kind, about how anybody might have been fooled. On the contrary, the most common strain of critical response condemned the panickers as poor listeners and worse citizens, as incompetents, idiots, and failures. A man who was a freshman in college in 1938 still recalled clearly 50 years later that the event was not about war scares: "The panic Welles provoked was caused by the simplicity of John Doe."[5] The dominant topic of public debate after the panic broadcast was the stupidity of the American people, and what that might mean for the place of radio in a democracy.

Recent scholarship reads the panic broadcast as fundamentally about radio. Sconce interprets the panic as expressing anxieties about "the public's newly forged relationship with the central authority of network radio."[6] Miller argues that the broadcast referenced radio's affinities with disaster and emergency, and "places the listener on the precipice of disaster."[7] Alpers identifies the theme of failure of authority more generally—noting that in the program, experts are "almost always incorrect."[8] The Welles adaptation was indeed from the very beginning a radio play about listening to the radio. One of the key dramatic moments was the on-the-spot interview with farmer Wilmuth, who was meant to be talking about the Martians he had seen, but insisted on framing his testimony within a description of how it interrupted his radio listening. Much of the play is indeed framed in just this self-referential way, as a series of increasingly rapid "interruptions" to previ-

4. "Women Are Urged to Act on Nazis," *New York Times,* November 16, 1938: 11.

5. "Martian Invasions," *New York Times,* December 11, 1988: BR46.

6. Jeffrey Sconce, *Haunted Media: Electronic Presence from Telegraphy to Television* (Durham, NC: Duke University Press, 2000): 111, 114.

7. Edward D. Miller, *Emergency Broadcasting and 1930s Radio* (Philadelphia: Temple University Press, 2002): 113.

8. Benjamin Alpers, *Dictators, Democracy and American Public Culture: envisioning the totalitarian enemy, 1920s-1950s* (Chapel Hill: University of North Carolina Press, 2003): 123.

ously announced content. The *Mercury Theater*'s "War of the Worlds" enacted a drama about listening, and the public event that unfolded in the ensuing days was a national discussion of radio listening as a civic practice. That will be the theme of this chapter, but I need first to identify two relevant contexts—the 1930s educational movement to teach the population to deal critically with broadcast propaganda, and the prevailing national concern with the intelligence of the American population.

DEFENDING THE POPULATION AGAINST PROPAGANDA

The reaction to the panic broadcast, as several scholars have recognized, makes sense only in the context of the general 1930s anxiety about radio and propaganda. The broad concern about propaganda discussed in chapter 2 provoked some quite particular responses from American educators and intellectuals. I focus here on the movement to educate Americans about propaganda, to make them critical and self-reflexive enough to resist it. The anticipation and onset of war in Europe only intensified this concern—in February 1940, the *People's Platform* was asking the key question "Is the United States Propaganda Proof?" That was consistently the aspiration of educators, and it was again progressive educators who took the lead in thinking about the kinds of adult education that would be necessary to achieve that goal.

There were two major ways of thinking about propaganda prevalent among American intellectuals and educators. The most influential position was that of the propaganda critics, who argued that while propaganda was bad and endemic, its worst effects were preventable. They concluded that their task as intellectuals was education about and against propaganda. There was a second and more covert view, held by those intellectuals who became propaganda managers, who concluded that propaganda would be a permanent feature of modern life and who wanted to make sure it was used for desirable ends. This group was less concerned with educating against propaganda than with monitoring and managing public opinion—their intellectual lineage is traced in innumerable studies back to Walter Lippmann's views on public opinion and democracy. Exemplifying this approach, Harold Lasswell in 1934 famously defined propaganda as "a mere tool...no more moral or immoral than a pump handle."[9] The existing historiography tells the story of the eventual triumph of these propaganda managers over the propaganda critics, but my attention in this chapter is to the critics, who in 1938 remained very influential.[10]

As the possibility of war loomed toward the end of the 1930s, the need to know about the whole population and its mental state, as a national resource or liability, grew. There would be little point in a modern democracy having an elite that could see through propaganda if any significant section of the people remained vulnerable to it. Concern about propaganda led to a cultural and intellectual climate in which the credulity and intelligence, the mental and emotional state of the population, were under scrutiny as

9. Harold Lasswell, "Propaganda," in Robert Jackall (ed.), *Propaganda* (New York: New York University Press, 1995): 17.

10. See especially J. Michael Sproule, *Propaganda and Democracy: The American Experience of Media and Mass Persuasion* (New York: Cambridge University Press, 1997).

never before, as vital elements of national security. If the natural state of a population was vulnerability to propaganda manipulation, education about and against propaganda was essential. It was as individuals that Americans would have to deal with radio propaganda, and each individual in his or her own home bore the responsibility for listening attentively and critically. The propaganda theory made a clear and invidious distinction between potential victims of propaganda and those able to see through it. Ordinary Americans were usually reluctant to think of themselves as the objects or victims of propaganda, and they were not always sympathetic to the constant injunctions to remain critical, open-minded, and rational. Propaganda theory put radio listeners under suspicion; it was premised upon a low assessment of their capacity for unaided reason and discrimination.

Propaganda criticism was the concern of a particular stratum of educators and democratic reformers, whose vision of a better society was predicated upon the achievement of a more critical public, much more able than existing Americans to deal with flows of miscellaneous information of mixed quality, origins, and intentions. Propaganda critics saw their main task as public education and consciousness raising. In an attempt to gain respectability and a national profile for the mission of propaganda education, some distinguished social scientists in 1937 established an Institute for Propaganda Analysis in New York. Among the founders were Hadley Cantril, Clyde Miller of Teachers College, and Kirtley Mather, a Harvard geologist with a strong interest in adult education. They sought funding from Boston department store owner Edward A. Filene's Good Will Fund. Filene had long used his money to support progressive education and consumer movements, and he was now interested, because of his concern about propaganda, in promoting "education for democracy." In 1937, Filene, Mather, and Miller met with George Denny, Lyman Bryson, and Edward Bernays. As a result, Filene gave Miller $10,000 to set up an antipropaganda organization. The Institute for Propaganda Analysis was incorporated in September 1937, with Cantril as president and Miller as secretary.[11] Its aim was "to help the intelligent citizen to detect and to analyze propaganda, by revealing the agencies, techniques and devices used by propagandists." Right at the outset, then, intelligence was named as an essential prerequisite for the capacity for critical scrutiny and self-management in the modern sea of propaganda.

The institute published the monthly bulletin *Propaganda Analysis*, and prepared teaching materials. The bulletins were aimed particularly at schools and discussion groups, and each issue provided helpful suggestions for awareness-raising activities—for example, that each group member choose a newspaper or magazine or radio commentator for intensive analysis and make a file for later presentation to the group. A workshop held in 1939 canvassed propaganda analysis activities suitable for elementary schools, including gossip games to show how "stories are distorted," and visits to courts to observe firsthand the "unreliability of witnesses."[12] The institute offered the materials for a

11. The best account of the history of the Institute is Sproule, *Propaganda and Democracy*, ch. 5.

12. Transcript of discussions at Institute summer workshop, n.d., folder 1, box 1, Institute for Propaganda Analysis records, NYPL.

comprehensive education in skepticism, and in how to manage one's own reading and listening in a propaganda-saturated age.

Clyde Miller, in the institute's first bulletin, defined propaganda very inclusively as the "expression of opinion or action by individuals or groups deliberately designed to influence opinions or actions of other individuals or groups with reference to predetermined ends."[13] This broad definition made sense to many of those who had thought for a long time about propaganda. The almost inevitable trajectory of propaganda criticism was toward this kind of inclusivity, seeing propaganda as simply endemic to modern life. Thus Leonard Doob, in an influential 1935 work, asserted that "an attempt to identify propaganda with the untrue and education with the true must be likened to a pretty soap bubble, the life of which is brilliant and extremely short."[14] Propaganda, he argued, was inescapable, "and its abolition could be secured only by rupturing practically all of the complicated social bonds through which men associate on friendly or hostile terms with one another."[15]

The inclusive definition had the virtue of bringing home to all that they were inevitably involved with propaganda themselves. Clyde Miller argued in a lecture at Town Hall in 1939, "If we stand on either one side or the other and express our opinions or commit acts intended to influence the acts and opinions of others, we are propagandists."[16] This realization then led to reflection on one's own implication in the production and reception of propaganda. But it had some limitations as the basis of a strategic and fundable program to render the population propaganda-proof. That seemed more and more, on the propaganda analysts' own argument, to be a chimerical task. It was surely neither conceivable nor desirable that people might live sheltered from or immune to all attempts to influence them.

If removal from the world of propaganda was impossible, all that could be provided was a stronger suit of armor, usually understood to be mental toughness and unyielding rationality—a rationality agile and robust enough to combat the emotionalism of propaganda. Clyde Miller advised, "Teachers and students especially should know how to deal with propaganda unemotionally."[17] That seemed a powerful and timely capacity. Implicit or explicit nationalist comparison with the emotionalism and extremism of European politics also underpinned many of the new calls for a cooler and more rational public life in the United States.[18] We might note the appearance in June 1938, at the height of this concern, of the first Superman comic, featuring a new kind of unemotional superhero.[19] In an early institute teachers' workshop, Miss McTammany from East Denver High School enthused: "Why have we been so excited about propaganda analysis? Father Coughlin' speeches when analyzed by an individual with reason become

13. *Propaganda Analysis* 1, no.1 (October 1937): 1.

14. Leonard W. Doob, *Propaganda: Its Psychology and Technique* (New York: Henry Holt, 1935): 9.

15. Doob, *Propaganda: Its Psychology and Technique*: 5.

16. Clyde Miller, *How to Detect and Analyze Propaganda* (New York: Town Hall, 1939): 15.

17. Miller, *How to Detect and Analyze Propaganda*: 26.

18. See Peter N. Stearns, *American Cool: Constructing a Twentieth-Century Emotional Style* (New York: New York University Press, 1994): 103.

19. *Action Comics*, June 1, 1938.

impotent."[20] Propaganda criticism provoked anxiety, but it also stimulated among some Americans this kind of ardent enthusiasm about a new and more rational future.

The discussion of emotions and propaganda was always gendered. Clyde Miller insistently used masculine pronouns as he explained that "the intelligent citizen" did not want the propagandist "to utilize his emotions.... He does not want to be gullible. He does not want to be fooled. He does not want to be duped."[21] There was a persistent assumption in discussion of propaganda that women were more susceptible than men, and that the increasing vulnerability of all Americans to propaganda was an index of a kind of feminization of the whole population. Lyman Bryson, at a 1940 session of the Institute for Education by Radio conference, raised the gender question with his four guests—a Presbyterian minister (Harry Cotton), a professor of journalism (Edward Doan), a taxi driver (Ted Moran), and a "housewife" (Florence Horchow):

Mr. Cotton: I think women are more susceptible to propaganda than men. They are more emotional and therefore tools of propaganda.

Mrs. Horchow: It is perfectly true that emotions make persons tools of propaganda.

Mr. Bryson: But women do not have any?

Mrs. Horchow: Women have lots of emotions, but you do not suppose for one minute that we accept as cold and beautiful logic all the ideas you men hand out, do you?[22]

The conventional wisdom remained, however, that feminine emotion rendered one susceptible to propaganda, and a part of the war on propaganda was combating any kind of feminization within mass society that might render the population more emotional and hence vulnerable to propaganda.

Broadcasters, of course, were both expert at and crucially dependent on the manipulation of commercial propaganda aimed specifically at women. They did not want the public to hear too much exposure or criticism of persuasive radio techniques. When in June 1938 the Propaganda Institute's bulletin turned its attention to "Propaganda on the Air," it sought the assistance of leftist critic James Rorty, whose main concern was commercial propaganda, but then asked Hadley Cantril to revise Rorty's text. The published version acknowledged some freedoms in the American system of broadcasting, but noted that advertisers had a commercial interest in "pleasing a maximum number of listeners and offending nobody."[23] NBC executives remained very concerned about the institute, seeing in it a concerted attack on the advertising and public relations businesses. Franklin Dunham wrote, "I believe their avowed purpose is to drive the publicity counsel such as Edward Bernays and Ivy Lee—T. J. Ross, out of business, or at least, to

20. Box 1, Institute for Propaganda Analysis records, NYPL.

21. Miller, *How to Detect and Analyze Propaganda*: 31.

22. "Are We Victims of Propaganda? A Program in the Manner of 'The People's Platform,'" in Josephine H. MacLatchy (ed.), *Education on the Air* (Columbus: Ohio State University, 1940): 32.

23. *Propaganda Analysis* 1, no. 9 (June 1938): 3.

limit the activities of this new profession."[24] Too many parallels between political and commercial propaganda, too much skeptical education about advertisers and their techniques, would, the networks feared, be detrimental to the broadcasting business.

The next year NBC executives were trying to make something more positive for commercial radio out of the concern about propaganda. Walter Preston and Margaret Cuthbert argued that the chief result of "propaganda consciousness" to date had been "frustration" and "anxiety," and that "more fear of the propagandist will increase the fear of the radio, and the distrust of what it has to offer." As an alternative, they proposed a radio series to be called "The Great Game of Propaganda," which would stress how the "foreign teams who play over here are outsmarted all along the line—when we keep our eyes on them." The desire to shift attention to foreign rather than domestic propaganda evidences NBC concerns that the intense anxiety about propaganda could damage public perceptions of the American system of broadcasting.[25]

The concern about propaganda meant that the emotional state of radio listeners— most commonly, their level of excitement—became an important issue. Adults as well as children were considered at risk of excessive emotional stimulation from their listening. A Rochester man wrote to the *New York Times* in May 1938 arguing that "the nerves of adults, too, might be benefited by reducing the air of high tension" surrounding programs such as news flashes. This listener also thought that the "constant conflict in expression of opinion" on the radio contributed to the "atmosphere of high tension": "Why not replace the prevalent heatedly argumentative spirit by putting on more speakers who are neither 'pro' nor 'con' but who think objectively and coolly?"[26]

The institute publicized the inclusive definition of propaganda, but the animus behind its activities was clearly to uncover the workings of propaganda for undesirable ends. For the liberal intellectuals of the Institute, that meant a focus on right-wing propaganda and an underlying hope that, freed from the grip of emotion, the people would reject fascism and war. A perceptive member of the institute board, F. E. Johnson, pointed out to Clyde Miller in 1938 that while the institute's definition of propaganda was carefully written "to make it inclusive, as a definition, of wholesome as well as mischievous efforts to influence opinion," the examples of propaganda analyzed by the institute were almost always negative:

> What we have said is that the evil in propaganda is its appeal to the emotions instead of to reason. Now this seems to mean that a non-rational appeal is unjustifiable.... Are we prepared to say that an effort to win sympathy for the cause of organized labor or the Jews in Germany or unpopular radical agitators must be strictly rational in order to be valid—that is, must appeal to intelligence exclusively and never to an emotional set or a habitual attitude....[27]

24. John Royal to Lenox Lohr, July 25, 1938, folder 68, box 61, NBC records, WHS. John Royal's earlier career had been as a public relations man for the B. F. Keith theaters.
25. W. G. Preston to John Royal, June 8, 1939, folder 59, box 94, NBC records, WHS.
26. *New York Times*, May 8, 1938: 10.
27. Letter F. E. Johnson to Clyde Miller, September 8, 1938, box 2, Institute for Propaganda Analysis records, NYPL.

Johnson's criticism was astute, but he missed one other important strand of the institute's program: the argument that individuals had to be taught to scrutinize themselves for the signs of their own vulnerability to irrational persuasion. Propaganda critics became strong advocates of self-reflexivity. There were, advised the institute, two main ways to acquire the "mental alertness and independence of thought" needed to deal with propaganda. The first was simply to "study and analyze" propaganda. The second was to attempt to observe oneself and one's friends "engaging unconsciously in propaganda when discussing some vital controversial problem." It was insufficient merely to understand propaganda as a problem inflicted on society by political extremists and vested interests, to view it rationally from the outside as though one could step beyond its reach. To comprehend propaganda as it worked in society, one had to understand one's own implication in it, to make one's own vulnerability to persuasion an object of study and reflection.

The institute frequently advocated this conscientiously self-reflexive mode of propaganda analysis. The early bulletins were written mainly by Clyde Miller, who brought some of his background in progressive education and progressive journalism to the task—he had taught courses in "Public Opinion and Education" and "Propaganda Analysis in General Education" at Teachers College. Miller advocated self-reflection and self-analysis as essential preliminaries to recognizing and engaging critically with propaganda. "If we are to understand propaganda, we must catch ourselves using it."[28] Responsible citizenship required rigorous self-scrutiny and self-censorship: "Each member of the group should carry a notebook or stiff card with him and conscientiously attempt to check himself every time he uses 'good' or 'bad' names by writing them down."[29] Institute publications insisted that propaganda existed only when people were receptive to its messages and were unreflective in their adoption of them: "We must, therefore, see that we ourselves are the fertile soil in which propaganda flourishes; that without us there can be no propaganda; that we create it and propagate it."[30]

In a democracy, propaganda criticism thus had to be, above all else, self-criticism. The public sphere imagined in propaganda criticism was never separable from the private lives of citizens. And because of the "weakest link" logic of national defense thinking, all had to become involved in this new self-scrutiny. In October 1938, the institute thus advised its subscribers to "examine your own emotions concerning the present European crisis." The institute's advice more generally was to practice by choosing some sentences from a radio orator's address and speaking them out loud in different tones of voice—in order really to understand by experience and experiment the persuasive tools that the voice and the radio afforded.[31]

Self-scrutiny of radio listening became a civic duty; propaganda criticism was one of the key currents of thought that contributed to radio's civic paradigm. The intimacy of

28. Institute for Propaganda Analysis, *Propaganda Analysis: Volume 1 of the Publications of the Institute for Propaganda Analysis, Inc.* (New York: Institute for Propaganda Analysis, 1938): ix, xiii.
29. *Propaganda Analysis: Volume 1 of the Publications*: 69.
30. *Propaganda Analysis* 2, no. 4 (January 1939): 10.
31. *Propaganda Analysis: Volume 1 of the Publications*: 83.

radio listening thus became a space of self-government as ideal listeners monitored themselves, reflected on their propensity to believe what they heard, for the sake of the greater good. Self-scrutiny was part of a governmental process, in Foucault's sense: "This contact between the technologies of domination of others and those of the self I call governmentality."[32] Propaganda analysis advocated a kind of self-reflexivity that now came to seem not merely a sign of intellectual sophistication or superiority, but a civic and national duty. The propaganda critics were then partly responsible for the more general sense by the later 1930s that radio listeners bore onerous responsibility for their own listening.

INTELLIGENT LISTENERS

The relatively sophisticated, progressive education derived arguments of the propaganda critics made up one strand of 1930s scrutiny of the radio listener. Out of the pervasive interwar concern about intelligence came a much blunter and less reflexive set of questions, about whether the mass of people were actually intelligent enough to undertake the tasks of radio listening responsibly. The *Mercury* radio version of *War of the Worlds* was a war story, but it was also a story about intelligence—a play about the attempted subjugation of mentally inferior beings by mentally superior ones. While H. G. Wells was writing the *War of the Worlds,* his brother had asked him what would happen if a superior and ruthless civilization arrived on earth to exterminate humanity, just as (so the world had been told) the Tasmanian indigenous people had been, as Wells put it in the novel, "entirely swept out of existence in a war of extermination waged by European immigrants."[33] The *Mercury* version opens with the narrator describing the Martians watching Earth: "Across an immense ethereal gulf, minds that are to our minds as ours are to the beasts in the jungle, intellects vast, cool and unsympathetic, regarded this earth with envious eyes."[34] This theme had numerous historical and political resonances. The coverage of the 1938 panic broadcast sat on newspaper pages side-by-side with stories about the expulsion of Polish Jews from Germany. One letter writer to the *Washington Post* observed that while the world had little to fear from Martian invaders, there was much to fear about the regimes in Berlin, Tokyo, and Rome that were threatening to "compel races of people to wander over the face of the globe like hunted animals."[35] The drama of the *War of the Worlds* story was centrally about intelligence and domination,

32. Michel Foucault, "Technologies of the Self," in Luther H. Martin, Huck Gutman, and Patrick H. Hutton (eds.), *Technologies of the Self: A Seminar with Michel Foucault* (London: Tavistock, 1988): 19.

33. Paul Heyer, *The Medium and the Magician: Orson Welles, the Radio Years, 1934–1952* (Lanham, MD: Rowman and Littlefield, 2005): 83; H. G. Wells, *The War of the Worlds* (Rockville, MD: Phoenix Pick, 2008): 10–11. For a recent assessment of the Tasmanian history, see Henry Reynolds, "Genocide in Tasmania?" in A. Dirk Moses (ed.), *Genocide and Settler Society: Frontier Violence and Stolen Indigenous Children in Australian History* (New York: Berghahn Books, 2004): 127–49.

34. Film director Stanley Kubrick memorized these words and thought they "set the tone for public consideration of extra-terrestrial life for years to come." Gene D. Phillips (ed.), *Stanley Kubrick: Interviews* (Jackson: University Press of Mississippi, 2001): 53.

35. Morton Jerome Jacobs, letter to the editor, *Washington Post*, November 10, 1938: 11.

and about the very survival of subjugated peoples. It triggered a debate in American society that was full of eugenic interest in the place of the less intelligent within modern, mass-mediated society.

The intelligence of citizens had become by the 1930s a public and national issue. "A new kind of scrutiny was being applied to the mental state of the population," argues Nikolas Rose, and the prospective interest in wartime morale "signalled an extension of this concern to a wider and more complex subjective territory."[36] The intelligence, critical ability, and alertness of individual citizens thus became in the 1930s civic matters—everybody's business. Population was a national resource, or liability, depending upon how successfully citizens kept themselves informed and able intelligently to process the flows of contradictory and possibly deceptive information confronting them.

In the United States, social psychologists were central to these debates about population, intelligence, and propaganda. Psychological "rebels within the ranks," such as Gordon and Floyd Allport and Hadley Cantril, were shaping a new area of expertise and advice—one to which the U.S. government would turn gratefully during World War II when propaganda management was needed.[37] Psychologists in the United States had earlier popularized the notion that a section of the population might have dangerously low intelligence. The most publicized use of intelligence measurement, pioneered by Henry Herbert Goddard, was in the testing of recruits to the U.S. Army in 1918, and the finding that the average mental age of the white draftees was 13.08 years, only barely above the level of "feeble-mindedness."[38] Zenderland argues that the tests confirmed for Goddard "what he had gradually come to suspect: that most of the country's problems were caused by a large class of persons of low mental power."[39] American psychologists, Ellen Herman reports, led the way after WWI in giving scientific credence to the view that "public opinion was a real threat to rational planning, even to moral order itself."[40] This sense was reinforced by interwar American psychologists' readings of European crowd psychology.[41] By the 1930s, the strict hereditarian and eugenicist interpretation of the army intelligence tests was academically contested and even discredited. But a popular memory of the sensational findings lived on, and the emphasis that Goddard and others placed on education and training as a way of managing the low intelligence of the majority lies in the background of much academic and popular discussion of propaganda and radio in the 1930s.

36. Rose, *Governing the Soul: The Shaping of the Private Self*: 23.

37. Blair T. Johnson and Diane R. Nichols, "Social Psychologists' Expertise in the Public Interest: Civilian Morale Research During World War II," *Journal of Social Issues* 54, no. 1 (1998): 53–77.

38. Stephen Jay Gould, *The Mismeasure of Man* (New York: Norton, 1981): 222; Leila Zenderland, *Measuring Minds: Henry Herbert Goddard and the Origins of American Intelligence Testing* (Cambridge: Cambridge University Press, 1998): 289.

39. Zenderland, *Measuring Minds*: 295.

40. Ellen Herman, *The Romance of American Psychology: Political Culture in the Age of Experts* (Berkeley: University of California Press, 1995): 55.

41. Herman, *The Romance of American Psychology*: 23. See also Eugene E. Leach, "'Mental Epidemics': Crowd Psychology and American Culture, 1890–1940," *American Studies* 33, no. 1 (Spring 1992): 5–29.

The rhetoric of intelligence pervaded public discussion of radio audiences on every side. When psychologist James Rowland Angell took up his position at NBC, a journalist asked him about the suggestion that the average mental age of the radio listener was 13. "I think that is putting it high," Angell replied. "I believe the average intelligence of the radio audience is below the 13-year level."[42] Others worried that radio's low estimation of the intelligence of the population could become a self-fulfilling prophecy. In March 1938 the chair of the physical education department at New York University warned about children's radio: "It's the moronishness, the stupidity, the inactivity of it, rather than the badness, that gives us the greatest concern."[43] The specific concern was that radio could be producing morons as well as addressing them. In 1937, FCC commissioner George Henry Payne observed that "the average program of the broadcasters is addressed to an intelligence possessed by a child of 12. It is important to raise this average to the adult age; otherwise there is the danger that radio will perpetuate mental immaturity in the grown-up. There is the danger that radio and the movies will in time make us a nation of grown-up children."[44] Damon Runyon warned about a radio commercialism that "seems so essential to the operations of the business in the United States that it can dictate programs that sometimes seem a direct bid for the attention of the mentally deficient."[45] There was an established public concern in 1938, then, that the intelligence of the population was dangerously low, and that radio might have something to do with keeping it that way.

The army intelligence tests also played a part, Zenderland argues, in gaining attention to the social problems of the especially intelligent.[46] There was a fear in the 1930s that there might be a correlation between high intelligence and low civic virtue. A eugenicist from New Jersey argued in 1937 that the "intelligence quotient" needed to be supplemented by a "social quotient" that would measure a person's ability to fit in to a changing world; he raised the possibility that a highly intelligent person might be found to be socially incompetent and "unfit for society."[47] In December 1937, the president of Union Theological Seminary, Henry Sloane Coffin, warned that intelligence could be used for destructive ends: "Wisdom, which is a much higher capacity than intelligence, is a combination of brains and faithfulness."[48] In November 1938, a professor at Teachers College reported her finding that highly intelligent children were often unhappy, suffering from "an inferiority complex, loneliness, and a cynical attitude towards life."[49] This amounted to a significant and matching level of concern about the social understanding and values of the highly intelligent—relevant to the panic broadcast in that Orson Welles was consistently publicly identified as either highly intelligent or a genius.

42. "From Yale to Radio," *New York Times,* September 26, 1937: 184.
43. "Radio Denounced as Peril to Young," *New York Times,* March 31, 1938: 25.
44. "Calls for Raising Radio Standards," *New York Times,* December 2, 1937: 28.
45. Damon Runyon, "The Brighter Side," *San Antonio Light,* July 11, 1938: 7.
46. Zenderland, *Measuring Minds*: 293.
47. "Yardstick Tests Social Fitness," *New York Times,* August 22, 1937: N2.
48. "Misdirected Intelligence Greatest Danger in World of Today," *New York Times,* December 6, 1937: 28.
49. "Children With an I. Q. Above 150 May Be Too Smart for Own Good," *New York Times,* November 1, 1938: 25.

FROM MARS

The producers of the *Mercury Theater on the Air* series were 23-year-old Orson Welles and John Houseman. The Mercury Theater and its radio project grew from Welles and Houseman's collaboration on the Federal Theater Project. Welles had a left, Popular Front aesthetic, and a commitment to the development of a people's theater.[50] He appreciated radio's potential as a "popular, democratic machine." John Houseman brought to radio from his New Deal theater work a technical interest in agitprop and propaganda. In 1942, he became the founding director of propaganda broadcaster, the Voice of America.[51] Those behind the panic broadcast then had a particular interest in the power of radio to persuade, and in the politics of radio listening. In developing adaptations for *Mercury Theater on the Air*, Welles was also particularly interested in the intimacy of radio: "Listeners should be considered as small groups of two or three....Intimacy is one of radio's richest possessions." A "first-person singular" narrator who was also a part of the story was Welles's chosen technique to overcome the distancing effect of conventional radio drama that cast the listener only as eavesdropper.[52] Figure 6.1.

The "panic" broadcast was understood at the time to be the product of Orson Welles's imagination, and has been popularly associated with him ever since. Much of the public debate after the broadcast centered on the persona of Welles and the appropriateness of a young genius experimenting on the radio audience. It is clear, however, that the radio play was produced by a team, and that Welles, as was his usual practice, became actively involved only quite late in the production. Houseman recalls, "Orson Welles had virtually nothing to do with the writing of the script and less than usual to do with its preliminary rehearsals." He added, "Yet first and last it was his creation."[53] Welles had, for example, in rehearsal dragged out the length of the opening sequences way beyond what anyone else had thought reasonable, thus tightening the dramatic effect of the later events in the story. It was also Welles's idea, according to Houseman, to tell the story in news bulletin form, using the new form of "on the spot" radio news reporting familiar to Americans in 1938 from the Czechoslovakian crisis, "faithfully copying every detail of the new technique—including its imperfections."[54] The script was largely written by Howard Koch, although when Hadley Cantril made that attribution in print, Welles vehemently objected, insisting that Koch was only part of a team and that he himself had played the important role as "creator and responsible artist."[55]

50. Michael Denning, *The Cultural Front: The Laboring of American Culture in the Twentieth Century* (New York: Verso, 1998): 363–65.

51. See Holly Cowan Shulman, "John Houseman and the Voice of America: American Foreign Propaganda on the Air," *American Studies* 28 (2): 23–40, and Holly Cowan Shulman, *The Voice of America: Propaganda and Democracy, 1941–1945* (Madison: University of Wisconsin Press, 1990).

52. Richard O'Brien, "'The Shadow' Talks: Mr. Welles Turns to a New Art Form," *New York Times*, August 14, 1938: 10.

53. John Houseman, "The Men from Mars," *Harpers* (December 1948): 76.

54. John Houseman, "Introduction," in Howard Koch, *As Time Goes By: Memoirs of a Writer* (New York: Harcourt Brace Jovanovich, 1979): xiii; John Houseman, "The Men from Mars": 79.

55. See Heyer, *The Medium and the Magician*: 107–11; Hilmes, *Radio Voices*: 225–27.

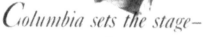

Columbia sets the stage—

SINGULAR FIRST PERSON

Orson Welles and his Mercury company are the theatre's reigning First Persons. Their new venture, "Julius Caesar", which opened so triumphantly last November, rocketed them to immediate success, was bulwarked by three consecutive hits, "Shoemaker's Holiday", "The Cradle Will Rock" and "Heartbreak House". At Columbia's invitation, Welles and his troupe bring their vivid originality and imagination to radio. In *First Person Singular*, Orson Welles writes, adapts, casts, directs and acts to the great "first person" stories of literature for radio. Old and new, from "The Tale of Two Cities" to "The Thirty-nine Steps", they are taken out, brushed off and broadcast to the nation in all their original excitement and newness.

... and action is the cue!

Whether it be the first poetic drama written for radio, Archibald MacLeish's *Fall of the City*; or a glowing re-creation of *Hamlet* by "Buzz" Meredith; or the brilliant adaptation of *The Red Badge of Courage* by the Columbia Workshop, the CBS curtain rises on a living, on an *active* theater. ¶ This summer, CBS tops its playbill with the brightest sensation of the drama season—Orson Welles and his Mercury Theater. But the distinguished CBS summer guest is only one of *eight* dramatic programs heard *each week*; ranging from the new *Four Corners Theater* to the eight-year-old program for children of all ages, *Let's Pretend*. To these, the nation is now listening, right times a week, in millions of the most comfortable, intimate theaters of the land.

BRAVOS FROM THE NATION'S PRESS

SUPERB "Welles does it too Welles"... "Dracula"...The offering was superb... It was a happy meeting between expert cast and sensational material. *New York Daily News*

ELECTRIC It seemed as if the "mike" was actually being held to the lips of the marvelled genius Bob Green, as it is in the cast and up to microphone prize-fighters and sound-effects will do it...So it was with "Treasure Island"...The transport had electricity. *New York Times*

GRATIFYING The gratifying thing about the hour was that we thought we deserved. *New York Journal*

VERY SMELL INDEED Welles wants to review the storyteller's art. He narrates right through the dramatized portions, drops in characters aloud as they cast the make-believe work and the effect he's chopping so you might imagine, but very well indeed. *New York Post*

CONSUMMATE The work was sure, consummate, sure and effective at the moments being interpreted by its own emotions, this Welles case. *Memphis Times Press-Scimitar*

VIVID Welles' use of the first person makes radio drama... as vivid as the stage... Before we knew it came a prize-fight, the story becomes the play... *Jonathan Hale, Record*

PERFECT Everything was so high pitched...Emotionally, it told you in the city of CBS. *Radio Daily*

STIMULATING CORNER Orson Welles launched his new WABC series of Monday evening dramas...It is a good mark it clear that each is one of the most stimulating series of radio offerings. *New York Herald-Tribune*

NEW HIGH It was some drama, this Welles. He reached a new high. *Cleveland Plain Dealer*

Mercury Theater on the Air was drawing only small audiences up against the very popular Edgar Bergen and Charlie McCarthy on NBC. The week before, the *Mercury* had rated 3.6% of the listening audience while Bergen and his puppet had scored 34.7%. The *Mercury Theater* was intended as minority fare radio—it was at that stage unsponsored, commercial-free, high cultural radio. Each episode opened with the opening theme from the first movement of Tchaikovsky's First Piano Concerto, then in the early episodes an announcement that this was "a unique new series dramatizing famous narratives by great authors."[56] Welles argued that radio had been underestimating the intelligence of the radio audience: "While the intelligence of the radio audience has been estimated at 11 years old, that does not mean that those who write for the microphone should be of similar mental stature."[57] Welles thus consciously packaged the *Mercury Theater* series for an "intelligent" audience.

Intelligent people, it was assumed, listened seriously, not distractedly. A play such as "War of the Worlds" demanded the kind of rapt attention that audiences for sacralized high culture were used to according valued performances. In the aftermath of the panic, *New York Times* radio critic Orrin Dunlap remarked that one of the things that broadcasters had learned was that "drama too is listened to carelessly; it also is background noise out of which some fragment hits the ear and starts rumors flying."[58] As the Hopewell, New Jersey, newspaper commented, one problem was that "those listening to the radio program rushed out immediately, or at least stopped listening, the moment they heard about the meteor."[59] In a subsequent Gallup Poll, 60% of those who reported listening to the program said they tuned in after it began and 19% said they stopped listening before the end.[60] This is reflected in newspaper accounts, in which people often said they were fleeing meteors—but only a few minutes into the drama, it became clear that the problem was not meteors but Martian invaders. Distracted listeners were much more likely to panic—a Trenton newspaper pointed out the next day that "part-time listeners" were among those most liable to have been fooled.[61] Many of the late-tuners-in came from the McCarthy show on NBC, and switched stations at about 12 minutes past the hour as the opening comedy routine came to an end. These people began listening to the *Mercury Theater* just in time to hear what many cited as one of the most "realistic" moments of the play, the interview with farmer Wilmuth.[62] Having missed the opening framing of the play as fiction, these listeners stayed on to be drawn into the increasing horror of the drama. Hadley Cantril's study of the panic concluded that "some people do not listen attentively to their radios until they are aware that something of particular interest is being broadcast."[63] The evidence of inattentive radio listening was not lost on newspaper proprietors. The *Trenton Evening Times* editorialized, "The permanency

56. Introduction to Mercury Theater broadcast of "The Thirty Nine Steps," August 1, 1938.

57. "'The Shadow' Talks," *New York Times*, August 14, 1938: 10.

58. Orrin E. Dunlap Jr., "Message from Mars," *New York Times*, November 6, 1938: 12.

59. "No Terror Here as 'Meteor' Kills," *Hopewell Herald*, November 2, 1938: 1.

60. American Institute of Public Opinion poll, December 16, 1938, in Mildred Strunk (ed.), *Public Opinion, 1935–1946* (Princeton: Princeton University Press, 1951): 711.

61. *Trenton Evening Times*, October 31, 1938: 2.

62. Heyer, *The Medium and the Magician*: 85.

63. Hadley Cantril with Hazel Gaudet and Herta Herzog, *The Invasion from Mars: A Study in the Psychology of Panic* (Princeton: Princeton University Press, 1940): 80.

of printed news reports, which can be read and re-read if desired, is the best assurance of accuracy and the difference between fact and fiction. The newspaper...mirrors life in all its phases in a way that leads to knowledge rather than hysteria."[64] The *Washington Post* took out a full-page advertisement in an advertising trade paper claiming that the panic broadcast proved how little attention people paid to radio announcers: "Who listened to him? Who listens to what your announcer tells them about your product?"[65]

PANIC

If newspapers clearly had an interest in exaggerating the panic, they did not press the advantage very far. There has been considerable subsequent skepticism about the actual extent of the panic. Newspapers the next day carried accounts in notably general terms—"a wave of mass hysteria reminiscent of war time."[66] The *Washington Post* reported the morning after that hundreds had fainted, men and women had fled their homes, and "hysteria swept the nation."[67] But several scholars make the point that, when viewed with knowledge of the subsequent fame of the panic incident, the newspaper coverage seems relatively minor, and confined to the few days after October 30.[68] One man wrote to the *Washington Post* to say he had been walking down K Street and "there was nothing approximating mass hysteria."[69] Socolow concludes that "the panic was neither as wide-spread nor as serious as many have believed at the time or since."[70]

But we must be careful not to slide from the almost certainly correct observation that there was not mass hysteria to a conclusion that there was very little panic at all. At least one panic-related death was reported—a 60-year-old Baltimore man died from a heart attack while listening to the broadcast, and his doctor diagnosed "sudden excitement precipitating a heart attack."[71] Here is one of many letters to the FCC that eloquently evidences real panic:

> We were all scared to death. Our daughter was up all night. A Gas station here 6 people was all frightened one fainted and the others would not tuch him he was black with fear a doctor came. A saloon keeper gave away all the stuff their was so many cars driving to another gas station he said take all you want no money it won't be any good any how so you see how bad it was.[72]

The *Mercury* writers had the Martians land in the small town of Grovers Mill, New Jersey, and there were several accounts of New Jersey panics. State troopers reported traffic at a

64. *Trenton Evening Times*, November 1, 1938: 8.
65. *New York Times*, November 15, 1938: 41.
66. "Nationwide Hysteria Caused by Radio Drama," *Tyrone Daily Herald*, October 31, 1938: 1.
67. *Washington Post* October 31, 1938: 1.
68. See, e.g., Sconce, *Haunted Media*: 115.
69. A. McK. Griggs, letter to the editor, *Washington Post*, November 3, 1938: X10.
70. Michael J. Socolow, "The Hyped Panic Over 'War of the Worlds,'" *Chronicle of Higher Education*, 55, no. 9 (October 24, 2008): 35–35.
71. "'Mars Invasion' Heart Attack Fatal to Baltimore Man," *Washington Post*, November 13, 1938: M8.
72. Letter to FCC, November 6, 1938, box 238, RG 173, FCC, Office of the Executive Director, General Correspondence 1927–46, 44–3, NACP.

standstill around Grovers Mill as people tried to flee; 20 families in the Clinton Hills area of Newark were found by police huddled in the street, faces covered with water-soaked handkerchiefs as protection against the gas.[73] In Hopewell, while there was no mass hysteria, telephone exchanges were swamped, and some people did leave.[74] Trenton's police department received 2000 phone calls in two hours and the City Manager complained that "all communication lines were paralyzed." The Trenton Electrical Bureau fielded many inquiries from "weeping women and frantic men."[75] One Grovers Mill resident recalled 60 years later how a neighbor with a young baby came running up on the porch that night screaming and pounding on the front door—he said he had never seen such fear in a person's eyes.[76] The New York Times reported that people in Harlem were shaken by the news: "The parlor churches in the Negro district, congregations of the smaller sects meeting on the ground floors of brownstone houses, took the 'news' in stride as less faithful parishioners rushed in with it, seeking spiritual consolation. Evening services became 'end of the world' prayer meetings in some."[77] The African American Amsterdam News corroborated: "Strong men who had forgotten all about the meaning of prayer dropped to their knees to spend their last few minutes with God. Children half frightened out of their wits screamed in terror and women fainted."[78] But there was also panic far away from New Jersey. In Lincoln, Nebraska, the police headquarters, newspapers, and radio stations were flooded with calls. One caller to the Nebraska State Journal said that her son had been killed in the war and that the broadcast had brought her "to a state of nervous shock."[79] In Boise, the Idaho Daily Statesman's four telephones "rang incessantly," with apparently well-informed callers warning that the death-ray machines would be in Boise by dawn.[80]

It is impossible now to say how many panicked; most accounts repeat Cantril's estimate of probably 1 million Americans. That is of course a small minority of listeners to the program, and an even smaller minority of the nation's population. So there were also plenty of accounts of people not panicking. In Grovers Mill, residents were reported to have gone peacefully back to sleep once satisfied that scenes of devastation were not occurring around them.[81] The Trenton Evening News reported some local concern but asserted with hometown pride that the panic was worse in New York City, where "thousands rushed into the streets and parks, spreading their infectious alarm as they milled around waiting for the destruction to overtake them." [Figure 6.2. and Figure 6.3.] [Companion website link 6.2.]

73. "Probe on as Protests Mark Program that Spread Panic," Trenton Evening News, October 31, 1938: 1–2.

74. "No Terror Here as 'Meteor' Kills," Hopewell Herald, November 2, 1938: 1.

75. Letter to FCC, October 31, 1938, box 238, RG 173, FCC, Office of the Executive Director, General Correspondence 1927–46, 44–3, NACP.

76. "60 Years after Invasion, Some Revisionist History in Grovers Mill," New York Times, October 25, 1998: NJ3.

77. New York Times, October 31, 1938: 4.

78. "War of Worlds Scared Harlem," Amsterdam News, November 5, 1938: 1.

79. Nebraska State Journal, October 31, 1938: 1; Abilene Reporter-News, November 1, 1938: 1.

80. Ogden Standard Examiner, October 31, 1938: 2.

81. New York Evening Post, November 1, 1938: 2.

Figures 6.2. Orson Welles is interviewed by the press after the radio broadcast of *War of the Worlds*, October 31, 1938, in New York. Figure 6.2. CBS/Landov.

Figure 6.3. *New York Daily News* photo archive.

THE PUBLIC DEBATE

The "War of the Worlds" broadcast provides one more reminder that in the late 1930s, the American settlement of the broadcasting question was fragile enough to be questioned. The newspapers immediately made the FCC response the main story. "US Probes Radio Shocker," read one banner headline in Iowa. The Trenton *Evening Times* front-page story was headed "US Board Starts Probe as Protest Marks Panic Spread by Radio Drama." Newspapers, even those close to the geographic heart of the panic, were clear that the real story was the regulation of radio. The Associated Press led its initial report with the observation that the radio industry had glimpsed a "hobgoblin more terrifying to it than any Halloween spook"—the prospect of "increasing federal control of broadcasts."[82] The panic broadcast took place just two weeks before the commencement of the FCC's major inquiry into network broadcasting and monopoly. The commission was known to be in an activist mood, and the surprise demonstration of the persuasive capacity of network radio was inevitably seen in the context of the question of regulation and the future of the American system. Senator Clyde Herring of Iowa was in almost all October 31 newspaper stories announcing his intention to introduce a bill into the next Congress "controlling just such abuses," and forcing radio stations to submit proposed broadcasts to the FCC for approval. He said, "Programs of that kind are an excellent indication of the inadequacy of our present control over a marvelous facility."[83] Herring's proposal was for a board within the FCC, to which broadcasters would submit programs for prior checking on obscene or horror content.[84] Newspaper editorial response to Herring's proposal was generally hostile—shared fear of government censorship was stronger than the much-publicized press-radio rivalry. In Herring's home state, the *Estherville Daily News* reasoned that "if it becomes government policy for some hireling to decide what the public should or should not hear it is only another small step to dictate what should and should not be read."[85] The *Oakland Tribune* contended that "any trend toward governmental control of speech is to be opposed within a democracy."[86] The *New York Times* on November 1 was already sure that the problems of broadcasting "can only be cured by a deeply searching self-regulation."[87] A *New York Times* story on November 6 placed the panic broadcast alongside the recent call from the Bach Society of New Jersey to prohibit the "swinging" of classical music on the air, and argued that in both situations free speech had to be preserved.[88] The *Milwaukee Journal* opined that "public reaction…is a good deal better and safer than bureaucratic censorship."[89] Cheekily, the *Chicago Tribune*

82. "Men of Mars Spread Havoc in Radioland," *Dallas Morning News*, October 31, 1938: 1.

83. "The Martian Attack," *Augusta Chronicle*, November 1, 1938: 4.

84. "Herring Discloses Letters Approving 'Clean Up' of Radio," *Carroll Daily Herald*, February 12, 1938: 1.

85. "Radio Censorship," *Estherville Daily News*, November 26, 1938: 4.

86. "Radio Censorship," *Oakland Tribune*, November 15, 1938: 36.

87. *New York Times*, November 1, 1938: 22.

88. Charles W. Hurd, "Will the Radio Be Censored?" *New York Times*, November 6, 1938: 7, and "Let Freedom Swing: Protest against Jazzing the Classics Stirs Listeners in War against Censorship," *New York Times*, November 6, 1938: 12.

89. Reprinted in *Chicago Tribune*, December 5, 1938: 14.

warned that it would be "extraordinarily difficult to write a law forbidding the broadcasting of hoaxes which would not at the same time prevent some of our most successful politicians from using the radio to address their constituents."[90] The industry journal *Broadcasting* predictably found in the panic further proof of the virtues of the "American system." If a fictitious broadcast could "throw some Americans into a frenzy, what would happen if radio were ruled by a Government dictatorship?"[91]

To the FCC, the panic event was in some ways peripheral to its then major concerns—decency and monopoly. As the *New York Times* reported, "The program was obviously far removed from the single pressing question of monopoly.... Likewise, it raised no question of obscenity."[92] The commission was, however, divided. The progressive George Henry Payne commented that "certainly when people are injured morally, physically, spiritually and psychically, they have just as much right to complain as if the laws against obscenity and indecency were involved."[93] The industry-friendly T. A. M. Craven, on the other hand, warned that the FCC should not do anything that would "discourage the presentation of the dramatic arts" or create a "'spineless' radio."[94] On October 31, Chairman Frank McNinch issued a statement of concern: "Any broadcast that creates such general panic and fear as this one is reported to have done is, to say the least, regrettable. The widespread public reaction to this broadcast, as indicated by the press, is another demonstration of the power and force of radio and points out again the serious public responsibility of those who are licensed to operate stations." He called an informal conference with the heads of the three networks, but stressed that the meeting would focus narrowly on the fictional use of news flashes.[95] *Broadcasting* reported that the meeting "went deeply into voluntary action by broadcasters in eliminating undesirable program matter."[96] The networks happily agreed that the terms *flash* and *bulletin* would in future be used with great discretion in drama. The FCC then reassured all parties that "complaints received regarding this program will not be taken into account in considering the renewals of licenses of stations which carried the broadcast."[97] The *New York Evening Post* succinctly summarized the proceedings: "Chains Decurdle Air Shockers to Bar U.S. Control."[98] NBC president Lenox Lohr cabled David Sarnoff at parent company RCA: "Had satisfactory three hour conference with Chairman McNinch and he showed attitude of helpful cooperation. Stated flatly he did not want to dictate anything which we should or should not do."[99] The regulatory aftermath was thus mild. This was largely because both sides could agree that someone else was to blame—the listener.

90. "The Gullible Radio Public," *Chicago Tribune*, November 10, 1938: 16.

91. *Broadcasting* 15, no. 10 (November 15, 1938): 40.

92. *New York Times*, November 1, 1938: 26.

93. *Washington Post*, November 1, 1938.

94. *Broadcasting* 15, no. 10 (November 15, 1938): 28.

95. Telegram Frank McNinch to William S. Paley, November 5, 1938.

96. *Broadcasting* 15, no. 11 (December 1, 1938): 14.

97. Frank McNinch, "A New Communications Program—Address of Frank McNinch...Over the Mutual Broadcasting System," FCC Press Release, February 10, 1939: 9.

98. *New York Evening Post*, November 1, 1938.

99. Lenox Lohr telegram to David Sarnoff, November 8, 1938, box 358, NBC history files, LOC. On the FCC response, see Justin Levine, "A History and Analysis of the Federal Communications Commission's Response to Radio Broadcast Hoaxes," *Federal Communications Law Journal* 52, no. 2 (2000): 273–320.

Blaming the Listener

It was in part the shared civic paradigm that limited the regulatory response. The dominant scrutiny was of the way people listened to radio, not of who decided what was broadcast. CBS placed responsibility for the turmoil squarely with the individual panicked listeners, suggesting that the problem was skittish listening: "We can only suppose that the special nature of radio which is often heard in fragments, or in parts disconnected from the whole, has led to this misunderstanding." *Radio Guide* more colorfully blamed "dial-twiddlers who dart all over the kilocycles like water-bugs."[100] Distracted, agitated listeners were widely perceived to be a significant cause of the problem, and various attempts were made to explain why distracted and emotional listening had apparently become so common. Psychologist Rudolph Acher diagnosed a "mass case of jitters" stimulated by the World War and the "persistent economic chaos."[101] The *Salt Lake Tribune* editorialized:

> The recent war scare in Europe, the constant booming of cannon on two continents, the roar of bombing planes and screech of descending missiles of death, the moans of dying mothers in hovels and marketplaces, the wail of starving babies beside mangled forms that gave them birth, echoing and flashing around the earth, filling people's ears from radios and staring at them from every issue of the daily press, has made the reading public apprehensive, jittery and hysterical.[102]

A letter writer to the *Washington Post* argued that the conditions that had produced jitterbugs had also made the panic: "The all-night life, the senseless barbaric swing music, questionable songs, drinking parties, wild, drunken driving and other poise-wrecking activities have brought forth so many disgraceful and tragic results that in a great number mental stability has been almost destroyed."[103]

Harsh as these judgments were, this kind of sociological and historical account at least gave listeners some credit for managing life in complex and risky times. Far more common, and far less charitable, were arguments about intelligence, deriding the audience and its mental capacity. The *Chicago Tribune* editorialized: "By and large the radio audience isn't very bright. Perhaps it would be more tactful to say that some members of the radio audience are a trifle retarded mentally, and that many a program is prepared for their consumption."[104] The *Tribune* thought no great harm had been done by the Mars broadcast: "The incident may have jolted a few persons into a realization of their intellectual limitations. Possibly some hundreds of citizens have learned that they are not as smart as they thought they were."[105] Influential syndicated columnist Dorothy Thompson also took up the issue of the intelligence of the radio audience. Three days after the broad-

100. *Radio Guide*, November 19, 1938: 1.
101. "Radio Play Hysteria Laid to 'Jitters' Era," *Miami News Record*, November 1, 1938: 6.
102. "Wars of Imagination Cause Hysterical Casualties," *Salt Lake Tribune*, November 1, 1938: 6.
103. I.L.G., letter to the editor, *Washington Post*, November 3, 1938: X10.
104. "The Gullible Radio Public," *Chicago Tribune*, November 10, 1938: 16.
105. "The Gullible Radio Public" 16.

cast, she wrote that Welles and company had "demonstrated more potently than any argument, demonstrated beyond question of a doubt, the appalling dangers and enormous effectiveness of popular and theatrical demagoguery." They had "cast a brilliant and cruel light on the failure of popular education. They have shown up the incredible stupidity, lack of nerve and ignorance of thousands. They have proved how easy it is to start a mass delusion."[106] This, Thompson concluded, was "the story of the century." It made a "greater contribution to an understanding of Hitlerism, Mussolinism, Stalinism, anti-Semitism and all the other terrorisms of our time than all the words about them that have been written by reasonable men." Thompson argued, against all the evidence to the contrary, that "nothing whatever" about the broadcast was "in the least credible, no matter at what point the hearer might have tuned in." The panic evidenced a "complete failure of logic." Even more telling, for Thompson, was that the deceived "of course demanded that the state protect them, demonstrating that they were incapable of relying on their own judgment." She expressed disdain at this apparent incapacity for self-government—the panickers had failed in their civic duty of listening skeptically and self-reflexively.[107] Radio had been let down by the people, whose stupidity and inability to take responsibility for their own listening threatened democracy.

All over the country, newspapers wrote of the panic broadcast in similar terms, echoing the themes enunciated by Thompson and the *Tribune*, listing the failures of listeners and questioning their intelligence. In Paris, Texas, a columnist observed, "Often times it's been said that the average radio listener has the intelligence of a 14 year old, but the behavior of thousands of supposedly sane citizens of these United States during that broadcast makes me doubt that they have much between the ears."[108] Columns and editorials offered such explicit judgments, but news reports also conveyed the prevalent scorn. The *New York Times* front-page story detailed the mistakes and omissions of the panickers: "The radio listeners, apparently, missed or did not listen to the introduction....They also failed to associate the program with the newspaper listing of the program....They ignored three additional announcements made during the program."[109] The next day, the paper editorialized: "The inability of so many, tuning in so late, to comprehend that they were listening to the account of an imaginary catastrophe has its ridiculous, even its pathetic, aspects."[110] New York's *Radio Daily* agreed, stating bluntly that the problem was that CBS had thought it was putting on a program for a "high-brow overflow audience," but that "lesser lights were listening too and couldn't take it."[111] Writers of letters to newspapers were also concerned to put the panicked listeners in their place. The hysteria was "a clear-cut example of the stupidity and ignorance that exists in the minds of some people," one man wrote to the *New York Evening Post*.[112] A listener

106. Dorothy Thompson, "Mr. Welles and Mass Delusion," *New York Herald Tribune*, November 2, 1938: 21.

107. Thompson, "Mr. Welles and Mass Delusion,": 21.

108. Henry Moore in *Paris, Texas News*, November 2, 1938: 2.

109. *New York Times,* October 31, 1938: 1.

110. *New York Times,* November 1, 1938: 22.

111. *Radio Daily*, November 1, 1938.

112. Daniel Feerst, letter to the editor, *New York Evening Post*, November 2, 1938.

wrote to the *New York Evening Sun* saying that it seemed "impossible that any one could take so highly imaginative and improbable a story seriously," but that the American people had become "extremely gullible in the past few years."[113]

Few of the frightened answered back. It was difficult to respond as a member of a derided and embarrassed group. One frightened listener did write to Thompson, detailing how his educated household had heard the broadcast: "Despite the fact that of eight people present six were university graduates, two have doctorates in philosophy...during a period of ten minutes and before published programs were checked, the group was thrown into a state bordering on panic."[114] Only a few newspapers took the side of the frightened. The *Chicago Daily News* argued that it was the broadcasters who lacked human intelligence. Radio, it said, "may be the most powerful means of arousing mass brain storms that humanity has ever encountered," and hence "none but trained, responsible hands should be entrusted even momentarily with such powers.... Morons and mikes do not mix."[115]

Print-media humorists were even freer to scorn listeners than editorial writers. A cartoon in the urbane *New Yorker* depicted a radio broadcast: "At this point, we interrupt the performance to inform the radio audience that the script of our play now calls for a revolver shot. We wish to assure all who may be listening in that the shot will be fired by our sound man, using an ordinary prop revolver and blank cartridges. There is no cause for alarm."[116] The cartoon dramatizes the moment when a cultural elite pulls away from the rest, demonstrating its greater fluency with forms and genres. The unintelligent literalism of the masses, unable to see things from other points of view, was unkindly mocked on all sides. The panic broadcast is most often today remembered as a quaint novelty from the days of less sophisticated understanding of media. It ought to be remembered also as an instance of a breakdown of civility, a culture wars moment, when elites felt unembarrassed about unleashing a torrent of scorn against those of their fellow citizens who had different expectations and experiences of the way the media worked.

Radio comedians tried to have fun with the invasion scare, but were constrained by the broadcasting industry's high anxiety about the whole incident. Comedians created jokes that invited knowing radio listeners to join them in ridiculing naïve and inexperienced, frightened listeners. But NBC prohibited lighthearted reference to the scare. John Royal issued this order: "There are to be no comic references whatsoever to last night's Columbia – Martian incident.... We must not risk recriminations or kidding a public that will grow angry and vindictive on the realization of being duped. Also know that FCC is moving cautiously on this and we must do likewise."[117] This gag was cut from Fred Allen's script, because NBC would not allow him to poke fun at a rival network:

Allen: In view of recent happenings in radio, I think it might be better, before we start, if I made sort of an announcement.

113. "A. R.," Letter to *New York Evening Sun*, November 3, 1938.

114. Letter to Dorothy Thompson, November 2, 1938, box 238, RG 173, FCC, Office of the Executive Director, General Correspondence 1927–46, 44–3, NACP.

115. *Chicago Daily News*, November 1, 1938.

116. Reprinted in *Broadcasting* 15, no. 10 (November 15, 1938): 14.

117. John Royal telegram, October 31, 1938, folder 76, box 59, NBC records, WHS.

Von Zell: It would be safer, Fred.

Allen: I think I will. We ought to take every precaution. Ladies and gentlemen, before this radio presentation starts, I would like to announce that this is a comedy program. Any dialogue or sound-effects heard during the next hour will be purely imaginary and will have no relation to any living sounds.... If you hear a phone ringing—like this—[phone rings] do not rush to pick up your receiver. If you hear a knock—like this—[door knock] do not run to open your door.[118]

The humor here mocks simple and trusting listeners, and points to the impossibility of radio entertainment in a world without aural play and fiction.

So just as the newspapers rallied to oppose censorship on radio, NBC came to the defense of its network rival against any possible regulatory backlash. Commentator Lowell Thomas, on the night after the panic broadcast, used his 6:45 p.m. slot on NBC Blue to absolve CBS of any blame—it "could not have foreseen" the panic, it had taken measures "to prevent any possibility of such a thing ever occurring again," and its prompt action had certainly rendered any FCC action unnecessary. NBC commentator Edwin Hill the same evening stated on air that "a similar error could never occur again," and assured listeners that "radio is patriotically American, clean, fair and utterly devoid of class feeling."[119]

Always behind the debate about the panic broadcast loomed the issue of prepared- ness for war. The *New York Post* worried that: "the public mind was...so prepared to accept anything, that it could accept this particular 'realism' as truth....So insecure do millions feel in a civilization constantly menaced by threats of a new world war."[120] The Associated Press reported that "military listeners" in the United States regarded the panic as highly significant: "What struck the military listeners most about the radio play was its immediate emotional effect. Thousands of persons...exhibited all the symptoms of fear, panic, determination to resist, desperation, bravery, excitement or fatalism that real war would have produced."[121] European coverage tended to ridicule—the London *Times* expressed surprise at a nation that "suddenly believes itself—and for little enough reason" under attack from another world, while Hitler in a speech on November 8 in Munich alluded to the panic, asserting that the German *Volk* "shall not succumb to a fear of bombs, falling—let us say—from either Mars or the moon."[122] Perhaps in anticipation of such criticism, the *San Antonio Express* creatively recast the event as a story about American openness to new possibilities, claiming that the panickers' response "evidenced an attitude which has made America the world's most progressive country: a deep-rooted conviction that nothing is impossible."[123]

118. Martin Lewis, "Airialto Lowdown," *Radio Guide*, November 26, 1938.

119. Edwin Hill script, October 31, 1938, folder 76, box 59, NBC records, WHS.

120. *New York Post*, November 1, 1938.

121. "Military Lesson Taught," *Nebraska State Journal*, November 1, 1938: 2.

122. Max Domarus (ed.), *Hitler—Speeches and Proclamations* 1932–1945: *The Chronicle of a Dictatorship* Volume 2, The Years 1935 to 1938 (London: I.B. Tauris, 1992): 1238; "Panic Caused by Broadcast," *Times*, November 1, 1938: 14.

123. *San Antonio Express*, November 2, 1938.

LISTENERS RESPOND

The "War of the Worlds" broadcast generated much letter writing. While the letters to individual stations, to the Mercury Theater, and to CBS are not available to researchers, those to the FCC are. They do not form a large collection by radio standards, and may represent an atypical group of listeners—writing to the FCC was probably not the first thing that would occur to the average disgruntled listener. But on the other hand, listeners who wrote to any federal official, from the president down, had their letter redirected to the FCC, so the collection does certainly represent more than those with detailed knowledge of the federal bureaucracy.

The FCC summarized the 625 letters it received on the panic broadcast as 253 endorsements and 372 protests. Endorsements included:

213 requests for rebroadcast
24 congratulations to CBS for "obtaining reaction of people in emergency"
36 commending Orson Welles's "excellent performance"
49 opposing censorship
29 opposing any action by the FCC
8 opposing governmental ownership of stations
9 opposing Senator Herring's proposed bill

Protests contained:

87 suggestions that the FCC take action to prevent a repetition of programs of that type
56 recommendations that the participants be barred from the air
21 calls for CBS to have all sketches censored
83 calls to have the licenses of the stations carrying the program revoked
59 protests against using the designations of government officials
16 protests against use of the names of actual cities
17 favoring censorship of radio programs and a number of other single letters on different themes.[124]

The two groups of letters were very different in tone and content.

Contempt

The pro-Welles letters were full of contempt for the listeners who had been fooled. Letter writers were freer than published commentators to pursue the point about the mental incapacity of radio listeners to its antidemocratic conclusion. These writers were clear that the credulity of the American people was the relevant issue, and they had a simple

---

124. Memo from Grace Miner, Correspondence Section, FCC, December 3, 1938, box 237, RG 173, FCC, Office of the Executive Director, General Correspondence 1927–46, 44–3, NACP.

explanation to offer—it was the stupidity of the masses that made them so vulnerable and credulous. "It is a sad commentary on the intelligence of the average radio listener," observed a listener from Yakima, Washington.[125] "The country must be full of nit wits," concluded another.[126] "It is regrettable that any part of our population, however small, should thus demonstrate the level of their positively moronic intellects," wrote a New York listener.[127] Others were even less charitable: "It is beyond my comprehension that anyone could possibly believe this fantastic tale.... Inhabitants of Mattewan, the Psychopathic Ward at Bellevue and other homes of the mentally deficient might possibly believe that this was so, and anyone who was frightened by this broadcast certainly deserves to be frightened."[128] The primary intention of such writers was to dissuade the FCC from censoring radio. A New Jersey man wrote to the *New York Times*, "Condemnation of the network for the childish hysteria and panic on the part of many listeners would place the Communications Commission on a par with those emotional and somewhat moronic individuals who, in shame at their own credulity and panic, are now indignant and vindictive."[129] A faculty member from the State Teachers College in Trenton, New Jersey, added, "I have no sympathy for the feelings of listeners who do not take pains to find out what they are listening to."[130] Rational and reflexive listening was, these writers made clear, an individual responsibility, not a matter for the state. "If people behave like a lot of sheep and choose to translate fiction into fact," opined a St. Paul listener, "that is a matter of their own concern."[131] Instead of regulating radio, government should concern itself with educating the masses, whose dangerous stupidity had caused the panic in the first place. "In radio, as well as on many other topics, the public needs education," wrote one woman. "They need to be taught to check radio broadcasts."[132]

Some listeners knew that the World War I intelligence tests had been somewhat discredited, but the panic seemed to many to reaffirm the earlier findings: "I have heard it stated that the old story of the Army Intelligence tests that gave the average I.Q. of our population as thirteen years is a myth," wrote a Pennsylvania listener. "Perhaps. After Sunday, one wonders."[133] Very many letter writers took the broadcast as clear proof of the low IQ of ordinary Americans. "The facts are self-evident," argued one letter. "A well presented and realistic play caused a number of sub-morons to become panic stricken." A professor of astronomy and mathematics wrote, "We are harboring a great many people of weak mentality and positively unbelievable stupidity and erratic judgment." One terse telegram asserted: "Nations hysteria laughing stock of the world. Indicative of average citizens low mentality are we a nation of morons? Legislate to raise average

125. All letters discussed below are from the FCC files: boxes 237 and 238, RG 173, FCC, Office of the Executive Director, General Correspondence 1927–46, 44–3, NACP.
126. Letter to FCC, received November 15, 1938.
127. Letter to FCC, November 1, 1938.
128. Letter to FCC, November 1, 1938.
129. Alvin J. Bogart, letter to the editor, *New York Times,* November 2, 1938: 22.
130. Letter to FCC, November 1, 1938.
131. Letter to FCC, November 1, 1938.
132. Letter to FCC, received November 4, 1938.
133. Letter to FCC, November 1, 1938.

mental capacity." A telegram writer from Long Island worried most about the world's judgment: "I feel that the low mentality of some of our public proved by their recent reaction to a fantastic broadcast has made us the laughing stock of many nations."[134]

Many listeners maintained that professional expertise was needed to fix the problem. "It seems deplorable there should be so many unthinking and hysterical people in our midst," wrote a New York woman. "We certainly need more neurologists."[135] A woman from New Jersey offered the thought that: "This unnecessary commotion shows plainly that the average Am. Mind is mentally immature" and in need of "plenty of Adult Education."[136] The fact that so many were deceived by the broadcast became to these listeners simply evidence of the failure of mass education. "At no time was it the least credible no matter when one tuned in," wrote one couple. "Perhaps our educational system is failing to train reason or logic."

The apparent inability of many listeners to distinguish fact from fantasy was taken as definitive evidence of low mental capacity. "Individuals shocked by this play certainly must be very infantile and obtuse, if they could not distinguish fact from fiction," wrote a man from Cincinnati. An Indiana man asked, "Are we a nation of four year olds or are we intelligent enough to know, especially when we are told four times, what is the difference between the real and fiction?"[137] One North Carolina listener wrote, "We should hang our heads in shame to know that such a great number of the citizens of these United States have the Mentality and emotional stability of an EIGHT Year Old."[138]

Pro-Welles listeners had a clearly gendered understanding of the intelligence problem. One man wrote to the *New York Times*: "Unless the American average of intelligence is lower than some people suspect, I for one refuse to believe that any but children, old ladies and mental deficients were seriously perturbed by what struck my family and self merely as a boring and rather inane production."[139] Supporters of the broadcast were not only of the opinion that the mass of the American people was dangerously stupid and ill-educated, they argued that the broadcast had also revealed American men to be so feminized by their participation in mass culture that they were unable to "take" the realism of a drama that several writers described as particularly masculine or virile. One listener asserted strongly, "This is no reason why intelligent people should be deprived of viril [sic] entertainment." The panicked listeners were "too soft and effeminate for safety," as an Indiana man put it, a "bunch of jitterbug softies," as a man from Texas observed. And that, of course, had implications for the safety of the nation. A man from upstate New York argued, "The first line of our defense of the Republic stands embodied in the minds of the citizens, that clear perception; steadiness and calmness of mind. True, it has been a minority displaying this weakness. But it is a minority that can, in times of crisis,

---

134. Letter to FCC October 31, 1938; letter to FCC November 1, 1938; telegram to FCC November 15, 1938; telegram to FCC, November 1, 1938.
135. Letter to FCC, November 1, 1938.
136. Letter to FCC, November 2, 1938.
137. Letter to FCC, October 31, 1938.
138. Letter to FCC, November 1, 1938.
139. *New York Times*, November 2, 1938: 22.

affect the morale of a nation." Pro-Welles listeners thus saw the national security threatened by the low intelligence and incipient hysteria of the now emasculated population, and worried what would happen in a real crisis. "It will show us what we can expect if some national emergency does occur," wrote a Missoula lawyer. "We can talk about order during a crisis but once it comes the less intelligent mass of our citizens will be so hysterical that we shall become easy prey."[140] Andreas Huyssen has argued that 20th-century "mass culture is somehow associated with woman while real, authentic culture remains the prerogative of men."[141] An association of this kind was clearly behind many Americans' thinking in the late 1930s. One writer from New York's Park Avenue observed that he would hate to see "all future broadcasts emasculated, on account of a lot of hysterical women and lily-livered men." Radio, wrote a man from Indiana, was already "too much emasculated, to meet the requirements of the feeble-minded element."

A man from Michigan bluntly summed up the implication of all of the criticism of listener intelligence: "People so stupid should not be allowed access to a radio."[142] A Philadelphia listener suggested: "Would it not be well to reserve certain designated channels for the broadcast of

1) programs for adults
2) programs for children
3) programs for morons"[143]

Or perhaps, as a doctor from Indianapolis argued, the unintelligent should be removed from society altogether: "You must be aware that those who were upset by that broadcast represent that small minority whose dullness prevents their distinguishing phantasy and reality in any phase of their existence. There may be a solid argument for their institutionalization."

Defenders of the broadcast also understood that a population so stupid would struggle to sustain a democracy. A Pennsylvania listener commented on "the wave of besotted idiocy and almost inconceivable witless mental degeneration revealed by the now famous radio panic," and added this pessimistic assessment of the future of American democracy: "Certainly I am a venomous and whole-hearted hater of the collective guts of all the Mussolini-Stalin-Roosevelt-Hitler type, and will certainly be one of the first to be shot after Mr. Roosevelt gets his third term in 1940, but I must admit that the boys have the right slant on how to govern humanity.... Let's have a dictator, and get it over with."[144] If these relatively elite listeners were ready to abandon democracy, they were determined fiercely to defend art. The pro-Welles letters insisted on the literary and dramatic merits of the broadcast. Many of them observed that *War of the Worlds* was one of the best plays they had heard on radio, and that such creative efforts should be supported, not stifled because of the foolish

140. Letters to FCC, November 1, 1938.

141. Andreas Huyssen, *After the Great Divide: Modernism, Mass Culture, Postmodernism* (Bloomington: Indiana University Press, 1986): 47.

142. Letters to FCC October 31, 1938; letter to FCC, November 1, 1938.

143. Letter to FCC, November 1, 1938.

144. Letters to FCC, November 1, 1938.

reactions of the ignorant. "This was a clever fantasy in a clever medium," wrote a Pennsylvania woman: "This was just *fun*. The fault lies not with CBS or Orson Welles but with a number of stolid listeners with little or no imagination."[145] "It was a splendid work of art, and any effect it may have had upon superstitious, short-sighted people should be regretted but ignored," argued a woman from Nashville. These listeners were clear that Welles's art should not be held back by the failings of the audience. "Mr. Welles is a mature and brilliant young artist," wrote a Pittsburgh woman, "and cannot be blamed for failing to realize that so many people were mentally living in the fifteenth century."[146]

Some identified the problem of the panicked as an incapacity to recognize and then enjoy fiction. For Alice Keliher, chair of the Commission on Human Relations of the Progressive Education Association, the problem was that "Mr. and Mrs. America should take fiction and, above all things, the drama so unimaginatively."[147] Eddie Cantor sent a telegram from Los Angeles, describing the program as a "melodramatic masterpiece intended to thrill not terrify the public." Pro-Welles writers emphasized that the realism of the program was its great artistic achievement: "one of the GREATEST DRAMATIZATION RADIO PERFORMANCE OF THE CENTURY and certainly deserves the highest praise of the whole world for its vivid life-like actuality," argued a man from New Hampshire. Pro-Welles listeners also stressed the genius of the young Orson Welles. They praised his "originality, imagination and vitality," his great skill in "fitting his material to his medium."[148]

There are plenty of signs of the relatively elite status of the authors of these letters. Many wrote on personalized notepaper or sent telegrams.[149] They displayed a kind of cosmopolitan embarrassment at the naiveté of ordinary Americans. One of their constant concerns was about how the United States would look to the rest of the world: "It is appalling to have such colossal ignorance of a great number of citizens exposed to the whole world," exclaimed one writer from Charlotte, North Carolina. "A law should be passed or a committee appointed to do something about it."[150] Both the form of the letters and this cosmopolitan perspective, I think, mark these pro-Welles letters as coming from a relative social and cultural elite. Several letters pointed out that the press had an interest in stories that appeared to discredit radio, its competitor, which also suggests a knowledge of business practice and a skeptical relationship to common public discourse that was also often an elite characteristic.

THE VICTIMS

"Strangely enough," wrote a journalist in the *Washington Post*, "questioners who learned they were listening to a Nation-wide broadcast of H. G. Wells' fantastic story . . . were not relieved. They were angry, fiercely angry, and many demanded that police be called to

145. Letter to FCC, November 1, 1938.

146. Letter to FCC, n.d.

147. Alice V. Keliher, "Radio 'War' Stirs Educators," *New York Times*, November 6, 1938: 8.

148. Letters to FCC, November 1, 1938.

149. For a contemporary analysis of radio fan mail which emphasizes such distinctions see: Jeanette Sayre, "Progress in Radio Fan-Mail Analysis," *Public Opinion Quarterly* 3, no. 2 (April 1939): 272–78.

150. Letter to FCC, November 1, 1938.

halt the broadcast."[151] In the incomprehension of that "strangely enough" lay much of the story of the response to the broadcast. It was difficult to live as a subject, let alone a victim of propaganda. Few Americans understood themselves as dangerously open to seduction and persuasion, and hence there was little language available, other than that of personal failing, to talk about the experience of being duped or inappropriately persuaded. Panic victims did feel that radio had betrayed them, and they argued that the broadcasters responsible had reneged on their side of the civic bargain. A Montana man wrote to CBS, observing simply, "Words cannot express the contempt for a public servant such as you should be for violating the public confidence."[152]

The anti-Welles letters then were simpler and angrier. The writers regarded the broadcast as one of the worst things that had ever happened to them and the nation. It was "the most awful crime ever perpetuated on the American Public," wrote one listener. "I am a widow—in poor health and almost died from shock."[153] An insurance agent from New York stated, "I never hope to see my family go through such a trying 45 minutes as long as I live. It was by long odds the most dastardly thing I have ever experienced or encountered."[154] It is impossible to read these often poignant letters and conclude that there was no significant panic, or that the panic was narrowly confined to New Jersey and New York.

The protesting letters testified to the pain that the broadcast had created, and to the writers' incomprehension that anybody would choose to cause, or run the risk of causing, such suffering. Several reported that family members had suffered heart attacks, or hysteria, or other symptoms of extreme stress. A New York man wrote, "My wife developed an hysteria that is impossible for me to describe."[155] "From the bottom of my heart," wrote one woman, "I protest the cruelty of allowing the broadcast of any such program as was put on by CBS Sunday night!" For three quarters of an hour, she "listened with the most *abject horror* to one of the most inexcusably (and I believe intentionally) horrifying, broadcasts any one could possibly conceive of."[156] A man from California reported that his wife, on learning that the broadcast was only a play, "fell over in my lap shook and cried like a baby."[157] Six World War I veterans from a U.S. veterans hospital in California wrote to say that, although they were well acquainted with the horror of war and its effects on human nerves from their time in the trenches in France, they found "the realistic depiction" of the broadcast "profoundly more horrifying and gruesome than any conceivable nightmare."[158] "My children and myself were frightened nearly to death," wrote an Arkansas woman, "and even now you can tell by this writing I am in such a

151. Marshall Andrews, "Monsters of Mars on a Meteor Stampede Radiotic America," *Washington Post*, October 31, 1938: X1.

152. Letter to CBS from FCC files, November 10, 1938.

153. Letter to FCC, October 31, 1938.

154. Letter to FCC, October 31, 1938.

155. Letter to FCC, October 30, 1938.

156. Letter to FCC, n.d.

157. Letter to West Coast President, CBS, from FCC files, October 31, 1938.

158. Letter to FCC, November 1, 1938.

nervous state that I can hardly eat, sleep or work. It seemed all so real to me that I was on my knees waiting for the end of everything."[159] A Los Angeles woman wrote vividly of what she had seen:

> A young girl of 14 trembling, her eyes almost bulging out of her head screaming Mamma dear I don't want to die, I want to live hold me Mamma darling, the Mother near collapse herself. I begged them to keep cool but of no avail. I saw a young mother who had run home 2 blocks from a store, to her 2 babies, white as a ghost and trembling, run and get clothes to dress them so she could go to her mother with her family, so they could die together. If you dear Sir, could have seen all the people, stark with fear run and scream with fear and no control at all over themselves you could understand what a horrible Panic this broadcast had caused....[160]

Stressing the involuntary nature of genuine panic, these letters pleaded for empathy, but also implicitly defended the plausibility and even rationality of their responses.

Several victims reported that symptoms of shock remained long after they discovered that the broadcast was a play. "We are still nervous and unable to sleep," reported a man from Knoxville, Tennessee later that night.[161] A Brooklyn man wrote, "My wife became hysterical and has been in a nervous state ever since."[162] A Washington State woman wrote, "I only wish I could forget it, especially how the monsters emerged from the cylinder."[163] A Newark woman reported, "I am still a bit hysterical from what I have just experienced. But after all, death at the hands of monsters is no pleasant thing to look for."[164] Several writers reported ongoing physical symptoms: "My right arm is still dead and numb as a result of the shock I received," wrote a Los Angeles listener.[165]

The rationality and skepticism expected of listeners under the civic paradigm conflicted with the actual beliefs of many listeners, most notably their religious faith. Some of the protesters had heard in the broadcast, in particular its depiction of fire and destruction, all the expected signs that the end of the world was at hand. "As we believe this world to be destroyed by fire some day," wrote a Michigan woman, "such an act by God would not be impossible."[166] "The Bible says the world will be destroyed by fire," wrote a Baltimore listener, "and I said I guess this is the end."[167] Such listeners experienced the civic paradigm's deeply secular listening expectations from the outside, as quite alien to their own belief structure and expectations. Recognizing the same connection, an Oregon listener helpfully suggested to the FCC that "now is your opportunity to put preachers of

159. Letter to FCC, November 2, 1938.
160. Letter to President Roosevelt from FCC files, November 1, 1938.
161. Letter to FCC, October 30, 1938.
162. Letter to FCC, November 1, 1938.
163. Letter to FCC, November 1, 1938.
164. Letter to FCC, October 30, 1938.
165. Letter to FCC November 3, 1938.
166. Letter to FCC November 4, 1938.
167. Letter to FCC, October 30, 1938.

the End of the World off the air": "These dervishes and their antics certainly had their part in preparing a not inconsiderable section of the public to react as it did."[168]

The anti-Welles writers defended themselves with some dignity against the charges that they were lacking in intelligence, or habitually hysterical. "Remember, we had not heard of 'Mars + the little men,'" reasoned one listener. "We were not morons to believe that."[169] Such listeners sought to establish both their mental normality and their intelligence. "The above is the opinion of a university graduate," wrote one listener, "a CPA and by all these tokens a sane and normal person."[170] "I assure you," a Minnesota woman wrote, "both of us who listened here are college graduates and are known in the community as intelligent and reliable citizens and we were seriously affected."[171] "I was near hysteria," wrote a Minneapolis woman. "I am a normal person, over 30 years of age; and this was too much for me." A Michigan woman wrote,

> In the first place I must let you know that my husband and I are college graduates. We are not hysterical, superstitious or easily stirred up.... Our reason told us it could not be true yet we were convinced by the fact that there was no announcement to the contrary.... The hell we lived through was an eternity. Our oldest child grew hysterical and we were so weak with terror and apprehension that we were unable to quiet her.... We have been through a lot of hard and shocking moments in our married life but absolutely nothing could compare with the state of mind we were in Sunday night.... It will be a long time before we really recover from the experience.[172]

The protesters were less elite than the defenders of the broadcast. The FCC's own summary of its mail found among the protest letter writers 15 attorneys, 5 college graduates, 3 schoolteachers, 15 businessmen, 3 newspapermen, 2 engineers, 2 judges, 2 clergymen, and 9 others in assorted professional occupations—a total of only 66 out of 372 who appeared to be professionals.[173] Many of these protesting listeners neatly turned the low intelligence argument back against the broadcasters. Those who created the scare, one listener told the FCC, were "a group of imbeciles who evidently should be incarcerated in a padded cell."[174] It was inconceivable, wrote a Missouri doctor, "to believe that the Broadcasting Company could be so unintelligent as not to realize the effect on persons" who tuned in after the initial announcement of the program.[175] The problem, another Missouri listener wrote, was that the "supposed entertainers" on the radio were "of varying degrees of intelligence and morality," and that indeed a "very large percentage of them are below a 12-year age of mentality." These defective entertainers were then a threat to the rest of the population: "Children insist on listening to that variety of slush and are being developed into a race of

168. Letter to FCC, October 31, 1938.
169. Letter to FCC, November 13, 1938.
170. Letter to FCC, October 30, 1938.
171. Letter to FCC October 31, 1938.
172. Letters to FCC, November 1, 1938.
173. Grace Miner Memo December 3, 1938.
174. Letter to FCC, October 30, 1938.
175. Letter to FCC, October 30, 1938.

morons and jitter bugs."[176] "It is incredible," argued a woman from Alexandria, Virginia, "that there should be in authoritative positions in radio, persons so devoid of the understanding of human emotional reactions that they would sanction such a broadcast." She added sinisterly, "If programs are made up by enemy aliens, that would explain it."[177] A Chicago businessman felt that the participants in such broadcasts "are in the same class as humans who pull the wings off flies to see them suffer."[178] Such thoughtless, emotionally immature cruelty, these listeners argued, belonged to children or adolescents, not responsible, intelligent adults. Intelligent persons who were "devoid of the understanding of human emotional reactions" were themselves a threat to society.

Those who panicked felt betrayed by radio itself. They were confident that they themselves could readily distinguish fact from fiction, but wondered whether the broadcasters could. "We have become accustomed to believing radio bulletins and in spite of their serious nature we did believe them."[179] "Hoax it was," wrote a New Hampshire listener, "because its 'success' was due *entirely* to the trust and good will built up by Columbia's recent news flashes."[180] An Arkansas man reported, "My family and myself are accustomed to treat Radio News with great respect, and to believe them, this custom growing out of the many valuable services received from them in the past, notably the recent way in which your company handled news bulletins on the European crisis, and in which accuracy and dependability were the key note."[181] After all, wrote a Pennsylvania man, "a vast majority of the people of the United States listen to the Radio and depend upon the News Broadcasts and your News Flashes as being True and not of the nature of Fiction."[182] "I couldn't understand it of course," wrote a North Carolina woman, "but who was I to question Princeton scientist the War Department at Washington the Red Cross and other names for which we have the greatest respect and reverence?"[183] These listeners clearly expected truth from radio, not play, and they felt that their trust had been scorned.

Very many of the anti-Welles listeners cited the impersonation of a government official in the broadcast as the reason for their believing in it and for their keenest sense of betrayal. The Secretary of the Interior, played by Kenneth Delmar, sounded eerily like Franklin Roosevelt. Does "the government allow broadcasting stations to use, or borrow the cloak of dignity which the U.S. Government is the sole possessor" asked a Michigan man.[184] "How anyone in their right mind would dare to perpetrate such an outrage on our citizens and have persons of high authority in our Federal, State and City Governments impersonated for such a base purpose is incomprehensible and justice should be meted out to them," asserted a Long Island woman.[185] One Brooklyn listener wrote to FDR:

176. Letter to FCC, November 11, 1938.
177. Letter to FCC, October 31, 1938.
178. Letter to FCC, November 2, 1938.
179. Letter to FCC October 31, 1938.
180. Letter to FCC, November 1, 1938.
181. Letter to FCC, November 1, 1938.
182. Letter to FCC, October 31, 1938.
183. Letter to FCC, received November 3, 1938.
184. Letter to FCC, November 5, 1938.
185. Letter to FCC, n.d.

We tuned in just as a person impersonating yourself read his lines....Of course we believed it was all pure truth, the "news flashes" speeches etc. and were prepared for utter destruction. There were absolutely no announcements until the very end that it was all fictions. By that time our family were in utter collapse....In justice to right living and right thinking Americans, I trust this will never happen again.[186]

Such listeners rejected the idea that it was their low intelligence that allowed them to mistake the drama for news. Some wanted an unambiguous sign to assure them in future that an important broadcast was true. A St. Louis man suggested a "faint bell signal, just a slight sound every two or three seconds," to identify "an authentic news item."[187] A Michigan man requested that from now on he be advised by registered mail if "some high government official" was going to broadcast important news.[188]

Many of the anti-Welles letters were written by women, defending their families from the charges of low intelligence or hysteria. "Let me assure you," wrote a woman from Minnesota, "that we are not 'hysterical women' in this home but we were terrified by the reports."[189] A Maine woman wrote, "I refuse to believe myself a complete moron for listening to an interruption in a regular Sunday evening program for a news bulletin."[190] Many of the men who wrote did so to seek an apology or compensation for the effect of the broadcast on their wife or children. One Massachusetts man wrote to FDR—"as one father to another"—that "there is no excuse for the mental horror and acute anguish which millions of fine-minded children, mothers and others experienced unnecessarily."[191] The men who admitted to fear wrote to deny that they were deficient in masculinity. "I work on the railroads," explained a Texas man. "And just happened to be at home that night. My small family was terrified and I'll admit that I myself was quite uneasy for sometime. I dread to think what might have happened to my family had I been away that night out on the road...."[192] The broadcast raised issues about how people listened to radio, and this was also understood in gendered terms. Radio listeners in the 1930s surfed around the dial with a residual technical pleasure in their ability to pull in stations far and near; their attention wandered in and out as other events in their homes intervened— they listened distractedly much of the time.[193] One Arkansas man said the broadcast came on at his house while he, his wife, and two guests were eating dinner, and "we did not notice particularly the transition from one program to another."[194] The pro-Welles

186. Letter to president Roosevelt, from FCC files, October 31, 1938.

187. Letter to FCC, October 31, 1938.

188. Letter to FCC, November 5, 1938.

189. Letter to FCC October 31, 1938.

190. Letter to FCC, November 1, 1938.

191. Letter to President Roosevelt, from FCC files, October 30, 1938.

192. Letter to FCC, October 31, 1938.

193. See David Goodman, "Distracted Listening: On Not Making Sound Choices in the 1930s," in Susan Strasser and David Suisman (eds.), *Sound in the Age of Mechanical Reproduction* (Philadelphia: University of Pennsylvania Press, 2010): 15–46.

194. Letter to FCC, November 1, 1938.

listeners accused the frightened of being poor listeners, having limited concentration, little respect for art. Orson Welles himself said on the morning after the broadcast, "I have long maintained...that dramatic presentations over the radio would never be wholly successful....Musical programs do not require strict attention, but in the case of a drama, the average listener hears only the highlights."[195] This lack of "strict attention" to the drama being broadcast was often at the time understood as a feminine characteristic. The busy distracted housewife stood as the personification of distracted listening, and it was the radio soap opera that enacted an endless melodrama to which she could listen interruptedly.[196] The *Mercury Theater* was, however, not soap opera; it had the mission of putting serious literature on the air. The defenders of the broadcast argued that a careful, responsible listener would not have been fooled. "Let the gullible listeners admit the laugh is on them and resolve to listen more carefully next time," wrote one Pittsburgh listener.[197]

Almost all of those who wrote in to say that they had been terrified by the broadcast said that they had tuned in after the beginning of the program—for many, contingent personal, familial, or even technical reasons. "We listened a short while to Columbia's Boston station 'WEEI' at 8 pm, but found the Faneuil Hall Forum of the Air disinteresting," reported one Massachusetts listener. "Swung down the band picked up a report that the seismograph recorded shocks were probably caused by the meteor that landed in Jersey etc., then faded in the static."[198] Such listeners thus provided in self-defense detailed descriptions of their listening experiences that night, explaining how joining the program late had led them ineluctably down a path of terror. A man from California, in a wonderful rush of testimony, wrote,

> Last evening, we were sitting quietly reading and I was watching the clock for 8:30, there was to be a Democratic speech on KFI. I tuned in and he said just a moment there is a slight delay. I turned the dial to KHI and a voice said there are five enemy planes flying high over New Jersey dropping big steel tanks of gas and germs and he said that they were broadcasting from on top of a high building in New York and that buildings were falling and the streets were choked with people running over each other and he was telling them which roads to take. Bombs were bursting and hundreds of bells were ringing and whistles were blowing and sirens, my dear wife she has a weak heart....[199]

Such listeners specified their listening experience with some precision. They were laying claim to the normality of their reactions and understandings, given the way they had heard the broadcast. A woman in Iowa wrote that her family had also tuned in late:

195. *The Daily Princetonian*, November 1, 1938: 5.
196. See Susan Smulyan, "Radio Advertising to Women in Twenties America: 'A Latchkey to Every Home,'" *Historical Journal of Film, Radio and Television* 13, no. 3 (1993): 299–314.
197. Letter to FCC, October 31, 1938.
198. Letter to FCC, November 5, 1938.
199. Letter to President Roosevelt, from FCC files, October 30, 1938.

And when they told of the discs falling at St. Louis and in Chicago, we knew that was getting pretty close to home and comparing the destruction that was caused in such a short time and the distance covered in that little while we knew our time had come, that we would never go to bed another night; and that we would all have passed into eternity before morning. Our main thought was getting our folks and families together and getting home in time to die....[200]

Anti-Welles listeners were particularly offended by the argument that the program was justified because of its status as art. A Los Angeles woman reported that "when we called KNX here—the young man at the information desk...told us if we had ever read anything we would have known the book."[201] "I have a little over 200 books in my own library," wrote a Trenton man, "but sorry to say I never read H. G. Wells book so it seemed too dam [sic] real to us to be allowed on the air."[202] A woman teacher from Louisiana reported the following: "As a result of Mr. Welles' broadcast children were almost killed by distressed parents who sought to save them from a death more horrible than a pistol shot could inflict. Does Mr. Welles hold his art more dear than the lives of our American children?" Several letter writers said they had been so terrified by the broadcast and so convinced that a horrible death was imminent, that they had contemplated taking their own lives. "Had we weapons in the house," wrote one man, "we may have blown ourselves to pieces. My little girl was stricken with hysteria and grown man that I am, I blanched with fear."[203] "Should we be on the verge of murdering our little girl and then committing suicide for the sake of entertainment?" asked a Baltimore man.[204] Orson Welles and H. G. Wells "may be in the prodigy class," wrote a California listener, "but I think their warped minds are in the fiendish class....These men are not to blame...for being endowed with more than a usual quotient of intelligence, but neither should they be placed in a position to panic a country with their peculiar brand of fun."[205] These ordinary, often nonmetropolitan Americans wrote in to say that they thought the especially intelligent could be a menace, and in particular that they might lack an understanding of ordinary American values.

Some anti-Welles listeners pointed to reasons why the wealthy or well educated might have been less scared. A man from Missouri said that citizens deserved "protection, against those who would impose upon their credulity—and then gloat because of 'superior and broader information' on scientific subjects." A woman from New York said that "it may not be so bad for the rich" who have cars to escape such an invasion, "but what about the poor people who have a lot of children and nothing that looks like a car."[206] These writers also suspected that the voice of the wealthy and educated would be

200. Letter to FCC, n.d.
201. Letter to FCC, October 31, 1938.
202. Letter to FCC, October 31, 1938.
203. Letter to FCC, November 30, 1938.
204. Letter to FCC, n.d.
205. Letter to FCC, November 1, 1938.
206. Letter to FCC, October 31, 1938.

better heard in the controversy. A woman from Iowa wrote, "Mr. McNinch says he has not received many telegrams, there are probably millions like myself, who cannot afford the price of a telegram. I have heard several people say 'if they could write well enough, they would write concerning that Broadcast.'" And she concluded that if "a Negro or a poor man would have done this, I doubt if they would be alive at this time to hear any complaints against them."[207] These listeners wanted revenge. "If such programs continue I will make kindling wood of my receiving set," wrote a man from West Virginia—and added that if he could have gotten within gun-shot range of Orson Welles after the broadcast, "I can swear to you it would have been his last."[208]

Children were seen to be particularly vulnerable to the kind of excitement the broadcast provoked. There was an existing concern about radio overexciting children, and the *Mercury* broadcast seemed but the latest and most dramatic instance of the problem. One New York woman wrote to President Roosevelt of her son: "Billy is 15, Nov. 19th this yr. Is 6 ft. 2 1/2 tall and we try to keep him from over excitement and this was terrible because my husband and I were both terrified. You read of how in years to come they say most people will be insane or in 'nervous sanitariums.' What can we expect Mr. Roosevelt if such things as this be experienced?"[209] An attorney from Akron, Ohio, wrote to say that his nine-year-old son was so excited by the "wild, shrieking mystery stories" he heard on the radio that "he gets up in his sleep and screams and walks around the room, dreaming about the thrills he has heard on the radio." The Welles broadcast had been "very little more thrilling" than this routine radio fare. The writer concluded by assuring the commissioners that his son was "regularly examined by the doctor and I am sure that he is normal in every way."[210]

Others used the troubled state of the world and the constant news of disaster as reason for having believed the broadcast. "During the past few years," wrote a Maine woman, "we have seen horrible depression visit our wealthy nation, we have lived through unbelievable floods and droughts, war has threatened which we were told would wipe civilization from the earth, and secure little New England has been overwhelmed by a tidal wave and hurricane."[211] The troubled state of the world was also a reason that such broadcasts should never be allowed again. A Texas hardware store owner argued that "such things should under no circumstances be permitted to disturb the homes of the country over the air, as this thing did, and more particularly at a time when people are restless and disturbed over too many things that are real."[212] Some even thought the broadcast might hasten a war. "Permitting such a broadcast as last night," a New York man warned the FCC, "it might be alleged that you played deliberately into the hands of munitions makers which might mean war."[213] Those who had been frightened also had to defend themselves against the suspicion that they would be too nervous to deal with an

207. Letter to FCC, n.d.
208. Letter to FCC, November 2, 1938.
209. Letter to President Roosevelt, from FCC files, October 31, 1938.
210. Letter to FCC, November 1, 1938.
211. Letter to FCC, November 1, 1938.
212. Letter to FCC, November 1, 1938.
213. Letter to FCC October 31, 1938.

actual war. "We are not pacifists," read a telegram from a couple in Pennsylvania, "but red blooded Americans and...we protest against such unwarranted programs."[214]

Many complainants assumed that radio was ordinarily censored, and requested that the censors be more vigilant in future. In their requests for more overt policing of the air, these listeners registered their distance from the self-regulating ideals of the civic paradigm, which placed such stress on listener responsibility. One listener suggested that "'G' men be assigned to radio stations to police program in future."[215] Another wrote directly to the FBI to say she had thought that "presentations via Radio had to be thoroughly investigated and censored before public presentation" and requesting that the author of the play "be thoroughly examined mentally."[216] A New York lawyer complained of what he termed "the disgraceful lack of supervision which permitted an effeminate actor, by the name of Orson Welles, to terrorize the people of New York City."[217] "This is the cruelest hoax to be played upon the American People EVER," wrote a woman from Memphis. "All the people responsible for last night's CRIME of MENTAL CRUELTY TO THOUSANDS, should be banned from RADIO, FOREVER. Columbia Broadcasting System and OTHERS should be fined enough to provide a government police at every broadcast to protect the innocent listeners."[218] "Where are our policemen of the air?" asked a Colorado woman.[219] That was perhaps the logical end of the complaints at the broadcast—the felt need for public protection and direct policing of the air. To many Americans, the relatively self-regulating nature of both broadcasting and listening to the radio in America was still difficult to comprehend—and when comprehended, it was disapproved.

American elites were much more likely to defend free market radio against a more regulated system. The radio listening audience was deeply divided on the question of regulatory control. Gallup reported in February 1938 that 59% of Americans opposed censorship on the radio, while 41% approved it—which seems a high number given the pejorative connotations of *censorship*. The poll also discovered that "federal censorship is particularly opposed by radio owners in the upper levels, whereas those of below-average income are divided about evenly."[220] That indication of a class divide about radio regulation—a sense that the absolute commitment to freedom of speech was of greater importance higher up the income scale—is an important context for understanding the public debate provoked by the panic episode. On Gallup's figures, about half of poorer Americans were in favor of stronger supervision of radio program content, even when it was proposed to them as *censorship*.

Anti-Welles listeners understood that the American system of commercial and lightly regulated radio was one of the central things at issue in the aftermath of the panic. "It seems to me," wrote an Oregon man, "that more material involving patriotism, loyalty and Americanism should be put out. Lunacy, pills, soap powder and mouth wash fill the

214. Letter to FCC, October 30, 1938.
215. Telegram to FCC, October 31, 1938.
216. Letter to FBI, from FCC files, October 31, 1938.
217. Letter to FCC, October 31, 1938.
218. Letter to FCC, October 31, 1938.
219. Letter to FCC October 31, 1938.
220. *New York Times,* February 11, 1938: 4.

day and far into the night with very little that is of educational value." He advocated a "more rigid control of the air-waves" and the imposition of a "rigid censorship of all material broadcasted to the public."[221] The panic broadcast seemed to these listeners to cast doubt upon the wisdom of the American system. A Brooklyn attorney concluded that the broadcasters would find that "it is only going to be a short time before their business will have to be taken from them and handled for the many and not for the few."[222] A California man wrote directly to FDR to say, "Really I think the Government should take over the Broadcasting Companies and stop a lot of this dam [sic] foolishment."[223] "If many more such broadcasts are permitted," wrote a Michigan woman, "the people will begin to believe England has the right idea about the radio, after all."[224] One listener offered a commonsense analogy: "When we in Pennsylvania exceed the speed limit on our highways, they take away our driver's license from us—because it is not safe for others to be anywhere near us. Your program was like a maniac on the air, spreading fear, terror and panic over the countryside."[225] This was all further evidence that the American system was far from invulnerable even by 1938. When things went wrong with American radio, plenty of Americans were willing to rethink the whole basis of the system. "Those of us who love our country don't want that kind of hoax put over the air," wrote an Oregon man. "We want government regulation of radio. We are opposed to every little town in the country getting a radio station and putting on the air what they want. We need a radio dictator...."[226] Some of the victims' letters expressed anger at what they perceived to be control of American broadcasting by foreign-born or Jewish Americans, and asked for government intervention to restore control of broadcasting to the "real" American people. "I have also heard rumors," hinted "a citizen," "as to the ownership of Columbia System! A widow near us nearly had a heart attack, during this program. It seemed deliberately planned."[227] A man from Philadelphia complained that those who owned or controlled broadcasting had "foreign ideas and philosophy." The problem was that "the Mr. Levy's, the Sarnoff's, the Gredstein's, the Fishbein's, etc., are not the right class of people to censor radio programs that enter into millions of homes of real Americans. I doubt if any of them were born in this country." He went on to suggest that FCC officials "investigate the reason *all* foreign governments, including Great Britain, Switzerland etc., are removing all persons from public office belonging to the race of the persons who control the CBS, the NBC and Mutual systems."[228]

The *War of the Worlds* broadcast dramatized radio's cultural divide. On one side were the elites who embraced the dominant civic paradigm ideal and its goal of listener self-regulation, who wanted to protect art from censorship, and who wondered in their frankest moments whether the masses were really capable of self-government. On the

221. Letter to FCC, October 30, 1938.
222. Letter to FCC, October 31, 1938.
223. Letter to president Roosevelt, from FCC files, October 30, 1938.
224. Letter to FCC, November 1, 1938.
225. Unsigned copy of letter to CBS, from FCC files, November 1, 1938.
226. Letter to FCC, October 31, 1938.
227. Letter to FCC, October 31, 1938.
228. Letter to FCC, November 1, 1938.

other side were those ordinary Americans who were angered at continual criticisms of their intelligence, who felt more simply that the broadcast was irresponsible and should not have been allowed, that radio should transmit truth and that government should police it to that end, and who were moved by the panic controversy to provide detailed justifications of themselves as both listeners and citizens. It seemed to many of these people that radio was just not worth the trouble it had caused. "If you allow radio announcers to make special announcements that cannot be accepted as truthful, to find out after the public has been scared to death that it was merely a hoax, then I say cut out every radio broadcasting unit in this country," wrote a Wisconsin man.[229]

THE PRINCETON STUDY

The Institute for Propaganda Analysis immediately recognized the significance of the panic broadcast. The event seemed to confirm many of its central ideas about the dangers of radio and vulnerability to propaganda. The institute (it seems likely Hadley Cantril was one author) proposed a study of the panic: "Our thesis is that the free-floating anxiety on the part of many individuals is a very real danger to the continuance of democracy. We point to the release of comparable anxieties in the German people—to their ready acceptance of the Nazi Party program." The study would, it was promised, illuminate both the psychological state of the populace and the prognosis for democracy in such an anxious and credulous society.[230] Cantril had begun thinking about the invasion scare very quickly—on November 2, he was already discussing the panic in his Psychology 303 class at Princeton, telling them that "almost any type of person could have been 'taken in' by the broadcast."[231]

Paul Lazarsfeld also saw an opportunity for some fast research that would shed light on issues of trust and people's relationship to radio. He and Cantril were stimulated by seeing the results of a hastily commissioned CBS poll ordered by Frank Stanton.[232] Cantril and Herta Herzog, then married to Lazarsfeld, worked together in November on an "Outline for the Welles Study" to submit to the Rockefeller Foundation.[233] They proposed a series of personality and intelligence tests on listeners to the broadcast, seeking information on factors such as age, proximity to scene of invasion, sex, educational level, religion, race, family status, reading habits and taste, intellectual maturity, emotional maturity, neurotic inventory, and "questions getting at the extent to which individuals attempt to give meaning to life."[234]

229. Letter to FCC, n.d..

230. "A Clinical Study of Social Crisis," box 2, Institute for Propaganda Analysis papers, NYPL.

231. *The Daily Princetonian*, November 3, 1938: 1, 3.

232. See Michael Socolow, "The Behaviorist in the Boardroom: The Research of Frank Stanton, Ph.D.," *Journal of Broadcasting and Electronic Media* 52, no. 4 (2008): 538.

233. Although Paul Lazarsfeld much later recalled that Cantril "forced me to make him co-author of the *Invasion from Mars* while he had practically nothing to do with it": Lazarsfeld letter to Ann Pasanella, September 6, 1975, in Ann Pasanella, *The Mind Traveller: A Guide to Paul F. Lazarsfeld's Communication Research Papers* (New York: Freedom Forum Media Studies Center, 1994): 30.

234. Folder 6, box 26, Lazarsfeld papers, CRBM.

On Lazarsfeld's advice, Cantril shifted the emphasis to analysis of the reasons why some listeners panicked and others did not.[235] After meeting with John Marshall of Rockefeller, Lazarsfeld wrote to Cantril that he thought the emphasis of the study should be "very strongly on checking up": "the most important object of study...is not that people became scared...what is so extremely interesting and deserves all generalizations is the fact that after people were scared they were not able or willing to check up to see whether it was true or not." Lazarsfeld reported that the foundation saw more utility in a study with the potential for some practical conclusions, some insight into other situations of "mass hysteria," such as race riots and lynchings, in which "the main thing is whether people are willing to check up upon rumors...whether they find out and make sure first that the raping has actually taken place before they lynch the Negro." Displaying his usual canny sense of the kind of conclusions that would be most valuable, Lazarsfeld argued that if the study was centered on "the fact that we are full of anxiety and therefore believe everything, you can't help much because our anxiety will remain for a long time and dangers will happen all the time." It was around the process of the checkup, he advised, that "the possibilities of educational or social interference is greatest." He also suggested that Cantril think of a word other than "check-up"—"I wish you could find a better word for it so that this whole idea could be more easily merchandised."[236]

Cantril received $3000 from Rockefeller for the study.[237] He was a busy man ("I'm trying to budget my spare time very carefully...it is so precious") and had considerable assistance with the writing of the book. He sought the help of Herta Herzog for the interviews: "God knows what her reward will be—except my continued admiration for her ability and a eulogistic footnote in the last chapter."[238] *Invasion from Mars* was based on interviews with 135 people in the New Jersey area, most of them known to have panicked.

Intelligence was one of the central concerns of the study, which promised to show "why some people reacted unintelligently in this instance."[239] "Critical ability," the Princeton researchers found, was most closely related to level of education—there was "a tendency for people with low education to misinterpret the broadcast *irrespective* of their economic status."[240] A second important personal characteristic was "susceptibility." Here again, "educated people were less susceptible than relatively uneducated people."[241] Susceptibility encompassed a range of emotional conditions—including insecurity, phobias, worry, lack of self-confidence, fatalism and religiosity—that might render a person's critical ability "ineffective."[242]

235. Hadley Cantril, "Proposed Study of 'Mass Hysteria,'" folder 6, box 26, Lazarsfeld papers, CRBM.

236. Memorandum Lazarsfeld to Cantril, October 12, 1939, folder 6, box 26, Lazarsfeld papers, CRBM.

237. *New York Times*, December 20, 1938: 29.

238. Cantril to Lazarsfeld, undated, folder 6, box 26, Lazarsfeld papers, CRBM.

239. Hadley Cantril with Hazel Gaudet and Herta Herzog, *The Invasion from Mars: A Study in the Psychology of Panic* (Princeton: Princeton University Press, 1940): viii.

240. *The Invasion from Mars*: 113.

241. *The Invasion from Mars*: 135.

242. *The Invasion from Mars*: 139.

The book set out a rather unself-consciously classed view of psychologically healthy behavior, placing under critical scrutiny the lives of those Americans who were less literate, less rational, more religious, more materialistic, and less curious than the educated and socially secure ideal. Cantril bluntly summarized his conclusions in a 1939 article: "People of higher socio-economic status have frames of reference which are better structured, more highly rationalized, more readily applicable to a variety of situations."[243] Such exemplary personal rationality—flexible, modern, portable—was more than usually difficult to maintain, the Princeton researchers did acknowledge, in the United States in 1938. Poverty, and the status anxiety that so often afflicted the socially mobile, were both found to be disruptive of a feeling of security in the world. Historical conditions had created a turbulence and uncertainty that complicated the cognitive tasks faced by citizens, as "many social norms, with their corresponding personal habits, were in a state of flux and change," and many individuals were left "perplexed and confused."[244]

A disturbing general conclusion did remain in the study: "There is every reason to believe that the anxiety and fear revealed by the panic were latent in the general population, not specific to the persons who happened to participate in it."[245] The book held out some hope for the diffusion of enlightened rationality: "If this skepticism and knowledge are to be spread more widely among common men, they must be provided extensive educational opportunities." But, more radically, to achieve such skeptical rationality, they would need to be "less harassed by the emotional insecurities which stem from underprivileged environments."[246] That—the concluding sentence to the book—suggested residual traces of the more socially critical stance evident in the Propaganda Institute document.

As we have seen, many Americans had less time for environmental explanations. The *War of the Worlds* broadcast ought to be remembered not as a quaint novelty, but as a moment in a rather disturbing fundamental conversation about what radio could be, and what forms of self-government were necessary or possible in the age of broadcasting. It was a moment when the less attractive side of the civic paradigm contract was exposed—when it seemed to many of the best educated, most wealthy, and influential people in America that ordinary citizens were just not capable of the kind of self-regulated, self-reflexive, rational, and critical citizenship required in mass-mediated, propaganda-soaked modernity. It was a distressingly undemocratic moment, in which the civic paradigm values of tolerance and empathy were quite forgotten in an excess of zeal about rationality, intelligence, and national security.

243. Cantril comment in P. F. Lazarsfeld, "The Change of Opinion during a Political Discussion," *Journal of Applied Psychology* 23, no. 1 (February 1939): 136.

244. *The Invasion from Mars*: 154.

245. *The Invasion from Mars*: 202.

246. *The Invasion from Mars*: 205.

7

Populism, War, and the American System

POPULISM AND MONOPOLY

The class divided response to civic paradigm radio found political expression in concerted populist challenges to the American system of broadcasting from the late 1930s. Civic paradigm invocations of the ideal of active citizens, open to reasoned persuasion, new knowledges, and points of view, were through the 1930s challenged by another—more American and more popular—kind of criticism of commercial and networked broadcasting. Populists, unlike elite educational radio reformers, could at times mobilize a vast constituency. Fundamental criticism of the American system was by the later 1930s more likely to come from populist critics of national centralization and internationalism than from the education lobby or from advocates of the establishment of an American BBC. Challenges in the name of popular control did for a time look as though they might lead to a reshaping of the American system of broadcasting.

The populist critique of radio had both radical and conservative implications. Populists spoke of wresting control of radio back from corporations *and* government, of restoring broadcasting to the people. From the late 1920s, populist reformers and critics had been suspicious of the centralizing influence of network broadcasting, arguing that ownership and programming were falling into too few hands. For that reason, populists were equally hostile to proposals for government-funded or government-operated broadcasting. They wanted to see radio move away from centralization and national coordination, not toward it, in part because they saw national coordination as but a prelude to internationalization. Populists' preoccupation with economic monopoly of all kinds led them to favor the breaking up rather than the formation of large broadcasting organizations. Another significant shaper of the distinctive American system of broadcasting, then, was that one of the most potent critical traditions was not at all likely to promote the establishment of a national public broadcaster, because it understood the dangers of the existing commercial radio system to lie in its networked, national, and international character rather than in its commercialism. In this tradition, actual or incipient monopoly, rather than commercialism itself, was the most commonly identified problem.

Populism offered a language admirably suited to criticizing the centralizing potential of network broadcasting, but it had practical limitations as a program of radio reform. While educational and civic paradigm reformers generally knew what they wanted, populist critics of network radio were far clearer about what was wrong with the status quo than about what should replace it. The language of populism gave them a way to talk about the new conditions of networked and mediated modernity, a means of identifying its dangers, but not necessarily a practical plan of reform action.

Populism kept alive the dream of radio as a common carrier, available to all who wanted to address the people. Speech on the street corner and speech on a nationwide radio network reached such clearly incomparable numbers of people that to treat the two together as instances of free speech seemed patently inadequate. But positing a general right to broadcast, while attractive in theory, raised insuperable practical difficulties—not least the question of who would listen. The argument that restoring radio to the people had to mean actively as broadcasters, not just passively as audience, was always vulnerable to some simple and fatal objections. The FCC's Frank McNinch observed, "If it be suggested that a right should be recognized and protected in every person to speak over the radio, simple arithmetic would make it plain that this right to speak would be only for a matter of seconds or minutes in a lifetime." But the manifest practical absurdity of the idea of a right to broadcast—a consequence of the vast asymmetries of mass communication—did not prevent the question from being raised repeatedly through the 1930s. Former Federal Radio Commission member Ira E. Robinson, for example, still in 1934 wanted radio made a public utility so that licensees would not have a "private long-range mouthpiece" for their own views while denying such facilities to the American public more generally.[1]

The sheer utopian impracticality of the idea of a right to broadcast was a gift to the broadcasters defending the commercial, civic paradigm status quo. Broadcasters had a standard response to any suggestion of a right to broadcast—simply threatening to abandon discussion of public affairs entirely if common carrier or equal time provisions were forced upon them, and arguing that such an impost would make well-proportioned and entertaining broadcasting impossible. "Program balance would be ruined," wrote NBC's A. L. Ashby, "speeches unfit for the American home would be broadcast wholesale."[2] The dominant language of criticism of the American system in the later 1930s—populism—sounded a roar but ended with few viable proposals for radio reform.

What made the situation in the United States distinctive was that populism—the rhetorical claim to speak on behalf of the people—was not only a language of plebeian critique of radio, but also increasingly the language of official regulation of it. On one side, populist radicals such as consumer activist Ruth Brindze argued that American radio had become "a private monopoly dominated by government."[3] On the other, populist FCC chair McNinch warned broadcasters that "all radio frequencies belong to the people" and that their judgments must prevail.[4] The broadcasters' dilemma was thus that they were being assailed by populism from both critical and regulatory sources. Figure 7.1.

1. Ira E. Robinson to C. C. Dill, March 10, 1934, in *Hearings Before the Committee on Interstate Commerce United States Senate on S. 2910* (Washington DC: U.S. Government Printing Office, 1934): 71.

2. A. L. Ashby, "Legal Aspects of Radio Broadcasting," *Air Law Review* (1930): 346.

3. Ruth Brindze, *Not to Be Broadcast: The Truth about the Radio* (New York: Vanguard Press, 1937): 5–8. On Brindze, see Kathy M. Newman, *Radio Active: Advertising and Consumer Activism, 1935–1947* (Berkeley: University of California Press, 2004): 63–70.

4. "Public Owns Air, McNinch Cautions," *New York Times,* November 23, 1938: 12.

Figure 7.1. Frank McNinch, chairman of the FCC, at a Senate committee hearing, Jan. 13, 1939. Harris and Ewing collection, Library of Congress, LC-H22-D- 5483

The failure of the most radical populist proposition—that free speech in the broadcast age entailed a right to broadcast—eventually led some populists in government to a middle ground of compromise on the idea that citizens had a right to listen rather than a right to broadcast. The consumer right to hear all points of view marked the end of one trajectory of the 1930s civic paradigm. Frank McNinch proposed that Americans had a right to listen, and specifically to hear all sides of controversial questions.[5] It is important to remember that this idea emerged in the later 1930s as a kind of liberal second-best to the more radical but impossible populist dream of a right to access the microphone. "The vital requirement for the protection of listeners," McNinch maintained, "is that all sides be given, if any side is given, on any important social, political, economic or religious subject that is controversial."[6] His successor Lawrence Fly elaborated further on the theme, arguing in 1943 that there had to be recognition of a right to listen, and that "complete freedom to listen demands that divergent views be aired."[7] Figure 7.2.

5. Frank McNinch, "Radio and the Bill of Rights—Address of Frank McNinch, Chairman, FCC…Over the Blue Network of the National Broadcasting Company," FCC Press release, January 26, 1939: 5–8.

6. Frank McNinch, "A New Communications Program—Address of Frank McNinch…Over the Mutual Broadcasting System," FCC Press Release, February 10, 1939: 13.

7. "Freedom to Listen Basic Counterpart of Freedom of Speech, Fly Tells Club," *Broadcasting* 25, no. 14 (October 4, 1943): 30.

Figure 7.2. Frank McNinch, new chairman of the Federal Communication Commission, was reported to have become a "rabid radio listener" since his appointment. He is shown "dialing in one of his favorite programs on his office set." Harris and Ewing collection, Library of Congress, LC-H22- D-2245.

The radical edge of populist concern about radio lay in the warnings about monopoly control of broadcasting and the threat it posed to listeners' rights to hear diverse points of view. Both major political parties housed numbers of people very actively concerned with radio and monopoly. There were repeated calls in Congress like that made by Massachusetts Democrat William Patrick Connery, whose 1937 House resolution argued that "a monopoly exists in radio broadcasting...profiting illegally at the expense and to the detriment of the people through the monopolistic control and operation of all clear-channel and other highly desirable radio-broadcasting stations."[8] The populist language here very typically counterposed the interests of "the people" to those of the commercial monopolies. A flurry of resolutions was introduced to Congress in 1937 and early 1938 calling for investigations of possible monopolistic control of radio—provoked in part by Republican fears of an alliance between the networks and the Roosevelt administration.

8. Cited in Hearings before the Committee on Interstate Commerce, United States Senate, Seventy-Seventh Congress, First Session, on S. Res.113: 14.

Responding to these concerns, McNinch, with his public utility regulation background, announced that the FCC would investigate the existence of monopoly in broadcasting. Commission Order No. 37, calling for an investigation of the radio chains, was issued in March 1938. A committee of the FCC held public hearings for 73 days over a period of six months, from November 1938 to May 1939. Ninety-six witnesses were heard from, the evidence filled 27 volumes, including over 8000 pages of transcript and more than 700 exhibits. NBC witnesses were quizzed closely about the competition claimed to exist between the NBC's two networks, the Red and Blue. John Royal was asked by a skeptical FCC lawyer, "And you try to attract as many listeners as you can to the Blue and take them away from the Red to listen to the Blue, and as many to the Red as you can and take them away from the Blue?"[9] The most tangible outcome of the monopoly inquiry was the set of regulations—shaped by FCC chair Lawrence Fly—forbidding a network to have two stations in the same area. This forced NBC to divest itself of one of its networks, leading to the sale of the NBC Blue network and its reemergence as the American Broadcasting Company. Figure 7.3.

Figure 7.3. Commissioners Frank McNinch, Thad Brown, and Eugene O. Sykes at the FCC hearings into alleged radio monopolies, Washington DC, Nov. 15, 1938. Harris and Ewing collection, Library of Congress, LC-H22-D- 4954.

9. FCC chain broadcasting hearings, box 1400, Docket 5060, RG 173, NACP: 617.

The FCC decision to force NBC to sell its Blue network set some reform minds dreaming again of a national public broadcaster. George Denny wrote a hopeful memo in May 1942, outlining an argument for the transfer of ownership of the Blue network to Town Hall.[10] President Roosevelt asked on December 11, 1941, for advice on a government takeover of the Blue network for the duration of the war, but his key radio advisers, including Byron Price and Lawrence Fly, dissuaded him.[11] Archibald MacLeish remembered that "there were a lot of people trying to persuade the President to buy the Blue Network, but they never persuaded him."[12] The monopoly inquiry, a response to populist unease with the increasingly centralized nature of the American system, briefly put the question of fundamental change of American broadcasting back on the national agenda. As a consequence of the inquiry, debate and litigation about the future of American broadcasting was taking place from 1941 to 1943, just as the war emergency provided powerful new reasons to leave American broadcasting as it was, to work with its strengths rather than experiment with new modes of organization.

RADIO AND WAR

The considerable populist reform momentum of the late 1930s was to be stilled by the war. Broadcasters successfully made the case that radio needed to continue entertaining its audience in order to keep it listening to war-related messages. NBC president Niles Trammell observed a couple of weeks after Pearl Harbor that, despite the FCC monopoly crusade, "since the declaration of war other high authorities of the government have expressed to us their wish that nothing be done to disturb the present network structures."[13] Figure 7.4.

Figure 7.4. "Washington, D.C. Listening to a murder mystery on the radio in a boarding house room." Esther Bubley took this photograph in the Washington boarding house in which her sister lived—it housed young women who had come to the capital for wartime jobs. Office of War Information photograph, January 1943. Available: http://memory.loc.gov/cgi-bin/query/r?ammem/fsaall:@field(NUMBER+@band(fsa+8d33602)).

10. Memorandum "The Blue Network and Town Hall," May 11, 1942, box 103, President's Office Correspondence, Town Hall Inc. papers, NYPL.

11. Michael Socolow, "'News Is a Weapon': Domestic Radio Propaganda and Broadcast Journalism in America, 1939–1944," *American Journalism* 24, no. 3 (2007): 110.

12. Meeting in New York March 22, 1944, Document 15, folder 4, box 1, Commission on Freedom of the Press papers, UCSC.

13. Trammell statement, December 31, 1941, folder 10, box 83, NBC records, WHS.

It was obvious to all that radio—as a propaganda instrument and a means of disseminating emergency information—would be crucial to the nation in wartime. Section 606(c) of the 1934 Communications Act empowered the president, in the event of "war or a threat of war…or in order to preserve the neutrality of the United States," to "suspend or amend as he sees fit" the rules of broadcasting, and to "close any studio" or authorize its "use or control by any department of government."[14] "I am not confiding any state secret," said Frank McNinch in a 1939 speech, "when I tell you that our plans for national defense are to a very considerable extent built around radio."[15] The continuation of the commercial American system during war was surprising to many, who understandably assumed that modern war would require much closer governmental control because of the ever-present risk that enemy propaganda or coded messages would slip by an open microphone. Lowell Mellett, director of government reports, had argued in March 1941 that "definite control of radio is necessary" in wartime, but director of the Office of Censorship, Byron Price, disagreed.[16]

Radio's undeniable strategic importance became a bargaining chip for the broadcasters, aware that no one wanted to upset the nation's communications at such a critical time. The importance of news broadcasting during the war years, and radio's willingness to take on morale and propaganda roles, were effective counters to renewed talk of closer government control or a government network.[17] The 1942 code for radio self-censorship signaled that a government takeover was no longer contemplated.[18] The code called for extra caution with audience participation shows—an end to vox pop street interviews, musical request shows, quiz shows from remote locations, and to lost-and-found notices received by telephone or telegraph.[19] There was also to be closer supervision of forum discussion programs—on the *People's Platform*, Lyman Bryson had to drop the "man in the street" guest.[20] Figure 7.5. [Companion website 7.1.] *Broadcasting* magazine reported that the code was a "bitter pill" for smaller stations, some of which had derived "a substantial amount of income" from open microphone features. But, the industry publication warned, the code could have been much worse, and war was no time for complacency about defending the American system: "Broadcasters should keep in mind that there exists in Washington a radical fringe still fostering Government ownership. There are adherents of this view on the FCC. The staff is permeated with them."[21]

14. Communications Act of 1934, Section 606; Max D. Paglin, James R. Hobson, Joel Rosenbloom (eds.), *The Communications Act: A Legislative History of the Major Amendments, 1934–1996* (Silver Spring, MD: Pike & Fischer, 1999): 384–86.

15. Frank McNinch, "Radio and the Bill of Rights," broadcast on the NBC Blue Network January 26, 1939, Library of American Broadcasting, University of Maryland.

16. Lowell Mellett in *Censorship* (New York: Council for Democracy, 1942): 11–12, as quoted in Robert E. Summers, *Wartime Censorship of Press and Radio* (New York: H. W. Wilson, 1942): 16.

17. Michael J. Socolow, "To Network a Nation: NBC, CBS, and the Development of National Network Radio in the United States, 1925–1950," (PhD diss., Georgetown University, 2001): 217.

18. Michael S. Sweeney, *Secrets of Victory: The Office of Censorship and the American Press and Radio in World War II* (Chapel Hill: University of North Carolina Press, 2001): 8–10.

19. John K. Hutchens, "Radio Gets a Code," *New York Times,* January 25, 1942: X12.

20. "Reminiscences of Lyman Bryson," Columbia Oral History Research Unit: 133, box 40, Lyman Bryson papers, LOC.

21. Editorial, "It Could Be Worse," *Broadcasting* 22, no. 4 (January 26, 1942): 24.

Figure 7.5. The *People's Platform* broadcast, August 19, 1944, on the topic "United Nations Discuss Small Nations." Speakers, from left: Brooke Claxton, parliamentary secretary to Prime Minister Mackenzie King of Canada; Carl J. Hambro, president of the Norwegian Parliament; Lyman Bryson, CBS director of education; and Andre Miochalopoulos, former minister of information of Greece. CBS/Landov.

Just as the civic paradigm was a product of the settlement of 1934, so now the broadcasters entered a new implicit contract with government. In return for being left alone, they voluntarily took on, under the Network Allocation Plan, the task of communicating government-nominated themes, cooperating with government propaganda, censorship, and morale objectives.[22] War-related messages were worked ingeniously into regular commercial programming—radio comedians and soap opera writers were recruited to explain, for example, the need for rationing, reducing travel, buying war bonds.[23] Archibald MacLeish argued that wartime government needed radio not just to make its facilities available, but "to apply to the doing of the job all of its skill, all of its experience, all of its tremendous resources of ingenuity and imagination."[24] Former network executives Douglas Meservey and William B. Lewis at the Radio Division of the Office of War Information, given the role of coordinating radio propaganda, were important in ensuring relatively smooth cooperation in working key messages into scripts of drama and comedy programs—although their network connections brought continuing

22. See Gerd Horten, *Radio Goes to War: The Cultural Politics of Propaganda during World War II* (Berkeley: University of California Press, 2001).

23. Horten, *Radio Goes to War*, chs. 5, 6; *Address by Donald D. Stauffer Before the NAB War Conference April 28, 1943* (Washington: NAB, 1943).

24. Archibald Macleish, *Radio and War* (Washington, DC: NAB, 1942): 4–5.

accusations that OWI favored the networks over smaller stations.[25] War messages were, however, communicated effectively. Donald Stauffer of OWI reported that, while in mid-1942 only 24% of the population in the Midwest had believed that gas mileage rationing was necessary, after a radio campaign, that proportion rose to 67%.[26]

It is impossible to understand where this close relationship with government came from if we think of American radio after 1934 as simply what it repeatedly said it was—a free enterprise broadcasting system that gave its audience what it wanted and had nothing to do with government. Under the civic paradigm, radio was already well used to thinking about shaping citizen behavior and cooperating with government. When Frank Mullen reminded NBC affiliates that "we are essential to every activity of Government....We are essential to the maintenance of public morale and the service of public information," he spoke in fact as a veteran of cooperation between broadcasters and government.[27] The demands of the war situation were then not entirely novel to broadcasters who had worked through the New Deal era—civic paradigm cooperation provided a model for wartime cooperation with government. The broadcasters' proven civic paradigm skill at combining educational messages with entertaining form was once again vital. Former assistant secretary of war Louis Johnson addressed the NAB in San Francisco in 1940: "You broadcasters of America, who are expert phrase and slogan makers, I urge you to coin a national motto to keep constantly before the American people as a reminder, every day, in every way, of the necessity for national teamwork."[28] The message was new, but the idea that American broadcasting required a marriage of showmanship with attempts to change the thinking of individual Americans was not. Figure 7.6.

Even before U.S. entry into the war, Americans were staying closer to their radios and paying them more attention than ever before. The number of sets in use increased by between 10% and 20% during 1940, compared to the average of the previous three years; by 1940, news was overwhelmingly the favored program type of both men and women.[29] The share of the radio audiences garnered by presidential addresses went up from 31% in 1941 to 66% by mid-1942.[30] The broadcasting industry had sensed from the beginning of the war in Europe that the war emergency would be good for business, and the predictions were accurate. Advertising increased even more rapidly than audiences. Under 1942 changes to the tax code, businesses could claim tax deductions for up to 80% of their advertising costs so long as the campaign assisted the war effort, and this produced an even greater tide of radio advertising.[31]

25. Socolow, "To Network a Nation": 201–9.

26. "Global Effort, 'Nerve' Warfare," *Billboard*, May 8, 1943: 7.

27. "More Realistic View of War Needed, NBC Tells Affiliates," *Broadcasting* 22, no. 12 (March 23, 1942): 14.

28. "Johnson Urges Broadcasters to Feature Patriotic Message," *Broadcasting* 19, no. 4 (August 15, 1940): 28.

29. "How the War Affects Radio Listening," *Broadcasting* 19, no. 3 (August 1, 1940): 76; "Ladies First...As News Listeners Too," *Broadcasting* 19, no. 3 (August 1, 1940): 86.

30. A. W. Lehman, "War Listening Since Pearl Harbor," *Broadcasting* 22, no. 19 (May 11, 1942): 27.

31. Barnouw, *The Golden Web*: 165–67; Horten, *Radio Goes to War*: 92–93; "Net Time Sales Hit $191,000,000 in 1942," *Broadcasting* 24, no. 6 (February 8, 1943): 7.

It's right in his lap

The subject of the photograph is named John.

He is the Average American.

A very *un*-average person he is. He and his wife and kids (in the service or not) are 'what makes America go'. He works for somebody or other—maybe himself, even—but he runs the country. Increasingly it becomes apparent to him that his responsibilities and those of his kids are not limited by our national boundaries.

He runs the country?

Yes. What is perhaps more urgent is that HE RUNS YOU.

He's got the major problems of the world squarely in his lap. He realizes that if he doesn't tackle and solve them he will have to take orders from who-ever tackles and solves them first. *He is thinking very hard these days.*

He doesn't like to sound off an opinion without plenty of facts to fortify his instincts.

He relies on radio, enormously and increasingly, for the facts and impres-sions on which he bases his judgments. He and his family listen some 5 hours a day. He is cagey as a fox about believing—or disbelieving—the information, argu-ment and emotion he gets from the air. But out of his weighing, accepting and rejecting of everything he hears, he forms an opinion, and acts on it. This is called *public* opinion. *Radio* public opinion is 31 million families strong.

His personal opinion—no matter what the captains and the kings may say—will decide what happens to the USA in the factory, the military field, and the home.

He is not to be trifled with, nor deceived—especially on the air. He is "open to argument", and in the long run he is just. He is grateful for a good time, bountiful in his generosity, scornful of fraud —and loyal to tried friends.

He's worth taking up your case with. In 28 million homes he and his family listen to CBS. After all, he's your boss.

Figure 7.6. On the first page of this CBS advertisement, a middle-aged man in a business shirt with tie loosened, sits at home with a globe of the world in his lap. He is the emblematic civic paradigm member of radio's public—critical, rational, cautious, responsibly working toward developing his own personal opinion. The invitation to advertisers, in the somber wartime environment, is to make their sales pitch in this same judicious mode. "It's Right in His Lap," *Broadcasting* (Dec. 7, 1942): 6.

As a consequence, of course, the tensions characteristic of the American system were even more starkly apparent during war. The mix of war news and commercial advertising was noxious to many: "I once heard the Campbell's soup announcer describe the destruction of several Russian army divisions and immediately afterwards exclaim, 'Lady, do you like real chicken noodle soup? Ha! Ha!,'" recalled a writer in the *New Republic*, who described the conjunction as "barbarous."[32] Psychologist Erich Fromm, who had lived in New York since 1934, was nevertheless in 1941 alarmed at the wartime juxtapositions: "The announcement of the bombing of a city and the death of hundreds of people is shamelessly followed or interrupted by an advertisement for soap or wine. The same speaker with the same suggestive, ingratiating, and authoritative voice."[33] Such complaints, however, sparked no serious political attention to radio reform, in part because of defensive industry self-regulation. "Do not allow sponsors to use the news as a springboard for commercials," warned the NAB's code. "Such practices as starting commercials with 'And now here's some good news, etc.' should *never* be permitted."[34]

The FCC was very concerned, however, that broadcasters' successful fulfillment of the implicit wartime contract seemed to entail neglect of their longer standing civic paradigm responsibilities. Wartime increases in radio advertising meant that both the number and reach of sustaining programs was greatly reduced. Heistad calculates that the proportion of sustaining programs on the networks fell from 42% of all programming in 1935–41, to just 30% during WWII.[35] The crowded and profitable schedule had little time left for worthy sustaining programs. Sidney Strotz, John Royal's replacement as vice president for programs at NBC, wrote to the managers of the Red and Blue networks in 1941, suggesting that they "review with Walter Preston our Public Service situation and reduce the number of Public Service programs wherever possible."[36]

In this environment, the leading forum programs struggled to keep their times and stations. William Benton learned from Norman Thomas in 1943 that "Town Meeting is losing a lot of stations.…Detroit and Chicago, as examples." The *University of Chicago Round Table* was also losing outlets and hence audience: "Our stations have dropped from 119 to 47." The problem was that "as the demand for time for advertising has mounted, local stations have cancelled the sustaining programs."[37] The ideological climate within the networks was also shifting—Sidney Strotz confided to Judith Waller in 1941 that "confidentially, I have always considered the Town Hall crowd a bit 'pinkish.'"[38] FCC chair Lawrence Fly wrote to *Billboard* in 1944 to express his concern about the "fundamental problem" of the "dwindling of sustaining time and of educational programs."[39] Fly told the Commission on the Freedom of the Press in June 1944 that

32. Jesse Rainsford Sprague, "Slaughter, Sponsored by—," *New Republic* October 6, 1941: 435.

33. Erich Fromm, *The Fear of Freedom* (London: Routledge and Kegan Paul, 1942): 216.

34. "NAB Guide for Wartime Broadcasting," *Broadcasting* 1942, Yearbook no. 92.

35. Mark J. Heistad, "Radio without Sponsors: Public Service Programming in Network Sustaining Time, 1928–1952," (PhD diss., University of Minnesota, 1998): 177.

36. Strotz to Carlin and Hillpot, April 25, 1941, folder 1, box 354, NBC records, WHS.

37. Benton to Hutchins, November 15, 1943, folder 4, box 176, Office of the President records, Hutchins administration, UCSC.

38. Strotz to Waller, August 11, 1941, folder 5, box 354, NBC records, WHS.

39. "Fly Says He Had Something to Buzz Around About," *Billboard*, January 29, 1944: 6.

"sustaining time is weakening under the attraction of more money": "In short, though the broadcasting industry is making 50% more money than ever before, it is giving less public service than it ever did. The question of public service seems to have no impact on the broadcaster." Fly affirmed again, however, that a government broadcaster was "not feasible politically."[40]

So the United States faced the postwar world with a dilemma—the civic paradigm contract seemed broken, at a time when the creation of a national public broadcaster was further than ever from being a political possibility. Those lamenting the situation had little idea where to turn for a solution. In 1945, James Rowland Angell wrote to NBC vice president Frank Mullen that the public service staff of NBC harbored a "deep and sincere conviction that broadcasting is top-heavy with commercialism."[41] "Whatever interests the programs may serve, the chap with the big bank account is apt to get far the best hours for his purposes and he is certain to be able to put the most money into programs to attract his clients."[42] FCC commissioner Clifford Durr warned a symposium in 1944 that radio was becoming less free as it became more commercial: "You need only turn on your radio to be aware of the trend toward the almost complete commercialization of radio programs. The good sustaining programs are becoming fewer and fewer and during the evening hours have just about disappeared from the air."[43] Those most alert to the condition of radio in the United States were acutely aware that the civic paradigm compact had broken.

The radio forums struggled in the war environment to maintain the ethos of toleration and good will, and their capacity to demonstrate that aural exposure to diverse opinions bred tolerance. I have described elsewhere the conflict that beset *ATMA* from the time possible U.S. participation in the European war became a bitterly divisive issue.[44] Isolationists accused Denny, with some justification, of internationalist and interventionist sympathies. More fundamentally, the relativist and cosmopolitan edge to *ATMA*'s conception of democracy divided listeners. A stream of virulent letters and cards alleged that the program had become a forum for internationalist elites, Jews, and foreigners who held un-American views. To these populist listeners, real identities were fixed and ultimately racial in origin. Here the hard and exclusive edge of populism became apparent—the "people" whose ownership of radio had to be defended was a group somewhat smaller than the whole population. A listener wrote to complain in 1940 about sentiments expressed during *ATMA*'s question time: "I was not surprised in the least at the thoughts expressed in some of them, especially when one takes into consideration the decided foreign accent of those making them. This has been noted quite frequently of late...especially since the great influx of alien-minded, constitution-hating foreigners

40. Commission on Freedom of the Press, Meetings of June 19–20, 1944, New York City, Commission on Freedom of Press Records, UCSC.

41. James Angell to Frank Mullen, June 1, 1945, folder 69, box 114, NBC records, WHS.

42. James R. Angell to Frank E. Mullen, May 25, 1945, folder 69, box 114, NBC records, WHS.

43. Clifford Durr, "How Free Is Radio," speech at 15th Institute for Education by Radio, Columbus, Ohio, May 5, 1944, in box 25 James Lawrence Fly papers, CRBM.

44. David Goodman, "Programming in the Public Interest: *America's Town Meeting of the Air*," in Michele Hilmes (ed.), *NBC: America's Network* (Berkeley: University of California Press, 2007): 44–60.

who seek to carry on their personal war of hate from these shores."[45] Such populist listeners challenged the very idea of an inclusive radio forum. When isolationist John T. Flynn spoke on *ATMA* in May 1941, a supporter wrote to him with this supportive comment: "I have always thought that none but American citizens should be admitted to a 'town meeting.'"[46] One observer noted a change in the Town Hall audience—their manner was now "inflammable," their questions "bitterly phrased." Denny, on one broadcast, feared for the first time that "the audience would get completely out of control," and he struggled in this environment to continue to separate personal from public considerations.[47] For years one of Denny's favorite methods of explaining the Town Hall idea had been to produce a ball that was black on one side and white on the other. Things appear differently to us from our different vantage points, he would say, but discussion can help us understand and overcome our differences. By 1943, Denny had a profoundly more pessimistic conclusion to draw from the black-and-white ball: "The tragedy is that we cannot turn our problems around so simply. Each of us is bound by all of his yesterdays."[48] He had lost much of his earlier confidence that discussion could trump history.

Even those most identified with the forum movement were beginning to conclude that democratic public morale would require some greater guidance and assistance than the open forum model provided. Among the more reflective forum proponents there was worry that badly managed forum talk in such a tense environment might lead to what the University of Chicago's Sherman Dryer called a "contempt for talk." It had to be "a supreme concern," he argued, of all who directed discussion programs, to work out how to avoid producing this kind of contempt for democratic public deliberation.[49] Dryer sent Robert Hutchins a November 1942 *Variety* editorial, saying he thought it justified their policies for the *Round Table*. "The whole notion," *Variety* observed, "that a debate is 'educational' simply because it's a debate falls pretty flat when the public hears a continuous jumble of crosstalk, interruptions, rude hecklings, baitings, sarcastic cracks and general peevishness."[50] As early as June 1939, executives at NBC were thinking about the limitations of the radio forum as a means of building up the "faith and confidence of the citizens of the United States in a democratic form of government." Walter Preston and Margaret Cuthbert argued that while *ATMA* discussed important public questions with entertaining contrasting personalities, it nevertheless constituted "a subtle danger to democracy" because it created "a sense of frustration—rather than achievement—as a result of public discussion." They proposed a new program that, instead of leaving listeners to decide for themselves, would have an examiner question the speakers on their arguments and evidence: "This would tend to make the listener join in the adventure of

45. Letter to George Denny, January 10, 1940, box 18, Town Hall Inc. papers, NYPL.

46. Letter to John Flynn, Chicago, May 9, 1941, box 16, John T. Flynn papers, University of Oregon library.

47. Herbert Lyons Jr., "Free Speech in Action," *New York Times*, May 25, 1941: X8.

48. Box 26, Series 1, Denny papers, LOC. Denny recycled his stories and speeches often, and some of the same sentences appear in an interview with Denny in the *New York Times*: S. J. Woolf, "The Umpire of the Town Meeting," *New York Times,* June 6, 1943: 16.

49. Sherman Dryer, *Radio in Wartime* (New York: Greenberg, 1942): 169.

50. *Variety*, November 11, 1942.

searching out the truth…and in the process learn to think for himself." Finally, a judge would be introduced, who would sum up for the jury.[51] This elaborate formula, with its introduction of authoritative opinion directors, was one expression of growing disillusion with the open-ended discussion that *ATMA* and the forum movement had been fostering. Charles Siepmann, who had gone from being director of talks at the BBC to working for the FCC and undertaking radio research at Harvard University, also had significant reservations about *ATMA* by 1941. "I think you are over-generous in your praise of the Town Meeting of the Air," he wrote to William Benton, arguing that the program "by playing up emotionalism and exploiting mob psychology, defeats the very aim of the round table technique….The Town Meeting, in fact, for me illustrates perfectly what happens when so-called educational objectives are associated with publicity techniques of the kind which Denny dexterously exploits."[52] Denny himself was beginning to worry that the *ATMA* techniques were failing in the new environment. In a September 1942 article, he retold yet again the story about walking home one night and hearing about his neighbor who would not listen to Roosevelt on the radio. But this time, instead of concluding that Americans "must" listen to the other side, he posed the problem as one of motivation and desire: "How could people be made to *want* to give their minds a chance by listening to other than congenial views? How could people be made to *want* to hear both sides?"[53]

Elsewhere, radio was abandoning even the attempt at fostering civil public discussion. The 1946 FCC "Blue Book," *Public Service Responsibility of Broadcast Licensees*, was, as noted in chapter 2, the culmination of FCC concern about the relationship between the station promises and performance. Clifford Durr, Charles Siepmann, Edward Brecher, and Dallas Smythe worked on the report, which noted a tendency for commercial pressures to take stations away from discussion of news and public affairs:

> Any vigorous discussion of a point of view will of necessity annoy or offend some listeners. There may be a temptation, accordingly, for broadcasters to avoid as much as possible any discussion over their stations, and to limit their broadcasts to entertainment programs which offend no one. To operate in this manner, obviously, is to thwart the effectiveness of broadcasting in a democracy.[54]

This had been brought home to the commission during its investigation of radio's coverage of the vexed question of isolation or intervention in the war. While George Denny had been dismayed by the difficulties of tackling the war question head on, many other broadcasters had chosen to stay out of trouble by avoiding it altogether. A study of

51. W. G. Preston to John Royal, June 8, 1939, folder 59, box 94, NBC records, WHS.

52. Charles Siepmann to William Benton April 10, 1941, folder 1, box 1, University of Chicago, Office of the Vice President Records 1937–46, UCSC.

53. George V. Denny Jr., "'Town Meetin' Tonight!': The Revival of a Great American Institution," *Atlantic Monthly* (September 1942): 63.

54. John A. Salmond, *The Conscience of a Lawyer: Clifford J. Durr and American Civil Liberties 1899–1975* (Tuscaloosa: University of Alabama Press, 1990): 86; Federal Communications Commission, *Public Service Responsibilities of Broadcast Licensees* (Washington DC: FCC, 1946): 40.

network and local programs broadcast during the critical period of January and May 1941 showed that the networks addressed the pressing issue of possible intervention on average only every third day, and that even then, not all affiliates carried the programs. Local programs rarely discussed the war issue at all. All this at a time when "there are no economic considerations to prevent the rendering of a considerably broader program service than the public is currently afforded."[55] The Blue Book provoked some discussion but little major change. Socolow observes that "with the end of the Blue Book controversy, the last vestiges of the New Deal regulatory environment…evaporated."[56] The influence of the civic paradigm waned because of the exhaustion of the line of thought it represented, but also because the radio industry itself began to change in the new environment.

Intellectual interest was shifting toward making propaganda rather than protecting citizens from it. Lyman Bryson participated in a communications seminar funded by the Rockefeller Foundation, which began meeting just as war broke out in Europe in September 1939. Looking ahead, the distinguished group (which included Bryson, Lasswell, Lazarsfeld, Lynd, and Siepmann) concluded that "a state of full emergency" would necessitate "the deliberate formation and control of public opinion."[57] In this atmosphere, spontaneous group discussion came to seem too relativistic—the urgent task now was to create national consensus, not to inculcate skeptical distance and encourage open-ended discussion, or to produce elaborated and nuanced personal opinion. But direct government broadcasting was less acceptable than ever during a war against propaganda states. Increased political scrutiny of government broadcasting led to budget cuts to those agencies that had been most active in radio production. In 1941, Congress imposed a ceiling on the relief money that could be used for radio broadcasting, and there was consequently a rapid diminution in government radio production.[58] So American radio by the end of World War II was delicately poised. The civic paradigm was becoming neglected as one of its conditions of existence, the constant threat of government intervention in broadcasting, receded. Populist reform—breaking up radio "monopoly"—held little realistic promise of fundamental reform. And radio programming was changing in ways that seasoned civic paradigm advocates found difficult to comprehend.

55. *Public Service Responsibilities of Broadcast Licensees*: 47.

56. Socolow, "To Network a Nation": 351.

57. Rockefeller Communication Seminar, "Public Opinion and the Emergency," in box 18, Lyman Bryson papers, LOC.

58. Sayre, *An Analysis of the Radiobroadcasting Activities of Federal Agencies*: 77.

Postlude
From Toscanini to Sinatra

The Commission on Freedom of the Press originated from a suggestion by Henry Luce to his Yale classmate, University of Chicago president Robert M. Hutchins. Luce supplied $200,000 for the project, and the commission conducted its work from 1944 to 1946. The members of the commission were all men: Beardsley Ruml (chair of the New York Federal Reserve Bank), Robert Hutchins (president of the University of Chicago), Zechariah Chafee (legal scholar), Arthur M. Schlesinger (historian), George Shuster (college president and expert on Germany), Robert Redfield (anthropologist), Reinhold Niebuhr (theologian), Charles Merriam (political scientist), Archibald MacLeish (poet, Librarian of Congress), Harold Lasswell (psychologist), William Hocking (philosopher), John Dickinson (legal scholar), and John M. Clark (economist). There were in addition four 'foreign advisers'. For three years, some of the most influential social scientific, legal, historical, and philosophical intellectuals of the era discussed the freedom of the press broadly considered. Commission members interviewed 58 media industry owners and practitioners, and staff interviewed 225 more. The commission produced seven books of its findings.[1] [Companion website link 7.2.]

The commissioners—steeped both in the civic paradigm and populist concern about monopoly—worried a good deal about radio's future. It was clear to them, looking ahead to the postwar world, that the civic paradigm was not working and that the populist recipe of monopoly breaking did not provide a solution. Some of their key informants reinforced their sense that all was not well with American radio. Robert Leigh of the commission staff asked Lyman Bryson about "the actual outlook of the leadership in the radio business"—did the men really see its social significance, the necessity of taking a professional point of view and serving the public interest? "Off hand Bryson could name only two people at the head of the business whom he thought had the social point of view."[2] This pessimism was highly significant from someone who had been so close to the shaping of American radio's civic programming.

The commissioners decided to confine their deliberations to the civic paradigm question of the "role of the agencies of mass communication in the education of the

1. An earlier version of this section appeared in a volume of conference proceedings: David Goodman, "'We Know So Little': Civic Ideals and Emotional Engagement in Post-war Debate about American Radio," in Sianan Healy, Bruce Berryman, and David Goodman (eds.), *Radio in the World: Papers from the 2005 Radio Conference* (Melbourne: RMIT, 2005): 331–41.

2. Document 57, folder 12, box 2, Commission on Freedom of Press Records, UCSC.

people in public affairs."[3] An initial sketch of concerns dwelt upon the possibility of the media providing a common public sphere for citizens, to combat the fragmenting "tendency for every industrialized society to develop separate sections of the community on an economic or occupational rather than the former neighborhood basis." Strikingly, this early document concluded that free enterprise alone would not solve the problem: "No member of our Commission shares the Utopian faith that the uncoordinated pursuit of the purposes and interests of individuals and groups automatically serves the public interest."[4] While that statement did not survive the drafting process, the final commission publications did make clear that the group was very worried about cultural and social fragmentation and inequality, and was interested in the media as means to ameliorate some of these tendencies.

The commission also addressed the populist questions, and wrestled continually with prescriptions for maintaining freedom of expression in the face of declining diversity of ownership and participation in media. Seeing no viable solution to the problem of concentration, despite the FCC's monopoly campaign, members of the commission looked forward with some trepidation to the postwar world. Harold Lasswell asked gloomily in 1944 whether the "incipient conflict between the United States and Russia would lead to the suppression of freedom in the United States":

> One possible sequence is the following: Fear of the masses on the part of our monopoly-business and related groups will lead to perpetual "red scares" utilized to crack down on labor unions and to reestablish "white supremacy" in the South. These scares will also be utilized to attack fighting liberals who take the offensive against privately owned monopolies and other abuses. Concentration tendencies will go rapidly forward.[5]

Many of the commissioners thus accepted the populist diagnosis that economic concentration was at the root of lack of freedom in the media. Continuing and developing the traditions of thought about economic monopoly that had been so important in the second New Deal, they extrapolated them into the unknown dangers of the postwar future, while also clinging to their civic paradigm concerns about preserving diversity of opinion.

The commissioners spent much time on the populist argument that freedom of expression for media owners was less socially important than the right to free expression of ordinary people, and that the right to speak had to include some right to be heard over the mass media. This populist idea was identified and denounced by the more conservative members of the commission, but it nevertheless remained through all the drafting and discussion and into the final report. "When an instrument of prime importance to all the people is available to a small minority of the people only," the published report

---

3. Commission on Freedom of the Press, *A Free and Responsible Press* (Chicago: University of Chicago Press, 1947): vi.

4. "Definition of the Inquiry," Document 20, Commission on Freedom of Press Records, UCSC.

5. Discussion on April 26, 1944, Document 16, folder 4, box 1, Commission on Freedom of Press Records, UCSC.

maintained, the freedom of the press was in danger.[6] Freedom of speech in an era of mass media had to take account of the difference between owning a newspaper and standing on a corner with a megaphone.

The more conservative members of the commission mocked the idea of a right to broadcast or publish: "I should suppose that if this were the conception of freedom of the press toward which our report is aiming, we would have to end up with some proposal whereby any individual so desiring could become the proprietor of a newspaper," observed John Dickinson acidly.[7] Reflecting this skepticism, the published report raised the question of access to audience, but then made it clear that "this does not mean that every citizen has a moral or legal right to own a press or be an editor or have access as of right to the audience of any given medium of communication." The report talked of the right to an audience more abstractly, as something accruing to ideas rather than persons—"an idea shall have its chance" to be heard by the public.[8] This was the site of one of the commission's most intractable disagreements, and the issue that, left to themselves, the commissioners were most likely to end up debating. The commission's primary reform concerns were thus both civic paradigm and populist, to do with the obstacles in the American system to citizens using the media actively—as speakers as well as listeners. There was much illuminating talk about the economic and informational preconditions for active citizenship, and a dislike of whatever seemed to stand in its way.

The civic paradigm and populist analysis of the commission led it, however, to internal dissension and stasis. Discussion went around and around a familiar set of arguments about ownership and control and public service. The commissioners diagnosed some core problems very clearly, but could not agree on any fundamental set of recommendations. This was a matter of frustration and even embarrassment to men who clearly felt that, give the generous endowment of their work, they ought to be coming up with original solutions.

The more liberal members of the commission included Archibald MacLeish, who wrote the first draft of the general report. He focused on the economic concentration issue and tried to bring the commission's deliberations on that question to a head. He failed to get a clear resolution. Commission members retreated to the idea that the problem was complex or insoluble, but also began to express doubt that their heated arguments about ownership and control were going to lead them to any new ways of thinking about the problem. Posing the economic problem as part of a more general issue of concentration in modern society helped them rule out more firmly something they had already rejected— government operation of the media. They sought solutions that would produce more diversity, not greater central control, either by business or government. But they had no idea how to obtain it. When they were pushed on the question of whether small media operations were really better than big ones, all had to admit that they themselves preferred metropolitan to small-town papers and network radio to local programs, and that there were advantages as well as costs to media centralization.

---

6. Commission, *A Free and Responsible Press*: 2.

7. "Comments on the Revised Draft of the General Report, February, 26, 1946," Document 91B, folder 2, box 5: 1–4, Commission on Freedom of Press Records, UCSC.

8. Commission, *A Free and Responsible Press*: 9.

MacLeish asked his colleagues one day, "Would you feel that the Commission had jumped over the fence if it came out with the conclusion that the business motive, as such, is no longer a sufficient motivation to provide the service of information that the American people now need?" Told that the problem was "awfully complex," MacLeish replied that "unless your analysis is simple enough to make a recommendation, we are going to be one of the funniest groups of people who have met for three years." Reinhold Niebuhr reiterated that "actually we have an insoluble problem" and that there could be no "very tremendous solutions which will shock the whole world." Charles Merriam thought there was a need to relate the freedom of the press a little more to "our modern industrial society." The "increasing concentration of power" was not peculiar to the media but was "a common characteristic of our society." He argued that there was an anachronistic quality to some of the commission's language and thinking, but found it difficult to articulate the kind of analysis that was needed: "It would seem to me that if we could get a form of analysis that would be a little more up to date, a little more modernistic and futuristic, by looking into our present industrial system and technology, it might be helpful."[9] But in the end, the most surprising thing about the commission's findings, Hutchins remarked in the final report, was that "nothing more surprising could be proposed."[10] The commission was working on the cusp of two eras. Its inherited civic paradigm concern about the possibilities of greater coordination in broadcasting, how to protect the public interest amidst the chaos and self-interestedness of the marketplace, led naturally to an increased interest in government activism and regulation. But the war and Cold War climate, a residual conviction that state-owned media were liable to become merely instruments of government propaganda, and the resurgent populist concerns of the later 1930s about centralization and monopoly, all led them firmly to reject those solutions as well. No commission member called for anything remotely like an American BBC. There was increasing concern by the end of the life of the commission—from, for example, John Dickinson—that recommending greater government involvement would be seen as support for the "Russian" model of broadcasting. In the language of the final report,

> If modern society requires great agencies of mass communication, if these concentrations become so powerful that they are a threat to democracy, if democracy cannot solve the problem simply by breaking them up—then those agencies must control themselves or be controlled by government. If they are controlled by government, we lose our chief safeguard against totalitarianism—and at the same time take a long step towards it.[11]

The main issues preoccupying the commission, then, led it to admitted defeat. It could not formulate an adequate solution to the problem of economic concentration in the media, and hence felt it could not provide any simple recipe for a better and more

9. Document 90, folder 9, box 4: 18–28, Commission on Freedom of Press Records, UCSC.
10. Commission, *A Free and Responsible Press*: viii.
11. Commission, *A Free and Responsible Press*: 5.

democratic media. Even those commissioners who thought that economic concentration lay at the root of the major problems of the media acknowledged that the New Deal language of monopoly breaking was not providing them with the intellectual tools they needed to think about a civically satisfactory radio. They also groped somewhat uncertainly toward a language more adequate to talk about emotional connections to media, about the affective, rather than civic, reasons people had for reading and listening.

At their most instrumental, the members of the commission talked about the problems they were investigating as being about the dissemination of accurate information to the public. Occasionally, commission members acknowledged that there was another, more emotional level, to communications. But each time such a discussion began, it was abandoned with a confession of ignorance or inadequacy. Commissioners had in general neither the intellectual training nor the life experience to begin talking descriptively or analytically about the emotional aspects of communication or interaction with popular entertainment media.

American social science had thus far had little to say about the subjective dynamics of response to popular music, and the extraordinary civic paradigm emphasis on broadening the audience for classical music had left the popular appeal of popular music relatively unexamined, as something both self-evident and undesirable. "It is a form of social stimulus," reported one wartime study, "for which, in its production, the music, advertising and radio industries spend millions of dollars each year. However, despite these vast expenditures and the psychological effect on people of what is produced, this whole sphere of social dynamics has been but barely touched by social scientists."[12] The author ventured one significant conclusion: "The overall picture is that *women* generally prefer popular music programs slightly more often than men."[13] That was perhaps a further reason that the all-male members of the commission felt a little lost with this topic.

Members of the commission did make brief explorative forays into the terrain of emotional response to media, at least far enough to indicate their awareness that there was a large and significant territory out there. Robert Redfield talked of the importance of "the symbol-creating and symbol-perpetuating function."[14] Beardsley Ruml, thinking of a positive and democratic kind of propaganda, tentatively suggested that perhaps truth telling was not always the most important thing, that sometimes a "romantic view…a view biased toward improvement" would be better. The prevailing faith in democracy was "from a factual standpoint…unwarranted…. We are probably one of the most bigoted, race-conscious peoples of the world but it is better not to stress the fact." Philosopher Kurt Riezler, one of the Commission's foreign advisers, thought this argument was heading in a very dangerous direction in its tacit abandonment of truth telling as an absolute: "even if the possibility of truth-telling is a fiction, this fiction must be upheld and not unmasked as fiction."[15] But Ruml persisted in his attempts to supplement the account of communication

12. Peatman, "Radio and Popular Music": 391.
13. Peatman, "Radio and Popular Music": 354.
14. Document 91, folder 1, box 5: 7, Commission on Freedom of Press Records, UCSC.
15. Record of discussion September 18/19, 1944, New York City, Document 21, folder 9, box 1, Commission on Freedom of Press Records, UCSC.

as truth telling with something else. He later distinguished the defensible, even admirable, "unfactual representation by symbol of what is essentially true," from the indefensible "deliberate use of error." Buck Rogers and Orphan Annie, he said, "are probably more truthful…than many of the facts which, though accurately reported, are misleading as symbols when applied back to the community." He even remarked that "we should reexamine the approach of the USSR to the press from this point of view because it may be that their notions of what is 'useful truth' may in fact not be so different from our own."[16]

The commissioners sought some guidance on the more emotional aspects of communication from psychologists Paul Lazarsfeld and Eric Fromm. MacLeish posed the commission's question to them:

> We find ourselves continually coming back to the question of whether on the affirmative side you demand enough of the press if you demand a very complex service of factual information, plus the provision of a forum in which controversy can take place, whether it isn't perhaps necessary to have something further, to demand of the press a use of the instruments of mass communication for some affirmative kind of what I would call—symbol perpetuation and the creation of symbols of validity.
>
> On the other side, we find ourselves faced with the question of whether the introduction into modern journalism in the United States of a communication of information through symbols which are highly emotive, and many of which are at a sub-rational level, isn't deleterious to the whole process of self-government, whether it doesn't undercut the operation of reason which, in theory at least, is necessary.

The commissioners frankly acknowledged that they lacked the intellectual tools that would be needed to weigh these important alternatives—each inadequate on its own—or to carry out the kind of investigation required. "It is very difficult for me personally to ask these questions," said MacLeish, "because I don't know in what language to ask them."[17] In reply, Fromm began to talk about the importance of "the emotional appeal of a kind of daydream satisfaction," which might be "entirely different and contradictory to the aim one has as a citizen in active participation in a democracy."[18] Fromm's skepticism about the overly rational and individualized civic paradigm had already been expressed in his wartime book *The Fear of Freedom*. There he had questioned the centrality of individual opinion formation in liberal democracies: "*the right to express our thoughts, however, means something only if we are able to have thoughts of our own.*" Like Adorno, Fromm thus skillfully skewered civic paradigm assumptions, writing instead of the "illusion of being self-willing individuals."[19]

16. Document 91C, folder 2, box 5, Record of discussion, September 28, 1946, Commission on Freedom of Press Records, UCSC.

17. Document 90A, folder 11, box 4, Commission on Freedom of Press Records, UCSC.

18. Document 90A, folder 11, box 4, Commission on Freedom of Press Records, UCSC.

19. Erich Fromm, *The Fear of Freedom* (London: Routledge and Kegan Paul, 1942): 207, 218.

It was, however, documentary filmmaker John Grierson, then working in Canada, who provided the most eloquent pleas to the commission for greater attention to the emotional and symbolic aspects of communication. He criticized MacLeish's draft general report for its "meat-axe cleavage between entertainment and the 'fare of fact and thought'" and for its "one string fiddle" repetition of the need to preserve "variety and diversity" in the supply of information: "MacLeish conceives it [entertainment] as come-on stuff and sugar for the pill, but dammit it isn't. Men don't live by bread alone, nor by fact alone and much of this entertainment is the folk stuff… of our technological time; the patterns of observation, of humor, of fancy, which make a technological society a human society." Grierson lamented that the American intellectuals on the commission remained deaf and blind to the considerable creative and symbolic achievements of American popular entertainment: "America may have lagged in the political forms which make for order in a technological society, but not in the imagery which makes for vitality, initiative, endurance and boldness of experiment in a technological society."[20] He castigated his fellow commissioners for their failure to understand the connections between pleasure and communication. As a working propagandist rather than a critic, he had a much surer sense of the relationship between affect and knowledge.

The commissioners were men of middle age and older, all but one of them born in the nineteenth century. None had grown up with radio. There were some things they knew they were in danger of just not understanding. Discussing television, John Dickinson said, "The thing that is puzzling me is why a man should be interested in seeing a man's mouth working as he makes a speech over the radio."[21] Brought together as experts, there were telling moments when the commissioners acknowledged their ignorance of popular media forms and the opacity of popular relationships to mass communication to their modes of analysis.

Debating civic paradigm and populist questions, the commission had little to say about music. In September 1944, however, in New York City, Arthur Schlesinger asked "whether music engenders social attitudes and hence whether the Commission should study its effects." Beardsley Ruml replied, "We don't know enough about it": "For instance, what causes the mass hysteria of young people who swoon to the music of Sinatra. Something very important may be going on here involving the communication of attitudes, but because we know so little, it must be beyond our scope. Lasswell agreed."[22] The commissioners thus acknowledged their bewilderment at certain kinds of new relationship to the media. In the published general report, *A Free and Responsible Press*, there was the recognition that "the utterance of critical or new ideas is seldom an appeal to pure reason, devoid of emotion, and the response is not necessarily a debate; it is always a function of the intelligence, the prejudice, the emotional biases of the audience…."[23] But the book as a whole demonstrated again that the commission was far more comfortable with the issues of regulation, the legal bases of free speech, the role of government in

20. Document 91, folder 1, box 5: 15, Commission on Freedom of Press Records, UCSC.

21. Document 108A, folder 3, box 8: 37, Commission on Freedom of Press Records, UCSC.

22. Record of discussion, September 18/19, 1944, New York City, Document 21, folder 9, box 1, Commission on Freedom of Press Records, UCSC.

23. Commission, *A Free and Responsible Press*: 7.

communication, preserving diversity of opinion, and the dangers of economic centralization than it was on this terrain of emotional communication. In part this was because the propaganda model had habituated American intellectuals to thinking of the dangers rather than the pleasures of emotional capture by radio. It led them to predict that too much communication addressed to the emotions and "irrational desires" would "eventually result in an audience unable to distinguish between true and false information so that people will lose faith in the medium as a whole."[24]

The puzzled reference to the Sinatra phenomenon is of course an allusion to a situation quite the opposite of this endemic disillusionment. It is a story about the enchantment of radio and the pleasures people found in adoring rather than doubting. Here was a case where radio had been instrumental in creating an intense, almost overwhelming emotional response in a particular audience. Through 1943, Sinatra had been performing at New York's Paramount Theater to crowds of bobby-soxed teenagers. It was only a few weeks after the commission's September meeting—on Columbus Day, October 11, 1944—that 30,000 teenagers, mainly girls, had tried to attend the Sinatra concert at the Paramount Theater, provoking something close to a riot. They screamed and swooned at the sight and sound of Sinatra, who was known from radio, primarily as a voice—"The Voice." Bruce Bliven wrote in the *New Republic*, "Thousands of girls profess to be spellbound just from hearing The Voice over the radio, never having seen him in the flesh."[25] There was at the concerts much discussion of Sinatra's appearance—thin, fragile. Bliven observed with surprise that "there is a solidity and sureness about him that are out of all proportion to his physical frailness."[26] [Figure P.1; Figure P.2]

Quite apart from the fact that these teenagers were skipping school to attempt to attend the concerts, mass behavior of this kind caused understandable public anxiety in the not-quite-postfascist era. A letter to the editor of the *New York Times* defending the young fans nonetheless observed, "Thank God that they line up for a Sinatra instead of for a Hitler."[27] Critical public discussion of the Sinatra phenomenon focused on this question of the public display of emotion. George H. Chatfield, member of the New York Board of Education, called for the board and the police and the courts to deal with the problem: "We can't tolerate young people making a public display of losing control of their emotions." His concern was truancy from school, but also this loss of control and perspective.[28] Another letter to the *Times* contrasted the "young people in Europe who are in camps or forced to do labor in Germany" with the hysterical behavior of the New York Sinatra fans who were "wasting" time outside the Paramount.[29] The fan behavior was thus not only emotionally excessive, it was a conspicuous waste of

24. "Definition of the Inquiry," Document 20A, folder 8, box 1: 7, Commission on Freedom of Press Records, UCSC.

25. Bruce Bliven, "The Voice and the Kids," *New Republic* 1944, reprinted in Steven Petkov and Leonard Mustazza (eds.) *The Frank Sinatra Reader* (New York: Oxford University Press, 1995): 33.

26. Bliven, "The Voice and the Kids": 33.

27. Narciso Puente Jr., letter to the editor, *New York Times*, October 19, 1944: 22.

28. "Sinatra Fans Pose Two Police Problems and Not the Less Serious Involves Truancy," *New York Times*, October 13, 1944: 21.

29. "Teenager Disapproves," *New York Times,* October 16, 1944: 18.

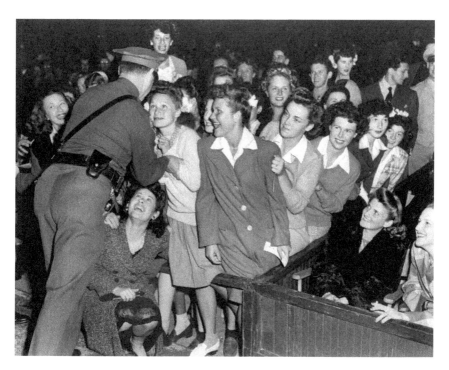

Figure P.1 Fans at a Frank Sinatra concert, Hollywood Bowl, August 14, 1943. CBS/Landov. The concert was a benefit for the Hollywood Bowl and the Los Angeles Philharmonic. *Los Angeles Times* music critic Isabel Morse Jones denounced the whole idea, claiming that "swooner-crooners" such as Sinatra purveyed a kind of "musical drug," an "opium of emotionalism" that did not belong in the Bowl. *Los Angeles Times*, Aug. 1, 1943: C6.

valuable time and effort—a national resource during wartime—comparable to the symbolic waste of material in zoot suits (the Sinatra fans were described as "sweatered and zoot-suited teenagers").[30] Only a little more sympathetically, one expert noted a tendency for youth during the war to "desire to herd," a "marked increase in the desire to be with crowds."[31]

The Sinatra phenomenon called out for explanation and interpretation. But the leading social science intellectuals in the United States lacked a language with which to talk about it. Their focus on information and the formation of personal opinion and the civic paradigm benefits of multiple perspectives meant that, while they could recognize in the Sinatra phenomenon a significant development in the history of media usage in the United States, they literally did not know what else to say about it. Their intellectual heritage fitted them to identify emotional engagement with radio only as negative and potentially fascistic. They sensed that both more and less was going on in this case.

30. "Mob Runs Riot in New York," *Washington Post*, October 13, 1944: 1.

31. Roy Sorenson, "Wartime Recreation for Adolescents," *Annals of the American Academy of Political and Social Science* 236 (November 1944): 147.

Figure P.2 Frank Sinatra fans at the Paramount Theater, New York, Oct. 15, 1944, just a few days after the widely reported "riots" at the venue. *New York Daily News* photo archive.

As the United States entered the Cold War, with its intense scrutiny of the slippery slide from liberal statism to communism, civic paradigm thinking about broadcasting became further embattled. Colonel McCormick, owner of the *Chicago Tribune*, denounced the commission's report and its members as "more or less obscure professors and crackpots mentioned in the report of the Committee on Un-American activities for Communist front activities no less than 67 times."[32] New Deal civic paradigm analysis was becoming politically untenable. The urgent need for democratizing American society became a less acceptable theme than the need to bring American democracy, understood now as a solid achievement rather than a work in progress, to the rest of the world. But alternative languages for talking about a mass medium such as radio were not ready to hand. American intellectuals concerned with the mass media were thus conscious at the end of WWII of the need to find ways to talk about the emotional dimension of radio's appeal, but had no idea how to link their exploratory thoughts on that subject to their major concern with radio's civic ambition. Their uncertainties and dissatisfactions with their own ability to reach conclusion displayed the exhaustion of the civic paradigm and a casting about for a new way of thinking.

32. "Col. McCormick Reacts," in Louis M. Lyons, "A Free and Responsible Press," *Nieman Reports* 1, no. 2 (April 1947): 3.

Radio itself was changing in the postwar period. As the new medium of television soaked up much of the national advertising dollar, the format of local spot advertising and recorded music that had been so lamented in the Blue Book was to become radio's mainstream future. Civic paradigm expectations shifted to television, which had through the 1950s its own era of heightened civic concern and a golden age of attention to "serious" drama and music. But by the 1960s, broadcast political discussion between people of opposing views had become routinized, not something that was going to change the world, just as classical music broadcasting became a niche market, not a reform movement. As William Boddy has observed, in television's case, the years between the golden age and the "vast wasteland" of the early 1960s were "few in number"—the cycle from high civic expectation to disillusion seemed even faster and more extreme than in the case of radio.[33] By the 1990s, it was the Internet that was going to revive civic life in America. The cyclical history should lead us not to cynicism, but to an attempt to understand what has happened in each cycle of hope and disillusion that might help us with the next big medium.

33. William Boddy, *Fifties Television: The Industry and Its Critics* (Urbana: University of Illinois Press, 1992): 107.

Conclusion

The American broadcasting industry in the 1930s attempted with some success to persuade the public that the free market in broadcasting was the only guarantee of freedom of speech on the air. But in radio's golden age there were also countervailing restraints—a set of ideas about the public sphere that radio could or should create—that shaped and constrained broadcasting. As broadcasting in the United States has moved since 1996 toward an even less restrained free market, still employing some of the arguments first elaborated by the industry in the 1930s, it is important to understand that American radio in its golden age was rather more civically minded and more closely responsive to government than we have remembered.[1] The American system of mainly commercial but regulated broadcasting survived in the years after 1934 because broadcasters—and especially the networks—made what now look like very significant efforts to comply with the spirit of a regulatory regime that did claim the capacity to discern what kinds of broadcasting were in the public interest. Programs made under the influence of what I have identified as the civic paradigm were intended to encourage the formation of an active, responsive, opinionated, and individualized public. This was, I have argued, a distinctive U.S. inflection to an international conversation about how to make radio work in the public and national interest.

For all the compromises and conflicts, there was and is a great deal to admire about the civic paradigm era in U.S. radio history. The practices of and ideas about radio developed in that era still stand today as fresh and creative. The attempts to find ways to make radio audiences active, to persuade them to discuss what they heard about politics and society, to combine their music listening with music making, were significant interventions. Radio might, more speculatively, be some of the context for political scientist Robert Putnam's much-discussed finding that the WWII generation—reared in the heyday of civic paradigm radio—was more civically engaged than those that came after. *Bowling Alone* named television as part of the cause of decline in social capital, but had little to say about radio's shaping of the earlier generations whose civic engagement Putnam rated more highly.[2] As a new generation debates discursive democracy, and tries forlornly to rescue commercial broadcast media from hitherto undreamed of levels of centralization and homogenization, we would do well to pay a little more attention to

---

1. Robert W. McChesney, "Theses on Media Deregulation," *Media, Culture & Society* 25 (2003): 125–33.

2. Robert D. Putnam, *Bowling Alone: The Collapse and Revival of American Community* (New York: Simon and Schuster, 2000).

what was said and done in the civic paradigm era, to listen carefully enough that we hear what they said—not just subsume them into our own era's sometimes cruder debates about high and popular culture, active and passive audiences, agency and submission.

Civic paradigm radio was premised on the assumption that exposing the radio audience to different points of view was a public good. While cloudily formulated populist claims of a right to broadcast went nowhere, the liberal response—the formulation of a right to hear all sides of public questions—remained for decades a pillar of broadcasting's contribution to American society. John Hartley has asked, in relation to audiences from the network television era, whether "generations-long enforced exposure to the others of our world" might have produced "a level of diplomatic sophistication, a Venusian skill in negotiating 'partial' and 'compromised' meanings."[3] Social scientists are beginning to investigate empirically the effects of low choice broadcast era television on political understanding and behavior—did the decades when three-quarters of the television audience watched the evening news produce more political engagement and less intransigent polarization than our current niche market media landscape?[4] Scholars and public intellectuals worry that continual exposure to only self-selected agreeable views on cable television or the Internet fosters extremism, accounts for some of the much remarked polarization of American political life in recent decades.[5] No one would want to turn back the clock or put the Internet genie back in its bottle, but there are nonetheless things to be learned from the realization that earlier generations had similar issues and dangers in mind. Much recent discussion of the media's role in producing intolerant dogmatism probably unknowingly echoes similar concerns in the 1930s. George V. Denny Jr. and John Studebaker would be nodding in agreement if we could sit them down to read the current literature on the connections between niche media specialization and political intolerance.

But nostalgia for the broadcast era would obviously be an unhelpful response to draw from the history I have tried to sketch in this book. It is also important to remember that the civic paradigm divided radio audiences, because some Americans rejected its valuing of cosmopolitan openness and readiness to change. A significant part of this book has attempted to explicate and understand those divisions and conflicts. We also need to understand and remember the divisiveness of the civic paradigm. This is much more uncomfortable territory, in part because today accusations about the divisiveness of liberal elites come most loudly and objectionably from the TV news channel Right.

I admire many of the civic paradigm radio activists I write about in this book, and would certainly have been a part of their audience had I lived in the 1930s. But the cultural history of media has to include consideration of conflict, of the unintended consequences of benign actions, of miscommunication as well as communication. I have tried hard not just to accept and repeat the self-assessment of the civic paradigm activists. Their story

3. John Hartley, "Flowers Powers: Mars or Venus?" *Flow* 2, no. 7 (June 24, 2005). Available: http://flowtv.org/?p=446. [January 21, 2010].

4. See Markus Prior, *Post-Broadcast Democracy: How Media Choice Increases Inequality in Political Involvement and Polarizes Elections* (New York: Cambridge University Press, 2007).

5. See Cass R. Sunstein, *Going to Extremes: How Like Minds Unite and Divide* (New York: Oxford University Press, 2009).

was about tolerant liberal elites battling popular prejudice and close-mindedness. Ordinary radio listeners have indeed at several points appeared in these pages as racially and religiously discriminatory populists. But I have also gone out of my way to try to show this cultural conflict from the other side—those moments when civic paradigm elites intolerantly rejected popular beliefs as evidence only of ignorance, stupidity, and limited experience of the world. When liberal elites went too far in valuing openness, empathy, tolerance, and compromise, they risked losing touch not only with ordinary American worldviews, but even with the crucial historical importance of moral certainty—as civic paradigm true believers often discovered when they took on ideological work for the nation during WWII.

The dialectic of moral certainty and perspectivalist empathy is a universal drama, but I have tried here too to make an at least occasionally comparative argument about the specificity of the U.S. case. Deweyan progressive ideas shaped American civic paradigm radio in both obvious and subtle ways. This book is also intended as an invitation to others to develop further the comparative and transnational history of radio—a field still in its infancy. Comparative approaches highlight the importance of writing contextualized media history, of setting the radio in the middle distance, not just creating more narratives of internal developments in broadcasting in one nation. Radio history should of course be contextualized in a broader cultural and social history, but radio also needs to be—as Kate Lacey has put it—"radically decentered" in radio history.[6] Radio, like other new media, always entered existing social and cultural worlds and created the possibility of significant changes, and in almost every case, people had already been thinking about the problems to which radio seemed to offer a new solution.

Much of this book has been about the production of personal opinion in response to mass media. The history of radio has important things to tell us about the history of individualism, and the development of ideas of self in everyday life. Personal opinion is so ubiquitous now, as individuals create "personal opinion blogs" on the web, or post videos of themselves speaking opinions on YouTube, obeying its injunction to "broadcast yourself," that it is easy to forget that the idea of personal opinion, and the practice of developing personal opinion in and against the mass media, has a history. Not so long ago, influential Americans perceived a need to school their fellow citizens in the art and craft of opinion formation. We have not well remembered that, just before the age of rock and roll and its new fears about listening and conformity, radio had been used in a concerted attempt to mass-produce individualism. That was the distinctive ambition of the civic paradigm, expressing some of the best hopes and qualities of a hard-working but imaginative liberalism that flowered for all too brief a time in the twentieth-century United States.

6. Kate Lacey, "Ten Years of Radio Studies: The Very Idea," *Radio Journal: International Studies in Broadcast and Audio Media* 6, no. 1 (Feb. 2009): 22.

Bibliography

Archival Materials

BBC Written Archives Centre:
BBC North American representative records.

Columbia University Library, Rare Book and Manuscript Library:
Bureau of Applied Social Research records.
James Lawrence Fly papers.
Paul F. Lazarsfeld papers.

Franklin D. Roosevelt Presidential Library, Hyde Park, NY:
President's personal file.

Library of American Broadcasting, University of Maryland:
Pamphlets and photos from the collections.

Library of Congress:
NBC history files, Recorded Sound Reference Center.
Lyman Bryson papers, Manuscript Division.
George Vernon Denny papers, Manuscript Division.

Music Educators National Conference Historical Center, University of Maryland, College Park:
Frances Elliott Clark papers.

National Archives at College Park:
Records of the Office of Education, RG 12.
Records of the Federal Communications Commission, RG 173.

New York Philharmonic Archives:
New York Philharmonic records.

New York Public Library, Manuscripts and Archives Division:
Town Hall Inc. records.
Institute for Propaganda Analysis papers.

Ohio State University Archives:
Institute for Education by Radio and Television records.

Princeton University Library, Manuscripts division:
Radio Broadcasting Collection.

Rockefeller Archive Center:
Rockefeller Foundation Archives.

Special Collections Research Center, University of Chicago Library:
Commission on Freedom of the Press Records.
University of Chicago, Office of the President, Hutchins Administration Records 1892–1951.
University of Chicago, Office of the Vice President Records 1937–46.

University of Oregon Library:
Chester S. Williams papers.
John T. Flynn papers.

Wisconsin Historical Society:
National Broadcasting Company Records.
H. V. Kaltenborn papers.
Allen Miller papers.
William Saxby Hedges papers.

Published Works

Adorno, Theodor W. "Analytical Study of the NBC Music Appreciation Hour." In *Current of Music: Elements of a Radio Theory*, ed. Robert Hullot-Kentor, 163–215. Cambridge: Polity, 2009.
———. "Analytical Study of the NBC Music Appreciation Hour." *Musical Quarterly* 78, no. 2 (Summer 1994): 325–77.
———. "The Radio Symphony: An Experiment in Theory." In *Radio Research* 1941, ed. Paul F. Lazarsfeld and Frank N. Stanton, 110–39. New York: Duell, Sloan and Pearce, 1941.
———. "Scientific Experiences of a European Scholar in America." In *The Intellectual Migration: Europe and America, 1930–1960*, ed. Donald Fleming and Bernard Bailyn, 338–70. Cambridge, MA: Harvard University Press, 1969.
———. "A Social Critique of Radio Music." In *Current of Music: Elements of a Radio Theory*, ed. Robert Hullot-Kentor, 133–43. Cambridge: Polity, 2009.
———. "Some Remarks on a Propaganda Publication of NBC." In *Current of Music: Elements of a Radio Theory*, ed. Robert Hullot-Kentor, 469–76. Cambridge: Polity, 2009.
———. "Radio Physiognomies." In *Current of Music: Elements of a Radio Theory*, ed. Robert Hullot-Kentor, 41–132. Cambridge: Polity, 2009.
Adorno, Theodor W., and George Simpson. "On Popular Music." *Studies in Philosophy and Social Science* 19 (1941): 17–48.
Albig, William. *Public Opinion*. New York: McGraw Hill, 1939.
Alpers, Benjamin. *Dictators, Democracy and American Public Culture: Envisioning the Totalitarian Enemy, 1920s–1950s*. Chapel Hill: University of North Carolina Press, 2003.
Angell, James R. *American Education: Addresses and Articles*. New Haven: Yale University Press, 1937.
———. "The Influence of Radio." In *Broadcasting and the Public: A Case Study in Social Ethics*, ed. Federal Council of the Churches of Christ in America. Nashville: Abingdon, 1938.
———. "The Moral Crisis of Democracy." *Vital Speeches of the Day* 2, no. 22 (Aug. 1936): 670–74.
———. "Radio and National Morale." *American Journal of Sociology* 47, no. 3 (Nov. 1941): 352–59.

Axtell, James. *The Making of Princeton University: From Woodrow Wilson to the Present.* Princeton: Princeton University Press, 2006.

Baker, Kenneth H. "Radio Listening and Socio-Economic Status." *Psychological Record* 1, no. 9 (Aug. 1937): 97–144.

Baldwin, Lillian. "Music Appreciation." *Music Educators Journal* 25, no. 2 (Oct. 1938): 30–31.

Barker, Chris. *Cultural Studies: Theory and Practice.* London: Sage, 2003.

Barlow, William. *Voice Over: The Making of Black Radio.* Philadelphia: Temple University Press, 1999.

Barnouw, Erik. *The Golden Web: A History of Broadcasting in the United States, 1933 to 1953.* New York: Oxford University Press, 1968.

———. *A Tower in Babel: A History of Broadcasting in the United States, to 1933.* New York: Oxford University Press, 1966.

Batts, H. Lewis. *History of the First Baptist Church at Macon.* Macon: Southern Press, 1968.

Beck, Ulrich, and Elisabeth Beck-Gernsheim. *Individualization: Institutionalized Individualism and Its Social and Political Consequences.* London: Sage, 2001.

———. *The Normal Chaos of Love.* Cambridge: Polity, 1995.

Benjamin, Louise M. *Freedom of the Air and the Public Interest: First Amendment Rights in Broadcasting to 1935.* Carbondale: Southern Illinois University Press, 2001.

———. *The NBC Advisory Council and Radio Programming, 1926–1945* Carbondale: Southern Illinois University Press, 2009.

Bensman, Marvin R. *The Beginning of Broadcast Regulation in the Twentieth Century.* Jefferson, NC: McFarland, 2000.

Bergreen, Laurence. *Look Now, Pay Later: The Rise of Network Broadcasting.* New York: Doubleday, 1980.

Bernays, Edward L. "Manipulating Public Opinion: The Why and the How." *American Journal of Sociology* 33, no. 6 (May 1928): 958–71.

Berube, Maurice R. *American School Reform: Progressive, Equity, and Excellence Movements, 1883–1993.* Westport, CT: Praeger, 1994.

Beville, H. M. "The ABCDs of Radio." *Public Opinion Quarterly* 4, no. 2 (Jun. 1940): 195–206.

——— *Social Stratification of the Radio Audience.* Princeton: Office of Radio Research, 1939.

Bianchi, William. *Schools of the Air: A History of Instructional Programs on Radio in the United States.* Jefferson, NC: McFarland, 2008.

Bineham, Jeffrey. "A Historical Account of the Hypodermic Model." *Mass Communication* 55, no. 3 (Sept. 1998): 230–47.

Bloom, Allan. *The Closing of the American Mind.* New York: Simon and Schuster, 1987.

Bonfiglio, Thomas P. *Race and the Rise of Standard American.* New York: Mouton de Gruyter, 2002.

Botstein, Leon. "Music of a Century: Museum Culture and the Politics of Subsidy." In *The Cambridge History of Twentieth Century Music*, ed. Nicholas Cook and Anthony Pople, 40–68. Cambridge: Cambridge University Press, 2004.

Boudon, Raymond, ed. *Paul Lazarsfeld, on Social Research and Its Language.* Chicago: University of Chicago Press, 1993.

Bourdieu, Pierre. *Distinction: A Social Critique of the Judgment of Taste.* London: Routledge, 1998.

Boyer, Paul S. *Urban Masses and Moral Order in America 1820–1920.* Cambridge: Harvard University Press, 1978.

Brehony, Kevin J. "From the Particular to the General, the Continuous to the Discontinuous: Progressive Education Revisited." *History of Education* 30, no. 5 (2001): 413–32.

Briggs, Asa. *The Birth of Broadcasting.* Oxford: Oxford University Press, 1961.

————. *History of Broadcasting in the United Kingdom: Volume I: The Birth of Broadcasting.* Oxford: Oxford University Press, 1995.

Brindze, Ruth. *The Truth About Radio: Not to Be Broadcast.* New York: Vanguard, 1937.

Brooker, Will, and Deborah Jermyn, eds. *The Audience Studies Reader.* London: Routledge, 2003.

Brown, Robert J. *Manipulating the Ether: The Power of Broadcast Radio in Thirties America.* Jefferson, NC: McFarland, 1998.

Bryson, Lyman. "Education, Citizenship and Character." *Teachers College Record* 42, no. 4 (1941): 297–300.

————. *A State Plan for Adult Education.* New York: American Association for Adult Education, 1934.

Buehler, E. C., ed. *American vs. British System of Radio Control.* New York: H. W. Wilson, 1933.

Buxton, William J. "The Political Economy of Communications Research." In *Information and Communication in Economics,* ed. Robert E. Babe, 147–75. Boston: Kluwer Academic, 1994.

————. "Reaching Human Minds: Rockefeller Philanthropy and Communications, 1935–1939." In *The Development of the Social Sciences in the United States and Canada: The Role of Philanthropy,* ed. Theresa Richardson and Donald Fisher, 177–92. Stamford, CT: Ablex, 1999.

Camporesi, Valeria. *Mass Culture and National Traditions: The BBC and American Broadcasting 1922–1954.* Florence: European Press, 2000.

Cantril, Hadley. "The Effect of Modern Technology and Organization upon Social Behavior." *Social Forces* 15, no. 4 (May 1937): 493–95.

Cantril, Hadley, and Gordon W. Allport. *The Psychology of Radio.* New York: Harper & Brothers, 1935.

Cantril, Hadley, Hazel Gaudet, and Herta Herzog. *The Invasion from Mars: A Study in the Psychology of Panic.* Princeton: Princeton University Press, 1940.

Carlat, Louis. "Sound Values: Radio Broadcasts of Symphonic Music and American Culture 1922–1939." PhD diss., Johns Hopkins University, 1995.

Chaffee, Steven H. "Differentiating the Hypodermic Model from Empirical Research: A Comment on Bineham's Commentaries." *Communication Monographs* 55, no. 3 (Sept. 1988): 247–50.

Chaffee, Steven H., and J. L. Hochheimer. "The Beginnings of Political Communication Research in the United States: Origins of the 'Limited Effects' Model." *Mass Communication Review Yearbook* 5 (1985): 75–104.

Charlesworth, Hector. "Broadcasting in Canada." *Annals of the American Academy of Political and Social Science* 177 (Jan. 1935): 42–48.

Chase, Gilbert, ed. *Music in Radio Broadcasting.* New York: McGraw Hill, 1946.

Chotzinoff, Samuel. *Toscanini: An Intimate Portrait.* New York: Alfred A. Knopf, 1956.

Clark, Frances E. "Music Appreciation and the New Day." *Music Supervisors Journal* 19, no. 3 (Feb. 1933): 12–20.

Cloud, Stanley, and Lynne Olson. *The Murrow Boys: Pioneers on the Frontlines of Broadcast Journalism.* Boston: Houghton Mifflin, 1996.

Cohen, Lizabeth. *Making a New Deal: Industrial Workers in Chicago, 1919–1939.* New York: Cambridge University Press, 1991.

Commission on Freedom of the Press. *A Free and Responsible Press.* Chicago: University of Chicago Press, 1947.

Corbett, Krystilyn. "The Rise of Private Property Rights in the Broadcast Spectrum." *Duke Law Journal* 46, no. 3 (Dec. 1996): 611–50.

Cox, Megan. "Chicago Radio Outlet Gets a Lot of Static." *Wall Street Journal,* Sept. 17, 1985, 1.

Craig, Douglas B. *Fireside Politics: Radio and Political Culture in the United States, 1920–1940.* Baltimore: Johns Hopkins University Press, 2000.

Craig, Steve. "How America Adopted Radio: Demographic Differences in Set Ownership Reported in the 1930–1950 U.S. Censuses." *Journal of Broadcasting & Electronic Media* 48, no. 2 (Jun. 2004): 179–96.

———. *Out of the Dark: A History of Radio and Rural America.* Tuscaloosa: University of Alabama Press, 2009.

Cramton, Peter. "The Efficiency of the FCC Spectrum Auctions." *Journal of Law and Economics* 41, no. 2, part 2 (Oct. 1998): 727–36.

Cremin, Lawrence A. *The Transformation of the School: Progressivism in American Education, 1876–1957.* New York: Alfred A. Knopf, 1964.

Culbert, David H. *News for Everyman: Radio and Foreign Affairs in Thirties America.* Westport, CT: Greenwood, 1976.

Czitrom, Daniel J. *Media and the American Mind: From Morse to McLuhan.* Chapel Hill: University of North Carolina Press, 1982.

Damousi, Joy. "'The Filthy American Twang': Elocution, the Advent of American 'Talkies,' and Australian Cultural Identity." *American Historical Review* 112, no. 2 (Apr. 2007): 394–416.

Day, Patrick. *The Radio Years: A History of Broadcasting in New Zealand.* Auckland: Auckland University Press in association with the Broadcasting History Trust, 1994.

Denning, Michael. *The Cultural Front: The Laboring of American Culture in the Twentieth Century.* New York: Verso, 1998.

Dennis, Everette E., and Ellen Wartella, eds. *American Communication Research: The Remembered History.* Mahwah, NJ: Lawrence Erlbaum, 1996.

Denny, George V. Jr. "Bring Back the Town Meeting!" In *Capitalizing Intelligence: Eight Essays on Adult Education,* ed. Warren C. Seyfert, 101–28. Cambridge, MA: Graduate School of Education, Harvard University, 1937.

———. *Town Meeting Discussion Leader's Handbook.* New York: Town Hall, 1940.

Dewey, John. "American Education Past and Future." In *The Later Works of John Dewey 1925–1953, Volume 6,* ed. Jo Ann Boydston, 90–98. Carbondale: Southern Illinois University Press, 1990.

———. "Anthropology and Ethics." In *The Later Works of John Dewey 1925–1953, Volume 3,* ed. Jo Ann Boydston, 11–24. Carbondale: Southern Illinois University Press, 1990.

———. *Art as Experience.* London: George Allen and Unwin, 1934.

———. *Democracy and Education: An Introduction to the Philosophy of Education.* 1916. Reprint, New York: Macmillan, 1929.

———. "Individualism Old and New." In *The Later Works of John Dewey 1925–1953, Volume 5,* ed. Jo Ann Boydston, 41–65. Carbondale: Southern Illinois University Press, 1990.

———. "Liberalism and Social Action." In *The Later Works of John Dewey 1925–1953, Volume 11,* ed. Jo Ann Boydston, 1–41. Carbondale: Southern Illinois University Press, 1990.

———. "Philosophies of Freedom." In *The Later Works of John Dewey 1927–1928, Volume 3,* ed. Jo Ann Boydston, 92–114. Carbondale: Southern Illinois University Press, 1990.

———. *The Public and Its Problems.* New York: Henry Holt, 1927.

———. "Radio's Influence on the Mind." In *The Later Works of John Dewey 1925–1953, Volume 9, 1933–1934,* ed. Jo Ann Boydston, 309. Carbondale: Southern Illinois University Press, 1990.

———. "What I Believe." In *The Later Works of John Dewey 1925–1953, Volume 5,* ed. Jo Ann Boydston, 267–78. Carbondale: Southern Illinois University Press, 1990.

Doerksen, Clifford. *American Babel: Rogue Radio Broadcasters of the Jazz Age*. Philadelphia: University of Pennsylvania Press, 2005.

Doob, Leonard W. *Propaganda: Its Psychology and Technique*. New York: Henry Holt, 1935.

Douglas, Susan J. *Listening In: Radio and the American Imagination*. New York: Times Books, 1999.

———. "Mass Media: From 1945 to the Present." In *A Companion to Post-1945 America*, ed. Jean Christophe Agnew and Roy Rosenzweig, 78–95. Oxford: Blackwell, 2002.

———. "Notes toward a History of Media Audiences." *Radical History Review* 54 (1992): 127–38.

Downes, Olin. "Be Your Own Music Critic." In *Be Your Own Music Critic: The Carnegie Hall Anniversary Lectures*, ed. Robert E. Simon Jr., 3–40. New York: Doubleday, Doran, 1941.

Dryer, Sherman. *Radio in Wartime*. New York: Greenberg, 1942.

Dryzek, S. "Opinion Research and the Counter-Revolution in American Political Science." *Political Studies* 40 (1992): 679–94.

Dunning, John. *On the Air: An Encyclopedia of Old-Time Radio*. New York: Oxford University Press, 1998.

Dykema, Peter W. *Radio Music for Boys and Girls*. New York: Radio Institute for the Audible Arts, 1935.

Ely, Mary L. *Why Forums?* New York: American Association for Adult Education, 1937.

Ely, Melvin P. *The Adventures of Amos 'n Andy: A Social History of an American Phenomenon*. New York: Free Press, 1991.

Fiske, John. *Television Culture*. London: Methuen, 1987.

———. "TV: Re-Situating the Popular in the People." *Continuum* 1, no. 2 (1987): 56–66.

Fiske, Marjorie. *Survey of Materials on the Psychology of Radio Listening*. New York: Bureau of Applied Social Research, 1943.

Foner, Eric. *The Story of American Freedom*. New York: W. W. Norton, 1998.

Fones-Wolf, Elizabeth. "Promoting a Labor Perspective in the American Mass Media: Unions and Radio in the CIO Era, 1936–56." *Media, Culture & Society* 22, no. 3 (2000): 285–307.

Foucault, M. "Technologies of the Self." In *Technologies of the Self*, ed. L. Martin, H. Gutman, and P. Hutton, 16–49. Amherst: University of Massachusetts Press, 1988.

Frank, Glenn. "Radio as an Educational Force." *Annals of the American Academy of Political and Social Science* 177 (Jan. 1935): 119–22.

———. "The Role of Music in the Life of the Time." *Music Supervisors Journal* 20, no. 1 (Oct. 1933): 6–7.

Frank, Mortimer. *Arturo Toscanini: The NBC Years*. Portland: Amadeus Press, 2002.

Frith, Simon. "The Pleasures of the Hearth: The Making of BBC Light Entertainment." In *Formations of Pleasure*, ed. Fredric Jameson, Victor Burgin, and Tony Bennett, 101–23. London: Routledge, 1983.

Fromm, Erich. *The Fear of Freedom*. London: Routledge and Kegan Paul, 1942.

Frost, S. E. Jr. *Education's Own Stations: The History of Broadcast Licenses Issued to Educational Institutions*. Chicago: University of Chicago Press, 1937.

———. *Is American Radio Democratic? A Study of the American System of Radio*. Chicago: University of Chicago Press, 1937.

Gary, Brett. *The Nervous Liberals: Propaganda Anxieties from Word War I to the Cold War*. New York: Columbia University Press, 1999.

Gasher, Mike. "Invoking Public Support for Public Broadcasting: The Aird Commission Revisited." *Canadian Journal of Communication* 23, no. 2 (1998). Online. Available: http://www.cjc-online.ca/index.php/journal/article/view/1032. [Jan. 27, 2010].

Giddens, Antony. *The Consequences of Modernity.* Stanford, CA: Stanford University Press, 1990.

Gienow-Hecht, Jessica C. E. "Trumpeting Down the Walls of Jericho: The Politics of Art, Music and Emotion in German-American Relations, 1870–1920." *Journal of Social History* 36, no. 3 (Spring 2003): 585–613.

Gilbert, James. "Midcult, Middlebrow, Middle Class." *Reviews in American History* 20, no. 4 (Dec. 1992): 543–48.

Gitlin, Todd. "Media Sociology: The Dominant Paradigm." *Theory and Society* 6, no. 2 (1978): 205–53.

Glander, Timothy. *Origins of Mass Communications Research during the American Cold War.* Mahwah, NJ: L. Erlbaum, 2000.

Glenn, Mabelle. "National Music Discrimination Contest: Results and Conclusions." *Music Supervisors Journal* 18, no. 5 (May 1932): 34–35.

Godfried, Nathan. *WCFL, Chicago's Voice of Labor, 1926–78.* Urbana: University of Illinois Press, 1997.

Goodman, David. "Democracy and Public Discussion in the Progressive and New Deal Eras: From Civic Competence to the Expression of Opinion." *Studies in American Political Development* 18, no. 2 (Fall 2004): 81–111.

———. "Distracted Listening: On Not Making Sound Choices in the 1930s." In *Sound in the Age of Mechanical Reproduction,* ed. Susan Strasser and David Suisman, 15–46. Philadelphia: University of Pennsylvania Press, 2010.

———. "Programming in the Public Interest: America's Town Meeting of the Air." In *NBC: America's Network,* ed. Michele Hilmes, 44–60. Berkeley: University of California Press, 2007.

Griffen-Foley, Bridget. "The Birth of a Hybrid: The Shaping of the Australian Radio Industry." *Radio Journal* 2, no. 3 (2004): 153–69.

———. *Changing Stations: The Story of Australian Commercial Radio.* Sydney: University of New South Wales Press, 2009.

Gustafson, Ruth. "Merry Throngs and Street Gangs: The Fabrication of Whiteness and the Worthy Citizen in Early Vocal Instruction and Music Appreciation." PhD diss., University of Wisconsin-Madison, 2005.

———. *Race and Curriculum: Music in Childhood Education.* New York: Palgrave Macmillan, 2009.

Habermas, Jürgen. *The Structural Transformation of the Public Sphere: An Inquiry into a Category of Bourgeois Society.* Translated by Thomas Burger and Frederick Lawrence. Cambridge, MA: MIT Press, 1991.

Halper, Donna. *Invisible Stars: A Social History of Women in American Broadcasting.* Armonk, NY: M. E. Sharpe, 2001.

Hard, William. "Radio and Public Opinion." *Annals of the American Academy of Political and Social Science* 177 (Jan. 1935): 105–13.

Hart, Floyd T. "The Relation of Jazz Music to Art." *Music Educators Journal* 26, no. 1 (Sept. 1939): 24–25, 73.

Hays, Arthur G. "Civic Discussion over the Air." *Annals of the American Academy of Political and Social Science* 213 (Jan. 1941): 37–46.

Hazlett, Thomas W. "Assigning Property Rights to Radio Spectrum Users: Why Did FCC License Auctions Take 67 Years?" *Journal of Law and Economics* 41, no. 2, part 2 (Oct. 1998): 529–75.

———. "The Rationality of U.S. Regulation of the Broadcast Spectrum." *Journal of Law and Economics* 33, no. 1 (Apr. 1990): 133–75.

Heistad, Mark J. "Radio without Sponsors: Public Service Programming in Network Sustaining Time, 1928–1952." PhD diss., University of Minnesota, 1998.

Herman, Ellen. *The Romance of American Psychology: Political Culture in the Age of Experts.* Berkeley: University of California Press, 1995.

Herzberg, Max J. "Tentative Units in Radio Program Appreciation." *The English Journal* 24, no. 7 (Sept. 1935): 545–55.

Herzog, Herta. "Children and Their Leisure Time Listening to the Radio: Typescript Paper B0001." In *Reports of the Bureau of Applied Social Research on Microfiche.* New York: Clearwater, 1981.

———. "Professor Quiz: A Gratifications Study." In *Radio Research* 1941, ed. Paul F. Lazarsfeld and Frank N. Stanton, 34–45. New York: Duell, Sloan and Pearce, 1941.

Hesser, Ernest G. "Music in the New Social Order." *Music Educators Journal* 22, no. 5 (Mar. 1936): 21–23.

Hettinger, Herman, S. "Broadcasting in the United States." *Annals of the American Academy of Political and Social Science* 177 (Jan. 1935): 1–14.

———. "The Future of Radio as an Advertising Medium." *Journal of Business of the University of Chicago* 7, no. 4 (Oct. 1934): 283–95.

———. "Review of 'Radio's Listening Groups: The United States and Great Britain.'" *Annals of the American Academy of Political and Social Science* 218 (Nov. 1941): 239–40.

Heyer, Paul. *The Medium and the Magician: Orson Welles, the Radio Years, 1934–1952.* Lanham, MD: Rowman and Littlefield, 2005.

Hill, Frank E. *The Groups Tune In.* Washington, DC: Federal Radio Education Committee, 1940.

———. *Listen and Learn: Fifteen Years of Adult Education on Radio.* New York: American Association for Adult Education, 1937.

———. *Radio's Listening Groups: The United States and Great Britain.* New York: Columbia University Press, 1941.

Hill, Frank E., and W. E. Williams. *Radio's Listening Groups: The United States and Great Britain.* New York: Columbia University Press, 1941.

Hilmes, Michele. "British Quality, American Chaos: Historical Dualisms and What They Leave Out." *Radio Journal* 1, no. 1 (2003): 13–27.

———. "Front Line Family: 'Women's Culture' Comes to the BBC." *Media, Culture & Society* 29, no. 1 (2006): 5–29.

———. *Hollywood and Broadcasting: From Radio to Cable.* Urbana: University of Illinois Press, 1990.

———, ed. *NBC: America's Network.* Berkeley: University of California Press, 2007.

———. *Radio Voices: American Broadcasting, 1922–1952.* Minneapolis: University of Minnesota Press, 1997.

Hirsch, Jerrold. *Portrait of America: A Cultural History of the Federal Writers Project.* Chapel Hill: University of North Carolina Press, 2003.

Hofstadter, Richard. *The Paranoid Style in American Politics and Other Essays.* New York: Knopf, 1965.

Holter, F. "Radio among the Unemployed." *Journal of Applied Psychology* 23, no. 1 (1939): 163–69.

Horkheimer, Max, and Theodor W. Adorno. *Dialectic of Enlightenment.* 1944. Reprint, London: Allen Lane, 1973.

Horowitz, Joseph. *Classical Music in America: A History of Its Rise and Fall.* New York: W. W. Norton, 2005.

———. "'Sermons in Tones': Sacralization as a Theme in American Classical Music." *American Music* 16, no. 3 (Fall 1998): 328–29.

———. *Understanding Toscanini: How He Became an American Culture-God and Helped Create a New Audience for Old Music*. New York: Alfred A. Knopf, 1987.

Horten, Gerd. *Radio Goes to War: The Cultural Politics of Propaganda during World War II*. Berkeley: University of California Press, 2001.

Howe, Sondra W. "The NBC Music Appreciation Hour: Radio Broadcasts of Walter Damrosch, 1928–1942." *Journal of Research in Music Education* 5, no. 1 (Spring 2003): 64–77.

Hull, W. H. N. "The Public Control of Broadcasting: The Canadian and Australian Experiences." *The Canadian Journal of Economics and Political Science/ Revue Canadienne d'Economique et de Science Politique* 28, no. 1 (Feb. 1962): 114–26.

Hullot-Kentor, Robert, ed. "Second Salvage: Prolegomenon to a Reconstruction of 'Current of Music.'" *Cultural Critique* 60 (Spring 2005): 134–69.

———. *Theodor Adorno: Current of Music: Elements of a Radio Theory*. Frankfurt: Suhrkamp, 2006.

Huyssen, Andreas. *After the Great Divide: Modernism, Mass Culture, Postmodernism*. Bloomington: Indiana University Press, 1986.

Hyman, Herbert H. *Taking Society's Measure: A Personal History of Survey Research*. New York: Russell Sage Foundation, 1991.

Inglis, K. S. *This Is the ABC: The Australian Broadcasting Commission 1932–1983*. Carlton: Melbourne University Press, 1983.

Jackson, Joseph G. "Vintage Broadcasting: The End of an Era—WMAZ AM." *Antique Radio Classified* 15, no. 3 (March 1998). Online. Available: http://www.antiqueradio.com/wmaz_03-98.html. [Jan. 27, 2010].

Jenemann, David. *Adorno in America*. Minneapolis: University of Minnesota Press, 2007.

Johnson, Blair T., and Diane R. Nichols. "Social Psychologists' Expertise in the Public Interest: Civilian Morale Research during World War II." *Journal of Social Issues* 54, no. 1 (1998): 53–77.

Johnson, Lesley. "The Intimate Voice of Australian Radio." *Historical Journal of Film, Radio and Television* 3, no. 1 (1983): 43–50.

———. *The Unseen Voice: A Cultural Study of Early Australian Radio*. London: Routledge, 1988.

Kaltenborn, H. V. *I Broadcast the Crisis*. New York: Random House, 1938.

Karl, Barry. *The Uneasy State: The United States from 1915 to 1945*. Chicago: University of Chicago Press, 1983.

Katz, Elihu, and Paul F. Lazarsfeld. *Personal Influence: The Part Played by People in the Flow of Mass Communications*. Glencoe, IL: Free Press, 1955.

Keith, William M. *Democracy as Discussion: Civil Education and the American Forum Movement*. Lanham, MD: Lexington Books, 2007.

Keliher, Alice V. *Life and Growth*. New York: D. Appleton-Century, 1938.

Kerby, Philip. "Radio's Music." *The North American Review* 245, no. 2 (Summer 1938): 300–314.

Kirkpatrick, Bill. "Localism in American Media 1920–1934." PhD diss., University of Wisconsin-Madison, 2006.

———. "Localism in American Media Policy, 1920–34: Reconsidering a 'Bedrock Concept.'" *Radio Journal: International Studies in Broadcast and Audio Media* 4, nos. 1, 2, and 3 (Oct. 2007): 87–110.

Koch, Howard. *As Time Goes By: Memoirs of a Writer*. New York: Harcourt Brace Jovanovich, 1979.

Kunzman, Robert, and David Tyack. "Educational Forums of the 1930s: An Experiment in Adult Civic Education." *American Journal of Education* 111, no. 3 (May 2005): 320–40.

Lacey, Kate. "Ten Years of Radio Studies: The Very Idea." *Radio Journal: International Studies in Broadcast and Audio Media* 6, no. 1 (Feb. 2009): 21–32.

———. "Towards a Periodization of Listening." *International Journal of Cultural Studies* 3, no. 2 (2000): 279–88.

LaFount, Harold. "Should the US Adopt the British System of Radio Control?" *Congressional Digest* 12, nos. 8/9 (Aug./Sept. 1933): 193–93.

Lagemann, Ellen C. *An Elusive Science: The Troubling History of Education Research.* Chicago: University of Chicago Press, 2002.

Lanza, Joseph. *Elevator Music.* New York: St. Martins Press, 1994.

La Prade, Ernest. *Broadcasting Music.* New York: Rinehart, 1947.

Lazarsfeld, Paul F. "An Episode in the History of Social Research: A Memoir." In *The Intellectual Migration: Europe and America, 1930–1960,* ed. Donald Fleming and Bernard Bailyn, 270–337. Cambridge, MA: Harvard University Press, 1969.

———. "Interchangeability of Indices in the Measurement of Economic Influences." *Journal of Applied Psychology* 23, no. 1 (1939): 33–45.

———. *Radio and the Printed Page: An Introduction to the Study of Radio and Its Role in the Communication of Ideas.* New York: Duell, Sloan and Pearce, 1940.

———. "Remarks on Administrative and Critical Communications Research." *Studies in Philosophy and Social Science* 9 (1941): 3–20.

———. *Should She Have Music?* New York: Bureau of Applied Social Research, paper B-0135, Bureau of Applied Social Research microfilm collection. New York: Clearwater, 1981.

———. "Some Remarks on the Role of Mass Media in So-Called Tolerance Propaganda." *Journal of Social Issues* 3, no. 3 (Summer 1947): 17–25.

Lazarsfeld, Paul F., and Harry H. Field. *The People Look at Radio: Report on a Survey.* Chapel Hill: University of North Carolina Press, 1946.

Lazarsfeld, Paul F., and Robert K. Merton. "Mass Communication, Popular Taste, and Organized Social Action." In *The Communication of Ideas: A Series of Addresses,* ed. Lyman Bryson, 95–118. New York: Harper & Brothers, 1948.

Leach, Eugene E. "'Mental Epidemics': Crowd Psychology and American Culture, 1890–1940." *American Studies* 33, no. 1 (Spring 1992): 5–29.

———. "Tuning out Education: The Cooperation Doctrine in Radio, 1922–38." Originally published in *Current* in January, February, and March 1983. Online. Available: http://www.current.org/coop/index.shtml. [Jan. 27, 2010].

———. "'Voices out of the Night': Radio Research and Ideas about Mass Behavior in the United States, 1920–1950." *Canadian Review of American Studies* 20 (1989): 191–209.

Lears, T. J. Jackson. *Fables of Abundance: A Cultural History of Advertising in America.* New York: Basic Books, 1994.

Lee, Alfred McClung, and Elizabeth B. Lee. *The Fine Art of Propaganda: A Study of Father Coughlin's Speeches.* New York: Harcourt Brace, 1939.

LeMahieu, D. L. *A Culture for Democracy: Mass Communication and the Cultivated Mind in Britain between the Wars.* Oxford: Clarendon Press, 1988.

Lenthall, Bruce. *Radio's America: The Great Depression and the Rise of Modern Mass Culture.* Chicago: University of Chicago Press, 2007.

Levin, Thomas Y., and Michael von der Linn. "Elements of a Radio Theory: Adorno and the Princeton Radio Research Project." *The Music Quarterly* 78, no. 2 (Summer 1994): 316–24.

Levine, Justin. "A History and Analysis of the Federal Communications Commission's Response to Radio Broadcast Hoaxes." *Federal Communications Law Journal* 52, no. 2 (2000): 273–320.

Levine, Lawrence W. *Highbrow/Lowbrow: The Emergence of Cultural Hierarchy in America.* Cambridge, MA: Harvard University Press, 1988.

Levine, Lawrence W., and Cornelia R. Levine. *The People and the President: America's Conversation with FDR.* Boston: Beacon Press, 2002.

Lewis, Tom. "'A Godlike Presence': The Impact of Radio on the 1920s and 1930s." *OAH Magazine of History* 6, no. 4 (1992): 26–33.

Lippmann, Walter. *The Phantom Public* New York: Macmillan, 1927.

———. *Public Opinion.* New York: Harcourt, Brace, 1922.

Lott, R. Allen. *From Paris to Peoria: How European Piano Virtuosos Brought Classical Music to the American Heartland.* New York: Oxford University Press, 2003.

Loviglio, Jason. *Radio's Intimate Public: Network Broadcasting and Mass-Mediated Democracy.* Minneapolis: University of Minnesota Press, 2005.

———. "Vox Pop: Network Radio and the Voice of the People." In *The Radio Reader: Essays in the Cultural History of Radio,* ed. Michele Hilmes and Jason Loviglio, 89–112. New York: Routledge, 2002.

Maltin, Leonard. *The Great American Broadcast: A Celebration of Radio's Golden Age.* New York: Dutton, 1997.

Marchand, Roland. *Advertising the American Dream: Making Way for Modernity, 1920–1940.* Berkeley: University of California Press, 1985.

———. *Creating the Corporate Soul: The Rise of Public Relations and Corporate Imagery in American Big Business.* Berkeley: University of California Press, 1998.

Marcus, Kenneth H. *Musical Metropolis: Los Angeles and the Creation of a Music Culture 1880–1940.* New York: Palgrave Macmillan, 2004.

Markowitz, Michael. "The Slow Death of Classical Music." *Media Life,* June 21, 2002. Online. Available: http://www.medialifemagazine.com/news2002/jun02/jun17/5_fri/news3friday.html. [Jan. 27, 2010].

Marsh, C. S., ed. *Educational Broadcasting 1937: Proceedings of the Second National Conference on Educational Broadcasting.* Chicago: University of Chicago Press, 1938.

Mattson, Kevin. *Creating a Democratic Public: The Struggle for Urban Participatory Democracy During the Progressive Era.* University Park, PA: Pennsylvania State University Press, 1998.

McChesney, Robert. *Rich Media, Poor Democracy: Communication Politics in Dubious Times, the History of Communication.* Urbana: University of Illinois Press, 1999.

———. *Telecommunications, Mass Media, and Democracy: The Battle for the Control of U.S. Broadcasting, 1928–1935.* New York: Oxford University Press, 1993.

———. "Theses on Media Deregulation." *Media, Culture & Society* 25 (2003): 125–33.

McFadden, Margaret T. "'America's Boy Friend Who Can't Get a Date': Gender, Race, and the Cultural Work of the Jack Benny Program, 1932–1946." *Journal of American History* 80 (Jun. 1993): 113–34.

———. "'Anything Goes': Gender and Knowledge in the Comic Popular Culture of the 1930s." PhD diss., Yale University, 1996.

McGerr, Michael. *The Decline of Popular Politics: The American North 1865–1928.* New York: Oxford University Press, 1986.

McKay, Anne. "Speaking Up: Voice Amplification and Women's Struggle for Public Expression." In *Technology and Women's Voices: Keeping in Touch,* ed. Cheris Kramarae, 198–203. New York: Routledge, 1988.

Merton, Robert K. *Social Theory and Social Structure.* New York: Free Press, 1968.

Meyrowitz, Joshua. "Media and Behavior: A Missing Link." In *McQuail's Reader in Mass Communication Theory*, ed. Denis McQuail, 99–108. London: Sage, 2002.

Miller, Clyde. *How to Detect and Analyze Propaganda.* New York: Town Hall, 1939.

Miller, Edward D. *Emergency Broadcasting and 1930s American Radio.* Philadelphia: Temple University Press, 2003.

Miller, Neville. "The Place of Radio in American Life: A Free People Can Never Tolerate Government Control." *Vital Speeches of the Day* 4, no. 23 (Sept. 1936): 715–17.

Miller, Thomas W. "The Influence of Progressivism on Music Education." *Journal of Research in Music Education* 14, no. 1 (Spring 1966): 3–16.

Mills, C. Wright. *The Sociological Imagination.* New York: Oxford University Press, 1959.

Morgenstern, Sheldon. *No Vivaldi in the Garage: A Requiem for Classical Music in North America.* Boston: Northeastern University Press, 2001.

Morley, David. "Active Audience Theory: Pendulums and Pitfalls." *Journal of Communication* 43, no. 4 (Autumn 1993): 13–20.

Morris, Meaghan. "Banality in Cultural Studies." In *Logics of Television*, ed. Patricia Mellencamp, 14–43. Bloomington: Indiana University Press, 1990.

Morrison, David. "The Beginning of Mass Communication Research." *European Journal of Sociology* 19 (1978): 347–59.

———. "Kultur and Culture: The Case of Theodor W. Adorno and Paul F. Lazarsfeld." *Social Research* 45, no. 2 (1978): 331–55.

Mueller, John H., and Kate Heynes. *Trends in Musical Taste.* Bloomington: Indiana University Press, 1941.

Mugglestone, Lynda. *Talking Proper: The Rise of Accent as Social Symbol.* Oxford: Oxford University Press, 2007.

Murray, Matthew. "'The Tendency to Deprave and Corrupt Morals': Regulation and Irregular Sexuality in Golden Age Radio Comedy." In *The Radio Reader: Essays in the Cultural History of Radio*, ed. Michele Hilmes and Jason Loviglio, 135–56. New York: Routledge, 2002.

Nachman, Gerald. *Raised on Radio.* New York: Pantheon Books, 1998.

Napoli, Philip. "Empire of the Middle: Radio and the Emergence of an Electronic Society." PhD diss., Columbia University, 1998.

National Broadcasting Company. *NBC Interprets Public Service in Radio Broadcasting.* New York: NBC, 1940.

———. *The NBC 1937 Yearbook: A Report of the National Broadcasting Company's Service to the Public in Its Eleventh Year.* New York: NBC, 1938.

Newman, Kathy. "The Forgotten Fifteen Million: Black Radio, the 'Negro Market' and the Civil Rights Movement." *Radical History Review* 76 (2000): 115–35.

———. *Radio Active: Advertising and Consumer Activism, 1935–1947.* Berkeley: University of California Press, 2004.

Ostrander, Marie C. "Music Education by Radio." *Music Educators Journal* 25, no. 3 (Dec. 1938): 28–29.

Overstreet, Harry O., and Bonaro W. Overstreet. *Town Meeting Comes to Town.* New York: Harper & Brothers, 1938.

Paglin, Max D., James R. Hobson, and Joel Rosenbloom, eds. *The Communications Act: A Legislative History of the Major Amendments, 1934–1996.* Silver Spring, MD: Pike & Fischer, 1999.

Paley, William S. "Broadcasting and American Society." *Annals of the American Academy of Political and Social Science* 213 (Jan. 1941): 62–68.

———. "Radio and the Humanities." *Annals of the American Academy of Political and Social Science* 177 (Jan. 1935): 94–104.

Pandora, Katherine. "'Mapping the New Mental World Created by Radio': Media Messages, Cultural Politics, and Cantril and Allport's the Psychology of Radio." *Journal of Social Issues* 54, no. 1 (1998): 7–27.

———. *Rebels within the Ranks: Psychologists' Critique of Scientific Authority and Democratic Realities in New Deal America*. New York: Cambridge University Press, 1997.

Passanella, Ann. *The Mind Traveller: A Guide to Paul F. Lazarsfeld's Communication Research Papers*. New York: Freedom Forum Media Studies Center, 1994.

Peatman, John G. "Radio and Popular Music." In *Radio Research* 1942–1943, ed. Paul F. Lazarsfeld and Frank N. Stanton, 335–93. New York: Duell, Sloan and Pearce, 1944.

Pegolotti, James A. *Deems Taylor: A Biography*. Boston: Northeastern University Press, 2003.

Perry, Stephen D. "Securing Programming on Live Local Radio: WDZ Reaches Rural Illinois 1929–1939." *Journal of Radio Studies* 8 (2001): 347–71.

Perse, Elizabeth. "Herta Herzog." In *Women in Communication: A Biographical Sourcebook*, ed. Nancy Signorielli, 202–11. Westport, CT: Greenwood, 1996.

Peter, Paul, F. "The American Listener in 1940." *Annals of the American Academy of Political and Social Science* 213 (Jan. 1941): 1–8.

Peters, John D. *Speaking into the Air: A History of the Idea of Communication*. Chicago: University of Chicago Press, 1999.

———. "The Uncanniness of Mass Communication in Interwar Social Thought." *Journal of Communications* 46, no. 3 (Summer 1996): 108–23.

Petersen-Perlman, Deborah S. "Opera for the People: The Metropolitan Opera Goes on the Air." *Journal of Radio Studies* 2, no. 1 (1993): 189–204.

Petkov, Steven, and Leonard Mustazza, eds. *The Frank Sinatra Reader*. New York: Oxford University Press, 1995.

Pickett, Paul C. "Contributions of John Ward Studebaker to American Education." PhD diss., State University of Iowa, 1967.

Pooley, Jefferson. "An Accident of Memory: Edward Shils, Paul Lazarsfeld and the History of American Mass Communication Research." PhD diss., Columbia University, 2006.

———. "Fifteen Pages That Shook the Field: Personal Influence, Edward Shils, and the Remembered History of Mass Communication Research." *Annals of the American Academy of Political and Social Science* 608, no. 1 (2006): 130–56.

Prior, Markus. *Post-Broadcast Democracy: How Media Choice Increases Inequality in Political Involvement and Polarizes Elections*. New York: Cambridge University Press, 2007.

Putnam, Robert D. *Bowling Alone: The Collapse and Revival of American Community*. New York: Simon and Schuster, 2000.

Raboy, Marc. *Missed Opportunities: The Story of Canada's Broadcasting Policy*. Montreal: McGill-Queens University Press, 1990.

Randolph, David. "Lewisohn Intermission Talk." *Music Educators Journal* 38, no. 2 (1951): 31–60.

Razlogova, Elena. "True Crime Radio and Listener Disenchantment with Network Broadcasting, 1935–1946." *American Quarterly* 58, no. 1 (Mar. 2006): 137–58.

———. "The Voice of the Listener: Americans and the Radio Industry 1920–1950." PhD diss., George Mason University, 2003.

Reith, J. C. W. *Broadcast over Britain*. London: Hodder and Stoughton, 1924.

Reese, William J. *America's Public Schools: From the Common School to "No Child Left Behind"*. Baltimore: Johns Hopkins University Press, 2005.

―――. "The Origins of Progressive Education." *History of Education Quarterly* 41, no. 1 (Spring 2001): 1–24.

―――. *Power and the Promise of School Reform.* New York: Teachers College Press, 2002.

Richardson, Theresa. "Rethinking Progressive High School Reform in the 1930s." *American Educational History Journal* 33, no. 1 (2006): 77–87.

Robinson, Glen O. "The Federal Communications Act: An Essay on Origins and Regulatory Purpose." In *A Legislative History of the Communications Act of 1934*, ed. Max D Paglin, 3–24. New York: Oxford University Press, 1989.

Robinson, William S. "Radio Comes to the Farmer." In *Radio Research 1941*, ed. Paul F. Lazarsfeld and Frank N. Stanton, 224–95. New York: Duell, Sloan and Pearce, 1941.

Rogers, Everett M. *A History of Communication Study: A Biographical Approach.* New York: Free Press, 1994.

Rorty, James. *Our Masters Voice: Advertising.* New York: John Day, 1934.

Rose, Nikolas. *Governing the Soul: The Shaping of the Private Self.* London: Free Association Books, 1999.

―――. *Inventing Our Selves: Psychology, Power and Personhood.* New York: Cambridge University Press, 1996.

―――. *Powers of Freedom: Reframing Political Thought.* Cambridge: Cambridge University Press, 1999.

Russo, Alexander. *Points on the Dial: Golden Age Radio Beyond the Networks.* Durham: Duke University Press, 2010.

Sachs, Harvey, ed. *The Letters of Arturo Toscanini.* New York: Alfred A. Knopf, 2002.

Salmond, John A. *The Conscience of a Lawyer: Clifford J. Durr and American Civil Liberties 1899–1975.* Tuscaloosa: University of Alabama Press, 1990.

Sanders, Constance. "A History of Radio in Music Education in the United States." PhD diss., University of Cincinnati, 1990.

Savage, Barbara D. *Broadcasting Freedom: Radio, War and the Politics of Race 1938–1948.* Chapel Hill: University of North Carolina Press, 1999.

Sayre, Jeanette. *An Analysis of the Radiobroadcasting Activities of Federal Agencies.* (Studies in the Control of Radio, No. 3). Cambridge, MA: Radiobroadcasting Research Project at the Littauer Center, Harvard University, 1941.

―――. *The Audience of an Educational Program.* New York: Columbia University Office of Radio Research, 1939.

―――. "Progress in Radio Fan-Mail Analysis." *Public Opinion Quarterly* 3, no. 2 (April 1939): 272–78.

Scannell, Paddy. *Radio, Television and Everyday Life: A Phenomenological Approach.* Oxford: Blackwell, 1996.

Scannell, Paddy, and David Cardiff. *A Social History of British Broadcasting: Volume One 1922–1939—Serving the Nation.* Oxford: Basil Blackwell, 1991.

Schneider, James C. *Should America Go to War? The Debate over Foreign Policy in Chicago, 1939–1941.* Chapel Hill, NC: University of North Carolina Press, 1989.

Schwoch, James. *The American Radio Industry and Its Latin American Activities 1900–1939.* Chicago: University of Illinois Press, 1990.

Sconce, Jeffrey. *Haunted Media: Electronic Presence from Telegraphy to Television.* Durham: Duke University Press, 2000.

Sheats, Paul H. *Forums on the Air.* Washington, DC: FREC, 1939.

Shulman, Holly C. "John Houseman and the Voice of America: American Foreign Propaganda on the Air." *American Studies* 28, no. 2 (Fall 1987): 23–40.

———. *The Voice of America: Propaganda and Democracy, 1941–1945*. Madison: University of Wisconsin Press, 1990.

Siepmann, Charles A. *Radio, Television and Society*. New York: Oxford University Press, 1950.

Simonson, Peter, and Gabriel Weiman. "Critical Research at Columbia: Lazarsfeld's and Merton's 'Mass Communication, Popular Taste, and Organized Social Action.'" In *Canonic Texts in Media Research: Are There Any? Should There Be? How About These?* ed. Elihu Katz, John D. Peters, Tamar Liebes, and Avril Orloff, 12–38. Cambridge: Polity, 2003.

Slotten, Hugh. "Commercial Radio, Public Affairs Discourse and the Manipulation of Sound Scholarship: Isolationism, Wartime Civil Rights and the Collapse of the Attractiveness of Communism in America, 1933–1945." *Historical Journal of Film, Radio and Television* 25, no. 3 (Aug. 2005): 371–98.

———. *Radio and Television Regulation: Broadcast Technology in the United States, 1920–1960*. Baltimore: Johns Hopkins University Press, 2000.

———. *Radio's Hidden Voice: The Origins of Public Broadcasting in the United States*. Urbana: University of Illinois Press, 2009.

———. "Universities, Public Service Experimentation, and the Origins of Radio Broadcasting in the United States, 1900–1920." *Historical Journal of Film, Radio and Television* 26, no. 4 (2006): 485–504.

Smulyan, Susan. "Radio Advertising to Women in Twenties America: 'A Latchkey to Every Home.'" *Historical Journal of Film, Radio and Television* 13, no. 3 (1993): 299–314.

———. *Selling Radio: The Commercialization of American Broadcasting 1920–1934*. Washington DC: Smithsonian Institution Press, 1994.

Socolow, Michael J. "The Behaviorist in the Boardroom: The Research of Frank Stanton, Ph.D." *Journal of Broadcasting and Electronic Media* 52, no. 4 (2008): 526–43.

———. "The Hyped Panic over 'War of the Worlds.'" *Chronicle of Higher Education* 55, no. 9 (Oct. 24, 2008): 35–35.

———. "To Network a Nation: NBC, CBS, and the Development of National Network Radio in the United States, 1925–1950." PhD diss., Georgetown University, 2001.

———. "'News Is a Weapon': Domestic Radio Propaganda and Broadcast Journalism in America, 1939–1944." *American Journalism* 24, no. 3 (2007): 109–32.

———. "Psyche and Society: Radio Advertising and Social Psychology in America, 1923–1936." *Historical Journal of Film, Radio and Television* 24, no. 4 (2004): 517–34.

Sproule, J. M. *Propaganda and Democracy: The American Experience of Media and Mass Persuasion*. New York: Cambridge University Press, 1997.

Stearns, Peter N. *American Cool: Constructing a Twentieth-Century Emotional Style*. New York: New York University Press, 1994.

Sterling, Christopher H., and John M. Kittross. *Stay Tuned: A Concise History of American Broadcasting*, 2nd ed. Belmont, CA: Wadsworth, 1990.

Stocking, George. "Introduction: Thoughts toward a History of the Interwar Years." In *Papers from the American Anthropologist*, ed. George Stocking, 1–74. Lincoln: University of Nebraska Press, 2002.

Stokowski, Leopold. *Music for All of Us*. New York: Simon and Schuster, 1943.

Streeter, Thomas. *Selling the Air: A Critique of the Policy of Commercial Broadcasting in the United States*. Chicago: University of Chicago Press, 1996.

Strunk, Mildred, ed. *Public Opinion, 1935–1946*. Princeton: Princeton University Press, 1951.

Studebaker, J. W. *Education for Democracy*. Washington, DC: U.S. Office of Education, 1936.

———. *Forum Planning Handbook*. Washington, DC: U.S. Office of Education, 1939.

———. *Plain Talk*. Washington, DC: National Home Library Foundation, 1936.

Suchman, E. A. "Radio Listening and Automobiles." *Journal of Applied Psychology* 23, no. 1 (1939): 148–67.

Summers, Robert E. *Wartime Censorship of Press and Radio*. New York: H. W. Wilson, 1942.

Sunstein, Cass. "Democracy and Filtering." *Communications of the ACM* 47, no. 12 (Dec. 2004): 57–59.

———. *Going to Extremes: How Like Minds Unite and Divide*. New York: Oxford University Press, 2009.

Sweeney, Michael S. *Secrets of Victory: The Office of Censorship and the American Press and Radio in World War II*. Chapel Hill: University of North Carolina Press, 2001.

Toro, Amy. "Standing up for Listeners' Rights: A History of Public Participation at the Federal Communications Commission." PhD diss., University of California, 2000.

Vaillant, Derek. "Bare-Knuckled Broadcasting: Enlisting Manly Respectability and Racial Paternalism in the Battle against Chain Stores, Chain Stations, and the Federal Radio Commission on Louisiana's KWKH, 1924–33." *Radio Journal* 1, no. 3 (2004): 193–211.

———. *Sounds of Reform: Progressivism and Music in Chicago, 1873–1935*. Chapel Hill: University of North Carolina Press, 2003.

———. " 'Your Voice Came in Last Night ... but I Thought It Sounded a Little Scared': Rural Radio Listening and 'Talking Back' during the Progressive Era in Wisconsin, 1920–1932." In *The Radio Reader: Essays in the Cultural History of Radio*, ed. Michele Hilmes and Jason Loviglio, 63–88. New York: Routledge, 2002.

Vipond, Mary. "British or American? Canada's 'Mixed' Broadcasting System in the 1930s." *Radio Journal* 2, no. 2 (2004): 89–100.

———. *Listening In: The First Decade of Canadian Broadcasting 1922–1932*. Montreal: McGill-Queen's University Press, 1992.

Warren, Donald. *Radio Priest: Charles Coughlin the Father of Hate Radio*. New York: Free Press, 1996.

Wartella, Ellen. "The History Reconsidered." In *American Communication Research: The Remembered History*, ed. Everette E. Dennis and Ellen Wartella, 169–80. Mahwah, NJ: Lawrence Erlbaum, 1996.

Wertheim, Arthur F. *Radio Comedy*. New York: Oxford University Press, 1979.

Westbrook, Robert B. *John Dewey and American Democracy*. Ithaca: Cornell University Press, 1991.

Wheatland, Thomas. "Critical Theory on Morningside Heights." *German Politics and Society* 22, no. 4 (Winter 2004): 57–87.

Wheatley, Parker. "Adult Education by Radio: Too Little? Too Late?" *Journal of Educational Sociology* 14, no. 9 (May 1941): 546–53.

White, Llewellyn. *The American Radio, a Report on the Broadcasting Industry in the United States from the Commission on Freedom of the Press*. Chicago: University of Chicago Press, 1947.

Wiebe, Robert H. *The Search for Order, 1877–1920*. New York: Hill and Wang, 1967.

———. *Self-Rule: A Cultural History of American Democracy*. Chicago: University of Chicago Press, 1995.

Wiesengrund-Adorno, Theodore. "Memorandum: Music in Radio." Copy in Paul F. Lazarsfeld papers, Box 26, Series 1. Rare Book and Manuscript Library, Columbia University, 1938.

Wiggershaus, Rolf. *The Frankfurt School: Its History, Theories and Political Significance.* Cambridge, MA: MIT Press, 1994.

Zenderland, Leila. *Measuring Minds: Henry Herbert Goddard and the Origins of American Intelligence Testing.* Cambridge: Cambridge University Press, 1998.

Index